Under THE VINE

תחת הגפן

Messianic Thought
Through the
Hebrew Calendar

PATRICK GABRIEL LUMBROSO
פטריק גבריאל לומברוזו

Lederer Books
A division of
Messianic Jewish Publishers
Clarksville, MD 21029

ISBN: 978-1-936716-65-4

Library of Congress Control Number: 2013938114

Cover: istockphoto 12-15-07 © Todd Bates

Illustrations: Original pen and ink drawings by Christine Lumbroso

17 16 15 14 13   6 5 4 3 2

Published by:

Lederer Books
A Division of Messianic Jewish Publishers
6120 Day Long Lane
Clarksville, MD 21029

Distributed by:
Messianic Jewish Publishers and Resources
Order line: (800) 410-7367
Lederer@messianicjewish.net
www.messianicjewish.net

Printed in the United States of America

As I wrote these pages, I always had an imaginary audience in view. One morning as I was pondering on the parasha of the week, I took the time to ask myself who is that audience. Who am I writing to, and most of all, why am I writing to them.

Then it came to me that my main audience was the Jewish Messianic community around the world, and most especially that of Israel.

I view the Jewish Messianic community in Israel as the spearhead of the Nazarene movement in our day, as 'ground zero' of all the follower disciples of Yeshua, the rabbi from Nazareth.

I pray that these words envision, encourage, strengthen, and quicken the spiritual walk of all those, Jew and Gentile who disciple themselves after the Jewish Messiah Yeshua, in the Land and in Diaspora

I wish to thank my wife for her editing work, and whose vision and faith in my ability to write anything is at the birthing of this project. I wish also to thank everyone who had a hand in helping edit these pages, especially Carolyn Hathaway who has also put many hours going over these pages.

TABLE OF CONTENTS

TISHREI 3

CHESHVAN 35

KISLEV 67

TEVET 99

SH'VAT 131

ADAR 163

NISSAN 195

IYAR 227

SIVAN 259

TAMMUZ 291

AV 323

ELUL 355

GLOSSARY 386

INTRODUCTION

THE IDEA BEHIND THE BOOK

As I was publishing my first book, *Under the Fig Tree,* I also started a new set of writings. In my first devotional, using the Levitical festivals as a calendric backbone, I attempted to find messianic concepts in the words of the Jewish prophets. In *Under the Vine,* I felt that my mission was one of restoration; restoration of the movement started by Yeshua, the rabbi from Nazareth, to its Davidic messianic context. In *Under the Vine,* I hope to add my contribution to the worldwide resurrection of Messianic Judaism started in 19th century Eastern Europe.

It is the view of this writer that, in the Tanach's own wording concerning the messianic era (1 Kings 4:25; Micah 4:4; Zechariah 3:10), Israel's fig tree is brought to perfection and fruition through the Davidic messianic vine. Even as expressed by Chassidic writers, Judaism truly comes alive and culminates to the fullness of its beauty only when mixed with messianic faith. This principle was very much understood by pioneers of modern Messianic Judaism such as Rabbi Yechiel Lichtenstein and Paul Philip Levertoff. Reading through the pages of my Tanach, I one day realized that Messianic faith was the motor and what gave substance to Abraham's new beliefs, hope to Job, trust to Isaac, vision to Jacob, resilience to Joseph, courage to David, wisdom to Solomon, knowledge to Daniel, and divine messianic authority to Yeshua.

THE ILLUSTRATIONS OF THE BOOK

A hand-drawn illustration introduces each month in this devotional. Tishrei brings us the messianic king who will read the Torah for all Israel during Sukkot. Chesvan reminds us of Isaac's messianic offering. Kislev hosts Hanukkah, the festival of lights, and sheds on us the light of a Havdalah candle. Tevet, a month of desolation in both the Babylonian and Greek era, reminds us of the branch growing from the stump of Jesse, the messianic hope that grows even from seeming death. Sh'vat leads us to a new season of potential growth and fruition. Adar tells us of the victorious Jerusalem exiles in leadership position after an attempted annihilation. Nissan offers us the broken Afikomen and redemption cup of the resurrected body and blood of Messiah. Iyar presents us a scene from the resurrection encounters during the counting of the Omer. Sivan tells us of Hashem, the mighty El-Shaddai speaking to his people through tongues of fire both on Mt. Horeb and in Jerusalem at Shavuot. Tammuz, a summer month reminds us of our responsibility to the fields of the Master before the return of the fall harvest. Av, a month seemingly cursed with defeat, tragedy, and desolation reverses its evil omen into a vibrant messianic Jerusalem. Elul takes us on a visit to the Judean desert where the Master first defeated his mortal enemy.

THE HEBREW CALENDAR, THE TORAH PORTIONS, AND THE LEVITICAL FESTIVALS IN THE BOOK

The Hebrew calendar has been defined of old from the words Hashem spoke to Moses, "This month shall be for you the beginning of months. It shall be the first month of the year for you" (Exodus 12:2). Since the time of this statement refers to the time when the barley is ready to harvest in that part of the world (Exodus 9:31), the new moon at the time of barley harvesting defines the arrival of the new year. This time generally falls around the last weeks of March in the Gregorian calendar. In Judaism this is called the Spiritual Year.

Working side by side with the Spiritual New Year starting in the spring, Judaism also refers to the first of Tishrei, Rosh Hashana, as the Civil New Year. This new year is mostly concerned with

1

tithes, the end of one harvest cycle and the beginning of another. It is at that time also that we come to the end of one Torah reading cycle and roll up the Torah scrolls in order to start them again for a new cycle.

This book follows the calendar starting with the first of Tishrei and with the first of what is called Parashah, or Torah portion.

After the return from Babylon, the prophet Ezra realized that the children of Israel went to exile because of disobedience. As it stood, the children of Israel were only exposed to the Word of Hashem in the Torah once every seven years, at the time of the jubilee. Ezra felt that the solution to the disobedience problem was 'more exposure to the Torah.' He then had the idea for synagogues, meeting places in every city where people would read the Torah weekly on the Sabbath. Ezra then developed the first system of reading the Bible in a year, dividing the Torah into weekly reading sections according to the Hebrew calendar. While over the centuries this system has been altered, it remains until today at the heart of the weekly Sabbath synagogue service. It is after these divisions called 'parashiot,' portions, that I built this devotional.

The texts in Elul leading to Rosh Hashana are meant to prepare the reader's heart for the coronation of the king on the first of Tishrei. The reader will then be encouraged to continue reflecting and searching his/her soul in order to come to a spirit of repentance in view of Yom Kippur, the day when some say Messiah comes to rescue his people and to establish his throne in Jerusalem.

During Sukkhot, day after day you will recline with the traditional heavenly visitors in their order from Abraham to Messiah.

From Pesach to Shavuot, The fall feasts will take you though the events that transpired in Jerusalem 2,000 years ago among what was then an obscure messianic sect.

WHY ARE SOME PASSAGES USED MORE THAN ONCE

It has been said that like a polished diamond, the Torah has many facets. Talmudic books *Shabbat 115b and 116a* claim that any part of the Torah of 85 verses or more constitute a 'book'. By inference, each of these 'books', like a polished diamond, also reflect many facets of truth.

The Torah is rich by its whole and by each of its parts. It is my wish to dig and find more facets within it in its whole, and in each of its parts.

THIS AND THAT

The reader may notice at times unusual capitalization for the words 'Day,' and 'Place.' This unusual capitalization is done on purpose in order to mimic the Talmud which adds a definite article in front the word 'Yom' when it refers to the 'Day' of Messiah, and to the word 'Place,' when it refers to the 'Place' in Jerusalem where he writes his name.

When writing about what transpired with the children of Israel by the mountain in the desert after the exodus from Egypt, I have chosen to use the Horeb appellation of the Mount where the Torah was given. The reasoning behind this is to avoid confusion due to newly discovered evidence that, as is mentioned in the apostolic letter Paul wrote to the Galatian congregations, this famous mountain might be situated on the East side of the Gulf of Aqaba (Galatians 4:25) and not in the southern tip of the Sinai desert as is presently assumed.

Tishrei ~ תשרי

Tishrei

More than the promise of meeting the Judge of all the earth, more than a priestly atoning service, more than an anticipation of Hashem's Tabernacle on earth, we yearn for that day when our Messiah King will fulfill the Torah command to read its sacred words to the people of Israel.

Matthew 24:48–51   **Rosh Hashanah/ראש השנה**   **Tishrei 1/ א בתישרי**

But if that servant is wicked and says to himself, 'My master is taking his time'; and he starts beating up his fellow servants and spends his time eating and drinking with drunkards; then his master will come on a day the servant does not expect, at a time he doesn't know; and he will cut him in two and put him with the hypocrites, where people will wail and grind their teeth!

Those of us who acknowledge Yeshua as our Master and Rabbi have been given responsibility over his heritage. As disciples we are expected to behave as responsible leaders over his flock. He left us in charge while he is gone on a journey, but at the time appointed, our Master will return. At that time, we will sit down with him for an audit. He will look at what he left us and require the increase. If there is no increase, he will examine the situation and demand an explanation. This is the time when the priorities that led our lives will be thoroughly examined and evaluated.

We all mean to do well and I doubt if any person reading this actually beats his fellow servants or drinks with the drunkards. On the other hand, we can all admit to neglecting our responsibilities towards others by just being selfish, negligent, self motivated, and over-concerned with our personal pleasure, entertainment, comfort, and reputation.

As we prepare for rehearsing the Day of the Lord through the festival of *Yom Kippur* הכיפורים יום, we may need to do a little self-auditing. Here are several questions we can ask ourselves that can help get us back in line: What does Yeshua expect of me? Have I been fulfilling his will and wishes for my life? If not, why? Where am I in my relationship with my family, my brothers, and my sisters? Are there any sour relationships that I need to sweeten? Would I want him to ask me the questions: Why is your relationship with so and so in such a state of negativity? Are there people in either your social or biological entourage that you are expected to look after? Are you fulfilling your responsibilities with them? If yes, how? And if not, why?

James the apostle exhorts us in this way,

> For if anyone is a hearer of the Word and not a doer, he is like a man who looks intently at his natural face in a mirror. For he looks at himself and goes away and at once forgets what he was like.

James' 'mirror' is the Torah. Using the word of truth, the Torah points out what we ought to be like. It is a bit like the truth-telling evil witch's mirror in the fairy tale *Snow White*; we are meant to look in it and compare our lives with the beauty of his words. The mirror faithfully points out our blemishes so we can fix them through repentance, prayer, and emulation of the Master. Sad to say though, like in the famous story, many of us use it to retaliate against anything that challenges the erroneous righteous image we have of ourselves. The apostle continues his exhortation and says,

> For whoever hears the Word but doesn't do what it says is like someone who looks at his face in a mirror, who looks at himself, goes away and immediately forgets what he looks like. But if a person looks closely into the perfect Torah, which gives freedom, and continues, becoming not a forgetful hearer but a doer of the work it requires, then he will be blessed in what he does. (James 1:23–25)

May we look in the 'mirror', learn, repent, and change, that our names may be written in the Book of Life!

Matthew 24:45–47   **Tishrei 2/** ב בתישרי

Who is the faithful and sensible servant whose master puts him in charge of the household staff, to give them their food at the proper time? It will go well with that servant if he is found doing his job when his master comes. Yes, I tell you that he will put him in charge of all he owns.

Since the days of John the Immerser we are told, "Repent, for the kingdom of heaven is at hand (Matthew 3:2). *At hand*, means easily reachable. Isn't it strange that more than 2,000 years have passed and this *at hand* Kingdom of God has not yet been established on the earth?

Every generation learns that the kingdom of heaven is *at hand*. In fact, many generations have been convinced that they were going to see the return of the Master in their own days but didn't. In a way, it is right that it should be so. If it weren't, how would we, in each generation, feel the necessity to ready ourselves for that great and awesome final Day? Even more important; we would not have passed this feeling of urgency on to our children? If in every generation we did not apprehend the return of our Master Yeshua, within two generations, the whole endtime preparation message would be lost.

Each year during the High Holidays we rehearse and anticipate this return of our Master. We look forward to his judgment, his vindication, and his final take-over of the kingdoms of this world as he ushers us into 1,000 years of restoration. All wrongs will then be made right; the day will conquer the night; the lost will be restored, and injustice will be rectified. In the glory of his ruling majesty, as Solomon of old, the great King will listen to our pleas, wipe our tears away, vindicate the souls of those persecuted for righteousness' sake, and challenge all who destroy the earth.

May it be soon Abba, even in our days!

PRAYER:
May it be your will Abba that we may be ready for that great Day.
May it be your will that we may at that time be found doing those things which pertain to your commands, not in lip service but from the heart.
May we start today living a life that reflects unswerving love and dedication to your commandments.
May we be found worthy of the title of disciple: one who emulates his Master.
Blessed are You ADONAI our God King of the universe, who rewards righteousness, punishes iniquity, and most of all, brings the disobedient to your rectitude.

My Personal Thoughts

_____

_____

_____

_____

_____

_____

_____

_____

Hebrews 13:15   **Tishrei 3/** ג בתישרי

Through him, therefore, let us offer God a sacrifice of praise continually. For this is the natural product of lips that acknowledge his name.

As we continue searching our hearts in preparation for that great Day, let us use some of the admonitions and exhortations from the early apostles.

When the Messianic Jewish community was in disarray, an apostle wrote to them to give them guidance. Having been rejected from the Temple and synagogues as Yeshua had prophesied to them, it was easy for disillusionment to settle in. "What's the use?" one may ask. "First our Master dies unjustly at the hands of the authorities, and now we are nothing more than pariahs of society, rejected from Israel's social life." This social rejection is a reality for many in today's society. For others, it may come tomorrow.

And what did the Apostle say to help these people? What kind of advice did he give them? Did he give them empty promises and affirmations? Did he fill them up with positive words to keep them going until such time when hope was no more?

The Apostle gave many exhortations to the Israeli Messianic Jewish community in the first century, and he also made sure their spiritual lives stayed on track. The Day of ADONAI is sure to accompany such trials and tribulations, so it behooves us to review some of the words given to these pioneers of our messianic tradition.

The Apostle said, "Keep your lives free from the love of money; and be satisfied with what you have" (Hebrews 13:5). In times of trials and tribulations, gratefulness is very important. A lack of it leads to complaining and the covetousness by which all the other commandments are transgressed. The Apostle then implores the community's disciples to remember the word of the Master and said, "I will never fail you or abandon you.'"

In such times, we should follow the example of King David, who, in his times of trouble confidently said, " ADONAI is my helper; I will not be afraid—what can a human being do to me?" (Hebrews 13:6).

Trying to suggest more current role models for the believers, the Apostle directs the believers towards the sample of Yeshua's disciples and says, " Remember your leaders, those who spoke God's message to you. Reflect on the results of their way of life, and imitate their trust" (Hebrews 13:7).

The great Day is coming soon. May we take the advice of the Apostle in emulating the pioneers of our faith, the disciples of the Master, and learn as they did just to be thankful.

My Personal Thoughts

_____

_____

_____

_____

_____

_____

Acts 24:14–16   **Tishrei 4/** ד בתישרי

But this I do admit to you: I worship the God of our fathers in accordance with the Way (which they call a sect). I continue to believe everything that accords with the Torah and everything written in the Prophets. And I continue to have a hope in God—which they too accept—that there will be a resurrection of both the righteous and the unrighteous. Indeed, it is because of this that I make a point of always having a clear conscience in the sight of both God and man.

Hear these words spoken by Paul, Yeshua's chosen apostle, several years after his encounter with the Master: "I worship the God of our fathers in accordance with everything that accords with the Torah (my edition) and everything written in the Prophets (Acts 24:14). In other words, Paul's defense against the Sadducee high priests' accusations of sedition and profanation was that he never swayed from practicing Judaism; that he believed and practiced the commandments written in the Books of Moses, as well as the teachings of the prophets.

Judaism is not a creed; it is a way of life. It is not something that can be believed nor somehow practiced on the outside. The high priest knew it and couldn't refute Paul's confession so he added false accusations of seditions to the package of 'evidence' against Paul. Ananias knew that the Roman governor couldn't care less about religious squabbles, but disturbing the peace of the Empire was a very serious offense, especially in Jerusalem.

Paul proclaimed his innocence by insisting that he always took pains to have a clear conscience toward both God and man. To Paul, this meant that he stayed clear of offenses, by his sincere efforts to serve God and obey his commandments. By bringing these facts to the forefront, Paul hoped to close the mouth of his accusers.

In a certain way, each of us finds ourselves daily in the same predicament as Paul. The Accuser is always in front of us. He daily accuses us, not to the Roman emperor, but to Hashem, the Creator of the universe. It is difficult enough to be accused of an evil that we have done, and we all have done plenty. But there is something we can do to close the mouth of the Adversary. To the best of our ability, we can strive to have a clear conscience before both God and man: before God by our obedience to Torah, and before men by submitting to the ordinances of earthly authority. We can also strive for *shalom* שלום with everyone, and for the holiness without which no one will see ADONAI (Hebrews 12:14).

We may agree to obey God, but there are times when we feel that man's command goes against Hashem, and it may be so at times, but what I have observed is that it is more often our personal extreme application of both that creates the conflict.

Let's take the stand today to close the mouth of he who stands in front of Hashem accusing us of evil. Let us have the conviction that despite the sin of our human nature, which we cannot avoid, we do follow in the footsteps of the apostle in, "striving for peace, and taking pains to have a clear conscience toward both God and man."

My Personal Thoughts

_____

_____

_____

_____

Matthew 5:21–22   **Tishrei 5/ ה בתישרי**

You have heard that our fathers were told, 'Do not murder,' . . . But I tell you that anyone who nurses anger against his brother will be subject to judgment; that whoever calls his brother, 'You good-for-nothing!' will be brought before the Sanhedrin; that whoever says, 'Fool!' incurs the penalty of burning in the fire of Gei-Hinnom!

Paul, Yeshua's apostle, reminds us that according to the Torah, "what one earns from sin is death" (Romans 6:23). Furthermore John, another apostle of the Master, also reminds us that sin is the violation of the Torah (1 John 3:4). Yeshua himself was against even the relaxing of the commandments (Matthew 5:19), and challenged us to be even more righteous than his very conservative brothers (Matthew 5:20). Is that feasible?

Because the breaking of the Torah was so dangerous, the teachers of Israel decided to make fences around the commandments. The idea was to teach the people of Israel practical ways to make it less likely to break commandments. It's like having an important meeting at six thirty, but aware of people's procrastinating nature you declare it at six o'clock. There is nothing wrong with that. It's called wisdom and knowing human nature. We do it all the time. We tell children, "Don't go in the kitchen" when all we really don't want them to do is touch the knives or the hot stove.

After their return from Babylon, the sages of Israel understood that they had gone to exile because of their breaking of the commandments. They realized that it wasn't very fun to go to exile, so they adopted the principle of *fences* around the commandments in order to safeguard themselves from breaking them. We must remember that the responsibility of the elders of the Hebrew nation was very great. People did not have Torah scrolls around in their homes during these days. The teachers were the only means by which people could even know what the commandments were.

Hashem allowed Cain, the first murderer, to live. As a result, when Lamech, Cain's great grandson, also committed murder he thought that he should get away with it (Genesis 4:23–24). Eventually, after the Great Flood, the Father made it a universal law that murder warranted the death penalty (Genesis 9:6). The idea is that to kill a man is to kill something made in the image of the Almighty; it is like the reverse action of the Creator. If someone kills your son, it is typical to want revenge for his shed blood. Through Moses, the Father reiterated his position about murder (Numbers 35:30–31). Yeshua also spoke about it. He even established a fence around the sin of murder by teaching people to check the anger in their heart (Matthew 5:21–22). The sages of Judaism teach that when we kill unlawfully, we actually commit murder against ourselves. If the law doesn't catch us, Messiah, the true avenger of blood, will. God is a God of justice and mercy: justice for the offender, and mercy for the offended.

I asked my students once: "How would you feel if you lived in a world where you never had to worry about people lying, killing, stealing, hating, and all the likes?" My students said, "It would be like heaven!" to which I responded, "We can have it, by just deciding to obey the Ten Statements written on stone by the finger of God himself at Mt Sinai. By the way . . . why don't we?

My Personal Thoughts

_____

_____

_____

9

John 3:3   ו בתישרי **/6 Tishrei**

I tell you that unless a person is born again from above, he cannot see the Kingdom of God.

In Hebrew the word translated from the Greek as baptism which in English means immersion is *tevilah* טבילה. This tevilah is done in a *mikveh* מקוה pool. The etymological meaning of mikveh is "gathering," as in the gathering of waters. From long ago, Jewish sages have equated this ritual to the idea of being born-again. As a child is born from inside a water-sack, they say that people, "immerse in order to emerge a born-again new creature in God" (Yevamot 47b and 48b). As a result, the flooding of the planet in the days of Noah has been understood as Hashem's effort towards the renewal of a degenerated humanity.

In Genesis we read, "In the days of Noah, ADONAI saw that the wickedness of man was great in the earth, and that every intention of the thoughts of his heart was only evil continually" (Genesis 6:5). Humanity had really blown it. The Father could have opted to destroy us, but he chose instead to fix us. I lived ten years in Asia. Upon my arrival in the US, I told a relative about the miserable state of many places in rural India. My relative reacted by saying, "Just blow it up and start again!" The Father could have had a similar reaction in the days of Noah and said, "Let them all drown and let's be done with it!" . . . but no. The Father wanted to fix us instead and give us a chance, to give a chance to humanity. This *fixing* took the form of a planet-wide immersion while preserving a remnant of humanity for posterity.

Here are a few extra details from the Book of Enoch as to what happened in the days of Noah. Angels renounced their heavenly station in order to settle down on earth with women. In the process, these spiritual beings taught mankind knowledge that corrupted the earth with wickedness and violence. These unions of women with angels created offspring who wreaked havoc on the earth; thus the earth was filled with violence. Josephus tried to explain the nature of these offspring, comparing them to those of Greek mythology (Antiquities 1:3:73). Needing to purify humanity and the earth it came from, Hashem then orchestrated a planet-wide immersion preserving Noah's family, Noah whom Hashem called "blameless in his generation" Genesis 6:9).

Later, when Hashem wanted to separate a people through whom he would teach the world about himself and finally redeem humanity, he brought the Israelites out of Egypt. He needed them to go through a *tevilah* (an immersion as a type of rebirth) so he brought them all the way to the eastern arm of the Red Sea (1 Corinthians 10:1–2). As they crossed, the people shed their Egyptian culture and emerged on the other side as the new nation of Israel. They had become God's people. Before entering the Promised Land, the Red Sea scenario was repeated, this time in the Jordan River. That area of the Jordan River became the place where later John the Immerser would immerse people unto repentance. People would have to cross the Jordan out of the Land to meet John, immerse, and then re-enter the Land as born again, new creatures.

Friends; the message is clear. Unless we shed behind the *Egyptian* culture that keeps us in idolatry, as well as the doubtful disobedient behavior that keeps us in the desert, we cannot call ourselves born again, and we cannot enter the Promised Land.

May we daily immerse in his words (John 15:3), shed our old selves behind, be born again, and live new lives as his creatures.

My Personal Thoughts

Luke 1:18   **Tishrei 7/** ז בתישרי

How can I be sure of this? For I am an old man; my wife too is well on in years.

For centuries, through diligent searching in the text of the Torah, Israel understood that the redeemer would someday come; that he would rule supreme on earth and govern the world by Hashem's word of Torah. This coming Savior was the only hope of final lasting independence for the tiny Jewish nation. So many have come whom they thought were the one; so many that it even produced cynicism on the part of the people of Israel.

As he was serving his course at the Temple (Luke 1:5), Zechariah had an encounter with an angel. Angels did not necessarily appear as flying beings or as ethereal lights. In both cases of Abraham and Lot they appeared as people, as guests you can host for a meal (Genesis 18:1; 19:1). No one but the serving priest was supposed to be in the Holy, the first chamber of the Tabernacle, so it was quite a surprise to Zechariah not only to have company there, but also to hear an oracle telling him that his wife would conceive in their old age. He was also given instructions on how to raise the miracle child. Luke also tells us that Zechariah doubted the angel who therefore punished him with muteness (Luke 1:5–24).

Throughout the whole Biblical narratives, Hashem has always made a point to draw our attention towards certain individuals by making their birth a blessing out of barrenness. Such was the case for many patriarchs, judges, and prophets. First Temple classic Judaism even considered that the Messiah would come from a young maiden who had not yet been with a man.

As per the Torah's instruction, Jews are trained to try the spirits, demanding a sign to confirm prophecy even from angels. To ask for a sign was not a bad thing. It is the norm in testing prophecy (Deuteronomy 13), and I think we may be well advised to follow that injunction today. Hashem himself wants to provide the necessary signs to prove his points to the people. Zechariah was not punished for asking for a sign, but for cynical incredulity concerning the message, and Gabriel, being the angel of judgment, didn't seem to appreciate that. This attitude of incredulity was even pointed out by Yeshua later. Notice that Yeshua did nevertheless give the people the sign of his resurrection, which he prophesied ahead of time using the story of Jonah (Matthew 12:29).

Even as his return seems to be lingering, we also could become incredulous. Yeshua gave us signs wherewith to identify his coming (Matthew 24), the biggest one of course being the restoration of the State of Israel. As we see the signs fulfilled today, let us not be incredulous, but remember the predictions of the holy prophets and the words of his apostle,

> First, understand this . . . scoffers will come . . . asking, "Where is this promised 'coming' of his? For our fathers have died, and everything goes on just as it has since the beginning of creation." But . . . dear friends, do not ignore this: with the Lord, one day is like a thousand years and a thousand years like one day. The Lord is not slow in keeping his promise, as some people think of slowness; on the contrary, he is patient with you; for it is not his purpose that anyone should be destroyed, but that everyone should turn from his sins. (2 Peter 3:3-9)

We are thankful for his patience in waiting for us!

1 Corinthians 10:4   **Tishrei 8/**ח בתישרי

. . . that Rock was the Messiah.

All throughout the Sacred Scriptures, prophets and kings call Hashem their *Rock*. While projecting a beautiful image, the most awesome theme flowing from this expression is the undercurrent of God's justice when he disciplines us for our sins or trains us through seemingly very unfair situations.

Moses initiated the idea when he said, "The Rock! His work is perfect, for all his ways are just" (Deuteronomy 32:4). The weary and wise leader and prophet knew that the generation of people he would lead to the Promised Land would eventually corrupt themselves with sin and idolatry. He sees the future exiles, the persecutions, as well as the bloody and sad history of Israel. So right away he establishes the idea that no matter what will happen, Hashem is a *rock*, a God of faithfulness without iniquity, just and upright (Deuteronomy 32:4). King David understood that. He even complains to the Rock, "I say to God, my Rock: Why have you forgotten me? Why must I go about mourning, under pressure by the enemy?'" (Psalm 42:9), but later he also says, "I love you, ADONAI, my strength! ADONAI is my Rock, my fortress and deliverer, my God, my Rock, in whom I find shelter, my shield, the power that saves me, my stronghold" (Psalm 18:2). In these words we picture a desperate David in the caves of Ein-Gedi (1 Samuel 24:2).

Centuries later through Isaiah, Hashem encourages an Israel whom he thoroughly rebuked with these words about his unfailing compassion and eternal mercies,

> Don't be frightened, don't be afraid—Didn't I tell you this long ago? I foretold it, and you are my witnesses. Is there any God besides me? There is no other Rock—I know of none. (Isaiah 44:8)

Habakkuk also struggles to see God's justice in the Babylonian invasion,

> ADONAI, haven't you existed forever? My God, my holy one, we will not die. ADONAI, you appointed them to execute judgment. Rock, you commissioned them to correct us. Your eyes are too pure to see evil, you cannot countenance oppression. So why do you countenance traitors? Why are you silent when evil people swallow up those more righteous than they? (Habakkuk 1:12–13)

During the days preceding Yom Kippur we usually check our hearts for bitterness against others, but do we also check our hearts for bitterness against Hashem and his ways in our lives? A lifelong affliction, loss of a loved one, bankruptcy, or trouble with our teenagers can cause us to wonder if God is really in control or if he is just letting things go awry in our lives without rhyme or reason. Do we fully understand that these things are the chisel strokes to make us into the image of Messiah, the wind that drives the reed closer to the protection of the great and mighty oak?

May we always remember that whatever happens, Hashem is our Rock; that his works are perfect, for all his ways are just (Deuteronomy 32:4).

My Personal Thoughts

_____

_____

_____

Matthew 25:1–7   **Tishrei 9/** ט בתישרי

> *The Kingdom of Heaven at that time will be like ten bridesmaids who took their lamps and went out to meet the groom. Five of them were foolish and five were sensible. The foolish ones took lamps with them but no oil, whereas the others took flasks of oil with their lamps. Now the bridegroom was late, so they all went to sleep. It was the middle of the night when the cry rang out, 'The bridegroom is here! Go out to meet him!' The girls all woke up and prepared their lamps for lighting.*

Behold the night is far advanced. It has been a long wait and drowsiness has taken hold of the congregations. The Master has finished his work; he has prepared a place for the bride and he now comes for her (John 14:2–3). The ten virgins, the friends of the bride, are to stay awake with her to serve and help her, but just like the disciples in that fateful night on the Mount of Olives, their eyes are heavy (Matthew 26:43).

Will we watch one hour with him? Will we stand guard, watch, and pray?

On the eve of the manifestation of his messianic nature, Yeshua asked his disciples to watch with him, to stand guard in prayer denying themselves of the sleep they so much needed. Even today, as we await his manifestation in the world, as we wait for the time of the wedding ceremony, we must watch, pray, and stand guard. Are our eyes heavy? Can we deny ourselves needed sleep for a moment? Can we wait even though we do not know at which hour he will come?

A sudden cry pierces the night, "The Bridegroom is coming; the Bridegroom is coming!" See him! He is majestic riding on a white horse (2 Samuel 2:1–20). He is coming for his bride. The friends of the bride rise from their drowsiness to fix their lamps. They must trim their wicks to make sure their lamps burn clear and bright, without smoke.

Even so, now the time has come; even now we hear the sound in the horizons. There will soon be a shout in the heavens, "The Bridegroom is coming; the Bridegroom is coming!" Let us rise from sleep. Let us shake our drowsiness. "Awake, awake," the prophet says (Isaiah 52:1, 9).

It is time now for us to rise from our sleepiness and appear before the King of the universe. He comes to take the bride and to bring his people to the greatest party ever thrown. He has sent his servants to cry in the streets, the highways, and the byways compelling people to come in. He has sent white robes to each one to wear at the feast.

Let us now be ready; let us trim our wicks that the light of our love through our keeping of his commands may shine bright and unequivocally, distinctly, and without smoke. Let us now answer the Master's request, "Let your light shine before others, so that they may see the good things you do and praise your Father in heaven" (Matthew 5:16).

My Personal Thoughts

_____

_____

_____

_____

_____

Matthew 24:31   **Yom Hakippurim/ יום הכיפורים**   **Tishrei 10/ י בתישרי**

He will send out his angels with a great shofar; and they will gather together his chosen people from the four winds, from one end of heaven to the other.

Behold the great Day has come. We have fasted for it over the centuries. Each year on that same day we afflict our souls in prayers of repentance. Now Hashem hears our voices; the blood of his many martyrs reaches his nostrils; he inclines his ears to our cries. Blessed is he who brings Israel back to himself for truly, he who scattered Israel will gather him, and will keep him as a shepherd keeps his flock (Jeremiah 30:10).

On this day, see the reward of our work over the centuries. See him who comes from Edom, in crimsoned garments from Bozrah, he who is splendid in his apparel, marching in the greatness of his strength?

"It is I, who speak victoriously, I, well able to save." Why is your apparel red, your clothes like someone treading a winepress? "I have trodden the winepress alone; from the peoples, not one was with me. So I trod them in my anger, trampled them in my fury; so their lifeblood spurted out on my clothing, and I have stained all my garments; for the day of vengeance that was in my heart and my year of redemption have come." (Isaiah 63:1–4)

The galloping of his white horse echoes Moses' song,

Next I saw heaven opened, and there before me was a white horse. Sitting on it was the one called Faithful and True, and it is in righteousness that he passes judgment and goes to battle. His eyes were like a fiery flame, and on his head were many royal crowns. And he had a name written which no one knew but himself. He was wearing a robe that had been soaked in blood, and the name by which he is called is, "THE WORD OF GOD." The armies of heaven, clothed in fine linen, white and pure, were following him on white horses. And out of his mouth comes a sharp sword with which to strike down nations—"He will rule them with a staff of iron." It is he who treads the winepress from which flows the wine of the furious rage of ADONAI, God of heaven's armies. And on his robe and on his thigh he has a name written: KING OF KINGS AND LORD OF LORDS. (Revelation 19:11–16; Deuteronomy 32:34–43)

As Moses and all the prophets sang of the deliverance of Israel, of his return to his land and to his God, let us foresee and rejoice of his mighty works

For ADONAI has ransomed Ya`akov, redeemed him from hands too strong for him. They will come and sing on the heights of Tziyon, streaming to the goodness of ADONAI, to the grain, the wine, the olive oil, and the young of the flock and the herd. They themselves will be like a well-watered garden, never to languish again. "Then the virgin will dance for joy, young men and old men together; for I will turn their mourning into joy, comfort and gladden them after their sorrow." (Jeremiah 31:11–13)

Mark 13:27   **Tishrei 11/** יא בתישרי

He will send out his angels and gather together his chosen people from the four winds,
from the ends of the earth to the ends of heaven.

Many centuries ago, Hashem had punished his people by banishing them from his Land. Now that Hashem's favor has returned to his people, the world needs to finally realize that the strip of land by the Mediterranean Sea, historically called Israel but the Romans renamed *Palestina*, ultimately belongs to God and that he gives it to whoever he pleases, regardless of world opinion.

Hashem did banish his first-born son to exile, but that never gave license to these hosting nations to also chastise Israel. Can you imagine disciplining your son and suddenly the whole neighborhood joining in on it? Hashem's discipline is measured, "For his anger is momentary, but his favor lasts a lifetime. Tears may linger for the night, but with dawn come cries of joy" (Psalm 30:5).

All the prophecies of what would happen to Israel if they stubbornly disobeyed have already been fulfilled under the Roman invasion, occupation, as well as with the sacking and destruction of the country and the current Great Exile (Deuteronomy 28; Matthew 24). As the Assyrians and the Babylonians were moved by God to punish Israel, so were the Romans. But whereas these powers had sort of a divine mandate—which they abused—to punish Israel, it has never been a mandate for the Catholic and Protestant Churches, Germany, or today's radical Islam.

Ancient history teaches us that every world power that persecuted God's people lost their right to domination, even if they were doing it by divine mandate. Egypt, Assyria, Babylon, Greece, and Rome all saw their downfall as God's retribution for their oppression of his people, Israel.

The prophecies in the Tanach teach us that a Day comes when Hashem reinstates his people in the Land he promised to give them through Abraham (Deuteronomy 30:1–7). Scriptures also tell us that at that time many nations rise against re-instated Israel (Ezekiel 38; 39), and that these nations pay a devastating price for it (Deuteronomy 32:40–42; Ezekiel 39:4; Matthew 24:28; Revelation 19:17–18).

Countries today are faced with very important decisions. A simple study of the Torah should show the world that Hashem has again turned his favor toward his people of old, on Israel, his first-born son. Whereas the world is already indebted to God for the unwarranted persecution of his exiled people, those who stand in the way of his present will of Israel's reinstatement most certainly will be the recipients of his great wrath.

Whatever anyone else does: God's will be done!

My Personal Thoughts

_____

_____

_____

_____

_____

_____

Revelation 20:1–3   Tishrei 12/ יב בתישרי

Next I saw an angel coming down from heaven, who had the key to the Abyss and a great chain in his hand. He seized the dragon, that ancient serpent, who is the Devil and Satan [the Adversary], and chained him up for a thousand years. He threw him into the Abyss, locked it and sealed it over him; so that he could not deceive the nations any more until the thousand years were over. After that, he has to be set free for a little while.

I heard it said once, "When you leave sin behind, don't leave a forwarding address!"

At the time of his coming, Yeshua, the Messiah-King, will rule on earth. The Adversary will be under Yeshua's control so, therefore, the evil inclination that causes us so much trouble will be greatly diminished. Living by Hashem's commandments and avoiding sin will be much easier then. But at the end of these 1,000 years of relief from the Adversary's work, *HaSatan* השטן will be released. At that time, he will again be allowed to tempt us as he is today.

Here is something we must ask ourselves, "The Messiah may rule the earth then, but does he rule my heart now? Is he my King today?" During the High Holidays, we go through deep introspection; we confess our sins and we deny ourselves on the Day of Atonement. But what happens after that? Does life continue as usual? Mashiach may do the atoning work, covering our balance of sinful debt to the Father, but there is a chilly warning for going back into the works of darkness after Messiah did the hard work of cleaning us up. The writer of the book of Hebrew puts it in these following words,

> For if we deliberately continue to sin after receiving the knowledge of the truth, there no longer remains a sacrifice for sins, but only the terrifying prospect of Judgment, of raging fire that will consume the enemies. (Hebrews 10:26–27)

As we prepare for *Sukkot* סוכות, the Feast of Tabernacles, which is the next festival on our calendar, we are told to look back at the time of our sojourn in the desert, at the time when we lived in *sukkot* סוכות, in temporary flimsy shelters remembering our vulnerability as we were in the desert, totally dependent on the Father's mercy.

As well as reminding us of times past, this festival also speaks to us about our temporal situation on this earth, looking forward to the time when we will enter what John called New Jerusalem, Hashem's *mishkan* מישכן with men. It is a place where nothing shall hurt or destroy; sin, death, and corruption will not be allowed.

In preparation for that day, may we learn today to stay away from sin; like Joseph of old, to flee temptation when it comes with its sensual attires, even leaving our *coat* behind when it cleaves to us (Genesis 39:12). That is our work, and one of the ideas behind the apostle's words: "keep working out your deliverance with fear and trembling" (Philippians 2:12).

My Personal Thoughts

_____

_____

_____

_____

Revelation 20:4–6 **Tishrei 13/ יג בתישרי**

Then I saw thrones, and those seated on them received authority to judge. And I saw the souls of those who had been beheaded for testifying about Yeshua and proclaiming the Word of God, also those who had not worshipped the beast or its image and had not received the mark on their foreheads and on their hands. They came to life and ruled with the Messiah for a thousand years. (The rest of the dead did not come to life until the thousand years were over.) This is the first resurrection. Blessed and holy is anyone who has a part in the first resurrection; over him the second death has no power.

Concerning this time of future restoration and reorganization of the world, Paul, our Master's apostle, specified, "Don't you know that we will judge angels, not to mention affairs of everyday life" (1 Corinthians 6:3)!

We are not given too many details about this judging of angels that we are to do (Deuteronomy 29:29); we are simply told in this and other passages that at the time when Messiah will physically reign on earth, the faithful will share in his exaltation and in the judging of the universe. This logically implies judging angels. This idea of mankind judging angels was birthed in the Book of Enoch when he became the first scribe ever and was given an active role in the judgment of the disobedient angels (Genesis 6:1–5). The narrative of Enoch was a widespread publication in the 1st century CE, which the early believers seem to have been familiar with (Jude 14).

What is revealed to us though—and the things that are revealed belong to us and our children forever, as noted by Moses (Deuteronomy 29:29)—is that if we are to judge angels in the future, we should today be able to righteously judge in earthly disputes among ourselves (Isaiah 11:3–5 tells of the way to judge righteously). In essence, our training for judging angels tomorrow starts today with learning to maturely take care of our own issues between ourselves, with godly counsel from our learned elders.

The problem is that today, as with many other things, we are not encouraged to manage our own affairs and disagreements. We are told to go to the police, to the spiritual leader, to get a lawyer, or a psychologist. As far as I can understand from his epistles, in the eyes of Paul, the fact that those who called themselves by the name of Yeshua could not manage their own problems by themselves and had to go to ungodly lawyers for justice, was a disgrace and a bad representation of Messiah's congregation in front of the non-believers. Paul suggests that it would be more valuable to be defrauded by others than to allow such a poor testimony in front of unbelievers (1 Corinthians 6:7).

It is high time that we take control of our lives; that we take responsibility over our affairs. Just as in ancient times the Hebrew nation was taught to establish its own courts of Torah legislation, we, as Messianic congregations, must organize ourselves into a coherent movement that is self sufficient in every way. Then and only then, will we ever be able to fulfill our destiny of entering the Promised Land of his divine will and be an example to all nations of life under the rule of Mashiach.

My Personal Thoughts

Revelation 20:5   Tishrei 14/ יד בתישרי

(The rest of the dead did not come to life until the thousand years were over.) This is the first resurrection.

Following the logical flow of text in the Book of Revelation, Those who first resurrect are those who refused to receive the mark of the beast; those who "did not come to life" are those who received such a mark.

Much is speculated about this mark. We may not, at present be sure of its form, but we know its function. We are told that he that is called the Anti-Messiah

> forces everyone—great and small, rich and poor, free and slave—to receive a mark on his right hand or on his forehead preventing anyone from buying or selling unless he has the mark, that is, the name of the beast or the number of its name. (Revelation 13:16–17)

In biblical terms, the head, especially the forehead, represents the will; the hands represent the actions birthed by the will. That is why even today when Jews pray, they wrap *t'fillin* תפילין, prayer boxes with a Scripture scroll inside, on their heads and arms. It serves to remind them of what should be the focus and direction of both their thoughts and their actions. In the same way, the Adversary also tries to control our thoughts and actions by attempting to replace Hashem's mark on our hands and foreheads with his mark, and in the eyes of the Eternal God, this means death.

We are used to thinking of death as a permanent state. Looking at the verse in Revelation though, it seems the dead await resurrection in order to go to their reward, good or bad. We are obviously then talking about something different than the mere corruption of the body, or even its non-existence. There are people who are alive and yet who are deader than the dead, while there are those who are dead, but who are more alive than those still in the body (Matthew 22:32)!

What is then a life that is more substantial than an active biologically functional state? And what is a death that is more empty and void than the mere corruption of the body? King David put it in these wonderful words, "I shall dwell in the house of ADONAI forever' (Psalm 23:6). In other words, presence with Hashem is a life that is more alive than this biological functionality; but absence from God is a state of death that is lower than the mere corruption of the body.

As long as we are alive, the flame of the life of El-Shaddai, however small at times, still lives in us. Its light is manifest in our hearts via the twinges of our conscience. When we *die*, that flame is set on *pilot*, until the time of resurrection and judgment when we come to either more than life in what Yeshua called "the bosom of Abraham", or to less than death, in the *she'ol* שאול.

We must take this life more seriously. "The good, the bad, and the ugly" of this life do follow us in the world to come. We may then shed many tears of regret, which Hashem will surely wipe away, but that doesn't mean that we will not still have to learn the substance of the lesson from the disobedience that caused these tears (Revelation 7:17; 21:4).

If we are truly sealed with the mark of the Messiah, let us make sure that in each day of this life, both our will and hands are synchronized with those of our Master. Then and only then will the prayer, "Your will be done, on earth as in heaven," be answered!

Hebrews 13:2   **Sukkhot 1** סוכות   **Tishrei 15/** טו בתישרי

But don't forget to be friendly to outsiders; for in so doing, some people, without knowing it, have entertained angels.

The Feasts of Tabernacle carries in itself a beautiful tradition of hospitality. The idea is to entertain a distinguished guest each night of the festival. These guests include in order, Abraham, Isaac, Jacob, Joseph, Moses, Aaron, King David, and Messiah. Of course, the patriarchs do not actually physically come to the sukkah, but their presence is invited through reading, talking, and learning about them.

Hospitality was a fundamental virtue at work in the Middle East of our patriarch Abraham. When a guest visited your house, he was automatically under your wings and protection. If an enemy came to hurt him, you were to use all resources at your disposal to protect your visitor. No matter what the cost, your company could find total sanctuary in your house. A very good example of that is found in the story of Lot who even offered his daughters to the people of Sodom in order to protect his angelic guests.

In traditional Jewish writings, Abraham is the gold standard of hospitality. To be invited to the table and tent of Abraham was a great honor. Whoever you were, he would treat you to the best of his flock as if you were a high dignitary. Tradition describes that the patriarch would send his servant Eleazer to the highways and byways—and we are talking great distances in the desert—to compel people to honor him by finding rest and restoration in his tent. In Middle Eastern tradition, guests didn't just stay for a cup of coffee and cookies to quickly be on their way. Their feet were washed; they maybe stayed several days at the host's expense while they, their company, and their animals were also cared for. Aside from Melchizedek, Abraham seemed to have been one of the rare persons acquainted with God. This act of hospitality from Abraham was his outreach program in the midst of an idolatrous world. He would invite people and treat them like God would. Abraham wanted to show people the favor of Hashem.

Come to think of it, as we invite Abraham as a guest in our sukkah on this first day of Tabernacles, we must remember that he invited us first as guests at his table. The tent of Abraham represents God's favor as well as an invitation to come to the Messiah, his descendant. Abraham was Hashem's representative and prophet, and through him, all the families of the earth are blessed (Genesis 28:14). The whole world is blessed as they come to the table of Abraham to have a foretaste of the world to come. That is why in the synagogues of Paul's day, those of the Gentiles who joined themselves to the God of Israel were called "those of the family of Abraham" (Acts 13:26).

May those that meet us on our daily path and who get to know us as the children and representatives of the Almighty Creator of heaven and earth also find in us, and through us, the bounty, the beauty, and the restoration Messiah would give them. May all those who come in touch with us get a foretaste, however small, of the world to come, of what Hashem has prepared for them.

Like with Abraham, may this be our witness, our sharing of his favor and light in this sad and dark world.

My Personal Thoughts

Hebrews 11:19   **Sukkhot 2 סוכות**   **Tishrei 16/ טז בתישרי**

For he had concluded that God could even raise people from the dead! And, figuratively speaking, he did so receive him.

Of all the patriarchs, Isaac may be the most mysterious. It is a miracle that he even lived at all. He was born out of time from a sterile womb; his life was challenged by his stepmother and stepbrother; and if that was not enough, God asked for his life on the altar of sacrifice. The big question though is, "What happened to him after Mt. Moriah?"

On their way to Mt. Moriah, the text constantly reminds us of Isaac's presence alongside Abraham. Before the last stretch climb, Abraham even asks for the servants to wait at the foot of the mountain until he and the lad return to them. But after the offering scene, all we are told is that Abraham returned to the servants and went to live in Beersheba (Genesis 22:19). But what happened to Isaac? We do not hear of him until Abraham decides to marry him off over twenty years later (Genesis 24:3; 25:20) when we are told that Rebecca falls off her camel when she sees him (Genesis 24:64). Some translations write that Rebecca *dismounted* her camel, but the Hebrew says *fall*.

Many Jewish sages have pondered the question and came up with various answers and parables about it. Here is one that I find most amazing. The hope of every Jewish father is for his son to become a Torah scholar, so a Jewish scholar supposed that Abraham may have sent Isaac to Salem to learn at the feet of Melchizedek, or even went to heaven to learn at the feet of Messiah. Of all of them, I like the one about Isaac going to learn at the feet of Messiah in heaven. The parable tells us that at the offering scene, the knife touched Isaac's throat who then, for a moment only, died, but revived right away and went to heaven to learn Torah. He would only return later to marry the bride brought to him from Babylon, by Eleazer—which means: my God is my help—Abraham's servant.

In Jewish literature, Isaac foreshadows the Messiah. We talk about it every year with the Passover Afikomen. It seems that the early believers knew about the parable of this old rabbi. The Book of Hebrews says,

> For he had concluded that God could even raise people from the dead! And, figuratively speaking, he did so receive him. (Hebrews 11:19)

The Greek text from which this verse is taken doesn't say *figuratively speaking* but, *as in a parable*. Abraham must have had mixed feelings; even knowing that his son was a *goner*, he still told the people at the foot of the mountain that he would return with him.

What sounds amazing to me is that as a foreshadow of Messiah, the picture in this parable fits perfectly. Hasn't Messiah died on the wood, on Mt Moriah, resurrected right away, disappeared from the scene as he went to the Father, and he will return soon to marry his bride brought to him from Babylon—this world—by the *Ruach HaKodesh* רוח הקודש, (the Holy Spirit/ God's helper)?

My Personal Thoughts

_____

_____

_____

John 4:12   **Sukkhot 3** סוכות   **Tishrei 17/** יז בתישרי

You aren't greater than our father Ya`akov, are you?

Jacob has been honored in so many ways. The name given to him became the very name by which Hashem would later be identified: the God of Jacob, the God of Israel.

As such, the life of Jacob merges with the destiny of the country and the people bearing his name. His very birth springs from a potential annihilation and throughout his lifetime, he has to contend in order to inherit and keep what Hashem has rightfully given him. Later on, under the threats of his brother Esau, Jacob leaves his birthplace of Canaan for Babylon. There he finds employment with his uncle as a shepherd. He marries the two daughters of that same uncle and twenty-one years later secretly leaves with his new family to return to Canaan. As Jacob reaches the Land, before meeting his brother who stills seeks his life, an angelic host welcomes him. It is also at that time that a mysterious, powerful messenger meets Jacob, changes his name, and thereby his heart (Genesis 32).

Is it possible to not see in Jacob's life story the birth of the nation of Israel—who sprung out of Egyptian slavery and persecution, pursued by Pharaoh and fought by the Amalekites? Throughout its history, Israel always struggled to preserve its independence and autonomy, only to be expelled from its own country not for twenty-one years, but as of today, twenty-one centuries. Now Israel is returning to his land. There again, Esau meets him and wants to kill him. This battle will end in a bloody war with all the countries in the world gathered against Israel (Zechariah 12). At that time, the Messiah, Hashem's messianic messenger, will return and . . .

The rest of Jacob's story tells us the end from the beginning. Jacob prevails over the messianic messenger/wrestler. Jacob does not let him go; he hangs on to Messiah at any cost until he gets the blessing, causing him a deep wound in his thigh, thus transforming him into a new person. When Jacob, now called Israel, meets Esau, they make up and Israel enters Canaan, the Land of his future, the Land promised to his grandfather Abraham.

In the distance, we already hear the galloping hooves of the messenger's horse. He comes in greatness and strength from Bozrah in a garment dipped in blood (Isaiah 63:1). He will fight, wound, and bless Israel and change his heart as that of his brother; he will carry him to his country with an angelic welcoming committee.

That my friend is Messiah's roadmap to peace in the Middle East. May it come soon, even in our days.

My Personal Thoughts

_____

_____

_____

_____

_____

_____

_____

_____

Matthew 2:15   **Sukkhot 4 סוכות**   **Tishrei 18/ יח בתישרי**

Out of Egypt I called my son.

Just as the life of Jacob merges with the destiny of Israel, the life of Joseph, Jacob's son, merges with that of Yeshua.

Joseph was born of a barren womb and his brothers rejected his God-appointed leadership over them. When their jealousy got the better of them, they decided to throw him in a pit where according to Jewish literature, Joseph stayed three days and three nights. Later, they sold him as a slave telling his poor father Jacob that a wild beast had killed Joseph. As proof, the brothers brought to Jacob Joseph's famed coat soaked in the blood of a goat as a substitute to his own. Joseph then spent time in a prison where he became steward, to eventually rule over the gentile world of his day.

Doesn't that tell us of the story of Yeshua whose birth was also miraculous; whose God-appointed leadership was rejected by his brothers because of jealousy; who spent three days in a pit; who was sold for a price; who spent time in the prison ministering to the imprisoned spirits (1 Peter 3:19), and who later became the ruler over most the gentile world?

Since the life story of Joseph tells us of the beginning of Yeshua's life, could the end of it reveal to us the future? Wise King Solomon said, "What has been is what will be, what has been done is what will be done, and there is nothing new under the sun" (Ecclesiastes 1:9). We must not fail here to mention that not all of Joseph's brothers were against him. Benjamin was not part of the plot. Benjamin loved and believed in his big brother Joseph.

When Egypt faced a famine so dire that it threatened the very life of the Empire, God raised Joseph to save Egypt. The Egyptians looked to Joseph as he who saved them. Cana'an also suffered so Joseph's brothers came to buy grain from the new Egyptian viceroy, who was of course Joseph. The brothers didn't recognize him as he looked, acted, and spoke like an Egyptian. On the other hand, Joseph recognized his brothers and proceeded to test them by creating a situation where Benjamin would be enslaved. At that moment, Judah offered his own self as a ransom for the life of Benjamin. This showed Joseph the change of heart in his brother Judah who had been instrumental to his fate. Whereas before, Judah, his brother from Leah, sold Joseph the son of Rachel, to save his own inheritance, Judah was now ready to give his life to save his Benjamin, Joseph's brother from Rachel, and save his father from grief. At that time, Joseph revealed himself to them and said, "I am your brother, Joseph!"

What does this tell us? Who is Benjamin today? Would he be the Jew who did not reject Yeshua? Could he be the Messianic Jew? Will there then be a time in the soon future when Hashem will again test Judah, the brother who did not accept Joseph's leadership with Benjamin, the brother who did? In present-day Israel the conflict between Orthodox and Messianic Jews is fierce. It is a 2,000-year-old conflict. Will Judah pass the test so that eventually, Yeshua reveals himself to them and will say, "I am your brother, Yeshua!" The Tanach says he does.

May it come quickly, even in our day!

My Personal Thoughts

_____

_____

Luke 1:17   **Sukkhot 5** סוכות   **Tishrei 19/** יט בתישרי

He will go out ahead of ADONAI in the spirit and power of Eliyahu to turn the hearts of fathers to their children and the disobedient to the wisdom of the righteous, to make ready for ADONAI a people prepared.

As Moses foresees the rebellious future of the nation he helped birth, he speaks to the future generation that will see the most tragic punishment and the longest exile: the generation of the Master (Deuteronomy 32:5; Matthew 16:4). Moses tells the people, "Remember how the old days were; think of the years through all the ages. Ask your father—he will tell you; your leaders too—they will inform you" (Deuteronomy 32:7).

The Torah devotes whole chapters to genealogies. People used to memorize them. It was their main education, their link with the past and their guidance to the future. As these texts unfold, they teach us lessons. They help us peer into our ancestry and discover our personal fiber so to speak. It tells us who we are and where we're from, which in turn helps us to know where we should go and how to get there. Very important lessons are imbedded in the genealogies.

Today many people have what they call an identity crisis. This is the epitome of foolishness, but even more, of rebelliousness. We live in a generation that desperately tries to disconnect itself from its past. Since the 1960s, it seems that every generation tries to define itself as an antithesis to the one that birthed it. This creates a very unhealthy and unstable social and cultural environment.

Every generation stands on the shoulders of the former ones. Cars would never have filled our streets, appliances never found our homes, and computers never been on our desks if it were not for the ancients who gave us the wheel, mathematics, and taught us how to harness electricity.

Come to think of it, this rebelliousness goes back much further, especially when it comes to our faith. Already in the second century CE the messianic movement among the Gentiles defined itself against the Jewish matrix that birthed it. This eventually created a religion with no legs and no feet: a house with no foundation (Luke 6:47–49). As always though, as depressing as looking into the past can be, the Torah offers us the hope of a more connected future when in the Messianic Age, generations will be reconnected (Malachi 4:6; Luke 1:17).

Today, may we hear Moses' cry and learn!

My Personal Thoughts

_____

_____

_____

_____

_____

_____

_____

_____

Hebrews 5:4   **Sukkhot 6 סוכות**   **Tishrei 20/ כ בתישרי**

And no one takes this honor upon himself, rather, he is called by God, just as Aharon was.

Aaron and Moses may have been brothers but they each had a very different childhood. Aaron was raised by father Amram and mother Jochebed, who was also Amram's aunt (Exodus 6:20). While Moses was raised in the cool shade of Pharaoh's palace, received an education, and became an army officer and a skillful international diplomat, Aaron escaped Pharaoh's deathly edict by little and learned to live as a slave making bricks in the hot sun for Pharaoh's building projects.

Through the story of Moses and Aaron, we are given the definition of a prophet. Moses felt inadequate to speak to the people of God, so Hashem sent Moses' brother saying, "He will be your spokesman to the people, in effect; for you, he will be a mouth; and for him, you will be like God" (Exodus 4:16). Aaron's job was to be Moses' mouth not only to Hashem's children, but also to the incredulous world of his day: "And ADONAI said to Moses, "I have put you in the place of God to Pharaoh, and Aharon your brother will be your prophet" (Exodus 7:1). According to these statements, the definition of a prophet is someone who has the ability to effectively communicate God's messages to a desired audience.

Later Aaron was given another function to execute for the people of Hashem. He became high priest. As high priest, he continued his function as Moses' mouthpiece and executive. People also came to him to find the will of God, which Aaron communicated using the Urim and Thummim, the stones on Aaron's breastplate by which he judged Israel:

> You are to put the urim and the tumim in the breastplate for judging; they will be over Aharon's heart when he goes into the presence of ADONAI. Thus Aharon will always have the means for making decisions for the people of Isra'el over his heart when he is in the presence of ADONAI. (Exodus 28:30)

When Aaron spoke by the Spirit, the right one lit up. As you can see, for the Hebrews, prophecy was a very pragmatic matter. The children of Israel didn't always obey the words they heard, but there was very little doubt as to who said them.

As a high priest, Aaron led the priesthood. The priesthood dealt with the sins of Israel. Though punishments and restitutions were to be executed as the result of sinful acts, offerings also had to be brought to the Temple for the restitution of fellowship with ADONAI broken because of sin. The *offerer* killed the animal, not the priest. The priest only brought the blood to the altar. Also, once a year, Aaron the High Priest brought an offering for the whole nation of Israel in the Holy of Holies of the Tabernacle/Temple. In a certain sense, the function of the priesthood served to remind us of our sinful state; it convicted us of sin and helped us make peace with Hashem. In Talmudic writings, Aaron is not only known as an accessory to peace between man and God, but also as a peacemaker among mankind (Psalm 133).

Aaron's role was therefore one of communicator between Hashem and us, and thus, we are reminded of our sin. How like the *Ruach-HaKodesh* רוח הקודש, (the Holy Spirit) Aaron was!

My Personal Thoughts

_____

_____

Under the Vine

Revelation 5:5   **Sukkhot 7 סוכות**   **Tishrei 21/ כא בתישרי**

One of the elders said to me, "Don't cry. Look, the Lion of the tribe of Y'hudah, the Root of David, has won the right to open the scroll and its seven seals."

King David is our penultimate guest for this season of Tabernacles. The ruddy looking David became the standard by which all ensuing Judean kings would be measured.

Finishing the job started by Joshua, King David is the one who finally completed the conquest of the Land. He subjugated Israel's neighbors, brought Jerusalem under his control, and got rid of idolatry. These were his greatest accomplishments along with planning and financing the building of the Temple and organizing its priesthood and liturgy.

A careful study of David's life teaches us about Messiah. David's older brothers despised him; when Samuel visited David's father, Jesse, in search for a king, David was passed up. His brothers shamed him for his indignation about Goliath's challenge until the young shepherd boy showed them that the spirit of Hashem was with him. After he killed Israel's main enemy, David had to flee the country, and even spent time living with the gentile Philistines until such a day when he made his triumphal entry in Jerusalem. David also orchestrated bringing the Holy Ark to Jerusalem. All this speaks to us about Messiah who after slaying the devil fled the scene and even until today lives in exile alongside his people even though they ignore him. One day Yeshua will make a triumphal entry in Jerusalem where he will rebuild the temple. The ensuing period will be one resembling the Solomonic era. Israel will live in peace and prosperity and all the nations of the earth will come to bring it their glory as well as to hear the words of God. The prophet Zechariah tells us that at that time, under the threat of impending drought, all the nations will be required to come to Jerusalem for the Feast of Booths (Zechariah 14:16–19)!

David has been accused of having been a lenient father, that he didn't discipline his sons and therefore brought trouble to Israel. It could be so, but one must not forget that when he started making a family, the prophet Nathan stated that David's son would build the Temple and become the Messiah (2 Samuel 7), but David didn't know which of his five would fulfill this prophecy. To kill one of his sons could have been disastrous and would have thwarted God's plan. David felt responsible for his family, for the Jerusalem that God had given him, but also for the glorious future of the Jewish nation and its Messianic role of teaching about the one true God to the world.

Solomon may have built a temporary temple, but Yeshua, David's Messianic son, is now building the final Messianic Temple. He is doing it the same way he did it before. First he gathers his congregation out of Egypt, brings it to his place, then builds the Temple. For over 2,000 years now Messiah has been gathering a congregation of Jews and Gentiles and he will eventually bring them to his place: Jerusalem. He will rebuild the Jerusalem Temple, which will then truly become a House of Prayer for the whole world.

May it come speedily even in our days!

My Personal Thoughts

_____

_____

_____

_____

Luke 2:21 **Sukkhot 8** סוכות **Tishrei 22/** כב בתישרי

On the eighth day, when it was time for his b'rit-milah, he was given the name Yeshua, which is what the angel had called him before his conception.

We are now drawing to the last day of the Feast of Tabernacles. The traditional guest to receive in our midst on this day is Messiah. A Messianic tradition holds that this eighth day of the Feast of Tabernacles is the day of Yeshua's *brit-milah* ברית מילה (Luke 2:21). Ritual circumcision is an outward sign of belonging to Hashem. One of the ideas of circumcision is to create an outward sign in our flesh that represents our belonging to God. We alter our body so that we literally become a new creature (2 Corinthians 5:17); quite an idea! People couldn't claim to believe in the God of heaven in a solely ethereal fashion. They couldn't just quote a statement of faith or an affirmation. They had to be able to present a sign in their flesh that proved and showed that they were different from the rest of the world.

In his letters to the Messianic congregation in Diaspora, Paul told the Gentiles that joined themselves to the Jewish Messianic movement, "Also it was in union with him that you were circumcised with a circumcision done by the Messiah" (Colossians 2:11). Paul therefore did not enforced physical circumcision on these Gentiles who turned to the God of Israel through Yeshua, but he did nevertheless expect the proof of their commitment through an outward change of lifestyle. They could not get away by just quoting an affirmation, statement, or creed as a proof of their faith. They had to show that they drew away from their idolatrous former lifestyles. In first century ethics, to turn away from Roman idols unto the God of Israel was as dangerous as today when a Muslim becomes a follower of Yeshua. Since the God of Israel was not recognized by Rome, a person could be prosecuted for the crime of atheism. Paul made no mention of circumcision issues to Jewish believers on Messiah. He didn't need to since they already had the commandment in the Torah.

Jewish circumcisions are usually followed by festivities among relatives and friends, following the traditions of the eighth day of Tabernacles.

When after her purification Miriam came to present her first-born to God in the Temple, an old man called Simeon, took the baby in his arms and blessed God saying the following words: "for I have seen with my own eyes your yeshu`ah (ישועה salvation ending with the Hebrew letter 'ה', thus a play on words with the similarly pronounced name of the Master Yeshua, ישוע without the ending letter 'ה', and which means 'he will save'), which you prepared in the presence of all peoples — a light that will bring revelation to the Goyim and glory to your people Isra'el." (Luke 2:29–32) Simeon said that Yeshua will be a light for revelation to the Gentiles. Therefore on this day of Yeshua's circumcision, on this day when his flesh enters the Covenant of Israel as a Jew, it is not only incumbent for Jews to rejoice, but also for the Gentiles who know him. Yeshua is the Jew mentioned by the prophet Zechariah—the one whose *tzit-tzit* (the name given to fringes the children of Israel are required to wear on the corner of their clothes Numbers 15:38) the nations would take hold of because they heard that God was with him (Zechariah 8:23).

Hear, O nations this lone baby's cry in the Temple. Hear, O nations the groaning of he who brings all people into covenant with the Almighty. From the very beginning of his life, the cuts in his body and the drawing of his blood are signs in his flesh of his invitation at the table of the Almighty. Will you come to him? Will you change your lives and your habits so you can be found sitting at the table of the God of Israel? Will you follow him, live like him, and be found worthy of the high calling whereby he has called you?

26

John 1:14   **Simchat Torah/ שמחת תורה**   **Tishrei 23/ בג בתישרי**

The Word became a human being and lived with us, and we saw his Sh'khinah, the Sh'khinah of the Father's only Son, full of grace and truth.

Today is the day after the last day of the Festival of Tabernacles. This day is called in Hebrew *Simchat Torah שמחת תורה Simcha* means: joy, *Torah* means: teaching/instruction. Translated into English, that day could be called: *The Day of the Rejoicing of the Torah/Teaching.*

Isn't it strange to give a human virtue to something that is not biologically human? O my friend, come with me and peer in the wisdom of the sages of old. There is a tradition in Judaism that on the twenty-third day of the month of *Tishrei,* in synagogues all around the world, Torah scrolls are taken out of their arks and put in the arms of congregants. On that day, you see otherwise austere rabbis laugh and dance with Torah scrolls in their arms. People then have a great party surrounding the dancing of the Torah. What is this party all about?

Upon returning to Jerusalem from Babylon, Ezra the High Priest understood that the country had gone into exile because of their disobedience to God's commands. He then felt concerned for the people. He believed that they needed more exposure to the Torah so he established a national reading schedule. This schedule took the people of Israel through weekly sections that completed the reading of the Torah and most of the prophets' in a year's time. The twenty-third of *Tishrei* is the day when this schedule is completed, and Torah scrolls are rolled back to their beginnings to start a new cycle of reading and studying.

It is said that on that day, the Torah rejoices that it has been read and studied through for a whole year. The Torah is now looking forward to teaching God's people again for another reading cycle. The Torah wants to dance, laugh, and rejoice but it has no mouth, no legs, and no arms. The Torah wants to dance, but it has no body.

On *Simchat Torah*, we take the Torah in our arms and we become the singing and rejoicing mouth, the dancing legs, and the waving arms of the Torah. In essence, we give a body and become an incarnation of the Torah to allow it to dance, to rejoice in us, and through us.

This application of the rejoicing in the Torah shows that Jewish sages understood the idea of the Torah incarnate in us as Jeremiah taught it (Jeremiah 31:31–40). All the more, it shows that they understood the idea that the Messiah would be a Son of Man—which would be translated into Hebrew as Son of Adam—who would be the incarnation of the Torah, of the Commandments of God spoken at Mount Horeb, Mt. Sinai.

Yeshua, the son of Joseph and Miriam was truly the Son of Adam who became the incarnation of the Torah, who also lives in us causing us to dance, laugh, and rejoice.

My Personal Thoughts

_____

_____

_____

_____

_____

_____

Luke 24:50   **Tishrei 24/** כד בתישרי

Then he led them out as far as Bethany, and lifting up his hands he blessed them.

In all things Yeshua was a 'prophet' like Moses. Before ascending the mountain where Hashem would bury him, Moses blessed the people of Israel with a personal blessing to each one of the tribes (Deuteronomy 33:1). In the same manner, before ascending to the Father, Yeshua lifted up his hands and blessed his disciples. We do not know what he said but the description of his actions in the text gives us a clue.

In the Book of Numbers, Hashem gives instructions on how his people should be blessed. Aaron and the Levites—Moses was also a Levite—were to lift their two hands up in the air in the form of the Hebrew letter *shin* שׁין in representation of one of the names of God: *El Shaddai* אל שׁדי, Then they were to say,

> May ADONAI bless you and keep you. May ADONAI make his face shine on you and show you his favor. May ADONAI lift up his face toward you and give you peace. (Numbers 6:24–26)

In Mishnaic writings, this blessing known as the Aaronic blessing, was also called the *Blessing of the Lifting of the Hands*. So every time the Bible text mentions that the priests lifted up their hands to bless the people, we know what they did and said. It is therefore very likely that this is also the very blessing wherewith Yeshua blessed his disciples as he lifted up his hands before ascending to the Father (Luke 24:50–51).

When Yeshua prayed, he was praying for his Father to bless and keep us, for Hashem to shine upon us, for God to be gracious unto us, to lift his countenance upon us, and give us peace. This is really the whole reason why Messiah came: to put us back in good standing with the Father through the agency of his righteousness. The Aaronic blessing therefore can only be fulfilled through the agency of Messiah. When we pray it on people we pray that they find Messiah.

As it was then, so it is now. From creation's days, the Messiah has been the Father's executive agent (John 1:1–3). Even before the days when he came to the Tabernacle with us (John 1:14) the Messiah was alive, well, and active. It is he who came to Abram in the Plain of Mamre, he who spoke to Moses on Mount Horeb, he who fought with Jacob, and he who appeared to many people doing many mighty acts even before the time of his sojourn and great manifestation on earth. Forever and always, he has been the "radiance of the glory of God and the exact imprint of his nature, and he upholds the universe by the word of his power" (Hebrews 1:3).

As Messiah prayed this blessing over his disciples before ascending to his Father and our Father (John 20:17), doing just as Moses did unto the children of Israel before he left them, may we receive the imprint of Messiah; may we be formed, and conformed according to his will by the work of his righteousness. May we be yielded clay that we may become like him.

My Personal Thoughts

_____

_____

_____

_____

John 1:1–3

In the beginning was the Word, and the Word was with God, and the Word was God.

Here is John's prelude to his accounts of the life of Yeshua. He starts the chronicle not with "Once upon a time . . ." but rather in the same manner and wording as the chronicles of creation, with the words: "In the beginning . . ." The Genesis account tells us of creation in the following terms,

> In the beginning God created the heavens and the earth. The earth was unformed and void, darkness was on the face of the deep, and the Spirit of God hovered over the surface of the water. (Genesis 1:1–2)

The consistency of the imagery is perfect. In the beginning, when the earth was without form, the spirit of Hashem hovered over the face of the earth. About fifteen hundred years later, at the time of another beginning, we see a repetition of this imagery when Noah's dove hovers upon the face of the water (Genesis 8:8–9). At first she could find nothing where to rest her feet. The Spirit of God always looks for someone, a host to rest upon. Unlike the raven that did not come back, the dove couldn't just rest with death and corruption. At the opportune time though, she found the olive tree and brought a torn branch to Noah (Genesis 8).

At another time when the world was in the confusion of the *Pax Romana* (enforced peace), there was another primeval beginning. In the latter days of John the disciple, Yeshua introduced himself as the beginning of the creation of God (Revelation 3:14). That is why at the beginning of his ministry, the spirit of God also hovered upon the immersion waters of the Master (Matthew 3:16); a beautiful fulfillment of Isaiah's Messianic prophetic words, "And the Spirit of ADONAI shall rest upon him" (Isaiah 11:2).

Noah's dove rested upon he who is called the branch (Zechariah 6:12), the *torn branch* of the olive tree of Israel. Through him the nations learn to praise the God of Israel as the rest of Isaiah's oracle says,

> On that day the root of Yishai, which stands as a banner for the peoples—the Goyim will seek him out, and the place where he rests will be glorious. On that day ADONAI will raise his hand again, a second time, to reclaim the remnant of his people who remain from Ashur, Egypt, Patros, Ethiopia, `Eilam, Shin`ar, Hamat and the islands in the sea. He will hoist a banner for the Goyim, assemble the dispersed of Isra'el, and gather the scattered of Y'hudah from the four corners of the earth. (Isaiah 11:10–12)

My Personal Thoughts

_____

_____

_____

_____

_____

_____

John 1:4–5, 9   **Tishrei 26/ כו בתישרי**

In him was life, and the life was the light of mankind. The light shines in the darkness, and the darkness has not suppressed it. This was the true light, which gives light to everyone entering the world.

The first creation mentioned in the first chapter of the Book of Genesis is the primeval light. The Hebrew gives two different words for *light* in this chapter. The *or* אור of verse three refers to the primeval light of the beginning of creation, and the *ma'or* מאור of verse fourteen refers to the two great luminaries in the firmament.

The primeval light was the beginning of God's creation. Without it, nothing would have been created. The Hebrew word translated as *beginning* is actually a derivative of another Hebrew word *rosh* ראש, or 'head.' In Hebraic understanding, a *beginning* is understood as the *head* of something, like the engine is the beginning/head of a train. It leads the rest and without it nothing goes anywhere. Yeshua introduced himself to the Laodicea congregation as the *beginning/head* of Hashem's creation (Revelation 3:14), the *head* without which nothing else moves or exists.

John's introduction of Yeshua in the first chapter of his chronicle mirrors the account in Genesis of creation. The *word* John referred to was the Aramaic *memrah* ממרה of Jewish Targumic literature. This *memrah* existed with the Almighty as his executive agent, as the *head* of creation, the light by which everything else would be done right from the beginning. How fitting this is with the account of John who from his studies under the sages of Israel understood what they said by the Talmudic statement that, "God said 'let there be light' (Genesis 1:3) to reveal that God will ultimately illuminate Israel with the Light of Messiah." This was John's hinted message embedded in the format of his introduction. He was mirroring the text of the first chapter of Genesis. John wanted to reveal that Yeshua was the incarnation of that Messianic primeval light. God revealed the light in the very beginning of creation.

Hashem also revealed a light provoked phenomenon at another beginning through Noah's rainbow, and finally revealed it as a human 2,000 years ago fulfilling the promise made in Mt. Horeb that Hashem will come live among his people (Exodus 25:8).

As we try to do things in our own effort, as we attempt to lift ourselves up by our own bootstraps by trying to change our environment, may we learn to realize that nothing is done nor can be done without the light of Messiah. He is the *beginning/head* without which nothing else is done; by him and him only can anything be done. He pulls, and as we yield to his command we let ourselves be pulled.

May we learn to be fully satisfied simply basking in the light of his greatness and beauty, solely obeying his commands. Who knows, if we do, it may actually change the world for the better!

My Personal Thoughts

_____

_____

_____

_____

_____

John 7:37   **Tishrei 27/ כז בתישרי**

If anyone is thirsty, let him keep coming to me and drinking!

This world can be compared to a giant outdoors market place not unlike those you see in Europe. The merchants are all shouting to advertise their wares and their foods. Water bearers also invite people to quench their thirst at their brews. The prophet Isaiah walks around the marketplace and observes people buying food that does not satisfy and water that does not quench. These vital items are also priced way above their actual cost. Frustrated the prophet cries,

> All you who are thirsty, come to the water! You without money, come, buy, and eat! Yes, come! Buy wine and milk without money—it's free! Why spend money for what isn't food, your wages for what doesn't satisfy? Listen carefully to me, and you will eat well, you will enjoy the fat of the land. (Isaiah 55:1–2)

Such is the world today. Everyone competes in the market of ideas, philosophies, and religions. As a humble merchant among them the Spirit of God also

> calls aloud in the open air and raises her voice in the public places; she calls out at streetcorners and speaks out at entrances to city gates: "How long, you whose lives have no purpose, will you love thoughtless living? How long will scorners find pleasure in mocking? How long will fools hate knowledge?" (Proverbs 1:20–22)

How pathetic that Hashem, that he who offers the only food that satisfies and the only water that quenches, has to humble himself to beg and shout for our attention amidst a market of lies and falsehoods. Yet he does. He does in Mashiach who "made himself of no reputation" (Philippians 2:7, KJV), that he may reach us with what he knows we need, even when we seem distracted by the shiny plastic pretend gold of man's philosophies and religions. When will we let go of the junk jewelry and reach for the real pearl of the Kingdom of God, even at the cost of losing everything else, of losing the wealth that does not satisfy (Matthew 13:35–36)?

Hear his Voice now, As Abraham who was known to send Eleazer his servant (Eleazer means: My God is my help) in the highways and the byways to invite perfect strangers into his master's tent so he could host them and tell them about the magnificent *host* whose world we enjoy. Messiah daily sends the Spirit of God to shout in our ears saying,

> Everyone who drinks this water will get thirsty again, but whoever drinks the water I will give him will never be thirsty again! On the contrary, the water I give him will become a spring of water inside him, welling up into eternal life! (John 4:13–14)

And again,

> See, I have prepared my dinner, my oxen and my fat calves have been slaughtered, and everything is ready. Come to the wedding feast. (Matthew 22:4)

Will it be also said of us, "but they paid no attention" (Matthew 22:5)?

My Personal Thoughts

_____

_____

31

Matthew 24:37   **Tishrei 28/ כח בתישרי**

For the Son of Man's coming will be just as it was in the days of Noach

The Master compared the coming apocalyptic events surrounding his return to the times of Noah (Matthew 24:37). Much teaching has been drawn from this comparison, but one in particular may need to be reviewed, the one surrounding the idea of *left behind*, where our Master says, "Then there will be two men in a field—one will be taken and the other left behind. There will be two women grinding flour at the mill—one will be taken and the other left behind" (Matthew 24:40–41).

This passage is usually viewed as the people taken being those going to be with the Master (1 Thessalonians 4:17), while the ones remaining on earth endure the final wrath of God. The disciples felt that Yeshua's statement was important so they asked for clarification. They asked him, "Where, Lord?" To which Yeshua answered, "Wherever there's a dead body, that's where the vultures gather." (Luke 17:37). (Other English translations say 'eagles', but the Hebrew word used in the text is *nesher* נשר, which can be translated as either *eagle* or *vulture*.)

The *vultures* referred to by the Master give us an invaluable clue as to the meaning of the verse. The Master uses the Days of Noah as a microcosm foreshadowing future events. As floodwaters rose on the earth, many corpses floated to the surface becoming food for scavenger birds such as vultures. Both Ezekiel and John had visions of end-time events where scavengers came to clean up the mess left by an apocalyptic war. Here is Ezekiel's:

> As for you, human, ADONAI Elohim says that you are to speak to all kinds of birds and to every wild animal as follows: Assemble yourselves and come, gather yourselves from all around for the sacrifice I am preparing for you, a great sacrifice on the mountains of Isra'el, where you can eat flesh and drink blood! (Ezekiel 39:17)

And now John's:

> Then I saw an angel standing in the sun, and he cried out in a loud voice to all the birds that fly about in mid-heaven, "Come, gather together for the great feast God is giving" (Revelation 19:17)

Applying Yeshua's statement to his own explanation, we can easily conclude that the ones remaining are in fact the ones who will enjoy Yeshua's Kingdom on earth (Matthew 6:10), while the others will be taken to a less pleasant future by the birds of prey.

The Kingdom of God is not somewhere in space. It is on the earth. We may only have a little bit of it right now, like a guaranty (Ephesians 1:14) that we find in obeying his commandments, but one day it will cover the earth as waters cover the sea (Isaiah 11:9).

On that day, do you really want to be 'left behind'?

My Personal Thoughts

_____

_____

_____

_____

1 Peter 2:9   **Tishrei 29/** כט בתישרי

But you are a chosen people, the King's cohanim, a holy nation, a people for God to possess!

Whereas evolution wants to tell us that life started sporadically anywhere and at anytime, Hashem tells us that he is the author of life. He also tells us that he started life in one place, at one time, and that the earth is fully populated from one man: Adam (Genesis 1). All of us are related to Adam through one of the sons of Noah. Japheth fathered the Caucasian race; Ham the black race, and from Shem came all those related to the Asian races including our father Abraham (Genesis 10).

As it is in the physical, so it is in the spiritual. Whereas New Age teachings try to teach us that all the gods worshipped on earth are individual, local, and cultural deities and should be respected as such, the *Tanach* תנך teaches us that faith solely comes from the God of Israel, and that all the others are idols designed to snare the heart of man away from the one true God who created the heavens and the earth (Deuteronomy 7:16).

In fact, according to the text, the goal is that, as the tribe of Levi was established as the priesthood for Israel, Israel will eventually be established as the priesthood for the whole world. God has even divided the world according to the numbers of the children of Israel (Deuteronomy 32:8). Jewish sages claim that number to be seventy; why?

The children of Israel were seventy when they entered Egypt (Genesis 46:27). Also in Genesis 10, we read the list of the seventy sons—and grandsons—of Noah. This all may be arguable, but the facts remain that as physical humanity comes from one man, the spiritual faith also comes from one man, Abraham, solely through whom all the families of the earth are blessed with the knowledge of God, through his son: Yeshua from Nazareth (Genesis 12:3).

This gives a whole new theme to the idea of being in Messiah. In the days of Yeshua there were only two types of people on earth: those who knew Hashem and those who didn't. The children of Israel, who are the children of Abraham, already knew Hashem. They had been introduced to him at Mt Horeb long before Yeshua's manifestation on earth, while the rest of the world remained in the darkness of ignorance and idolatry for another several hundred years. As Moses received the mission to Israel, Yeshua initiated the mission to the Gentiles, which Paul successfully conducted.

This all should give a new sense of mission to the idea of being grafted into the olive tree of Israel as Paul puts it (Romans 11). Before Yeshua, only people from Israel who knew God could exercise spiritual leadership within the congregation, but when one is grafted into Israel through Messiah, he, along with Israel, becomes a recipient of the promise made to Moses to be part of a nation of priests (Exodus 19:6; 1 Peter 2:9). In fact, anyone who through Messiah becomes grafted into Israel also becomes a part of God's peculiar nation, what he called, "His portion" (Deuteronomy 9–10).

May we be found worthy of the great calling whereas he has called us!

My Personal Thoughts

_____

_____

_____

_____

Matthew 15:4   **Tishrei 30/** ל בתישרי

> *For God said, 'Honor your father and mother,' and 'Anyone*
> *who curses his father or mother must be put to death.'*

The Torah tells us that after the Great Flood, Noah was a farmer and the first to plant a vineyard. We are told that,

> He drank so much of the wine that he got drunk and lay uncovered in his tent. Ham, the father of Kena`an, saw his father shamefully exposed, went out and told his two brothers. Shem and Yefet took a cloak, put it over both their shoulders, and, walking backward, went in and covered their naked father. Their faces were turned away, so that they did not see their father lying there shamefully exposed. When Noach awoke from his wine, he knew what his youngest son had done to him. He said, "Cursed be Kena`an; he will be a servant of servants to his brothers." (Genesis 9:21–25)

What Ham did was very serious. Many have speculated as to the actions that caused Noah to so severely curse his grandson for the sake of his son's actions, but the Bible tells us exactly what happened, and if it does, why speculate?

What the text tells us about Ham is that he saw the nakedness of his father and told his two brothers outside; that when Ham saw his father in a vulnerable disgraceful position, he went and publicized it. His brothers to the contrary, going in and out of the tent with their back toward their father so that they would not see him, respectfully covered his shame with a blanket of discretion.

Today's lack of high reverence and respect towards parents and elders is not seen as a very serious sin; that's why we feel the need to find something more, something else that is not in the text in order to justify Noah's strong punishment of Ham. But according to Biblical standards, honoring parents is what caused longevity and prosperity in the Land. The idea also meant to care for them in their old age as they cared for us in our young age.

As young children we adore our parents like gods, but as we grow older, we become critical of them and see their faults. Should we then go and gossip about them to others publicizing their shortcomings? Or should we respect them by doing what love does, which is to "cover all kinds of transgressions" (Proverbs 10:12)?

We wonder today at our kids' attitudes towards us, but maybe they are emulating our very own attitudes towards our parents. How do we talk about or treat their grandparents in front of them? This is a commandment without if, ands, or buts, without the option of "only if my parents are respectable and honorable." We are not asked to obey them, only to respect and honor them, as well as care for them in their old age.

A very important blessing that influenced all of history until today ensued from Shem and Japheth's discreet and respectful actions. Hashem said,

> Then he said, "Blessed be ADONAI, the God of Shem; Kena`an will be their servant. May God enlarge Yefet; he will live in the tents of Shem, but Kena`an will be their servant. (Genesis 9:26–27)

Indeed, the way we treat and honor our earthly parents is a hint about our relationship with our heavenly Father.

34

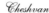

Cheshvan

*A father and a son
walk up a mountain.
One reveals the other
One brings in the other
This is the Messianic
truth of Cheshvan!*

John 1:18 (DHE)   Cheshvan 1/ א בחשון

No one has ever seen God; the only son who is in the Father's lap has made him known.

We all want peace in the world. The Torah teaches us that peace comes from studying its precepts. Foreseeing the role of the Torah in the World to Come, Isaiah prophesizes and says, "All your children will be taught by ADONAI; your children will have great peace" (Isaiah 54:13). (The Hebrew text uses the Tetragrammaton for the word ADONAI in this verse; it therefore refers to direct interaction with Hashem.)

John the disciple claims that in this present time, "No one has ever seen God," but Isaiah prophesies that in the established Messianic Age "your teacher will no longer hide himself, but with your own eyes you will see your teacher." In another place the prophet also adds, "Then the glory of ADONAI will be revealed; all humankind together will see it" (John 1:18; Isaiah 30:20; 40:5).

Yeshua made mention of this prophecy from Isaiah. When speaking of the dynamics of his relationship with the one whom he called Father, Yeshua compared himself to manna coming from heaven. In the Talmud, bread and rain from heaven also symbolize the coming of the Torah: the word of God's teaching coming to God's people. Yeshua compared his teaching of God—whom he had seen (John 1:18)—to the manna that came down from heaven to feed the people in the desert. When people who had known Yeshua from a young age challenged his claim of coming down from heaven, Yeshua, who is at the Father's side (John 1:18), answered using Isaiah's prophecy and said,

> It is written in the Prophets, 'They will all be taught by ADONAI.' Everyone who listens to the Father and learns from him comes to me. Not that anyone has seen the Father except the one who is from God—he has seen the Father. Yes, indeed! I tell you, whoever trusts has eternal life: I am the bread which is life. Your fathers ate the man in the desert; they died. But the bread that comes down from heaven is such that a person may eat it and not die. I am the living bread that has come down from heaven; if anyone eats this bread, he will live forever. Furthermore, the bread that I will give is my own flesh; and I will give it for the life of the world." (John 6:45–51)

In essence, Yeshua was saying, "In me is fulfilled Isaiah's prophecy" (Isaiah 54:13). Since no one can see the Father and live, if all God's children are to be taught of the Father, it needs to be done by proxy. "I am the *proxy,*" Yeshua says. This resonates with the words the children of Israel said: "Let me not hear again the voice of ADONAI my God or see this great fire any more, lest I die." Hashem responded with, "They are right in what they are saying." So to solve the problem, Hashem then added, "I will raise up for them a prophet like you from among their kinsmen. I will put my words in his mouth, and he will tell them everything I order him" (Deuteronomy 18:16–18).

May we all be taught the words of the Father through his Messiah. Only then will we finally have peace in our hearts . . . and in the world!

My Personal Thoughts

_____

_____

_____

Hebrews 11:8   Cheshvan 2/ ב בחשון

By trusting, Avraham obeyed, after being called to go out to a place which God would give him as a possession; indeed, he went out without knowing where he was going.

Do you hear the voice? Do you hear the call? How many times does Hashem call us to go somewhere with him but we don't go?

He is a jealous God (Exodus 20:5). To be with him requires a total abandonment of everything else. He requires that we completely strip ourselves of our personal attempts at righteousness, protection, security, and sustenance. He wants us to lie bare and prostrated before him, down, down to our utmost vulnerable point because without faith, it is impossible to please him (Hebrews 11:6).

Where is Hashem taking you today? Has he asked you like Abraham to, "Get yourself out of your country, away from your kinsmen and away from your father's house, and go to the land that I will show you" (Genesis 12:1)? Has he asked you to leave the comfortable place of familiar surroundings, to venture out from the comfort zone of familiar beliefs and into the unknown? When he does, are you willing to go like Abraham or do you whine because things are not 'the way they used to be'?

In this day of fundamental changes in the society of man, in this time of economic, political, and societal international upheavals we may feel as though the rug has been pulled out from under us. We may feel insecure and uncomfortable. For the person of weak faith, it is a test, but for the person of mature faith, it is a joy. The world is becoming a place we are not familiar with and God forbid that we should become at ease with the direction it is taking.

It is now high time for us to do like Abraham and hear the call of Hashem's voice,

> For he is our God, and we are the people in his pasture, the sheep in his care. If only today you would listen to his voice: "Don't harden your hearts, as you did at M'rivah, as you did on that day at Massah in the desert, when your fathers put me to the test; they challenged me, even though they saw my work." (Psalm 95:7–9)

Let's go with Abraham, away from our comfort zone and walk in the new dimensions of faith he leads us to; who knows, it may take us to the Promised Land!

My Personal Thoughts

_____

_____

_____

_____

_____

_____

_____

Hebrews 11:9–10   **Cheshvan 3/ ג בחשון**

By trusting, he lived as a temporary resident in the Land of the promise, as if it were not his, staying in tents with Yitz'chak and Ya`akov, who were to receive what was promised along with him. For he was looking forward to the city with permanent foundations, of which the architect and builder is God.

We are on a journey. We presently live as strangers in a world that will eventually be under our ruling. Until that day we must not lose the vision. Oh, how easy it is in the constant uncertainly of the roaming to want to settle down somewhere, anywhere, even before the fullness of Hashem's vision is accomplished in our lives.

Both Lot and Abraham prospered, but their reactions were different. The Tanach tells us that they increased so much that the Land could not bear them. Their servants quarreled. This situation resulted from prosperity. Prosperity often brings with it discontentment and a perverted sense of justice and fairness. Worst of all, there is a tendency to associate success with numbers. We *count* and we become so obsessed with numbers that eventually we lose the original vision. Little by little, we lose the true perspective: that individual people are more important than numbers and wealth. That's what happened to Lot as he was lured by the prosperous life of the city folks to the area of Sodom. He was tempted by their vain lifestyle. Little did he know that as in the case of this generation, Sodom's false sense of security was about to be shaken. Its days were numbered.

Abraham on the other hand kept the heavenly vision. He was not at home in this world; he had already found that the prosperity of his former worldly station had left him feeling spiritually empty. He therefore followed Hashem looking for the true riches that come with desiring and putting first the Kingdom of God. The king of Sodom even tried to reward Abraham, but again Abraham made the right choice and turned himself towards the true King, Melchizedek, the King of Salem; the King of Jerusalem.

As we hear his voice today, may we learn to turn away from the call of this world's false wealth. May we reject its adulterated sense of justice and fairness where gains and numbers are more important than people. May we turn our heads instead towards the obedience of the true king who owns the true wealth of the true Kingdom that will last forever.

My Personal Thoughts

_____

_____

_____

_____

_____

_____

_____

_____

_____

_____

Romans 2:29   **Cheshvan 4/** ד בחשון

On the contrary, the real Jew is one inwardly; and true circumcision is of the heart, spiritual not literal; so that his praise comes not from other people but from God.

When it was time to honor and bless Abraham, Hashem made a covenant with him. This covenant took the form of a legal contract (Genesis 15) where God and Abraham became venture partners. The culture of the day required that contracts between parties be signed through some sort of blood producing cut in the flesh that would then become an outward visible sign of this new relationship. The idea was that since this new contract gave you new assets, liabilities, strengths, weaknesses, and responsibilities, you had become a new person; you had become in essence a new creature. That societal change needed to be visible and therefore applied to your flesh by altering your body in some way. The cutting alteration required by God of Abraham was that of circumcision. The terms of the contract Hashem makes with us is his word, that's why the Hebrew word for circumcision is: *Brit-milah* ברית מילה: the Covenant of the word.

The Torah teaches that concerning our relationship with Hashem, it wasn't enough to be circumcised in the body. Our hearts also needed to be circumcised thus curbing our old appetites and desires (Deuteronomy 10:16). Our ears needed a similar alteration so we would receive a new pure sense of hearing, a hearing provoking obedience. When Gentiles joined the local synagogues in first century Asia Minor, Paul made sure that people did not solely focus on the physical part of their new lives, but rather that their hearts were right as he said, "For neither circumcision counts for anything, nor un-circumcision, but a new creation" (Galatians 6:15). For Paul, the outward show of works, even Torah works, meant nothing if the heart was not changed. As far as he was concerned, the change of heart came first and Torah works came second.

Today we have the opposite problem. People feel that they can have a change of heart without involving any change of behavior. People surely expect God to do his part of the physical elements of the contract by protecting, supplying, loving, and most of all forgiving, while we seem to not want to take upon ourselves any term of the contract that would cramp our lifestyle.

Anyone who comes to Yeshua becomes a new creature. Paul, a great rabbi was also a great disciple who wanted so much to be like his Master. He made sure to receive in his body the marks of the cost of true discipleship. He did not try to shirk away from them.

Can people see the marks of your covenant with him in your flesh? Is your life the living testimony of a change that reflects that you belong to Hashem? Do you carry the marks, the cuts of Yeshua not only in your heart but also in your body? When the time comes, will you enter the fellowship of his suffering (James 5:10; 1 Peter 2:19)?

My Personal Thoughts

_____

_____

_____

_____

_____

_____

1 Peter 2:19–21   Cheshvan 5/ ה בחשון

For it is a grace when someone, because he is mindful of God, bears up under the pain of undeserved punishment. For what credit is there in bearing up under a beating you deserve for doing something wrong? But if you bear up under punishment, even though you have done what is right, God looks on it with favor. Indeed, this is what you were called to; because the Messiah too suffered, on your behalf, leaving an example so that you should follow in his steps.

Abraham was called a friend of God. Did Abraham click the digital *like* button on God's Facebook? Or did God click the digital *like* button on Abraham's Facebook? In ancient Semitic societies to be a friend meant something much deeper than a digital click or a casual acquaintance. The bond of friendship was as strong as a marriage. David and Jonathan had such a bond (1 Samuel 18:1–4)!

In a friendship covenant, two parties merged their assets and liabilities. They even pledged military support to each other. The covenant could only be annulled by the death of either one of the parties and could be passed on to the children. To break its terms was a serious issue that could even lead to war between the two factions. Here is the question now: whereas I may find benefits in making such a covenant/merger with Hashem, what would God gain in making one with me? Do I have anything to give him? Will I protect God in his day of trouble? In fact, God needed a man to bridge the divide between his holy realm and the human sinful one; a man with integrity who would show himself unconditionally loyal towards that covenant; a man who would initiate a family line to carry the seed of Messiah.

The man who Hashem would entrust needed to have a certain amount of *chesed* חסד. This word is usually translated as *mercy, lovingkindness*. It also means devotion, as devotion and faithfulness to a covenant. Ten times Hashem tested Abraham's *chesed* towards the covenant even to the point of requiring the life of his only begotten son, and ten times Abraham proved himself worthy of Hashem's trust and investment.

Covenants are passed from fathers to sons. When we accept Yeshua as our Messiah, the responsibilities and assets of the Abrahamic Covenant fall upon us. Should we then also be tested? Life does seem to be a series of tests where we each are faced with decisions pertaining to the terms of the covenant. The Torah given on Mt. Horeb contains the terms of our covenant with Hashem.

Most of us have trials and tests in our lives. Some are our fault, while some seem totally random. Jewish sages taught that when the sinner suffers, it is for his own sake, but that when the righteous suffers, it is for the sake of others. Yeshua did say that as the Father sent him, so he sent us.

Could it be that our random trials operate virtue credit for others who need it? This principle is why prophets who interceded for Israel always reminded God of someone else's virtue such as that of Abraham or King David. We ourselves are redeemed not by our own virtues but by that of Messiah. If anything, it may give purpose to those bad things we feel happen to us for seemingly no reason at all!

My Personal Thoughts

_____

_____

Romans 11:17–18   **Cheshvan 6/ ו בחשון**

But if some of the branches were broken off, and you — a wild olive — were grafted in among them and have become equal sharers in the rich root of the olive tree, then don't boast as if you were better than the branches! However, if you do boast, remember that you are not supporting the root, the root is supporting you.

Before leaving earth, Yeshua told his disciples to immerse people in his name. It is from this Torah ritual of immersion that we understand the idea of rebirth. In Judaism, ritual immersions had to do with being born-again into repentance or renewal after a disease such as leprosy, but for a Gentile, ritual immersion meant conversion from paganism into monotheism. It meant becoming a part of the House of Israel. Such people in synagogues were called proselytes or *Sons of Avraham* (Acts 13:26).

Why *Children of Abraham?* Let me now engage you in a little Hebrew wordplay. The sages of Israel loved these! Hashem said to Abraham, "I will bless those who bless you, but I will curse anyone who curses you; and by you all the families of the earth will be blessed" (Genesis 12:3). It is because of this verse mentioning that those of the nations would be blessed through Abraham that Judaism always looked at converts from the nations as Children of Abraham. Yeshua followed the same idea in his admonition to make "make people from all nations into talmidim" (Matthew 28:19–20). You see, the word blessing in Hebrew is *b'rachah* ברכה, which is the same word used for an immersion pool. In this sense, Abraham becomes an *immersion* pool for the Gentiles to repent and turn to the God of Israel. Of course, this is what is called in Hebrew a *midrash* מדרש, or a creative interpretation to explain a spiritual principle. Yeshua, Paul, and all the writers of the Apostolic Scriptures generously indulged in the use of such a literary tool.

Here is another midrash, also related to our subject. The Hebrew word for 'shall be blessed' in our Genesis verse is *nivrechu* נברכו. This verb is in a conjugated form of the verb *levarech* לברך, to bless, from which many other words derive. The word for knees for example *berkayim* ברכים, is a derivative from the verb to bless and speaks of the position in which we bless or are blessed. Another derivative of *levarech* is the term *mavrich* מבריך meaning "to intermingle," or "to graft." This latter derivative is quite amazing because in his midrash about the nations entering the Covenant of Israel, Paul speaks of the Gentiles' inclusion into Israel using the concept of grafting (Romans 11). He must have gotten the idea from an ancient midrash stating the grafting of Rachab the Amonite and of Ruth the Moabite into Israel by conversion (Yavamoth 63a). The conversion of these two women into Judaism is all the more amazing because the Torah implicitly forbids Amonites and Moabites to enter the congregation of Israel up to the tenth generation (Deuteronomy 23:3). This shows that they were not thought of as foreigners anymore, but proselytes with complete rights in Israel. It also teaches us that if Hashem accepted them, he will certainly accept you!

Today we are sent by the Master not only to make disciples of all nations, but also to teach them to observe all things that he has taught us. At his coming may we be found being faithful Torah teachers not only in words, but in deeds also, teaching all who come to us by the example of a godly life.

My Personal Thoughts

_____

_____

Revelation 18:2   **Cheshvan 7/ ז בחשון**

She has fallen! She has fallen! Bavel the Great!

Abraham was brought up as one coming from the East to deliver Lot his nephew from the captivity of foreign kings. Abraham would not take a blessing from the heathen king of Sodom; the patriarch had better rewards than that of the world in its mire. His faith was duly rewarded when Melchizedek, the King of Righteousness, came to bless the old patriarch with the recompense no one could ever take from him (Genesis 14).

In the same manner, King Cyrus, whom Hashem called "My shepherd" over two hundred years before his birth, also came from the East (Isaiah 44:28; 45:1). Not desiring a bounty from God's people, he captured the city of Babylon. Isaiah prophesied of him: "If he sees the cavalry, horsemen in pairs!" And the watchman answered, "She has fallen! She has fallen—Bavel! All the carved images of her gods lie shattered on the ground" (Isaiah 21:9). After his valiant conquest of the impregnable city, Cyrus' hand was moved to free Judah and Israel from captivity and he allowed them to return to their country and rebuild their beloved city Jerusalem along with its Temple (Ezra 1:1–3).

God's children are still in captivity. This world is certainly not our home. We, along with all the holy elected ones who died before us, declare plainly that we seek a better country, that is, a heavenly country solely ruled by the Messiah King and his Torah. And Hashem is not ashamed to be called our God: for he has prepared for us a city (Hebrews 11:13–16, KJV).

Even so our Messiah redeemer comes with dyed garments from Bozrah. He is glorious in his apparel, travelling in the greatness of his strength. He speaks in righteousness. He is mighty to save. You may ask,

> Why is He red in His apparel, and His garments like him that treads in the winefat? And He answers "I have trodden the winepress alone; and of the people there was none with me: for I will tread them in mine anger, and trample them in my fury; and their blood shall be sprinkled upon my garments, and I will stain all my raiment. For the day of vengeance is in mine heart, and the year of my redeemed is come." (Isaiah 63:1–4, KJV)

Yes, as Abraham of old who flew upon the heathen kings to deliver Lot; and as God himself who formed a king to conquer Babylon in order to deliver his people, the social and economic collapse of today's' societies recall the distant cry heard 2,000 years ago by Yochanan the beloved disciple of the Master saying,

> She has fallen! She has fallen! Bavel the Great! She has become a home for demons, a prison for every unclean spirit, a prison for every unclean, hated bird. For all the nations have drunk of the wine of God's fury caused by her whoring—yes, the kings of the earth went whoring with her, and from her unrestrained love of luxury the world's businessmen have grown rich. Then I heard another voice out of heaven say: "My people, come out of her! So that you will not share in her sins, so that you will not be infected by her plagues." (Revelation 18:2–4)

May it be soon Abba, even in our days!

2 Corinthians 7:10   Cheshvan 8/ ח בחשון

Pain handled in God's way produces a turning from sin to God which leads to salvation, and there is nothing to regret in that.

At the time of Jechonias, the last Davidic king to ever sit on the throne of Jerusalem, we find the following words in an oracle pronounced by the prophet Jeremiah,

> This is what ADONAI says: "List this man as childless; he is a lifetime failure— none of his offspring will succeed, none will sit on David's throne or rule again in Y'hudah." (Jeremiah 22:30)

These words are troubling because according to the prophets Samuel and Nathan, the lineage of David was to be a never-ending one culminating to the Messiah. If this Davidic king was to remain childless, the hope of Israel was gone and with it the hope of the world.

As we continue looking into the Davidic genealogy, we realize that Jechonias had a son: Salathiel, who dies. Pediaiah, the brother of Salathiel fulfills the levirate law and marries his brother's widow thus raising seed to him in Zerubabel, whom God chooses to continue the Davidic line (Haggai 2:23). Did Hashem reverse the curse he put on Jechonias? Did the prophet get it wrong? Would Hashem really annul the covenant made with the Davidic line concerning world redemption because of the iniquity of one? These are very serious question imbedded in the reading of the genealogies.

Hashem is faithful to his covenant. Even at Mt. Horeb when he wanted to annul the whole Covenant because of the sin of worshipping the golden calf, he would have made good on his promises to Abraham even through Moses alone (Exodus 32:10). What we learn from these events is that even "If we are faithless, he remains faithful, for he cannot disown himself" (2 Timothy 2:13). Blessed be Hashem's name.

Jewish sages knew that about Hashem, so in Talmudic literature, they conclude that Jechonias must have repented while in exile. The sages speculate that even though Jeconiah's son died, Hashem reversed the curse through the accepted Toratic practice of the levirate marriage. The repentance of Jechonias cannot be documented but this tells us that the people of Israel looked at Hashem as one full of mercies; one who looks dearly at our repentance to reverse the fruits of our disobedience. *T'shuvah* תשובה, or repentance therefore becomes essential to renewal and fulfillment of God's promises.

Come to think of it, it is not the first time that levirate law comes to the rescue of the covenantal Davidic lineage. It happened with Judah and Tamar, Boaz and Ruth, and in the immediate family of the Master himself [Julius Africanus].

The Davidic Messianic line is filled with people of disrepute who desperately needed absolution and renewal through sincere and true repentance. So when you feel that you've really blown it this time and that there is no hope left for you, look at whom God chose. Reflect on the illustrious descendance of Messiah and know that Hashem is a God who rewards true and sincere repentance more than perfect sinlessness. David, more than anyone else knew it. He was destined to death because of murder and adultery, so he said, "Yah, if you kept a record of sins, who, ADONAI, could stand?" (Psalm 130:3).

My Personal Thoughts

Hebrews 11:10   **Cheshvan 9/ ט בחשון**

For he was looking forward to the city with permanent foundations, of which the architect and builder is God.

At Mt. Horeb, Hashem instructed the people of Israel about the different types of offerings. The first one mentioned in the Book of Leviticus is the *burnt offering* or the *offering of ascent*—in Hebrew called the *olah* עולה (Leviticus 1:3). Unlike the other offerings, no one else receives any benefit from this. It is fully and totally burnt and dedicated to God. This speaks of total abandonment to Hashem without reservations. This is what Abraham was asked to do with Isaac on Mt. Moriah, which he did, with the ram provided by ADONAI.

This event took place at Mt. Moriah, the place occupied by the city of Salem where Melchizedek was king. This was also the place where later, at the time when David sinfully decided to take a census of the nation of Israel, an angel destroyed many people with a plague (2 Samuel 24). Under the instructions of Gad, the prophet David bought the place to build an altar so he could make an offering for ADONAI. We must remember at this point that God had forbidden altars to be built in random places. The only altar to be used so far was the one in Shiloh where the Holy Ark was located. This was therefore a strange command from God, but David also knew that at some point in time, Hashem would have a place in the land of Cana'an where he would write his name. A traditional source tells us, in order to honor both Melchizedek and Abraham, David later renamed the place, *Yireh-Salem* ירא שלם, or Jerusalem, meaning 'He will provide peace'. What a name for a city that has seen more than its share of war and conflict . . . while still waiting for the *big one*!

Oh, but Hashem will provide peace. Like Abraham we must not stop our eyes at this imperfect world. We must seek for our true homeland; desire a better country, that is, a heavenly one. That's why Hashem is not ashamed to be called our God. He has prepared for us a city (Hebrews 11:16), a city that will finally see and know peace; a peace like no other city or even country in the world has ever known or seen. Not a 'Pax Jerusalema' enforced type of peace, but a peace from within originated by Yeshua the Messiah, the Prince of Peace himself.

This Jerusalem is the city with foundations, of which the architect and builder is Hashem. He has the true peace-plan and roadmap to peace in Jerusalem. Yes, Jerusalem will see peace; Hashem promised it (Hebrews 11:10, 16).

My Personal Thoughts

_____

_____

_____

_____

_____

_____

_____

_____

Hebrews 11:14–16

For people who speak this way make it clear that they are looking for a fatherland. Now if they were to keep recalling the one they left, they would have an opportunity to return; but as it is, they aspire to a better fatherland, a heavenly one. This is why God is not ashamed to be called their God, for he has prepared for them a city.

A young man at a university was expounding his beliefs to me about the end of the world. He was very excited and convincing in his arguments that the end was coming soon and that we should get ready. He explained to me that there will be an economic collapse that will cause a downright breakdown in society and that seismic activities also were on the rise so we should learn to survive without modern conveniences. He was showing me that it was all in the Bible, and there is nothing we could do about it. When the conversation shifted, I asked him what he was presently studying. He said he was going for some sort of law degree in economics. This is when I stopped listening.

This man may have been right in his conjectures, I do not know, but whatever our beliefs may be, our arguments seem very hypocritical when our lifestyle projects values directly opposite to our rhetoric. If this young man believed that the whole social and economic system was on the brink of collapse and that there was nothing he or I could do about it, why in the world was he investing in a long term college education on man's economics? Why doesn't his lifestyle reflect his rhetoric?

We are taught in Scriptures that we are all in exile here. That our true home is in the *Olam Habah* עולם הבא, the "World to Come," where all is to be restored the way it should be. Apostolic writings actually teach us that here, we are really like the Children of Israel in the desert (1 Corinthians 10; Hebrews 11). As believers, we are like Abraham who was told to leave his home looking for a better place. Many of us may believe this, but how much do we live by it?

Do we talk the language of pilgrims while living like settlers? Do we take part in this world's Canaanite culture? Do we let its influence shape our thinking? Does unnecessary baggage weigh us down and clutter our journey? Or do we live the lifestyle of the passing-through pilgrim?

Here is a story about a poor rabbi, whose name I forgot but bless him for this lesson. This rabbi was so poor he had nothing in his house, just some straw that he used for a bed. One day as he was visiting a wealthy neighbor, his host challenged his poverty and said, "But Rabbi, is it wrong for us to own things or to be comfortable?" The rabbi said, "Of course not; King Solomon was the richest man on earth, but let me ask you a question now, do you always travel with all your things?" "Of course not," replied the host, "when I do, I usually travel light; but I am home now." That's when the wise old rabbi answered, "Aaah, but I am not home yet; I'm not home!"

Are you 'home'?

My Personal Thoughts

_____

_____

_____

_____

_____

Hebrews 13:2   Cheshvan 11/ יא בחשון

Do not neglect to show hospitality to strangers,
or thereby some have entertained angels unawares.

It is very common in hot countries for people to take a break from work around noon. Due to the heat, they break at twelve and sometimes do not work again until mid-afternoon. In the case of Genesis 18, Abraham was not taking a midday nap due to the "heat of the day." He was convalescing from undergoing circumcision (Genesis 17). The fever lasted three days with the third day incurring the highest fever (Genesis 34:25). The first verse therefore of Genesis 18 infers that it was the third and highest day of Abraham's fever.

While Abraham was convalescing, the Torah tells us that ADONAI came to visit him (Genesis 18:1). This notion of Hashem's personal visit to Abraham to check up on him is the true origins of the Master's injunctions to visit the sick (Matthew 25:34–40). True discipleship is the desire to become like one's master. If Hashem therefore took the time to visit Abraham when he was sick, we should also practice the visiting of the ill.

This visit resulted in several tests.

1. **Hospitality**: The hospitality of Abraham was legendary. His table was like no other. To be at the table of Abraham was like being at the table of ADONAI. When we receive brethren in our homes to share with us, we should also do our best to honor them. The meal that Abraham served was composed of dairy and meat; a full meal worthy of a King. Did Abraham know who he was serving? All the text tells us after the verse's beginning narrative is that Abraham saw three men, strangers in the plain of Mamreh. Even the apostolic letter to the Hebrews seems to indicate that Abraham did not know at first (Hebrews 13:2). We should always share our best with strangers and consider it a high honor to host the saints, those for whom our Master died.

2. **Belief**: ADONAI had a message for Abraham. When Sarah (89 years old) heard that she would give birth, she laughed a cynical laugh for which the guest reproved her. Abraham did not laugh. He already had that conversation with Hashem a few days before when Hashem confirmed his promise through the sign of the circumcision (Genesis 17:17). Similarly, we should learn not to laugh at the impossible doings of God. The Talmud compares Sarah to Jerusalem. If Hashem is able to take an old woman, rejuvenate her, and make her fruitful throughout generations, he is also able to take a broken down seemingly barren city such as Jerusalem and resurrect her to be a blessing to all forever. Jerusalem's resurrection has already started.

3. **Motives**: How was Abraham going to use his new standing with God? Since he and ADONAI were now covenanted together, Abraham right away used his new assets as a blessing towards the incredulous world around him, not without motive though. For the sole sake of saving Lot, his wayward nephew, he pleaded for the sparing of Sodom and Gomorrah. How do we use our covenanted standing with the Master? Are our prayers a repetition of *gimme's*, or are our eyes turned toward those in need?

I think Abraham passed the test.

Would we?

My Personal Thoughts

Hebrews 11:19   יב בחשון /Cheshvan 12

For he had concluded that God could even raise people from the dead! And, figuratively speaking, he did so receive him.

NOTE: The Greek text for 'figuratively speaking' says: 'as in a parable', thus referring to an ancient Jewish parable by Pirkei de R. Eliezer. In the parable, the rabbi suggests that as the knife touched Isaac's throat, the young man's spirit actually left his body, only to come back at the sound of the voice of the angel. According to that midrash, while Abraham did not kill him, Isaac actually died and resurrected when on the altar. The author of the apostolic letter to the Hebrews was aware of this ancient tradition to which he referred in order to make his point.

Oh, for the provision of our Almighty Abba! When we don't bring in our part of the bargain, he provides the missing elements. He provides the missing elements and yet teaches us a lesson in faithfulness. Abraham was ready to go though the whole of God's plan. He let go of his own plans for Isaac to accept the plan of Hashem instead.

One could blame Abraham for being a fanatic and a lunatic; a religious nut of some sort but wait . . . ! Abraham was not bringing an innocent unsuspecting young boy to an untimely death. Isaac was actually a young bachelor, a young man who willingly, in full knowledge of what was going to happen to him, allowed himself to be tied up on this altar at Mt. Moriah. He had seen his father do it many times before and probably had done it himself.

In the days of the Tabernacle and of the Temples, animals brought to the altar were to be calmed down before going through the whole offering process; they had to be willing victims. Such was Isaac; a young man who utterly trusted his father and who lived solely to do his father's bidding. That is why Isaac was, in the minds of Jewish people, a representation of the coming Messiah, a representation alluded to in Jewish literature and most of all, in the tradition of the Afikomen of the Passover Seder.

Abraham's confession of faith came with a test that provoked in him immense turmoil. Did he really believe, as is suggested in the text, that God would resurrect Isaac and provide something else for the offering on Mt. Moriah (Hebrews 11:17–19)?

What if Hashem would ask us to make testimony of our dedication to Torah in such a way? What if he were to ask us to sacrifice our son and told you, "Don't worry; it's just to teach a lesson to the generations to come; I am going to resurrect him right away!" The same could be said of Isaac when he realized what was happening. His faith in his father was tested then, but he still relied entirely on the faith of his father who told him, ADONAI Y'rei יי ירא, "Hashem will provide." For generations to come, this test provides a standard to quantify the value of our commitment, a touchstone to define the caliber of our faith.

From one to a hundred how would you grade Abraham's test? Probably off the charts.

And what about Isaac's? Probably off the charts too.

How about yours?

My Personal Thoughts

_____

_____

Hebrews 11:17–18   Cheshvan 13/ יג בחשון

By trusting, Avraham, when he was put to the test, offered up Yitz'chak as a sacrifice. Yes, he offered up his only son, he who had received the promises, to whom it had been said, "What is called your 'seed' will be in Yitz'chak."

Here is a conversation I often have with my Torah students, "Do you believe in Yeshua being the Messiah?" When they reply positively I say, "That means that you believe in a man who was resurrected from the dead." I continue with, "Do you really believe that God can resurrect someone from the dead?" They say yes a bit less self-assured and I then ask, "What if today God would say to you, 'I want to use you for a little skit that will teach the generations to come about resurrection. Take your little sister, put her on a table, stab her with a knife, and burn her up completely to ashes. I know she is the little sister I promised you but don't worry because I will resurrect her. You do believe I can resurrect her right?'" There is usually a silence among the students then I ask again, "Do you believe in the bodily resurrection of Yeshua the Messiah? After all, you bank your whole faith system on that very fact!"

Much ink has been shed about the subject of Hashem asking Abraham to sacrifice his promised son Isaac. Most of what is written denotes the extreme love Abraham had for God, a love that gave him the strength to even sacrifice the most precious thing he owned: his son Isaac, the son of promise. This story is usually offered to encourage people of whom God seems to require great loss or sacrifice. There is a problem with this idea though, because human sacrifice is not acceptable to God. The Father had defined what he accepted as offering and humans are not on the list. They are actually forbidden, non-kosher, not fit for offering. That's the whole idea and why Leviticus teaches us that to approach God, we need the blood mediation of an innocent fit animal of which the list is given. Abraham also knew that Hashem's repugnance for human sacrifice was one of the main differences between him and the idolaters of his days.

What ADONAI was asking of Abraham was not a proof of his love by giving up Isaac, but a proof of his faith in the belief of resurrection. When he went up the mountain, Abraham said to his servants, "Stay here with the donkey; I and the boy will go over there and worship and come again to you" (Genesis 22:5). The Hebrew translation is more specific; it says, "We will come again to you." Why did he say that if he was on his way to sacrifice Isaac? The author of the Book of Hebrews tells us that Abraham considered that God was able to raise him from the dead, from which, figuratively speaking, he did receive him back (Hebrews 11:19). (The Greek for *figuratively speaking* says: *as in a parable*; referring to the ancient Hebrew parable on the potential death and resurrection of Isaac.)

In this case, Abraham, the father of all believers in the Messiah, Jews and non-Jews, believed in God in the same way that we do now: through believing in a non-human mediated resurrection.

My Personal Thoughts

_____

_____

_____

_____

_____

49

Hebrews 6:10 Cheshvan 14/ יד בחשון

For God is not so unfair as to forget your work and the love you showed for him in your past service to his people—and in your present service too.

The itinerant prophet Elisha often traveled through the Jezreel Valley also called the Plain of Megiddo in the Northern Kingdom. A prominent barren woman from the village of Shunem noticed that this oftentimes wanderer was a prophet of God, so she and her husband, who were part of a small remnant who had not gone the way of Jeroboam, decided to offer him hospitality whenever he passed through. They added an extra bedroom on the roof of their house equipped with a bed, a chair, a table, and an oil lamp. (The first Hebrew letters of each of these elements in the room spell the word, *Mishkan* מֹשׁכן, which is the term used for the area where the Ark of the Covenant used to rest. This teaches us the very important principle that he who practices hospitably transforms his house into a Sanctuary for the Divine Presence to dwell in.) The Master remembers this Shunamite woman when he said,

> Anyone who receives a prophet because he is a prophet will receive the reward
> a prophet gets, and anyone who receives a tzaddik because he is a tzaddik will
> receive the reward a tzaddik gets. (Matthew 10:41)

Against the woman's protests, knowing how God rewards those who care for his saints without personal motives but just because they are God's people, Elisha desired to reward the woman for her kindness. When Elisha's servant pointed out to him that she was barren, the prophet proceeded to tell her that by next year, at the *time of life* (same Hebraic expression used by the angel who spoke to Abraham about Sarah in Genesis 18:10), she will embrace a son, a son which Elisha later raises from the dead. Not only did these events carry an uncanny resemblance to those mentioned in the Book of Genesis—concerning Sarah after Abraham practiced hospitality to strangers (Genesis 18)—but they also closely follow those that Elijah, Elisha's master, performed in that very same area.

These local stories were still recounted in those towns of Israel when the Master arrived on the scene. They were still fresh and people encouraged each other with them as they waited for the final Messiah who would deliver them. They knew that he would do the same miracles and even more. What a surprise then it must have been for the people of Nain when this new prophet who was born not too far from them in Nazareth crashed one of their funeral processions, and being moved with compassion, brought a young man back to life (Luke 7:11–15).

If you want Hashem's will to be done on earth as it is in heaven; if you desire to make a sanctuary of your heart and of your house for the Presence of God to dwell in; if you want to see the life-giving blessings of the Almighty fill your life: practice hospitality, especially on the Sabbath!

My Personal Thoughts

_____

_____

_____

_____

_____

John 14:9   **Cheshvan 15/ טו בחשון**

Whoever has seen me has seen the Father.

Our dear sages who compared Jerusalem to Sarah our matriarch could not have foreseen the extent of their analogy. In the midrash of the barren woman, Hashem reveals the messianic future of his dear city to the prophet Isaiah. Since its sacking by the Romans in the first century CE, many have looked at Jerusalem just as Isaiah described her, a barren woman sitting on a heap of ashes, ostracized and rejected by her husband because of her many infidelities (Isaiah 54; Jeremiah 26:6).

My favorite legend of Jerusalem is the one about the weaning of Isaac. It is said that Abraham called for a great feast (Genesis 21:8). The rumor had gone around that Isaac was actually Pharaoh Abimelek's child (Genesis 20:2). Not only could people not believe that old Abraham sired a boy, but they also could not conceive of the idea that Sarah could lactate at ninety years old. The point of the feast was to vindicate Hashem's miracle and put these rumors to rest. Great Sheiks came from all around in great caravans to attend Abraham's feast. To prove her point, not only did Sarah nurse her son, but she offered to nurse every baby in the camp. She did, and the story goes on to say that every child Sarah nursed eventually became a king or a person of great influence and integrity. Also, in order to erase any doubt that the child was truly Abraham's, God had made the face of Isaac similar to that of his father, so that it was said that *he who saw the son saw the father*. Sounds familiar, doesn't it (John 14:9)?

Now we see why our sages compared Sarah to Jerusalem. Just like Sarah, Jerusalem was twice conquered by foreigners and taken captive, first by the Babylonians, then by the Romans. With the re-establishment of the State of Israel, the Roman captivity shows signs that it may be coming to an end. Looking at Jerusalem's destiny through Sarah's life, we can now see its future.

After Sarah returned from her second captivity, Isaac, the promised child, the foreshadow of Messiah, was born. Sarah, who was old, barren, and past the age, finally bore fruit. In the same manner today, Jerusalem, one of the oldest cities in the world, a city that has been used, abused, rejected, redeemed, to be rejected again and re-redeemed, prides itself of a new vibrant Messianic community rising all over Israel. It is what John called the "remnant of the seed of the woman" (Revelation 12:17), preparing the way for the soon return of the King (Revelation 19). The same miracle that rejuvenated Sarah to conceive Isaac and generously lactate happens in our day through Jerusalem. Think of it: a whole country was re-born in a day with a new generation of messianic believers preparing the way for the soon-coming King who will rule the earth with the justice and righteousness of the Father. Will they become the kings of integrity nursed to rule in the Jerusalem of the World to Come? May it be soon, Abba, even in our days!

Those who would try to interfere with the miraculous plan of God are playing with the unstoppable spiritual and natural forces that created the heavens and the earth.

May they beware!

My Personal Thoughts

_____

_____

_____

Romans 11:12, 18

Moreover, if their stumbling is bringing riches to the world . . . how much greater riches will Isra'el in its fullness bring them! Then don't boast as if you were better than the branches! However, if you do boast, remember that you are not supporting the root, the root is supporting you.

> You find that as long as Sarah lived, a cloud hung over her tent . . . her doors were wide open . . . there was a blessing on her dough, and the lamp used to burn from the evening of the Sabbath until the evening of the following Sabbath . . . (Genesis Rabah 60:16)

In this scrap of tradition, *Sarah's tent* is homiletically compared to Jerusalem, typified by the Temple. The cloud is symbolic of the *Shechinah* שכינה of Hashem's presence; the wide open doors to the temple being an open invitation to the world to come to the House of Prayer (as Yeshua calls it). The blessed dough compares with the showbread, which as tradition says, miraculously never spoiled And Sarah's lamp compares to the candelabrum that burned continuously in the Holy Place.

In the Book of Galatians, Paul builds on this illustration. Using the concept that Judaism views Sarah as the great matriarch, he says, "But the Yerushalayim above is free, and she is our mother." Then, using Isaiah's allegory and adding the fact that Sarah was barren, Paul continues with, "Sing, barren woman who has never had a child! Burst into song, shout for joy, you who have never been in labor!" Though Paul doesn't quote it, the rest of the oracle says, "Enlarge the space for your tent, extend the curtains of your dwelling; do not hold back, lengthen your cords, make your tent pegs firm" (Isaiah 54:1–2; Galatians 4:26).

This midrashic interpretation of Isaiah's text represents an illustration that Jerusalem—the center of Jewish religion—is one day to open its doors to all nations. The next chapter of Isaiah actually goes on to call all nations to drink and be fed from the fountain of Jerusalem (Isaiah 55; Zechariah 14:16).

Referring to modern history, I also will build on this concept. In their impatience, while waiting on Hashem to fulfill the messianic promise of the birth of Isaac, Abraham and Sarah brought Hagar into the picture. After Hagar bore fruit, she despised and boasted to Sarah who was still barren and dry. In his own time, Hashem miraculously caused Sarah to bear the fruit of the messianic promise. In the end, though blessed by God because of beloved Abraham, Hagar paid for her attitude and had to leave Sarah's presence.

For 2,000 years while waiting for the 19th century when *Jerusalem* would miraculously birth the present-day worldwide Messianic movement, the nations bore fruit unto Yeshua. But sad to say, they have done against the warning of the apostle, "don't boast as if you were better than the branches . . . remember that you are not supporting the root, the root is supporting you" (Romans 11:18), thus adopting a similar attitude as that of Hagar. This arrogance against the natural branch of Israel has often taken the form of horrible persecutions or of silence in the face of it. Will the nations suffer the same fate as Hagar? The *Tanach* תנך tells us that they won't, but that instead, Jerusalem will return to its rightful original owners, and that these nations will come and serve and worship the God of Abraham, Isaac, and Jacob in Jerusalem. On that day, they will bring their glory to the city of the Great King (Isaiah 66; Haggai. 2:7). For what it's worth, there is an ancient Jewish teaching which suggests that Keturah, Abraham's second wife after Sarah died, is actually Hagar returned (Genesis 25:1–6).

Matthew 1:20   Cheshvan 17/ יז בחשון

But while he was thinking about this, an angel of ADONAI appeared to him in a dream and said,
"Yosef, son of David, do not be afraid to take Miryam home with you as your wife; for what has
been conceived in her is from the Ruach HaKodesh."

When instructing Moses about the future mediator that will stand between him and Israel, Hashem spoke of a prophet *like* Moses (Deuteronomy 18:15–18). Looking therefore at the life and ministry of Moses, we should be able to define our mysterious prophesied mediator.

Let us look at Moses' conception. Feeling threatened by the proliferation of the Hebrews in his country, Pharaoh enslaved the Israelites to his building ambitions. One of Pharaoh's wise men came to him one day with a star-omen that a boy is to be born to the Israelites that would deliver them from his hand. Our angry Pharaoh then decided to kill all newborn males, throwing them into the Nile River.

We are told in certain Talmudic sources that at that time, Amram who already had a son, Aaron, and a daughter, Miriam, divorced his wife because he didn't want to be faced with the possible tragedy ordered by Pharaoh. Because of his clout as a Levite, many of Israel followed Amram's example causing Miriam, a child, to be an angelic voice of rebuke chastising him with the following words: "What you have done is worse that Pharaoh. Pharaoh's decree was only against males, yours is against males and females alike. His decree may not come to pass, but yours certainly will!" Upon these words, Amram returned to his wife only to find that she was miraculously three months pregnant.

I cannot ascertain that this Talmudic story is the report of true events, but it certainly offers a very uncanny parallel with the Master's conception. Actually, Jewish sages refer to Moses as the first redeemer, and Messiah as the second.

In the accounts about the conception of the Master, we also have wise men, Chaldean astronomers, who come to Herod, a Pharaoh-like king, with an indication from the stars that the Savior of Israel is born in Bethlehem. This in turn provokes Herod to kill all the babies in Bethlehem who were two years old and younger. A little while before, Joseph, thinking that Miriam, his fiancé, committed adultery, found himself with no other option but to divorce her, but like Amram, he returned to her after the intervention of an angelic messenger.

These events also take us all the way back to Isaac whose birth was prophesied through the stars and his untimely death prevented by an angelic intervention.

Oh, for the wonders of the Torah! Why do so many seek wisdom and wonder north and south, east and west, high and low? All the secrets of heaven above and earth below, as well as past, present, and future, are imbedded right there in the words of theTorah.

My Personal Thoughts

_____

_____

_____

_____

_____

1 Corinthians 11:1   Cheshvan 18/ יח בחשון

Try to imitate me, even as I myself try to imitate the Messiah.

When Abraham arrived in the Land, an idol worshipping Philistine ruler took notice of the patriarch's godly ways. Impressed, the Philistine initiated an inter-generational covenant with Abraham in the following terms,

> Therefore, swear to me here by God that you will never deal falsely with me or with my son or grandson; but according to the kindness with which I have treated you, you will treat me and the land in which you have lived as a foreigner. (Genesis 21:23)

Several years later, due to a famine, Isaac, the inheritor of Abraham's legacy, finds himself in the position of claiming the privileges of this covenant. There was a problem though: the new Philistines of that generation did not really know Isaac, so they plugged his wells and contended with him. Finally, feeling threatened by Isaac's prosperity, the Philistines asked him to leave. For all good purposes, the covenant made between Abraham and the Philistine ruler was broken and now invalid.

The Genesis narration continues. We learn that Phicol continued watching Isaac and his tribe. After awhile, the Philistine general concluded that the God of Isaac was the same as the God of Abraham so he asks for the treaty to be re-enacted as if nothing had happened with the wells. As ludicrous as it sounds, Isaac accepts.

This teaches us that the deeds of the parents are portents for the children. It teaches us that though we may automatically inherit the reputation and hard work of our fathers, we must show ourselves of the same spirit if we want to enjoy their privileges. In this case, it is not until Phicol carefully observed Isaac that he recognized that the God of Isaac was the same as the God of Abraham, and that Isaac could therefore be trusted with the same covenant.

Maybe this is a lesson for our people today. It may not be until the powers of the world recognize the ways of Messiah in Israel that they will see in them the ways of the God of Abraham and that they will concede to the re-instatement of the covenant (John 8:56)!

Shlomo Carlebach, an Orthodox rabbi, was known in Israel and the US as the singing and dancing rabbi, but in Apartheid South Africa, he was known as *Master Jesus*. In fact, the black population in South Africa surnamed Rabbi Shlomo Carlebach, *Master Jesus*. They did so because of his loving and caring interaction with them. Just as by observing Isaac, Phicol recognized the God of Abraham, the people of South Africa saw Yeshua in the loving and caring interactions of this Orthodox rabbi who seemed to know about Messiah's nature and character solely by studying the word and obeying it.

Someone once said that discipleship is the art of imitation. Wouldn't it be nice if someone mistook us for Yeshua because of the way we lived and acted?

My Personal Thoughts

_____

_____

_____

Hebrews 11:9

By trusting, he lived as a temporary resident in the Land of the promise, as if it were not his, staying in tents with Yitz'chak and Ya`akov, who were to receive what was promised along with him.

Abram is told by Hashem to leave his cozy comfortable home in Babylon. Along with Lot, his nephew who decided to go with him, the patriarch is lead by Hashem to Cana'an, a land already occupied. They settled south and were driven to Egypt by a famine. Abram's wife was then taken captive by Pharaoh, who God punished with plagues. Pharaoh then released Sarai and showered Abram with gifts; they both returned to the Land, separated from Lot, and it is then that Hashem made an eternal covenant with him concerning his ownership of the Land. Later, Abram had to fight to keep that Land away from five foreign invaders and to free Lot, his relative. He then met with the King of Salem to whom Abraham honored and gave tithes.

After these events, Hashem renewed his covenant with Abraham and promised him a son. Sodom was destroyed. Sarah was taken captive for a second time, then released in the same manner as before. Isaac was born, brought to the altar, and *resurrected* (Hebrews 11:19). The text then tells us that Sarah died.

Abraham then needed to buy a piece of land to bury his wife. His only ownership of the Land was in the promises Hashem gave him, which sadly did not constitute a valid currency for Hephron the Hittite. At first, the Cana'anite seemed to make an altruistic offer, but pragmatic Abraham saw the strings attached to the gift and wanted nothing of it. He therefore yielded to an exorbitant price for a piece of land in Hebron. Abraham wanted this to be a closed undisputable affair. To this day, this biblically recorded transaction serves as a record of the indisputable Jewish ownership of that Land. Hashem allowed these to be recorded in the Torah so there would be no doubt about it.

We may wonder at the encrypted message in this story. The prophet Isaiah said it so well, "At the beginning I announce the end, proclaim in advance things not yet done!" (Isaiah 46:10).

Read with me now in the lives of Abraham and Sarah the life and destiny of Jacob, who shares his name with that of the Promised Land (Genesis 32:28). Coming out of Babylon Jacob/Israel came to an occupied Promised Land. Israel was later made captive in Egypt, freed after plagues raged upon her captor and then showered with gifts. When Israel returned to the Land, he still had to fight kings who wanted to dominate him. Israel is again taken into captivity, this time in Babylon, from where he returns with gifts from the King of Persia. The whole story takes us to the miraculous birth of Yeshua and to his resurrection. Eventually, the Land will be legally owned by its God-ordained inhabitant but, as with Abraham, for an exorbitant price!

Here is now the rest of the verse from Isaiah, "and I say that my plan will hold, I will do everything I please to do" (Isaiah 46:10).

My Personal Thoughts

_____

_____

_____

_____

_____

Galatians 4:26　　　　　　　　　　　　　　　　　　**Cheshvan 20/ כ בחשון**

But the Yerushalayim above is free, and she is our mother.

"Then Yitz'chak brought her into his mother Sarah's tent and took Rivkah, and she became his wife, and he loved her" (Genesis 24:67). It is said that in seeking a wife a man looks for another mother. Today, our stubborn demand for individuality makes potential wives want to distinguish and define themselves against their husband's mothers. On the other hand, a man will often refer to his mother's cooking as the best, and new wives who haven't sat learning at the feet of an older seasoned matriarch often can't compete, which can create serious problems within families.

In the ancient world, a betrothed woman would spend her time learning about the things that please her future husband. She would learn from mostly his mother and others who knew him well. She would prepare his favorite foods, wear clothes, and do her hair in the manner that he liked, as well as behave in the way that he approved. Today the mentality for both men and women is more, "if you really love me, you'll take me as I am." There is little respect for continuity, traditions, or culture, so grandchildren end up living in a completely different world than that of their grandparents. This creates fragmented families. That's why it is hard for older people today; they feel that everything they know and have taught their children is obsolete and as a result, they feel useless.

Sarah was the matriarch. Whole traditions of hospitality, care, wisdom, and even of the prophetic gift had developed around her. She was a tough act to follow. That's why Eleazer's mission of finding Isaac a wife was so crucial. Though coming from the idolatrous culture of Babylon, she had to have the right spirit and endorse the traditions of Sarah, and she did. Isaac wanted and needed her to enter into his *mother's tent* and continue in the godly traditions his mom had instituted. Things would have been different if she would have said, "Look, I'm not living in your mother's tent! Can't you give me my own tent? I am my own person after all! I left my parents house for you so you take me as I am . . ."

Jewish prophetic eschatology compares Sarah to Jerusalem. After her second captivity, Sarah birthed Isaac. Following the binding of Isaac, Sarah (Jerusalem) died and many years later, Isaac married Rebecca. This order of events is not coincidental. Classic Judaism always looked upon Isaac as a foreshadowing picture of the coming Messiah. Like Isaac, Yeshua had a miraculous birth and was sacrificed on the altar; the sacking and consequent dying of Jerusalem follows and one day, after many years, Yeshua will return to marry his bride.

Even today, like Eleazer, the Spirit of Hashem roams in the earth in search of the bride who will enter *Jerusalem/Sarah's tent* and continue in the Jewish traditions of his mother; the bride where the Sabbath candle burns continually and where the *dough* is blessed.

My Personal Thoughts

_____

_____

_____

_____

_____

Hebrews 11:9

By trusting, he lived as a temporary resident in the Land of the promise, as if it were not his, staying in tents with Yitz'chak and Ya`akov, who were to receive what was promised along with him.

The Almighty El-Shaddai swore to Abraham, "All the land you see I will give to you and your descendants forever" (Genesis 13:15). Yet, after decades of wondering, and even going to war with five kings to protect his divine inheritance, when it came time to bury his wife, the patriarch still claimed to be a *foreigner* in the Land of Promise (Genesis 23:4). He even had to haggle to get a burial place from a mocking Cana'anite.

The *Tanach* תנך records three important places purchased by Abraham and his offspring. Abraham bought the Cave of Machpelah (Genesis 23:17–18), Jacob acquired the parcel of ground where Joseph was eventually buried (Joshua 24:32), and David purchased the place where the Temple was built (2 Samuel 24:24). While today, these very places are claimed by some to be Muslim holy sites stolen by the Jewish nation, the narratives of the *Tanach* solidly records these transactions in favor of the Jewish nation.

Abraham believed in the divine reality of Hashem's promises and acted upon them as much as he could. But he also knew how to live within his earthly present reality, the very present reality of having to buy what already belonged to him by divine right. He even refused Hephron's offer of a gift. Abraham bought the land, and he bought it at an exorbitant price. This teaches us the difference between promise and reality.

Four thousand years later, as an echo to a distant past, the descendants of the Children of Abraham moved into this land and re-conquered what was already theirs by divine right. Until today this small strip of land by the Mediterranean Sea, that Pleasant Land (Jeremiah 3:19; Daniel 8:9), is being bought at an exorbitant price. It is being bought not only at the price of the lives and deaths of many victims of war and terrorism, but also at the cost of the world's anger and the resurgence of anti-Semitism. Haggling with the *Cana'anite* seems to continue, not only with one king this time, but with the world and the United Nations. Sometimes Israel is so tired of this *haggling* that it is tempted to offer *land for peace*.

We must learn something from Abraham our father. While being aware of the promise of our divine destiny, we must also learn to live within our present earthly reality. Our souls have been bought and purchased; Yeshua paid the exorbitant bride price to live within the walls of our hearts, but daily the haggling goes on with the *Cana'anite*, the *old man* who does not let go. We sometimes get so tired of the *haggling* that we are tempted to compromise with the evil one, offering him terms of peace in the form of land from our heart. But wait, Messiah bought that land; it belongs to him. As Israel does today, we must remember the price and the promises, and as such, expect the total fulfillment of these promises in the Messianic Era.

As the offspring of Abraham, we must learn to fight knowing that what Hashem is able to accomplish fully what he has promised (Romans 4:21).

My Personal Thoughts

_____

_____

_____

Under the Vine

Luke 3:4   **Cheshvan 22/ כב בחשון**

Prepare the way for ADONAI! Make straight paths for him!

This challenge from John the Immerser echoes the prophetic words of Isaiah as he calls, "Go on through, go on through the gates, clear the way for the people! Build up a highway, build it up! Clear away the stones! Raise a banner for the peoples" (Isaiah 62:10). In the same manner as John, Isaiah was preparing the people of Jerusalem for the arrival of the promised messianic king. The call of Isaiah sounds like the language of landscapers calling for road improvements and reparation projects in light of the arrival of a great dignitary, projects that had to be started before the onset of a great event. Isaiah's message continues with these words,

> ADONAI has proclaimed to the end of the earth, "Say to the daughter of Tziyon, 'Here, your Salvation is coming! Here, his reward is with him, and his recompense is before him.' They will call them The Holy People, The Redeemed of ADONAI. You will be called D'rushah *[Sought-After]*, `Ir Lo Ne`ezvah *[City-No-Longer-Abandoned]*. (Isaiah 62:11–12)

In the ancient world a young maiden chosen to marry a king would ready herself for sometimes up to a year (Esther 2:12). She would go through body *improvements* and *reparations* so to speak. She would regularly immerse herself in baths filled with aromatic herbs and plants with skin conditioning properties. She was also given food from the king's table until the appointed time when she would finally marry him.

Rebecca left her past behind to marry he who is a shadow of Messiah. She became a new creature, as she left her kinfolks behind in Babylon to be part of a new family. She entered the tent of her mother-in-law Sarah to continue in the matriarchs' venue. We today are this bride, the bride of the King to come, and we ought to prepare as such. We are to make ourselves ready and immerse in the baths of repentance to present ourselves to him in splendor, without spot or wrinkle or any such thing, that we might be holy and without blemish (Ephesians 5:27); betrothed to one husband, as a pure virgin (2 Corinthians 11:2).

Immersion in waters filled with his cleansing words (John 15:3) is our preparation before we come to him at the end of the age. May we let it clean us each day from the Cana'anite culture that surrounds and snares us. As we do, may we sincerely and honestly pray in the same manner as King David, the great messianic foreshadow:

> God, in your grace, have mercy on me; in your great compassion, blot out my crimes. Wash me completely from my guilt, and cleanse me from my sin. Sprinkle me with hyssop, and I will be clean; wash me, and I will be whiter than snow. Create in me a clean heart, God; renew in me a resolute spirit. Then I will teach the wicked your ways, and sinners will return to you. (Psalms 51:3–4; 9; 12; 15)

My Personal Thoughts

_____

_____

_____

2 Corinthians 6:14 Cheshvan 23/ כג בחשון

Do not yoke yourselves together in a team with unbelievers. For how can righteousness and lawlessness be partners? What fellowship does light have with darkness?

Or what fellowship has light with darkness?

We have mused with the idea of Abraham's son Isaac foreshadowing Messiah. We have noticed Isaac bound to the wood and destined to a certain death, which Hashem averted, thus he did not see the Abyss (Psalm 16:10). Things then take a different turn.

As we continue reading the text of Genesis, Isaac seemed to disappear from the narration of the Torah. We also notice that Abraham did not return to Sarah, his wife. He went back only many years later to bury her. After the death of his loved one, Abraham's most immediate concern was the choice of a wife for Isaac who was now nearing forty. Keeping our analogy in mind, let's see what happened.

Abraham sent his servant Eleazer to find a wife for his son Isaac. First, the old patriarch extoled two promises from Eleazer: 1) to not choose a woman from among the Canaanites around them (Genesis 24:3), 2) to not take Isaac out of the land (Genesis 24:6). Isaac was to stay pure. Though his wife would come from an idolatrous home, she would take on the God of Abraham as her own. She was also from the same genealogic stock as Abraham. Isaac was to marry Rebecca, but she would be the one coming to him from Babylon; he would not go to her. It is Abraham's servant Eleazer—which means in Hebrew: 'the help of my God'—who goes to look for her.

Today, as was required of Eleazer, the Spirit of Hashem runs to and fro through this Babylonic confused world seeking to gather the bride. The Spirit is commissioned to bring to the Master a pure and undefiled bride. The bride is to come out of Babylon; she is to clean herself from her Babylon-ish ways and culture in order to meet her husband. Isaac did not go to Babylon and try to assimilate to its culture so he could be agreeable to a potential bride. He stayed in the land and sent a messenger. It is the *bride* who came and changed her ways for Isaac. This teaches us something.

Because of Paul's injunction, "With all kinds of people I have become all kinds of things" (1 Corinthians 9:22), some tend to imagine Yeshua adapting himself to every way and culture. Whereas he is relevant to all, relevance cannot be taken to an extreme, as today, Yeshua seems to have become acultural. From the minute we remove Yeshua from his Hebraico-Jewish context, all that remains is an adulterated copy of the real thing. In the last 2,000 years, the world has created a Yeshua as a Western person with Western thoughts and ways. In every country, we want Yeshua to relate to us, but it is us who have to go to him and become like him. And whether we like it or not, he is not a Western Caucasian from Europe, but a Semitic Jew from the Middle East.

Let us therefore learn to not only come out of Babylon, but also not to carry Babylon with us. Like Rebecca, let us rid ourselves of our Canaanitish/Babylonish/Helenistic Western ways and learn to endorse the culture of Messiah, which is Torah culture, the culture of the Bible. Let us allow Hashem's Spirit to teach us through the word all the ways of the Master so that we may come to him at the end of days a pure bride, undefiled from the ways of the world.

Revelation 19:16   Cheshvan 24/ כד בחשון

And on his robe and on his thigh he has a name written:
KING OF KINGS AND LORD OF LORDS.

Luminaries and sages of the past have established relationship themes between the Torah and the prophetic books. Look at the following passages that our sages have put together: "By now Avraham was old, advanced in years, and, King David grew old, the years took their toll" (Genesis 24:1; 1 Kings 1:1). In the Hebrew text, these two sentences are expressed in similar sentences. It seems that the events behind these similar introductory clauses are conceived in a cosmic dimension.

In both of the following narrations, the old patriarchs establish one of their sons as the sole carriers of their dynasty. Both heirs also have an older brother from their father's previous wife, and both older brothers were jealous of the chosen position of their sibling.

In the Book of Kings, Samuel tells us that Adonijah, the oldest of David's living sons, tried to pull a fast one on his father by organizing his own coronation behind his back. When Bat-Shebah (Daughter of an Oath) found out, she quickly reminded her old husband of his oath that Solomon should be king after him—leave it to a mother to stand up for her son to be king. David immediately took action organizing Solomon's coronation ceremony.

The people of Jerusalem were seeing two concurrent coronations and were faced with a choice of leader: the one whom the king had appointed and the one who appointed himself. The choice was easy to make for those who were loyal to God in the House of David. Only Solomon had the king's prophet with him, the king's priest, the king's mule, and the oil from the Temple for the anointing. All Adonijah had was Joab, David's disgruntled general, and a corrupt priest. When the people who ignorantly followed Adonijah found out they had been fooled, they immediately gathered around Solomon who ushered in a time in Israel when everyone sat under their vine and fig tree, thus foreshadowing the Messianic era that will one day "cover the earth as the waters cover the sea" (1 Kings 4:25; Micah 4:4). May it come soon, Abba, even in our days.

This is such a repetitive theme. We find it in Ishmael who contended for Isaac's inheritance, in Esau for Jacob's, and in Adonijah for Solomon's. Even so, now there is one, who from the creation of man, contends for Messiah's kingship over us. Until today, much like Ishmael, Esau, and Adonijah, he tries to fool the ignorant, the rebellious, and the disgruntled into making him king over them, stealing the crown of the only legal heir of the throne of David, of the only legitimate ruler of our souls.

In ignorance, some may get fooled for a while by a counterfeit pretender, but when the true King descends from the throne of the Father, when the only one whom the Father sends, the one who is also called the prophet, the priest according to the order of Melchizedek, may we all gather together around him to give glory, loyalty, and honor.

Long Live the King!

My Personal Thoughts

_____

_____

_____

Hebrews 12:4   Cheshvan 25 / כה בחשון

You have not yet resisted to the point of shedding blood in the contest against sin.

When Abraham and Isaac reached Mount Moriah, the patriarch told the young men with him, "Stay here with the donkey. I and the boy will go there, worship and return to you" (Genesis 22:5). The Hebrew is a little more specific, translated, it says, "we will go, and we will return." Knowing that he was going to offer Isaac on the Mount, why did Abraham say, "We will return"?

The other question to ask is, "Why did he even go?" When I teach this story, I always ask my students, "If today God came to you and said, 'Son, I want to teach a lesson to the universe and I want you to help me. All you need to do is take your son or your little brother or sister and sacrifice them.'" Would you go? Would you even hear that type of language? Abraham had always been a willing instrument in God's hands so it is fair to assume the he was, in good conscience, going to literally sacrifice Isaac on the altar that day. But he did say to the young men, "we will return."

We get a little clue about the issue from the writer of the Book of Hebrews. Chapter eleven says, "By trusting, Avraham, when he was put to the test, offered up Yitz'chak . . . For he had concluded that God could even raise people from the dead! And, figuratively speaking, he did so receive him" (Hebrews 11:17–19). Because of Abraham's willing intentions, the text tells us that Abraham 'offered' Isaac. The text also reveals that Abraham believed in resurrection, and that was the belief that made him obey God. This faith in resurrection was the seal of Abraham's faith in Hashem and wherein he and us become potential heirs to all that is promised in the Book.

Let us return to our former scenario. What if today God came to you and said, "Son, I want to teach a lesson to the universe and I want you to help me. All you need to do is take your son or your little brother or sister and sacrifice them, but don't worry, I will resurrect them right away." Would you do it? Would you have that much desire to accomplish God's purpose, so much love as to kill what is dearest to you, even if he had told you that he would give it back? Our messianic faith does lie in that one idea that Hashem allowed Yeshua to die on the cross and that he resurrected him.

A problem also is that when Hashem allows us to be tested with the prospect of losing something dear, we usually rationalize the idea. We try to find a comfortable compromise so we don't really have to give it up. Abraham probably had his trial, but he didn't rationalize the issue into disobedience. Some people like to think that Abraham did it so we don't have to, but this is not my experience. I for one believe that faith in God though Yeshua is sealed in our conscience through many trials and tests (Acts 14:22). The chosen apostle of Yeshua does challenge us noting that "you have not yet resisted to the point of shedding your blood" (Hebrews 12:4).

Have you?

My Personal Thoughts

_____

_____

_____

_____

Galatians 5:6   **Cheshvan 26/ כו בחשון**

What matters is trusting faithfulness expressing itself through love.

I recently read a story about the mother of an Israeli soldier in the IDF. Like all good Jewish mothers, she had ambitions for her boy that defied the rules of the possible (Matthew. 20:20–23). When approaching the chief officer of her son's battalion to make her motherly impossible request, the officer replied, "Jewish mothers are one step above army chief officers in God's book, so we'll see what we can do."

When she saw that Hashem was lingering in fulfilling his own word, Sarah decided to help him out (sarcasm intended) using the stratagem with Hagar. Rebecca, who took over the role of matriarch after Sara's death, proved herself to be cut of the same cloth. She had received a personal prophecy that Jacob should be the recipient of the Abrahamic blessing through Isaac, not Esau. She was going to make sure God did not mess up again as he seemed to have done with Sarah (again, sarcasm intended!).

First we can wonder about God; "What takes him so long anyways?" (Don't our wives always get on our case for procrastinating on important projects?) It is easy also to wonder about these two women's ways. Did they not trust God? Other questions beg to be asked, "Did these women, by their actions, show unreserved dedication and faith in the prophetic destiny of their lineage, even at the cost of a seeming lack of integrity? Could they maybe have been more interested in the word of God being fulfilled than in themselves and their own reputation?" It takes a mother, a Jewish one at that, to fight for their sons with the devil himself on these kinds of terms.

We tend to judge people through the screening of personal virtue, but it seems that the way Hashem judges us is more by the virtue of the force of our dedication to his promises and of our love for him.

Yeshua mentioned that we break into the kingdom of God through forceful determination (Matthew 11:12). This is not to say that the end justifies the means; it is only to reiterate the words of the dear apostle Paul when he explains that the most important element of our spiritual walk is a faith working through love (Galatians. 5:6).

Our love for the Master needs to go beyond the concerns of our personal posture. Our love for him needs to expand; it needs to live in utter abandonment, above and beyond the restricted borders of the acceptable, breaking through the narrow confines of the possible. Does it in your life?

The Master left us an example to emulate. We are told that he,

> emptied himself, in that he took the form of a slave by becoming like human beings are. And when he appeared as a human being, he humbled himself still more by becoming obedient even to death—death on a stake as a criminal! (Philippians 2:7–8)

Can we do the same for him, in whatever he asks us to do?

My Personal Thoughts

_____

_____

Romans 9:13

Ya`akov I loved, but Esav I hated.

Jacob and Esau live in each of us. When in Rebecca's womb, before they had even done anything right or wrong, Hashem already knew the difference between the two brothers. Their nature was within them from conception, and its contrast left for us a pattern to be used today as a moral compass.

Esau, the wild man whose sword is against everyone especially his brother, is the resurrection of Cain. He lives, and he fights against all that is conformed to God. His very nature is to defy, reject, and challenge God and to endorse the very antithesis of everything that is good, true, and pure. We call him the *old nature* (Ephesians. 4:22), the "the old nature is hostile to God" (Romans 8:7). Esau is a microcosm of the anti-Messiah that is within each of us (1 John 4:3). Rebecca's complaint, "If it's going to be like this, why go on living?" (Genesis 25:22), expresses the cry of every man and woman who fervently desire to follow Hashem's ways of righteousness, yet, as the Master's apostle says, through trouble and persecution (2 Timothy. 3:12).

Jacob on the contrary allowed Hashem to search his heart. He allowed the Spirit, the flame of the Almighty God to search him through and through, to clean him from deceit, corruption, disobedience, rebellion, and all other forms of unrighteousness. He lived for twenty-one years in exile in the house of idolatrous Laban and returned home purer than before.

The narration tells us of a camp of angels welcoming him as he returned to the Land of Cana'an with his family, which he snatched from Babylonic Laban (Genesis 31:1). Though Hashem had already accepted him (Genesis 27:26–29; 28:11–21), Jacob worked out his "deliverance with fear and trembling" (Philippians 2:12), and when graduation time came, Jacob took hold of the kingdom's blessing with passionate love and violence (Genesis 32:24–32; Matthew 11:12).

In our generation, no one is a helpless victim of a godless environment. Each one of us is given the choice to emulate Jacob or Esau, to obey either one within us, to yield to the old self and the flesh within us, or to combat our innate human nature and live in Jacob, the resurrected new man who holds on to the angel until the blessing is bestowed, even at a price.

The choice is ours to make!

My Personal Thoughts

_____

_____

_____

_____

_____

_____

_____

_____

_____

Hebrews 11:20   Cheshvan 28/ כח בחשון

By trusting, Yitz'chak, in his blessings over Ya`akov and Esav,
made reference to events yet to come.

Rebecca's ruse in concealing Jacob and taking advantage of Isaac's blindness lends itself to much speculation. Does God endorse lying and deception? Certainly not! But the narration of this text can provide, for the unspiritual soul, an acceptable excuse for such practices. Far be it from Hashem to endorse the darkness of devilish lies. In presenting us with such a story, the God of light actually reveals to us an eternal messianic truth.

The Jewish people had certain expectations that would help to recognize their Messiah, expectations that are right and true. Many expected the messianic redeemer to be a great military hero like King David or like the judges of old, one who would deliver them from the tyrannical hand of Rome. The Messiah truly is all that, but as Balaam prophesied, "I see him, but not now; I behold him, but not soon" (Numbers 24:17). The Messiah's coming follows a pattern of concealment.

In musing on the concealed coming of the Messiah, we are reminded of Nehemiah. Before revealing his kingly mandate to rebuild Jerusalem, Nehemiah spent time incognito under the cover of night to scout out Jerusalem (Nehemiah 2:11–16). We see the same pattern in Queen Esther, who concealed her identity before she was able to put her life on the line to save the nation (Esther in Hebrew means: concealed). We also remember how Joseph received the brothers he would later save under the concealed identity of an Egyptian viceroy so he could test them (Genesis. 42–45).

Through his mother's ruse, Jacob teaches us that the Messiah will initiate his mission in a concealed manner. We also learn from the patriarch that the Messiah will spend a long time in the exile of the nations until he finally returns in glory to the land of his birth.

The Messiah did come to his people to fulfill their deepest yearning and expectation, but his coming was concealed. To this day, he appears to his fellow Jews under the identity of a stranger but oh, what a rejoicing day it will be for the whole world, the day he reveals himself to his people. It will dwarf the rejoicing of Joseph's brothers, even that of the Hebrew nation as they were saved from the evil clutches of Haman.

Far from teaching us to lie and deceive, the story of Jacob and Isaac teaches an eternal truth, a truth concealed under a seeming lie. Rebecca received the promise that Jacob should inherit the blessing of Abraham, so instead of deception, their story teaches us love, devotion, and faith for the commandment and the promises of God.

In our daily discoveries in the words of truth, may we do more than read and study. May Abba allow us to understand the truth that is concealed in the words.

My Personal Thoughts

_____

_____

_____

_____

Romans 11:25–26

Stoniness, to a degree, has come upon Isra'el, until the Gentile world enters in its fullness; and that it is in this way that all Isra'el will be saved. As the Tanakh says, "Out of Tziyon will come the Redeemer; he will turn away ungodliness from Ya`akov.

The Book of Genesis tells us the story of Isaac as a father blinded to his oldest son's wickedness. Isaac could have been fooled by Jacob's ruse, but Rebecca, his wife, had been given a prophecy about the future of her two children. Did Isaac know about this? And how could Isaac be oblivious to Esau's marriages with several Canaanite women? It seems also that Isaac was unaware of the *birthright-for-red-stuff* (that's what the dish is called in the Hebrew text) deal between Jacob and Esau.

Many Talmudic commentators attribute Isaac's blindness to an act of God's mercy to spare him the distress of seeing his oldest son Esau's wicked behavior. Some also suggest that Isaac was oblivious to Esau's wickedness because of his smoke screen of hypocrisy, pretending to be so righteous in front of his father. Isaac's blindness could have also been simply be because he was old and had cataracts.

Interesting elements are unveiled when we look at this story as the prophetic foreshadow of a future situation, as the microcosm of a larger concept. Not only was Isaac blinded to Esau's wickedness, but so was he to Jacob's righteousness. Here we have Isaac, the promised seed of Abraham, blinded to the righteousness of he who in essence would carry the seed of Messiah in him, blindness that caused Jacob to leave his mother's tent for exile. We must remember that Rebecca lived in Sarah's tent, which in the eyes of the sages compared to Jerusalem. Jacob therefore is exiled from Jerusalem, and we never hear of Rebecca again. Jacob later returns to the Land with an angelic escort (Genesis 32).

Two thousand years ago, Hashem also blinded the eyes of Israel to the early messianic movement (Romans. 11:7, 25). The apostle Paul too started out blinded to the fulfillment of the promises made to the fathers. This forced the Messianic believers of Israel, which were mostly a Temple sect of Jerusalem found gathering by Solomon's Portico, to leave the Land and go into exile.

Today, the seed of Jacob has returned to the Promised Land as a growing Messianic movement. They face many Esaus, but Hashem's angels escort them to destination. As in the story of old, they conquer the Land. And as it was before, the Messiah who is also called David (Hoseah 3:5) will arrive and establish his kingdom in Jerusalem from where the whole world will learn to live by the Torah of God.

May it be soon Abba, even in our days!

My Personal Thoughts

_____

_____

_____

_____

Kislev

Teach us O Kislev
of what shall be.
Hasn't the wise king said

"What has been is what will be,
what has been done is what will be done."

Ecclesiastes 1:9

Matthew 6:10   **Kislev 1/** א בכסלו

May your Kingdom come, your will be done on earth as in heaven.

Neither Abraham, Isaac, nor Jacob got a free pass into the Promised Land. All had to push and fight for their God-given inheritance.

And what does this teach us? The promises are given to us freely, but like Abraham, Rebecca, and Jacob, we have to show our desire to see them come to pass. We have to prove our worthiness to receive them by going in an all-out spiritual war for them. The promises of the world to come may be up for grabs, but it nevertheless takes a personal conscious push to receive what has been promised (Matthew 11:12). Yeshua the Master told us to,

> Go into all the world and proclaim the *Besorah* בשורה [*Good News/Gospel*] to the whole creation. Whoever believes and is immersed will be saved, but whoever does not believe will be condemned. And these signs will accompany those who believe: in my name they will cast out demons; they will speak in new tongues; they will pick up serpents with their hands; and if they drink any deadly poison, it will not hurt them; they will lay their hands on the sick, and they will recover." (Mark 16:15)

With this, the Master sent us on a mission to win the world for him, not to stay in the comfort of our fellowships. These signs that he gave us are also a hint of some may face: demons, serpents, and deadly poison. The uniform defines the mission.

We tend to think that Messiah establishes his kingdom on earth with the stroke of a magic wand; that all of a sudden, we will rule with him (Revelation 5:10). Rome was not built in a day, and neither will the Kingdom of God on earth be. Since his manifestation 2,000 years ago, we are meant to be building his kingdom on earth. I tend to think that those who will rule and reign with him in the World to Come are those who got involved in the building while in this world. Why should he choose those who today are too distracted, living for themselves and not choosing to get involved?

Just like our youth, many of us adults today are distracted from our calling. We are so engrossed in playing religion, in congregational activities and fellowships, that we leave very little time for our divine mission and calling to reach out to the world around us. We also haven't grasped the idea of living a life that shares with others. What people around us need today is not doctrine, but gentle edifying teaching of Messiah. We forget that our nice meetings are a means to an end, not an end in themselves.

We as adults need to show our teenagers the way to a godly life in reaching out to others. It is our responsibility to blaze the trail for them by doing like Abraham, letting go of home, and our personal baggage in order to engage in the mission Messiah called us to in establishing his kingdom on earth (Genesis 12:1).

Like Abraham, Moses, and all our fathers, our eyes and our hearts need to be so focused on the bright future of the Kingdom of God on earth that the present world and its concerns seem to us but husks (Luke 15:16). If not, why do we pray, "May your Kingdom come, your will be done on earth as in heaven" (Matthew 6:10)?

My Personal Thoughts

John 4:12

You aren't greater than our father Ya`akov, are you? He gave us this well and drank from it, and so did his sons and his cattle.

Today's children want anything but to follow in the footsteps of their fathers. They want to find their own paths, dig their own wells, and start all over again for themselves. Life has lost its generational continuity; therefore through generational fragmentation people have lost their sense of purpose and identity.

We must take example from Isaac. As a son, he wanted to emulate his father. He wanted to represent Abraham's dreams and visions. Isaac was willing and ready to accomplish the destiny his father had so dearly cherished and held on to.

When Isaac found himself in a dispute with his Philistine host over water rights, he could have said, "I don't need my father's wells, I am going to dig my own!" Instead, he took it upon himself to revive the wells of Abraham. He unplugged them and renamed them with the same names Abraham once did (Genesis 27).

This course of events in the patriarchs' lives lends itself to a very beautiful principle. From his miraculous birth, to carrying his own sacrifice wood on Mt. Moriah, Isaac foreshadows our Messiah, Yeshua. The vast majority of the people who claim to be disciples of Yeshua claim that he started a new religion; that he rendered Judaism obsolete and created Christianity. Nothing could be further from the truth. If anything, Yeshua taught the very heart of Judaism: the faith of Abraham.

As Isaac of old revived and drank from his father's wells, Yeshua also brought us to the waters of the wells of Abraham. He taught us to live the life of the patriarchs of our faith, to emulate their faith. Even his sermon on drinking the water of life was given at the sight of one of the wells Jacob dug (John 4).

As we learn to define our walk, as we learn to articulate our beliefs, may we be sure that the waters we drink come from the wells of Abraham. There is no need to re-invent the wheel, dig new wells, or find new doctrines and understandings of the old texts. All we need to do is revive the wells of Abraham that have been plugged with the sand of centuries of the doctrines of men who think they knew better than our patriarchs.

My Personal Thoughts

----

1 Corinthians 13:12   Kislev 3/ ג בכסלו

For now we see obscurely in a mirror, but then it will be face to face. Now I know partly; then I will know fully, just as God has fully known me.

Measure for measure is so real. So much of what happens to us is the returning of our own actions. The harvest we reap is surely the result our own sowing. By this standard, a man's life is easily assessed and his character thoroughly revealed. If someone has many friends, he must have been friendly. If others are generous with him, he must have been a sharing person. By the same token, if someone finds the heart of others like desert sand or a sky of brass, closed to his needs and pleas, maybe he lived his life as selfishly as a closed book. We are all too often to blame for the hell we create with our own two hands.

Jacob deceived his father Isaac by concealing his identity under a goat's skin. Several years later Jacob became victim of deceit as Laban concealed Leah's identity in the nuptial chamber. This would result in their family's long sibling rivalry that would cause Leah's children to later rid themselves of Joseph. When they did, they put the blood of a goat on Joseph's famous coat to pretend he had been killed by a wild animal, thus repeating the theme of being concealed under the identity of a goat. Joseph would also later trick his brothers by concealing his own identity as that of an Egyptian viceroy (Genesis 40–45).

When headed by Judah, Leah's children, returned from pasture with the news about Joseph. Judah showed Jacob the *hard evidence* of Joseph's bloody coat to prove their case. As he did, Judah used the Hebrew words, *haker-nah* הכר-נא meaning, *please, recognize these*. Many years later, Judah would be tricked and exposed by his own daughter-in-law using the very same words, *haker-nah*. These words must have pierced his heart as he remembered the treachery and lying to his own father (Genesis 37:32; 38:25)!

The concealed identity theme is a common one throughout our history. Kings, queens, and prophets used it, sometimes even under God's own purpose.

It could even be said that today Messiah hides his Jewish identity from both Israel/Jacob and the Gentiles. To the Western world he conceals his Jewish identity and appears to them as a Westerner, seeming to live as they do. This in turn makes him foreign and unrecognizable to his people.

But as with Joseph and his brethren, the day will come when Yeshua will throw off his Egyptian looking garb and say to them, "I am Yeshua, your brother" (Genesis 45:3). At that time, Yeshua will show the whole world who he really is: the King of the Jews. He will also reap the harvest of his own labor and doing. At that time he will reunite Rachel and Leah's family (the whole twelve tribes) under one banner (Ezekiel 37), and rule over the whole world from his throne in Jerusalem (Revelation 19 and 20).

In that day and in the word to come, we will each reap the harvest of the actions of our lives; what will this harvest be for you?

My Personal Thoughts

_____

_____

_____

John 1:51   **Kislev 4/** ד בכסלו

Then he [Yeshua] said to him, "Yes indeed! I tell you that you will see heaven opened and the angels of God going up and coming down on the Son of Man!"

Jacob flees from the face of his brother Esau. The received blessing now seems to have turned into a curse. He has to leave the Promised Land not knowing whether he will ever return. On his way to Paddan-Aram the patriarch makes a stopover for the night. The narrative says that he *gathers a stone* to use as a pillow and falls asleep.

During the night Jacob has a strange dream. He sees a ladder with angels descending and ascending upon him (as stated in the Hebrew text). Hashem stood above the ladder saying to him,

> Then suddenly ADONAI was standing there next to him; and he said, "I am ADONAI, the God of Avraham your *[grand]*father and the God of Yitz'chak. The land on which you are lying I will give to you and to your descendants. Your descendants will be as numerous as the grains of dust on the earth. You will expand to the west and to the east, to the north and to the south. By you and your descendants all the families of the earth will be blessed. Look, I am with you. I will guard you wherever you go, and I will bring you back into this land, because I won't leave you until I have done what I have promised you." (Genesis 28:13–15)

The message was clear: as Jacob left the Land, he would also return. With these words Jacob is comforted and rededicates himself to ADONAI (Genesis 28:20–22).

This story constitutes the main elements of Jacob's résumé as a patriarch for the House of Israel, as the leader of the people of Hashem. It is Hashem's irrefutable and undeniable endorsement of Jacob, which will find fulfillment in later years. From Laban's household, Jacob returned rich to the Land where the same angels welcomed him back (Genesis 32:1).

Yeshua introduced himself to Nathanael alluding to this story. Referring to his resurrection, in essence, Yeshua told Nathanael, "From where I came from, you will see me return." That fact was to be the proof of Yeshua's messianic claim, the sign by which all sincere Israelites with no deceit like Nathaniel should recognize him (John 1:47).

Yeshua mentioned seeing Nathanael under the fig tree. Fig trees speak of the world to come, the coming age called the Millennium (Micah 4:4), and were often used by people as the preferred place to pray and meditate. As Nathaniel, may we at his appearing also be found praying and watching (Luke 21:36) with sincere hearts and with no deceit in our mouth.

My Personal Thoughts

_____

_____

_____

_____

_____

_____

John 11:25   **Kislev 5/ ה בכסלו**

Yeshua said to her, "I AM the Resurrection and the Life! Whoever puts his trust in me will live, even if he dies."

Allow today to indulge in a Talmudic style analogy. Throughout the Biblical text there are many repeated themes. These are our heavenly author's way to get our attention towards some commonality. Twice in the apostolic writings we observe the rolling of a heavy or large stone: once in Bethany with Lazarus (John 11:39) and once at the resurrection of the Master (John 20:1). The common theme of these two events is obvious: resurrection.

When he arrives in the land of the people of the East and opens the well for Rebecca (Genesis 29:1), Jacob gives us a preview of this 'large' stone. The patriarch had just been given the promises bestowed upon the Abrahamic messianic line (Genesis 28). Because he became a forerunner of the Messiah of Israel, the events of his life are to be observed for messianic clues. His arrival in Paddan-aram is of utmost importance. The scene is set up like a well-written screenplay. It is a skit, an analogy with a prophetic message for future generations (Genesis 29:1–12).

Jacob arrives near a well at about noon. Three flocks wait for water before going to pasture but it is not time for them to drink yet as not all the flocks have come. The large stone also waits to be rolled from the mouth of the well. Rachel arrives. Jacob falls in love at first sight and opens the well for Rachel's flocks. Having watered the flocks of Rachel, the water is now available for those present at the scene, and for those still to come. (Note: Many years before, Rebecca, Jacob's mother, watered Abraham's camels; unbeknownst to him, Jacob now returns the favor and waters Rachel's flocks.)

Search this analogy with me and see the beauty of the Father's message in the life of Patriarch Jacob as reported in the Torah. The messianic redeemer is the one who opens the door to the waters of life-giving resurrection. When he, Yeshua, is manifested on the world's scene, people are already waiting for the resurrection; others will come later. First, the messianic redeemer had to be manifested coming out of what seems the wilderness of time to water Rachel's flock, who by interpretation is Israel. Only then would the water be available to the waiting flocks, and to those still arriving. Rachel's flocks were watered at noon; all throughout the rest of the day other flocks come to this water of life until such a time when night falls and the well is closed again.

Do you hear the cry of the prophet? He is calling to all the nations saying, "All you who are thirsty, come to the water! You without money, come, buy, and eat! Yes, come! Buy wine and milk without money—it's free!"(Isaiah 55:1). Sad to say, many false teachers have fouled the water with their feet (doctrines of man) (Ezekiel 34:18–19). City-folks drink stagnant water from man-made reservoirs filled with chemicals. At my house, I have well drawing water straight from Mt. Hood's snowy reserves. City people come to fill up at our well. In these days when there is a famine and drought for the pure words of the Father, we are commanded to be an oasis for the arriving flocks.

Are you?

My Personal Thoughts

_____

_____

Romans 11:26   **Kislev 6/ ו בכסלו**

And that it is in this way that all Isra'el will be saved. As the Tanakh says, "Out of Tziyon will come the Redeemer; he will turn away ungodliness from Ya`akov."

I can never wonder enough at the majestic heavenly foresight in the Torah. How many times have we seen the deeds of the father's portent to the children? This part of Jacob's life is nothing but a direct prophecy, something that relates to us today. It shows us God's plan and destiny for the world.

Deceitful worldly Laban owned everything. He ran his big business sleazily without any scruples or apologies. Kill, steal, lie, cheat; everything is allowed to *make a buck*. He sells his own daughters and consciously tries to manipulate God's blessing in Jacob to his own advantage. In spite of it all, for twenty-one years, Jacob showed a purity of spirit. Time and again he turned the proverbial *other cheek* as he allowed himself to be used and abused. Finally, like the gambler enthralled by the euphoria of several wins, Laban becomes so arrogant and sure of himself that he loses everything with one *throw of the dice* in a last attempt at treachery.

Jacob arrived in Babylon with nothing but returned from exile with the children that would later become the foundational families of the Kingdom of God. The sinner's wealth is truly laid up for the righteous (Proverbs 13:22). This same story will be repeated a few hundred years later when this time, Jacob's children will leave their Egyptian exile with spoils. Will there be another time when the descendants of Jacob will leave exile with the spoils of their persecutors? Is this an indication of things to come?

Yeshua our Master said no less. He said that if we, those who belong to him, while in this worldly Laban-like adulterous and perverse generation, if we live by the virtue taught us in the Torah instead of by the instinct of vengeance and greed, we would inherit the Land. And just like happened in Egypt, the nations would bring us their glory (Matthew 5:3–10; Isaiah 61:6).

In English texts, the book where we find Jacob's biography is called Genesis, but in Hebrew it is called by the first word of the text, *Bereshit* בראשית, meaning: *In the beginning*. Wise King Solomon teaches us that, "What has been is what will be, and what has been done is what will be done, and there is nothing new under the sun (Ecclesiastes 1:9). In the story of Jacob the Messianic patriarch, can we not see the universal redemption program of Messiah?

Like Jacob, Messiah is exiled in the nations due to the wrath of his brother. Like Jacob, Messiah takes a wife from among his exiled relatives. Like Jacob with the spoil of the nations (Jacob had Laban's sheep; Messiah has the people of the nations), Messiah eventually returns home to re-establish and populate the Land. Can you see the plan?

Who do you work with today? Righteous Jacob, who was later renamed, Israel? Or wicked Laban who represents the evil worldly systems of this day? The choice is yours. Your future depends on it!

My Personal Thoughts

_____

_____

_____

_____

Revelation 12:12   **Kislev 7/ ז בכסלו**

Therefore, rejoice, heaven and you who live there! But woe to you, land and sea, for the Adversary has come down to you, and he is very angry, because he knows that his time is short!

In the parasha this week, Jacob is in exile (he is not called Israel yet). His exile could seem the result of simple home feuding rivalries, but it is also part of a greater divine plan to create the foundational family that is to become the gates of the Kingdom of God for the rest of the world (Revelation 21:12).

Hashem's heavenly purposes do not settle on earth without struggle. The deceit and rivalries that sent Jacob in exile would follow him to Laban's house where Jacob would be deceived. On his wedding night, the man whose daughter he was to marry swapped her for her older sister. This created a feud between Rachel and Leah as they tried to out-birth each other in order to win Jacob's favor. But Jacob's heart was set on Rachel.

Laban for his part saw the favor of God on Jacob; whatever he put his hand on, turned to gold. This made his Babylonian taskmaster jealous; he wanted to keep Jacob no matter what the price. But whatever Laban did to out maneuver Jacob, Hashem always blessed his chosen-one. This didn't fail to infuriate Laban (Genesis 30).

See now the cosmic parallel: Jacob was in exile for twenty-one years fleeing from Esau (also called 'Edom'), and present-day Israel has been in exile for twenty-one centuries. The sages of the Talmud actually surnamed this present-day exile the *Edomite Exile*. Hashem made Jacob a prosperous man while in his exilic state, and so he made his people prosper in many ways while in Diaspora.

We see this very principle at work in Jacob and Laban, in the Children of Israel in Egypt and now, in the Jewish people scattered in the world. In every age, this has caused the *Labans* and the *Pharaohs* to despise the Children of Israel. As it did with Jacob, the world often envies Jewish success. Esau's problem was that of a sibling rivalry, an inheritance issue between two brothers, but Laban's problem with Jacob is different. It embodies the very heart of Anti-Semitism throughout the ages. To this day, the shrewd and heartless Jewish businessman *Jacob* stereotypes, as found in Shakespeare's work *The Merchant of Venice* and in the famed *Christmas Carol's* Ebenezer Scrooge and Jacob Marley, lingers on.

Today, as the divine plan of universal restoration comes to its completion, the devil screams and shrieks in fear. Anti-Semitism raises its ugly timeless head again as both *Esau* (the Arab world resisting Israel's right to return to its land), and *Laban* (the world at large in a growing Anti-Zionist movement) seem to mount an endless propaganda war against Israel and Jews worldwide.

Don't they know the story? Haven't they read it in the Book? No matter what anyone may do or say in the great institutions of man, God's will be done. Time may demand its due but as it was before, Jacob does return to his dear Promised Land, and he does under the name of Israel. There he lays the foundations of a kingdom that will eventually rule the entire world through one of his descendants: Yeshua.

May it be soon Abba, even in our days!

My Personal Thoughts

Matthew 28:19–20   **Kislev 8/ ח בכסלו**

Therefore, go and make people from all nations into talmidim, immersing them into the reality of the Father, the Son and the Ruach HaKodesh, and teaching them to obey everything that I have commanded you. And remember! I will be with you always, yes, even until the end of the age.

As Jacob fled his brother's wrath, Hashem came to our patriarch to reveal his overall plan. The Almighty planner of the destiny of Israel said,

> I am ADONAI, the God of Avraham your *[grand]*father and the God of Yitz'chak. The land on which you are lying I will give to you and to your descendants. Your descendants will be as numerous as the grains of dust on the earth. You will expand to the west and to the east, to the north and to the south. By you and your descendants all the families of the earth will be blessed. Look, I am with you. I will guard you wherever you go, and I will bring you back into this land, because I won't leave you until I have done what I have promised you. (Genesis 28:13–15)

Anyone who believes in the Bible has to accept that by divine mandate, the land that is now *Israel*—Jacob's future name (Genesis 32:28)—belongs to his descendants. Jacob fled from Esau, but also he was following in his father's—and grandfather's—footsteps; he was getting a wife from within the family clan. Talmudic tradition says that as he left Canaan, Hashem protected Jacob from Esau's son who pursued him. Hashem also reassured Jacob declaring that he will accomplish, through him, all the words he previously spoke to Abraham (Genesis 12:3; 28:14).

The spreading of the Children of Israel to the four winds is often referred to as the present-day Great Exile. This exile may appear as a curse to the Children of Israel, but it is the instrument Hashem uses to bless the nations. The first post-second Temple Jews to go in exile were the messianic believers who brought the teachings of our Master to all the nations of the Roman Empire. Later, as all Israel evacuated its land under Roman orders, they filled the rest of the pagan world with the knowledge of the one true God who created the universe. Thanks to the Great Exile, the majority of the world today is monotheistic, lives by a seven-day week, and derives its basic moral notions of right and wrong from the tenets of the Torah. Judaism has therefore become the most influential form of belief in the world. It is also fair to say that the whole world has heard of Messiah, so in that regards, one can also conclude that the whole world has been blessed through the descendants of Jacob, the grandson of Abraham to whom this prophecy was first given.

Jacob received this oracle as he himself went to exile. Jacob's fate then foreshadowed the future great Diaspora. Hashem assured the patriarch that the divine presence going with him in this exile will also bring him back to the Land promised to Abraham. In the same manner, Yeshua, our *Mashiach* משיח who has been with us all throughout this exile brings us back today to our Land.

Though as in the case of Jacob, God's heavenly purposes do not find their earthly fulfillment without troubles and tribulations, we are thankful to be a part of his great plan of blessing the earth.

My Personal Thoughts

_____

_____

Matthew 28:19–20   **Kislev 9/** ט בכסלו

Therefore, go and make people from all nations into talmidim . . . And remember! I will be with you always, yes, even until the end of the age.

By divine mandate and destiny, Jacob goes alone into exile for twenty-one years. That's bad news. By divine mandate and destiny, Jacob returns to the Land rich with a large family. That's good news.

In the oracle in the desert, Hashem not only reassured Jacob that his exile will not be forever, but also that he will not be there alone. Hashem says,

> Look, I am with you. I will guard you wherever you go, and I will bring you back into this land, because I won't leave you until I have done what I have promised you. (Genesis 28:15)

This promise foreshadows the cosmic truth that following the Great Exile will come the Great Ingathering of Israel. "ADONAI will bring you and your king whom you have put over yourselves to a nation you have not known, neither you nor your ancestors; and there you will serve other gods made of wood and stone" (Deuteronomy 28:36).

Chassidic teachings refer to this *king* as the presence of Messiah with his people in exile.

When Isaiah prophesied of Israel's future exile he said,

> But now this is what ADONAI says, he who created you, Ya`akov, he who formed you, Isra'el: "Don't be afraid, for I have redeemed you; I am calling you by your name; you are mine. When you pass through water, I will be with you; when you pass through rivers, they will not overwhelm you; when you walk through fire, you will not be scorched—the flame will not burn you. For I am ADONAI, your God, the Holy One of Isra'el, your Savior . . . Don't be afraid, for I am with you. I will bring your descendants from the east, and I will gather you from the west; I will say to the north, 'Give them up!' and to the south, 'Don't hold them back! Bring my sons from far away, and my daughters from the ends of the earth.'" (Isaiah 43:1–6)

Though Christian expositors like to take this passage and apply it to the universal redemption of the Gentiles, the original context of the prophecy follows Moses' theme of the return of the actual Children of Israel/Jacob to the Land promised to them by Hashem through Abraham. Similarly, knowing the Great Exile of all Israel was at hand, our Master sent his apostles away, along with Israel, with the assurance of his forever presence with them, even in exile, just as he did with Jacob. He tells them, "Therefore, go and make people from all nations into talmidim . . . And remember! I will be with you always, yes, even until the end of the age" (Matthew 28:19–20).

So you see, we have never been alone in our exilic state. ADONAI has been with us all along and he promises to bring us back as he certainly is doing in our days. It is a long and tedious process, but angels are waiting for us to lead us in the way in which we should go (Genesis 32:1–2) At that time, Esau will also quit seeking revenge against Hashem who from the beginning had given Abraham's inheritance to his brother Jacob (Genesis 25:23; 33).

May it be soon Abba, even in our days!

John 1:51

Then he said to him, "Yes indeed! I tell you that you will see heaven opened and the angels of God going up and coming down on the Son of Man!".

In the days of the Master, Galilee was a center for Torah learning. It was where many rabbis taught their disciples in Yeshivas (religious schools). The dream of every parent was for their child, especially the oldest boy, to be tutored as the disciple of a famous Rabbi. Usually an interested student would follow a Rabbi around and eventually ask him if he would take him as a disciple. The Rabbi would then tell him to stick around and that he will give him an answer later.

Yeshua broke with the traditional way of his contemporaries. Instead of waiting for potential disciples to pop the question "May I follow you, sir?" he himself did the choosing and proposing with the words, "follow me" (John 1:43). By his choice of students, it seems that Yeshua did not look for disciples already versed in the current contemporary teachings. It looks like he wanted folks who came straight from the 'streets', people who had never really learned at the feet of other rabbis. This way, he could start them from scratch without having to undo a lot of teachings. Reading about them, it seems that Yeshua's disciples were not refined in the ways and the mannerism of the disciples of other local rabbis; that's why some wondered about some of them (Matthew 9:14–17). It is the same problem with many people today; there is so much to unlearn, so many rocks of false teachings to rid the ground of before the truth can take root in people's hearts.

When in Judea, Andrew left John the Immerser and followed the Master, Andrew *fished* his brother, Peter. When the Master returned to Galilee to establish his itinerant Yeshivah of disciples, he found Philip and Nathanael. These were all local boys who roamed the streets of Bethsaida as youth.

Yeshua chose all sorts: despised tax collectors, a Roman collaborator, main stream working folks, zealot political activists, and even religious activists. When he saw Nathanael, the Master had a very particular comment for him. He said, "Here's a true son of Isra'el—nothing false in him" (John 1:47).

Whatever he was referring to, it is a great compliment to receive from he who is the Messiah. It seems that Nathanael was a religious man, a *just* or a *righteous* man like Yeshua's own earthly father was (Matthew 1:19), which in Judaism today would be called an Orthodox Jew.

When Yeshua saw Nathanael, he told him what he was doing. Some suggest that perhaps Nathanael was studying the Torah, which people often did in the shade of a fig tree. Some even suggest that Nathanael was reading the section about Jacob's Ladder, and that it is why Yeshua referred to that prophecy about himself in his comment to Nathanael (John 1:51).

Whatever it was that Nathanael was doing by the fig tree, he received a very nice compliment from the Master. Whereas we may not all be given that sort of accolade of being found *without deceit or guile*, may we all be told at the end of this age, "Excellent! You are a good and trustworthy servant. You have been faithful with a small amount, so I will put you in charge of a large amount. Come and join in your master's happiness" (Matthew 25:21).

My Personal Thoughts

_____

_____

1 Corinthians 3:13

But each one's work will be shown for what it is; the Day will disclose it.

The knowledge that every act, whether good or bad carries its own reward or punishment should create in us a certain fear of Hashem. When I say *fear of Hashem* I do not mean just respect, but the actual fear of the consequences of breaking his Torah rule. This system of *measure for measure* is actually meant to be a form of soul-policing imposed on us by the spirit of the Almighty God who created us.

There are many who claim that since the time they have been immersed in the name of Yeshua, they are regenerated into sinless being and are therefore impervious to sin. They claim that through this process, the Torah of God is written in their heart as it is said in Jeremiah (Jeremiah 33:31–33). If it were true, with the amount of people in the world who claim to have been immersed in the Master, we should see a substantial decline in crime and immorality, but it is not the case. Instead, man seems to be receiving upon his own head the fruit of his rebellious nature and unchecked actions.

Only one hope remains.

In the end, at the time when judgment calls and the books are opened, we will each stand before Hashem. In the presence of the Ancient of Days who created the heavens and the earth and all that is in it, we will stand on the scales of judgment and our lives will be measured and weighed for virtue (1 Corinthians 3:13). As the scales drastically tip to a negative balance, the accuser and prosecutor of our souls will shout, "*middah k'neged middah* מידה כנגד מידה or, *measure for measure*: this is the law of all the Heavens." In the deep silence and awe of the courtroom, the defender and redeemer of our soul will then approach and step on the other side of the scales adding to the balance and righteousness earned by virtue of his stripes and innocent suffering. As the scales now tip to the other side, he will again shout, "*middah k'neged middah*, measure for measure." With a knock of his gavel, the judge of the earth will then proclaim the final sentence: "The measure has been met."

I am saddened when I hear people talking flippantly about sin. Just because they don't pay for it they think that their redemption is so-called free. It is only free for them because someone else pays for it. In this case, Yeshua paid the price in the measure of his dedicated life and cruel suffering on the cross.

May we never forget it!

My Personal Thoughts

_____

_____

_____

_____

_____

_____

_____

Matthew 5:45   **Kislev 12/ יב בכסלו**

That you may be sons of your Father who is in heaven.

As Eleazer and his ten camels loaded with a bride price arrived in Padam-Aram, he asked the God of Abraham to help him identify she who would be the next matriarch of Israel. He stopped by the municipal well expecting the chosen maiden to remove a very heavy stone from the mouth of the well, and water his camels with one hundred and fifty gallons of water. This was a very unlikely sign but the calling and stakes were high. The chosen one needed to have the right heart, the heart of a servant. Many years later Jacob, who was that same maiden's son, would stand by that same well and return the favor to the House of Laban. This time he would roll the stone from the well and water Rachel's flocks (Genesis 24:12–20; 29:1–11).

The Torah teaches us the notion of measure for measure. It says, "But if any harm follows, then you are to give life for life, eye for eye, tooth for tooth, hand for hand, foot for foot, (Exodus 21:23–24). We may tend to conclude that type of tit for tat as Mosaic Law modus operandi, but our Master Yeshua expected us to also live within the notion of measure for measure. In his own words he said, "For if you forgive others their offenses, your heavenly Father will also forgive you; but if you do not forgive others their offenses, your heavenly Father will not forgive yours" (Matthew 6:14–15).

The Master's idea of measure for measure was not for us to demand the exact measure of justice for ourselves, but rather to realize that on that great Day, the God of Heaven will be the one to balance the scales of justice for us all. In his teaching about *measure for measure*, Yeshua re-affirms the tenets of the great luminary of Israel who said, "Whoever refrains from exacting his measure, the heavenly courts forgives his sins" (b.Rosh Hashana 17a). Another teaches the following:

> Regarding those who are insulted but do not return an insult, those who are rebuked without replying, they are the ones who do good out of love for God and rejoice in their suffering. . . . He who passes over an opportunity to retaliate has all his transgressions passed over. (b.Yoma 23a)

May we also learn to live by our Master's idea of measure for measure as he taught it: "How blessed are those who show mercy, for they will be shown mercy. . . . Don't judge, so that you won't be judged. . . . Forgive us what we have done wrong, as we too have forgiven those who have wronged us. . . . For the way you judge others is how you will be judged—the measure with which you measure out will be used to measure to you."

Here is how the Master taught us to apply measure for measure,

> You have heard that our fathers were told, 'Eye for eye and tooth for tooth.' But I tell you not to stand up against someone who does you wrong. On the contrary, if someone hits you on the right cheek, let him hit you on the left cheek too! If someone wants to sue you for your shirt, let him have your coat as well! And if a soldier forces you to carry his pack for one mile, carry it for two! When someone asks you for something, give it to him; when someone wants to borrow something from you, lend it to him . . . Therefore, be perfect, just as your Father in heaven is perfect. (Matthew 5:7; 7:1–2; 6:12; 5:38–45)

Colossians 4:6   Kislev 13/ יג בכסלו

Let your conversation always be gracious and interesting,
so that you will know how to respond to any particular individual.

Rachel our beloved matriarch died shortly after Jacob foolishly swore to Laban, "But if you find your gods with someone, that person will not remain alive" (Genesis 31:32). This should teach us about the power of words. Even though Jacob loved Rachel, this is the second record of his harsh speech to her, thus the saying, 'We often hurt most the people we love most,' might be true.

Rachel was certainly not guilty of idolatry while she was married to Jacob. The gods she had stolen were family heirlooms, an inheritance to which she might have been entitled. Tradition also teaches that Laban could have used them as means of divination, and that Rachel was keeping them away from her father to keep him from consulting them about Jacob's whereabouts. Whatever these *gods* were, this story should teach us about the power of words, especially under oath. Even though innocent of idolatry, Rachel dies in childbirth shortly after Jacob's utters his foolish vow. Like toothpaste out of a tube, words cannot be taken back.

I do not agree with the adage, "Sticks and stones can hurt my bones but words can never hurt me." Words are real things; they can kill or they can give life. Words pronounced in anger can leave indelible scars in someone's heart. People who get hurt because of words are accused of being sensitive, but where does it say that it is wrong to be sensitive? The truth is that we have to be sensitive enough if we want to be attuned to Hashem's voice in our hearts and aware of the needs of those around us. When people have to constantly protect themselves from verbal harshness and abuse, they naturally develop a shield of protection, which in turn makes them callous and insensitive even to God's voice.

The world needs not to be a place run by the law of the jungle where only the strong survive and the weak live in fear. This type of society reminds me of the school yard in the boarding school where I was raised. Because of fear of the bullying older kids who ruled the center of the yard, we younger kids remained in the perimeter. The world needs instead to be a place where the strong exerts their power in the protection of the weak, not to dominate them.

Mathematician Edward Lorenz posited that even a small change at one place in a complex system can have major effects elsewhere. In his famous example of the "butterfly effect," he tells us that the beating of a butterfly's wing in Brazil can cause a series of much greater changes in the weather, such as a cyclone hitting Japan, or a tornado touching down in Texas. In the same way, small acts, and even smaller words (positive or negative) can have large outcomes. Even the flickering of a candle can be seen very far when it is very dark.

With positive actions and words, as small as the fluttering of a butterfly wings or the flickering of a candle, we have the power to change the world. Let's do it, one good deed and one good word at a time!

My Personal Thoughts

_____

_____

_____

_____

Luke 21:29–31   **Kislev 14/ יד בכסלו**

Then he told them a parable: "Look at the fig tree—indeed, all the trees.
As soon as they sprout leaves, you can see for yourselves that summer is near.

In the same way, when you see these things taking place, you are to know that the Kingdom of God is near. Must history always repeat itself (Ecclesiastes. 1:9)? Let's hope it does!

When Abraham arrived in the Land with his family he was unpleasantly surprised by its Canaanite inhabitants. Even though divinely promised to him, Abraham could not possess the Land without warfare, which he wanted to avoid. Later, due to a famine, the patriarch left for Egypt where, after the captivity of his wife, he returned to the Land with great wealth. The text doesn't reveal it to us, but since the Canaanite still lived in the Land, they might have made a compromise with Abraham. Maybe the fact that Abraham was now wealthy and powerful enough to defeat five Amorite kings could have had something to do with it (Genesis 13).

Our father Jacob also left the Land for a long exile at Laban's house. When he returned with his big family, his brother, who had adopted the Canaanite way of life, only had evil intentions towards his returning wealthy and blessed brother Jacob. Esau intended to kill Jacob as soon as they met. Before the fatal show down, Jacob had a surprise encounter with the Messiah against whom he was not able to prevail. The Messiah blessed Jacob and gave him a new name: Israel. The patriarch has now become a new person. Through wisdom and humility, he was able to win his brother's heart, who then kisses him and allows him to settle again in his homeland.

When Moses, following in the footsteps of Abraham and Jacob led the children of Israel from Egypt towards Canaan, the Amalekites pursued them from the rear (Exodus 17:8) and later in Kadesh Barneah, Edom would not allow passage through its lands (Numbers 20:14–18). In spite of it all, Hashem's overall plan succeeded and Israel settled in Canaan. Today, like Abraham, Jacob, and the Children of Israel in the desert, the Jewish people from around the world are returning to the Land from where they have been exiled for so long. Ironically Esau the Canaanite, who was fully knowledgeable of Jacob's rightful inheritance, lay in wait for his brother to do him harm. Thank Hashem that we know the end from the beginning and that Jacob does settle in the Land. We must only pray now that Hashem's will be done. We must pray for the wisdom that comes from the Messiah.

In the meantime, we learn from history that the Jewish soul is like that of a homing pigeon. From wherever he is in the world, through hell and high water, he instinctively returns home to his ground zero: to the Land of Israel.

It is an awesome example teaching us about the very soul of man, the soul of all humanity. In the end, it must return to its Creator.

My Personal Thoughts

_____

_____

_____

_____

_____

2 Corinthians 5:17   **Kislev 15/** טו בכסלו

Therefore if any man is in Messiah, he is a new creation.

As he made ready to face Esau before entering the Promised Land, Jacob had another encounter to make. This was probably the most important encounter of his life, the one that changed him forever and confirmed his messianic destiny.

While Jacob was by himself, the angel of Adonai attacked him in the dark of the night. Jacob felt his blows but didn't see him. He heard the voice but could not make out the face. Jacob was the victim of a wild man attacking him under the cover of night and probably presumed it to be Esau until he heard the voice, which sounded like God. It was almost like the words of his old father— who said in the darkened sight of his old age, "The voice is Ya`akov's voice, but the hands are `Esav's hands" (Genesis 27:22), were returning to haunt Jacob in the form of this concealed adversary. Jacob's attitude towards this angel determined the next day's encounter with Esau. The angel finally revealed himself by changing Jacob's name. Jacob then names the place, *Peniel* פניאל (the face of God) (Genesis 32:30). Much later, the prophet Hoseah spoke of these events saying, "In the womb he took his brother by the heel; in the strength of his manhood he fought with God" (Hoseah 12:3).

For 2,000 years people have fought against a Messiah concealed in the dark of cultural misconceptions, a Messiah who, like Joseph, hid himself under an Egyptian cloak; who, like Jacob, hid himself under Esau's disguise in front if his father. There came a time though when the Messiah identified himself to Jacob, even at the cost of a crippling blessing.

Can Jews be accused of refusing the Messiah, also called, the *word*, or *the Memrah* ממרה *made flesh* (John 1:14)? What word are we talking about? Yes; it is the word of Torah. To be eligible, the Messiah must be Torah observant, which Yeshua was. He proclaimed that he did not come to reverse the Torah, and that whoever teaches against even the smallest of its commands is called least in the Kingdom of heaven (Matthew 5:17–19). But today Yeshua is described to the Jewish nation as one who cancels the very Torah that condemns to death any would-be prophet who even talks or teaches about disobeying it (Deuteronomy 13:5).

Jacob fought for what he knew was right. As he surrendered, he inherited a wound in his thigh. When Jacob met his match, it changed his life forever and sent him into his messianic destiny (Genesis 32). It is one thing to hear Messiah, but it is another to meet him. You know you've met him when your life changes. When the Jacob in you, is changed to Israel (the Prince with God), a person submits and yields to Hashem. When someone meets Messiah, he does not need to confess it with loud words, personalized T-shirts, or bumper stickers in order to make the point to others; his altered life is the proud testimony of the event.

Have you heard Messiah? Have you also met him? If so, can people around you testify of the event by just watching your changed life?

My Personal Thoughts

_____

_____

_____

_____

Matthew 5:48

Therefore, be perfect, just as your Father in heaven is perfect.

Jacob left the house of Laban. He reckoned with the angel of ADONAI as well as with his estranged brother, which shows that meeting with Hashem's angel generally provides us with the humbler attitude necessary to improve our relationships with our family, friends, and neighbors. The events at Sheshem left a bitter taste in the patriarch's mouth (Genesis 34), but then Hashem called unto Jacob (Genesis 35:1). The God of Heaven initiated a rendezvous with the patriarch at Beth-El, the very same place Jacob laid his head on a stone and received the vision of the ladder (Genesis 28).

See now the heart of an unassuming man, of a man who knew how to humble himself before his God. Like Abraham and Moses after him, Jacob did not assume that the Creator of the universe called unto him because of any sense of personal virtue. Jacob feared his God and in view of this awesome event decided to go on a spiritual house cleaning. "Oh no!" he said. "The Father wants to see us. He summoned us to his presence. We must prepare. We must get ready. Come on everybody! Let's get the house cleaned up. Let's wash up and put clean clothes on." It's a little bit like preparing to go on a date. We will see later that the way Jacob prepared for this very important encounter with the greatest VIP of all times, was the same way the Children of Israel prepared to meet Hashem by Mt. Horeb, as well as the way a priest would later sanctify himself before entering the Holy, the first chamber of the Temple.

While preparing for the special encounter Jacob told his people, "Get rid of the foreign gods that you have with you" (Genesis 35:2). We must not assume here that Jacob had fallen into idolatry. Jacob's whole family and all his servants came from the idolatrous household of Laban, and whereas Jacob certainly did not consciously permit the worship of idols, people always carry extra baggage with them.

So it is with us. The Messiah calls us. We are now on a spiritual journey to Beth-El (the House of God). One day we will meet him there on Mt. Moriah when he reigns over the whole world. In the meantime, we are meant to prepare for this awesome rendezvous. We must purify and sanctify ourselves in the living waters of the Torah. We must clothe ourselves with humility, and put away the foreign gods from among us. We do live in an idolatrous world where instead of worshipping Hashem and celebrating his sanctified days, people have created religions that fit more into their personal ways and perverted sense of right and wrong. Whether we like to admit it or not, we also carry a little bit of that baggage with us.

In our walk towards the messianic Age, let us all, like Jacob, learn to always keep with us the wounding blessing from the concealed Messiah which provokes us to reconcile with former enemies, clean and purify ourselves with the waters of the Torah, and clothe ourselves with the humility of his righteousness. As his bride, let us ready ourselves to physically meet our Messiah at the end of this age; let us not forget to put away the idols, the worldliness, the vanity, the pride, and the selfishness of the god of this world from among us.

My Personal Thoughts

_____

_____

_____

James 1:23–25

For whoever hears the Word but doesn't do what it says is like someone who looks at his face in a mirror, who looks at himself, goes away and immediately forgets what he looks like. But if a person looks closely into the perfect Torah, which gives freedom, and continues, becoming not a forgetful hearer but a doer of the work it requires, then he will be blessed in what he does.

Jacob may have inherited the promises made to Abraham but he nevertheless had to come clean before receiving them from the Almighty. He first had to meet Esau and face up to his former deception. He had to come to terms with his own demons before meeting the angels on the way to the Promised Land (Genesis 32–33).

These chapters may point us to the struggle Israel faces today as it returns to the Promised Land after a long exile in *Babylon*, but they also speak to the issues we face in our own lives.

As believers in Yeshua the Messiah, each one of us inherits a share of the elements of the promises made to Abraham. The fact that we are inheritors does not mean that we are not asked to work out this deliverance in fear and trembling (Philippians. 2:12). We may be eligible, but we still have to show our worthiness. Don't get me wrong; this does not come in the form of works to earn the already given blessing, but rather in the form of a living statement of personal integrity, like passing the entrance exam and getting acceptance into the university.

Granted, life is a fight, life is a struggle, and there is no way around it. But if we are to labor, may we labor for that "food that stays on into eternal life" (John 6:27). If we are going to contend, may we contend for the incorruptible price, for that crown of life Hashem has promised to them who love him (James 1:12). If we are going to be soldiers, may we fight for the city with permanent foundations, of which the architect and builder is Hashem (Hebrews 11:10).

Can we stand with Jacob and meet the angel of ADONAI in our lives? Can we meet he who makes us face the lies of our lives that we've ignored for so long? Can we face him with the rationalizations that make us deny his name daily in front of others through disobedience? Can we stand him to bless us by crippling our pride forever, change our name and truly make us a new creature, not fashioned after the pride we so dearly hold on to, but after the meekness of those who inherit the Land (Matthew 5:5)?

Jacob had to learn not to hold a grudge; do you hold grudges? Jacob had to learn to forgive his enemy; do you forgive your enemies? Jacob had to learn to solely rely on his God for vindication; do you try to vindicate yourself in front of others?

We are always so concerned about straightening up others that we forget that our primary duty is to be faced daily with the word of Torah, that we may learn to be fashioned according to the ways of Hashem. May we accept what the word of Torah tells us. May we allow it to even cripple us for life; to take our pride and our arrogance away, that we may inherit the eternal price reserved for those who put their trust solely in him.

My Personal Thoughts

_____

_____

_____

_____

Matthew 26:15   **Kislev 18/** יח בכסלו

"What are you willing to give me if I turn Yeshua over to you?" They counted out thirty silver coins and gave them to Y'hudah.

Joseph was sold by his brothers. Some ancient Jewish commentaries put the price of the transaction at thirty pieces of silver, the same price given for the Master to be delivered to the Sadducees.

Many years before the manifestation of the Mashiach, Amos cried out about it in the days of Uzziah King of Judea. The prophet, a former shepherd from Tekoah, received an oracle against all of the nations surrounding Israel (Amos 1–2:3). One can imagine the scene.

First he cried out against the sins of Damascus, then of the Philistines, Edom, Amon, and finally against the people of Moab. This was a safe prophecy. Everybody in Israel could not agree with him more. As he exposed the sins of the Gentiles and of the enemies of Israel, the prophet was on safe grounds and probably very popular. The oracle then turned towards Judea. The people of the Northern Kingdom may have cheered as they had had a long rivalry with the Southern Kingdom of Judah.

The oracle was not over. It continued on to expose Israel, the Northern Kingdom. The prophet then might have been less popular. It seems to be the ungrateful destiny of would-be-prophets to earn fame and popularity only as long as the disciplinary divine oracle focuses on the sins of others. One of the strongest accusations against Israel/Northern Kingdom/sons of Leah was, "they sell the upright for silver" (Amos 2:6), a stern reminder of Leah's children's sale of Joseph for silver.

It seems that the oracle employed some sort of a psychological oratory device on the audience. The people already knew the sins of the idolatrous nations around them. They did not need to be reminded of it. What purpose would it serve really? What it did though is that as long as he exposed the sins of others, it got the people of Israel to agree with him on the principles of sin. They were a bit taken aback though when he suddenly turned the focus on their own iniquity.

This attitude of not being able to see our own sins and mistakes because of being so focused on those of others is at the root of all sorts of bigotry. It is even at the root of the breaking down of families.

May we live in the remembrance of the Master, who reminding his disciples of the wisdom of their own sages, said,

> Don't judge, so that you won't be judged. For the way you judge others is how you will be judged — the measure with which you measure out will be used to measure to you. Why do you see the splinter in your brother's eye but not notice the log in your own eye? How can you say to your brother, 'Let me take the splinter out of your eye,' when you have the log in your own eye? You hypocrite! First, take the log out of your own eye; then you will see clearly, so that you can remove the splinter from your brother's eye! (Matthew 7:1–5)

My Personal Thoughts

_____

_____

1 Timothy 3:6   **Kislev 19/** יט בכסלו

Not a novice, lest being lifted up with pride he fall into the condemnation of the devil (KJV).

It is easy to see Joseph the son of Jacob as a Messianic foreshadow. Even classic Judaism presents Joseph as prefiguring the Messiah. Because of the messianic allusions to both Joseph and Judah, Judaism even believes in two Messiahs: first a suffering one, Joseph, and second a ruling one, Judah. We know now that the two ideas are resolved in Yeshua's first and second coming.

Joseph and Judah were the recognized heads over the families, each one by their respective mothers: Rachel and Leah. The tension between the two families resulted in a divided kingdom.

From the beginning, Joseph seemed rather unwise. He flaunted his father Jacob's preferential love, strutting around in his princely coat. He also probably didn't have to pull in as much of a workload as his brothers. He was treated like a first-born. To add insult to injury, Joseph publicly volunteered his seemingly narcissistic dreams, at which even Jacob seemed astounded. His brothers even surnamed him, *The Master of dreams*, which proved in fact, true, as the story confirms later (Genesis 37).

Joseph was truly the *Master of dreams*, for that matter; he was to be established over his family and the known world of his day. But in order to fulfill his destiny, he still needed the humiliations that only slavery and unjust incarceration could offer. It doesn't seem to be enough for Hashem that we fulfill our destiny for him. This is true of all of us. If we are to represent him through our life or even verbal messages, we are to represent him properly by exerting a life of humility and virtue he can be proud of. Before finally being given his God-given destiny, like Joseph, every man needs to go through rejection, slavery, and the cruel injustice of man. Only the distress and humiliation of wrong and unjust treatment provides the qualities needed for Godly leadership. Without it, any would-be leader of God's people is prone to the pitfalls of novices.

Come to think of it, the same was told of Messiah (Hebrews 5:8). Yeshua was not to be given the crown without the cross. As a nation, it is also true of God's people. For centuries, like Joseph and Messiah, the nation of Israel as a whole was afflicted by the world without as cause, just for being Jews. We are told though that it is God who put 'stoniness' on Israel for a while so that the nations could have their time (Romans 11:25). This time of humiliation of Israel serves therefore to prepare him for its priestly destiny in the World to Come (Exodus 19:6).

As we approach the time of the fulfillment of the Messianic era, the true followers of Messiah will all be unjustly treated, and that is only because they are God's people (Revelation 12:17). May this coming tribulation heal us from our arrogance, pride, and immaturity that we may be worthy to rule and reign with him in the World to Come (Revelation 20:4).

My Personal Thoughts

_____

_____

_____

_____

_____

87

2 Timothy 4:7   **Kislev 20/ כ בכסלו**

I I have fought the good fight, I have finished the race, I have kept the faith.

Genesis 36:43 ends all Biblical narrations about Esau and his family line stating: these are the chiefs of Edom (that is, Esau, the father of Edom), according to their dwelling places in the land of their possession. Genesis 37 takes up the story of Jacob's family line with the mention that Jacob lived in the land of his father's sojournings, in the land of Canaan.

Esau and his descendants are said to live in the *land of their possession*, while Jacob lived in the *land of his father's sojournings*. We are actually told that Jacob's fathers lived in the Land as in a foreign land (Hebrews 11:9). Esau is *home*, while Jacob still waits for the fulfillment of the promises of God.

In our desire for peace and security, in our desire to stop roaming, to put down our luggage and establish roots, it is so easy to settle for the here and now. What is it that made the patriarchs *the patriarchs* of our faith? What made their faith so special? It is that they, all "kept on trusting until they died, without receiving what had been promised" (Hebrews 11:13)?

I was talking with a friend recently about an idealistic project I wanted to get into. He asked me, "Can you really see it through?" I said, "Except by a miracle, I don't think so!" I explained to him that *victory* is not crossing the finish line, but *victory* is fighting with all we've got for the goal God set in our hearts until the day we die, to be consumed by it if necessary. We may not enjoy the fruits of our labor, but our children, our grandchildren, great-grandchildren, or future generations will. Most world-changers did not enjoy the fruits of their labors, but the generations after them did.

The fathers of our faith pioneered the way for us. Not having received the promises but having seen them and greeted them from afar (Hebrews 11:13). They left for us an example to follow.

May we also learn not to settle for the temporary *here and now* but set our eyes on the higher goals of the establishment of the Kingdom of God on the earth in the world to come. May we set our eyes on the Promised Land and not compromise for the sake of temporary peace and security.

My Personal Thoughts

_____

_____

_____

_____

_____

_____

_____

_____

_____

Romans 8:18   **Kislev 21/ כא בכסלו**

I don't think the sufferings we are going through now are even worth comparing with the glory that will be revealed to us in the future.

The Torah tells us,

> ADONAI was with Yosef, and he became wealthy while he was in the household of his master the Egyptian. His master saw how ADONAI was with him, that ADONAI prospered everything he did. Yosef pleased him as he served him, and his master appointed him manager of his household; he entrusted all his possessions to Yosef. (Genesis 39:2–4)

When in the prison, the jailor noticed the same things about the patriarch and he put Joseph in charge of the jail. It's almost like Joseph heard the very words of the Master, "Purchase friends for yourselves with mamon of wrongdoing, so that when it is finished they will take you into eternal dwellings" (Luke 16:9, DHE).

Through all his ordeals, Joseph's life under servitude remains an example to us all. His attitude was nothing short of divine. He never indulged in thoughts of revenge, sullenness, hatred, or anger. When he later saw his brothers, they probably thought Joseph would use his position of Viceroy of Egypt to exact vengeance upon them, but instead he told them,

> But don't be sad that you sold me into slavery . . . because it was God who sent me ahead of you to preserve life . . . God sent me ahead of you to ensure that you will have descendants on earth and to save your lives in a great deliverance. (Genesis 45:5–7)

In everything that happened to him, Joseph understood that the problems in his life were not the fault of his brothers or his father, but that they were the will of God in order to prepare him for the greater destiny of saving the world.

Yeshua, our Beloved Master also was sold by his brothers and was put in charge of the Gentiles. Later he will return and, like Joseph, unveil his identity to his brothers and tell them not to fear; he did not come to exact vengeance upon them but to save them.

And what does this teach us? In spite of our many problems, may we also refuse to indulge in thoughts of revenge, sullenness, hatred, or anger. May we learn that our lives are the result of Hashem's ultimate unfailing plan and that as we learn the lessons of the proverbial *school of hard knocks*, we are getting prepared for our glorious destiny in the World to Come.

May if be soon Abba, even in our days!

My Personal Thoughts

_____

_____

_____

_____

_____

_____

John 15:13   **Kislev 22/ כב בכסלו**

No one has greater love than a person who lays down his life for his friends.

The story of Judah's problems in engendering a proper posterity seems like a disconnected interlude between Genesis 37 and 39. One wonders, "What is the purpose of cutting of the narrative of Joseph's story with the outrageous story of Judah and Tamar?"

The writers of the *Tanach* often wrote thematically rather than chronologically. They did this in order to make a point. When reading the *Tanach*, missing the theme could mean missing important points of the story. In this case the theme is found in the connection between the lives of Joseph and that of Judah.

We are told that previously, Joseph had been *brought down* to Egypt (Genesis 39:1). Now we are told that Judah also *went down* from his brothers to marry a Canaanite woman. This union was a step-down for Judah because it disqualified him from the rights of first-born after his three older siblings also disqualified themselves (Genesis 38:1–2). The two stories tell us of the spiritual direction of the concerned person. In this case, the writer points out the theme of divine retribution. As Judah sent his brother Joseph *down*, so Hashem sends Judah.

Amos the prophet brings the idea of divine retribution for evil doing. He said, "For Isra'el's three crimes, no, four—I will not reverse it—because they sell the upright for silver" (Amos 2:6). This statement is reminiscent of Joseph and of the Master. Amos continued and asked, "Do two walk together, unless they have agreed to meet . . .? Does disaster come to a city, unless ADONAI has done it?" (Amos 3:3,6). Thus he reminds people, "the curse causeless shall not come" (Proverbs 26:2, KJV).

Sometimes we do not understand why our lives take certain turns and we wonder if Hashem really watches. It is at these times that we should ask ourselves if what is happening to us might only be a reflection of our own actions. One who can do that has really learned the fear of God.

Judah repented and understood what Tamar did and that it was because of love for the covenant of Abraham. Ultimately this course of events turned the tide for Judah and his whole family. We learn later that, as he had first sold his brother for his own benefit, he offers his life as ransom to save that of Benjamin's. This in turn started the course of events that would save all of Jacob's family from famine and death. We remember that from Judah also comes he who would also give his life as ransom for our sins.

May Abba grant us, like Judah, the ability to start on the way up and come to the understanding of our sins (Genesis 38:12, 26). This is the beginning of the way to the Promised Land!

My Personal Thoughts

Matthew 7:6

Don't give to dogs what is holy, and don't throw your pearls to the pigs. If you do, they may trample them under their feet, then turn and attack you.

Until this day, we Jews are persecuted for our stubborn adherence to the tenets of the Torah. We always hope that if we could get people to understand it better, they would understand us, so we try to teach it to them. Ironically, our Master used the Biblical Instruction of feeding only the ritually unclean meat to dogs (Exodus. 22:31; Matthew 7:6) to give us a warning about the dangers of teaching Torah to the spiritually ignorant.

Nowhere is the Master's warning better illustrated as in the traditionally told story of ten Jewish sages in the second century who were tortured and martyred on the orders of the Roman emperor Hadrian. The account is based on the medieval Midrash Eleh Ezkerah. According to the Midrash, the Roman ruler asked rabbis what the Jewish law prescribes as punishment for one who kidnaps and sells a fellow Jew. The rabbis informed him that the Bible stipulates that the criminal be put to death. The emperor then brought up the case of Joseph who was kidnapped by his ten brothers and sold as a slave to Egypt. He argued that since the brothers were not sentenced to death, ten sages of Israel must be put to death in their place. The problem is that the Roman Emperor, being ignorant of the Torah could not wisely balance its commandments. He did not know the verse that says ". . . nor are children to be executed for the fathers; every person will be executed for his own sin" (Deuteronomy 24:16).

Hadrian's rhetoric for anti-Semitism has remained within Christianity at large. Today many people still blame the tragic history of the Jewish nation on an accusation of deicide by Jews in the first century CE This accusation resonates the same way as one who would decide to hate all white Americans for the decisions of one white American president many years ago. This comfortable rhetoric helps the Christian world to shirk responsibility for 2,000 years of cruel persecution of Jews and provides the water needed to wash their bloody hands saying with Pilate, "My hands are clean of this man's blood; it's your responsibility" (Matthew 27:24).

Yes, the Father visits the sins of the parents onto the children, but only to the third or fourth generation (Exodus 34:7), and even then, God said that children should not be put to death for the sins of the fathers (Deuteronomy 24:16). So even if by the wildest stretch of one's imagination it were true that Jews were nationally responsible for the death of Yeshua, the Inquisitions and the Holocaust are no justifications for it. What remains now is the fact that people need to realize that the only reason for bigotry of any kind is man's unregenerate heart.

May the world think on these things as again it is faced with very serious decisions concerning the fate of Israel and of the Jewish nation.

My Personal Thoughts

_____

_____

_____

_____

_____

_____

John 10:10–11, 22

The thief comes only in order to steal, kill and destroy; I have come so that they may have life, life in its fullest measure. "I am the good shepherd. The good shepherd lays down his life for the sheep. Then came Hanukkah in Yerushalayim. It was winter,

Tonight is the first night of Hanukkah. This evening the majority of Jews around the world, believers and non-believers alike, will remember this joyous event by lighting the first candle of the nine-branch candelabrum. Since this week we are also looking at the story of Joseph, let us see if we can find a connection.

Just like there are many foreshadows of Messiah, there are also many foreshadows of the Anti-Messiah. Like many did before him and others continued after him, Antiochus Epiphanes established himself on the world of his day to bring darkness, fear, sorrow, and perdition to God's people (1 Maccabees). Joseph on the other hand was established on the world of his day to bring light, safety, joy, and the redemption of God's people. We could therefore think of the story of Joseph as a *Hanukkah in reverse*.

Yeshua our Master taught us that Hanukkah foreshadowed events yet to come (Matthew 24:15–31). When he went to Jerusalem to celebrate this glorious festival, he used the opportunity to teach us about the *evil one*, about the false shepherd and the thief that will one day manifest himself and devour Hashem's flock (John 10:1–22). In that day, there will be another *Hanukkah*.

The story echoes that of Passover with Moses, and that of Purim with Mordechai and Queen Esther. May we remember that as there was a Pharaoh, a Haman, and an Antiochus Epiphanes—who all willed the annihilation of God's people if they did not conform—there will also be a Moses, a Mordechai, and a Mathias Maccabee who will rescue us away from the hands of the evil one.

Yes, at that time, the Good Shepherd, Our Mashiach, like David of old who killed a lion and bear to protect the flocks of his father (1 Samuel.17:34–36), will come and rescue us from the hands of he who seeks our destruction.

When that time comes, may we be found on the right side of history!

My Personal Thoughts

_____

_____

_____

_____

_____

_____

_____

_____

_____

92

Matthew 24:15   כה בכסלו /Kislev 25

So when you see the abomination that causes desolation spoken about through the prophet Dani'el standing in the Holy Place (let the reader understand the allusion).

From Cain to Nebuchadnezzar, everyone who ever tried to conquer the Jewish people did it forcefully through political, financial, and military means. In his *Jewish Antiquities*, Flavius Josephus gives a detailed account of Alexander the Great's visit to Jerusalem and the transpiring events that caused him not to invade and destroy it. Alexander the Great did not conduct a military campaign against Jerusalem. In spite of this, the Hellenic Empire seems to have been the most successful at conquering the Jewish nation. They did not do it forcefully through political, financial, and military means, but like Balak of old, through enticing Israel into cultural assimilation (Numbers 25). In those days, Greece represented the West and a philosophy of life that was very different than that of Semitic Israel. Hellenism then became attractive to Israel, thus causing it to sin.

When Israel had gotten truly addicted to Hellenism and even had a Greek appointed corrupt Jewish high priest, all Antiochus Epiphanes thought he had to do was to send his emissary with a list of reforms to bring all of Judaism into his evil hands. He didn't expect the Maccabee Revolt. The Maccabees may have won the war and rededicated the Temple, Antiochus Epiphanes may be dead, but the form of Anti-Semitism that he taught is still alive and vibrant.

In his great graciousness and compassion, Hashem gave us his Messiah but as of now, this Jewish, righteous, and Torah-observant Messiah has been highjacked. In less than two hundred years, Greco-Roman believers displayed him as a Roman god dressed as a Greek Adonis and teaching Hellenistic philosophy. By a twist of irony, in today's mainstream Christianity, an interpretation of Paul's epistles advocates this identity theft of our Messiah by including in its theology the very same set of religious reforms initiated by Antiochus Epiphanes. These were to stop observing the seventh day Sabbath, the practice of circumcision, that of eating according to biblical dietary laws, and of studying theology as per the Torah, which is referred to as the Old Testament, as if it were old and obsolete.

As a Jewish believer, I find myself in awe that today, my non-Jewish brothers live by the same religious reforms as those pushed by Antiochus Epiphanes. I even sometimes find myself shunned from their fellowship as one whose theology is overly influenced by Judaism. I wonder what Yeshua would think of the fact that if his Jewish disciples want to fellowship with his non-Jewish disciples, they have to live by Antiochus Epiphanes theological surmises.

Jewish believers seem to need another Hanukkah Revolt where with Matthias Maccabee we say "no" to Antiochus Epiphanes' rules and live our faith in Messiah according to the terms of the covenant Hashem gave to his people at Mt. Horeb. Maybe that day will be the Day of Messiah. May Hashem give us another Matthias Maccabee who will stand for us and lead us into the cultural battle to defeat Antiochus Epiphanes once and for all!

May it be soon Abba, even in our days.

My Personal Thoughts

_____

_____

_____

Matthew 3:12   **Kislev 26/** כו בכסלו

He has with him his winnowing fork; and he will clear out his threshing floor, gathering his wheat into the barn but burning up the straw with unquenchable fire!

A king gave a very expensive coat to his son. The very ungrateful and careless prince spoiled the coat within a very short time. The king replaced the expensive clothing with an even more costly one. To the disappointment of the king, his son quickly soiled the second coat even more than the first one. The king then had prepared for the prince the most exquisite garment one could weave. He hired the best tailors and weavers of thread. The silver and gold threaded coat shined in the brightness of the sun. The prince was pleased at the new coat but the king decided that his son should only receive it after he showed himself worthy of it.

This parable is taught in the Talmud about the Jerusalem Temple. The first Temple was built by King Solomon. As the prince's coat, Solomon's Temple was defiled by compromise and disobedience in the pre-first exile era. The second Temple was built when Jews returned from Babylonian captivity. This Temple was even more defiled than the first one, causing the second exile. The prophet Ezekiel speaks of a return of Israel's families to the Land and of a third Temple: the Temple of the Messianic Age (Ezekiel 37–48).

The second Temple was the scene of the Abomination of Desolation spoken of by the prophet Daniel and referred to by the Master (1 Maccabee 1; Matthew 24:15). These events happened in the days of Antiochus Epiphanes and brought on the successful famous Maccabee revolt. After the rag-tag Israeli army led by the Maccabee family won the war, they purified and cleansed the Temple for use by the people of Hashem.

In teaching his disciples about the events that will usher the Messianic Era, Yeshua mentioned this Maccabee revolt. In some ways, it will be the same. The rebuilt Temple in Jerusalem will be desecrated by the nations, but when Yeshua returns from the clouds of the heavens (Acts 1:11) at the end of the Battle of Armageddon, he will purify the Temple for our use again.

As we light our third candle tonight, let us anticipate the Messianic Age of the Third Temple where all the families of the earth will bring their glory and offerings at the Feast of Tabernacles and be blessed by the God of Abraham (Genesis 12:3; 28:14; Zechariah. 14:16).

My Personal Thoughts

_____

_____

_____

_____

_____

_____

_____

_____

Revelation 2:23   **Kislev 27/ כז בכסלו**

I am the one who searches minds and hearts, and that I will give to each of you what your deeds deserve.

Being sorry is not enough. True repentance displays better choices when faced again with a situation that previously caused offense to God and/or man.

Before he was ready to bestow blessings upon them, Joseph tested his brothers to see if they really had a change of heart. For that, they needed to experience a little of what he had experienced at their hands. Using his brother Benjamin, Joseph then created a set of circumstances that would serve as a catalyst, a litmus test of his brothers' characters.

Joseph spent three days and three nights in the pit not knowing what would happen to him; so his brothers would also spend three days and three nights in the jail not knowing if they would live or die. Trying to preserve their inheritance away from Rachel's first son, Leah's children tried to rid themselves of Joseph. Now, one of the children of Leah will have to sacrifice himself in order to save Benjamin, Rachel's second son. All this would show Joseph if his brothers had truly learned and matured.

 The life of Joseph and that of the Master carry an uncanny parallel. In Judaism, one of the names of Messiah is, the *Son of Joseph.* Just as some of Joseph's jealous brothers left Joseph in a pit for three days, so the Master spent three days in the *pit* of the earth. Later, as Joseph was taken out of the pit to eventually appear in front of Pharaoh who was then the king of the earth, Yeshua ascended from the pit of the earth to appear in front of the Father, who is the Master of the universe. Just as Pharaoh appointed Joseph as his personal representative over the world, Hashem gave the government of the earth to Yeshua. The story also tells us that in the end, because of a famine, Joseph's brothers came to him for help.

Are these signs of future events? Will there be a time of sore trouble for Jacob/Israel that will force him to ask Yeshua for help? Israel has not only spent three days and three nights in the pit, but is in its third millennium in it. Will Messiah at the end of days test the heart of his brothers? Will there be a Benjamin? Because since then, like Joseph to his brothers, Yeshua has revealed himself to many of our people, some have suggested that the Holocaust was this *testing.* Our new Messianic Jewish movement could then represent Benjamin, the believing brother who did not despise Joseph. We can certainly see the end from the beginning in all these things.

Before sending them on their way to bring their father, Joseph had a festive royal meal with his brothers. This speaks to us of the Marriage Supper of the Lamb following the revelation of Messiah (Revelation. 19:9).

Even today, all our hearts are being tested. The Feast of Hanukkah should remind us of our brothers who stood firm refusing to compromise their faith with the corrupt standards of the world around them. May we be like those Maccabees of old who when tested came out without even the smell of smoke. May we refuse to assimilate to the ways of the world. May we bravely and zealously pass the test, come out clean on the other side, ready to recline for a festive royal meal at the table of the Master at the end of the age.

My Personal Thoughts

Acts 7:13   Kislev 28/ כח בכסלו

The second time, Yosef revealed his identity to his brothers, and Yosef's family became known to Pharaoh..

For centuries now the Jewish people have been accused of rejecting the Messiah, of being the force that provoked his execution. This accusation gains momentum each year in spring when people remember the crucifixion. This erroneous understanding of the Bible by Christianity has to do with an ignorance of history, of Jewish culture and religion, as well as with the English semantics used in English New Testaments. It repeatedly uses the expression, *And the Jews . . .* These sorts of statements have hung on the Jewish nation for two millennia and have been the source of much atrocious persecution from the beginning of the second century CE on. Paul, the chosen emissary of the Master, warned against this attitude of non-Jewish believers in his famous "do not be arrogant against the branches" (Romans 11:18) olive tree analogy. Could there be a misunderstanding? The events following Hanukkah may bring us some illumination.

After pushing away the Greco-Syrian army, the Maccabees set themselves on the throne of Jerusalem. Because only a descendant of David could sit on that throne, this created great tension among the people of Judea. One of the last Maccabee kings ended up begging Rome for help to end their civil war. Rome of course obliged by taking over Judea and its government, including Temple high priest appointments (Maccabees 1 and 2). At that time, Herod, the illegitimate Roman-appointed King over Israel, persecuted many who were from the lineage of David, so they fled to Galilee. Many in Judea resisted this whole situation, mainly the Zealots and the Assenes who wanted the return of the Davidic monarchy, of which Yeshua was eligible.

Only a few Roman collaborating Sadducees from the Judean leadership had a serious problem with Yeshua. The rest of the people loved him and were glad to debate the Torah with him as Jews always do. Most of the world's Jewry at that time lived outside of Israel. So how could the statement, "and the Jews . . ." refer to the Jewish nation in general?

In the narration of the story of Joseph, we see how the patriarch concealed his true identity from both the Egyptians and his brothers. We also see that Joseph did not reveal himself to his biological family until Benjamin, the brother who did not persecute, was present (Genesis 41–45).

In the same manner, for now 2,000 years, the Messiah's identity has been concealed from his brothers. As Paul mentioned, Israel has been as if it were *blinded* (Romans 11:25, KJV) to Yeshua. So just as Joseph's brothers could not recognize him until he decided to reveal himself to them, Yeshua also has not yet fully revealed himself to his brothers. Could he be waiting for the arrival of *Benjamin*, the brother who was not part of the persecution ordeal? Could *Benjamin* be today's Jewish Messianic movement? The Torah tells us that Joseph revealed himself to his brothers at their second visitation. Will then Yeshua reveal himself to his brothers at his return? Ezekiel told us he would (Ezekiel 39:22).

If the *blinding* (Romans 11:25) was part of Hashem's greater plan, persecutors of the people of God throughout history will have to answer to Abba for what they have done (Jeremiah 2:3).

My Personal Thoughts

_____

_____

_____

John 10:16

Also I have other sheep which are not from this pen; I need to bring them, and they will hear my voice; and there will be one flock, one shepherd.

Do you see Jacob by the well (Genesis 29:2)? Where did he come from? Fleeing from his twin brother's death threats, he crossed the desert alone. On his way out of the Promised Land, on his way to a long Diaspora, Jacob received a vision. The vision reassures our lone traveler of the constant presence, even in the Diaspora, of the one who is in control of our fate and destiny (Genesis 28). Even though on the preceding night things may have appeared bleak, by morning Jacob realized that there was a greater and divinely inspired purpose in his flight to Laban in Babylon.

Jacob arrived at the very well where his own mother Rebecca watered Eleazar's camels (Genesis 24:20). As Rachel arrives, Jacob's heart is filled with love, a love that gives him supernatural strength (as love usually does) to roll the stone from the mouth of the well and water Rachel's flocks (Genesis 29:10). As a favor returned, this story sends a messianic echo through time, an echo resounding until this day.

Jacob is the messianic foreshadow. The seed of Messiah lies in him and as a teacher acting out a lesson or principle, Jacob's life teaches us of the great messianic mission of our Master.

Like Jacob, our Master escaped a death threat, a death threat that took him out of Israel to look for a bride in the Diaspora. The chosen one is a distant relative. She is not all that unfamiliar with the Master's own customs, but she still comes from an idolatrous household. When Jacob sees her, he immediately helps water her flocks. What a beautiful picture of our Messiah who, while rejected by the Sadducee Temple leaders of Israel, takes his own body of Jewish disciples into the Diaspora to water the flocks, the flocks also made up of the *other sheep* which are not from *this fold* (John 10:16). From Jacob's messianic waters, the whole nation of Israel would be born. From the Master's word/water, the Congregation of Messiah would birth.

Rachel birthed Joseph whom the Egyptians called Savior. Joseph then married an Egyptian princess. To save his own people, Hashem lifted Rachel's son to a position where he was able not only to save his own family, but the world as well. In the same manner, Yeshua, the Anointed One, pours his redeeming oil upon his people of Israel at the time of Passover, and this oil overflowed on the world of the Gentiles as well.

This is not the end of the story. As they started to persecute God's children, Hashem's blessings withdrew from Egypt. May the world take notice today. As they withdraw their hands and hearts from blessing the seed of Israel, they also incur a curse upon themselves, a curse that will destroy them with the same plagues that destroyed Egypt. Sad to say, it seems to be an unavoidable destiny, and John the Disciple saw it in the revelation Yeshua gave him on the Isle of Patmos.

My Personal Thoughts

_____

_____

_____

_____

Tevet

Leaving the victorious Chanukiah behind
You take us to another tragedy
Also to one crucified upside down.
In all this, we find
"garlands instead of ashes."

(Isaiah 61:3)

Revelation 5:13   Tevet 1/ תבת ב א

To the One sitting on the throne and to the Lamb belong praise, honor, glory
and power forever and ever!

Y'hudah and Isra'el were as numerous as sand grains on the seashore . . .
Y'hudah and Isra'el lived securely, every man under his vine and fig tree,
throughout the lifetime of Shlomo. (1 Kings 4:20, 25)

King Solomon's era prefigures the Messianic Age. It points us to the time when Hashem's
Messiah will reign on the earth as king, priest, and judge. This will be a time when Judah and
Israel will finally live as one independent sovereign nation in peace and prosperity; a time when
the nations will come to Jerusalem to learn God's word and offer him tribute (Micah 4).

It is said that at that time the Messiah will judge the impoverished justly (Isaiah 11:1–5). The
wisdom of Solomon was heard worldwide and made famous by the unorthodox way he revealed
the truth during a difficult case. A difficult case because there were no witnesses, a must for any
biblical court case where circumstantial evidence is not easily accepted (Numbers 35:30). Here is
the case: two prostitutes lived in the same house and gave birth to a child. One night one of the
babies dies and its mother exchanges it for the live baby. Now both mothers claim the living child
(1 Kings 3:16–22). Solomon found the truth.

"Bring me a sword . . . Cut the living child in two; give half to the one and half to
the other." At this, the woman to whom the living child belonged addressed the
king, because she felt so strongly toward her son: "Oh, my lord, give her the
living child; you mustn't kill it!" But the other one said, "It will be neither yours
nor mine. Divide it up!" Then the king answered, "Give the living child to the first
woman, don't kill it, because she is its mother." (1 Kings 3:23–27)

Today the question rages between two proclaimed *mothers* of the movement of the followers of
the Nazarene, two mothers also guilty of harlotry. Was Yeshua born of a Jewish or a Christian
mother? Was he an Israeli Jew or a Greco-Roman Christian? Christian theology sustains that
God has rejected his people in favor of them, that Jews therefore need to convert to Christianity to
have the Messiah. On the other hand, Jewish believers stand on the everlasting promises of the
Good News as found in the Tanach, meaning the promise of the coming of the Messiah, and
Hashem's merciful restoration of Israel as a sovereign country. Jewish prophecies tell us that in
the end, the world comes to Jerusalem to finally enter peace in the Jewish Messiah (Micah 4). In
other words, it is the world that is grafted into Israel's 'olive tree' (Romans 11), not Israel who is
grafted into Christianity's 'Christmas tree.'

When Yeshua was brought to the Temple for the dedication of the firstborn ceremony, old Simeon
told Miriam, "This child will cause . . . to reveal many people's inmost thoughts." (Luke 2:34–35).
Solomon used his sword to search the heart of the two mothers. The sword of Messiah is this
discerning and revealing word of wisdom (Hebrews 4:12–13). As Solomon used his sword to
reveal who is the true mother, so when the Messiah comes, through the sword that comes out of
his mouth, he will also reveal and re-establish the rightful origins of the Nazarene movement
(Revelation 19:15).

May it be soon Abba, even in our days!

Luke 11:13

So if you, even though you are bad, know how to give your children gifts that are good, how much more will the Father keep giving the Ruach HaKodesh from heaven to those who keep asking him!

The story of Joseph seems to be the story of our lives. As Joseph's brothers did not recognize and even balked at Hashem's workings in their family dynamics, we often do not recognize all the bounties of the divine Creator in our lives. Though divine hands may so carefully plan them, they seem to us, oh so random.

Yeshua warned us of it. He said, "Is there any father here who, if his son asked him for a fish, would instead of a fish give him a snake? Or if he asked for an egg would give him a scorpion?" (Luke 11:11–12).

Hashem's *fish* sometimes look like *serpents* and his *eggs* like *scorpions*. But no matter what happens, in spite of the outcome of events and relationship dynamics in our lives, we must always believe that Hashem is ultimately in control. We unfortunately only see life through the limited scope of time and personal concerns. Abba to the contrary is the great planner who sees the past, the present, and the future of the whole world from the angle of the great eternal now. It is through that wider perspective that he orchestrates everything that happens, and our seeming flukes, tragedies, and disappointments often contribute to a greater purpose unseen by us (John 9:1–3).

As we process the events that daily affect and even afflict us, we must always remember what has been coined as the *God factor*. When we do, we automatically understand and liberate ourselves from the fear that can fall upon us; we also realize that we ultimately really have only very small control (if any) over anything that happens to us. When one lives a life independent from God, this realization usually dawns on the hardest on his deathbed.

Joseph, who for a long time saw his life seemingly to unravel, finally understood Hashem's purposes and eventually told his brothers, You meant to do me harm, but God meant it for good — so that it would come about as it is today, with many people's lives being saved." (Genesis 50:20).

This agrees with the faith of our Master, with the attitude of he who endured such hostility against himself (Hebrews 12:3). He is the one who proclaimed, "So if you, even though you are bad, know how to give your children gifts that are good, how much more will the Father keep giving the Ruach HaKodesh from heaven to those who keep asking him" (Luke 11:13).

May we learn today to discern Hashem's *good gifts* in our lives even when they look like *snakes* or *scorpions*.

My Personal Thoughts

_____

_____

_____

_____

_____

_____

Romans 9:1–3   Tevet 3/ ג בטבת

I am speaking the truth—as one who belongs to the Messiah, I do not lie; and also bearing witness is my conscience, governed by the Ruach HaKodesh: my grief is so great, the pain in my heart so constant, that I could wish myself actually under God's curse and separated from the Messiah, if it would help my brothers, my own flesh and blood.

As he hears Judah's impassioned plea for Benjamin (Genesis. 44:18–31) Joseph perceives the change of heart in his brothers. For over twenty years Joseph swallowed his pain, his anger, his pride, his natural desire for vengeance, as well as his longing to be reunited with his family. As Egyptian viceroy he could have himself engineered the reunion, but he preferred to wait for Hashem to do it.

This is the moment when the brother-in-exile-Egyptian-viceroy is ready to reveal his identity. As tears choke his speech (Genesis. 45:1–2), the words of Joseph echo Messiah's own longing to be reunited with his people. Joseph's sorrow is the sorrow of the exiled Messiah forced to live away from his people.

Jewish people today see Yeshua much like Joseph's brothers saw Pharaoh's viceroy: as a despotic foreign ruler who cares little about them. Little do they know that like Joseph, Yeshua himself longs to be reunited with his brothers and celebrate the feasts, his Father's appointed days with them again. Like Joseph, for a very long time Yeshua swallows his pain, his anger, his pride, and his natural desire for vengeance, until an opportune master-stroke moment of history when he will reveal himself to his people Israel. It was not the Egyptians who revealed Joseph to his brothers; his brothers did not figure it out themselves either. It was Joseph, who while removing his Egyptian headdress and speaking in their native tongue, revealed himself to them (Genesis. 45:3–5). In the same matter, it is not the evangelical efforts of gentile believers or the Talmudic calculations of Jewish scholars who will reveal Messiah to Israel; it is Messiah himself.

In the meantime, Messiah is still in exile. In the years preceding the destruction of the Temple, the Sadducee rulers of Jerusalem persecuted the Jewish disciples of Yeshua. Just as Benjamin did not have a part in the selling of his brother Joseph, the Jewish Messianic community did not have a part in the *selling* of Yeshua (Matthew: 26:15). Joseph tested his brothers with Benjamin, so today Yeshua, the Messiah in exile tests the heart of Israel with the Jewish Messianic communities sprouting up everywhere in the Land.

It is with the restoration of Israel under its rightful King and High Priest Yeshua the Messiah that the earth will be able to experience the world to come. That is why we are constantly admonished to "pray for the peace of Jerusalem" (Psalm 122:6), a peace that will not come until the restoration of the true Davidic King on the throne of Jerusalem.

My Personal Thoughts

_____

_____

_____

_____

_____

Luke 3:8   **Tevet 4/ ד בטבת**

If you have really turned from your sins, produce fruit that will prove it!

As he undertakes the task of speaking for his brothers, Judah approaches Joseph (Genesis 44:18). For a reason only known to Hashem, Judah recounts to the Egyptian viceroy the story of their long lost brother and of the pain it inflicted on their father. Joseph listens intently to this very precious inside information. Jacob's pain concerning Joseph seems to have been a crushing weight on that family. As Judah makes his plea before the viceroy, he reveals that he presently stands as safety for Benjamin in the eyes of his father (Genesis 43:9).

This is a pivotal moment for Judah and his family; this is the time of reckoning. Their sin has returned upon them and judgment from on high is about to be pronounced. They stand before Joseph as if it were before the court of heaven; the gavel is about to fall. At that moment, Judah makes the move that will change the wheels of justice: he offers himself as ransom for the life of Benjamin. This is exactly what Joseph was looking for: true repentance from a changed heart, repentance translated into acts of godliness and self-denial.

To be only repentant with the heart is not enough. If this repentance does not become the force and the engine that puts the body into motion towards godly behavior and actions, even into reversing a former misdeed, it is not true repentance; it is just being sorry, which while being somewhat emotionally comforting, is legislatively useless. When Judah offered himself as a slave for Benjamin, he showed concern for both the father and the House of Rachel, which he formerly despised. That was acceptable unto Joseph. The idea here is that no matter how sorry we are, we cannot improve our *grade* until we are faced again with the same test, with a similar situation giving us the opportunity to make different and better choices. In this case, Judah passed the test.

It is the same with us. We are daily faced with situations and choices. Some we pass, some we don't, and the Master tallies the grade. We are told that in the end Abba will judge the world according to the Master's deciding (Acts 10:42). Jewish sages teach us that a judge is unfit to judge a man unless he can find that man's sin within himself. Yeshua who taught the same thing (Matthew 7:3–5) came and was subject to every temptation just as we are; he is therefore the fit judge and one day, we will stand before him like Judah before Joseph and be required to not only speak repentance, but also show fruits in keeping with it (Matthew 3:8).

This is part of the restoration of our heart mind and soul. Restoration does not come by the stroke of a magic wand that instantly reprograms our nature and character. It comes by meeting again the situations that made us fall; it comes by taking the test again and hopefully earning a better grade.

Hashem is patient (2 Peter 3:9). May we therefore be faithful to do our homework, to "present" ourselves "to God as someone worthy of his approval, as a worker with no need to be ashamed, because he deals straightforwardly with the Word of the Truth" (2 Timothy 2:15).

My Personal Thoughts

_____

_____

_____

_____

Matthew 3:8   Tevet 5/ ה בטבת

If you have really turned from your sins to God, produce fruit that will prove it!

What is repentance? What does a true change of heart look like? John the Immerser told some who came to him, "produce fruit that will prove it" (Matthew 3:8), meaning that even before a confession of repentance is accepted, it must be proven with works documenting the statement.

In order to save their skin and inheritance, Joseph's brothers did not hesitate to sell him, breaking his and their father's heart. Foreshadowing Messiah, Joseph was sold to the Gentiles upon whom he eventually became ruler. Many years later during a famine that threatened to extinguish their family, Joseph's brothers sought help from Egypt. Unbeknownst to them, they had to deal with the Egyptian viceroy who by a twist of fate was actually Joseph. The brother turned ruler chose the opportune moment to test his brother's hearts.

Through a well-orchestrated ruse, Benjamin, Joseph's full biological brother, was accused of stealing the Viceroy's special cup. The Egyptian wanted to keep Benjamin as a slave, but Judah won't stand for it and pleads for his brother. Judah takes the lead and pleads for the uncomforted heart of his father who still mourns Joseph's loss. He pleads and offers his own self as a substitute for Benjamin's, the brother who did not sell Joseph. To his father Judah had said, "I myself will guarantee his safety; you can hold me responsible. If I fail to bring him to you and present him to your face, let me bear the blame forever" (Genesis 43:9), and to the viceroy he now says, "Let your servant stay as a slave to my lord instead of the boy, and let the boy go up with his brothers. For how can I go up to my father if the boy isn't with me? I couldn't bear to see my father so overwhelmed by anguish" (Genesis 44:33–34). It is at this moment that Joseph finally decides to reveal himself to his brothers (Genesis 45:1–3).

Even so today, while Gentiles have acknowledged him as Messiah, Yeshua's true identity is hidden from his brethren, the Sons of Israel. Even today messianic believers in Israel suffer intense harassment and persecution from a small but very vocal minority of their brothers. The questions we must ask now are, "Will there be a test? Will there be a test where the 'Judah' community of those who refused Joseph/Messiah's leadership and therefore sold him for silver in the end will at great cost come to the rescue of the 'Benjamin' community, of the messianic believers sons of Israel who believed in Joseph/Messiah and did not sell him away?"

The Israeli government is facing difficult choices about this issue. Will there be a time in the future when Judah is fully put to the test? Judging from the story of Joseph it seems to be a plausible course of events. May at that time, Judah show his true repentance by making right choices concerning Benjamin, his messianic believer younger brother, rather than break his Father's heart again!

May it be soon Abba, even in our days!

My Personal Thoughts

_____

_____

_____

_____

_____

Acts 1:6   **Tevet 6/** ו בטבת

"Lord, are you at this time going to restore self-rule to Isra'el?"

Through an undesired twist of fate, the patriarch Jacob found himself married to two sisters, Leah and Rachel, thus creating two main factions within Israel. Jacob favored Rachel and gave her firstborn Joseph the mantle of leadership over his whole household. The other brothers, the children of Leah, rejected Joseph's authority and position. Reuben was in fact the firstborn of Jacob through Leah, but his actions cause him to lose the right of first-born. The same happened to Simeon and Levy, the next ones in line. Leadership of Israel then fell on Judah, Jacob's fourth born. Israel's history is punctuated by the rivalry between the House of Joseph and the House of Judah. Prophets have expressed the world to come as the time when the two Houses born from Israel are finally united in peace.

Joseph had two sons, Ephraim and Manasseh. When Moses died, leadership of the newborn nation of Israel was given to the House of Joseph through Joshua the Ephraimite. Until the reign of Saul the Benjamite, leadership in Israel fell on judges who were mostly from either the tribes of Ephraim or Manasseh, the House of Joseph. It is King David from Judah who united the tribes under one rule and started the Davidic dynasty that was to fulfill Jacob's prophecy and usher in the Messiah (Genesis 49:8–12).

At the end of the Solomonic reign, the country was again divided into two camps: the Ephraim and the Judah camps. Most of the tribes from the House of Leah, joined with Ephraim and Judah, were left alone with Benjamin. Ephraim became the Northern Kingdom, and Judah the Southern Kingdom, with Benjamin stuck in between the two. Eventually the Assyrians conquered and deported the Northern Kingdom. Later, Nebuchadnezzar deported the Judeans to Babylon. At the end of the Babylonian exile, King Cyrus issued the order for all the captives of Israel from either North or South to be allowed to return to the Land.

In his prophecies of the *two sticks*, the prophet Ezekiel speaks to us of the Messianic Age, the time when the two houses of Israel are again united under the Judean Davidic leadership (Ezekiel 34–37). This comes in fulfillment of the Psalm that tell us, "Rejecting the tents of Yosef and passing over the tribe of Efrayim, he chose the tribe of Y'hudah, Mount Tziyon, which he loved" (Psalm 78:67–68). Ezekiel's prophecy of the two sticks united (Ezekiel 37) is actually an echo of the reunification of the two houses foreshadowed by Joseph who, as he reveals himself to them, embraces his brothers' lead by Judah (Genesis 45).

The reunification of the two houses is and has always been one of the main signs of the Messianic Age and of the coming of Messiah. Before Yeshua ascended to the Father, his disciples asked him, ""Lord, are you at this time going to restore self-rule to Isra'el?" (Acts 1:6), which meant, "Will you at this time restore the twelve tribes as a sovereign nation?" To which he answered, "You don't need to know the dates or the times; the Father has kept these under his own authority" (Acts 1:7–8).

May it happen soon Abba, even in our days!

My Personal Thoughts

_____

_____

_____

Mark 11:26 (DHE)   Tevet 7/ ז בטבת

> *But as for you, if you do not pardon, neither will your*
> *Father who is in Heaven forgive your transgressions.*

"When two brothers do not recognize each other, it is like each is exiled from the family unity." The sages who taught this truth also mentioned that God's Shekinah cannot dwell where there is no unity; in disunity, all are exiled. Joseph was exiled in Egypt. Jewish sages also taught that Hashem's Shekinah does not abide on a mourning soul, so through Jacob's continual mourning for Joseph, his whole family was exiled from Hashem's presence. Only joy, zest for life, and unity between brothers can bring it back.

King David so beautifully expresses these similar thoughts saying,

> Oh, how good, how pleasant it is for brothers to live together in harmony. It is like fragrant oil on the head that runs down over the beard, over the beard of Aharon, and flows down on the collar of his robes. It is like the dew of Hermon that settles on the mountains of Tziyon. For it was there that ADONAI ordained the blessing of everlasting life. (Psalm 133:1–3)

Aaron was known for being a peacemaking force who often worked reconciliation between people within the tribes of Israel. David knew that, so he used the anointed high priest as a metaphor to tell us that unity between brethren is fluid. It flows everywhere positively affecting everything in its path. From the head, it descends to every part enveloping all with its shine, smoothness, and healthy properties. It is like two mountains on two opposite ends of a country, one sharing its proverbial abundant dew (material blessings) with the other who shares its divinely appointed blessing (spiritual wealth); everything working in perfect harmony.

This is the picture that we can imagine in Joseph and his brothers kissing and reuniting (Genesis 45:15). The son of Rachel acted as a true godly leader. Joseph revealed himself thus putting an end to the four-generation-old game of concealed identities. He also forgave his brothers stopping the never-ending returning measure of evil for evil. Unity is restored; Hashem is now able to bless Israel and send it to its destiny of growing into the powerful nation that will eventually teach the whole world about him.

May we learn from this. As disciples of Yeshua, we have a job to do which is sharing the spirit of his mission to everyone. We therefore do not have the right to indulge in grudges; it is actually forbidden by the Torah (Leviticus 19:18). The sages mentioned that even entertaining grudges in our hearts was sinful, thus agreeing with the Master (Matthew 5:21) who even implied that holding grudges against our brothers nullifies our offerings and prayers (Matthew 5:23–24).

It is funny how in English we use the expression *holding* a grudge; all we have to do is let go of it!

My Personal Thoughts

_____

_____

_____

_____

_____

Revelation 19:7–8   Tevet 8/ ח בטבת

Let us rejoice and be glad! Let us give him the glory! For the time has come for the wedding of the Lamb, and his Bride has prepared herself—fine linen, bright and clean has been given her to wear. ["Fine linen" means the righteous deeds of God's people.]

Benjamin, who did not reject Joseph, was only a young child when his older brother was exiled. He was unaware of the tensions between Joseph and his brothers. He was even unaware of what his brothers had done to Joseph. Where does Benjamin stand in the prophetic picture? We understand Joseph's messianic prefiguring role. We also understand Judah and his brothers representing Israel at the time of the Master. But what, or who does Benjamin represent in this midrashic picture? Could he represent Messianic Judaism? Could Benjamin prefigure the disciples, those sons of Jacob who not only didn't reject Joseph but loved him; those of Israel who accepted Yeshua?

Even as Yeshua said that his disciples would drink of his cup, so Joseph hid his cup in Benjamin's sac (Genesis 44:2; Matthew 20:22). The Jewish believers have certainly drunk of Yeshua's cup. As that of the Master's life on earth, our history is one of rejection and intense persecution by our brethren, and by the world. By the early Middle Ages, Messianic Judaism had all but disappeared, only to resurrect in our days.

Benjamin ate from Joseph's table. Didn't the Jewish disciples of Yeshua also eat at his table? We still do; as disciples we only live by his bounty. Will we not eat at his table again and drink wine with him at the end of this age? After revealing himself, Joseph gave extravagant clothing to Benjamin, a repeat of what his own father did for him. Will not Yeshua also clothe us in white raiment (Genesis 43:34; 45:22; Revelation 19:7–8).

For centuries, the two families birthed by the two sisters and wives of Jacob warred against each other. At one point in time they even became two separate countries. The prophets and sages of Israel speak of the Messianic Era as a time of reunification of the two families. The disciples even brought it up to Yeshua before he left to sit at the right hand of the Father (Acts 1:6).

The geographical area of the tribe of Benjamin is situated almost like a buffer zone between Ephraim, the leader of the northern tribes, and Judah, the leader of the southern tribes. This should give us an idea of where we should stand as Messianic believers: as a neutral zone of reunification between the two. It may just be coincidence, but the Temple—which is to be rebuilt for the Messianic Era—is positioned in the area of Benjamin, which at the time of the Master had been assimilated by Judea. In the Messianic Era, the whole world will come to Jerusalem, in Benjamin/Judea to bring their glory (Revelation 21:24–26).

Though we can guess for some of them, except for Paul we do not know for sure the tribal origin of any of the disciples of the Master. In the case of Paul, the writing style veers from its regular pattern. This tells us that we must take notice. Paul was a Messianic Jew from the tribe of Benjamin. His mission by the Master was to bring the *Besorah* בשורה, or "Good News" to Israel and to the Gentiles. May we learn to follow Messiah emulating Paul's passion, zeal, wisdom, and knowledge to bring the Master's Good News to his brothers, and to the world.

My Personal Thoughts

_____

_____

John 8:31–32   **Tevet 9/** ט בטבת

So Yeshua said to the Judeans who had trusted him,
"If you obey what I say, then you are really my talmidim,
you will know the truth, and the truth will set you free."

The Torah teaches us as much by its narratives of the patriarchs as by its legislative code of law rhetoric. Jacob had been unjustly treated by his brother Esau, but at the end of the story, Jacob bites the bitter end and organizes a repentance party where all make peace (Genesis 32–33). They may not live together but at least enmity is somewhat put behind them.

Later, Joseph follows the pattern of his father Jacob. Having been unjustly treated by his brothers, he also organizes for them a way to properly repent. All this needed to happen before Hashem was ready to make Israel a great nation and fulfill the promises made to Abraham. The pattern of concealed identities, lying, vengeance, and measure for measure retribution needed to stop, and by revealing himself and forgiving his brothers, Joseph put an end to it all. This story of repentance and forgiveness then becomes the contextual cradle of the giving of the Torah to Israel.

Is there a lesson for us in this? Relationships in this world are often born of ulterior personal selfish motives and interests. As a result, we often live lives of pretence hiding our true self under a façade of *social correctness*. This may be good and well for the secular unbeliever, but it is certainly wrong for the children of the Most High and disciples of the Master.

Can the Father of truth and light bless us when we play social games with each other? Sad to say, in our modern society, this sort of hypocrisy has become a hallmark of religiosity and spirituality. This is often the reason why our teenagers reject the notion of God altogether because they see through the hypocrisy of their socially correct religious parents.

And why do people do that? Because they cannot look at themselves in a mirror. They are afraid of admitting to themselves that they are not as good as they claim to be. Because their theology teaches them that because they are redeemed, they now should be sinless, but every once in a while, the reality of their true sinful selves comes up to confront them with a reality check. When this happens, they hide behind a veneer of spiritual religiosity made up of cliché statements, clothing, adversarial loud opposition to sin, accompanied with charismatic pious attitudes and platitudes. But this self-righteous veneer is thin, brittle, and cracks easily. When faced with the awful truth about himself, one has two choices: to remain in the bondage of deception by lying to himself and others in order to sustain a false image, or to liberate himself by being honest, ask for forgiveness, and do works in keeping with repentance (Matthew 3:8).

Thankfully, in the case of the patriarchs, lessons were learned. In the days of Joseph, everybody repents and unites which then causes Israel to grow as a mighty people who are able to conquer the Land where Messiah would be born.

May it be the same with us! May we in our days stop playing *religion* and learn to worship Hashem as the Master taught us to: "spiritually and truly" (John 4:23).

My Personal Thoughts

Hebrews 11:16   י בטבת **/Tevet 10**

But as it is, they aspire to a better fatherland, a heavenly one.

Do you remember the story of the poor rabbi and the rich man? In the story a rich man confronts a poor rabbi asking him how he can speak so highly of Hashem's bounty when he is so poor. The rabbi then answered the rich man saying, "When you travel, do you carry all your furniture with you?" "Of course not!" the rich man replied, "I take a traveling bag; but when I am at home I live comfortably." "Ah, that is it Shlomo, I am not home yet, I am not home!"

When Jacob knew that his time had come, he told Joseph his son, "The time came when Isra'el was approaching death; so he called for his son Yosef and said to him, "If you truly love me, please put your hand under my thigh and pledge that, out of consideration for me, you will not bury me in Egypt. Rather, when I sleep with my fathers, you are to carry me out of Egypt and bury me where they are buried" (Genesis 47:29–30). Jacob spoke of death using the term, "sleep with my fathers," a Hebrew expression we also find in Abraham and David (Genesis 25:8; 1 Kings 2:10). It is an early expression referring to life in the hereafter and the world to come.

It was very important for Abraham to bury Sarah in the Land. It was very important also for Jacob and Joseph to be buried in the place Hashem had promised to his children. This shows that the patriarchs did not look at death as the end of anything but rather as the continuation of life where God's promises are fulfilled, but in a somewhat different dimension. Yeshua also confirmed (before his death and resurrection) that the patriarchs were alive (Matthew 22:32). You see, those who have gone before us are not dead, they are only resting, sleeping.

At the end of his sojourn on the earth, Jacob yearned to return to his ancestral land. He didn't even want his bones to remain in Egypt. This has to do with a belief in resurrection. The type of resurrection the patriarchs believed in was not just a spiritual one, but a very physical one with flesh and bones. It was much like Yeshua's resurrection. As he appeared to the disciples in his resurrected body the Master said, "A spirit does not have flesh and bones as you see that I have" (Luke 24:39). That is why it was important to the patriarchs to be buried in the Land. Even today devout Jews pay thousands of dollars to be buried in Jerusalem's Old Cemetery. They say that those buried there will be first ones to see the returning Messiah.

And what can we learn from this?

Have we settled down in this world, in this dimension, in this absurd, temporal reality? Do we live for what we can get today or do we use this life to prepare towards the more substantial and eternal reality of the world to come? Are we *home* here, or do we yearn with Jacob and the patriarchs, "Carry me out of Egypt" (Hebrews 11:10; 14–16)? Prisoner in this dimension of time and flesh, like the homing pigeon the soul of the true child of God constantly yearns to be reunited with the spiritual roots that birthed it. This is the meaning of the Hebrew word *Dror* דרור, liberty: freedom to go home (Isaiah 61:1).

May we all at the opportune time be found with our fathers in our ancestral home, in the eternal dimension of the world to come!

My Personal Thoughts

_____

_____

John 10:16   **Tevet 11/ יא בטבת**

> Also I have other sheep which are not from this pen; I need to bring them, and they will hear my
> voice; and there will be one flock, one shepherd.

Retelling the life story of Joseph we have played with the very important midrashic messianic analogy equating Joseph to Messiah. This has led us to observe that Benjamin represented the Jewish people who did not reject Messiah/Joseph. We are now at the part where Jacob meets his two grandchildren, conceived through Joseph by an Egyptian mother, the daughter of a priest of Egypt. At first, he does not know who these Egyptian looking children are. When he finds out, he adopts them as his own (Genesis 48:5).

The idea of redemption through adoption is a main theme throughout the whole Tanach. Starting with Abraham, each of us is an adopted son (Romans 9:4–5). In adopting Joseph's sons as his own, Jacob accomplished a very tricky maneuver. His showing favor to Joseph had already caused him much trouble so this time, instead of openly conferring to Joseph the right of first-born, Jacob adopts Ephraim and Manasseh, the sons of the son of his true chosen bride and love of his life, Rachel. This not only has the effect of these sons and nephews becoming brothers to their father and uncles, but for Joseph to receive the double-inheritance that is usually conferred to firstborns.

Ephraim and Manasseh can be compared to the offspring of Messiah while in Diaspora. Jacob actually said that Ephraim will become the *multitude of the nations* (The Hebrew text uses the definite article *ha* ה, "the"). In Hebrew, the same expression is used in Romans 11:25, "stoniness, to a degree, has come upon Isra'el until the Gentile world enters in its fullness." Judaism teaches that when the Romans evicted Israel from its land, Messiah went to exile with them. Just like Joseph, while in exile, Messiah has been busy raising himself an offspring among the Gentiles, an offspring to be adopted and inherit the Abrahamic promises alongside the Jewish people (Ephesians 1–2).

Today Judaism and Christianity are seen as two different religions. The truth is that Christianity outside of Judaism did not exist for the first three hundred years after Yeshua and the apostles. Today if a Jew wants his Messiah, Christians tell him that he has to convert. "Convert from what to what?" one may ask. It is the pagans who needed to convert from idolatrous paganism to the God of Israel.

It is very strange because originally the question was not whether a Jew could be part of the Congregation of Messiah, but whether a non-Jew could be part of Israel. In Acts 15, the Jewish disciples accepted the Gentile converts, but today, does the Church accept in its midst a Jewish believer living in Judaism? In the adoption of Ephraim and Manasseh, we see that in actuality, in Messiah non-Jews are grafted in the olive tree of Jacob/Israel, not Israel in the Gentile Roman Christmas tree (Romans 11).

Joel did prophesize that at the end of time Hashem will pour his spirit on all humanity (Joel 2:28), not just on Israel. In that day, there will truly be one shepherd and one flock.

May it happen soon Abba, even in our days!

My Personal Thoughts

_____

_____

Matthew 25:31–32

When the Son of Man comes in his glory, accompanied by all the angels, he will sit on his glorious throne. All the nations will be assembled before him . . .

Before being *gathered* to his people (Genesis 49:33), Jacob/Israel uttered his last prophetic outbursts. While he addressed his sons, Jacob/Israel prophesied of many things, especially of the return of the children of Israel to the Promised Land. Already the tension between the house of Pharaoh and the children of Israel was mounting. The famine was over for twelve years. The children of Israel had every right to return to their ancestral land; they were not Egyptians. Yet, we see that at this time, they had to ask permission to leave Egypt in order to bury Jacob. It was granted but with the company of dignitaries who probably required a military battalion and leaving their little ones behind, thus foreshadowing what another Pharaoh later tried to impose on Israel (Exodus 5).

The relationship between Pharaoh and Joseph is remarkable. Joseph is brought to Egypt a slave first to Potiphar. He then goes to prison, which eventually leads him to Pharaoh. We are never told he was given his freedom. Joseph offers his gift of wisdom and prophecy to Pharaoh, and becomes a leader in Egypt. Egypt owes its survival to that slave, a non-Egyptian who insisted on being faithful to his God. This story repeats itself through Daniel and Queen Esther. We can even see it in King David who was brought to Israel's courts as the servant of disobedient King Saul. As such, the world often values the gifts God's people have to offer, so they bring the anointed ones to their courts as captives. The problem is that the true child of God cannot live in captivity. The Spirit of God cannot operate under the ruling of man. It is like the story of the king who hears the beautiful song of a bird, but gets upset when the bird stops singing after he puts it in the captivity of a cage. It is also like trying to put a firefly in jar to enjoy its glow, eventually the bounds of captivity steals what made it beautiful.

God has a plan though, not through Joseph, but through Judah. Jacob/Israel prophesized, "The scepter will not pass from Y'hudah, nor the ruler's staff from between his legs, until he comes to whom *[obedience]* belongs; *[or: until Shiloh comes]* and it is he whom the peoples will obey" (Genesis 49:10). Judah is at the origin of the word *Jew*. Technically speaking, a *Jew* is a descendant of Judah, the others are children of Israel/Jacob, and those before Jacob are called *Hebrews*, after Abraham, the first one ever called by that name (Genesis 14:13). To Judah then was prophesied a kingly scepter who would never depart from him, a scepter where the roles were reversed. Whereas, in Egypt the nations attempted control over God's people, as did the world throughout history, the promise to Judah is that of an eternal scepter that will this time dominate over the nations, as it is written, "to him will be the obedience of the people," of the nations of the world.

The Davidic monarchy came to a stop with the Babylonian captivity, but through the Judean Jew Yeshua, Judah's scepter will be revived in the end of days when Yeshua will come to reign over the whole world and establish his Kingdom when righteousness will cover the earth as the waters cover the seas.

May it be soon Abba, even in our days!

My Personal Thoughts

_____

_____

Revelation 12:5

She gave birth to a son, a male child, the one who will rule all the nations with a staff of iron.

Believing the time of his departure was nigh, Jacob blesses his children. The pronounced words are not just blessings; they are insights into the future of Israel and thereby, of the world. About Judah, Jacob says, "The scepter will not pass from Y'hudah, nor the ruler's staff from between his legs, until he comes to whom *[obedience]* belongs; *[or: until Shiloh comes]* and it is he whom the peoples will obey" (Genesis 49:10).

Judah's scepter takes a prominent place in the Torah from Genesis to Revelation. The Hebrew word for it is *shevet* שבט, a word also related to "tribe," each tribe being represented by the staff, or *shevet* of the tribe leader.

In Genesis thirty-eight, Judah uses his staff as collateral and a token of identity. It was probably a shepherd's staff, a tool representing his ruling, shepherding, and even disciplining of the flock. Judah's staff foreshadows Messiah's ruling and victorious scepter as it is said in the Psalms, "ADONAI will send your powerful scepter out from Tziyon, so that you will rule over your enemies around you" (Psalm 110:2). This staff/scepter also represents Messiah's discipline of those who are disobedient, as the psalmist also says, "You will break them with an iron rod, shatter them like a clay pot" (Psalm 2:9). King David must have believed in this rod of discipline as his son Solomon often talks about it in his proverbs (Proverbs 13:24).

The *shevet* of Messiah is not only a tool of correction, it is also used for protection against those wolves that would eat us alive if they could. It is also Messiah's instrument of comfort as is said, "Even if I pass through death-dark ravines, I will fear no disaster; for you are with me; your rod [shevet] and staff reassure me" (Psalm 23:4), and the sign of our passage into covenant with him, "I will make you pass under the crook [shevet] and bring you into the obligations of the covenant" (Ezekiel 20:37).

The staff/scepter/rod/*shevet* of Messiah is powerful to chastise, to lead, to comfort, and represents a rite of passage of some sort. Isaiah speaks of the *rod of his mouth*,

> But he will judge the impoverished justly; he will decide fairly for the humble of the land. He will strike the land with a rod from his mouth and slay the wicked with a breath from his lips. (Isaiah 11:4)

This indicates that this rod/staff/scepter/*shevet* is also the spoken word of the Master.

May we pay attention to his word. May we obey his words carefully and emulate Abba by emulating the Master. The word Judah or Y'hudah יהודה, has the same etymological root as the words *todah* תודה, "thanks", as in thanks to Hashem. It is not enough to praise the Father in words only; we praise him best through our actions of obedience to his ways. Just like we as fathers feel praise and honor when our children emulate and obey us, the Father which is in heaven is also feels praised and honored when we obey and emulate him in following the Master. It is our choice then whether the *shevet* of Messiah is the gentle leading staff of the great shepherd or the heavy iron rod of correction.

My Personal Thoughts

John 17:14   **Tevet 14/** יד בטבת

I have given them your word, and the world hated them, because they do not belong to the world—just as I myself do not belong to the world.

When the famine was over, the children of Israel could have returned to Canaan; after all, they were not Egyptians! We notice though that when they wanted to bury Jacob in Canaan as he had requested, Joseph had to get special permission. Pharaoh granted the request but the flocks and the children had to stay behind, foreshadowing the request of a later Pharaoh. Pharaoh also sent an army with the Israelite procession through the desert. Though it had been twelve years since the end of the famine, it seems that the children of Israel were not free to go (Genesis 50:7–9).

We must remember that even as viceroy, Joseph was still a captive. The situation was similar to that of Daniel who, as a Judean captive held a prominent place in the affairs of Babylon, and later of Medo-Persia. As the children of Israel came to Egypt under the umbrella of Joseph, they seem to have inherited Joseph' status of slaves. We could almost say that whereas Joseph did not want revenge upon his brothers, through the famine, Hashem still brought retribution upon them. How was Joseph still a slave? He was a slave because he lived in a country that was not his own, within a culture that was foreign to him. He was a sort of minority group with different beliefs.

Had they planned to leave right at the end of the famine, the children of Israel might have been able to return to Canaan, but this is the problem with living in Egypt: we get comfortable. Then it becomes hard to leave, to uproot, and start again. Comfort and prosperity dulls our senses and lures us into a false sense of security until suddenly, one day we wake up and find ourselves bound with gold handcuffs. In the case of Israel, it might have been with cucumbers, melons, leeks, onions, garlic, and fish, which they got for free (Numbers 11:5).

The Master did warn us, we do not belong to the world and the worries of the world, the deceitful glamour of wealth, and all the other kinds of desire that choke us (John 17:16; Mark 4:19). We are not to live for the conservation and preservation of our life and comfort in this world, but as disciples our lives belong to him and we are expendables for the needs of his Kingdom.

May we live our lives in remembrance of that!

My Personal Thoughts

Revelation 3:21

I will let him who wins the victory sit with me on my throne, just as I myself also won the victory and sat down with my Father on his throne.

In the ancient Middle East, when a father bestowed his blessing on his children he laid his hands on them. In the case of Jacob blessing Ephraim and Manasseh, we are privy to the awkward picture of two grown young men sitting on the lap of a blind and frail older one who is over one hundred and thirty years old (Genesis 48:10–12).

In the ancient Middle East sitting on man's lap was part of a ritual of adoption. In this passage of text, Jacob/Israel does not only bless the children of Joseph born in exile from an Egyptian wife, but he adopts them as his own (Genesis 48:5–6). After this clever patriarchal maneuver, the two boys will technically become brothers to their father and to their uncles. They will inherit as brothers at the same level as the other children of Jacob. They also each will have a tribal allotment in the Promised Land and this indirectly allows Jacob to bestow upon Joseph the double-portion reserved to first-borns, thus circumventing Leah's children.

Judah inherited the scepter and the crown of the kings of Israel, but Joseph remained the first-born. Joshua who brought the children of Israel in the actual Promised Land was an Ephraimite, and so were most of the following judges after him. The tribe of Ephraim therefore played a strong leadership role in Israel at that time. Even the Holy Ark remained in Shiloh, Ephraim. King Saul was the first one to call the loose federation of Israeli tribes together, and David is the one who united the country as one. This unity of the tribes foreshadows the Messianic age of final peace and unity between the House of Leah and the House of Rachel (Ezekiel 37:15–22).

But what about the adoption program?

As Jacob prophesied, until this day, each Friday evening at the time of the welcoming of the Sabbath, Jewish fathers bless their boys with the words, "May Hashem make you like Ephraim and Manasseh" (Genesis 48:20). I know of a Jewish father who puts their boys on his lap as he says the blessing. This father of course doesn't need to adopt his boys but when Jacob pronounced Abraham's blessing upon Ephraim and Manasseh, he adopted them as full members of the patriarchal leadership of Israel. So were we all adopted by Hashem? Abraham was adopted and in him so are we. Joseph is highly looked upon, viewed as someone strong who did not compromise with Egypt. We want the Ephraim and Manasseh blessing upon us and to be like Joseph's children who probably inherited their father's virtue and strength.

To the Messianic community of Laodicea, Yeshua said, "I will let him who wins the victory sit with me on my throne, just as I myself also won the victory and sat down with my Father on his throne" (Revelation 3:21). I always pictured this as a child on the lap of his father or grandfather sitting on his armchair. In this case we have a three-generation adoption ritual. Yeshua the *begotten one* vested in all the powers of the Father (Psalm 2:7–12) endows these same powers to his victorious *overcomers* whom he adopts and in whom he invests his powers to rule.

May Hashem make you all like Ephraim and Manasseh, adopted in the House of Israel!

My Personal Thoughts

John 2:19

Yeshua answered them, "Destroy this temple, and in three days I will raise it up again."

As Jacob gets ready to be *gathered with his people*, he charges his sons. The Hebrew word translated as charged is actually the Hebrew word *vay'tsav* ויצו, a conjugated inflection of the verb "to command." Jacob/Israel gives his children a command to not bury him in Egypt. This passage is usually read in synagogues in concert with 1 Kings 2:1–12 where at the point of death, King David also charges, or commands his own son Solomon with unfinished business.

As Jacob/Israel asked to not be buried in Egypt, he was actually giving a subtle message to his children. He was saying, "The famine has been over for twelve years; what are we doing here? This is not our country, neither the place Hashem gave us. At least, don't bury me here!" At the point of death Joseph also alluded to the children of Israel's exodus from Egypt, which will constitute the laying of the first stone in the creation of the nation of Israel as an individual entity, a nation with the destiny of not only introducing God to the whole world, but to act as a nation of priests and firstfruits.

In the same manner, one of the charges of David to his son Solomon was to build the Temple of Israel, (1 Kings 5:5), a temple that will be called, *a house of prayer for all nations* as Yeshua reminded the people of his days while quoting the prophet Isaiah (Mark 11:17; Isaiah 56:7).

The main mission of Mashiach is to reunite all the tribes as one nation in their own land (Acts 1:6) a mission that he actually started 2,000 years ago. Let's say that there have been some setbacks to the program as for the last two millennia: the world has tried to annihilate Messiah's people through either violent ethnic cleansing or assimilation. It seems though that much progress has been made towards the reunification of Israel since the 20th century.

Another one of Hashem's charges to Messiah is to build the third Temple, the one described in Ezekiel's prophecies (Ezekiel 40–48). Only the Jewish people have the knowledge and understanding of the ritual concerns about the Temple. There is an organization in Israel in charge of the building of the third Temple. Many things are already in place and the seven-branch candelabrum designed for it is already available for public display.

May we pray for the time when all of Israel is united and the house of prayer for all people is rebuilt.

May it be soon Abba; even in our days!

My Personal Thoughts

_____

_____

_____

_____

_____

_____

Revelation 2:17

To him winning the victory . . . I will also give him a white stone, on which is written a new name that nobody knows except the one receiving it.

The Book of Exodus in Hebrew is called *Shemot* שמות, meaning "names." It is the Book of Names. *Names* is the first principal word that appears in the book's narrative and Judaism names the Books of the Tanach using the book's first main words.

The names of the different people involved in the scenarios of the book appear little by little, but what we discover most in the Book of *Shemot* is the names of Hashem. Hashem himself introduces his names first to Moses when he asks, "Look, when I appear before the people of Isra'el and . . . they ask me, 'What is his name?'" (Exodus 3:13) and to Pharaoh when he challenged Moses' divine message with, "Who is ADONAI, that I should obey when he says to let Isra'el go?" (Exodus 5:2). Hashem answered Moses' question by showing his great power to conquer and save and Pharaoh's by showing his great power to conquer and destroy.

In Western philosophically Greek culture, names are looked at as a sound bite by which we call people. Sad to say, this is also the way we look at the name of God: an identifying sound bite to which he should answer when called upon.

In the Semitic world of the Bible, names refer to what you are, to what you were created to be. Names also describe who you are, the reason and circumstance of your birth; your qualities and/or attributes. By knowing your name, people know something very important and special about you. In Exodus, the Father and Creator introduces himself by many names, not a sound bite we are supposed to use to make sure we are addressing the right person, but as a memorial of what he is in what he does.

Yeshua said that the name of the Father should be hallowed, sanctified (Matthew 6:9), which means set aside for special times and uses. Yeshua said these things quoting parts of an ancient Jewish prayer referring to the practice of only pronouncing the ineffable sacred name in the precincts of the Temple and during times of devoted prayer, never in common conversation. Yeshua followed that practice, and also taught his disciples to follow his example of simply calling Hashem, *Avinu* אבינו, or "our Father" (Matthew 6:9). Some people believe that Jewish application of respect toward protecting God's name comes from a rabbinic conspiracy to hide the ineffable name for themselves. This anti-Semitic idea still lingers.

Today each of us has a name given to us by our parents. In this world where truth is hidden under the fiction of a physical veil, this name may or may not have anything to do with us. In the world to come, Yeshua has promised us a new name revealing to the world our true attributes, our qualities, in a sense who we really are (Revelation 2:17). Come to think of it, it may be a scary thought for some of us. At that time, we will be fully known even as we have been fully known (1 Corinthians 13:12).

May it be soon Abba, even in our days!

My Personal Thoughts

_____

_____

_____

1 Peter 3:5

This is how the holy women of the past who put their hope in God used to adorn themselves and submit to their husbands.

I heard it said one time, "A woman can make or break a man". Another axiom among modern feminists is that, "Well-behaved women rarely make history." Let's look at some of the female heroes that populate the biblical narrative.

Pharaoh sees the Hebrew population getting too numerous. He enslaves them and decrees that all newborn males must die (Exodus 1:16). In spite of all this, the Hebrew population kept on growing. The sages tell this legend explaining the phenomena. They say that each day, as Hebrew wives would bring food and refreshments to their husbands, they would wash and attire themselves all pretty and ready to have relations with them in the fields. They would go to their men with words of encouragement and comfort. The men despaired under the weight of Pharaoh's decree, but through their initiative, the Hebrew women nursed a little flame of faith that eventually turned into the fire that destroyed even almighty Egypt (b.Sotah 11b).

Hashem knew his creation when he said, "It is not good that the man should be alone; I will make him a helper fit for him" (Genesis 2:18, ESV). In Hebrew אעשׂה־לו עזר כנגדו: (my literal translation of the text) I will make him a helper fit to be *against* him." The idea in the word *against* is not of opposition but of balance. It is another way of saying, "Behind every great man there is a great woman."

Truly, a woman *makes* a man by balancing him. She gives him wise and fit advice, encourages him when he is down and confused, and often reminds him of his divine earthly responsibilities. This helps him to properly focus and balance his life between idealism and practicality. On the other hand, she can *break* him if she tries to steal his focus away from his divinely ordained mission and towards herself. A woman will also destroy her man when she either nags him for his weaknesses, or fans his ego so that he gets unduly lifted up in pride and sees himself as the focus of everything.

The aforementioned legend should provide today's women with a good role model. At times when men feel crushed under the exilic weight of their responsibilities, they need the intuitive and bracing care of their life-long partner. They need to be working side-by-side with them to counter-act the effects of *Pharaoh's* ungodly edicts. The Exodus narrative also tells us of two brave women who feared God above Pharaoh, and therefore refused to kill the Hebrew baby boys (Exodus 1:17–20).

Even so today, our modern world has created a society where the weight of spiritual confusion crushes and discourages men. They eventually get distracted away from their spiritual responsibilities as fathers and husbands.

May Hashem give us great women who know how to use their godly lure to bring these discouraged men back into focus, into being the husbands, fathers, and leaders that will bring the next generation to the Promised Land of the world to come. "The hand that rocks the cradle rules the world."

My Personal Thoughts

_____

_____

1 Timothy 4:12

Don't let anyone look down on you because of your youth; on the contrary, set the believers an example in your speech, behavior, love, trust and purity.

Exodus 2:1–2 tells us, "A man from the family of Levi took a woman also descended from Levi as his wife. When she conceived and had a son, upon seeing what a fine child he was, she hid him for three months." This statement seems to imply that Moses was Amram and Jochebed's first child, but we discover later on that it is at least their third after Miriam the oldest who was five, and Aaron who was three years old at Moses' birth. Why this strange text rendition then?

Jewish tradition explains the text, noting that after Pharaoh's decree, Amram felt that it was useless to attempt raising a family so he divorced his wife. Because he stood as a Levite, Amram's decision created a snowball effect within the Israelite population. Miriam, who was very young at the time, rebuked her father telling him that he was worse than Pharaoh. Her reasoning was that, whereas Pharaoh sought to kill all the Israelite male children, Amram, through his example threatened to bring genocide to the whole Hebrew nation. If the Israelites stopped raising families, their population's numbers would decrease, possibly come to a standstill, and finally disappear. Miriam certainly had the gift of judging actions by their long-term effect; she went on to become a great leader in Israel. Tradition also tells us that Amram repented, remarried Jochebed, and sired Moses, and that is why the Torah text appears the way it is. One can argue about the veracity of this story but true or not, it gives us a window on ancient Israelites views of family, tribal dynamics, morality, goals, purposes, and methods of judgment.

Through the story of Moses who foreshadowed the first and second coming of Messiah, we are given the foundation stone of mankind's redemption plan. Imagine now that the events that formed Moses' life could have been thwarted because of one act of despair from one of the older generation of Israel. In the mean time, a youth with a fresh non-cynical look at life saw the calamitous results of her father's decision. She then confronted her father and provoked a reversal of action.

We complain much about youth today but could it be that perhaps they do not feel heard by the cynical so-called wise parental generation? We have our lives behind us but they have theirs in front of them and without the cynicism that so often sadly accompanies age and experience.

In preparing for tomorrow, may our children find their place. May we raise them in an atmosphere where they feel at liberty to change and prepare their future by being able to challenge us and expose our shortcomings. May Hashem give us the humility to hear the voice of conviction in their uncouth and unseasoned tone.

What is it the prophet said? ". . . with a little child to lead them" (Isaiah 11:6).

My Personal Thoughts

_____

_____

_____

_____

_____

Hebrews 11:23–27   Tevet 20/ כ בטבת

By trusting, the parents of Moshe hid him for three months after he was born, because they saw that he was a beautiful child, and they weren't afraid of the king's decree. By trusting, Moshe, after he had grown up, refused to be called the son of Pharaoh's daughter. He chose being mistreated along with God's people rather than enjoying the passing pleasures of sin. He had come to regard abuse suffered on behalf of the Messiah as greater riches than the treasures of Egypt, for he kept his eyes fixed on the reward. By trusting, he left Egypt, not fearing the king's anger; he persevered as one who sees the unseen.

"One day, when Moshe was a grown man, he went out to visit his kinsmen . . . " (Exodus 2:11).

We are not born *there*. We get *there* by starting where we are. In essence, like Moses we are all born in exile and then, we grow up to that divinely ordained place we are meant to occupy, to that perfect destiny Hashem created for us to gravitate to.

To get *there* is the compounding result of many of life's decisions and sad to say, the reason why many don't get *there* is because of wrong decisions. It is in old age or on our deathbed when the realization suddenly strikes.

Moses followed the exact pattern Hashem imposed on all the patriarchs. Abraham went through it as well as Isaac. I also like to compare Jacob's *School of Laban* to the proverbial *School of hard knocks*. They, and we, all have to experience a time of spiritual, if not physical Diaspora, exiled from Hashem's perfect will in our lives. It could be Hashem's way to help us appreciate the *Promised Land* of his perfect will when we get *there.*

It takes us a long time before we find that perfect place. We first have to travel in diverse endeavors, programs, ideologies, congregations, groups, and fellowships. Most of the time, we don't *grow up* and get *there* until our forties or fifties; Moses got there in his eighties (Proverbs 4:18).

In this age and in this world, we are all in Diaspora from the Kingdom of God. We have been away from our spiritual home since Adam and Eve. We get glimpses of *home,* when we study Torah and/or fellowship with one another. We get a glimpse of it when we pray, praise, and exalt the Father of us all (Psalm 22:3). One day as the children of Israel did, we will all have *grown up.* At that time, we will enter the Promised Land of the Kingdom of God.

Come to think of it, every Friday night as we welcome the Sabbath, we experience a little bit of the Kingdom of God on earth, a foreshadow of the world to come. After the Sabbath, we all spend the week in *Diaspora,* but oh wonder of wonders, Shabbat always comes back, and when it does, what a joy!

My Personal Thoughts

_____

_____

_____

_____

_____

Mark 15:17   **Tevet 21/ כא בטבת**

They dressed him in purple and wove thorn branches into a crown, which they put on him.

Thirty four hundred years ago the Creator of the universe revealed himself to Moses, a man who would in turn introduce him first to Israel, then to the world. For many years Hashem watched the affliction of his people; he was now ready to bring them out of Egypt to embrace their grand destiny. Whether we realize it or not, Hashem knows us and is always with us, even in this exilic world. Hashem also knows that our human frame causes us to judge by appearances so as a long awaited mysterious visitor, he carefully prepared his grand entrance on the scene of our history. Everything had to be right; especially the form of his appearance to us, for his message is not just words, but also his revelation.

In the Torah, we learn that Hashem appeared to us in sort of a paradox: a bush that burned, but yet was not consumed. None of it was illusionary: the thorn bush really burned, yet it really was not consumed. The Hebrew word for thorn is: *s'neh* סנה, carrying the same etymological Hebraic root as the word *Sinai*. According to Rabbi Yanni's perspective, God's appearance in the midst of a thorn bush was *emblematic of the anguish he suffered over Israel's affliction*. The revelation of the Almighty El-Shaddai within a lowly dry thorn bush was something akin to putting on sackcloth and ashes. The thorn bush then represents a royal messianic statement: Hashem's empathy and personal suffering over Israel's plight.

Isaiah the prophet was given an understanding of Hashem's emotional attachment with his people. He says,

> In all their troubles he was troubled; then the Angel of His Presence saved them; in his love and pity he redeemed them. He had lifted them up and carried them throughout the days of old. (Isaiah 63:9)

Rabbi Yanny expresses the same sentiments as Isaiah's using the following words, "If one has a pain in his head, the other feels it. Israel certainly had a pain in his head." Eventually, as if to illustrate for us Hashem's anguish and empathy over Israel, Mashiach wore the crown of thorns, the thorns of Sinai upon his own forehead (Mark 15:17).

A father naturally suffers when his child is afflicted, so naturally Hashem suffers when his people are afflicted. He takes upon himself all their suffering until the time when, in his fury, he awakes and desires vengeance, yes, vengeance on those who afflict him by afflicting his people (Isaiah 63:3). As we are afflicted, he is afflicted. On the other hand, parental love contains an element of hatred against our children's evil behavior. Parents should not be afraid of afflicting their children in order to set them straight, thus the uncomfortable love, hate, and affliction paradox returns.

If we succeed to solve the love, hate, and affliction paradox of the burning bush, we may have succeeded to rationalize ourselves into the greatest of all errors because Hashem revealed himself to us in a paradox: in the mystery of the burning bush, in the mystery of the suffering Mashiach.

My Personal Thoughts

_____

_____

_____

Hebrews 3:15

Now where it says, "Today, if you hear God's voice, don't harden your hearts, as you did in the Bitter Quarrel."

As Moses' divine oracle laid heavy upon Pharaoh's heartened heart, today the voice of Messiah cries out unto the Adversary: "Let my people go, so that they can worship me" (Exodus 7:16). As the plagues of God's judgments fell upon a defiant Egypt, today the torment of God's retributions afflict an arrogant world. As many of the Children of Israel chose to stay in the seeming safety of the culture of Egypt, many whom God calls choose to stay in the elusive dream of this world. As a great multitude of other nations followed Israel to the mountain where it would learn a brand new way of life, so today a great multitude follows the chosen few desiring to apply the words of the Creator of heaven and earth onto their lives (Exodus).

From the foundations of the world, the plan for man's redemption was defined and played out (Hebrews 4:3). The lone voice of God's word is heard (Exodus 3); the paschal ransom of our freedom is paid (Exodus 12:3); we leave the old country (Exodus 12:51); and we immerse unto rebirth (Exodus 14:29; 1 Corinthians 10:2) to go and meet God in a lonely place where we learn the parameters of our new life in him (Exodus 20). Finally, as new rewired individuals we enter the Promised Land (The Pentateuch).

The problem today is that, while many hear the lone voice of the word, they also covet the beautiful prospects of the Promised Land. They leave and immerse themselves out of the old country. They really want to go to the new country, but they never pass by the mountain. They never go and learn how to live a life acceptable unto him. They therefore remain forever stuck between their old culture and the new one. Not having completely rid themselves of their past, they are not entering into the future. They are like the bride who left her father's house and never got married. She heard the voice of the bridegroom, betrothed him, prepared for the wedding, but never went to the wedding ceremony nor to the bedchamber to consummate the marriage. Why? She wanted what the bridegroom had to offer, but without really ever belonging to him. Marriages today are much the same way. People live together without really belonging to each other.

Is that the way we are with God? Do we want the blessings of his treasury but do not want to be his? Do we want the protection of his right arm while we refuse to learn the ways of his Kingdom? Do we want the clout of being called by his name, yet do not want to live in his house?

Today again while the voice and culture of the world grows darker and darker, the voice of the Master calling his bride is made clearer and clearer. Let us together follow the trail that leads to higher moral and spiritual grounds. Let us be immersed unto the new life Hashem has for us and follow him to the lonely bedchamber at the mountain of his choice. When there, let us bask in his loving arms allowing him to renew our minds and hearts. Then we will enter the Promised Land of his house as his forever new creatures, as lights of everlasting life and wells of living waters for the nations.

My Personal Thoughts

_____

_____

_____

_____

John 17:21

That they may all be one. Just as you, Father, are united with me and I with you.

One thing I have discovered in my life with Hashem is that it is always subject to change. Changes are bound to be constant especially when we endeavor to follow him. Change is an unchangeable fact; it is inevitable because he doesn't change. Because he doesn't change we are the ones who have to do the moving and the changing in order to adapt to his unchangeable continuity. One time a man complained that he didn't feel as close to God as he used to, until his friend asked him, "Who moved?" Broken friendships and marriages work much the same way; we must sometimes ask ourselves, "Who moved?" or "Who changed their priorities?" Hashem doesn't, so when we feel further from him than we used to, we must have changed things somehow.

The Creator of all things expressed his unchangeable nature when he gave his name to Moses on the Mount. He introduced himself then as *Ehyeh asher Ehye* "אהיה אשר אהיה" roughly translated as "I WILL BE THAT I WILL BE," and meaning, "I, ADONAI, do not change" (Malachi 3:6).

Many people have fallen into the trap that the God of the Tanach is different than the one of the apostolic scriptures. A thorough understanding of God's name as introduced to Moses on the Mount claims the exact opposite. A solid grasp on God's unchanging nature spares us from falling into errant theology.

Yeshua himself directly disclaimed this theology of being different than the Father. He claims total unity of concepts with the Father when he says, "so that they may be one, just as we are" (John 17:11, 21). Yeshua teaches us here that because he is on the 'same page' with the Father, if we go on the 'same page' with him, we will also be on the 'same page' with the Father. This reflects the standard Jewish Chassidic theology of approaching God through your spiritual mentor.

God doesn't change. He remains the same from creation until today. From the beginning his standards of mercy, grace giving, patience, goodness, compassion, and forgiveness have been the core of his being. Now, and just as it was in the past, his people have always been able to rely on these attributes in order to come in his presence, but so are the rest of his name's attributes unchangeable: truth, justice, and retribution (Exodus 34:5–7). May we never forget it as we pray to him who never changes.

You may notice I didn't list 'love' as an attribute of God. It is a purposed omission in my listing. Love being abstract is better defined through the aforementioned attributes.

My Personal Thoughts

_____

_____

_____

_____

_____

_____

_____

Luke 22:18

For I tell you that from now on, I will not drink the 'fruit of the vine' until the Kingdom of God comes.

For two millennia, each year at the Passover Seder we drink the four cups of wine that tell the story of our Exodus from Egypt. The Seder is a meal that uses food elements and cups of wine to tell the story of the Exodus. It is a great tradition and children usually love it.

The four cups of the meal are: the cup of sanctification, the cup of deliverance, the cup of redemption, and the cup of praise. These cups define the four phases of the redemption of the children of Israel from Egypt: "I will free you . . . rescue you . . . redeem you . . . I will take you as my people" (Exodus 6:6–7). The children of Israel did not celebrate Passover again until their last year in the desert.

King Solomon teaches us, "What has been is what will be, what has been done is what will be done" (Ecclesiastes 1:9). During his early last Seder with his disciples, with a trace of melancholy, Yeshua informs his friends that he will not eat of the Passover Lamb again with them until it is fulfilled in the Kingdom of God (Luke 22:16). Then, he takes the first Seder cup, the cup of redemption, and says, "I will not drink the fruit of the vine until the kingdom of God comes" (Luke 22:18). This statement teaches us that there is another Passover coming up on the schedule, a Passover complete with sanctification through election of the bride, deliverance from deathly plagues, and redemption through marriage, ultimately belonging to the Almighty in his household.

Hear now: from before the foundations of the world the Passover's perfect lamb has been chosen in the heavens. Each day we hear the good news of his redemptive power. His blood now stands at the door of every heart (Revelation 3:20). What will it be for us when the plagues descend? Will we be of those protected in Goshen, or of those receiving the recompense of their evil deeds against the people of God? At the time appointed, will we be of those following him to a desert place for a marriage banquet, or will we be left behind? When the *wood hits the sand* (chariot adaptation of the expression: *when the rubber hits the road*), we will see. As is told in the story of old, many Israelites stayed in Egypt while many non-Israelites threw their lot with Hashem.

To be chosen and leave Egypt is not enough. The old Egyptian culture also has to be replaced by Hashem's new culture. Before entering the Promised Land we must follow him to the mountain and receive the ordinances that are to direct our new life. We must spend time in obedience to these in order to be ready.

Just before entering the Promised Land of Yeshua's reign on earth, we will see again a Passover complete with plagues, blood, and exodus (Revelation 19–20). At that time, we will recline with Messiah at the table where he will again drink wine with us.

See you there?

My Personal Thoughts

_____

_____

_____

_____

1 John 4:1–3

Dear friends, don't trust every spirit. On the contrary, test the spirits . . . every spirit which acknowledges that Yeshua the Messiah came as a human being is from God . . . in fact, this is the spirit of the Anti-Messiah. You have heard that he is coming. Well, he's here now, in the world already!

Egypt was on the way to meet her Endtime. After having been given a chance at godliness through the God of Joseph, choosing rather the ways of idolatry and of persecuting God's people, she had turned back on the God who saved her. Moses is sent to give her a last chance through repentance. The Pharaoh was to allow the Hebrews to go and worship Hashem. Even so, for 2,000 years the nations have been given a chance at godliness, but today, more and more, it is choosing the ways of secularism, sensuality, and even idolatry. As Egypt once did, our world will also one day chose a god-man leader who will persecute all those who desire to follow the God of Moses.

Using demonism to imitate the power of God is an earmark of the Anti-Christ. Pharaoh's magicians replicating Moses' staff metamorphosis miracle through their magic is actually a prelude to the Endtime period that is to come on the planet. Today our world is hungry for peace, health, tranquility, and prosperity. This state of affairs provides a breeding ground for the Jannes and Jambres of our days (Exodus 7:11; 2 Timothy 3:7–9), for magicians and false prophets claim to bring us the peace, the health, the tranquility and the prosperity that only the Messiah will provide in the world to come. Indeed, the medical and defense budgets are the largest expenses in many countries' economies. Many also succumb to the gambling of the stock market and other 'get rich quick' scams. Our materialistic world has created a society that is hungry for the spiritual. This provides scientists, quack revivalists preachers, and New Age groups the desperate audience they need to prosper.

It has been long foreseen that along with imitating the realm of Messiah (Revelation 13:4), including his death and resurrection (Revelation 13:3), the Anti-Christ will also be a political and military genius bringing for awhile peace and prosperity to the planet. It will take the form of a fake and enforced peace, not unlike the Roman peace era, coined by historians as the 'Pax Romana.'

If we take the model of Moses, Pharaoh, and Egypt, what can we speculate Hashem will do then? Here is a little English proverb to illustrate, "Bring herbs to Herbtown." This simply means that if you are a merchant, you bring your market where people need and appreciate your wares the most. This doesn't preclude that there will not be competition for your products, but this very competition can be the perfect place to prove the superiority of your goods. Hashem knew about Egypt's society's proclivity towards the supernatural; magic was widely practiced. Hashem then, as a good *marketer* of his ware, brought his *goods* to Pharaoh's court where his own staff morphing into reptilian show proved its superiority by devouring those of the magicians Jannes and Jambres (Exodus 7:10–12).

And what does this teach us?

May we not be so gullible as to follow in the footsteps of every peace, health and prosperity prophet. May we learn how to 'try' the spirits by a confession of faith that is not just verbal, but the demonstration of a life according to God's commands (1 John 4:1–3; James 2:14–26).

My Personal Thoughts

125

Revelation 19:21   **Tevet 26/** כו בתבט

The rest were killed with the sword that goes out of the mouth of the rider on the horse, and all the birds gorged themselves on their flesh.

I heard it said one time that reading the Bible through a translation is like kissing a bride through a veil. I would like to give an example of that.

When Hashem asked Moses for signs to help Hashem to identify himself to his people, the Almighty showed Moses that he could transform an ordinary wooden staff into a *nachash* נחש, "serpent." When came time to demonstrate the experiment in Pharaoh's court, Moses might have been surprised when instead of his wooden staff morphing into a *nachash,* it morphed into a *tannin* תנין (Exodus 7:10). Sadly, this distinction is not given to us in texts written in English. *Nachash* is the Hebrew word for serpent. *Tannin* is the Hebrew word for crocodile, or in biblical Hebrew, "sea monster." In Egypt the crocodile was sacred, so there was a very strong spiritual message in the fact that Moses' *tannin* swallowed those of Pharaoh's magician (Exodus 7:12).

We meet this *tannin* again in the prophecies of Ezekiel, and again, this sea monster is compared to Pharaoh.

> Human being, turn your face against Pharaoh king of Egypt; prophesy against him and against all Egypt; speak out; and say that ADONAI Elohim says: "I am against you, Pharaoh king of Egypt, you big crocodile [tannin] lying in the streams of the Nile!" You say, "My Nile is mine; I made it for myself." (Ezekiel 29:2–3)

Herodotus the historian tells us how you catch a tannin:

> A man puts the back of a pig upon a hook as bait, and lets it go into the midst of the river, while he himself upon the bank of the river has a young live pig which he beats; and the crocodile hearing its cry makes for the sound and when he finds the pig's back he swallows it down. Then they pull. (Jacobus Van Djik, *The Civilizations Of The Ancient Near-East.*)

Ezekiel's oracle tells Pharaoh, "But I will put hooks in your jaws and make your Nile fish stick to your scales. Yes, I will bring you up from your Nile, with all your Nile fish sticking to your scales" (Ezekiel 29:4). The Book of Revelation also describes the upcoming Anti-Messiah who will also persecute the children of Hashem as a monster coming out of the sea (Revelation 13:1). His end seems to meet that same end as that of Ezekiel's,

> . . . and leave you in the desert, you and all your Nile fish. You will fall in the open field and not be gathered or buried; but I will give you as food to wild animals and birds. (Ezekiel 29:5)

> Then I saw an angel standing in the sun, and he cried out in a loud voice to all the birds that fly about in mid-heaven, "Come, gather together for the great feast God is giving, to eat the flesh of kings, the flesh of generals, the flesh of important men, the flesh of horses and their riders and the flesh of all kinds of people, free and slave, small and great!" (Revelation 19:17–18)

Yes, Hashem is always victorious over every Tannin who tries to persecute and annihilate us. As it as been throughout history, so it will continue!

1 Timothy 3:2–6   Tevet 27/ כז בטבת

A congregation leader must be above reproach. . . . He must not be a new believer, because he might become puffed up with pride and thus fall under the same judgment as did the Adversary.

Pharaoh and the Exodus is a test-tube to show the world not only what happens in the days preceding the return of Messiah, but also the results of hardening our heart. Whereas while the plagues unfold, the narrative tells us that God himself hardens Pharaoh's heart; it is his own idea to challenge Moses and his God (Exodus 7). It's like the little boy who received a scolding from his Mom, "Johnny, why did you punch your brother in the face and kick him in the shin? Don't you know the devil made you do that?"

"Oh no Mom," Johnny answered, "The devil may have made me punch him in the face, but kicking him in the shin was my very own idea!"

In a sense, Hashem is like a parent who after giving us a stern warning, let's us learn by allowing us our own choices, and even setting before us the fruits of our own thinking. He then allows us to go the full length that we may learn by experience that he was right in the first place. It's a scary thought but there was no other choice for Pharaoh. One may say that he was a victim of his own environment and ignorant of the facts, but the remembrance of Joseph and of the famine was not so far in the annals of Egypt. This Pharaoh though belonged to another dynasty, a dynasty that did not recognize the works of Joseph in saving Egypt (Exodus 1:8).

Rashi the Jewish sage notes that for the first five plagues, Hashem did not harden Pharaoh's heart; the biblical text tells us that Pharaoh's heart was hardened. What Pharaoh was, is a victim of his pride; he thought he was God. Spiritual pride, the notion that we are something special is the worst of all prides. It causes us to have a narrow worldview where the world revolves solely around what's happening in our realm. As a result we step on everybody else's toes and then wonder why in the world they should be hurting. Pride makes a person very vulnerable to the Adversary's devices. There is a saying in whaling, "Don't harpoon until she blows!"

Sad to say, spiritual pride is a very rampant and contagious disease in the body of Messiah. Even though Peter, the close disciple of Rabbi Yeshua, strongly advised against autocratic oppressive leadership in the congregations in favor of teamwork among co-workers (1 Peter 5:3; Acts 6:2–3), people naturally fall back on their past habits and training. In his pride, man is naturally and wickedly ambitious, always desiring to establish himself in a position of power and authority over others, which is forbidden. It is even sicklier when spirituality is used as a vehicle to establish oneself above others.

Soon Messiah will return and help us establish leaders who are meek, not victims of the Adversary's pride in being desirous of authority and power in leadership. He himself chose meek men from Israel's working class instead of the pompous religious circles and told them that they will sit upon thrones judging the twelve tribes of Israel. May we all take notice and live by their example.

My Personal Thoughts

_____

_____

_____

John 17:26   **Tevet 28/** כח בטבת

I made your name known to them, and I will continue to make it known; so that the love with which you have loved me may be in them, and I myself may be united with them.

While on Mt. Horeb, Moses clearly hears the voice of the Almighty Creator of the universe telling him to go to his children. Fully aware of the cynical nature of man, Moses proceeds by asking the voice, "Look, when I appear before the people of Isra'el and say to them, 'The God of your ancestors has sent me to you'; and they ask me, 'What is his name?' what am I to tell them?" (Exodus 3:13). The voice cryptically answers, ""Ehyeh Asher Ehyeh *[I am/will be what I am/will be]*," and . . . say to the people of Isra'el: 'Ehyeh *[I Am or I Will Be]* has sent me to you'" (Exodus 3:14). In those preceding words, the mighty One reveals the fullness of his nature. Using a superlative conjugation of the Hebrew verb, 'to be', *l'hiyot* להיות, he calls himself the Everlasting Existential One that is, was, and ever shall be. This same connection with the verb *to be* is also found in the etymological root of the tetragrammaton *Yah* יה, used in the Tanach for the name of God.

The Almighty later tells Moses, "I appeared to Abraham, to Isaac, and to Jacob, as God Almighty, but by my name [tetragrammaton in the Hebrew text] I did not make myself known to them" (Exodus 6:3). This is strange because Abraham, praised Hashem using the tetragrammaton (Genesis 22:14). Are those contradictions? To add to the confusion, Yeshua comes and claims to reveal the name of the Father as if no one ever knew it before (John 17:26).

These are not contradictions. When the Tanach tells about the name of the Father, it doesn't talk about a sound bite attributed to Hashem to help us refer to him in conversation. These statements about his name in the Book of Exodus speak of his nature, of the particular character of his revelation, which is different in every column of the scroll. In Abraham, ADONAI is the one who provides; in Moses, he is the avenger; in Yeshua, he is the savior, the atonement, the shield who covers.

How does Yeshua then reveal the name of the Father?

Like Joshua was to Moses and Elisha was to Elijah, Yeshua is the model disciple of the Father. He is in such unity with the Father that he says they are "one." They are so much "one" that he who saw Yeshua saw the Father. It didn't mean that if you saw Yeshua in the market place you went home and said, "Hey, I saw God in the market place today!" It simply meant that Yeshua emulated the Father in such a way that one can understand who the Father is simply by looking at Yeshua. When Yeshua says that he came to reveal God's name, he simply says that by his lifestyle he reveals the Father's nature to us.

Yeshua also said that we should be one with him. That means that when people see us they should be able to see him, and through him, the Father (John 17:20–21; Matthew 5:16). It's a tall order for each one of us, but if we seriously live in the injunctions that the Master gave us directly, or indirectly, through his apostles, we should be able to shine some of the light of the Father on this poor spiritually dark earth.

My Personal Thoughts

_____

_____

_____

Romans 11:26–27   **Tevet 29/ כ״ט בטבת**

Out of Tziyon will come the Redeemer; he will turn away ungodliness from Ya`akov and this will be my covenant with them . . . when I take away their sins.

Moses arrived in Goshen and told Israel of God's promises. He told them that Hashem remembered the promises he made to Abraham, Isaac, and Jacob; that intending to make good on his promises, he has now called on them to be their God to serve him as his people instead of serving Pharaoh. The Israelites understood the message. Israel, who belonged to Pharaoh, the God of the world, is now being vied by another lover who says to her, "You are being abused, I will deliver you. You shall be mine now and I will take care of you." Was Israel ready for the fight between two *bucks* vying for her? As far as she was concerned, she could be jumping from the frying pan into the fire!

The Torah tells us because of their broken spirit and the harsh slavery, the children of Israel were not enthused at the message (Exodus 6:6–9). I like how the Hebrew text puts it. It speaks of Israel's spiritual condition using the term, *ketser ruach* קֹצֶר רוּחַ. The expression is an idiom for *despondency*. The literal meaning is *shortness of breath* or *of spirit*. They were spiritually exhausted. Their cruel bondage stole from them all strength for faith (Exodus 6:9). Hashem was going to have to do all the hard work.

How much like today. As it happened with Moses, who is also called in Judaism the *First Redeemer* (thus making allusion to Messiah the *Second Redeemer*), we are watching the fulfillment of the promises Hashem made to the patriarchs and the prophets concerning Israel. We have seen him resurrect the country where Messiah is supposed to make his landing at the time they will all see him (Zechariah 14). Just as in the times of the Exodus, Hashem today, spiritually and physically redeems Israel his people. Someone once told me, "If I was Jewish, I'd take the first plane out of exile, I'd be excited; why are they not?"

Same problem as with Moses! After 2,000 years of persecution first by the Romans, then the Catholics and the Spanish inquisition, followed by Luther's Protestants, the Germans, Tsarist and Communist Russia, and now the Muslims who imported anti-Semitism from Europe, the Jewish people again seem spiritually exhausted on the *Chosen People* idea. They seem to complain with Reb Tevieh looking at his lame horse (Fiddler on the Roof), "Why, why me? I know, I know, because we are the Chosen People . . . but sometimes couldn't you chose somebody else?" Nevertheless Hashem again saves his people with a great and mighty hand.

It is funny though. There are some who teach that because of their sins, Hashem forsook his people of old and replaced them with another: the Church. First, this doesn't add up with God's mathematics of covenant faithfulness. He said that he only remembers the wickedness of fathers for three or four generations. And as far I know, Hashem does not change and his covenantal promises are irrevocable (Malachi 3:6; Romans 11:29). The question is, "Is our history of disobedience worse than theirs? Why would he forgive their sins but not ours?" He either forgives or he doesn't. If he forgave yours, he also forgave mine. But if he replaced us because of our sins, then he is also apt to replace you because of yours.

The Hebrew word *chesed* חֶסֶד translated as grace means *covenant-keeping*. Hashem is gracious. Unlike mankind, he keeps his covenant and his promises in spite of us. He keeps them for me, and he keeps them for you.

Sh'vat

The time of rebirth
The rebirth of nature
The rebirth of a Land
The rebirth of a people
O what a time
To be reborn as a new creature!

Acts 17:30   Sh'vat 1/ א בשבט

*In the past, God overlooked such ignorance; but now he is
commanding all people everywhere to turn to him from their sins.*

The showdown between God and Pharaoh in Egypt could be coined *Hashem's Battle for the Souls of Men.*

The great Almighty Creator of the universe, he who only allows the nations to exist for the sake of his will, gave a direct command to Pharaoh. He said, "'Let my people go, so that they can celebrate a festival in the desert to honor me," to which Pharaoh replied, "Who is ADONAI, that I should obey?" (Exodus 5:1–2). Boy was Pharaoh about to get an answer to his question! Egypt lost world rld dominance and never recovered.

Through the plagues, ADONAI of hosts challenged each and every god of Egypt. It showed God's children and the vain Egyptians that the gods of Egypt were nothing. He showed the proud nation that they didn't owe their wealth to the flow of the Nile nor to their abundant stocks, but ultimately to the God of the very Hebrews whom they had enslaved. They had forgotten that it was through Hashem's blessing upon Joseph, a Hebrew slave, that the country had been saved from destruction through famine over two hundred years before. How quickly do people forget those who save them!

For decades the empire continued to partake of the blessing bestowed upon God's children. But like Laban, Egypt wanted to keep the *blessing catalyst* prisoner. This reminds me of the story of a king who, when he heard the beautiful song of a bird, captured it and set it in a cage. Expecting to hear the beautiful heavenly music at will, this king was very disappointed when he realized that the bird couldn't bless the king with his music while in captivity.

Now that Egypt had served its purpose of providing a place for God's people to grow and multiply, Hashem needed his people to go and establish the place that would eventually become the cradle of Messiah, the birthplace of he who would bring not only the Jewish nation, but also the whole world to repentance.

The message is the same today. He that is in the similitude of the Passover lamb calls to us. He calls us to repent and let go of our sinful leaven, of the gods of pride and rebellion. He invites us to follow him to a place of solitude far away from the vanity of this world. He longs to teach us his ways of love and humility.

As a groom lifts his bride over the threshold of his house, so Messiah, the bridegroom, lifts us up to carry us to his Kingdom where we will live with him forever.

My Personal Thoughts

_____

_____

_____

_____

_____

_____

John 11:50   Sh'vat 2/ ב בשבט

You don't see that it's better for you if one man dies on behalf of the people,
so that the whole nation won't be destroyed.

While enslaved in Egypt, our fathers were victims of a gross injustice. They had done no wrong, yet they were persecuted. They were persecuted solely because of man's fear and vanity; because of man's innate and perverted desire to control the fate of others.

As the children of Israel finally enacted Hashem's requirements for freedom, as they killed the lamb and applied its blood to their doorposts, they did not know they were part of a plan that would bring freedom not just to them, but eventually to the whole world. Jewish Chassidic sages believe that the suffering of a righteous person atones for the sins of the wicked. Could it then be that when we go through negative experiences that seem totally random, we may actually be going through something for the sake of others? It is certainly true that the suffering the Righteous One, of he who is called the *only begotten of the father,* serves an atoning role for our sins.

About eight hundred years after the Exodus, Jeremiah the prophet spoke of the return from Babylonian captivity in these terms,

> The day will come when people will no longer swear, "As ADONAI lives, who brought the people of Isra'el out of the land of Egypt," but, "As ADONAI lives, who brought the people of Isra'el out of the land to the north and out of all the countries where he drove them"; for I will bring them back to their own land, which I gave to their ancestors. (Jeremiah 16:14–15)

The return from dispersion has been a long-held Messianic promise and Cyrus the Persian king did allow all the tribes to return to Israel. In the days of the Master, there were representatives of all tribes in the Land, but like today, many remained in the Dispersion.

About six hundred years after the time of Jeremiah, Yeshua was born in the care of a righteous man, Joseph. The last time Yeshua enacted the long-held tradition of the Seder meal, he put himself as the element of the Seder (Luke 22:19–20). Creating a shadow picture, he helped the disciples understand the ancient teaching of the sages that *eating the Passover represents the suffering of the Messiah* (Tractate Pesachim). If you remember, in Egypt, he who splashed the blood of the Passover lamb on his doorposts (Jew and non-Jew) was freed from Pharaoh to go and serve the God of Israel. In the same manner, in the Jerusalem of the time of the Master, he who followed Yeshua (Jew and non-Jew) was freed from a greater Pharaoh. He was freed from the Prince of the power of the air (Ephesians 2:2) who like Pharaoh refused to let us go and worship our God.

The work of redemption has been done from the foundation of the world (Revelation 13:8). All the elements are in place. The only thing needed is our own free will to accept liberation from the seemingly secure shackles of this world to go into the seemingly insecure spiritual wilderness of his service.

It can be a hot, cold, lonely, windy, scary place out there; but none are more secure than one who follows the footsteps of the Master.

My Personal Thoughts

Matthew 12:8   Sh'vat 3/ ג בשבט

For the Son of Man is Lord of Shabbat!

In his encounters with the religious body of Israel, the Master often discussed the details of Torah observances, most especially those concerning the Sabbath. It is the common understanding of many believers that Yeshua broke the Sabbath because, as they say, *he annulled the Torah given on Sinai.* The problem with that is that it flies in the face of his own teaching,

> So whoever disobeys the least of these mitzvot and teaches others to do so will be called the least in the Kingdom of Heaven. But whoever obeys them and so teaches will be called great in the Kingdom of Heaven. (Matthew 5:19)

This idea also contradicts Hashem's injunction that anyone who breaks the Torah, not only cannot be the Messiah, but is also a false prophet (Deuteronomy 18). There is also another argument out there claiming that Yeshua did not break the Sabbath, he only broke the traditions of the Oral Law as taught by the Scribes and the Pharisees. That does not make sense either because the Master's justification for his actions came from the same mishnaic oral tradition the scribes and the Pharisees used.

The verse, "For the Son of Man is Lord of Shabbath" (Matthew 12:8), sheds some light on the situation. Yeshua often referred to himself using the expression *Son of Man* (Daniel 7:13). The expression *Son of man* in Hebrew is, *ben adam* בן אדם, and also means *human being* in general. In our text, Yeshua seems to use the expression in a very general way. As a recognized rabbi with disciples, it was perfectly legal for Yeshua, a *ben adam,* to establish rulings on Sabbath observance. Even in today's Judaism, religious leaders differ in their opinions of details of commandment applications and people are free to follow their favorite rabbi. The issue in the narrative was that a few particular rabbis simply did not agree with Yeshua (not all, as in the case of Nicodemus and Joseph of Arimathea).

The situation was very irritating for Yeshua's doctrinal opponents, but they could not do anything against him because even his justifications denoted a wide understanding of Jewish law and of the teachings of the Talmud. What the Master taught was simple. Even though it was already understood that any issues regarding life and death superseded Torah commandments, even the Talmud agrees that it is right to do good on the Sabbath. *Good* in Yeshua's teaching included alleviating human suffering such as hunger and disease. What we have here is typical religious legal debate.

The Apostolic texts tell us that Yeshua is "This Son is the radiance of the Sh'khinah, the very expression of God's essence" (Hebrews 1:3). What Yeshua teaches us through these conversations is that the Father in Heaven is full of mercy and compassion for his children (Exodus 34:6–7) and that the form of obedience he requires from us is not hard, rigid, and cold.

As Yeshua did, may we weigh the matters of Torah observance and know how to recognize the *weightier matters* (more important) and elements of the Torah, which are justice and mercy (Micah 6:6–8; Matthew 23:23).

My Personal Thoughts

_____

_____

Matthew 6:24 (KJV)   Sh'vat 4/ ד בשבט

No man can serve two masters: for either he will hate the one, and love the other;
or else he will hold to the one, and despise the other. Ye cannot serve God and mammon.

About 3,400 years ago the people of Israel learned that Egypt was an unreliable *staff* to lean on. Not only did they learn that Egypt was no match for Hashem, but that the fish, the cucumbers, the melons, the leeks, the onions, and the garlic weren't as free as they thought. They came at the price of servitude to Pharaoh, the god of the land (Exodus 11:5). Ultimately Hashem himself challenged Pharaoh's pride, destroyed his army, and took his country down several notches. The only option at freedom for Israel was to throw itself at God's mercy in total devoted obedience to his will.

About eight centuries later, both Israel and Egypt were faced with the same lesson. Judea had been told to submit to the Babylonian invasion and live (Jeremiah 27:12). They stubbornly refused, which eventually caused the destruction of the Temple and seventy years of captivity. Those left behind found themselves under repeated Babylonian attacks. Again, they rejected Jeremiah's advice who told them to stay put in Israel (Jeremiah 42). Instead, they sought refuge under Ophra, the Pharaoh of Egypt. So again, we have a Pharaoh, who thinks himself to be a god, and an Israel tempted by Egypt's provision and protection. What Israel didn't know was that Babylon would come and fall on Egypt like locusts and if that went there, they would end up sharing in Egypt's doomed fate. (Jeremiah 46:23; Exodus 10:4, 12–14). So as in the past, the only option for Israel will be again to throw itself at God's mercy in total devoted obedience to his will.

Today Israel faces the same dilemma. In its divine destiny to re-conquer and re-populate the Promised Land, Israel is discovering that the political credit and financial support it receives from the international community may come at the price of heavy compromises, including giving up Jerusalem. Again, Israel has to make hard choices, and throw itself at Hashem's mercy in total devoted obedience to his will.

Homiletically speaking, this lesson may apply to us all. In the global economy in which we live, when someone sneezes in Asia or the Middle East, our whole economy gets a cold. Suddenly, that far away *sneeze* echoes and sends shivers into our very pocket books and affects our ability to provide for our families here at home. The good news is that as believers and followers of Hashem, we have the admonition from Yeshua to not rely on the shaky uncertainty of a brain-dead international economy, only kept alive by the life support of political lies and pretences (Matthew 6; 19–34; Philippians 4:19).

Most of the time, successful businesses in a capitalistic society come at the price of aggressive financial maneuvers that go against the principles of Torah and of God's commandments. The Torah teaches us that usury is wrong and that we should rather give, in love, preferring the welfare of others before that of our own. These do not make for good coffer-filling financial rules, so we all have hard choices to make, and ultimately, the answer is to throw ourselves at Hashem's mercy in total devoted obedience to his will.

My Personal Thoughts

_____

_____

_____

1 Corinthians 10:11   Sh'vat 5/ ה בשבט

These things happened to them as prefigurative historical events,
and they were written down as a warning to us who are living in the acharit-hayamim.

After God delivered the children of Israel from Egypt with his mighty arm, he commanded that any future king of Israel should, not "have the people return to Egypt" (Deuteronomy 17:16). Because of this commandment, some among Jewish religious circles conclude that once a Jew returns to Israel, to the Land of his ancestors, it is a sin to leave it again, even temporarily. But was the commandment to be applied solely within a geographical understanding?

Eight centuries after the exodus, the children of Israel had gone full circle. Subject to a coup within their own royal house, they feared the fury of Nebuchadnezzar, so the remnant from the Babylonian deportation decided to seek refuge in Egypt. They sought the advice—or demanded the approval—of Jeremiah the prophet who by the word of Hashem told them to stay put in Israel. They rejected the counsel and went to Egypt anyway, taking Jeremiah with them as a prisoner (Jeremiah 46). Hashem foresaw this event, which explains why he warned them of this before they even entered the Promised Land (Deuteronomy 17:16).

It is easy to judge and criticize the children of Israel for this blatant bout of disobedience. Children are known to love judging their parents, especially teenagers. Yes; we can look at them and say, "Why? Why didn't they trust God and obey the commandment, especially when Jeremiah told them? Can't they remember all the bounty and power Hashem showed them in the past?"

Yes, it is easy to react that way, but the only way to have mercy and compassion on others is to have a good hard and honest look at ourselves. A rule for Jewish judges was that, if a judge could not see within himself the fault of the person he was to judge, he would not be fit to judge that person. The reason was that in such a case the judge would be self-righteous and unable to empathize. Seeing the fault of others in ourselves provides us with the spirit of Yeshua, who having not sinned, voluntarily took sin upon himself so he could be a fit judge who can judge us righteously (Isaiah 11:1–4). He still asks us, "Why do you see the splinter in your brother's eye but not notice the log in your own eye?" (Matthew 7:3).

We must remember that, "These things happened to them as prefigurative historical events, and they were written down as a warning to us who are living in the acharit-hayamim" (1 Corinthians 10:11). A good honest look at ourselves easily reveals the spirit of fear and compromise stifling our effectiveness as well as eating at our trust to obey his word. It is often only at the end of our lives that we realize where we have missed the boat. We see then how we have allowed fear and personal interest to provoke us to compromise and choose a life of apparent safety instead of launching out like Abraham into a bright future that could not be altered no matter what.

May we learn from the children who tried to find safety in returning to their old lives. May we learn that we are safer in a desert surrounded by enemies if Hashem is with us, than in that shady well supplied walled garden without Hashem. We need this lesson to help us face the days to come. We need to live it today so we can teach it to our children for their days to come . . . and that of their children's!

My Personal Thoughts

_____

_____

Matthew 25:13   Sh'vat 6/ ו בשבט

So stay alert, because you know neither the day nor the hour.

The Biblical calendar is a lunar calendar adjusted with the sun. Because of a statement in Paul's letter to the Colossians, some deduct that we are not to attach importance to certain calendar dates (Colossians 2:16). We need to remember that the people that Paul chided for calendar observances were superstitious, idol-worshipping pagans, not Torah observant Jews! Paul himself observed Sabbaths, Passovers, Jewish festivals, and the Yom Kippur fast which were all calendar-based festival dates. Hashem even required *sanctifying* the new moon (Exodus 12:2), to set it apart as a special calendar related event. Setting apart the new moon gets us all in sync celebrating festivals at the same time. The Hebrew word used for Levitical festival is *Mo'ed* מוֹעֵד, *appointed times, appointment*. At these times, it is like having a rendezvous with the Creator. Would we want to miss it?

Because of our undue independent nature, even something as simple as coordinating ourselves together with God in function of the cycles of moon has been a major issue over the centuries. A cloudy night could mess the whole thing up. Besides that, with Jews living more and more outside of Israel, it became more and more difficult to synchronize everybody. To top it all, in the fourth century CE, the Roman government, desiring to stop the believers from observing Passover on the fourteenth of Nissan, officially forbade the Sanhedrin in Jerusalem to convene and determine the new moon. This had the desired effect of leaving everyone to their own devices, creating division and chaos until today. As a result, the method of determining the moon by sighting fell into disuse and Jewish leadership started to do it through astronomical calculation. This is how the Hillel II calendar was born. Until Yeshua returns and re-organizes the whole thing, it needs to suffice.

Calendar dates are important. The door of Noah's ark was shut on a specific day. It was also on a particular day that ADONAI went through Egypt to kill the first-born, and that the children of Israel needed to put the blood of a lamb on their doorpost. That very specific day would become the signal for them to finally leave the slavery of Egypt. In these cases, a calendar fluke would have had disastrous consequences. The Master himself followed the calendar dates of the Passover spring feasts scrupulously in his death and resurrection. The Sabbath also is a set day with particulars. If everyone decides for himself when the Sabbath is, how do we intend to fulfill Yeshua's injunction, "Pray that you will not have to escape in winter or on Shabbat" (Matthew 24:20)?

Even now a day is coming, a day that is the culmination of all of our calendar dates, a day that has been foreseen and predicted by all patriarchs and prophets. We are told that the only people who do not know that day are the ones living in the night of ignorance, but that those who live in the light of knowledge, know it (1 Thessalonians 5:1–6). It is a very special day.

As signs and plagues punctuated the arrival of the day for the children of Israel to leave Egypt, so will the day of Yeshua's return to avenge his people and judge the whole world. These signs will not be esoteric or mystical; they will be real and tangible, so that everyone will be able to recognize them.

May we be ever faithful to study and obey the word that gives us the light to know that day!

My Personal Thoughts

138

Matthew 24:24   Sh'vat 7/ ז בשבט

For there will appear false Messiahs and false prophets performing great miracles—
amazing things!—so as to fool even the chosen, if possible.

As time and again Pharaoh hardened his heart against Hashem, the worried Israelites must have wondered how he could not see the light, change, and repent. They did not fully realize that through this event, he who created the universe was making his grand entrance on the scene of world history. To this day, Hashem is marveled at through the remembrance of these events.

The narrative of a king or nation standing against Israel trying to destroy it was going to be repeated several times in history. It is very possible that today we are getting ready for another Jewish persecution, albeit in another form. Egypt therefore needed to be Hashem's powerful showcase for his children, of all generations, to remember and use as a precedent.

I am reminded of Herod Antipas who lived a double life. While in Jerusalem he acted as an observant Jew in order to please Israel, but when he was in his palace in Caesarea he would live a totally ungodly Roman lifestyle. In Israel, he was acclaimed as the King of the Jews, but the believers, Hashem's true followers from the Nazarene Sect, were not fooled. They could see him for the hypocrite that he was. To top it all, Herod Antipas initiated a persecution against the very followers of Yeshua. In the end, Herod Antipas is recorded as having died eaten by worms, for not giving glory to God (Acts 12). Such is the fate of the hypocrite who pretends to be godly in order to attract people to himself while he is actually a fake and a farce. He is soon revealed, as he does not give glory to God but takes it all for himself.

As the world gets darker and darker, many nations, even those who profess to believe in the God Yeshua worshiped, are becoming spiritually darker and darker. These nations will give rise to the one who, while professing and promising messianic expectancies of peace and plenty, will be in direct challenge and opposition to God. He will also change times and seasons and take glory for himself (Daniel 7:25; 2 Thessalonians 2:4). In those days, only those who know Hashem will know the difference between him and the true Messiah King of the Jews (Daniel 11:32). For this reason, this Pharaoh-like/Herod and Antipas-like future king will also try to exterminate them.

Like Pharaoh who thought he was God and could challenge Hashem; like Herod Antipas who thought he could deceive the people and who did not give glory to God but took it for himself (Acts 12:23); one will soon rise to deceive the people. Many will be deceived in those days (Matthew 24:5, 11, 24), but not those who know Hashem (Daniel 11:32), not the true followers of God, those from the Nazarene sect, the disciples of Yeshua. As our brothers of old saw through Herod Antipas, we will recognize this anti-Messiah (counterfeit-Messiah) for who he is, as he will not give glory to God but take it to himself.

May we in those days remember the mighty victory of the God Hosts against Egypt.

My Personal Thoughts

_____

_____

_____

_____

_____

Luke 22:19 · Sh'vat 8/ ח בשבט

Do this in memory of me.

In order to be worthy of eating the Passover lamb, the children of Israel were to clean their houses from leaven. Leaven represents sin. Before celebrating the special meal initiating their departure from Egypt to follow Hashem in a new life and country, Israel needed to clean itself from the sin of Egypt.

Have you ever tried to remove all forms of leaven from your house after a year of cooking and baking? It is hard work to go through all the cracks and crannies of your house, and even after you are done, can you consciously say that for sure you did not forget one single grain? No. That is why traditionally we pray: "Any leaven . . . that is in my possession . . . which I have not seen . . . should be annulled . . . (Siddur). In the same way, Yeshua annuls that which we cannot consciously remove.

The disciples of the Master followed that tradition and the room where they celebrated their early memorial Seder was leaven-free. Judas was gone for most of the meal—to do his dirty work while Yeshua washed his disciples' feet. Now they would all be very clean for celebrating the Passover on the evening leading to the Sabbath of the fifteenth of Nissan, the very next day when they ate the Passover lamb, while the Master laid in the tomb having just been crucified.

Some adhere to the theology that because in Yeshua our sins are forgiven, we do not need to seek for *leaven* anymore. Nothing could be further from the truth. That would be like saying that because I discovered this new powerful cleaning agent, I no longer need to do the hard work of finding dirt and cleaning. Part of the job of *cleaning* our soul is seeking and finding the *dirt* and thereby being ashamed of ourselves. It doesn't happen without our conscious participation. It is not like an operation under full anesthesia where the surgeon removes the cancer while we are asleep.

After eating the memorial Passover meal with the disciples, the Master shared the Afikomen saying, "This is my body, which is being given for you; do this in memory of me." He then lifted the redemption cup, the third cup of the Passover Seder and said, "This cup is the New Covenant, ratified by my blood, which is being poured out for you" (Luke 22:19–20). The Exodus from Egypt was now associated with a Messianic Exodus from this world of sin.

Remembering him each time we drink this cup, we anticipate the marriage supper that we will all eat with him after he has come as the final universal *leaven remover* (Revelation 19:9). First, leaven will be removed from his assembly—as judgment starts with the house of God (1 Peter 4:17; Daniel 12:10; Matthew 24:15–22)—then the rest of the world will be purified.

As we benefit from his daily cleansing, may we walk worthy of our calling that we may be a good showcase to the world of the greatest *cleaning agent* on the planet, the only one who has been given the power to truly remove all leaven from our souls.

My Personal Thoughts

_____

_____

_____

_____

Romans 11:15   Sh'vat 9/ ט בשבט

For if their casting Yeshua aside means reconciliation for the world,
what will their accepting him mean? It will be life from the dead!

Israel could have gone from Goshen Egypt to Israel without having to cross the Red Sea. Had they walked straight Northeast, they would have been back home in a few days and the whole ordeal would have been over. But this wasn't Hashem's plan. Not only did Hashem need to bait Pharaoh's army into the Red Sea, but Israel needed to go through a cultural renewal before entering their restored independent lives as the people of God.

Part of the program was for Israel, and for the *mixed multitude* of nations following them to go through a rebirth process (Exodus 12:38). They needed to get *baptized*, rid themselves of their old Egyptian identity, and be reborn as new creatures. For the Israelites, it meant to be cleansed from *Egypt*, but for the strangers with them, it meant literal conversion. The process would be repeated forty years later when the second desert generation crossed the Jordan (Joshua 3).

In Judaism, the main staple of conversion is immersion in water. In keeping with Jewish ideas, Paul mentioned the crossing of the Red Sea as a baptism (Rabbi Kaplan: *The Waters of Eden*; 1 Corinthians 10:1–2). This was the gist of the conversation between Yeshua and Nicodemus. Just as the priests did with John the Immerser, Nicodemus boasted that, being already Jewish, he didn't need the conversion rebirth of immersion.

Judaism teaches that when the mixed multitude crossed the Red Sea with Israel, they became children of Abraham; they literally became Israelites. It is interesting because the whole time in the desert, no circumcision (an important part of conversion to Judaism today) was performed. They just had a mass circumcision as they entered the land (Joshua 5:2–8).

Another important event is Amalek intercepting Israel (Deuteronomy 25:18). It seems that the descendants of Esau always intercept Israel returning home. It happened with Jacob (Genesis 32:6), during the Exodus, and it is happening again today. The first time peace was reached (Genesis 33), the second time God ordered the destruction of Amalek (Deuteronomy 25:19; 1 Samuel 15:1–3). What will it be this time?

The Yeshua believing world needs to know that as believers in the Jewish Messiah, as true born again people, like the *mixed multitude* of the Exodus, they share the fate of Israel. Even today, Esau's children are intercepting us, trying to annihilate us as we return home to our Land. They have done so from the on start in 1948.

Can Israel count on the *mixed multitude* to fight at its side? This is not just Israel's fight; the future of all believers is at stake (Romans 11:15). It has been said that they that stand idly by while the rights of others are being violated will soon become victim to these same evil forces themselves.

My Personal Thoughts

_____

_____

_____

_____

_____

Luke 1:54   Sh'vat 10/ בשבט י

He has taken the part of his servant Isra'el, mindful of the mercy.

Through Moses, Hashem instituted that his people should remember the Passover, the great Exodus from Egypt to the Promised Land. In those days the Creator of the universe revealed himself to his people in the form of a burning, but non-consuming bush. This was the way that he chose to show his people his great love, care, and power to redeem. At that time, Hashem wrought great miracles, miracles we still talk about today, miracles that are even documented with evidence from land and sea. One of those great miracles was that as God redeemed his people, a great multitude of Gentiles cast their lot with Moses and Israel, following them to find refuge from tyrannical, doomed, and destroyed Egypt, and into the God of Israel.

During his last Seder, the Master enjoined his disciples to also remember him at the time of the Passover. For also in the days of the Master, the *consuming fire* (Deuteronomy 4:24), revealed himself to his people in a non-consuming manner, to show them his great love, care, and power to redeem them, not only from Egypt or Rome, but from the *world* and the ungodliness that has been in them since the Fall. When Hashem renewed his covenant with his people, a great multitude of Gentiles cast their lot with Yeshua and the disciples, following them to find refuge from tyrannical, doomed, and destroyed Rome, and in the God of Israel.

Since the time when Rome expulsed Israel from the country Hashem gave them, Israel sought refuge in those nations that came to know the Messiah of Israel. These nations, for the most part, oppressed them. But even before the days of the Master, the prophet Jeremiah uttered the following words,

> The day will come when people will no longer swear, "As ADONAI lives, who brought the people of Isra'el out of the land of Egypt," but, "As ADONAI lives, who brought the people of Isra'el out of the land to the north and out of all the countries where he drove them"; for I will bring them back to their own land, which I gave to their ancestors. (Jeremiah 16:14–15)

This will be the second great Exodus; the one Yeshua initiated 2,000 years ago.

In these days, the Creator of the universe will reveal himself to his people through his Mashiach in order to show them his great love, care, and power to redeem them from the nations that will surround them in an attempt to annihilate them. In these days, Hashem will valiantly perform again great miracles, miracles that will be documented and spoken about forever and ever over land and sea. One of those great miracles will be that as Hashem redeems his people, a great multitude of Gentiles will also be redeemed joining Israel in finding refuge in the great Kingdom of God to come.

May it be soon Abba, even in our days!

My Personal Thoughts

_____

_____

_____

_____

Revelation 15:3   Sh'vat 11/ יא בשבט

They were singing the song of Moshe, the servant of God, and the song of the Lamb:
"Great and wonderful are the things you have done, ADONAI, God of heaven's armies!
Just and true are your ways, king of the nations!

3,400 years ago, the children of Israel celebrated a great victory on the Eastern bank of the Gulf of Aqaba. Miraculously supplied with bread from heaven (John 6:31) and with Pharaoh's armies at their heels, they crossed the wilderness of the Sinai. They saw more of the majestic power of Hashem when the waters of the Red Sea stood as walls at their sides to give them passage. They then witnessed the same waters recede to swallow the whole army of their enemy dealing a deathly blow to the power that once was Egypt. The biblical records tell us that, of all the hosts of Pharaoh that had followed them into the sea, not one of them remained (Exodus 14:28). On the other side, in the Land called Midian, under the leadership of Moses and Miriam, the children of Israel erupted into a song of praise that will echo through the centuries (Exodus 15).

Over a hundred years after the initial conquest of the Land, the song of Miriam already finds an echo. After Joshua's death, Israel was left without central leadership. Everyone did what was right in his own eyes (Judges 17:6), so, "So ADONAI handed them over to Yavin king of Kena`an. He ruled from Hatzor; and the commander of his army was Sisra, who lived in Haroshet-HaGoyim" (Judges 4:2). Eventually, when Israel was ready to amend his ways, Hashem allowed Judge/prophetess Deborah and military leader Barak to muster an army to challenge Jabin. As Sisera, Jabin's general, positioned his army to intercept Israel, Hashem worked again in Israel's favor. He showed his great glory and power while unleashing from the sky a torrential storm flooding the Kishon waterway (Judges 4). The floodwaters and muddy ground rendered Sisera's chariots helpless and vulnerable to Israel's army. The biblical records tell us again that "Sisra's entire army was put to the sword; not one man was left" (Judges 4:16). Again, an army trying to trap Israel was rendered helpless through a flood of waters. Like with Moses and Miriam, Barak and Deborah celebrated with a song (Judges 5).

Will there be another echo?

Zechariah tells us of another war against Israel; a war where all nations will rise against Jerusalem (Zechariah 14). At that time, a flood of blood will render the armies of the enemy useless (Revelation 14:20). By the mountain of Megiddo, at the same place where Sisera's army fell, the armies of the Anti-Messiah will gather against Jerusalem and fall. Again, not a man will be left (Revelation 16:16; Revelation 19).

At that time, Miriam's song will echo in the mouth of the children of God of all ages, through a spontaneous eruption of praise and adoration to our mighty God (Revelation 5:9; 14:3; 15:3).

May it be soon Abba, even in our days!

My Personal Thoughts

_____

_____

_____

_____

_____

1 Corinthians 10:2   Sh'vat 12/ יב בשבט

And in connection with the cloud and with the sea they all immersed themselves into Moshe.

The children of Israel could have left Egypt, traveled directly northeastward and been in Canaan in less than a few weeks. Instead, Hashem had them make a small detour crossing the Red Sea by the Gulf of Aqaba. Were the reasons given for this detour (Exodus 13:17–18) the only ones?

The Israelites had just spent several generations in Egypt. They needed to be cleansed from idolatry and Egyptian culture. They needed to be reborn into Hashem's people, and into the culture of his Kingdom. This is where the idea of *born-again* came from: from two tractates written by Jewish sages that say that "total immersion into water is like being born again". To go into a body of water and to stop breathing is like being in a grave where we do not have breath anymore. It is also like returning to a mother's womb. We come out resurrected as a new reborn person. The sages mention the born-again idea mostly in regards to conversion to Judaism. They say, "They immerse in order to emerge a born-again new creature in God" (Yevamot 47b and 48b). This is what Hashem had in mind in this nation-wide immersion through the Red-Sea (1 Corinthians 10:2).

When Yeshua told Nicodemus that he needed to be reborn, the modern-day *born-again* Christian movement did not exist. Yeshua was using the term according to its Talmudic value, and Nicodemus answered the Master accordingly. What Nicodemus replied in essence was "Why do I need to convert when I am already Jewish?" To which Yeshua answered,

> Yes, indeed, I tell you that unless a person is born from water and the Spirit, he cannot enter the Kingdom of God What is born from the flesh is flesh, and what is born from the Spirit is spirit. (John 3:5–6)

In other words, the Master reiterated John the Immerser's message that biological descent into God's family was not enough, but repentance into a new creature for Hashem was also needed (Matthew 3:9). The Israelites crossing the Red Sea were already Israelites, but they needed to also be immersed into Moses in the cloud and in the sea (1 Corinthians 10:2).

Yeshua continued answering Nicodemus with,

> The wind blows where it wants to, and you hear its sound, but you don't know where it comes from or where it's going. That's how it is with everyone who has been born from the Spirit. (John 3:8)

Just like the wind cannot be seen and is only perceived though its effects, so are we. The virtues of the new life that we now live, its positive influences on others and its reflection of Hashem, are the only testimony given to others of our rebirth.

As we claim to have been reborn, as we claim to have been immersed unto Yeshua, let the effects of our rebirth be felt by others. May we live and walk in the newness of life that he has given us to be God's children, and as the healing reflection of his spirit on our poor world.

My Personal Thoughts

_____

_____

_____

1 Thessalonians 4:17   Sh'vat 13/ יג בשבט

Then we who are left still alive will be caught up with them in the clouds
to meet the Lord in the air; and thus we will always be with the Lord.

After over two hundred years in Egypt, the people of Jacob who had come in initially as economic refugees were influenced by Egyptian ways and culture. Through the plagues, in plain sight of the Egyptians and of Israel, Hashem took on each one of the main gods of Egypt. He was to show the world his ultimate superiority over all that is called *god*. This was a shock to Pharaoh, and a reminder to the people of Israel of the stories they had heard about El-Shaddai, the God of their ancestors.

A parallel lesson unfolds for God's people in the fifth century BCE Israel had already been invaded by Babylonian Emperor Nebuchadnezzar, and Gedaliah's provisional government governed the poor that were left in the Land. A plot from Amon caused Gedalliah to be killed, so the people feared Babylon's reprisals. Against Jeremiah's strong counsel from God, the people decided to flee to Egypt for refuge. Once there, they sought Pharaoh's protection and prayed to Egyptian gods. Nebuchadnezzar was now coming after them in Egypt, which he was going to also destroy. In the forty-sixth chapter of the Book of Jeremiah, God showed that through Nebuchadnezzar, his mighty hand was again going to destroy the Egypt in which his children had trusted.

Hashem took aim and mocked the futility of the gods of Egypt who were unable to do stand up and protect. He said,

> Proclaim in Egypt, announce in Migdol, announce in Nof and Tachpanches; say: "Take your stand! Get ready! For all around you the sword is destroying. Why has your strong one been overthrown? He failed to stand because ADONAI pushed him down. He caused many to trip; yes, they fell all over each other." Then they said, "Let's get up, let's return to our own people, back to the land where we were born, away from the sword that destroys." They cried there, "Pharaoh king of Egypt makes noise, but he lets the right time *[for action]* slip by." (Jeremiah 46:13–17)

And what shall we learn from these? It seems that the Father is on a constant crusade against our hankering for the false gods of this world. No matter what he does to show us his great power, we always seem to fall to the lure of the sensual and indulging gods of this world. As it was then, so it is today.

Today again he is calling us to leave *Egypt* and to never return. He is calling us away from the gods of this world, but how can we enter the Land with an unregenerate heart?

At a future time, the mighty El-Shaddai will return. This time he will destroy the *Babylon* of this age (Revelation 17–18). He will also show his great power not only to his children but to the whole world. He will expose the vanity of mankind and bring his people from all over the world unto him.

May we be ready at that time. Let us take off from our ears the ear buds that fill us with the sounds of this generation that we may hear his call. May we then be clean from our idols, a bride without blemish consecrated unto Messiah.

My Personal Thoughts

Mark 3:4   Sh'vat 14 / יד בשבט

What is permitted on Shabbat? Doing good or doing evil? Saving life or killing?

The Sabbath is the most repeated ordinance in the Torah. Like wearing a wedding ring informs people that we belong to someone, Sabbath observance informs our entourage that we belong to Hashem. From a simple mental cognition to a strict and severe application, people have a wide array of ideas on how the Sabbath should be observed. All the aspects of the spectrum of Sabbath application are covered, sometimes even at the cost of feuding division between family and friends. The question we need to ask ourselves is, "How did Yeshua observe the Sabbath?"

We are told that the evening the Master's death was a Sabbath so his disciples went to rest according to the commandments (Luke 23:56). What Yeshua taught his disciples was a healthy respect of the Sabbath and there is nothing in the apostolic texts telling us that he broke it. Remember, Yeshua was without sin, and sin is the breaking of the Torah (Hebrews 4:15; 1 John 3:4).

Yeshua did teach about the Shabbat. He actually spoke of many aspects of Torah observance. He said, "My yoke is easy" (Matthew 11:30). In Torah talk, the *yoke* the Master referred to was the yoke of Torah application in our lives. What Yeshua was in fact saying was that his type of Torah application was easy and light, not hard and oppressive, which included his application of Sabbath observance. For example: a donkey was a precious commodity for farmers in Israel, so it was agreed by the religious leaders of the day that if on the Sabbath a sheep were to fall in a pit, its masters could rescue it even though it broke some Sabbath prohibitions. Yeshua then went on to argue that the life of a man was much more precious than that of a sheep, so if it is permissible to rescue a sheep on the Sabbath, it should certainly be permissible to heal a whole man on the Sabbath day (Matthew 12:11–12).

Yeshua was not creating a new law and application but he certainly was arguing from within the contents of the Jewish oral tradition of his day. Yeshua tried in fact to teach us that not only the saving of a life was acceptable on the Sabbath, but also the alleviating of human suffering, which is what eventually became a doctrinal point of disagreement between him and some of his more rigid opponents.

The examples of Yeshua's handling of the Sabbath should give us a good idea of what is biblically permissible on the Sabbath day. When he asked them the rhetorical question, "What is permitted on Shabbat? Doing good or doing evil? Saving life or killing?" (Mark 3:4), Yeshua in fact reminded his audience that by their own teachings it was alright to do good on the Sabbath Day.

May we remember this principle and learn to make our Sabbath observances a blessing to us and to those around us.

My Personal Thoughts

_____

_____

_____

_____

_____

2 Corinthians 1:21–22   Sh'vat 15/ טו בשבט

Moreover, it is God who sets both us and you in firm union with the Messiah; he has anointed us,
put his seal on us, and given us his Spirit in our hearts as a guarantee for the future.

Five lessons did the father teach Israel even before they arrived in Horeb:

1. He who had the power to embitter Egypt's waters by turning them to blood, and thereby drive its people to thirst, also had the power to provide sweet waters for his own people in the middle of the desert.

2. He who had the power to starve the richest nation in the world by destroying their crops also had power to feed his people right in the middle of the desert.

3. He who had the power to kill Egypt's cattle so that they had no more of that free meat could provide meat for his people in the middle of the desert.

4. He who destroyed Egypt's armies could also strengthen Israel's ragtag armies against mighty Amalek.

5. He who saw the affliction of Israel in Egypt gave them the gift of the Sabbath.

The Sabbath is a sign of our appurtenance to Hashem. It is like an expensive wedding ring. It is a gift. As a future husband is proud of the beautiful ring he has purchased for his future bride and wants to display it to her ahead of time, Hashem offered the Sabbath to Israel even before the people arrived in Horeb. In a sense, Hashem is displayed his true nature and told Israel, "You see what I can, and will, do for you? I delivered you; I gave you sweet waters to drink from; I fed you; I even made your men mighty warriors in order to deliver you from your enemies!" Later, as he would declare his intention to wed Israel he would actually say to her,

You have seen what I did to the Egyptians, and how I carried you on eagles' wings and brought you to myself. Now if you will pay careful attention to what I say and keep my covenant, then you will be my own treasure from among all the peoples, for all the earth is mine; and you will be a kingdom of cohanim for me, a nation set apart. These are the words you are to speak to the people of Isra'el. (Exodus 19:4–6)

While in desert, even before arriving at Horeb, Hashem gave a sneak preview to the children of Israel of what he had in mind for them.

The Apostle said that today we are given the earnest of the spirit (2 Corinthians 1:22, KJV). This means that today we are only given a ten percent guaranty of what Hashem has in store for us. We should then look forward to the full glory of his intended gift to us in the world to come.

May we always refuse to look at the bogus enslaving dainties of Egypt, and learn to keep our eyes focused on what Hashem does for us today, and that as a sign of the mighty glory that is to befall us in the world to come.

May it be soon Abba, even in our days!

My Personal Thoughts

_____

_____

Revelation 11:15   Sh'vat 16/ טז בשבט

The kingdom of the world has become the Kingdom of our Lord and his Messiah,
and he will rule forever and ever!

As Moses arrived at Mt. Horeb with the people of God, his Father-in-law Jethro paid him a visit. Jethro is not really his name; it's a title defining a societal rank. The name of Moses' father-in-law was Reuel, "Shepherd of God" (Exodus 2:18).

With Reuel's visit, we realize the greater purpose for the Exodus program. Reuel was a descendant of Abraham through his third wife Keturah (Genesis 25:1–2). It is recorded that Abraham gave that side of his descendents the land that is today called Saudi Arabia. It seems that they did not continue in the faith of Abraham but adopted the paganism of the area, thus we find Jethro, a descendant of Abraham, and a pagan priest of Median.

Jethro witnessed the life of Moses as a seeker. Like Abraham in Ur, Moses was not satisfied with his life as an Egyptian (Hebrews 11:8–16; 24–28). Moses was not going to put up with the magic tricks of the Egyptian priests. He wanted the real thing. He searched for Hashem with all his heart; that's why he found him (Jeremiah 29:13). Jethro also was a seeker. He probably knew about the God of Israel but imagined he was dead, or maybe asleep.

Whatever the case, this God, this Creator of heaven and earth, was on the verge of meeting all those who seek him for all generations to come.

As Jethro received knowledge of all God had done to Egypt in order to free his people, he returned to the faith of his ancestor Abraham. The Torah tells us Jethro's reaction. He said to Moses,

> Yitro said, "Blessed be ADONAI, who has rescued you from the Egyptians and from Pharaoh, who has rescued the people from the harsh hand of the Egyptians. Now I know that ADONAI is greater than all other gods, because he rescued those who were treated so arrogantly." Yitro Moshe's father-in-law brought a burnt offering and sacrifices to God, and Aharon came with all the leaders of Isra'el to share the meal before God with Moshe's father-in-law. (Exodus 18:10–12)

A greater Exodus is coming. A time is coming when people will not say anymore, As ADONAI lives who brought up the people of Israel out of the land of Egypt, but rather, blessed be ADONAI who brought back his people from all the nations where He scattered them (Jeremiah 16:14–15). This will have the same effect as the first Exodus. Like Jethro, the whole world will then know that Hashem is the Lord of all the earth.

May it be soon Abba, even in our days!

My Personal Thoughts

_____

_____

_____

_____

_____

Acts 6:3

Brothers, choose seven men from among yourselves who are known to be full of the
Spirit and wisdom. We will appoint them to be in charge of this important matter.

Flabbergasted, Jethro looked at Moses single-handedly dealing with every problem in the camp. He foresaw disaster and even danger in that style of leadership. Jethro conjectured that eventually people would learn to lean too heavily on Moses and that his son-in-law would not last very long. Jethro, who was a spiritual leader in his own right, suggested a lower court to be established to care for simpler cases. Moses would then share the load of leadership with others.

God's leadership is not autocracy. In God's Kingdom, even a king has counselors, and a wise leader leans on the council of his advisers as a cripple does on a cane. God's style of government is not democracy either. The *will of the people* is not supreme; Hashem's will is.

Hashem's government is usually made up of a leadership teamwork; a group of upright people elected by the congregation. No one person is perfectly well rounded so this leadership teamwork should be composed of people exerting different views and ways of looking at things. They should also be filled with a spirit of humility so they can yield to each other's counsel and advice.

We can see this pattern as God's leadership all throughout the sacred texts. Even Yeshua used it. He did not keep the whole burden on himself but established a group of disciples, who also went to preach, exhort, exorcise, and heal people. He even said that they will sit on twelve thrones judging the tribes of Israel, just like Moses was advised to do. Even Yeshua shares the responsibility of judgment. Peter and the disciples followed that same example and asked the congregation to submit seven people that they could ordain as leaders (Acts 6:1–7). This type of congregation leadership follows the *Jethro* pattern. If Yeshua himself used it, why shouldn't we?

The answers to that question are varied and can be scary. We will try to answer them in later articles. In the meantime, may God give us leaders, men and women of integrity whose sole desire is to do whatever needs to be done, whether it be to step in or to step aside. May these leaders help establish his Kingdom on earth as it is in heaven.

My Personal Thoughts

---

1 Timothy 3:1   **Sh'vat 18/** יח בשבט

If anyone aspiring to be a congregation leader is seeking worthwhile work.

Mankind is of a rebellious nature. We are small, weak, vulnerable and as ironic as it may seem, we strive for independence at any cost. Human history teaches us that our thirst for freedom from even God-appointed human leadership has solely been quenched by the spilling of much blood. Mahatma Gandhi is known to have said to British officials—who were then controlling India—that every man would prefer to be run by his own bad government than the good government of others. Whereas countries do have their own right to self-determination, in theology this principle translates in that mankind prefers to be led by his own distilled spiritual errors, than by the truth taught him by a divinely appointed leadership.

The Father knows that we need leadership, that's why he inspired Jethro to advise Moses about a council of elders. This council was to be called the *Court of Judgment* or *bet-din* בית דין in Hebrew. Authority was granted to individuals to help people find answers for their everyday questions. This was done by interpreting the Torah by using the Torah. This council would later become what we know as the Sanhedrin.

Just as people today balk at answering to any human authority, it is not hard to imagine that some of the children of Israel resented the lower court in favor of the higher court: that of Moses (Torah). It is not hard also to imagine that a charismatic council member from this lower court would draw much attention to himself, thus provoking unbalanced loyalties from the people. These problems with human leadership exist today, and they certainly existed then. We see plenty of them in the Bible.

This is why these appointed leaders needed to be men known for their integrity, men from among the people who feared Hashem, men, who were trustworthy, men who hated a bribe, men to whom Moses would teach the statutes and the laws of God. Moses had the charge to teach them the way in which they must walk and what they must do (Exodus 18:20–21).

The disciples of the Master used the same blueprint to establish leadership in the Messianic congregations. At a time of crisis, they also established leaders to judge petty matters within the community (Acts 6:1). Again, as in the Horeb blueprint, these men were chosen for their integrity; they were men of good repute and full of the spirit and of wisdom (Acts 6:3). Also, according to the same parameters, Paul established leadership over each and every congregation. Hear his advice to Timothy on how to choose congregational leaders,

> A congregation leader must be above reproach, he must be faithful to his wife, temperate, self-controlled, orderly, hospitable and able to teach. He must not drink excessively or get into fights; rather, he must be kind and gentle. He must not be a lover of money. He must manage his own household well, having children who obey him with all proper respect. . . . Likewise, the shammashim must be of good character, people whose word can be trusted. They must not give themselves to excessive drinking or be greedy for dishonest gain. . . . Similarly, the wives must be of good character, not gossips, but temperate, faithful in everything. Let the shammashim each be faithful to his wife, managing his children and household well. (1 Timothy 3:2–12)

It is also noticeable that it was the people who chose these leaders who were afterward appointed and anointed by Moses or Paul.

1 Timothy 3:2–6

A congregation leader must be above reproach, he must be faithful to his wife, temperate, self-controlled, orderly, hospitable and able to teach. He must not . . . get into fights . . . he must be kind and gentle. He must not be a lover of money . . . if a man can't manage his own household, how will he be able to care for God's Messianic Community? He must not be a new believer, because he might become puffed up with pride and thus fall under the same judgment as did the Adversary.

In Genesis 2:18, Hashem's intentions towards Adam in creating Eve are either lost in translation, or in the personal bias of the translator. A more literal reading would say, "I will create someone to be *against him.* It seems that the help man most often needs is in the form of someone who is *against* him; not as in someone fighting him, but as in one acting as a balance to him. Because of this, Judaism advises to not trust the teaching of a rabbi who is not married.

A wise man will willingly invite the counsel of his wife. She is the one who knows him best. If he listens to her, not only will his life be more harmonious, but he will make wiser decisions. Therefore a wise woman needs to learn how to fitly advise her husband. If she nags him or makes him feel inferior, he'll turn off and she won't be able to fulfill her God-given duty. She also needs not to do it as an attempt to control him. If because of control issues, passiveness, or a lack of wisdom, a wife is not able to advise her husband, she fails in her main wifely duty. The same goes for a wife who inflates her husband's ego, which she usually does because she wants to bask in his glory. Such a woman will be responsible for her man's downfall. A beautiful example of a good marriage relationship in American history is that of the second president of the United States John Adams with his wife Abigail Adams. It is even said that at one time, then President George Washington asked Abigail Adams' help to try to convince her husband of an important piece of diplomatic strategy.

When Roman Emperor Tiberius started commandeering the Senate, one senator protested and compared his governing body to an unheard and ignored wife. If a man, if a leader, does not have a wife, he should at least be able to listen to the counsel of those wise people God put around him. He is wise he who surrounds himself with people who are wiser than him. Paul was not married, but he worked within counsel. Though he took some liberties, he went to Jerusalem to make sure that his race was not in vain. He sought the approval of his own apostolic leaders (Galatians 2:2).

Sad to say though, many leaders in their pride, fear, and insecurity surround themselves with passive people who adulate them, or with those who find an interest in the relationship, so they will not balance a leader or a teacher. Even if they try, they eventually will give in. The leader knows it and it will be his downfall in the sight of God if not in the sight of men.

May Hashem give us leaders, men who have a right spirit before him, leaders whom the position of office does not corrupt with pride, true humble ministers of Hashem's flock who only wish to serve.

My Personal Thoughts

_____

_____

_____

1 Corinthians 15:52   Sh'vat 20/ כ בשבט

. . . at the final shofar.

Paul, Yeshua's emissary, speaks to us about the "final shofar" (1 Corinthians 15:52). If there is a final blow, there must have been an initial blow. Through the passage of time, the final shofar is an echo of the initial shofar blown at Horeb.

The first shofar was blown to herald the grand entrance of the King in the lives of men. The King entered the created dimension and his feet touched the mountain (Exodus 19:11). Later, he who they saw as Hashem and who did not lay his hand on them enjoyed a meal with the elders of Israel sitting at his feet (Exodus 24:9–11; Exodus 33:20). In the same manner, the last shofar will herald the arrival of Hashem's King whose feet will touch the mountain. He will also recline for a meal with his true followers, with those who cared not to lose their lives for him (Zechariah 14:4; Revelation 19:7–9).

At the Exodus, after Egypt licked its wounds from the series of plagues and were drowned, our fathers were placed under the legislation of Hashem's eternal instruction. By these, they were to be a light to the rest of the nations of the world. At the last shofar, while the world will also lick its wounds from the plagues of God's judgments, through Instruction flowing from Jerusalem, those of the nations who remain will also be placed under the legislation of the light of Torah, the constitution of the world to come (Micah 4:2).

When a man blows the shofar, he starts out strong then grows weaker as he runs out of breath. It is not so with the God whose breath (in Hebrew: *ruach* רוח, meaning: spirit or breath) is infinite. The mighty El-Shaddai doesn't run out of breath; the text in Exodus tells us, "As the sound of the shofar grew louder and louder" (Exodus 19:19).

Looking at our sad world today, it can easily be concluded that all of its problems are the result of breaking the fundamental instructions taught at Mt. Horeb. One of the sages of Israel defined that just by keeping the last of Horeb's Ten Statements we keep all the rest of them. Indeed if we (10) do not covet the things that we do not have or even need, (1) we worship our One God and (2) are not tempted the dainties offered us by idol-worshipping; (3) we do not need to lie so we do not need to take his Name in vain by swearing falsely (Matthew 5:33–37); (4) we do not find it binding to take a day off from lucrative activities to spend it with Hashem and those created in his image such as family and friends, and (5) we have no qualms about morally and financially supporting our aged parents. The absence of covetousness also negates the need for (6) murder, (7) adultery), (8) stealing, and (9) lying.

Thus is the legislation of the Messianic Era now and in the world to come.

May it come soon Adon Yeshua, even in our days!

My Personal Thoughts

_____

_____

_____

_____

John 8:36   **Sh'vat 21/ כא בשבט**

So if the Son frees you, you will really be free!.

Our fathers were slaves in Egypt. Pharaoh ordered their lives. He told them what to do, where to work, and how to work. He told them to serve him and no one else. Pharaoh was to be obeyed and worshipped under punishment of death. When they cried under the cruel oppression, the Almighty El-Shaddai heard them. He delivered them, brought them to a mountain, and bound them to himself and to his Laws. Hashem's Law then ordered our fathers' lives. It told them what to do, where to work, and how to work; to serve ADONAI and no one else. ADONAI was to be obeyed and worshipped under the pain of death.

For those who have a tendency to think that living under the Torah is a form of bondage, it could be concluded that the children of Israel went from one bondage to another: from slavery under Pharaoh to slavery under God.

Let me indulge in a mariner's analogy. A sailor is at sea. He is in charge of an expensive vessel. He is also responsible for the life of a crew and he has a mission to accomplish. He is at the helm. He has a serious look on his face and does not make a move or a single decision without checking his compass. This reliance on the compass determines the success or failure of his mission, the safety of his vessel, the life and death of his crew. I heard it said that if a sailor wants to enjoy the high seas, he must become a *slave* to the compass.

My friend, thus it is with life. To keep our traveling vessel worthy, to preserve the life of those entrusted in our care, and to accomplish the goal for which we were sent on the high seas of life, we also must become a slave to the compass, and in this case, the compass is the Torah.

In the end, we truly always have to serve somebody. We either serve the idolatrous King of the land or we serve Hashem. And even if external forces do not regulate our lives, we eventually become slaves to the worse bondage of all: the bondage to our own passions.

Serving God under his Torah is the most wonderful freedom of all. It means freedom from human slavery, self-imposed or otherwise. In the Torah we find the wings that free us from even the bondage of gravity to take us to higher ground. It is the very substance that delivers us from the fear of death to bring us to eternal life. If that is bondage, may I live under it all the days of my life.

My Personal Thoughts

_____

_____

_____

_____

_____

_____

_____

_____

_____

Acts 2:3   **Sh'vat 22/ כב בשבט**

Then they saw what looked like tongues of fire,
which separated and came to rest on each one of them.

The English narrative that concludes God's uttering of his Ten Statements at Mt. Horeb tells us, "All the people experienced the thunder, the lightning, the sound of the shofar, and the mountain smoking . . ." (Exodus 20:18). The Hebrew on the other hand literally reads, "And all the people *saw* the voices and the torches." One may see a fiery flash, but how does one see a voice? The question may have pushed English translators to stray from a literal rendition of the verse, but not the Hebrew sages. Also, the congregation at Horeb was composed of people from many nations, so for everyone to understand Hashem's words, the Ten Statements would have had to be uttered in several languages.

How do you see a voice, and how does a single voice speak in many languages? When Moses recounted these events to the second generation of the children of Israel in the desert, he said, "Then ADONAI spoke to you out of the fire!" (Deuteronomy 4:12). One of the sages saw this verse through the lenses of the following passage, "Isn't my word like fire," asks ADONAI, "like a hammer shattering rocks?" (Jeremiah 23:29). The sages of Israel have always described these events as the voice of God splitting into seventy voices speaking seventy different tongues and that these voices were actually like hot sparks flying forth from a hammer's blow on a stone and becoming tongues of fire. This may sound farfetched, but is it really?

Fourteen hundred years after these events, Yeshua, the prophet, "like me (Moses)," (Deuteronomy 18:15) came to give his elucidation of the heavenly voices. When he was on earth, like Moses "Yeshua walked up the hill. After he sat down, his talmidim came to him" (Exodus 24:9; Matthew 5:1). Later, as the disciples were celebrating the festival of Pentecost—which is on the same Jewish calendar date as the Horeb events—they saw these voices in the form of tongues of fire that gave them the ability to speak in the languages of all the foreign pilgrims then present for the festival in Jerusalem (Acts 2:1–5). These voices were later to be sent to the whole world to reach out to the lost sheep of the House of Israel and to the nations with their message.

Today we, followers of the Jewish Messiah Yeshua HaMashiach, are these *voices* of fire from Sinai. Today, from wherever we are in the world, we are Hashem's emissaries and apostles of the great message spoken at Sinai. I usually teach my students that the words of the Ten Statements uttered at Horeb constitute the solution to all of the world's social problems.

But the people must not only hear the message, they must also see it. They must see it in the exemplary walk of our lives. A tall order maybe, but a lot is at stake and his spirit is ever present to help us. Truly, Yeshua ever lives to make intercession off us (John 14:26; Hebrews 7:25). May we not fail in our mission!

My Personal Thoughts

154

James 2:5   Sh'vat 23/ כג בשבט

*Listen, my dear brothers, hasn't God chosen the poor of the world to be rich in faith
and to receive the Kingdom which he promised to those who love him?*

Why does the Torah speak about people selling their daughters (Exodus 21:7–11)? It may sound
archaic but we must remember that these laws were given within the context of a Middle Eastern
society living 3,600 years ago. The literal reading therefore may seem useless to us today, but
what about the principle behind the text?

This law was formulated as a system of protection towards the vulnerable poor of the land. God
created the poor (Proverbs 22:2) and Yeshua said that the poor is always with us (Matthew
26:11). Caused by man's cruel and unfair economic systems, poverty is part of our present
society, and whereas the Father does not usually interfere with the general affairs of mankind, he
still desires to protect the poor.

As poverty today forces one out of his home, in the time of Moses, the practice was that a man
would sell his daughter for a price to pay his debts. But because she was a daughter of Israel, she
was to be respected, and this young girl was not to be used as the buyer's private property. If he
sexually approached her, he was to marry her and automatically grant her the full rights and
privileges of a wife.

This law and others are part of a sort of *Bills of Rights* for the poor of the land. Solomon wrote
much about the poor and of the judgment against those who abuse them. To have mercy and
respect towards the poor is as much a part of Torah constitution as keeping the Sabbath. All the
more, we will be treated in our time of trouble in the same way we treated others in theirs. Our
actions for or against the poor are measured in the heavenly balances of judgment in or against
our favor.

We cannot do much about the decisions made by selfish and wicked men in power, but we can all
share with those in need and we can certainly refrain from abusing them. Let's remember: we are
all poor in the eyes of Hashem. In Hebrew, the words *charity* and righteousness are synonyms.
Also James, the brother of the Master gave stern instructions concerning the poor to the
Messianic Congregations of his days (James 1:27; 2:2–6).

The law of the sold daughter includes another interesting clause. If the buyer abuses the young
girl but does not retain her as a wife, the father then retains the right to redeem her back from him.
This is very eschatological as even though Hashem sold the virgin of the daughter of Zion to
captivity and exile, he reserves himself the right to redeem her if she is abused. Israel therefore
having been abused by the nations, will still be redeemed!

My Personal Thoughts

_____

_____

_____

_____

_____

_____

Romans 11:29   Sh'vat 24/ כד בשבט

For God's free gifts and his calling are irrevocable.

As we read the commandments in Exodus, we may wonder what some of them have to do with us. We may even wonder about their current relevance. Somehow though, these things about buying and selling children, slavery, and polygamy are part of the great Horeb oracle, so to consider them irrelevant can be, and is in my opinion, disrespectful.

Let's look for example at the laws of polygamy.

> If he marries another wife, he is not to reduce her food, clothing or marital rights. If he fails to provide her with these three things, she is to be given her freedom without having to pay anything. (Exodus 21:10–11)

Read from our modern western cultural viewpoint, these rulings sound barbaric, but, reading them within their own merit and context, let's give them a fair try.

Polygamy was an accepted Middle Eastern lifestyle in the days of Exodus when marriage was often no more than a mere business transaction. If he could afford it, a man could marry a woman for financial, political, or just plain lustful selfish reasons and once she served her purpose, get himself a new one to the neglect of the first. Apparently Hashem did not approve of this practice, so he decreed that if a man re-marries, the food, the clothing and the conjugal rights of the first wife are not in any way to be diminished. If the husband doesn't hold to that, she has automatic legal grounds to leave him and even remarry. In a certain way, that makes polygamy impossible unless you are as rich as Solomon.

We are today a far cry from such days of healthy *woman's rights*. Today a man can take a woman, and if he has affairs on the side that cause him to neglect the first wife, she has little recourse. Even in our modern, advanced society, we have little to protect battered and abused women. This Torah ruling teaches about the heart of the Father against such cruelty as rejecting or abusing a wife.

A common teaching today is replacement theology: the ideology that because of sin, God rejected his first wife, Israel, in favor of the Church. For many, this explains our ongoing exile, the inquisitions, and the Holocaust. People usually see God through the filter of their own lifestyle and culture; that is why they easily understand and endorse Replacement Theology. It is the scenario of their own lives, of their own perverted divorce-accepting viewpoint.

According to the torahtic injunction, God hates divorce (Exodus 20:14; Mark 10:2–9). As far as Israel is concerned, Paul also explains, "the gifts and the calling of Hashem are irrevocable" (Romans 11:29). But If God were to practice the putting away of wives, such as the children of Israel because of sin, the Gentile Christians would also be in danger.

My point here is that this commandment reveals the true nature and character of the Father. He may chastise us for a while to help us know and trust him more but never in an attempt to drive us away from him. He doesn't go from bride to bride, as mankind seems to enjoy doing today. We can now see that this seemingly archaic rule teaches us much about our current value system and even our theology.

156

Matthew 18:35   כה בשבט /Sh'vat 25

This is how my heavenly Father will treat you,
unless you each forgive your brother from your hearts.

Because of an erroneous stubbornly recurring antithesis theology between the Hebrew and the apostolic writings, people assume that Yeshua overthrew the retributive Mosaic legal code of *an eye for an eye* and replaced it with a new law based on love and forgiveness (Exodus 21:24; Matthew 5:38–41). Let's examine the issues a little closer.

The expressions, *eye for an eye* and, *turning the other cheek* are not to be taken literally. These are Hebrew idioms; legal terms invoking damage restitution by liable parties. For damage restitution not to be demanded by God's court of law would be unjust, and Hashem cannot be unjust. *An eye for an eye* is a command for an offender to restitute what is lost, broken, or stolen as a chance to redeem himself, not an obligation for the offended party to demand justice. In fact, if a liable party were not to beg for an opportunity to demonstrate his true repentance for his foolish actions, it would show callousness and a total lack of the fear of Hashem. It would show that the repentance was not sincere.

When reading the Master's recommended application of the Torah legal code we must realize that Yeshua could not have been changing the Torah. That would automatically make him a false prophet to be shunned. It is because of the erroneous teachings that Yeshua broke and even obliterated the Torah that today many from the Jewish nation do not consider Yeshua as the promised Messiah of Israel. What Yeshua taught was absolutely in line with Rabbinic Judaism. He took the Torah and gave his personal opinion on how to apply its wise instructions. Most of the Master's recommended Torah application can also be found within the pages of the Talmud. He actually promoted much of Rabbi Hillel's teachings (Rabbi Hillel was Gamaliel's grandfather and Gamaliel was Paul's mentor and teacher). Of course, since Yeshua is the Mashiach, his chosen applications are the right ones.

The mistake people make when they read the Master's teachings is the failure to distinguish between obligations pertaining to Torah courts of Law, and imperatives given to individuals. Because of this, people often want to take the *law* in their own hands and apply it in a vigilante style with the desire to kill the adulteress, the idolater, and the criminals, when actually nothing of the sort can and should be done outside of a legal Sanhedrin ruling.

What the Master teaches us is greater than requiring the due course of justice. There is no commandment to litigate, and what Yeshua offers here is the idea of *not litigating* but rather to forgive a debt or offense from the heart; to not hold grudges, but instead, to rely upon Hashem for justice. This principle is the one found in the parables of the unjust servant (Matthew 18:21–35). To forgive in the legal code of Torah was not an emotional mental exercise; it was simply not to require the Torah's demand for material retribution. Even Paul advocated the benefits of being defrauded rather than press charges (1 Corinthians 6:7).

Come to think of it; could anyone of us be required the full mandate of the Torah for our trespasses against Hashem?

My Personal Thoughts

_____

_____

Luke 1:79   **Sh'vat 26/ כו בשבט**

To shine on those in darkness, living in the shadow of death,
and to guide our feet into the paths of peace.

The Torah provides us with much ruling having to do with man's inhumane behavior. Some of the things the Torah talks about would make very gory bedtime stories. One could easily wonder how could such a heavenly document be so besmirched with the filth of human sin?

King David said that the Torah is light (Psalm 119:105). Light is only useful when it shines in darkness. In essence, the Torah finds its true mission against the backdrop of the spiritual darkness of our human condition. Paul built on David's proclamation in the Psalms saying, "But everything exposed to the light [of Torah] is revealed clearly for what it is" (Ephesians 5:13). Paul also taught his spiritual son and disciple Timothy the following:

> We know that the Torah . . . is not for a person who is righteous, but for those who are heedless of Torah and rebellious, ungodly and sinful, wicked and worldly, for people who kill their fathers and mothers, for murderers, the sexually immoral—both heterosexual and homosexual—slave dealers, liars, perjurers, and anyone who acts contrary to the sound teaching. (1Timothy 1:8–10)

I think that includes all of us. The Torah is therefore a light made to reveal to us our sinful condition. As such, it is a help to direct our paths away from sinful behavior.

In studying Hashem's oracles, we must be careful to distinguish between what the Torah permits and what the Torah advocates. Failure to do so can be disastrous. Whereas the Torah advocates unbroken marriages, in the knowledge of the nature of man's heart it gave leeway for divorce (Matthew 19:8). Whereas it advocates monogamous marriages, in knowledge of the human practices of the day, it gave rulings concerning polygamy. It doesn't mean that the Torah advocates divorce or polygamy; it only means that the Torah strives to be and remain relevant to the society in which it was given. The same goes for slavery; whereas the Torah gives ruling for slaves, it does not advocate slavery. We must be careful to study Hashem's instruction according to its contextual values. Not understanding this could cause us to feel removed from its text because of seeming irrelevance.

On the other hand, many of us who would not consider polygamy as a lifestyle, practice it, but in a sequential, rather than simultaneous, manner, using one spouse and then *throwing him/her away* for another one. Many today, who would not consider enslaving humans, practice a different form of slavery through the commonly accepted practice of usury (lending for interest) and economic policies that offer less guaranties than those offered to slaves in the Bible.

The Torah is a light, and those who consider it obsolete, live in darkness. The Torah reveals the light of Hashem's nature and character to contrast it with ours. Those who in a cafeteria-style pick and choose what they want from it, are found to *edit*, in *essence to add or take away* from the Torah in their hearts, For centuries man has tried to find a better type of government than the one offered in the Torah, and the messy results are evident. In the world to come, the light of Torah will expose our sinful world for what it is and we will finally learn to rule and be ruled under the justice and righteousness of Hashem.

May it come soon Abba Father, this world can't wait any longer; too many are crying out for justice.

James 1:22   Sh'vat 27/ כז בשבט

Don't deceive yourselves by only hearing what the Word says, but do it!

The reading portion assigned for this week starts with the rulings of freeing slaves every seven years (Exodus 21:2). This law of release also applies to fields that are to be let fallow one year out of seven. The purpose of these rulings is to keep people from oppressing each other, as well as to establish a sense of priority in our hearts. Hashem doesn't want us to spend our lives aimlessly increasing our wealth at the cost of our relationships and responsibilities towards human beings. Our spiritual life also needs to be given attention.

When the people of Israel did not obey the law of release, God sent Babylon against them. The seventy years of Babylonian captivity correspond to the seventy Jubilees they did not observe (Jeremiah 25:11). The Land is God's and everything in it. He makes the rules and he gets his due, you can be sure of it.

The part that compliments this week's reading portion is in the Book of Jeremiah. As the Babylonians besieged Jerusalem, through the mouth of Jeremiah, Hashem condemns the people for not observing the Jubilee (Jeremiah 34:8–10). As they obeyed and liberated their slaves, word reached the Babylonian army that Hophra was coming up out of Egypt with an army to raise the siege. It is not that the Egyptians loved Israel so much, it is just that whoever controls Israel controls the Via Maris, the main trade route between Egypt and Assyria.

Here is where the story changes. When Israel sees Egypt coming to its rescue, causing the lifting of the Babylonian siege, they renege on their repentance. They bring their slaves back to labor. They thought they played a good one on God, until Jeremiah unveiled Hashem's retributive plan. You can read it in chapter thirty-four of the Book of Jeremiah.

In Abraham, Hashem made a covenant with mankind that cannot be broken (Genesis 15). But the fact that this covenant cannot be broken does not exclude retributions to us for breaking it. Though these retributions may not be fatal, they are nevertheless drastic (Jeremiah 34:13–22). This covenant may have been made with Israel, but, when a Gentile goes under Hashem's redemptive covenant through Yeshua the Messiah, that person becomes liable to the obligations of its contract. Inclusion under Hashem's covenant is free, but there are particulars to the terms.

As we study the Torah, it is important for us to understand the particulars of this contract. In this day and age of literacy, the only excuses we have for not knowing, is distraction, disobedience, or indifference, and all are dire.

James admonished the Israeli community of believers in these very pertinent words,

> So rid yourselves of all vulgarity and obvious evil, and receive meekly the Word implanted in you that can save your lives. Don't deceive yourselves by only hearing what the Word says, but do it. (James 1:21–22)

May we also take these words to heart!

My Personal Thoughts

_____

_____

_____

2 Peter 1:4   **Sh'vat 28/ כח בשבט**

By these he has given us valuable and superlatively great promises,
so that through them you might come to share in God's nature.

In ancient times, in Israel when a young man wanted to marry, he first consulted with the local matchmaker. He then went to the prospective girl's father or guardian and agreed to a price. The agreement was then sealed with a glass of wine, which allowed the young man to go and *prepare a place*, or build a house for them to live in. This period of betrothal was as binding as marriage itself.

A *ketubah* כתבה was also written. A *ketubah* is a legal document written in beautiful calligraphy. This document outlines the bride price paid for the girl and incorporates all the conditions of the marriage, especially the responsibilities of the groom towards his bride-to-be. It serves as a prenuptial agreement and deterrent in case the husband would leave her as it also makes mention of the money owed to the wife in case of divorce, unless of course the divorce was due to the wife's marital unfaithfulness. During the ceremony held under a *chupah* חפה, which is a cloth held by four poles above the couple, the terms of the *ketubah* are sealed again through the sharing of a glass of wine. The glass is then placed on the floor for the groom to smash with his foot saying, "Thus be done to me if I do not honor the words of this contract." The ceremony is usually followed by a celebration with music, dancing, entertainment, and a banquet.

When the Almighty wanted to marry Israel he was his own matchmaker. He also had a place prepared for his bride: The Promised Land of Israel. First, Hashem brought his prospective wife to a solitary place under the *chupah* of Mt. Horeb's shade. He did so because he wanted her full attention so he could bare his heart to her. After the heavenly bridegroom made his proposal, Israel agreed and said, "All that Hashem said we will do." The engagement was then rendered valid. Moses along with seventy-three other people (witnesses) climbed Mt. Horeb to get the *ketubah* written in stone by the finger of Hashem himself. The whole thing was sealed in blood and followed by a meal with the Almighty (Exodus 19–24).

When God took Israel as a bride, he entered a covenant with everlasting legal promises. Whereas it can be agreed that the marriage has been rocky, Hashem is not man, that he should lie, or a son of man, that he should change his mind (Numbers 23:19), and unlike many men, he is compassion and forgiveness itself. He repents from the evil he wants to do to his people. As Israel, we need to cling tightly to that *ketubah*, to the term of the marriage found in the Torah. We need to study it so we can hold our bridegroom to his terms and to his promises.

We also need to be a faithful wife and hold to our terms of faithfulness and obedience. A very wise mother one day instructed her kingly son in the choosing of a wife and said, "Who can find a capable wife? Her value is far beyond that of pearls" (Proverbs 31:10). In his search, her son ended up with almost a thousand women. As Israel, let us put on the regeneration offered by the righteous one, Yeshua the Messiah, and become the excellent wife sought after by the Almighty.

My Personal Thoughts

_____

_____

_____

_____

Matthew 7:21 Sh'vat 29/ כט בשבט

Not everyone who says to me, 'Lord, Lord!' will enter the Kingdom of Heaven,
only those who do what my Father in heaven wants.

The rulings contained in Exodus 21–24 provide us with a big window into the heart of the Father. How more sensible our world would be if it acknowledged Hashem's wisdom and his approach to government. This is the problem today with the Torah: so few ever tried it. Maybe they will one day, probably out of desperation when the best of man's efforts will have only led to catastrophe, as they seem to presently do.

For millennia the world has not been able to care for its poor. Even today, with all our sophistication, at its best, all the world has to offer is a *slave-master* type of economy based on cruel usury (Proverbs 22:7), which is forbidden in God's eyes (Exodus 22:25–27). In the Torah, lending to the poor in need is not an option, it is a commandment that Yeshua reiterated saying, "When someone asks you for something, give it to him; when someone wants to borrow something from you, lend it to him" (Matthew 5:42). What room is there for usury in this statement? An idea for the Messianic communities would be to emulate Jewish communities and create interest-free lending funds. As times worsen, we certainly need to pool our resources. Hashem is the generous one; he cares for the downtrodden; he has compassion for the poor and gives freely. As disciples, we should emulate him and be as he is.

Another ruling that we should be careful to observe is, "You are not to curse God, and you are not to curse a leader of your people" (Exodus 22:28). As a result of disobeying this commandment, Miriam was afflicted with Biblical leprosy (Numbers 12). If the English wording in this verse seems strange, it is because the original Hebrew text of this whole chapter merges the identities of God and of *Judges of the people* into one. This teaches that when we talk down or disrespect Hashem's divinely appointed authority over us, we talk down and disrespect Hashem. Paul gave due diligence to this commandment. After he mistakenly publicly reviled a corrupt Sadducee high priest who was trying to unjustly condemn him, the Apostle apologized saying, "I didn't know, brothers, that he was the cohen hagadol." Paul then justified his apology quoting from Exodus, "You are not to speak disparagingly of a ruler of your people" (Acts 23:5).

This is a commandment without conditions. Even if the ruler seems curse-worthy, you are not to curse him with gossip, criticism, or open challenge. Let's say you don't like the way things are in your congregation, after humbly presenting your point to the persons involved, if things don't change, just leave and go where you can feel happy. It is certainly a sin to openly challenge leaders and create a mutiny. If you do it, it will surely happen to you in return, either in your congregation or in your family. Hashem will surely see to it.

May we learn to live by his rulings; Yeshua did!

My Personal Thoughts

_____

_____

_____

_____

Colossians 2:9   Sh'vat 30/ ל בשבט

For in him, bodily, lives the fullness of all that God is.

After successfully receiving the stone tables where Hashem engraved his first Ten Instructions to Israel, Moses was asked to levy from them a freewill contribution (Exodus 25:1). This voluntary contribution will serve to build what will eventually become the Tabernacle, the very place the almighty El-Shaddai will use as a sort of communication center with Moses. Remember, the children of Israel confessed that they could not hear the voice of God; they ask Moses to act as an intercessor for them (Exodus 20:18–19). I think it's strange that today many people casually say that they hear *God* speak to them. Even the children of Israel couldn't. They asked for a mediator to hear God for them and later in the Torah we learn that Hashem very much approved (Deuteronomy 18:16–17).

Sages from ancient Israel saw the future and imagined Moses asking God, "Will not the time come when Israel will be deprived of a Tabernacle or of a Temple? What will happen then?" According to the sages, the Divine reply was, "I will then take one of their righteous men and retain him as a pledge on their behalf, in order that I may pardon all their sins" (Midrash Rabbah Shemot 35:4). The agricultural ancient Israelites were familiar with the custom of dedicating a whole harvest to God by presenting one sheave, the first and purest drop of oil from their olives, or even the firstborn of animal and mankind. They understood the principles of the first and best given to Hashem for the sanctification of the whole.

The Tabernacle and Temple housed the Ark, which represented God's covenant presence among man. At the time when Hashem knew the Temple would disappear for a long time and the children of Israel would go for a long exile, the Almighty took one righteous man to hold as a pledge for the sanctification of the people. His name was Yeshua from Nazareth. By the end of the first century, there were over one billion believers in Israel.

Chassidic Jews seemed to understand these mechanism by which Hashem operates.

They believed that their righteous men, their 'tsaddik', their *rebbes* (rabbis) housed the Shekinah of God; they acted as the Temple or the Tabernacle. They were not far off. *Yeshua Ben Yoseph Hanotsree* (Yeshua Son of Joseph from Nazareth) is that righteous Jewish man, that rebbe whom God held as a pledge for the sanctification of the Jewish people and through whom the whole world is redeemed: "In him, bodily, lives the fullness of all that God is. And it is in union with him that you have been made full—he is the head of every rule and authority" (Colossians 2:9–10).

He is the first sheave of the harvest (Numbers 28:26), the pure first drop of olive oil from the press (Gethsemane, the place where the Master was pressed measure means: the olive press). He is also the perfect lamb offered as voluntary contribution from the heart.

My Personal Thoughts

_____

_____

_____

_____

_____

Adar

*In a story never revealing its divine author;
and a queen who concealed her identity,
you reveal to us he who though hidden,
is the glory and redemption of Israel.
O Adar; did you know?*

John 2:21   Adar 1/ א באדר

But the "temple" he had spoken of was his body.

We learn so much about the role of Yeshua in our lives when we study the different elements of the Tabernacle (Exodus 25). The Tabernacle was nothing less than a portable temple, a temporary dwelling place for the *Shechinah* שכינה, until such a time when King David would plan the first Jerusalem temple, to be built by his son, Solomon. Reminding us of the words given to Isaiah the prophet, Yeshua himself called the Temple a *House of Prayer* (Isaiah 56:7; Matthew 21:13).

By definition, Hashem is thrice *kadosh* קדוש, (Holy: Isaiah 6:3: Tanach), meaning that he is set-apart and cannot be approached by a human, which is by definition, common. Hashem wants to live among us but as the Holy King, there is a protocol to be respected, with a death penalty for breaking it (Leviticus 10:1-2). The Tabernacle and its protocol represent the means by which Hashem is to be approached. Even today, we have learned to approach the Almighty solely through the agency of Yeshua. Just as through obedience and submission Yeshua kept himself holy and without sin so he could house the Spirit of God in him, the Tabernacle was also kept holy in order to house the *Shechinah* (Hebrews 4:15).

As Yeshua debated Temple use (or misuse) with Judean leaders, he compared it with his own body or his own self (John 2:13-21). Learning therefore about Tabernacle/Temple protocol is learning about our own relationship with Hashem through Messiah. As we do, we should realize that though we may refer to him as *Father*, there is nothing casual about our relationship with Hashem. This term *Father* has nothing to do with the casual manner some fathers have with their children today. It is used with a sense of awe and respect. The relationship is not like one between peers, but rather reflects the idea of someone we can strongly lean and count on, someone we should pattern ourselves after in order to learn integrity and righteousness.

The role of Messiah is to sanctify us, to set-us apart from the world with his words that through his agency, we may approach our holy father (John 15:3). We are therefore sanctified not only by listening and reading his words, but also as we set ourselves apart to obey Hashem in the manner Messiah has taught.

May we therefore learn to serve and obey; to let our lives be transformed by Yeshua that he may testify on our behalf as those who have cleansed themselves, washed their robes, and set themselves apart from the impurities of the world to be presented unto him (Revelation 7:14).

My Personal Thoughts

_____

_____

_____

_____

_____

_____

Matthew 6:10

May your Kingdom come, your will be done on earth as in heaven.

Many teachings follow the Catholic idea that the final goal of our natural state is to eventually leave this earth and go dwell in a place far away called heaven. Part of this school of thought concludes that God's Kingdom is a place where we all go after we die, or shortly after, unless of course we go to the other place. Some also report having had dreams about being in this heavenly realm or even encountered loved ones living in it. Apostolic writings are not clear on this, but what is clear is that the Kingdom of Messiah comes to us (Revelation 21–22).

When Moses entered the cloud on the mountain, Hashem instructed him to tell the children of Israel to build him a sanctuary (Exodus 25:89). Jewish sages teach that at that moment Moses actually entered the heavenly realm; that he saw the pattern after which he was to build the Tabernacle and all its elements. Hashem had brought his realm down on earth to show Moses.

The idea of the Tabernacle was to establish the necessary protocol so that the Holy One may dwell among us on the earth (Exodus 25:8). We often speak of the restoration of all things. Restoration implies the return of something that was before, of the original model and prototype of Hashem's creation when he fellowshipped with us on the earth (Genesis 3:8). The Garden of Eden is the ideal we all desire to return to; living in complete unobstructed fellowship with Hashem within the realm of his marvelous unadulterated creation. That is *heaven*.

You may ask, "But what about these people who claim to have had dreams of a wonderful place or have even sojourned there?" Well, maybe they are just reacting to their experience with the only information they had (we often do). Maybe they have simply gone to the place where the soul sleeps or rests, awaiting the final resurrection (1 Samuel 28:15; Daniel 12:2; Revelation 6:9–11).

Yeshua spoke of resurrection as a time following biological death. He also spoke of the place where people await resurrection as a place corresponding to our works on the earth (Luke 16:19–24). Remember, he told the thief at his side that he would be in paradise with him that very night. But three days, later Yeshua hadn't yet gone to the Father (Luke 23:43; John 20:17). Paul also speaks of several levels of heavenly dimensions.

From the beginning, Hashem's work has been to restore the world to its original condition as it was at the time of the Garden of Eden. The way Josephus describes the first 1,000 years on earth under Seth the son of Adam and Eve sounds very heavenly (Antiquities. 2.3.68–69).

Later, when the world has gone astray, Hashem chooses a people through whom he makes a covenant so he is able to dwell among them. These people built the Tabernacle and the Temple that housed the *Shechinah*, the very presence of Hashem. From this same people, Yeshua came to show how godliness is experienced and lived. He taught us how to pray to the Father saying, "May your kingdom come . . . on earth as in heaven (Matthew 6:10). The whole story ends with Yeshua spending 1,000 years restoring all things on earth to prepare it for the arrival of New Jerusalem, again, on the earth (Revelation 21–22).

May it be soon Abba, even in our days!

My Personal Thoughts

Matthew 6:12

Forgive us what we have done wrong, as we too have forgiven those who have wronged us.

"For the life of a creature is in the blood, and I have given it to you on the altar to make atonement for yourselves; for it is the blood that makes atonement because of the life" (Leviticus 17:11). What a mystical verse! Much is spoken about blood atonement in the *Tanach* תנך. In the Book of Hebrews, the writer even tells the readers about the blood of Abel, murderously killed by his brother, calling for atonement and vindication (Genesis 4:10; Hebrews 12:24).

Much has been lost in our understanding of the Torah, some due to translations—which can never be perfect—but most are due to our failure to acknowledge the Semitic cultural context. The issue we have here is with the word *atonement*. The word atonement is very important in the Torah. It is the main theme of the document, so we surely must make an effort to understand this word properly according to its own cultural context, values, and merits.

Let's look at the origins of the word *atonement*. Its Hebrew root is the word *kaphar* כפר, from which we derive the words *lid, cover,* and *covering*. The word *kapporeth* כפרת for the golden lid of the Ark covered by the wings of the cherubs, and called in English *mercy seat,* has the same etymological root (Exodus 25:17). *Kippur,* for *Yom Kippur* יום כיפור, or the *Day of Atonement* (Leviticus 23:27) is also a derivatives of *kaphar*. What does *kaphar* mean then? To understand, let's look at the following scenario: let's say that like many of us, you have contracted a very large balance on your credit card and you are unable to pay it. You risk losing your credit, even losing your car, or your house, until a generous soul comes around and says, "Don't worry; I'll *cover* your credit card balance" (Wouldn't that be nice).

It is not that the balance never existed or that it has been deleted from the records, it is only that it has been covered. The credit card company then doesn't look anymore at your failure to pay your debts—which is a biblical command—but at the covering that expunged it. Even Matthew quotes the Master on the forgiveness of sin using financial terminology when he says, "Forgive us our debts, as we also have forgiven our debtors" (Matthew 6:12, ESV).

Indeed, because of sin, we have a bad credit rating; we have even lost all credit in the sight of the Father. He is ready to yank the rug out from under us but someone comes to the rescue and covers the balance of our sins. It is not like we never sinned, but all the Father sees now is the balance covered by Yeshua. King David related to this principle calling Messiah a *shield*. Here are a few of his statements,

> But you, ADONAI, are a shield for me; you are my glory, you lift my head high.
> For you, ADONAI, bless the righteous; you surround them with favor like a shield.
> My shield is God, who saves the upright in heart. (Psalms 3:3; 5:12; 7:10)

As Ruth by kinsman redeemer Boaz, may you be *covered* (atoned) under the *wings* of Yeshua the Messiah (Ruth 3:9).

My Personal Thoughts

_____

_____

_____

John 9:5

While I am in the world, I am the light of the world.

ADONAI said to Moses,

> You are to order the people of Isra'el to bring you pure oil of pounded olives for the light, and to keep a lamp burning continually. Aharon and his sons are to put it in the tent of meeting, outside the curtain in front of the testimony, and keep it burning from evening until morning before ADONAI. This is to be a permanent regulation through all the generations of the people of Isra'el. (Exodus 27:20–21)

This lamp was a seven-branch candelabrum called the *menorah* מנורה. This menorah was to be perpetually lit in the first chamber of the Tabernacle, usually called the Holy Place. In the apostolic letter addressed to the Messianic Jews, known as the Book of Hebrews, this chamber was also called the *First*, in front of the *Second,* which was the Ark's chamber (Hebrews 9:2, KJV), representing the very presence of God. It is important here to note that in Hebrews 8:13, the word covenant was added in the text by KJV editors thus considerably changing the context of Hebrews 9; this is the reason why that word is italicized in KJV and other English Bibles.

When the Temple was built, this lamp was again placed in the *First*, right in front of the *Second*. The Aaronic priesthood alone had the charge to care for it, making sure it was perpetually lit, but all of the people had the charge to provide the oil. In this manner, all of Israel was represented before Hashem and had a part in being the light of the world in Jerusalem. Presently, because there is no temple, the command cannot be performed. But in the days of the Third Temple, the practice will again resume since it is a forever commandment given to Israel (Exodus 27:21).

In the meantime, the menorah is charged with messianic symbolism. Several prophets and servants of God were privy to enter the Father's throne room. The first one we know of is Moses who upon being asked to reproduce what he saw, put this seven-branch candelabrum in the room in front of the Ark (Exodus 25:40). The last one we know of is John who wrote what he saw in the following words, "Then I saw standing there with the throne and the four living beings . . . a Lamb that appeared to have been slaughtered. He had seven horns and seven eyes, which are the sevenfold Spirit of God sent" (Revelation 5:6).

Yeshua proclaimed, "While I am in the world, I am the light of the world" (John 9:5). Yeshua is now with the Father, but before he went there he told his disciples, "You are the light of the world" (Matthew 5:14).

We are on a mission. We who proclaim the name of the Messiah, the Almighty's agent of redemption, have a role to perform, a duty to be the menorah, or the light of the world. When he was on earth, the light of Messiah shone for all to see. He did not hold back no matter how dangerous it was. Now the staff (the baton) is passed on to us and we must also perpetually let our light (the light of Messiah in us) shine before others, so that they may see our *mitzvot* מצות, (good works of obedience to Torah) and praise your Father in heaven (Matthew 5:16).

As the light of Messiah, we stand as his representative to the world. When the day of reckoning comes, may we not be found to have hid our light under a bushel (to have been a believer in secret for fear of man). Instead may we have set it on a lampstand so that it shines for everyone in the house (Matthew 5:15).

Hebrews 7:17

You are a cohen FOREVER, to be compared with Malki-Tzedek.

In this apostolic letter addressed to the Messianic Jews, Yeshua is spoken of as ushering in a new priesthood; it even seems to say there is a change in the Torah. It says, "For when there is a change in the priesthood, there is necessarily a change in the Torah as well. For the one of whom these things are spoken belonged to another tribe . . . altar" (Hebrews 7:12–13). This poses a problem because the Aaronic priesthood, as well as the Torah itself, stems from an eternal covenant (Exodus 29:9; 24:8). Hashem also doesn't change (Malachi 3:6). How then could the Levitical priesthood and the Torah be terminated? Here is more from that apostolic letter, "For on the one hand, a former commandment is set aside because of its weakness and inefficacy" (Hebrews 7:18). What?! The Torah: weak and inefficacious? Remember: context, context, context!

The writer of this letter did utter these words. At that time the Messianic Jews of Israel had just witnessed the assassination of their leader James, Yeshua's brother, by a wicked Roman-appointed high priest. As Yeshua had forewarned them (John 16:2), the disciples were now being evicted from the synagogues where they had continued worshiping. The congregations were at a loss. The author of the epistle tries to comfort the Israeli believers. He says, "For the Torah appoints as cohanim g'dolim men who have weakness; but the text which speaks about the swearing of the oath (Psalm 110:4) appoints a son who has been made perfect forever (Hebrews 7:28). The weakness of the earthly priests was that they themselves, being human, were impure, and needed to do offerings for themselves. In essence, the disciples are being instructed that though they have now lost the *weak high priest* and the Temple below, they can still look up to the perfect High Priest and Temple above. The apostle continues by explaining that whereas the Aaronic priesthood was efficacious for the ritual purifying of the flesh, the priesthood of Yeshua serves to purify the conscience (Hebrews 9:8–14). The Levitical service is therefore not to be replaced, but simply completed. That was the weakness of the Aaronic priesthood; it could never bring redemption to the soul. In fact, salvation was never the goal of the Levitical services hosted by the Aaronic priests. But Yeshua, as he does not need to offer sacrifices for himself every year as levitical priests do, holds his priesthood permanently, and because he continues forever, he is able to save those who draw near to Hashem through him, since he is forever able to intercede on their behalf (Hebrews 7:24–25). Now the equation is solved.

There is still one problem in the apostle's comforting argument to look to the resurrected Yeshua at the right hand of the Father as their high priest: Yeshua is not a Levite, as he was from the tribe of Judah. He is therefore not eligible to be a high priest in Israel; not even a priest for that matter. As such, he is not fit to serve in the Temple (Hebrews 8:4). The apostle then reminds the believer that the Messiah is not a priest from the Order of Aaron, but a priest according to the Order of Melchizedek, one who serves not in the Temple, which is below, but who serves in the Temple, which is above. The problem is that whereas people do read the word, they read it with the glasses of an already established theology. Consequently, they read into the text instead of letting the text instruct them.

Jeremiah the prophet tells us of the Messianic age when a third Temple, with the two priesthoods serving together (Jeremiah 33:22). May that time come, ADONAI, even in our days! In the meantime, may we, like our brethren from the Book of Hebrews, find comfort in lifting our eyes upwards (Hebrews 7:25).

Luke 2:49 Adar 6/ ר באדר ו

Didn't you know that I had to be concerning myself with my Father's affairs?

The US has become the icon of Western civilization, and as a teacher in the US, I notice that its people have become very casual. I was raised in France, and in my school days, I would have never dreamed of addressing my teachers, or any other adult, without using their title, such as Mr. or Mrs. I would have certainly gotten slapped if I would have called my parents or any relative anything other than *Papa, Maman, Tonton, Tata,* etc. *(*Daddy, Mommy, Uncle or Auntie).

I am of the belief that our style of rapport in human relationships reveals our style of rapport with God. We serve God the way we serve humankind, those made in his the image. You cannot say that you have a good relationship with God while you have trouble living and working with others or if your behavior is so obnoxious that others have a hard time getting along with you. You cannot tell me that you hear the voice of God when you have difficulty hearing those around you whom God has placed to advise you. You cannot tell me that you have respect for God and his will when you are not reverent of his word and of the people around you whom he has called *kedoshim* קדושים, or saints.

Because we live in a society that has rejected many ideas of protocol and respect of individuals placed in a position of authority, it seems we also want to have a very casual and familiar relationship with Hashem, and even with the Master, but is that right? During the time of his manifestation on earth (2 Timothy 1:9–10), the Master compared himself to the Temple. An understanding, therefore, of Temple and Tabernacle protocol as described in the Book of Exodus helps us understand what kind of relationship we are to have with him.

God is not content to merely peer down at us from above. He desires to engage in a relationship with us, but because of his status of holiness and ours of non-holiness, there are protocols to be respected and accommodations to be organized for the relationship to work. The Tabernacle/Temple system became this protocol and accommodation, and the Master compared himself to it (John 2:21). That should tell us that our relationship with the Master is anything but casual. Look at what happened when people of a much greater spiritual caliber than you and I—like in the case of the prophet Daniel and that of John, the disciple—encountered the Master (Daniel 7:13–28; Revelation 1:10–17).

After Yeshua's death and resurrection, the disciples became a Temple sect, spending a great deal of time there (Acts 2:46; 3:1–3; 5:42). They were in what the Master coined as the *House of Prayer* (Matthew 21:13), doing his Father's business (Luke 2:49). Their base of operation was Solomon's Porch (Acts 3:11; 5:12).

While creation is described in one chapter in the book of Genesis, the description of and measurement of the Tabernacle takes a large chunk of the book of Exodus. May we learn from the study of the Temple; there is a blessing in it (Ezekiel 43:10).

My Personal Thoughts

_____

_____

_____

_____

Revelation 3:12   **Adar 7/** ז באדר

I will make him who wins the victory a pillar in the Temple of my God.

While the children of Judah were exiled in Babylon, they witnessed the capture of their king, the devastation of their beloved Jerusalem, and the destruction of God's Temple. Ezekiel the prophet was among the captive who, after all hopes were gone for the deported nation, was given the ministry of encouragement. Hashem used Ezekiel to encourage the exiled in the Babylonian dispersion by telling them of the wonderful future of a rebuilt Jerusalem hosting a magnificent glorious temple where the Messiah himself will serve (Ezekiel 40: and forward).

Oddly enough, as particular as Hashem can be on these things, the architectural plans and service details of the Messianic era Temple are different than those of the first Temple. When the captives returned and started rebuilding, it would have seemed natural that they would follow the blue print of Ezekiel's prophetic temple but they did not. The prophets of the day believed that the temple they were to build right after their return from Babylon would not last forever. So they stuck close to the layout of the first temple. They understood that the Temple of Ezekiel's vision belonged to another time, to the time pertaining to Messiah's actual reign on earth.

Since Ezekiel's Temple has not been built, prophecies have therefore not been fulfilled, they now serve as an encouragement for us who are still in dispersion, for all believers are aliens and temporary residents on this earth (Hebrews 11:13) waiting for the time when we will reside in the kingdom of Hashem.

So whatever upheaval we see in the Middle-East, we must keep our eyes fixed on these prophecies telling us of the glorious future of the Messianic age when Messiah himself, who has the true roadmap for peace in the Middle East, will reign from his Temple in Jerusalem.

The Torah will then be the Law of the Land and will flow out of Zion to fill the nations of the world who will bring their glory to Jerusalem. It will be a time of great restoration when Messiah himself will wipe our tears away while bringing true justice to this world.

May it come soon Abba, even in our days!

My Personal Thoughts

_____

_____

_____

_____

_____

_____

_____

_____

_____

_____

171

2 Corinthians 2:16

The sweet smell of life leading to more life.

Three offices in the Torah require oil anointing: that of the priest, king, and prophet. The Hebrew word *Mashiach* מָשִׁיחַ, from where we derive the English *Messiah* and the Greek anglicized word *Christ,* simply means: *anointed one; one upon whom oil has been poured.* Yeshua is the Messiah, the anointed one; he upon whom oil has been poured, and he fulfills the three offices that require anointing. He first came as the promised prophet (Deuteronomy 18:15); he performs the function of High Priest (Hebrews 9:11); and he returns as the King of kings (Revelation 19:16).

Whereas the priests were simply sprinkled with the fragrant oil, the precious ointment was poured upon the head of the high priest. It anointed him from head to toe, thus the high priest emanated the special oil's sweet fragrance. In those days, oil, especially olive oil, was used for washing and as a perfume. It provided a shine and a shining sweet fragrance of the bearer.

Hear David's poetic description of the anointing of Aaron,

> Oh, how good, how pleasant it is for brothers to live together in harmony. It is like fragrant oil on the head that runs down over the beard, over the beard of Aharon, and flows down on the collar of his robes! (Psalm 133:1–2)

Jewish sages saw Aaron as the quintessential man of peace. He would go to two enemies and say to one, "Would you agree that in spite of all his faults, (his enemy) is a good carpenter?" When the man agreed, Aaron would go to his enemy and say, "Hey do you know what (first man) said about you? ("I can imagine . . . !" he would reply) "He said that you were a good carpenter. I know you don't like him too much but you can agree that he is a good cook!" When the second man heartily agreed, Aaron would take the precious statement back to the first man. When the two met each other next, they were able to have a positive rapport. It is because of this reputation of Aaron that in the Psalms, David compared the sweet fragrance of Aaron's anointing to brethren united and in peace together (Psalm 133:1).

Hear now Paul's praise, about the fragrance of Messiah,

> But thanks be to God, who in the Messiah constantly leads us in a triumphal procession and through us spreads everywhere the fragrance of what it means to know him! For to God we are the aroma of the Messiah, both among those being saved and among those being lost; to the latter, we are the smell of death leading only to more death; but to the former, we are the sweet smell of life leading to more life. Who is equal to such a task? (2 Corinthians 2:14–16)

Let us spread this sweet fragrance of peace throughout the whole world. Let us be examples of the sweet fragrance of the peace of Messiah because really, if our application of Torah doesn't bring us to the nitty-gritty of being at peace between each other as families, communities, and congregations, we are totally missing the point.

May our heads, faces, hands, and feet, be filled with the radiant fragrance of Messiah, the prince of Peace. May we be part of those whom the Master called *peacemakers* that we in turn may be called *sons of God* (Matthew 5:9).

My Personal Thoughts

2 Corinthians 2:14–15 ט באדר /**Adar 9**

> *But thanks be to God, who in the Messiah constantly leads us in a triumphal procession and through us spreads everywhere the fragrance of what it means to know him! For to God we are the aroma of the Messiah, both among those being saved and among those being lost.*

There is a fragrance reserved for the anointing of the holy. It is a fragrant scent distinguishing the consecrated from the profane (Exodus 29:7; 30:22–33). As a man distinguishes his wife's perfume personalized by her own scent, it is a sign for all to recognize what has been consecrated to God.

This oil has a special name. It is called: *Shemen HaMashiach* שמן המשיח: the *anointing oil*. *Mashiach* in Hebrew simply means *anointed one*, and the use of this oil was reserved to anoint the offices that required it such, as a priest, king, and prophet. Only three people were known to carry the three offices: Moses, King David, and Yeshua. There is a decree of banishment for whoever replicates this oil or pours it on a common person (Exodus 30:31–33).

Exodus speaks of this fragrance in sacrificial terms, but in Song of Songs it appears in a lover's language. "Let him smother me with kisses from his mouth, for your love is better than wine. Your anointing oils have a wonderful fragrance; your name is like anointing oil poured out. This is why young women love you—" (Song of Solomon 1:2–3). The Torah's fragrant oil speaks of someone being anointed. The context of the Song of Solomon is about King Solomon's kingship, the son of King David. Therefore, this verse from the Song of Solomon alludes to the future coming one, the Messianic King who will be known as the Messiah, or the *Anointed One*. It is remarkable that one of the steps of his anointing was a passage at a place called *The Olive Press*: *Gethsemane*.

The apostolic writings also take up the theme of the anointing oil as Paul thanks Hashem for the "fragrance" of the knowledge of Messiah in all places. He compares the people of Hashem and the "aroma of Messiah" (2 Corinthians 2:14–15).

Through Moses, Hashem promised that Israel would become a nation of priests. As the Levites are the priesthood for Israel, Israel is the priesthood for the world. About fifteen hundred years after Moses, Galilean Jewish fisherman Peter tells the mixed congregation of Jews and Gentiles that they are a royal priesthood (Exodus 19:6; 1 Peter 2:9).

As a nation of priests dedicated unto God, we are now carriers of the holy scented oil. May our lives truly exhale his fragrance in every case and every situation we meet throughout the day lest we profane the spirit that is vested in us.

My Personal Thoughts

_____
_____
_____
_____
_____
_____

Matthew 5:15   **Adar 10/** י באדר

Likewise, when people light a lamp, they don't cover it with a bowl but put it on a lampstand, so that it shines for everyone in the house.

From the time of its introduction to Israel, the world has been rich in speculations concerning the seven-branch candelabrum of the Tabernacle. Since Hashem hasn't told us what its seven mysterious lights are about, studies abound with menorah enthusiasts desirous to fill this knowledge void. They may all be right, they may all be wrong. Hashem certainly has a way of teasing our curiosity.

In the words of Jewish sages, the Hebrew word *or* אור which stands for *light*, not only refers to physical illumination, but also to mental understanding and mostly, spiritual enlightenment.

The menorah was fueled by scented oil specially prepared for that purpose (Exodus 25:6). In the mouth of the Torah sages, this oil represents our earthly works of obedience to commandments. In telling us "Let your light shine before others, so that they may see your good works and give glory to your Father who is in heaven" (Matthew 5:16), the Master encourages our obedience to Torah in a way that it becomes a light bearing witness to Hashem in the world. In that *light*, the Master's parable of the ten virgins waiting for the bridegroom becomes clear. They all had the light, but without the oil of obedience, the five foolish virgins' lamps quit burning, exposing the shame of their dark spiritual state in which they could not face the bridegroom.

Scholars taught that Hashem's *shechinah* שכינה (indwelling presence) rested on children like the wick of an oil lamp. To burn bright and strong this wick not only needs to be trimmed, but also to be deeply immersed in oil.

May our lives present this oil that the presence of God in us through the agency of his Mashiach may be seen and felt by all, providing light and warmth to the very dark and cold world around us.

My Personal Thoughts

_____

_____

_____

_____

_____

_____

_____

_____

_____

_____

_____

_____

_____

John 14:26　　　　　　　　　　　　　　　　　　　**Adar 11/ יא באדר**

But the Counselor, the Ruach HaKodesh, whom the Father will send in my name, will teach you everything; that is, he will remind you of everything I have said to you.

One of the mysteries of ancient Israel is the *Urim* and the *Thummim* אורים ותאומים: *lights* and *perfections* (Exodus 28:29–30). According to tradition, these referred to the twelve stones set in the high priest's breastplate and were often used to consult God's will. Only the high priest would wear them and only a king or prominent leader could inquire of them. The high priest and the inquirer would stand in the *Holy*, the first chamber of the Tabernacle, and the answer would be given by the light of the menorah shining on certain letters from the names of the tribes written on the stones of the breastplate.

One of the most popular examples is with King Saul. A priest deprived him from the linen ephod and carried the Urim and Thummim to David. As a result, Saul turned to the witch of Endor for oracles. On the other hand, it seems then that by consulting it, David was able to stay one step ahead of Saul (1 Samuel 23:6; 28:6).

Hashem wants us to consult him (Proverbs 3:5–7). Why then did he allow the *Urim* and *Thummim* to disappear? Only he knows, but during the time of the Babylonian exile, Israel filled the void by developing systems of studies that kept them close to the Torah and thereby to Hashem. After the exile, Ezra established these systems in rural center synagogues in a yearly Torah reading program.

When the people returned from the Babylonian captivity, Ezra also worked at re-establishing the Temple priesthood. When some families could not prove their Levitical descent, they were refused the offices of the priesthood (Ezra 2:61–62). Their name was not enough. They needed to be found written in the registry. Disobedience had had a disastrous effect on the country and Ezra was therefore determined to stick to the Torah commands about Levitical priesthood. Circumstantial evidence was not accepted. Ezra then told potential priests not to partake of the most holy food, until such a time when there will be a priest able to consult the *Urim* and *Thummim* (Ezra 2:63). This stands as a prophetic insight from Ezra as it lends itself to the idea that one day, a high priest will return with the *Urim* and *Thummim*.

Only that high priest, he who is light and perfection, truly knows whose name is written in the priesthood registry (Hebrews 5:5; Revelation 20:15). He promised through Moses and confirmed through Peter that we are a nation of priests (Exodus 19:6; 1 Peter 2:5, 9). As Yeshua returns with the *Urim* and *Thummim*, he will confirm whose name is written in the *Book*. We will then be able to partake of the most holy food, that of the peace offering (Leviticus 7:31–32).

In the meantime, may we, through the agency of the spirit of Hashem, learn to consult him about all our affairs. May we learn to seek his advice and follow it no matter what it says.

My Personal Thoughts

_____

_____

_____

_____

_____

Matthew 5:9

How blessed are those who make peace!

As Aaron is anointed high priest, he became a foreshadow of Messiah. The one time anointing of Aaron is remembered in Psalm 133 in the following words,

> Oh, how good, how pleasant it is for brothers to live together in harmony. It is like fragrant oil on the head that runs down over the beard, over the beard of Aharon, and flows down on the collar of his robes. It is like the dew of Hermon that settles on the mountains of Tziyon. For it was there that ADONAI ordained the blessing of everlasting life. (Psalm 133:1–3)

Why did David compare Aaron's anointing to peace and unity? We have learned before of the little scheme Aaron used to get people at odds with each other back in fellowship. Jewish sages taught that we should emulate Aaron in our efforts to bring peace within our families and communities.

We all search for peace and unity but seem to be plagued with division and conflicts. Maybe we have the wrong idea of what peace and unity are. Peace and unity do not mean absence of conflict and uniformity. Debates from differences of opinions are healthy. They keep us intellectually alive and sharp while seeking better answers. Also, as humans, we are naturally divided into cultural groups and thought patterns. Who said that we were all supposed to be uniformed zombies, all thinking the same thing? Hashem made us human beings with free will, not preprogrammed robots.

What creates our inability to be together is not our natural state, but the way we chose to react to those that are different from us. We generally fear what we do not understand and do not have control over, and that is what causes the problem. We all believe in unity but because of our fear, mixed with intolerance, we want that unity to orbit around us.

The Master had twelve men around him who came from diverse walks of life, having different cultures and different religious affiliations. He taught them to love, accept, and understand each other, so they could work together. As a result, they taught about the God of Israel to the whole world. Let us therefore learn not to concentrate on what divides us but on what unites us; not on what we dislike but on what we appreciate about each other; not to merely see each other, but see Yeshua, the image of the Father in our brethren.

Didn't our Master say, "How blessed are those who make peace! for they will be called sons of God" (Matthew 5:9)?

My Personal Thoughts

_____
_____
_____
_____
_____

Mark 4:40   Adar 13/ יג באדר

Have you no trust even now?

The Master sails on a small fishing boat with his students. They are crossing the Sea of Galilee (Mark 4:35). As a great storm arises almost filling the boat with water (Mark 4:37), the disciples begin to be swamped and feel in danger (Luke 8:23). The Master sleeps soundly in the stern of the boat. This passage alludes to Jonah's story:

> However, ADONAI let loose over the sea a violent wind, which created such stormy conditions that the ship threatened to break to pieces. The sailors were frightened, and each cried out to his god. They threw the cargo overboard to make the ship easier for them to control. Meanwhile, Yonah had gone down below into the hold, where he lay, fast asleep. (Jonah 1:4–5)

In both stories the main character sleeps peacefully during a dangerous storm; terrified sailors awaken the sleeper and rebuke him; the principal character has the solution to the danger; the storm miraculously calms down; the sailors are amazed; and the boats in both stories are on route to a gentile city; the fact that in Mark's account the disciples meet a pig herder tells us so.

Let's continue with our narrative of the Master and his disciples on a boat. From their cave carved in the rock, two demoniacs tremble as they look down towards the lake with fear. The spirits in them are panicking. They know exactly who is coming,

> When Yeshua arrived at the other side of the lake, in the Gadarenes' territory, there came out of the burial caves two men controlled by demons, so violent that no one dared travel on that road. They screamed, "What do you want with us [Hebrew idiom for, 'don't meddle with us'], Son of God? Have you come here to torture us before the appointed time?" (Matthew 8:28–29)

Evil spirits know that they look forward to a time of everlasting judgment (1 Enoch 10:13; 55:4). They were surprised to see Yeshua a bit early so they panicked and reminded the Master that their time had not arrived yet. Yeshua took pity on the poor victims and delivered them, which created a mixed reaction among these Gentiles. They rejoiced for the healing, but it came at the cost of their herd.

Even so, today the Master's footsteps are heard and evil spirits fear in anticipation of their eternal fiery future. His people are being restored to the Land and his message crosses borders reaching all nations creating mixed reactions. Because he knows his time is at hand, the enemy fills the world with political, financial, social, theological, and physical storms, which creates fear but again, the Master says to his disciples, "Why are you so afraid? Have you still no faith" (Mark 4:40)? The worst I fear is the storm of new technologies that floods our youth with evil media and ungodly relationships. The evil one cleverly tries to destroy the generation that will have to maybe face him before they even get a chance. He will actually succeed in establishing himself for a while, but only for a while, for the King of Kings eventually rises to deliver his people (Revelation 19:11–21).

May it come soon Abba, even in days!

My Personal Thoughts

177

John 10:3   **Adar 14/ יד באדר**

He calls his own sheep, each one by name, and leads them out.

The Torah tells us that when a census is taken, each man is to bring the price of his atonement to avoid the plague (Exodus 30:12–13). A census in the Bible is a very serious and dangerous thing. It means to be counted and recognized as a full subject of the Kingdom of God. In that moment, king and servant have equal worth in the sight of God, each is fully recognized in his own rights in front of all Israel

The price of a man's ransom is universal: half a shekel. The half a shekel price is not to be understood as a payment for salvation, similar to the old Catholic indulgences said to redeem us from our sins. The Hebrew word used here is *kaphar*, a word meaning: *covering* or *atonement* (Exodus 30:12). It is an awesome thing to come into the presence of God to be counted, and as we do, we need a covering. In the *Tanach*, Messiah is often called the *Shield* (Psalm 5:12). Messiah truly is our shield whose agency connects us safely to the Almighty. The money collected is to be used for the maintenance of God's sanctuary. Through it, we each take personal responsibility for our enrollment into Israel and for the care of the Temple. Our giving makes us a part of the work of God.

Censuses were often taken for the purpose of military enrollment, in which case only males twenty-years-old and older were counted. The reasons a census incurred a plague are not given to us clearly in the Torah text, so they have been left to scholars' personal deductions and speculations. From Genesis to Ezra, Israel was numbered on nine occasions. The tenth time will be in the future when "flocks will again pass under the hands of the one who counts them" (Jeremiah 33:13). One thing is sure: we want to be part of such a census!

In that day, the Messiah will count his sheep from both Israel and the nations. He is our *half-shekel*, whose confession is priceless as the shield of our souls while dangerous in the world of men. In my case, a long time ago, it caused me the scorn and separation of my family. Hasn't he said that he came stumbling (1 Peter 2:6–8)?

No matter what anyone does to them, of those counted in this final census, he says, "I give them eternal life. They will absolutely never be destroyed, and no one will snatch them from my hands" (John 10:28).

My Personal Thoughts

_____

_____

_____

_____

_____

_____

_____

_____

John 14:8

Lord, show us the Father.

The children of Israel blew it. Impatient for the return of Moses they made themselves a god of gold. Unfamiliar with the idea of an unseen god with no image or temple, they concretized the unseen One, who had qualified himself by taking them out of Egypt, into the similitude of a calf.

Israel played the harlot during her betrothal, so God called off the wedding. The first covenant made at Horeb is already broken. Israel, the bride, is technically eligible for the death penalty. Justice is an invariable concept. When justice is not paid, we give way to injustice and God cannot be found to be unjust. Justice has to be given its due but here is where Moses found a legal loophole. It doesn't matter by whom it is paid. In this case, Moses negotiates with Hashem. Moses drives a hard bargain. Knowing that the Father wants to destroy Israel but that he also found favor in the sight of God, Moses places himself on the side of Israel. He stops talking in *I, you, and them* terms, but uses *we, and us.* Therefore if Hashem kills Israel, he has to also kill Moses. Moses saves the day by identifying himself with Israel, by putting his own life on the line alongside Israel. As a result, by the righteousness of one, the whole nation is saved. This is a very important concept foreshadowing Messiah's mission.

Having heard Moses' pleas, Hashem rewards his sacrificial stand and shows his true compassionate nature through a covenant. It will be the same covenant but renewed and as such, this *renewed covenant*, this *brit hachadasha* ברית החדשה carries the same terms as the first one.

Hashem does so because of his own character and desire. In the third chapter of the Book of Exodus, as the almighty Creator of the universe reveals his identity to Moses, he uses the words *HEHIYEH ASHER HEHIYEH* אהיה אשר אהיה or *I Will Be That I Will Be* (Exodus 3:14), which means something to the essence of *I am the eternal existential being that changes not and I keep covenant forever,* or *I am that I am.* In Exodus thirty-four, Hashem continues revealing his identity. He does so using a list of thirteen attributes. These attributes represent the Father's compassionate nature and are a central motif in Jewish liturgies. Because Hashem is forgiving and compassionate, there will be a wedding in Horeb after all.

It is so funny that so many people think that divine grace and forgiveness is something our Master Yeshua brought, and that it didn't exist before. Yeshua's grace was only a reflection of the Father's never-changing willingness to atone and forgive. Yeshua came to show and represent the Father's eternal compassion to us.

Do we forget that it is actually Hashem who so loved the world that he gave his only son that whosoever believes in him should not perish but have everlasting life (John 3:16)?

My Personal Thoughts

_____

_____

_____

_____

_____

1 Corinthians 8:4　　　　　　　　　　　　　　**Adar 16/ טז באדר**

An idol has no real existence.

When Israel made the golden calf, they were not transferring their worship of Hashem to that of another deity. In their mind, they were still serving Hashem, albeit in a syncretized version. A literal translation of what Aaron said to the people of Israel in Exodus 32:4 reads, "Isra'el! Here is your god, who brought you up from the land of Egypt!" They thought they could worship Hashem by the medium of something familiar, in this case the calf. Contrary to the claimed deities of the day, being the Creator, Hashem did not want to be represented through the medium of one his creations.

Let's look at idolatry in religion today. Catholicism and the Eastern Orthodox Church seem to be a mixed bowl of ancient Messianic Judaism and their respective local pagan cultures. Western Protestantism also seems to have the charismatic religious form that is reminiscent of Hellenic ascetic transcendentalism. In the latest decades, Protestantism has also gotten mixed up with an anti-Biblical materialism philosophy that over glorifies independence, wealth, and prosperity over the virtues of generosity, humility, and a submissive spirit.

There seems to be another form of idolatry in the West; one that empowers words of affirmation, astral bodies, and geometric shapes through fear and superstition. Hashem indeed has created all languages, geometry, and the astral bodies, in order to glorify him (Revelation 4:11), and that is why the enemy is intent on highjacking creation for his own purposes. In the end, people fear them as if these things had power themselves. Fear is a form of worship. Witches today center their worship on new moons, and call some of their feast days *Sabbaths.* Does it mean that we should stop obeying Hashem's command to sanctify the new moon and remember the Sabbath just because the Adversary has perverted these things and uses them to his own purposes (Numbers 29:6; Exodus 20:8)? Should we stop recognizing God's Holy Days just because pagans also have special days (Colossians 2:16)? In the *Tanach,* Hashem uses a brazen snake on a pole to heal his people; the people were told that if they'd just gaze at it, they would live. Several hundred years later, a Judean King Josiah had to destroy that symbol because people had transformed it into an object of worship (Numbers 21:8; 2 Kings 18:4).

As a French-born naturalized American, as long as I am on American soil, the laws of France cannot affect me. In the same manner, when we renounce allegiance to the Adversary, as long as we remain on the realm of Hashem's spiritual territory, none of the devil's trinkets have power over us. Idols, astral bodies, and geometric shapes only have the power we allot them through fear, or ignorance.

Judaism teaches that when we use an element of creation for the glory of God, we capture it from the hands of the enemy. Wood can make an idol, but also an Ark to house a Torah scroll. Metal can make money, the love of which is the source of all evil, but it also can be fashioned into a headpiece to crown the King of Kings. Mathematics, geometry, physics, and astronomy are all related as sciences proving God's ownership of creation.

It is high time we recapture God's creation and give it back to him, along with our own hearts, minds, souls, and spirits. May we fear him, and him alone!

1 Corinthians 10:14   **Adar 17/ יז באדר**

Run from idolatry!

IDOL SOUP RECIPE: You will need: 1 freshly worshipped golden calf; 1 angry prophet; a large rock; a big stick; a pestle and mortar; 1 blazing open-flame fire; a generous supply of water.

> Remove idol from its elevated platform; meanwhile, heat open fire to full strength. Handling roughly, toss idol into open flames. Allow image to thoroughly melt. Wait till gold has assumed a shapeless mass. Poke with stick to make sure it is completely melted before extinguishing fire. Allow gold to cool. Once cold, crush gold with big rock into medium size chunks. Thoroughly grind gold chunks with pestle and mortar until they reach a powder-like consistency. Spread powder over surface of the water. Serve cold. Serves 603,550. (D. Thomas Lancaster, Torah Club Volume Five: Depths of the Torah (Marshfield, MO: First Fruits of Zion, 2012))

In the incident of the golden calf, God treated the Israelites like the woman suspected of adultery (emphasis on *suspected*). Here is the passage about it,

> Then, if a spirit of jealousy comes over him [the husband] . . . he is to bring his wife to the cohen . . . The cohen will put holy water in a clay pot, and . . . some of the dust on the floor of the tabernacle and put it in the water . . . When he has made her drink the water, then, if she is unclean and has been unfaithful . . . the water that causes the curse will enter her and become bitter . . . But if the woman is not unclean but clean, then she will be innocent and will have children. (Numbers 5:14–28)

In the last part of the section, in the place of 'shall conceive children,' the Hebrew says, "She shall bear seed." I believe that Hashem is knowledgeable of human biology and that he knows that women do not bear seed. The *Tanach* תנך makes another mention of a woman bearing seed, "I will put enmity between . . . your offspring and her offspring (Hebrew for offspring: *zerah* זרע)" (Genesis 3:15), so this is not the first time that idea surfaces. Both these references about women bearing seed are formidable Messianic expressions. The first one speaks of the final demise of the devil by the only woman (Miriam) to ever conceive seed without the agency of a man (Matthew 1:18–20), while the other speaks of the future destiny of Israel. How does that work?

The woman in question is merely suspected of adultery; she has not been caught in the act. If she had been, she would not be brought to the priest for verification. The cause of the accusation is probably because of uncomely behavior. She shall then be put to the test of the bitter water. If she really is guilty, she should become deadly sick and her people will be cursed. At Horeb, Israel as a nation was put through the bitter waters test—and for nearly 2,000 years, to the bitter test of exile. In the end though, Israel comes out victorious. Looking at the full story, we see Israel again, the Israel of the believers in the woman of Revelation 12 bearing seed from among the Gentiles as a sign of her restoration.

Sometimes Hashem allows us to go though bitter times. If our heart is pure towards him, these passing moments of our lives only enhance our station. Bitter times are coming to test all those that live upon the earth (Revelation 3:10). As in Horeb, these bitter times will also take the shape of an idolatrous image (Revelation 13:14). May we keep our heart pure from the world, that we may be found guiltless and bear *seed* unto him.

2 Corinthians 3:5–6   **Adar 18/** יח באדר

> *He [God] has even made us competent to be workers serving a New Covenant,*
> *the essence of which is not a written text but the Spirit.*

Because of the golden calf issue, the tablets containing the words of the contract between Hashem and man are broken. Moses' intercession appeases Hashem's anger who then renews the covenant with his people, albeit with the same terms as before (Exodus 32–33). The difference is that the first time the tablets were given under a contract of obedience, but the second time under God's compassionate mercy. But while Hashem's compassionate mercy remembers our sins no more, it does not seem to exclude a cleansing, and even sometimes a punitive process in between (Exodus 32:26–28; Jeremiah 31:34).

Moses' ordeal with the tablets serves to illustrate the two main manifestations of Messiah. In the same manner as the precious tablets, Yeshua the *word,* the *Davar,* the *Memrah* made flesh came and was *broken* due to our idolatrous sin. As Moses did, he then went back to plead with the Father (Hebrews 7:25; Isaiah 53:12) and at a future date he will return in a renewed fashion after a cleansing of the idolatrous world (Revelation 17–20). Jeremiah the prophet speaks of this return, and even speaks of a renewed covenant reflecting the idea of mercy (the Hebrew word *chadash* חדש, *new* also means *to renew)* (Jeremiah 31:31). This is why the prophet mentions that the renewed covenant will not be as the covenant that was made with the fathers in the desert. The terms are the same, but the conditions are different (Jeremiah 31:31–40).

Going over the full prophecy of Jeremiah concerning the New/Renewed Covenant shows us that the time has not yet come for it to be fully in force. All we have now is a promise (Ephesians 1:12–14 KJV).

Paul also explains the difference between the two covenants using the terms *letter* and *spirit* (1 Corinthians 3:1–6). These terms do not refer to the terms of the contract, as they are the same in both cases, but to the operating dynamics behind the contract. Because of our disobedience, the first became as a *letter* of condemnation (the report of accusation; the charges against us), the second was given in an act of Hashem's mercy. The idea seemed to work as is seen in the changed lifestyle of the Corinthians (2 Corinthians 3:2).

Hashem again closes the case. We have shown ourselves unworthy but he remained faithful to his word of promise to take us as a people unto him. We deserve the boot, but he still receives us, not because of righteous works that we have done, but because of his faithfulness towards his promises (Ephesians 2:8–9).

May we show ourselves worthy of his grace and goodness, living lives according to the standards of his Torah, thus reflecting his wisdom though living in a world of darkness brought through ignorance of his word (Deuteronomy. 4:5–9).

My Personal Thoughts

_____

_____

_____

_____

_____

Luke 21:19

By standing firm you will save your lives.

The episode of the golden calf finds a parallel in the days of the Kings of Israel. In the ninth century BCE, Ahab marries the Tyrian princess Jezebel who reintroduces devotion to Ba'al worship in Israel. Before long, Israel is deep in apostasy and God sends Elijah the prophet to minister to the wayward Northern Kingdom. Elijah's efforts culminate at the test on Mt. Carmel where again we have, as in the golden calf incident, Israel worshipping a false god at a wild dance party (Exodus 32; 1 Kings 18).

The events on Mt. Carmel ended a three-year drought inflicted on the country through Elijah as the result of their Ba'al worship. Rabbinic historians say that the drought only lasted fourteen months. Why then did both Yeshua and James mention that it lasted three and half years (Luke 4:25; James 5:17)? Joseph Fitzmyer explains that the drought lasted fourteen months straddling over a three and half year period. What is remarkable about this is that the duration of this drought parallels the length of the period of distress in apocalyptic literature (Daniel 7:25; Revelation 12:6).

In both the golden calf incident and the Mt. Carmel episode we have an impatient people turning to wild idolatrous parties. In the one they wait for Moses to return with the Torah, in the other they wait for the rain (the Hebrew words for *rain* and *Torah* are of the same etymological family). Will it be the same at the end of time?

Let us hear now these words of warning from the Master,

> For the Son of Man's coming will be just as it was in the days of Noach. Back then, before the Flood, people went on eating and drinking, taking wives and becoming wives, right up till the day Noach entered the ark; and they didn't know what was happening until the Flood came and swept them all away. It will be just like that when the Son of Man comes. (Matthew 24:37–39)

> It will go well with that servant if he is found doing his job when his master comes. Yes, I tell you that he will put him in charge of all he owns. But if that servant is wicked and says to himself, "My master is taking his time"; and he starts beating up his fellow servants and spends his time eating and drinking with drunkards; then his master will come on a day the servant does not expect, at a time he doesn't know; and he will cut him in two and put him with the hypocrites, where people will wail and grind their teeth! (Matthew 24:46–51)

These last 2,000 years of waiting for the return of the Master may seem long, but not as long as to those from whom the revelation of Messiah has been withheld. We have the assurance that after two days he will revive us; on the third day he will raise us up, that we may live before him (Hosea 6:2) (a day is a thousand years to the Lord (Psalm 90:4; 2 Peter 3:8)).

May we patiently wait for him, each day doing our best to follow in his footsteps and shine the light of his Torah to all those around us. May he find us and ours doing so at his return.

May it be soon, even in our days!

My Personal Thoughts

_____

_____

Matthew 26:41   **Adar 20/** כ באדר

The spirit indeed is eager, but human nature is weak.

It is so easy for us to look at the children of Israel making a golden calf in the desert with criticism. "How could they?" we say. "After all Hashem did for them; after witnessing the power of his great mighty hand, how could they so easily transfer their loyalties?"

What we have to realize is that in their minds, they were not transferring their loyalties. They were just reacting to what they knew, to the culture around them, to the familiar ways. Yes, these people were Hebrews, but they were Hebrews who had lived a long time in Egypt, among idol-worshippers. The whole world around them was an idol-worshipping world. On top of it, they were joined by a *mixed multitude*, a large amount of non-Hebrews who saw the power of the God of Israel in Egypt and decided to throw their lot with him (Exodus 12:38).

We are creatures of habit you and I. We do not realize how much we respond to life by just following a natural instinctive course. When we drive in our car somewhere out of our routine, don't we often take the habitual road and miss where we are going? This is one of the ways that, as the Master says, "the spirit indeed is eager, but human nature is weak" (Matthew 26:41). The *spirit* and the mind may agree to something, but *human nature* likes to naturally revert to the *old ways*. It does so because the *old way* provides the security of familiar surroundings. A person my change religion, but will subconsciously continue to relate to God in the same ways as before. The physical elements, the names, the days, the building, the clothing, even the language may change, but the spirit, the way they relate to God, the worship, and their relationship with him may remain unchanged. People can blame the children of Israel for their sin, but following the Master's teaching of trying to remove the log in our eyes before trying to remove the splinter in someone else's, they must first take a hard look at themselves (Matthew 7:3).

How many people from the world join Hashem and bring with them worldly and pagan concepts of business, politics, and lifestyles? How many also, as they grow to a fuller understanding of the Jewish Messiah, bring with them much baggage from their former persuasion? We often criticize our former leaders and teachers only to turn around and recreate the same thing they did. We may change the outside look, but the spirit, or the inside, remains the same. We generally can't see it, but the *mirror* of someone else uninvolved and outside of the picture will reveal it to us. It is like when a person is trapped in a non-violent oppressive and abusive relationship; they often do not even realize it until they come out and have a taste of freedom or someone shows it to them. We often need a breath of fresh air from the outside to help us realize the stench of our present living conditions.

May we, as we daily walk with the Master, discover all the golden calves areas of our lives. May we learn to shed from us the former culture of the world and put on the 'new man' (2 Corinthians 5:17) he has reserved for us.

My Personal Thoughts

_____

_____

_____

_____

Ephesians 5:18   Adar 21/ כא באדר

Be filled with the Spirit.

Moses comes down the mountain for the second time. He carries with him a renewed copy of the terms of the covenant between Israel and Hashem. The Horeb wedding is on again, the Tabernacle therefore needs to be built to house the tables of the covenant and for Hashem to indwell his people. Moses is not the one to build the Tabernacle, instead the Father directs him to two skilled workers whom the Torah says, are *filled with the Spirit* (Exodus 35:30–35).

In contemporary charismatic circles, the infilling of the spirit is mainly a pneumatic or emotional experience. As a result, today, many Bible teacher's claim to be *led of the Spirit* in their studying, spiritual walk, and teaching, but at the same time they refuse to learn from the work of previous expositors, such as the Jewish sages from which our messianic faith derives. They therefore read and study the Torah ignorantly and feed themselves with erroneous doctrinal conclusions. Over the millennia, they have redefined the understanding of the infilling of the Spirit, of Hashem's indwelling in man, of immersion, and of redemption, which are all Jewish concepts exhaustively expounded in the *Tanach* תנך as well as in Jewish commentaries. Those people refuse to study from the knowledge of others and instead, they feed on their own errors from their own head. They are in essence the epitome of the *blind leading the blind*, and not only do they lead themselves into a pit but they bring others along with them.

What we learn in this appointment of the two spirit-filled Israelite workmen is that the infilling of the Spirit has more to do with divine inspiration in the understanding and application of a learned skill than with the clairvoyant-type mystic who is led by vague pneumatic feelings and tingling sensations. The Spirit-filled biblical person is a person of study, ability, and pragmatic understanding. This person is knowledgeable in the complex intricacy of their skill, understands it, and is animated by the spirit of the Almighty in the accomplishment thereof. One can possess divine musical inspiration and love music, but if he doesn't take the time to learn how to play the instrument, he will only produce dissonant noises. Such are the teachings of those who solely rely on inspiration (so-called) without the aid of education.

What we need today is more than the empty hot air of charismatic teachings. What we need instead is true solid spiritual education based on the pragmatic and practical wisdom of the fathers of our faith. Maybe that's what it means that in the end of time Elijah will come " to turn the hearts of fathers to their children and the disobedient to the wisdom of the righteous, to make ready for ADONAI a people prepared" (Luke 1:17).

May Hashem give us true teachers who are not full of themselves and their own errors, but teachers filled with his spirit, with skill, with intelligence, with knowledge, and with all craftsmanship (Exodus 35:31); teachers who study the Torah and who acknowledge that they stand on the shoulders of others wiser than they.

My Personal Thoughts

_____

_____

_____

_____

John 1:14   **Adar 22/** כב באדר

The Word . . . lived with us.

What does the Tabernacle teach us? Let me now take you on a journey at the feet of Jewish sages who have pondered the question for hundreds of years.

Many have suggested that as he built the Tabernacle, Bezalel saw it as a microcosm of the creation of the universe. Here is how it works. King David describes the first day of creation when God created the heavens and the Earth using the following words, "You spread out the heavens like a curtain" (Psalm 104:2). So we find that a curtain (similar to that of a tent) was stretched out above the Tabernacle, the colors of which also corresponded to the colors of sky and earth. On the second day of creation, God made the firmament as a separation between the waters above and the waters below. Similarly, in the Tabernacle there was a curtain separating one part from another. Just like on the third day of creation God gathered the waters into one area, in the Tabernacle there was also a designated place to gather water in a basin. Corresponding to the luminaries created on the fourth day, we find the menorah with its lights in the Tabernacle. On the fifth day of creation, God created the birds. Similarly, there were birds brought as offerings on the altar of the Tabernacle. And corresponding to the creation of man on the sixth day, the service in the Tabernacle was led by the High Priest Esther. The Torah describes how the work was completed on the seventh day of creation and how that day was blessed and sanctified by God. The idea of the Tabernacle was to make a place for Hashem to live on earth. It represents therefore the restoration of all things to the day when the voice of ADONAI could be heard in the Garden of Eden.

Some have also viewed the Tabernacle as a microcosm of the human body with the Ark as the heart of a person and the cherubs with their wings over the Ark as the lungs that spread out around the heart. They saw the table with the showbread as a person's stomach and the menorah with its oil lamps as a person's mind. The frankincense reminded them of the sense of smell and the water basin of the fluids in the human body. Finally, the curtains were to them a person's skin and the beams represented the ribs. Jewish sages taught that every person is a microcosm of the entire universe just like the Tabernacle.

Just like it is the light of the world and of the body, the goal of the making of the Tabernacle was to house the Shekinah, for the indwelling presence of Hashem to come dwell within it, and thus within Israel (Exodus 25:22).

As farfetched as these musings may seem, we can't help but realize that our Jewish sages were on the right track in their understanding of the Tabernacle. After all, did not Paul say that, to their advantage, the Jewish people had been entrusted the oracles of God (Romans 3:1–2)? As the spirit of Hashem came to fill the earthly Tabernacle, so it filled the earthly *tabernacle* of the human body Yeshua who is the representation of the presence of God among us, in God's created universe (Hebrews 1:3; John 1:4; 8:12).

As we study these things, may we look forward to the time when Messiah will once again walk the earth among us.

May it be soon Abba, even in our days!

Matthew 22:37

You are to love ADONAI your God with all your heart
and with all your soul and with all your strength.

Before starting the construction of the Tabernacle, the children of Israel were commanded to cease from all sort of creative activity and observe the *Shabbat* שבת. "Oh but, how can we observe the Sabbath? There is no synagogue, no Tabernacle, no Temple . . . !"

Faith based on worship in certain places on certain days is common to most religious systems. For community sake, it is good, and even needed to have regular meetings and fellowships—I wonder if that was Hashem's core original idea. After all, the synagogue service was only a post-exilic organizational attempt to expose people to the Torah in order to avoid another exile. The problem is that with such systems, religion gets removed from home and daily life and revolves around what we do in the place of worship. Our teenagers then see the difference between who we are at home and who we are at the place of worship and feel that we are hypocrites, and maybe we are. What was then Hashem's core idea?

> These words, which I am ordering you today, are to be on your heart; and you are to teach them carefully to your children. You are to talk about them when you sit at home, when you are traveling on the road, when you lie down and when you get up. Tie them on your hand as a sign, put them at the front of a headband around your forehead, and write them on the door-frames of your house and on your gates. (Deuteronomy 6:6–9)

Regardless of our other fellowship activities, our religious lifestyle should be a home-based worship system, where Hashem is involved in every aspect of our lives from the time we wake up until the time we go to sleep. The Jewish Friday night custom of sanctifying (separating/distinguishing) the Sabbath day is a microcosm of the Tabernacle; it represents Hashem's presence among us. The two candles on the table remind us of the Menorah; the challah bread speaks of the bread of presence; the wine of the daily libation; the festive meal of the Sabbath double-offering portion; and the prayers of the altar of incense. It is home-base service officiated by the father as the priest for his congregation composed of direct and extended family, as well as friends. The Saturday fellowship at the synagogue is good but it is an extra. I would paraphrase Yeshua and say that, 'it is the Friday night *Kiddush* קדוש which sanctifies the synagogue service, not the synagogue service which sanctifies Friday night *Kiddush*." To go to Saturday service and not sanctify the Sabbath at home on Friday night with our families misses the whole purpose. Worship is a family thing. On Friday night, it is customary for the husband to give an ode to his wife using Proverbs 31; the wife does the same to her husband and they both bless their children.

Hashem doesn't just want a fellowship with us in a building somewhere when we are on our best behavior. He wants to be invited to live at the very core of our lives, to hear how we talk to each other at the table, witness how we interact and treat each other during the commonest of household functions. How else can we get his correction input if we just play games, if we play *religion* in front of him (which he is actually not fooled by anyways)?

As we live our lives, may we allow him to be present in all our thoughts. May his word be in our mouth when we sit in our house, and when we walk by the way, and when we lie down, and when we rise. May we bind them as a sign on our hand, and may they be as frontlets between our eyes. May they be written on the doorposts of our house and on our gates . . . and on our hearts.

Luke 10:42   **Adar 24/** כד באדר

But there is only one thing that is essential. Miryam has chosen the right thing, and it won't be taken away from her.

Moses gathers the congregation of Israel to give them instructions concerning the building of the Tabernacle. No matter how important this work is, they first must stop everything to honor the Sabbath (Exodus 35). To cancel the Sabbath because of Hashem's work reminds me of a story I read one time about a little girl who canceled the time she usually spent with her father in the evening in order to knit him bedroom slippers. The father missed the time with his daughter and was broken-hearted by it. Hashem may appreciate the bedroom slippers, but he'd rather have us!

This training on the importance of Sabbath-keeping continued in the Jewish messianic congregations from the time of the early disciples until today. Joseph of Arimathea and Nicodemus made sure Yeshua was entombed on Friday before *kabalat Shabbat* קבלת שבת, the welcoming of the Sabbath. The women who took care of his body waited till *motzei Shabbat* שבת מוצאי, till the end of the Shabbat to embalm him. If Yeshua had made the Sabbath obsolete (as some people claim), Yeshua's disciples didn't seem to know.

In the first century CE the historian Josephus reports that in his days, there was not a single city in the whole Roman Empire, where the Jewish custom of Sabbath-keeping was not practiced. This was due to the disciples of the Master being disseminated throughout the whole Roman Empire. Up to the fourth century, Anti-Semitic Emperor Constantine was passing laws against the Yeshua believers, forbidding any form of Jewish practice, especially that of Sabbath-keeping. From the disciples' recorded texts, it is evident that Yeshua expected his followers to continue the practice of Sabbath-keeping (Matthew 24:20).

In Sabbath observant homes, each Friday night the idea of Moses gathering the children of Israel to first keep the Sabbath before instructing them about the Tabernacle is repeated when a father gathers his family around the table. At that moment, the father is like Moses, and his family is like the congregation.

Throughout the Bible, the congregation is compared to a bride. On Friday night the father traditionally speaks Proverbs 31 to his wife. Sad to say, this proverb is often used by abusive and oppressive men to keep their wives under submission. They put their own twist under the word *virtuous* as if it were to describe a mousy, yielded, and submitted woman, who lives only to serve her husband. Reading the whole proverb actually reveals that this *virtuous woman* is anything but mousy. The Hebrew word for virtuous in this passage is actually *chayeel* חיל (as a noun, not an adjective) meaning having valor, or valiant. Along with being a mother, she is a businesswoman working hard not behind, or under her husband, but alongside him. The *wife* language in the proverb is actually an analogy; the same analogy Paul uses with the Ephesians (Ephesians 5:25–32). Both Proverbs 31 and Paul's admonition to the Ephesians speak of the Congregation and its responsibility as the *bride* to work this endtime harvest alongside our *husband*: Mashiach משיח. In this respect, since men are to take a lead in the congregations, Proverbs 31 may be more about men and their jobs of leading their families and congregation and the work of the Master than about women.

As faithful brides coming from the harvest in the wings, may Hashem grant us the joy and freedom to come and *shavat* שבת in his loving arms, for as long as possible.

188

Hebrews 9:10 (KJV)

> *. . . until the time of reformation.*

Many people want to find the Ark of the Covenant, but better than finding the actual ancient artifact, would be to understand what it stands for and more importantly, what it doesn't stand for. Let us therefore continue our archeological work of removing the debris of the doctrines of man and rediscover the truth of the word of Hashem according to its own value.

Misunderstanding the Letter to the Messianic Jews of Israel, many Western Bible editors have added the word *covenant* in the eighth chapter of the text of the Letter to the Hebrews. That is why that word is in Italics in the KJV edition. As a result, the text is read as an anti-thesis between the pre and post Yeshua eras. When we remove that unfortunate edition everything changes. From an erroneous dispensational argument, it becomes a midrashic revelation of the meaning of the two chambers of the Tabernacle. The KJV text reads in the thirteenth verse of chapter eight, "In that he saith, 'A new *covenant*', he hath made the first old. Now that which decayeth and waxeth old is ready to vanish away" (Hebrews 8:13, KJV).

What is it in our text that *decays and waxes old*, that becomes in fact *obsolete*? The terms of the Toratic covenant given on Mt. Horeb? How is that possible since the Torah is fixed forever in Heaven (Psalm 119:89)? The Levitical priesthood? How could that be since the eternal Torah says that theirs is a perpetual priesthood (Exodus 40:15)? Aaron's priesthood only stopped because the Temple was destroyed thirty years after Yeshua's resurrection, but both the prophets Ezekiel and Jeremiah speak of its reinstitution when the Temple is rebuilt. For that reason, it cannot be the Temple either that has become obsolete in our text. What is it then that *decays and waxes old*, becoming *obsolete* in verse thirteen?

When we read the text without the added edition, we realize that it is not at all about *covenants*, but that section is a midrash using the *first* and *second* chamber of the Tabernacle to tell us about the coming Kingdom of Heaven. Chapter nine then says,

> Now even the *first* (chamber) had regulations for worship and an earthly place of holiness. For a tent was prepared, the *first* section, in which were the lampstand and the table and the bread of the presence. It is called the Holy Place. Behind the second curtain was a second section called the Most Holy Place, having the golden altar of incense and the ark of the covenant . . . into the second only the high priest goes, and he but once a year, and not without taking blood, which he offers for himself and for the unintentional sins of the people.

Here is our midrash now,

> By this the Holy Spirit indicates that the way into the holy places is not yet opened as long as the first section is still standing—which is symbolic for the present age. (Hebrews 9:1–9, KJV)

What we are told is that it is this present age which *decays and passes away*, that becomes *obsolete* as it recedes giving way to the Kingdom of God slowly but surely established since the manifestation of Messiah.

Beloved: why do you fret? This present age, this age of the futile rule of man on the earth is coming to an end. Do you hear the footsteps of Messiah on the horizons? He is coming to take his bride and to establish with her the Kingdom of his Father on earth.

May it come soon, Abba, even in our days!

189

Hebrews 12:12–13

Wherefore lift up the hands which hang down, and the feeble knees; and make straight paths for your feet, lest that which is lame be turned out of the way; but let it rather be healed.

Here's to those who battle sickness, to those who find themselves losing faith in the midst of financial or domestic battlegrounds. You out there whose hands droop in discouragement and whose knees weaken under the weight of the heavy load Hashem seems to have unmercifully allowed to be placed upon your weak shoulders (Hebrews 12:12): has this world gotten you down?

A lady I recently met and who had a full life of serving the cause of the people of Hashem realized that she is approaching the last years of her life. After being a very active social creature, she is now handicapped and stuck in the small room of an adult care facility. Feeling sick, lonely, and abandoned even by friends, she confessed to me that two days before, she contemplated suicide. She then asked me, "Is it worth it? Is it worth it to wait it out, or should I just end it now?" Another lady friend of mine faced with a cancer resurgence cried in my arms the other day, "Why? Why doesn't Hashem heal me?" On the other side, my wife presently cares for her sick ninety-nine year-old Swedish aunt who does not believe in God or in an after-life. As she realizes that she may not reach the meaningful landmark of one hundred years, she faces her fate with uncanny pragmatism, barely falling short of comforting the doctors who care for her. What is the difference? Why does this lady who does not even believe in God seem to have more peace in the face of sickness and probable death than the ones who do?

Hope; hope is the difference. Those who believe have learned to have hope, but as wise King Solomon said, "Hope deferred makes the heart sick" (Proverbs 13:12). Deferred hope may make the heart sick, but is a cynical life without the life and light of hope better? I don't think so.

The very design of the Tabernacle teaches us about the present and tangible hope that Hashem fulfills all his promises; that if he doesn't do it now in the *Olam Hazeh* עולם הזה (this age) he will do it in the *Olam Habah* עולם הבא (the Age to Come, the Messianic Age). The great divine plan for the destiny of the world is imbedded in the geography of the Tabernacle. Through it the Holy Spirit teaches us that as long as the *protos* (the first part of the Tabernacle, which represents this present age) pursues its unfinished course, the *deuteros* (the second part which represents the World to Come where the full atonement of the Master our heavenly High Priest rules, the place where promises are all fulfilled) cannot come (Hebrews 9:8–9). Our patriarchs understood that they died in faith, not having received the things promised, but saw and greeted them from afar (Hebrews 11:13).

As we look into this beautiful shadow picture in the design of the Tabernacle, may we look for the World to Come with the hope and assurance from he who fulfills all hopes, as the finishing statement of King Solomon's proverb claims, "but desire fulfilled is a tree of life" (Proverbs 13:12).

My Personal Thoughts

_____

_____

_____

John 14:6 **Adar 27/ כז באדר**

No one comes to the Father except through me..

The Book of Exodus ends on the most depressing note: Moses tries to approach the Almighty in the Tabernacle but the glorious Presence forbids him. What went wrong? He previously had access to the throne room while on the mount, so what happened? We are faced here with the greatest paradox in the whole Torah. God is to live with us on earth yet we cannot approach him as long as we are in our human nature.

I sometimes use a trick question with new students. I ask them, "How do you approach God?" I usually get all kinds of answers covering the whole spectrum from the pragmatic to the esoteric. Then I usually shock them by saying, "Actually, we don't, because we can't." Jewish sages have pondered on this paradox for centuries. The way our sages saw it is, "Why does Hashem desire that we stick to him, if he is a *consuming fire*?" (Deuteronomy 4:4,24). After all, this is a fair question. The sages ultimately came up with an answer, which John the Disciple expresses in his narrative about Yeshua.

What Jewish scholars came up with was the idea of the burning bush. The Torah tells us, "The angel of ADONAI appeared to him in a fire blazing from the middle of a bush. He looked and saw that although the bush was flaming with fire, yet the bush was not being burned up" (Exodus 3:2). Here we have Hashem in his Angel coming as a fire, but a fire that does not consume. This represented God in his all-consuming form, yet non-lethal to man. This idea gave birth to the Hebrew/Aramaic *Memrah* ממרה, later expressed by John and translated in most English translations as *the word* (John 1). Like Yeshua, the burning bush/Angel of ADONAI represented the power of God in a non-lethal form for human beings; Hashem coming to us at our level, so to speak. The story is not finished though. The Book of Leviticus will take us through the process and protocol through which we are to approach God, so stay tuned!

A study of all the instances where the *Tanach* תנך in English mentions *the Angel of the Lord* seems to reveal important truths about the role of Yeshua in the Torah. Some verses even call this *angel* by his Hebrew terminology *Malach panav* מלאך פניו, The Angel of his *face* (Isaiah 63:9).

We realize that from the time Adam and Eve lost their place in the presence of ADONAI in the Garden of Eden until today, no sinful natural man approaches Hashem directly; it is always done through some sort of agency. Even though he appeared and was represented through many different venues before his ultimate manifestation 2,000 years ago, Messiah was, is, and will always be the quintessential agent through whom we approach the Father. Yeshua's own words, "no man cometh unto the Father, but by me" (John 14:6), represent a fundamental truth prepared at the foundation of the world for all humanity from the days of Adam and Eve until now.

He was, and is, the ultimate burning bush, the presence of Hashem, which does not consume; the angel of ADONAI who brings in the presence of the Almighty. From eternity to eternity, it is through and in him that we approach Hashem.

My Personal Thoughts

_____

_____

_____

Hebrews 4:14, 16   **Adar 28/ כח באדר**

Therefore, since we have a great cohen gadol who has passed through to the highest heaven,
Yeshua, the Son of God, let us hold firmly to what we acknowledge as true . . .
confidently approach the throne from which God gives grace,
so that we may receive mercy and find grace in our time of need.

During our whole narrative in the Book of Exodus, Moses had unlimited access to Hashem. Now that the Tabernacle is completed and that the glory of Hashem fills it, Moses cannot go in (Exodus 40:34–35). What happened? This is the great paradox concerning the glorious presence of Hashem inhabiting among us; God is to live within us but the sinful nature we contracted through disobedience in Eden forbids us communion. Hashem therefore must *tweak the system*, find a loophole so to speak, in order to make this fellowship happen.

In the first verses in the Book of Leviticus, the Almighty reveals his plan and says, "The man who approaches me needs to bring Me a *token of approaching* from his flocks or from his herds" (Leviticus 1:2: Literal translation by me). It is unfortunate that for *token of approaching* most English texts use the word *sacrifice*, as it does not convey the idea meant in the Hebrew text. The Hebrew word used here is *Korban* קורבן, a Hebrew word left un-translated from Hebrew in Mark's narrative of the life of Yeshua (Mark 7:11). What is a *Korban*?

The Torah teaches that life is in the blood, "For the life of a creature is in the blood, and I have given it to you on the altar to make atonement for yourselves; for it is the blood that makes atonement because of the life" (Leviticus 17:11), so the blood of a biblically clean animal is brought forward instead of ours, which is corrupted by sin. The Hebrew word *korban* is actually a derivative from the Hebrew verb *lekarev* לקרב, *to approach* or *to come near*. Therefore the animal brought forward to the altar is not a gift or a bribe to gain brownie points with Hashem. Neither is it a payment for a sin, but it is a token that helps us come near to Hashem by proxy.

It seems that since the time of Abel, both in heaven and on earth, the principles of approaching Hashem have remained the same; in essence, we don't. We only approach the Almighty God Creator of Heaven and earth by proxy, through the agency of an acceptable token, in the Tabernacle/Temple on earth, through the agency of a clean animal, in the throne in heaven, through the agency of Yeshua the lamb slain from the foundation of the world (Revelation 5:6; 13:8; John 14:6).

The Torah (as in Hashem's commandments found in the five books of the Pentateuch) is truly a tutor which teaches us this principle (Galatians 3:24). In a sense this confirms the idea that, "I Adonai, do not change" (Malachi 3:6).

May we all grow close to our agent, *Yeshua HaMashiach* ישוע המשיח; as we confess him on earth, he confesses us to his, and our Father (Matthew 10:32; John 20:17).

My Personal Thoughts

_____

_____

_____

_____

192

Matthew 11:29   Adar 29/ כט באדר

I am gentle and humble in heart.

The Torah contains several letters that differ in size, some bigger than the overall text, some smaller; there is even one that is broken in two. We find such a scribal oddity in what corresponds in English to the last letter of the first word of the Book of Leviticus, *Vayikra* ויקרא, which is noticeably smaller than the rest of the text. The extreme scrutiny Jewish scribes used in replicating this text throughout millennia forbid us to assume a scribal error. Why would Moses then have diminished the *ahlef* אלף, the first letter of the Hebrew alphabet and the last letter of the word *Vayikrah* , meaning, "And he [Hashem] called"?

The oracles Moses wrote down cannot just be read as a chronological string of words giving instructions. In the Hebrew biblical text, everything matters; repetitions have their value in emphasis as well as the placement of certain clauses within the text. The particular choice of certain words and their lexical root also tells us much about the underlying meaning behind the text. We are not used to paying such attention to these things while reading the Bible, but this is part of the cultural context of the writing, and sad to say, many of these vital details are lost in translation.

Scholars do not really have a satisfying answer concerning the diminishing of the *aleph* in *Vayikra,* the first word of the Book of Leviticus, but since Torah students hate a vacuum, it has left room for speculation and here is the most widely accepted reason for it. *Vayikra* means, "And he [God] called . . ." (Leviticus 1:1). Moses whom Hashem defined as the humblest of all men did not think himself worthy of being singled out and called by God, so he originally wrote *Vayikar* (same word without the last *ahlef*), a much more impersonal inflection of the verb also used when the Angel of ADONAI meets with the idolatrous prophet Balaam. Hashem disapproved of Moses' writing style and of the comparison with the address to Balaam, so Moses reluctantly acquiesced and added that last aleph, but smaller. This story is probably not true, but thus being so, it has it does have its own homiletic value in teaching us the values endorsed by the fathers of the Judaism and of our Master and Rabbi Yeshua.

The sages here describe Moses, the man blessed with the highest form of divine revelation one could ever be blessed with, as a person who did not even feel worthy of his calling. This sets Moses, the greatest of the teachers and prophets of Israel, as a trend setter, a blue-print for teachers and would-be prophets for all ages; one by which even the coming Messiah should be identified (Deuteronomy. 18:15). There is a dictum in Judaism that our Master Yeshua used, "With the same measure that a man uses, it will be measured to him" (Matthew 7:2). It is believed that because Moses humbled himself, God also humbled himself as he called Moses from the Tabernacle (Leviticus 1:1). In a certain sense, Hashem is not afraid of humbling himself as he did also in sending Yeshua, the *prophet* like Moses (Deuteronomy 18:15), "who, being found in fashion as a man, humbled himself, and became obedient unto death" (Philippians 2:8).

Many desire to be teachers and prophets and these are good callings. May these called to such offices never forget the blueprint of self-effacement and humility that is to be the earmark of all those Hashem chooses to teach and lead his flock. That is the standard measure that should be used, not eloquence, depth, or intelligence, but the spirit of utter humility because, "He dwells in the high and holy place, and also with him who is of a contrite and lowly spirit, to revive the spirit of the lowly, and to revive the heart of the contrite" (Isaiah 57:15).

Nissan - נ׳סן

Nissan

The lion became a lamb.
The righteous ranked with the criminals.
The covering exposed.
The invincible was made vulnerable.
The rich were made poor.
The high priest offered.
The king served.
The anointed anoints.

Hebrew 4:16

Therefore, let us confidently approach the throne from which God gives grace, so that we may receive mercy and find grace in our time of need.

This week we are studying the gory details in the beginning of the Book of Leviticus concerning the Levitical offerings. These consist of an uncomfortable text seemingly more worthy of a conversation between butchers than a spiritual manual on the concepts of approaching God. Yet, it may surprise many to know that Leviticus used to be the first book required of Jewish children to learn for their spiritual education, which began at the age of five.

Today, because there is no temple, the Book of Leviticus is *tossed under the bus* of irrelevancy. Yet, in full knowledge of what will happen to the Temple, Hashem gave these important words as part of the main oracles of his manifestation on Mt. Horeb. They constitute therefore a very substantial part of the Torah. How come so many people dare to claim that the words of Hashem are irrelevant and obsolete just because they sometime seem so far removed from their current culture and they don't understand them?

In spite of Paul's statement that the Levitical offerings were not intended for the perfecting of the conscience (Hebrews 9:9, ESV), many people still hold to the belief that the main function of these sacrifices was to receive atonement. This leads people to believe that in the post Yeshua-death-and-resurrection days, these commands are obsolete. If this were so, it would seem that somehow Yeshua forgot to inform his disciples because in the Book of Acts, we are told that they attended the twice daily worship times at the Temple, which consisted of a Levitical animal offering (Acts 3:1). Also, when Paul came to Jerusalem, he paid the price of the Levitical offerings that would terminate not only his own Nazarite vow but that of four other Jewish believers in Yeshua (Acts 21). History books tell us that Jewish believers in Israel actually continued Temple attendance until it was destroyed. The sacrificial system was never an issue for them; they always understood that for the Jewish people, these were perpetual ordinances. Yeshua himself said that he did not come to abolish the Torah—which included the sacrificial system of worship—but to complete it (Matthew 5:17).

A closer look at the etymology used in the text reveals that Leviticus is primarily a lesson on approaching God with the protocol, honor, and respect he deserves, not about atonement. The Levitical text also illustrates the role of Yeshua in our lives. Even the Hebrew word for atonement *kaphar* כפר reveals the nature of the offering as not being a ransom, or a price for sins, but a protective covering; a shield. Hashem is holy and a consuming fire towards all that is unclean and impure. That is why, in order to approach Hashem, we need the protective shield of *Mashiach* משיח, and this is what the Levitical offerings teach us in many levels. David actually called the Messiah the shield of salvation (Psalm 18:35).

Thanks be to Hashem. He has provided us the shield/covering of the Lamb to cover our nakedness (Genesis 3:21) so we may approach him confidently with our requests. Yeshua simply brought the final piece of the puzzle that activated the whole system: his innocent death as a righteous person.

May you and yours also come under his covering, that you may approach the Father with confidence.

Ephesians 2:14   **Nissan 2/ ב בניסן**

For he is our peace.

The beginning of the Book of Leviticus presents us with five types of offerings to facilitate approaching Hashem, each representing their own venue. Because of translation issues, some meanings have been lost, but their imagery still reveals their message. These offerings are the physical outward expressions of the longings of the inward heart of man, seeking to approach God in full communion.

The sin and guilt offerings are mandatory (Leviticus 4; 5:15). There is a difference between the two. The sin offering concerns itself with our natural state of being a sinner. In essence, we are not sinners because we sin; we sin because we are sinners. The guilt offering is for sins involuntarily committed. There are no offerings for voluntary sins (Hebrews 10:26). God and priests share in these offerings.

After we have acknowledged our innate sinful state and the sinful actions and thoughts that result from it, we have the burnt or ascent offering called the *olah* עולה, or *the acending one* (Leviticus 1:3). The *olah* represents our desire for complete dedication. After this testimony of commitment through the *olah*, comes the voluntary meal offering. Now that we've dedicated ourselves to Hashem, this offering represents our commitment to strive to live a leaven-less/sinless walk with God. Only priests and God share in it.

After admitting to our sinful nature, confessing our faults, and dedicating our lives to walk with Hashem, we celebrate the peace offering, the one we all look forward to as it expresses the completion of our union with Hashem. Everyone gets to share in the peace offering, he that offers the sacrifice, the priests, and Hashem. It is an enactment of complete communion. Peace offerings usually were followed by lavish festivities.

Fellowship with God has always been expressed by a meal. It was true on Mt. Horeb and it will be true at the end of the age (Exodus 24:9–11; Revelation 19:9). That is why I think that one of the most spiritually important things we can do in this world, the highest act of spirituality we can practice on this earth, is to have a peaceful and joyful meal with our families. It represents our union with God. Our home life really does expose the depth of our spiritual walk.

It is no wonder that the Adversary works like mad to break up families. The breakdown of the family unit in Western societies is a tool in the Adversary's hands against God's plan. For decades now, the devil's biggest attacks have been against the family units. First he got everybody distracted from the daily dinner table and onto the computer, T.V. and so many evening school activities, that now the very idea of family is being redefined; ugh!

May our Master soon return, even in our days, that we may recline with him at that peace offering meal with all our brothers and sisters (Revelation 19:9) and start the work of bringing sanity back to this world.

My Personal Thoughts

_____

_____

_____

_____

2 Corinthians 5:21 Nissan 3/ ג בניסן

For our sake he made him to be sin who knew no sin,
so that in him we might become the righteousness of God.

Reading much differently from its English translations, the original Hebrew text of Leviticus 1:2 presents interesting messianic insights. I do not believe that the English misreading is due to any conspiratory, voluntary, or malefic action, but rather to people reading the text with an already established theological understanding. They read into the text, instead of letting the text instruct them. We must also realize that a translation always carries the bias of its translator. As such, a translation merely becomes a commentary in another language. I heard it said one time that reading the Bible through a translation is like kissing a bride through a veil.

The usual translations of Leviticus 1:2 read something to the effect of: "When any of you brings an offering to ADONAI . . ." Another possible way to read the text in English would be, "When an Adam from among you desires to come near Me with an offering . . ." The word for *man* in the Hebrew text is *adam* אדם, the same as the name of the first man Adam. This did not pass the attention of Chassidic teacher Rabbi Schneur Zalman. In 1812, the rabbi suggested a deeper meaning in the verse; he came to the messianic conclusion of the existence of a supernatural/spiritual Adam who approaches Hashem on the behalf of Israel. Based on the vision of Ezekiel in which he saw "a figure with the appearance of an *Adam*," Jewish teachings sometime offer the idea of a heavenly Adam. It is to this spiritual Adam that the rabbi makes his reference (Ezekiel 1:26).

This may sound far-fetched, but Paul teaches something along the same lines in his letter to the Corinthians. He says, "The first man is from the earth, made of dust; the second man is from heaven" (1 Corinthians 15:47). Understanding that everything on earth was created after an a heavenly pattern, Paul's accounting of first and second does not refer to importance, but only to the chronology of this Adam's earthly manifestations.

The rabbi was right. Israel does have an Adam who approaches Hashem on our behalf, and who "lives to make intercessions for them" (Hebrews 7:25 referring to Isaiah 53:12). He is our burnt offering in Hebrew called *olah* עולה or *he that ascends*, an image of total submission and consumption in God and ascending to him (Leviticus 1:3; Matthew 26:39; John 3:13–15). He is our grain offering (Leviticus 2:2; Matthew 26:26); our peace offering, which is an image of communion and fellowship with Hashem through a meal (Leviticus 3:1; John 14:27; Revelation 19:9). He also is our sin offering for our involuntary sins (Leviticus 4:2; 2 Corinthians 5:21 Hebrews 9:28); and our guilt offering (Leviticus 5:19; Isaiah 53:10–11).

In studying the eternal offering ordinances in the Book of Leviticus, we learn about Yeshua's eternal intercessory role in our lives. It is one and the same thing, and since he completes them (Matthew 5:17), if the offerings become obsolete as some teach, Yeshua also becomes obsolete, God forbid!

May we always be granted to confidently approach Hashem through him who is our eternal intercessory offering, in a spirit of submission and humility, in full knowledge of our sin, and personal unworthiness.

My Personal Thoughts

_____

_____

Luke 22:46   **Nissan 4/ ד בניסן**

Why are you sleeping? Get up and pray that you won't be put to the test!

The first chapters of the Book of Leviticus teach us about the importance of *Korbanot* קורבנות, or offerings, as means of approaching God. In the forty-third chapter of Isaiah, God *complains* that Israel has become weary of him, that his people give their attention to idols of metal, stone, and wood, and that when it comes times to serve him, they are not available. They are like a spouse who has become bored in their relationship with their lover.

The Sages of Israel put it this way,

> A man stands engaged in his business transactions all day long without getting weary, but if his friend says to him, "come and pray", he replies that he is not able to do so. A man will sit all day long without getting tired, but as soon as he gets up to say prayers he feels tired. A man will sit all day long without growing drowsy, but as soon as he sits down to study he feels drowsy. (Lamentations Rabbah chapt 10; Ester Rabbah 4:8)

I am a married man of over thirty years. My wife and I have raised 6 children. One thing we have learned is that it takes work to keep a marriage alive and interesting. One of the best pieces of marital advice I ever received was, "Your wife loves Hashem, so become the man Hashem wants you to become and your wife will fall in love with you; she will fall in love with the Spirit of Hashem within you." I think it works both ways. A man who loves Hashem will also fall in love with the Spirit of Hashem in his wife.

In the case of Israel's relationship with God, I believe that Hashem did not fail to do his part. The problem was that Israel got its eyes off him; it got distracted and snared by the lure of idols.

Today idolatry is not such a problem, or at least not in the same venue, but distraction is. It is very easy nowadays to let our attention be stolen from Hashem by an over active social, professional, or *religious* life. We allow ourselves to be distracted from Hashem and then we feel that Hashem is not enough. Could it be that the problem really is that we haven't invested enough in the elements of our relationship with him? Our eyes are somewhere else, on the things of the world instead of focused on the things he has for us. What kind of response do we get when we treat our spouses like they are second place?

May we learn to return to him; to say with the psalmist, "Give light to my eyes, or I will sleep the sleep of death" (Psalm 13:3) and, "My eyes are always directed toward ADONAI, for he will free my feet from the net (Psalm 25:15).

My Personal Thoughts

_____

_____

_____

_____

_____

_____

John 14:6

No one comes to the Father except through me.

From new-age type meditations, to charismatic theology, to quantum physics: many books have been written on how to approach God. Why don't people just read the Torah? In the Tabernacle, which later evolved into the Temple, we are taught all the details concerning the protocol to observe when desiring an audience with the Almighty. Here is how it goes as explained in my own words:

Our sinful nature prohibits us from approaching God. We only do it by proxy through the mediation of the blood of a kosher animal that we bring as an offering to the altar. The offering was not designed to atone for sin; it only served as an acknowledgement and a confession of sin (Hebrews 10:4; 9:13). It is the same today. From Genesis until now, the formula never changed; we approach the Father through the sole mediating agency of the Son (John 14:6; Hebrews 4:14–16; Psalm 2:12).

Here is how it worked in the Temple. Someone brings the animal to the priest at the altar and offers it. After that, only the priest can go further into the precinct of the Temple. To do so, he first has to go through the laver and wash his hands and feet. He probably washed at home that morning, but this washing is not for hygiene; it is a ritual washing against ritual contamination. This ritual is designated for priests only. We remember how Yeshua did the same to his disciples on the night before he died. The disciples had already washed their bodies as well as their hands before eating as was done in Jewish customs. All they needed now was to wash their feet, which the Master did for them that night. In essence, Yeshua was treating his disciples as priests, fulfilling messianic prophecies (Exodus 19:6; 1 Peter 2:9). Yeshua himself is the laver wherewith we are clean to approach the Father (John 15:3).

Finally, as the high priest approached the Holy (of Holies), near the continual incense burning in front of the Ark, the prayers offered went up to Hashem. We can see this very principle when Zechariah came to the Temple, the angel who said, "Your prayer has been heard," appeared to him as he was offering the incense (Luke 1:13). Our prayers are brought before Hashem and he scrupulously answers each one of them. He never fails to vindicate his people (Revelation 5:8; 8:3–4).

May we then, having laid our sin on the altar, trust in the righteousness of our High Priest in heaven *Yeshua HaMashiach* ישוע המשיח, and through him have the confidence to draw near to the throne of grace, that we may receive mercy and find grace to help in time of need (Hebrews 4:16).

My Personal Thoughts

_____

_____

_____

_____

_____

_____

Hebrews 13:15–16   **Nissan 6/** ו בניסן

Through him, therefore, let us offer God a sacrifice of praise continually. For this is the natural product of lips that acknowledge his name. But don't forget doing good and sharing with others, for with such sacrifices God is well pleased.

In the sixth chapter of Leviticus, we discover the daily offering called the *Tamid* תמיד, meaning, *the perpetual offering* (Leviticus 6:8–13). This twice daily offering is supposed to be continuous before ADONAI. It represents the intercessory lamb perpetually standing before the Father; the one killed in the morning when Yeshua was hanged on the tree, and the second killed in the afternoon when the Master remitted his spirit into the hands of the Father.

Even after the death and resurrection of the Master, the Jerusalem disciples, as well as all these new Jewish believers from the nations, continued attending the twice-daily service at the Temple (Acts 2:46). The theology that Yeshua had replaced all offerings never existed in the disciples' mind; it was never an issue for them. We see it in the warning Yeshua gave them that they eventually would get kicked out of the Jewish places of worship. The theology that taught that Judaism was obsolete and replaced was fabricated later by non-Jewish Christian apologists, and it lingers until today.

So when the disciples became barred from temples and synagogues, they were very distraught. To them, it was a religious disaster. They had to learn to meet in homes and open spaces. The rest of the Jewish nation and the world were soon to meet the Nazarenes outside the Temple when in 70 CE all Jews were barred from it as the Romans burned it to the ground.

Jewish people, believers and non-believers alike, then turned their eyes to the sages who seemed to have anticipated the issue. A homiletic interpretation of a verse in the prophecies of Hoseah offered an answer to the crisis. The verse says, "Take words with you, and return to ADONAI; say to him, 'Forgive all guilt, and accept what is good; we will pay instead of bulls *[the offerings of]* our lips'" (Hoseah. 14:2). Jewish sages and religious leaders used this verse to teach the people that when they recite the *words* of the order of the offerings, it is as if they offered them as *bulls* on the altar (b. meguilah 31a). Jewish sages had that idea because the word *bulls* in Hebrew is spelled the same way as the word *fruits*, thus connecting the idea that offerings made in *words* are the *fruits of the lips*. Until this day, Synagogue services consist of the reciting of the offerings at the appropriate times.

This idea was actually endorsed by the writer of the Book of Hebrews. Referencing Hoseah, the epistle writer encourages the Jewish believers that while barred from the synagogue and temple, they should offer to God sacrifices of prayer, praise, good deeds and sharing. He says, "Through him, therefore, let us offer God a sacrifice of praise continually. For this is the natural product of lips that acknowledge his name." Along with verbal offerings, they were also exhorted to do good deeds and to share: "But don't forget doing good and sharing with others, for with such sacrifices God is well pleased" (Hebrews 13:15–16).

May we through our mouths and actions continually offer our offerings of prayer, praise, good deeds (obedience to the Commandments), and sharing, for these are pleasing to him.

My Personal Thoughts

Hebrews 7:25 ז בניסן/Nissan 7

He is alive forever and thus forever able to intercede on their behalf.

Contrary to what is commonly assumed, the five *korbanot* קורבנות, offerings described in the beginning of the Book of Leviticus are not meant for sin atonement. While the sin and guilt offerings portray an acknowledgment and confession of sin, the others are statements of thankfulness, gratefulness, praise, and dedication. The main atonement offering in the Levitical system is what is called the *Tamid* תמיד, the daily perpetual morning and evening offering (Leviticus 6:8–13).

Like two book ends, the Tamid opened the day's offerings in the morning, and closed it in the evening. These two offerings are the foundation of the two main prayer services in the Temple, and are still today the theme from where the synagogue service and daily personal prayers were conceived. Luke informs us that the disciples attended these lamb offering based services (Acts 2:26). Peter and John are also mentioned going to the temple's evening service (Acts 3:1). This is important information as it teaches us that the disciples of the Master continued to attend temple services and liturgies even after Yeshua's resurrection. They had never stopped.

Two lambs were offered each morning and evening, providing a continual lamb presence on the altar before God. Those who did not come to the Temple prayed in synchronicity in their homes facing Jerusalem.

At his last Passover on earth, our Master was nailed to the cross at the time the priests offered the morning offering. All day while Yeshua was on the cross, throngs of local people and pilgrims offered their Passover lambs. The Mishnah records that at the end of the ordeal—towards mid-afternoon—the high priest who worked hard in the hot Jerusalem sun said, "I thirst," and was offered a drink. At the end of the day, this same high priest declared, "It is finished." Our Master, the high priest from above, uttered these very words while on the cross, then remitted his spirit to his Father at the very time of the evening offering that closed the day's services (Mark 15:25,33,34). As Yeshua was put in the tomb just before dusk, Jewish families put their striped and pierced unleavened bread in their ovens.

The *Tamid* is therefore a perfect picture of the intercessory role of Messiah in our lives. As the writer of the letter sent to the Messianic believers of Jerusalem says, "[Yeshua] is totally able to deliver those who approach God through him; since he is alive forever and thus forever able to intercede on their behalf" (Hebrews 7:25).

Yeshua, the innocent righteous victim, truly stands at the right hand of the Father always ready to intercede for us because "the prayer of a righteous person is powerful and effective" (James 5:16).

My Personal Thoughts

_____

_____

_____

_____

_____

1 Timothy 2:15   **Nissan 8/ ח בניסן**

Nevertheless, the woman will be delivered through childbearing.

The subject of ritual uncleanliness in Leviticus is very extensive and complicated. It tells us that we are born in order to get close to God but that we can't because we are born. It is the greatest paradox in Leviticus but without a basic understanding of its workings, we miss many key elements of the *Tanach* תנ"ך, and even more of the apostolic writings.

Because of sin in Eden, humanity is born unclean and is bound to remain so. This unclean state raises an uncrossable wall between us and Hashem. Many stories try to explain what happened in the Garden of Eden but the literal one is that Eve was tempted to disobey, and because of her disobedience, humanity was sent away from the presence of Hashem. To this day, we are reaping the results of this event. In the Book of Genesis we are told that Hashem tells the woman, "I will greatly increase your pain in childbirth. You will bring forth children in pain" (Genesis 3:16), and to the man: "The ground cursed on your account; you will work hard to eat from it as long as you live" (Genesis 3:17). Since that time, things have not changed. Even man's attempts in averting childbirth pain through painkillers and caesarians are just an effort to circumvent what God has decreed. Mankind is continually trying to invent some sort of *get rich* scheme that would somehow help him to succeed in making a living without working hard.

Paul continues the "you will work hard to eat from it" rhetoric by advising the congregations of his days with, "if someone won't work, he shouldn't eat" (2 Thessalonians 3:10). The early teachings of the Apostles mention that even an itinerant rabbi or spiritual teacher should not be in charge of congregations for more than two days. After three days he needs to work for his stay (The Didache).

For women, things seem to fare a little differently. The apostle mentions that though she brought sin and impurity in the world, "The woman will be delivered through childbearing provided that she continues trusting, loving and living a holy life with modesty (1 Timothy 2:15). It seems therefore that the suffering of a woman in childbearing has atoning values. The messianic concept of atonement through one's suffering is very prevalent in the Talmud. It is remarkable to notice that it is through the process of childbearing that the Messiah comes to the world to make his redemptive work manifest to mankind.

Of all the stories I have heard about Eden here is, in my narration, the one I like the most:

> Eve sinned and was rejected from the garden. Adam loved Eve so much that he did not want to be separated from her, so he agreed to eat of the fruit of the knowledge of good and evil so he could stay with her and help her.

Whereas some so-called 'modern' minds may criticize this Jewish version of the story as sexist, it nevertheless may stand as the earliest version of messianic lore. It is the story of a man, made sinless, accepting ritual impurity and sin upon himself for the sake of his beloved bride. It is not only a romantic story, but very messianic. Isn't it what Yeshua—who Paul refers to as the *last Adam*—did for us, his bride (1 Corinthians 15:45)? Paul even says that *Adam* "prefigured the one who was to come" (Romans 5:14).

My Personal Thoughts

Matthew 3:11   **Nissan 9/ ט בניסן**

> *It's true that I am immersing you in water so that you might turn from sin to God;*
> *but the one coming after me is . . . he will immerse you in the Ruach HaKodesh and in fire.*

The fire of the altar was to be kept burning continuously (Leviticus 6:12). It was to never be put out. Even when travelling, the Mishnah tells us that the fire of the altar was to be kept low under a brass cover with coal still seething in order to use them to light a new fire at the time of the next offering.

The whole idea was to preserve the original fire where Hashem lit the original first offering (Leviticus 9:23–24). That first fire was not of human origin. It came from the altar above, from Hashem himself, and became the medium by which everything was burnt, and on it, everything transcended back to the heavenly realm. Without this divine flame, the altar was no more than a glorified barbecue pit and nothing burnt on it would go any higher than our atmosphere. It is the meaning behind Yeshua's mystic saying, "No one has gone up into heaven; there is only the one who has come down from heaven, the Son of Man" (John 3:13). This is also why the sons of Aaron were punished for bringing to the altar *strange fire*, a fire that did not originate from the altar above.

Homiletically speaking, this fire teaches us much. It teaches us that faith in Messiah cannot be something originated from earthly personal emotions. Our faith must be something kindled by the spiritual reality of Hashem, from the spiritual fire that is from above. This is the whole difference between *living faith* and *dead religion*. Our obedience to commandments may be all good and well but without being enflamed by redemptive messianic faith, it is nothing more than meaningless rote rituals. We can see this faith in the patriarchs; in Abraham whose faith was based on belief in the resurrection (Hebrews 11:19), in King David who in the Psalms incessantly speaks of Messiah, in Job who proclaimed, "But I know that my Redeemer lives, that in the end he will rise on the dust" (Job 19:25), and in a host of others.

Godly actions, even in obedience to Torah, but consumed by any other element other than this all-consuming faith in Messiah's work actually becomes idolatry. Maybe this is the idea behind Yeshua's rejection of many who will come to him in the end all proclaiming their good works for him while lacking faith in his power to redeem them (Luke 13:26-27; Matthew 7:21–23); like Nadab and Abihu, the sons of Aaron, whose offerings of strange fire were not accepted by Hashem (Leviticus 10:1–2).

May our faith be more than an earthly, emotional high originating from the mechanics of sounds and lights over-used in today's pulpits. May our faith come from an all-consuming fire (yet safe and controlled like Moses' burning bush) to challenge the powers that be, to deliver us from the Pharaoh outside of us and the one inside of us as well and lead us, even by night, through to the Promised Land.

My Personal Thoughts

_____

_____

_____

_____

Ephesians 2:14   **Nissan 10/ י בניסן**

For he himself is our shalom—he has made us both one and has broken down the m'chitzah (dividing wall) which divided us.

Everything about the Tabernacle was designed to mirror immortality. It is the reason why offerings were salted and why honey and leaven were forbidden on the altar. Even the resinous shittim wood it was made from was like cedar, which is resistant to corruption. Corruption was not allowed on it. To avoid any kind of spoilage of the meat left on the altar, any meat from peace offerings was to be burnt completely on the third day. Anyone who partook of the meat of a peace offering on the third day invalidated the offering and was regarded as cut off (Leviticus 7:16–21).

This brings us into the *third day,* a reoccurring theme of the *Tanach*. Rather than seeing corruption, meat from a peace offering is burnt on the third day. The idea here is that as the divinely originated fire from the altar consumes the meat of the offering, it lifts it back to Hashem in the form of smoke (Leviticus 9:23–24). This teaches us a symbol of the *corruptible* putting on *incorruptibility*. In the story of Samson, we see an example of the Angel of ADONAI, rising back to heaven through the smoke of a burnt offering called the *olah* or *that which rises* (Judges 13:20).

The peace offering is the only one in which the offerer partakes. It is a meal symbolizing our communion and fellowship with Hashem. Hospitality was a big thing in the East and to invite someone to eat showed a great level of acceptance and relationship. In the same way, eating with Hashem displayed a great level of acceptance and relationship. It shows that he accepts us. Moses and seventy-three other people ate with Hashem on the mountain and similarly, the whole congregation of Messiah's people will eat with him at the Marriage Supper of the Lamb (Exodus 24:11; Revelation 19:9).

The Passover Lamb is a shadow of Messiah, a peace offering that people partake of. Paul often used the imagery of the peace offering to describe Messiah's role in our lives (1 Corinthians 10:18; Romans 5:1; Ephesians 2:14; Colossians 1:20). In the manner of a peace offering, the Master's body was not allowed to see corruption (Psalms 16:10; 49:9) but rose from the tomb on the third day.

Hoseah prophesied on the resurrection of Israel's great Diaspora (exile) in the following words,

> Come, let us return to ADONAI; for he has torn, and he will heal us; he has struck, and he will bind our wounds. After two days, he will revive us; on the third day, he will raise us up; and we will live in his presence. (Hoseah 6:1-2)

Understanding that with Hashem, one day is as a thousand years, and a thousand years, one day (2 Peter 3:8), Hoseah the prophet prophesied the resurrection of Israel on the third millennium of the present exile, which we have seen. This resurrection of the Jewish State is also accompanied by a strong Messianic first fruit element of believers within the Land itself, bringing within it incorruptibility.

In this day, in our day, the peace offering is finally being consumed. At the time appointed, at the sound of the great shofar of the last day, it will rise to him in immortality and find fellowship with Hashem. All those who partake of Messiah's offering of peace are part of this everlasting promise.

My Personal Thoughts

1 Corinthians 15:53

For this material which can decay must be clothed with imperishability,
this which is mortal must be clothed with immortality.

Three days is such a repeated theme in the Torah. It is on the third day that Abraham and Isaac climbed the mountain (Genesis 22:4). Israel had to purify itself, and then God came in their sight on Mt. Horeb after three days (Exodus 19:16). Jonah was spewed out of the fish after three days (Jonah 1:17). Joshua crossed the Jordan as on dry land on the third day (Joshua 3:2,17). And the remainder of the flesh of any offering needed to be burned after three days (Leviticus 7:17).

The theme of the third day points to the idea of resurrection, when corruptibility, or that which is dead or dying, puts on incorruptibility, or the status of the resurrected in God (1 Corinthians 15:53). It is also on the third day that there was a wedding in Cana (John 2:1) and that the Master rose (Matthew 16:21).

On the other hand, Yeshua waited four days to go to Lazarus (John 11:17). It could be that the Master wanted to wait that long because he knew that the third day is actually the time when unrefrigerated flesh starts to decompose (John 11:39). The disciples hesitated to open the tomb not only because of the smell, but it represented a desecration and exposure to ritual contamination. Even in the Temple, meat from peace offerings was not allowed to remain on the altar more than three days; after that it had to be burned (Leviticus 7:16–18). The Master waited till the fourth day so the people would know that Lazarus was truly dead and not just *sleeping*.

The *three days* theme speaks to us of the most wonderful process and miracle in our redemption program: that of corruptibility putting on incorruptibility. The corruptible is transformed into an incorruptible state before it is allowed to decompose. This also represents the greatest promise Hashem made to his people. Through the prophet Hoseah came the following words for an apostate Israel who would soon face exile and deportation,

> Come, let us return to Adonai; for he has torn, and he will heal us; he has struck, and he will bind our wounds. After two days, he will revive us; on the third day, he will raise us up; and we will live in his presence. (Hoseah. 6:1–2)

One day for God is 1,000 years. In the third millennia of exile, Israel is resurrected to its former Salomonic grandeur as when nations brought their glories to Jerusalem and came to learn from the wisest king in the world. We can see the beginning of it even now.

All these scriptural themes foreshadow our passing from mortality to immortality, from the corruptible to the incorruptible, from death to resurrection.

May we always live in the understanding of these things. No matter what life throws at us in what seems at times tsunamis of troubles, may we, as children of the Most-High, be perfect (Matthew 5:48) and not have a morbid attitude towards the ending of our temporal passage in this earthly dimension. May we always remember that the end of the vanity of our sad temporal life is the fullness of eternal joy, that the end of death is life, and that in due time, corruptibility puts on incorruptibility; death is swallowed up by life.

My Personal Thoughts

John 1:4

In him was life, and the life was the light of mankind.

Studying the biblical laws of clean and unclean seem to take us to a world far removed from our present society. We cannot, though, read these passages in the Book of Leviticus and assess them according to the dynamics of our present world; we need to understand them according to their own context.

All the issues of ceremonial contamination in the Bible have to do with separating the holy—what is set-apart for the service of Hashem—from death, decay, and corruption. All the regulations mentioned concerning ritual purity in the Torah can be understood in the idea that God, being life itself, cannot, and does not have anything to do with whatever decays and dies. All the earthly elements therefore that represent him must be free—at least symbolically—from corruption. We easily understand these concepts through the gold covered acacia wood that makes the Holy Ark, a wood with the properties of cedar that fights corruption. Salt also, which is a preservative, has to be added to meat offerings and the meat discarded within three days before it turns rancid. Of course, as long as we are in this mortal body and on this temporal earth, we cannot fully get rid of corruption; the whole idea is therefore a message from the Father to teach us about himself.

Ritual contamination has nothing to do with us committing any particular sin. For example, a woman has done nothing wrong when she enters her monthly time and even less when she has a baby, the fulfillment of one of Hashem's greatest commandment, but yet, at these times she is considered ritually contaminated. Being ritually contaminated is a mere acknowledgment of our mortal human condition, and is a condition that mostly concerns the Temple and its service. All one needs to do to be ritually pure again is immerse in a *mikveh* (ritual immersion pool).

The best way to it is to relate it to protocol. There is a certain protocol to enter for example in the presence of a president or king of any country.

In the days of Yeshua, some people went overboard in their concerns with ritual purity. The Master tells us about it in the story about a dying wounded man on the road to Jericho. Both a Levite and a priest pass him by but choose not to help him because they were concerned about the possibility of ritual contamination, which comes by the touching of blood (Luke 10:25–37). The Levite and the priest in the story were used to portray a misapplication of this principle. The Master himself, who is sinless and came from the halls of heaven, was not reluctant to put on the impurity of humanity and contaminate himself in order to rescue us from our mortality. Again, ritual purity is not about having committed a sin. One can obey every dictum of the Torah and still be impure. It is solely about our human condition.

May we not be found to be like the aforementioned Levite or priest who, because they were so concerned about their own purity, failed to obey the commandment to reach out to those in need. The Master did not discard the practices of ritual purity, which came from him to start with, but he does teach us to have a proper balance and perspective in our commandment observance. He says, "These are the things you should have attended to—without neglecting the others" (Matthew 23:23).

My Personal Thoughts

Luke 22:17–18   Nissan 13/ יג בניסן

Then, taking a cup of wine, he made the b'rakhah and said, "Take this and share it among yourselves. For I tell you that from now on, I will not drink the 'fruit of the vine' until the Kingdom of God comes. "

In the late afternoon of the thirteenth of Adar 30 BCE the Master saw the day of the *Pesach* פסח preparation approaching. The narratives left to us by Luke, Paul's faithful scribe who collected his information from those who were first hand witnesses, tell us about the Master's Seder preparations with the disciple that year. As they get ready, the Master informs them, " I have really wanted so much to celebrate this Seder with you before I die! For I tell you, it is certain that I will not celebrate it again until it is given its full meaning in the Kingdom of God" (Luke 22:15–16).

Yeshua said that he would not eat that Passover with the disciples until he eats it in the kingdom … at the Marriage Supper of the Lamb (Revelation 19:9). In the meantime, he had to prepare his disciples for the next day's Passover Seder without him. Many people in Israel were ready one night ahead. It seems that that year, the master decided to follow the sometimes-traditional pre-Seder celebration. Adding a new wrinkle to the age-old tradition, he,

> Then, taking a cup of wine [the Kiddush Cup], he made the b'rakhah and said, "Take this and share it among yourselves. For I tell you that from now on, I will not drink the 'fruit of the vine' until the Kingdom of God comes." (Luke 22:17–18)

Notice that Yeshua did not drink it; did he take a Nazarite vow?

As the time came of the Seder's traditional hand-wash, the Master added a new 'wrinkle.' He started to wash the disciple's feet, to which Peter objected (John 13:5–10).

It is the priests who washed their hands and their feet before they entered the Holy (of Holies), the first chamber of the Tabernacle. That could be the reason of Peter's objection. The Master on the other hand could have been enacting Moses' ancient prophetic words, "And you shall be to me a kingdom of priests" (Exodus 19:6). Oddly enough, this same Peter later bestowed the same unction on the disciples—Jews and Gentiles—of the Roman congregation, "But you are . . . the King's cohanim" (1 Peter 2:9).

At the time of the dipping in the charoset, which is the mixture of apples and nuts used in the Seder, John records that Yeshua shocked everyone with the announcement that one of the disciples present was going to betray him. He said, "It is he to whom I will give this morsel of bread when I have dipped it" (John 13:26). Then after dinner,

> Also, taking a piece of matzah [the Afikomen], he made the b'rakhah, broke it, gave it to them and said, "This is my body, which is being given for you; do this in memory of me." He did the same with the cup after the meal, saying, "This cup is the New Covenant, ratified by my blood, which is being poured out for you." (Luke 22:19–20)

It is at the Mount of Olive, on this night of the fourteenth of Nissan that Judas and the temple guards would meet Yeshua to bring him to his Sadducee enemies. During the course of the night he would face all the authorities of the land: Caiphas the high priest, Herod the Jewish leader, and finally Pilate the Roman governor who, washing his hands of his fate, would find no fault in himself (Matthew 27).

Luke 23:54   **Nissan 14/** יד בניסן

It was Preparation Day, and a Shabbat was about to begin.

It had been a long twenty-four hours for Yeshua the Master. As an innocent victim, he has been condemned to a cruel death by both religious and secular authorities. John the Immerser rightfully compared Yeshua to, "God's lamb! The one who is taking away the sin of the world!" (John 1:29). At the time of the morning lamb offering, Yeshua was nailed to a crossbeam and hanged on a stake; one of the most cruel forms of death of the day. He stayed there until the afternoon time of prayer, the time of the second lamb offering, before the throng of Passover lambs arrived to be slaughtered.

At the time when the Temple was bustling with activity, when in an assembly-line style the priests would kill the lambs of the thousands of people who had come for the pilgrimage festival, our Master committed his spirit to his, and our heavenly Father. As he entered the tomb, the prepared lambs and unleavened breads entered the ovens. Then,

> There was a man named Yosef, a member of the Sanhedrin. He was a good man, a tzaddik; and he had not been in agreement with either the Sanhedrin's motivation or their action. He came from the town of Ramatayim, a town of the Judeans; and he looked forward to the Kingdom of God. This man approached Pilate and asked for Yeshua's body. He took it down, wrapped it in a linen sheet, and placed it in a tomb cut into the rock, that had never been used. It was Preparation Day, and a Shabbat was about to begin. The women who had come with Yeshua from the Galil followed; they saw the tomb and how his body was placed in it. Then they went back home to prepare spices and ointments. On Shabbat the women rested, in obedience to the commandment. (Leviticus 23:6–7; Luke 23:50–56)

The disciples probably all had their Seder together. We can imagine Peter leading the event and how confused and distraught they must have been. According to the narratives, the events had not yet clicked in their minds as the fulfillment of prophecy. It would take the Master himself to come and explain it to them. For the first time since they knew him, they had a fifteenth of Nissan Seder without their beloved rabbi.

As they passed the Kiddush cup, they remembered what he said, "Take this and share it among yourselves. For I tell you that from now on, I will not drink the 'fruit of the vine' until the Kingdom of God comes" (Luke 22:17–18).

As they washed their hands, they silently remembered the Master washing their feet. It was an even more somber moment as they passed the charoset and remembered that this was the cue for Judas to go do his work.

Then, after dinner, what must have gone through their mind as they passed the Afikomen, as they remembered the Master's words, "This is my body, which is being given for you; do this in memory of me." And likewise, when they drank the [3rd] cup after they had eaten, they were reminded of when he said, "This cup is the New Covenant, ratified by my blood, which is being poured out for you" (Luke 22:19–20).

The full meaning of these words would not be fully revealed to them yet. They were grieving for the loss of their Master and it must have been difficult to end the Seder with the customary Psalms of praise.

They would spend the second day (the fifteenth of Nissan) in this somber mood, until on the third day . . .

1 Peter 3:18–20   **Nissan 15/ טו בניסן**

> *For the Messiah himself died for sins, once and for all, a righteous person on behalf of unrighteous people, so that he might bring you to God. He was put to death in the flesh but brought to life by the Spirit; and in this form he went and made a proclamation to the imprisoned spirits, to those who were disobedient long ago, in the days of Noach, when God waited patiently during the building of the ark, in which a few people— to be specific, eight—were delivered by means of water.*

As the disciples of long ago, last night we experienced a Seder in the absence of Yeshua. Was he really absent?

It was a somber evening for them. Just the night before, the Master was teaching them a new way to celebrate the Seder. What they didn't know was that on the night of the Passover itself, they would be without him. On the night of the fifteenth of Nissan, as they go together for a customary Seder after the Mt. Golgotha events, they really didn't know what to make of everything. On this Sabbath of the fifteenth of Nissan, they attended the synagogue service with a mourning heart. All their hopes of salvation, of Yeshua taking over Israel, of him overcoming the Roman Empire, of establishing Israel back to the glorious days of Solomon were shattered. They did not understand what was happening and indeed, what *was* happening on that fifteenth of Nissan Sabbath?

When he wrote his letter to the Jewish/Gentile congregation of Rome, Peter gave us a clue. He said that Yeshua

> went and made a proclamation to the imprisoned spirits, to those who were disobedient long ago, in the days of Noach, when God waited patiently during the building of the ark, in which a few people—to be specific, eight—were delivered by means of water. (1 Peter 3:19–20)

Much is written in the Book of Enoch about the events surrounding Noah and the flood, and the early disciples were familiar with it.

May we take this Shabbat to reflect on these things.

What have we learned through the events of the two past days?

How have we understood the analogical parallelism the Master made of himself in the Seder elements?

How do these apply to those who "were disobedient long ago, in the days of Noach, when God waited patiently" (1 Peter 3:19–20)?

How does it apply to us today?

Or tomorrow?

Or to our children?

These questions would surely make good fifteenth of Nissan Sabbath discussions.

My Personal Thoughts

_____

_____

Luke 24:32   **Nissan 16/ טז בניסן**

Didn't our hearts burn inside us as he spoke to us on the road, opening up the Tanakh to us?

On the third day after the crucifixion, women came to the tomb to embalm the Master. To their great surprise, Yeshua's body had disappeared. Though incredulous, upon hearing the women's accounts, Peter and John ran to the tomb only to be faced with the same conclusions.

Did he really disappear? Coming to them on several occasions, Yeshua soon comforted the disciple's worries. He had resurrected and was now keen on giving them his instructions for the establishment of the Kingdom of heaven on earth. While all this transpired, two disciples who had come to Judea for the pilgrimage festival of Passover left Jerusalem for the village of Emmaus (Luke 24).

As Cleopas and his travelling companion were still grieving the death of their Master, a stranger joined them on their journey. As their new travelling companion wondered about their gloomy conversation, they asked, "Don't you know what happened three days ago in Jerusalem? We thought that the famous Galilean prophet, Yeshua Hanotzri ישוע הנוצרי was the Messiah. We thought he would be the one gathering back the children of Israel from the four corners of the earth and re-establish us as a sovereign country but alas, the Temple's authorities did not approve of him; they turned him in to the Romans to be crucified as a traitor and a criminal. To top it all, some our friends went to the tomb this morning and found it empty. We are still shocked at the whole thing; and also confused."

Upon hearing this account, starting with Moses and the prophets, the stranger demonstrated to the disciples that all had happened according to the Torah and the prophets and that they should not worry. Upon hearing the words of the old prophecies in their messianic perspective, the two discouraged disciples were filled with hope again. As they sat at the table, the stranger initiated the meal with a blessing; the disciples then realized that their travelling companion was the resurrected Master. Right away they decided to return to Jerusalem.

This story is everyone's story. In confusion and discouragement, we often leave Jerusalem to return to the same old ways. As with the other disciples, no empty tomb and no amount of convincing preaching could have changed the mind of these Jewish disciples. They needed to see the resurrected Master and he is the one who needed to open their eyes. As a matter of fact, It is also the only way that Israel as a nation can and will eventually see and recognize its Messiah, not through clever preaching or exposés of circumstantial evidence but when he comes in the clouds at the end of this age (Zechariah 12:10; Acts 1:11). As soon as they recognized their beloved Master, they repented and returned to Jerusalem.

Whether Jew or Gentile, meeting the resurrected Master should create in us a spirit of *T'shuvah* תשובה, or repentance, that brings us back to the origins of our faith, to the place where we belong, to Jerusalem. After three days of Yeshua's absence, the disciples were already straying from the faith, but the Master ran after them. He met them at the tomb, and in their house where he spoke with Thomas (John 20:27). He even met them on the road to Emmaus, just in order to bring them back, to bring them to Jerusalem where they were to remain until the next pilgrimage festival of *Shavuot* שבעות, Pentecost (Acts 1:4).

In these days of preparation leading to the awesome future times of his return, may our meditations grant us the presence of the Master that causes us to repent from our straying, and return to *Jerusalem* where we belong. On that day, may we be found doing his will.

1 Corinthians 15:54   **Nissan 17/ יז בניסן**

When what decays puts on imperishability and what is mortal puts on immortality, then this passage in the Tanakh will be fulfilled: "Death is swallowed up in victory."

Starting from the sixteenth of Nissan, the day after the Passover Sabbath, we are asked to count seven weeks and one day, fifty days, until Pentecost (Leviticus 23:15). On the fortieth day of this counting the Messiah ascended in the cloud in the plain view of his disciples. They were told at the same moment that in the same manner as Yeshua ascended in the clouds, he will return (Acts 1:11). As believers, for us this period between the resurrection and the ascension is very special. It is the period when, as we are told, Yeshua made all his resurrected appearances to up to five hundred disciples or more (1 Corinthians 15:6).

This fifty day period is called in Hebrew *s'phirat ha'omer* ספירת העומר, meaning, *the Counting of the Omer*. It could also mean the *Recounting of the Omer,* as if it were a story that was told, or even *the Shining of the Omer,* as in cleaning. I would say that all these translations are correct in their own rights. As we count the days of the Omer, we can tell the stories of the appearances of the risen Messiah, thus shining and preparing our souls for the great day of Pentecost when in the similitude of Mt. Horeb's events, through earthquake, wind, and fire, the Torah was sealed in the disciples' hearts 2,000 years ago (Acts 2).

I would even say that remembering the resurrection is vital to our faith. Up to the time of the resurrection, the disciples were weak in their faith. Many of those also who had previously believed in him because of the signs and miracles were easily swayed by the tide of prevailing public opinion. What sealed the deal for Israel was the resurrection. After the resurrection, the whole city of Jerusalem was filled with believers who had become quite a force and even a positive element in Israel until such a time when persecution started again under Herod Antipas (Acts 12) and the wicked Rome-appointed high priest who executed James (Josephus).

This belief in the resurrection is the corner stone of our belief system. It is this very same belief that made innocent victimized Job say, "But I know that my Redeemer lives" (Job 19:25). It is also the same belief that that brought Abraham to the mountain in the face of an insurmountable trial (Hebrews 11:17–19). Many people dare to challenge the authenticity of the apostolic texts, but their biggest vindication is the historically proven cruel martyrdom of each of the disciples who saw the resurrected Messiah. People can't go through that unless they are told to deny something that they have witnessed to be real.

Even today as the world gets darker, it is that same faith in the resurrected one that needs to be our beacon of light, hope, and faith in the face of the seeming irrationalities life deals us. Telling the stories of the resurrected one, particularly of the events surrounding his various apparitions during the Counting of the Omer, should give a *shine* to our faith and the assurance that even though death may seem prevalent, he has resurrected so that through his resurrection, corruption and death puts on incorruptibility.

My Personal Thoughts

Matthew 26:29   Nissan 18/ יח בניסן

I tell you, I will not drink this 'fruit of the vine' again until the day I drink new wine
with you in my Father's Kingdom.

Yoshiyahu was eight years old when he began his reign, and he ruled for thirty-
one years in Yerushalayim. He did what was right from ADONAI's perspective,
living entirely in the manner of David his ancestor and turning away neither to
the right nor to the left. (2 Chronicles 34:1–2)

As King Josiah undertook the restoration of the Temple of Hashem, the Temple's secretary
handed him a Torah scroll. The scroll was opened at Deuteronomy 28, the passage about the
blessings and the curses. As Shaphan read the text to the king, the king tore his clothes (2 Kings
22:11). In Josiah's days, most people in Israel had forgotten the Torah. They practiced religious
forms and traditions inherited from earlier generations and adopted from foreign nations. They did
not fully realize that their worship of God was polluted with idolatrous practices. Josiah's mother
had taught her son a healthy fear of Hashem, and the words of Torah worked in his heart.

The king wanted the land to repent, but instead of sending edicts and rebukes to the people, the
king made repentance something personal,

> The king stood on the platform and made a covenant in the presence of ADONAI
> to live following ADONAI, observing his mitzvot, instructions and regulations
> wholeheartedly and with all his being, so as to confirm the words of the
> covenant written in this scroll. All the people stood, pledging themselves to keep
> the covenant. (2 Kings 23:3)

Josiah also undertook a series of religious reforms where he disposed of the priests of Ba'al,
overthrew the altars to the foreign gods, and went on an all-out campaign against idolatry. This
campaign culminated in a renewing of the Passover observance like no other,

> The king issued this order to all the people: "Observe Pesach to ADONAI your
> God, as written in this scroll of the covenant." For Pesach had not been so
> observed since the days when the judges ruled Isra'el — not during the times of
> any of the kings of Isra'el or of the kings of Y'hudah. But in the eighteenth year
> of King Yoshiyahu this Pesach was observed to ADONAI in Yerushalayim.
> (2 Kings 23:21–23)

A similar situation exists for believers in Yeshua today. They have not totally forgotten Torah, but
because of erroneous theological assumptions many have declared it obsolete, as well as mixed
it with pagan religious elements. Like in the days of Josiah, today many are rediscovering the
Torah of Moses and are experiencing religious reforms in their hearts. Sometimes a whole
congregation will go through these reforms.

These attempts at restoration are great but they are very fragmented and confusing due to a lack
of leadership. The Tanach tells us, "At that time there was no king in Isra'el; a man simply did
whatever he thought was right" (Judges 21:25). But we know the King will return, as Josiah, and
lead us with a strong hand in this reformation. When he does, he will also lead us into the
marriage supper of the Lamb and partake with us from the Seder cup which he omitted to drink
when he celebrated an early Passover dinner with his disciples (Matthew 26:29; Revelation 19:9).

May it be soon Abba, even in our days!

John 5:28 יט בניסן / **Nissan 19**

Do not marvel at this, for an hour is coming when all who are in the tombs will hear his voice

This is the fourth day of the *S'phirat Ha'omer* ספירת העומר, the *Counting of the Omer*. The Master has appeared in his resurrected body to several of the believers. Cleopas and his companion who met him on their way to Emmaus are probably sharing notes with those to whom he appeared in the upper room and with the women who saw him at the tomb (Luke 24). The event that may have become the greatest conversation piece at that time might have been the fact that he committed his spirit unto the Father:

> But Yeshua, again crying out in a loud voice, yielded up his spirit. At that moment the parokhet in the Temple was ripped in two from top to bottom; and there was an earthquake, with rocks splitting apart. Also the graves were opened, and the bodies of many holy people who had died were raised to life; and after Yeshua rose, they came out of the graves and went into the holy city, where many people saw them. (Matthew 27:50–53)

It seems actually that all the resurrected apparitions of the Master appeared during the first forty days of the Counting of the Omer.

One of the days of *Chag Hamatzot* חג המצות or *Unleavened Bread* is usually a Shabbat. Ezekiel 37 is usually read in synagogues on that day. It is interesting because Ezekiel 37 is all about the resurrection of Israel in its own land, an event significant as the coming of Mashiach.

The schedule of the Book of Ezekiel provides us with a timeline of events that we can refer to as we see history unfolding. Ezekiel 34 exposes false shepherds who lead Israel astray and makes an announcement about the Good Shepherd, the *David* who comes to be the true king of Israel, a prince among us. Ezekiel says that at the time of the rule of this *David*, Hashem

> will make a covenant of peace with them; I will rid the land of wild animals; and they will live securely in the desert and sleep in the forests. I will make them and the places around my hill a blessing, and I will cause the rain to fall when it should — there will be showers of blessing. The trees in the field will bear their fruit and the soil its produce, and they will be secure in their land. Then they will know that I am ADONAI, when I break the bars of their yoke and rescue them from the power of those who turned them into slaves. No longer will they be prey for the Goyim, nor will the wild animals devour them; but they will live securely, with no one to make them afraid. I will make the productivity of their crops famous, and they will no longer be consumed by hunger in the land or bear the shame of the Goyim any more. They will know that I, ADONAI their God, am with them, and that they, the house of Isra'el, are my people,' says ADONAI Elohim. (Ezekiel 34:25–30)

What we learn from this oracle is that after the introduction of this *David*, Israel becomes a nation as if it were *resurrected* in its own land. This *David* refers to the Messiah, the one to whom John is introduced to on the Isle of Patmos as a resurrected one, "the Living One. I was dead, but look!—I am alive forever and ever! And I hold the keys to Death and Sh'ol" (Revelation 1:18). The next two chapters tell us about the war of Gog and Magog, and the Book of Ezekiel ends with the rebuilding of the Messianic third Temple.

May it be soon Abba, even in our days!

Matthew 12:37

For by your own words you will be acquitted, and by your own words you will be condemned.

Extreme tragedy often accompanies extreme glory. On the very day when Hashem accepts the hard work performed by the Israelites in building the Tabernacle and sanctifying the priesthood, two of Aaron's sons die (Leviticus 10:1–2).

Everything was in place. The children of Israel had performed beautifully. They were finished with the building of the Tabernacle and the priesthood was sanctified. Everything was ready for the great moment. Suddenly, fire came from heaven to light the wood on the altar and consume the offerings of the children of Israel. God was pleased. Whereas he had been refused entrance before (Exodus 40:35), now, with the offering accepted, Moses could approach Hashem again (Leviticus 9). Things have not changed very much today. We are still only allowed in the Divine Presence by virtue of the death of an innocent victim.

No sooner was the ecstasy of joy settled that Nadab and Abihu, Aaron's sons, decide to make an offering of *esh zarah* אֵשׁ זֹרה, foreign fire to ADONAI. As suddenly as before, Hashem's fire came out from heaven, but this time to devour the two young men. The Torah does not give us many details about the event. Speculations by commentators abound as to God's apparent irrational reaction. What I would like to bring out today is the reaction of Aaron, the young men's father, to Moses' attempt to comfort him. The text says, "Aharon kept silent" (Leviticus 10:3). Maybe that is the reason why the Torah itself remains silent; because Aaron was silent.

Aaron suffers this tragedy in the middle of a service when he is not allowed to mourn nor get out of character. Whereas he later acknowledges his grief and mourning heart (Leviticus 10:19), Aaron does not permit himself to blot Hashem's reputation and name by expressing his own feelings during the service. His two boys die, but he remains silent.

Jewish texts have commented on this with the statement, "By your silence you shall live." The idea is related to Aaron's lofty position of honor as the high priest of the people. As spiritual leaders, when inexplicable tragedy strikes, when what seems unreasonable and irrational happens to us, we are not forbidden to mourn or be sad, but we may not publicize it through words of personal anger or doubts about Hashem's wisdom and absolute justice and righteousness. We also may wait until our service to Hashem's congregation is finished.

The Master agreed to that. He taught his disciples that "by your own words you will be acquitted, and by your own words you will be condemned" (Matthew 12:37). He himself, in the image of the innocent lambs daily offered on the altar, was subject to a cruel and inhumane death for crimes he did not commit and yet, "He did not open his mouth. " (Isaiah 53:7).

May we learn from Aaron's godly attitude. Though our hearts may be bleeding, may we learn to have control over our mouths, souls, and spirit when inexplicable tragedies strike. Hashem knows our hearts, but our mouths need not to seal our burdens on those around us who may be carrying a heavy burden of their own. Ours may be the one to make them stumble and fall.

My Personal Thoughts

_____

_____

_____

Hebrews 5:8

Even though he was the Son, he learned obedience through his sufferings.

There is an expression in English: "The devil is in the details." It is funny that the enemy is given this attribute. *Hasatan* השטן, the Adversary doesn't know anything. All he does is copy God. He only tries to be a counterfeit in order to deceive us. God is the one really into details as is revealed in this week's reading sections. In one place we have Aaron's sons, Nadab and Abihu, who perish for offering *unauthorized incense,* and in the other one Uzzah who dies for touching the Holy Ark while not being authorized, probably because of not being in a ritually clean state. (Leviticus 10:1–2; 2 Samuel. 6:6–7). These two stories are very similar; that is why they are read together. Their similarity lies in the lesson that they teach.

Both stories happen at a time of spiritual ecstasy and jubilation. In the incident with Nadab and Abihu, it was on the eighth day of Aaron and his son's dedication. Fire had just come from heaven and the people saw the glory of ADONAI. Can you imagine the jubilation and the spiritual ecstasy? We can easily picture the joy, the shouts, the dancing, and the clapping of the hands (Leviticus. 9:23–24). It was the same when David was bringing the Ark into Jerusalem. We are told of musicians, of dancing, of joy, and merry-making (2 Samuel 6:5). In both cases tragedy strikes for what could be considered in our eyes, a breach in protocol.

These two events teach us a very important lesson, a lesson often forgotten and ignored by people of faith today. They teach us that religion without the instruction and the parameters of Torah is unacceptable to Hashem. Hashem teaches us how to come to him, how to worship and honor him. He also told us how not to (Leviticus). Oh, but that goes against our natural instinct and desire for spontaneity. Do you mean that we won't to be able to follow the *leadings* of our hearts? We will have to act only in obedience to commands? Oh, but that wouldn't be natural. Where is the spontaneity? You mean that it's not just the heart and the intent that counts? Form and format is also important in the eyes of the Almighty? Really though, when we ask these questions we doubt his ways. It is nothing more than pride acting out our inability to submit to instructions and wanting things our own way.

We understand that even in this world we cannot approach a high dignitary such as a king or a president without jumping through a few protocol hoops. If one were to just barge into the Oval Office in the White House without permission, he would surely be arrested. If he resisted, he might even get shot. The difference is that in the case of an earthly dignitary, they try to protect the dignitary; in the case of Hashem, the protection is for us.

We simply cannot approach God on our terms; it is his prerogative. Why can't we just obey? But no; people always want to find new ways to approach Hashem. They even borrow ways from the pagans in manifestations that are not from him. The simplicity in which he told us to do things is not enough; we must tweak it and give it our own imprint. It is pride, and the pride of man leads to destruction.

May we learn to be in the details as he is in the details. Obedience is not a small thing: in obeying God we emulate the Master. Even he had to learn obedience through the things which he suffered (Hebrews. 5:8).

My Personal Thoughts

John 15:3
כב בניסן **/22 Nissan**

Right now, because of the word which I have spoken to you, you are pruned.

Leviticus 11 tells us about food fit for consumption and teaches us the laws of pure and contaminated. Much has been misunderstood in this text. At first we are told about foods permissible for consumption (Leviticus 11:1–23) and it is pretty straightforward. We will refer to those as, *kasher* כשר, "edible," and *tareph* טרף, "non-edible." Whereas modern science continues to find health benefits to the Levitical diet of edible foods, the primary reason for these ruling is not health. If Hashem would forbid pork because of trichinosis, why doesn't he forbid chicken because of salmonella? The only reason we are given for this is sanctity (Leviticus 11:45).

Levitical 11 teaches us about another type of food fitness. Whereas the first was concerned with fitness regarding consumption, the second is concerned with ceremonial fitness. There are no perfect English words for the Hebrew *tahor* טהר, translated as "clean", and *tamei* טמא, translated as "unclean." *Ceremonially pure* or *contaminated* would be more appropriate. For the sake of textual integrity, we will keep these in Hebrew.

Tahor and *tamei* actually refer to an animal in its dead state, and technically speaking are only relevant as per approaching Hashem via the Tabernacle or later the Temple. Even the carcass of any animal killed improperly is ritually contaminating. It is not ritually contaminating to own a pig or a dog; ritual contamination is only in the carcass of an animal. Human carcasses are technically *tamei*—even if properly slaughtered—whereas the carcass of a properly slaughtered cow is *tahor*. This understanding gives a whole new twist on the story of Abraham going to offer his son. It also brings a new wrinkle to the narrative about Samson. Samson was a Nazarite from birth. He was supposed to stay in a state of continual *tahor-ness,* therefore eating honey from the carcass of a lion went against his Nazarite condition. This is why also certain animals are eligible for offering and others are not.

We must understand that the conditions of *tahor* and *tamei* have nothing to do with hygiene, personal sin, or morality. A woman is *tamei* after having a baby; that is not because of sin but of obedience to a fundamental divine command (Genesis 1:22). These conditions have only to do with the state of being human. As human beings we have dead cells, *tamei* particles in our body all the time, so that we can only enter the presence of the Almighty by proxy through the blood of a *kasher* animal, and/or immersion in a ritual pool. We must take into consideration though that these rulings only concern our relationship with the temple in Jerusalem, so until it is rebuilt, they are only applicable on a symbolic level

But here is the good news: Yeshua knew and anticipated a very long Temple-less exilic period of time. He told the Samaritan woman, "The time is coming when you will worship the Father neither on this mountain nor in Yerushalayim" (John 4:21). At his last Seder with his disciples Yeshua also said, "You are *tahor* because of the word that I have spoken to you" (John 15:3). So through Yeshua, the writer of the letter to the Messianic Jews (Hebrews) says to us, "Let us confidently approach the throne from which God gives grace, so that we may receive mercy and find grace in our time of need" (Hebrews 4:16).

May we always have the confidence that by virtue of the name, obedience, righteousness, and *tahor-ness* of Yeshua, we can always enter in the presence of the Father to obtain his favor.

Philippians 2:5–8

Let your attitude toward one another be governed by your being in union with the Messiah Yeshua: Though he was in the form of God, he did not regard equality with God something to be possessed by force. On the contrary, he emptied himself, in that he took the form of a slave by becoming like human beings are. . . . he humbled himself still more by becoming obedient even to death—death on a stake as a criminal.

Before even the end of the first century, many non-Jewish believers reading Paul's letters outside of their original Jewish contextual matrix misunderstood and forsook the Torah's dietary laws. They did this not only because of the ideas of food being *tahor* or *tamei* (ceremonially pure or contaminated), but also the idea of certain animal species not being fit for consumption. It is true that when read outside of their natural context, Paul's letters seem to indicate that faith in Yeshua makes these elements of Torah observance obsolete. The same problem actually appears with any text and ruling when read outside of its original context. Even the American Constitution ideas of freedom of press and religion suffer from an *identity crisis* when quoted today outside of their original context and intent.

The Jewish community of believers on the contrary had no issue with the whole idea of *tahor* and *tamei* (Acts 15:20, 29; 21:25). It always was part of their lives and of Torah and they understood Paul's letters within a Jewish contextual understanding. They also continued adhering to the injunction that sin is the breaking of Torah (1 John 3:4) and that a false prophet is one who teaches to disobey it. Consequently, they could not have imagined the Master or Paul teaching against these things (Deuteronomy 13:1–5; Matthew 5:19).

The very discussion about it in the apostolic letters tells us that there were concerns about the levels of obedience on that issue, especially concerning Gentile observance; but that there were no problems concerning the issue itself being obsolete or not. From the very start of the Nazarene movement, Yeshua himself rebuked two Asia Minor congregations for promoting the consumption of meat sacrificed to idols, which would then be *tamei* (Revelation 2:14, 20). I would even claim that nowhere in the apostolic texts are issues of relevance concerning consumable and non-consumable foods or of ceremonial fitness raised. Jews already knew these things as clearly defined in the Book of Leviticus. The only issues raised were concerning the levels of observance to these things concerning the new Gentile followers of Messiah. And what did both Yeshua and Paul say about it? That whereas these are legitimate Torah concerns to be observed, it should be done within the balanced perspectives of our obligation to love and fellowship, to help those in need, and of teaching the Torah. The Master also taught that these concerns did not require a spirit of self-righteous separatism, which was what was happening in the days when he walked the earth.

The whole idea of Torah wisdom rests on knowing how to apply Hashem's commandments with balance and the right spirit, especially when these commandments cross paths with each other. It is so easy to apply the outer letter of the Torah and forget its weightier matters of justice, compassion, and mercy. Yeshua reminded us of these very important principles. Using the exhortations of the former prophets he told the people of his days, "You pay your tithes of mint, dill and cumin; but you have neglected the weightier matters of the Torah—justice, mercy, trust. These are the things you should have attended to—without neglecting the others" (Matthew 23:23; Hoseah 6:6; Micah 6:8).

May we not be guilty of the same. May Abba give us the wisdom to apply his commands in his spirit, not forgetting that from the realms of sanctified glory, of his own volition, Mashiach came down. He put on the *Tamei* garment of humanity. Being *tahor,* he made himself *tamei* so he could bring us to the *tahor-ness* of the Father.

Acts 10:15   Nissan 24/ כד בניסן

Stop treating as unclean what God has made clean.

It seems that in the days of the Master, some in Israel had taken the considerations of ceremonial purity and contamination in Leviticus 11 to such an extreme that it rendered fellowship with common folks and non-Jews impossible. And in a way, separation from unbelievers may have indeed been the actual idea behind the commandment.

There is nothing wrong with giving due diligence to the commandments in the Torah; Yeshua himself taught extreme measures in order to avoid breaking them (Matthew 5:27–30). In all torah observance issues though, Yeshua was helping the leaders of Israel to understand that this due diligence has to be done with proper balance and perspective. In saying, "These are the things you should have attended to—without neglecting the others" (Matthew 23:23), Yeshua was trying to help people to adopt a more balanced attitude between ritual and relational commandments. Yeshua personally spoke to Peter about it in a vision telling him (my narration of the the text), "What God has *tahor-ed*, (considered ceremonially pure), do not *tamei* (consider ceremonially contaminated) (Acts 10:15). This allowed Peter to go to the house of the Roman centurion Cornelius, something observant Jews didn't usually do (Acts 10:28). By obeying the Master's vision, Peter initiated a revolutionary theological break with the Judaism of his day. He was throwing the newly born Nazarene movement into its universal mission of teaching Torah to the gentile world, a move that Paul followed in Syrian Antioch, later in Turkey, Greece, and finally, Rome.

Peter was the one chosen to challenge the stiff religious status quo of his day. As great as a disciple as he was, his weakness often surfaced. We saw him denying the Master the night of his arrest, and again in Antioch, to Paul's horror, withdrawing himself from fellowship with Gentiles (Matthew 26:75; Galatians 2:11–14). In both cases Peter yielded to peer-pressure and fear. He was afraid to stand up because he seemed to value the opinions of men.

It is easy to blame Peter, but what the Master was teaching here was of utmost importance. Whereas Yeshua retained the Torah ideas of holiness, of being *kadosh* קדוש, "set-apart" for Hashem, he was teaching it in an application that did not hamper the mission of being a light to our brothers, and to the world. The Master in effect was saying, "Do my will and trust me for your ceremonial sanctity; you can never attain it anyways" (Matthew 23:23).

Sad to say, I meet many today who, because of such concerns, separate themselves from even their relatives. I have seen people divorce on the same sort of imbalanced religious grounds. I think that from where he is, the Master sadly watches us wondering how is it that he was not afraid to put on the *tamei* (ceremonial contamination) of the world in order to reach us but we are too *holy* to do it in order to reach out to love others?

Even though Peter denied the Master in front of men (Matthew 10:33), the Master forgave Peter and reinstated him (John 21:15–18). Later Peter also repented from his self-righteous separatism in Antioch and died as a martyr while ministering to the believers in Rome, Jews and Gentiles. May we also, like Peter and Paul, learn from Yeshua's teachings and properly balance the commandments. A wise man may learn by his experiences, but a wiser man learns by the experiences of others!

1 Peter 1:15   **Nissan 25/ כה בניסן**

On the contrary . . . become holy yourselves in your entire way of life.

On the second Sabbath after Yeshua's second Passover with his disciples, Jerusalem Pharisees who came to check out this itinerant rabbi caught his followers not being particular about the ritual hand washing before eating (Luke 6:1, KJV/DHE). As they report the story, many English Bibles leave readers to understand that Yeshua declared all foods clean/edible, thus abrogating the Torah's dietary laws (Mark 7:19).

The aforementioned clause in the ESV is in parentheses. This was done to tell us that this particular clause is not part of the translated text, but an editorial addendum. This part of the text does not even exist in the KJV, which in general tries to keep a more literal translation of Greek sources. Before coming to these sorts of conclusions when reading the apostolic texts, we always need to remember that the instructions Hashem gave the children of Israel at Mt. Horeb are meant to be eternal and that according to his own words, Yeshua did not come to change them (Matthew 5:17–18).

Some of the mix-up may come from a poor choice of words in English translations. There are two forms of what English biblical texts of Levitical instructions call clean or unclean foods. 1) What meats are edible or non-edible defined today with the Hebrew words, *kasher* כשר or *taref* טרף. 2) What is ceremonially pure or contaminated defined by the Hebrew words *tahor* טהור and *tamei* טמא. The latter one concerns foods, walls, fabrics, and even skin afflictions. English texts usually use the expressions clean/unclean for both, which causes confusion.

In Judaism, one cannot come to the Temple or in the presence of the Almighty in a ceremonially contaminated state. As a fence commandment, some rabbis established that everybody should go though the ritual washing of hands before ingesting any food. This was not part of Torah commandments but rather an interpretative application of Leviticus 11. Rabbi Yeshua also took part in the conversation and gave it his own perspective, which reflected not only a better understanding of the laws of contamination, but also another side of the Talmudic teachings of the day. Rabbis always expected that the Messiah would one day come and settle their controversies and Yeshua did just that.

The editorial mention that Yeshua made all foods clean with an understanding of an abrogation of the laws of kasherut really is out of place. The concern of the discussion between Yeshua and the Pharisees was about the disciples eating grains, not meat, with unwashed hands. First of all, issues of edibility concern meats, not grains, so why would Yeshua have approached the issue of food being edible or not? Secondly, it seems that Yeshua's rebuke to those who questioned him was about disobeying Torah in favor of personal traditions (Mark 7:8), so why would he then teach that it was OK to break Torah's dietary laws even in concerns of ritual purity which are Torah based in Leviticus 11?

It is therefore crucial for one to know and understand the Levitical Laws, as well as the politics, the culture, and the linguistics present in the days of the Master in Israel in order to properly interpret the narratives left us by Matthew, Mark, Luke, and John.

The laws of *kasherut* and ceremonial fitness were not given to us for health nor for any other reason than as an identification of being holy/set-apart as the people of God (Leviticus 11:44). Even today, we can tell people's cultural background by their eating habits, thus the old adage is true: "you are what you eat!" May we learn to apply these rulings in the perspective of the Master just because *Daddy said so!*

Hebrews 9:28

So also the Messiah, having been offered once to bear the sins of many, will appear a second time, not to deal with sin, but to deliver those who are eagerly waiting for him.

Counting all the Hebrew words in the Torah, the half-way point is in the verse, "Then Moshe carefully investigated what had happened to the goat of the sin offering and discovered that it had been burned up" (Leviticus 10:16). To understand what happens in this passage we must go back to chapter 9 when the grand-priesthood inauguration begins.

Hashem, who is a *consuming fire* (Deuteronomy 4:24) had established a very serious protocol whereby Israel was to approach him. Moses gave very specific instructions about it. Nadab and Abihu, two of the sons of Aaron were careless in their application of the protocol and were utterly burned by the fire of God as they approached the Sanctuary in an unauthorized manner (Leviticus 10:1–3). Aaron was obviously devastated and in mourning but he and his other two sons were in the middle of the grand inauguration (Leviticus 9) so they couldn't stop for mourning; Aaron therefore held his peace (Leviticus 10:3).

Some may argue that God's punishment of Nadab and Abihu was out of proportion and could be qualified as the tantrums of a capricious deity, but instead of reviewing God's actions, maybe we should review our own sense of what is important and what is not. Intersection with God is not to be taken lightly. There may also be more to the event than meets the eye!

Part of the priesthood's inauguration was that Aaron and his sons were to eat sections of the goat offered as an *olah* עולה, burnt offering inside the Tabernacle precinct. Moses couldn't find that goat so he searched diligently for it until he discovered that it had been fully consumed. The patriarch then got angry and asked for an explanation to which Aaron answered,

> Even though they offered their sin offering and burnt offering today, things like these have happened to me! If I had eaten the sin offering today, would it have pleased ADONAI? (Leviticus 10:19)

What happens here is that Aaron reminds Moses that it was unpleasing to God for a priest to do office while in sadness or mourning (Deuteronomy 26:14; 16:11), a theme even found later among Semitic kings (Nehemiah 2:1–2). So because he was uncontrollably saddened at the death of his two sons, Aaron felt he could not do proper justice to that part of the service, which he then forewent. Moses was pleased with the explanation (Leviticus 10:20).

What is to be noticed here is that this center verse of the Torah tells us to "search diligently" for the goat of the sin offering which is an early representation of Yeshua's covering. Therefore the central goal of studying Torah is the search for Messiah's covering.

The Talmud explains that the death of Aaron's sons is not really justifiable, so that it can only be counted as the *death of the righteous, which creates atonement for others*, a very prevalent theme in Biblical text. Whether we agree with the Talmud's interpretation or not, since Yeshua is our High-Priest as well as our covering (Hebrews 9:25), this is an idea that very much fits the theme of the priestly inauguration.

May we also spend our lives seeking diligently to approach God through the atonement of Yeshua.

Luke 2:22

When the time came for their purification according to the Torah of Moshe,
they took him up to Yerushalayim to present him to ADONAI.

In the twelfth chapter of the Book of Leviticus we are told,

> Tell the people of Isra'el: 'If a woman conceives and gives birth to a boy, she will be unclean for seven days with the same uncleanness as in niddah, when she is having her menstrual period. On the eighth day, the baby's foreskin is to be circumcised. She is to wait an additional thirty-three days to be purified from her blood; she is not to touch any holy thing or come into the sanctuary until the time of her purification is over. (Leviticus 12:2–4)

Luke ties this verse to the birth of Messiah when he says, "When the time came for their purification according to the Torah of Moshe, they took him up to Yerushalayim to present him to ADONAI" (Luke 2:22).

Miriam therefore came to make an offering at the end of the days of her purification as was prescribed by Moses and that is when she meets Simeon (Luke 2:25). Luke actually makes sure to tell us how Miriam and Joseph did everything according to the Levitical process.

It is important here to note that even though most English Biblical texts relate to Miriam's post-natal state as *unclean* and therefore having to present an offering at the Temple; her condition has nothing to do with moral deficiency or spiritual unworthiness. A woman giving birth actually performs one of the highest of Hashem's commandments. She fulfills what she was created for. What the Torah refers to as the ritual *unclean* state is solely the reality of being human and therefore impure before. Ceremonial contamination is solely Temple related.

We are told in the Gospel of Luke that,

> When the time came for their purification according to the Torah of Moshe, they took him up to Yerushalayim to present him to ADONAI (as it is written in the Torah of ADONAI, "Every firstborn male is to be consecrated to ADONAI") and also to offer a sacrifice of a pair of doves or two young pigeons, as required by the Torah of ADONAI." (Luke 2:22–24)

We see in Luke's rendering of the story that Miriam and Joseph brought "a young pigeon or dove" and that is because they could not afford a lamb (Leviticus 12:6–8).

Little did young Miriam know, oh how little did she know, that whereas she could not afford to bring Lamb to the Temple for her purification, she actually brought with her the ultimate Lamb, he who would end up purifying not only her, but the whole world with her!

My Personal Thoughts

_____
_____
_____
_____

Mark 1:40   **Nissan 28/ כח בניסן**

A man afflicted with tzara`at came to Yeshua and begged him on his knees,
"If you are willing, you can make me clean."

The Torah spends a considerable amount of time detailing a condition called *leprosy*. It tells us about people's *leprosy*, but also about leprosy in beards, fabrics, and houses (Leviticus 13:18–59). Leprosy in the Bible seems to relate not only to the loathsome disease by that name, but also to other sorts of corruption and decay. The term seems to be used to refer to the advance of death and corruption in matter (Leviticus 13:4–8).

On a metaphorical level, Jewish sages referred to leprosy as the disease the snake inherited as part of the curse. Ritual contamination and mortality is part of the curse brought on by man because of sin, so the metaphor is certainly befitting.

Leprosy is also associated with one of the most important sins mentioned in the Tenach, the one called *lashon harah* לשון הרע which literally means the *evil tongue*. The term refers to gossip and slander because after slandering Moses, her brother and divinely appointed leader of Israel, Miriam was afflicted by this leprosy (Numbers 12). Leprosy and the state of ritual contamination are irrelevant today because they technically only relate to the Temple in Jerusalem, which does not exist at this present time.

At the time when religiosity accorded undue emphasis to ritual purity, Yeshua came to put it back in its proper perspective. In the days of the Master, priests and Levites were so obsessed with ritual purity that they would ignore the commandments about mercy and helping those in need for fear of contamination. We can see this in the parable of the Good Samaritan (Luke 10:33). Yeshua on the other hand was not afraid of being defiled by leprosy. On some occasions he voluntarily touched a leper to heal him (Matthew 8:2–3). He even entered the house of Simon the Leper to eat with him, and this is where he met Mary Magdalene (Matthew 26:6–7).

The Talmud tells of one called, *The Leper Messiah*. It presents a supposed discourse between the great Rabbi Joshua ben Levi and the prophet Elijah. The rabbi asks, "When will the Messiah come and by what sign may I recognize him?" Elijah tells the rabbi to go to the gate of the city where he will find the Messiah sitting among the poor lepers. The Messiah, says the prophet, sits bandaging his leprous sores one at a time, unlike the rest of the sufferers, who bandage them all at once. Why? Because he might be needed at any time and would not want to be delayed (Sanhedrin 98a). While this may seem to be a far-fetched story, it is not the only Jewish text that associates Messiah with leprosy. One of the names of the coming Messiah in Chassidic teachings is, *The Leper Scholar*.

Unlike the exclusive religious leaders of his days who stayed away, Yeshua came to us and voluntarily put on the decaying condition of mortality. He even contaminated himself by touching our *leprosy*. While we're still in our mortal decaying condition, he entered our house to fellowship with us. But the story doesn't end here; the most wonderful part of it is that as he goes back to his Father and our God, he takes us with him to partake of his pure resurrected body. What a wonderful Messiah we have. Amen, and Amen. May it be soon, even in our days!

My Personal Thoughts

James 4:6　　　　　　　　　　　　Nissan 29/ כט בניסן

God opposes the arrogant, but to the humble he gives grace.

At a time when Elishah was prophet in Israel, Naaman, a proud general of the Assyrian Empire, was afflicted with leprosy. A young Israelite girl in the service of his wife told him about the prophet in Israel who could heal him. This must have been hard to hear for this proud general because the Assyrians looked down at Israel and their seemingly backward religion. If that was not enough, Naaman also had to ask permission from his enemy, the king of Israel, before entering the Land in order to approaching Elishah.

Naaman desperately sought healing so he decided to give it a try. He took with him monies and rewards and set himself to visit the prophet in Israel. To the general's great humiliation, Elisha did not even come and see him but sent Gehazi his servant to talk to him. Here is the transcript of the story,

> Elisha sent a messenger to him, who said, "Go, and bathe in the Yarden seven times. Your skin will become as it was, and you will be clean." But Na`aman became angry and left, saying, "Here now! I thought for certain that he would come out personally, that he would stand, call on the name of ADONAI his God and wave his hand over the diseased place and thus heal the person with tzara`at. Aren't Amanah and Parpar, the rivers of Dammesek, better than all the water in Isra'el? Why can't I bathe in them and be clean?" (2 Kings 5:10–12)

Somehow it seems that Naaman's leprosy was related to his pride. What leprosy does to the flesh, pride certainly does to virtue. The story continues,

> Aren't Amanah and Parpar, the rivers of Dammesek, better than all the water in Isra'el? Why can't I bathe in them and be clean?" So he turned and went off in a rage. But his servants approached him and said, "My father! If the prophet had asked you to do something really difficult, wouldn't you have done it? So, doesn't it make even more sense to do what he says, when it's only, 'Bathe, and be clean'?" So he went down and immersed himself seven times in the Yarden, as the man of God had said to do; and his skin was restored and became like the skin of a child; and he became clean. (2 Kings 5:12–14)

What a miracle! But the greatest miracle of all is that Naaman returned to the man of God, he and all his company, and he came and stood before him. And he said, "Well, I've learned that there is no God in all the earth except in Isra'el" (2 Kings 5:15).

Hashem always seems to get good *mileage* out of things. In this case, Hashem healed the general of his sickness, he addressed the pride issue that created the disease, and he got Naaman to recognize the God of Israel. That, my friend, is complete healing!

My Personal Thoughts

_____

_____

_____

_____

Ephesians 2:12–13

You were estranged from the national life of Isra'el.
You were foreigners to the covenants embodying God's promise.
You were in this world without hope and without God.
But now, you who were once far off have been brought near
through the shedding of the Messiah's blood.

We are in the ninth century BCE Joram the son of Ahab rules in a Samaria besieged by Ben-Hadad, the Aramean king. This is the same Ben-Hadad who sent Naaman to Israel to be healed of leprosy (2 Kings 5). During a siege, people living in villages and encampments around the city took refuge within the walls, that is, except for lepers. As per the Torah, lepers had to live in special quarters outside the city (Leviticus 13:46). Even in the case of a siege, they were not allowed inside. Once all the people were in, all the invading armies had to do was to cut off food and water supplies. Famine and starvation followed and the city fell like ripened fruit.

Samaria was under siege and the famine devastated the city (2 Kings 7). Prices skyrocketed and, as was prophesied, people cannibalized their young trying to survive (Deuteronomy 28:53). Outside the gate were four lepers caught between a rock and a hard place—on one side a city that rejected them, on the other side the Syrian armies. Some people have suggested that among those four lepers was Gehazi, Elishah's servant who contracted leprosy by lusting after Naaman's rewards (2 Kings 5:27) and his four sons.

One day these lepers said to themselves,

> Now there were four men with tzara`at at the entrance to the city gate, and they said to each other, "Why should we sit here till we die? If we say, 'We'll enter the city, then the city has been struck by the famine, so we'll die there. And if we sit still here, we'll also die. So let's go and surrender to the army of Aram; if they spare our lives, we will live; and if they kill us, we'll only die." They got up during the twilight to go to the camp of Aram. But when they reached the outskirts of the camp of Aram, they saw no one! . . . When these men with tzara`at reached the outskirts of the camp, they entered one of the tents, ate and drank; then took some silver, gold and clothing; and went and hid it. Next they returned and entered another tent, took stuff from there, and went and hid it. But finally they said to each other, "What we are doing is wrong. At a time of good news like this, we shouldn't keep it to ourselves. If we wait even till morning, we will earn only punishment; so come on, let's go and tell the king's household." (2 Kings 7:3–9)

Lepers are the disfranchised of society and this story reminds us of the Master's special concern for lepers. Crossing Samaria on his way to Jerusalem, ten lepers cried out to the Master saying, "Yeshua, Adon, have mercy on us."

We are all lepers in the sight of God and as the four lepers in our story, we have cried to the Son of David for help and found the good news of God's victory over the enemy of our soul. We are now responsible to share it with all, even with those who showed no mercy to us.

My Personal Thoughts

IYAR   אייר

By the road
In the house
By the sea
In the field
Have you heard the Resurrected One?
He teaches of the Kingdom!

Mark 1:41

> *Moved with pity, Yeshua reached out his hand,*
> *touched him and said to him, "I am willing! Be cleansed!"*

Rabbi Yeshua touched the leper, declared him healed and therefore cleansed, then he told him to go through the purification process as instructed by Moses (Mark 1:41–44). Doing so, Yeshua purposely made himself ritually unclean and thus fulfilled the Messianic hope, "ADONAI laid on him the guilt of all of us" (Isaiah 53:6).

To declare a healed leper ritually pure is very mystical and the Torah does not give us any explanation to help us understand it. We are therefore left to define it by association. The ritual required that a bird should be killed over a clay vessel of water, thus creating a blood and water mixture. Another live bird was to be bound with hyssop and a scarlet yarn to a cedar wood board. The entire package was then dipped into the clay vessel of blood and water. The priest sprinkled the leper seven times with the blood and water mixture, then released the live bird—which did not need any more encouragement—so it could quickly flee the scene.

It was not finished. The priest then had to shave the healed/cleansed leper from head to toe and anoint him with the same markings as those of a priest. It is only after our now shaved and anointed man went to offer the required offering at the Temple that he was restored to full fellowship in the community of Israel (Leviticus 14).

Looking at this whole ritual, it is hardly possible to miss the messianic symbolism. The live bird tied to a piece of cedar wood with a tie of red yarn, then dipped in a vessel of blood and water from a dead bird brings to mind our dying Messiah with blood and water flowing from his side. The release of the live bird illustrates Yeshua's resurrection and ascension to the Father. This event, in connection with a totally shaved man ready to immerse in the renewing waters of the Mikveh, tells us of the death and rebirth of a man who will, like a priest, dedicate himself to Hashem as a sign of thankfulness.

Biblical leprosy represented death, corruption, and sin. It is a good illustration of how we are to Hashem in our unredeemed state. Yeshua, as he touched the lepers, took our sins and iniquity upon himself. The Messiah became a leper as the Talmud points out. He then subjected himself to stripes and his bloody body was tied to a wood from where he died shedding blood and water to finally rise and ascend to the heavens where he sits, interceding for us at the right hand of the Father (Luke 24:26).

My Personal Thoughts

_____

_____

_____

_____

_____

_____

_____

Romans 1:20   ב באייר /Iyar 2 ב באייר

For ever since the creation of the universe his invisible qualities—both his eternal power and his divine nature—have been clearly seen, because they can be understood from what he has made. Therefore, they have no excuse.

In Leviticus 15 we are instructed about the issues surrounding the women's cycle. We are told that she is to terminate her monthly cycle with a water immersion (Leviticus 15:19–24). These are commonly referred to as the laws of *Niddah* נדה. When read within the context of Western mentality, these passages often invoke feelings of misogynist archaism. We must remind ourselves that when our culture seems to clash with that of the Torah, we are the ones who need to change our position and look for some deeper meaning there.

Let's look now beyond the unpleasant physical details, and find spiritual reality in these words that Hashem obviously decided should be part of our religious instruction. We know that the Levitical festivals, which speak of redemption, are established in our calendar according to the movements of the moon. We also know that the movement of the moon affects water on earth and even creates the tides of the sea. Because a woman's body contains more water than that of man's (one pint), women are uniquely tuned to the moon. In places where people still practice natural childbirth, it is a common practice for hospitals to have more nurses on duty during full moon periods because they expect more deliveries.

The monthly waxing and waning of the moon leads us through the yearly redemptive festivals: first the spring festivals from Pesach to Shavuot, then the fall ones from Rosh Hashana to Sukkhot. Each month, the moon starts a new cycle. It is born and waxes each night until it comes to its full glory. The moon then wanes down and vanishes a little more every night until it disappears, to be reborn once more. The Hebrew term for the 'birthing" of the moon is *lidah* לידה, *to birth, to conceive*. This is very reminiscent of the cycle of a women's body. Each month a woman prepares to give life. This preparation comes to fullness after two weeks and then starts dying little by little until it finally sheds the lining of the uterus, only to start the same process a few days later.

All in all, in giving us the laws of *Niddah*, the Torah elevates the women's cycle from a mundane reality to the understandings of deep spiritual truths concerning life, death, and rebirth. Within the vastness of the movements of astral bodies to the narrow confines of the workings of the human body, Hashem daily reveals to us his own plan of redemption for mankind. He shows us how his mercies are new every morning, every month, and every year.

As Paul did say,

> Because what is known about God is plain to them, since God has made it plain to them. For ever since the creation of the universe his invisible qualities—both his eternal power and his divine nature—have been clearly seen, because they can be understood from what he has made. Therefore, they have no excuse. (Romans 1:19–20)

May we glorify him in all things!

My Personal Thoughts

Matthew 21:42   Iyar 3/ ג באייר

The very rock which the builders rejected has become the cornerstone!

A leper is an outcast. He is despised and rejected of men. He is looked upon as cursed and afflicted of God. He is vulnerable, dependent, and meek. But wait; aren't these the very words Hashem inspired the prophet Isaiah to describe the Messiah, our Master Yeshua (Isaiah 53)?

Indeed, even the ancient sages of Israel recognized the coming Messiah in the attributes. Within certain Chassidic academic circles he was even called The *Leper of the House of Study* (b. Sanhedrin 98b). While referring to the disease by that name, in Hebrew, the idea of being a *leper* can be an idiom for being rejected or ostracized. *The Leper of the House of Study* is a Hebrew idiom to speak of the Torah student who is rejected by the sages and by others in the religious and academic community.

The sages did not suggest that the Messiah would actually be a leper; the term is merely idiomatic and the text is to be taken figuratively. As we have discussed before, the term *leprosy* in the Torah is not necessarily related to the biological disease known today by that name, but rather relates to the general condition of man born under sin. Whereas that condition may be normal for us, it was not normal for Yeshua. He, of his own volition, decided to take that condition upon him in order to bring us back to the Father. He is like Father Damian, who after spending most of his life caring for the sick in a leper colony finally died of the disease himself. Our Master though conquered the corrupt, sinful condition of humanity and then resurrected. If we take on his identity, we also resurrect.

Today the fifty-third chapter of Isaiah is not recognized by mainstream Judaism as being about Messiah, but it was by ancient classic Judaism. Even the disciple Matthew knew it (Matthew 8:17). Again, I cannot help but be amazed at these ancient Jewish messianic concepts. In present-day Judaism, the Suffering Servant of the prophet Isaiah is interpreted as Israel, not as a nation but as a people. Again, the text works well as a metaphor. Here is how it works. Israel as a nation was born by God's will in the Middle East; existed with a mission to show surrounding countries about the one God who created the heavens and the earth; was rejected, killed, and died to finally resurrect two millennia later. During this whole time the nation of Israel was in exile among the nations, a reflection of what has been the Jewish Messiah's condition for the last 2,000 years. Today, Israel has returned to its land and so has Messiah in a constellation of Israeli Messianic congregations growing stronger by leaps and bounds.

While the rest of the world is going down because of its sin and disobedience, things can only get brighter now for obedient believers and followers of the *leper* Jewish Messiah. He returns to his rightful throne in Jerusalem, the eternal capital of Israel and of the people of God's choosing. His word will then flow from Jerusalem, the Jewish capital, to teach us all how to live in a world free from disease, war, and mankind's moral corruption. In that day the prophet says, many nations shall come, and say: "Come, let's go up to the mountain of ADONAI, to the house of the God of Ya`akov! He will teach us about his ways, and we will walk in his paths. For out of Tziyon will go forth Torah, the word of ADONAI from Yerushalayim" (Micah 4:2).

My Personal Thoughts

_____

_____

Matthew 19:16–19   Iyar 4/ ד באייר

*A man approached Yeshua and said, "Rabbi, what good thing should I do in order to have
eternal life?" He said to him, "Why are you asking me about good? There is One who is good!
But if you want to obtain eternal life, observe the mitzvot." The man asked him, "Which ones?"
and Yeshua said, "Don't murder, don't commit adultery, don't steal, don't give false testimony
honor father and mother and love your neighbor as yourself."*

This week we are studying about the observances that mark what is commonly called *Yom
HaKippurim* יום הכיפורים, the Day of Atonements. These come at the heel of the mishap with
Nadab and Abihu (Leviticus 10). After the premature death of the two young men, people now
realize the serious nature of what they were getting involved in. They realized that coming close to
God required specific precautionary measures. This is what the Book of Leviticus is mainly about:
the protocol whereby we come in the presence of Hashem.

In this text of Leviticus, Hashem tells the children of Israel that, "For on this day, atonement will be
made for you to purify you; you will be clean before ADONAI from all your sins" (Leviticus 16:30).
Did it really work? If it did, why was Yeshua still needed? Fifteen hundred years later, the writer of
the apostolic letter to the Messianic Jews of Israel, a man well acquainted with the Levitical
process, reminded his Jewish readers, "For it is impossible that the blood of bulls and goats
should take away sins" (Hebrews 10:4). Did he contradict the claims of the Levitical offering
process?

We ask these questions when we misunderstand the text because we're reading it with an already
established theology. Most people who read the apostolic letters read them with 'Old vs. New
Testament,' and 'Law vs. Grace' theological lenses, where apostolic writings negate the Torah.
Also, our present parameters of understanding these writings are very far removed from their
original texts, culture, and ideas, which makes it very difficult.

A clearer reading of these texts though reveals something different. Leviticus 16 for example
speaks of a national ritual cleansing by the priest approaching the Ark on the behalf of all the
people. This purification process has to be repeated year after year. On the other hand, the text
we read in the apostolic letter to the Messianic Jews speaks of national spiritual eternal
redemption done once and for all. The sages of Judaism understood that only repentance brought
expiation for sin, not offerings. They said, "Neither sin offering, not guilt offering nor the Day of
Atonement can bring expiation without repentance" (Tosefta Yoma 5.9). Repentance means the
return of the heart towards Hashem in the form of obedience to Torah, and it was the main
message brought by John the Immerser and Yeshua (Matthew 3:2; 4:17). We must also
remember that when the Levitical Festivals were given, which includes Yom HaKippurim
(Leviticus 23) they were given to the children of Israel as a perpetual command (Leviticus 23:31).

Today we have a Temple-less reality so we are only able to fulfill certain aspects of these
commandments. One day the Temple is to be rebuilt and inaugurated by Messiah. May we on
that day be as a bride who has prepared herself for the coming of her betrothed; one who is
physically and spiritually ready to enter his kingdom, familiar with his biddings and the ways of his
kingdom. May we continue studying the Levitical laws of offerings and the Levitical Festivals for
they teach us about the functions and roles of Messiah in our life.

My Personal Thoughts

Matthew 5:19

So whoever disobeys the least of these mitzvot and teaches
others to do so will be called the least in the Kingdom of Heaven.
But whoever obeys them and so teaches will be called great in the Kingdom of Heaven.

People invariably feel uncomfortable when I suggest to them that we owe some due diligence to Hashem's commandments. In order to soften the blow, they usually quickly protect themselves with the statement, "Oh yes, but he forgives me," or "We are not under the Law." These people usually understand very little about the Bible but they know how to use that statement like a theological security blanket. They allow themselves to be proud, to lie, to be selfish with their time or finances, while forgetting that these are the real offenses that are an abomination to Hashem (Proverbs 6:16–19),

There is a theology out there claiming that 2,000 years ago Yeshua came and abolished the need to obey the commandments of the Torah. Think about what this means. This means that 2,000 years ago, Yeshua came and abolished the moral code that helps us discern right from wrong, good from bad, holy from profane, and sanctified from common. That same theology also claims that the Torah has become obsolete to whoever recognizes Yeshua as his Messiah because he is the Torah written in their hearts. If it were all true, the facts on the ground show me a different reality, as those who claim to have Hashem's Torah written in their heart certainly don't act like it. If it were, our Yeshua believing Western world should be a paradise certainly not facing the sort of social issues it presently faces. Actually, the people who adhere to that theology are doubly guilty for their ungodly actions because they live in opposition to the Torah written in their conscience.

This notion that the Torah is obsolete not only takes away the understanding of right and wrong, but also the fear of God, which is the beginning of wisdom. It is therefore utter foolishness and *lawlessness*, which has the exact etymological root of the word *iniquity*. If 2,000 years ago, as people claim, Yeshua abolished the need to live by the Torah commandments, what need is there then today of a Savior to cover our sins?

My friend, the role of Messiah is and has always been to teach us the proper application of obedience to Torah. He came teaching, "Turn from your sins to God, for the Kingdom of Heaven is near" (Matthew 4:17), which means, "turn your ways towards God for the days of his kingdom are near; start living by his Torah and by his instruction."

In Yeshua, nothing of the sort becomes obsolete, not even the sentence of death is written against us because of our sins. What happens is that he takes it all upon himself. We therefore owe him our lives. From the Yom Kippur on Mt. Horeb when Moses brought down the Torah for the second time to today, when he is our atonement, our covering.

PRAYER:

Abba Father: may we understand that your Kingdom is ruled by the commandments that you have outlined in your word. May we realize that we are responsible to your Torah; that repentance means to turn back and start living by your teachings and principles. Forgive us for following erroneous teachings that negate the importance of obedience while we forget the teachings of the Messiah you sent to tell us that, "So whoever disobeys the least of these mitzvot and teaches others to do so will be called the least in the Kingdom of Heaven" (Matthew 5:19). Amen.

John 17:17   ו באייר /Iyar 6

Your word [Torah] is truth.

Biblical texts on offerings or about the Yom HaKippurim rituals in Leviticus 16 may today seem irrelevant without the existence of the Temple. They may feel to us like texts pertaining to a distant people of the past. As we follow this train of thought, we must remember the words of King David, "The Torah of God is perfect, pure and eternal" (Psalm 19). If these things are part of the divine oracle, they certainly have perpetual pertinence.

There are some who teach that Yeshua initiated a new Temple-less era. This is difficult to swallow when apostolic texts, as well as historical books pertaining to first-century life in Israel, tell us that for forty years after the resurrection of the Master, the Jewish disciples of Messiah continued Temple and synagogue attendance as a sect of Judaism. They continued in the Passover traditions, as well as in those pertaining to the atonement rituals of Yom Kippur. If they found relevancy in doing so, shouldn't we? Is there then something that we are missing—something we should learn from these long descriptions in Leviticus? Stepping aside a little from the realm of the ritual and entering that of the social, much indeed should be learned from Temple and offering protocols.

Here are some examples. The Torah acknowledges that appointed judges can sometimes err in judgment and therefore cause the people to sin. In such a case, a public admission of error is required through an offering (Leviticus 4:3). An offering is also required in the case that the whole congregation sins unintentionally (Leviticus 4:13). I am thinking right now of the court that wrongfully condemned our Master. There is a provision of reformation for both the priest and the congregation. In the Torah we also learn that Hashem understands our financial pressures and makes provisions for cheaper offerings to be made (Leviticus 5:1–11). Also, though Hashem understands involuntary mistakes, they still require acknowledgment and retribution. In our system, the punishment for a thief is incarceration. The Torah is concerned with retribution and as such a thief is required to restore that which he had gotten deceitfully, plus a fifth to the person he stole it from. He is also supposed to make amends with God for breaking his commands.

The offering process is quite interesting. The person comes to the altar and with his hand on the forehead of the animal to be offered confesses his sins to Hashem—not to the priest. Doing so, he in fact transfers his sinful identity on the poor animal. Then, except in the case of a bird offering, the one giving the offering is the one who has to kill the animal, hear it die, get splattered with its fluids, and feel its life's warm blood run through his hands. Along with having to pay for a good quality animal, one of the best of the flock, this becomes to him a very good illustration of the atrociousness of disobedience and sin, which should provoke in him a healthy fear of Hashem.

This makes me wonder about many who claim a theology that implies that they are no longer sinners. They say that under the atonement of Yeshua, their sinful condition has been voided and that therefore they do not need to observe the Torah, which was given because of sin. Unfortunately, through a mistake or the honesty of friends and relatives, reality sets in, and they realize that their sinful condition and habits are still with them. They realize at that moment that they need safeguards to keep themselves in check. The same principle seems to apply for individuals and for society. Eventually, they realize that in order to curb the effects of sin, they need rules as well as a social structure, moral guidance, and a penal system to act as their safeguards. This leaves them to institute their own sense of law and righteousness. The question is: Why didn't they keep God's system in the first place?

1 Peter 2:9   Iyar 7/ ז באייר

But you are a chosen people, the King's cohanim, a holy nation,
a people for God to possess! Why? In order for you to declare
the praises of the One who called you out of darkness into his wonderful light.

Though all Israel is liable to the whole Torah, not all of the Torah is incumbent upon each individual of Israel. Some rulings are solely incumbent on high priests, others on priests, some on Levites, some on Nazirites, or some on firstborns. Some commandments solely concern men, others women or children, and some also pertain to the stranger in the Land.

The children of Moses' brother Aaron are called Levites. They are called so because they are the descendants of the tribe of Levi, the son of Jacob. When Hashem divided the tribes of the new born Jewish nation into the land of Canaan, he decreed that the Levites should have no land inheritance in Canaan, but that he was their inheritance (Leviticus 18:20–24). In this manner the tribe of Levi obtained the spiritual oversight and responsibility of Israel. Not all Levites automatically became priests, but all priests were to be Levites.

Studying the lifestyle incumbent upon the Levite priests, it is easy to see that they were to live in a standard of purity and dedication higher than that of the rest of Israel. This standard was surpassed only by that of the high priest himself.

Some of the particularities of the Levite priest were that he could not own land nor busy himself with worldly affairs. His primary job was that of a Torah teacher to the people. Wealthy folks often had their own Levite living among them teaching them and their children. Most of the time though, the Levite taught in a village and people supported him with gifts and/or offerings in exchange for his services. He was the travelling, living word of Torah to the people.

In his definition of the higher calling of discipleship, the Master drew from the Levitical priestly standards. He told the twelve with him that their dedication to him was to be greater than that to their own families (Matthew 10:37), that they did not belong to the world—on the contrary, that they were picked out of the world (John 15:19), and that they were to shun material pursuits (Luke 12:16–35; Matthew 8:19–20). The Master encouraged his disciples to spend their lives in the study and teaching of the Torah and in prayer (Matthew 28:19–20). Yeshua did not ask for all who followed him to do that, but he left it there as an option. It seems that Peter understood the connection between a disciple of Yeshua and the Levitical priesthood; he referred to the people of the Roman congregation as a "royal priesthood" (1 Peter 2:9).

Many of us want to define ourselves as disciples of the Master. May we realize that this is not a title to be taken lightly. It is incumbent on whoever takes it to live like the Master did and obey his words. A higher standard of purity is required of us. If we don't apply ourselves to it, it would be better not to call ourselves disciples at all, lest we be judged more severely (James 3:1).

My Personal Thoughts

_____

_____

_____

_____

_____

1 Peter 1:14   **Iyar 8/ ח באייר**

As people who obey God, do not let yourselves be shaped by the evil
desires you used to have when you were still ignorant.

One of the laws of holiness, of the laws that set us apart from the world is, "Every one of you is to revere his father and mother" (Leviticus 19:3). Reverence towards our parents sets us aside from the world so we should be seen honoring and revering our parents. This was the first commandment given with a conditional promise, so that you may live long in the land which ADONAI your God is giving you (Exodus 20:12). There are two commandments with a longevity conditional clause, and they are both related to parenthood (Deuteronomy 22:7–8). Yes, to honor and reverence our parents is an integral law of the Kingdom of God; it will also be the rule of law in the world to come under the iron rule of Messiah when he reigns on earth.

It is easy to direct such a commandment towards our Western generation of teenagers. The society we have created around them seems to teach them very little respect for their parents. Could it be though that we need to direct this command towards ourselves? How much honor and reverence do we have for our parents? To *honor* our parents in the terms of the Torah means to support them. Exodus 20:12 basically says, (my suggested interpretation) "you shall support your parents in their old age, not send them to a government institution to be taken care of by strangers whose sole interest is to get paid for the job." If caring for them and helping to feed and assist them cramps our style, we must remember that they allowed their style to be cramped in order to care for us in the same manner that they now need us. We must also remember that one day we shall be in a similar situation.

Revering parents speaks of respect. It is understandable that some of us may have had abusive parents who seem unworthy of respect or even of the title but these are different situations that are outside of this commandment. Whereas our parents may not be respectable, our children should not hear negative feelings towards them out of our mouths. If they do, these same words will most certainly come back to us in their mouths because we are not perfect parents either. Forgiveness is not an option; it's a commandment from the Master who himself followed Hashem's commands to forgive by forgiving the abuse of his persecutors (Luke 19:18; Mark 11:25–26; Luke 23:24). Sad to say, in too many homes children hear their parents speak negatively, disparagingly, disrespectfully, or even mockingly about their older parents.

We often think of teaching as speaking, and of learning as listening, and as a result many of us try to teach others by telling them how to live. This was not the way of the Master. Like the rabbis of the day, the Master taught by exemplifying the Torah, by living it and encouraging his disciples to follow his example. Paul was cradled in the same pedagogy and taught it (1 Corinthians 11:1). Teaching is by doing, and learning is by emulating.

The way we react towards our parents is closely tied to the way we react to God. If we know how to trust our wiser parents, we will know how to trust the wiser leadership of the Master.

My Personal Thoughts

_____

_____

_____

_____

Matthew 7:12

Always treat others as you would like them to treat you;
that sums up the teaching of the Torah and the Prophets.

Leviticus 19:17 tells us, "Rebuke your neighbor frankly" (KJV). To rebuke our neighbor is actually a commandment. If we don't do it, we "carry sin." I would dare say that this commandment has no problem being observed. There is certainly no shortage of people readily willing to rebuke another. Our personal inferiority complex and sick craving for recognition constantly pushes us to want to be found as the one bringing everybody else on the right path. Let's look a little deeper at this commandment.

Whereas we do owe the truth to people around us (Ezekiel 3:17–19), I don't think this commandment applies to people who faithfully follow their understanding, however erroneous, of obedience to God. This commandment applies more to those who, knowing the truth, deliberately and willfully disobey it. Yeshua gave a good example on how to apply this commandment. He did not use it with the Sadducees and the Samaritans who were taught to reject pharisaic understanding of the Torah, as much as with the Pharisees themselves who were more enlightened. Yeshua himself was a Pharisee and he knew that they knew better. Another point to remind ourselves is that the Torah also forbids shaming others publicly. Our Master Yeshua reminds us of this. He even equates it with murder (Matthew 5:21–22).

Rashi, the medieval Jewish sage, had a particular take on the Torah command to rebuke others. In Hebrew the verse says, ‫הוכח תוכיח‬ which could roughly be translated as: 'rebuke yourself, rebuke others.' Rashi taught was that you must take a good look at yourself before you go on rebuking others as this will give you the dynamics of compassion that will help your brother to listen to you. Yeshua taught the same understanding of the commandment. He said, "First, take the log out of your own eye; then you will see clearly, so that you can remove the splinter from your brother's eye!" (Matthew 7:5). Judges from the Sanhedrin believed that they were unfit to judge a case if they could not find within themselves the sin of the accused. They felt unfit because in such a case they would not be equipped with the compassion necessary to judge the case in a godly manner.

Moses then ends the command to rebuke others with, "Love your neighbor as yourself" (Leviticus 19:18), a command which Yeshua commented on saying that it was the second most important in the whole Torah (Matthew 22:36–40). Also, another Jewish sage, Rabbi Akiva who lived after Yeshua, called the command to love others as ourselves "the fundamental rule of Torah" and paraphrased it in: "What is hateful to you, do not do to others" (Shabbos 31 a). Did he learn these words from our Master?

My Personal Thoughts

_____

_____

_____

_____

_____

_____

James 2:5   Iyar 10/ י באייר

*Listen, my dear brothers, hasn't God chosen the poor of the world to be rich in faith
and to receive the Kingdom which he promised to those who love him?*

Day after day newscasters from all sides of the political spectrum inform us of more signs of economic doom. Each side blames the other for the fate of their country's ill economy as they present what they consider is the best scenario to lead their country to a healthy financial recovery. Of course, political ethics of countries on the other side of the world are also to be blamed for these economic woes. It is always so easy to blame failure and bankruptcy on others. It sadly happens in domestic matters where in marriages one spouse blames the other for the family's bankruptcy, be it moral, social, marital, or financial.

Whereas the world's financial woes are complex, a thorough reading through the financial ethics of the Bible should show us where the crux of the problem is. Most Jewish and Christian religious organizations content themselves with a minimum ten percent tithe and call it good. Let us now examine the system taught us in the Torah. After thoroughly studying the work ethics, workers comps, and tithing system in the Torah, we can safely conclude that if thoroughly applied, between jubilee observances and tithing in every way he is required and suggested to, a man would never be opulently rich, wealth would be shared more equally, and the poor would be cared for and rehabilitated.

It is not what we give that the Father looks at, but what we've got left after we are finished giving. A Jewish sage even concluded that the tithing system was a protection against the moral corruption that comes through the hoarding of unnecessary wealth. Excess is best invested when wisely shared.

From this we can easily conclude that the biblical financial system is not based on capitalism but on sharing. The verses that suggest prosperity as a reward for obedience really speak of prosperity according to the currency of the Kingdom of God, which is virtue, not cash. The Bible does encourage the owning of private property (Micah 4:4), preparation for the future (Genesis 41), the wise handling of money (Luke 16:1–11), but it discourages the unnecessary selfish hoarding of wealth (Luke 12:15–21). It is to test our hearts that the great Father has allowed that some would be rich and able and others would be poor and insufficient (Proverbs 22:2).

"For you know how generous our Lord Yeshua the Messiah was—for your sakes he impoverished himself, even though he was rich, so that he might make you rich by means of his poverty." (2 Corinthians 8:9). This statement speaks of spiritual wealth and poverty, but if we are to pattern our lives according to spiritual truths, it is a good model of a proper use of physical wealth. The early believers of Jerusalem followed the pattern taught by the Master. That is why they were called the "Ebionites," in Hebrew Evionim אביונים, *the poor ones* (Galatians 2:10). They had shared everything for the sake of the kingdom and for the most part never financially recovered, at least not in this realm.

My Personal Thoughts

_____

_____

_____

Hebrews 4:14   Iyar 11/ יא באייר

Therefore, since we have a great cohen gadol who has passed through to the highest heaven,
Yeshua, the Son of God, let us hold firmly to what we acknowledge as true.

Leviticus 22 teaches us about the *Terumah* תרומה, the portion of foods only eaten by priests and their dependants. These portions may come from altar offerings or harvest tithes. Priests were not paid for their work at the Temple or for their teaching the Torah, so they were dependant on that tithe for their own survival and that of their dependants.

The instructions about who can eat or not eat of that portion of food are given in detail and they teach us how Hashem views family relationships and dependencies. When a priest's daughter, who is naturally eligible to eat the *Terumah*, marries one who is not a priest, she loses that right because she now belongs to the family she marries into. On the other hand, if she is widowed or divorced and returns to the full dependency of her father, she is again eligible. Also, a foreign servant bought with money and who becomes a permanent part of the priest's family can partake of the Terumah.

The inadvertent consumption of Terumah by someone not eligible incurred the punishment of the law of theft. It is considered robbing God (Malachi 3:8). People were taught to not eat anything that was not properly tithed or separated. Pharisees who were ultra concerned about it even made sure to tithe mint, anis, and cumin. They also lived a life excluding them from fellowship with others who weren't so particular on these things. The Master commended them for these practices though he rebuked them for their lack of wisdom in properly weighing the matters of Torah (Luke 11:42). While the Master obeyed the Torah, he also taught us wisdom in its application (Matthew 12:1–3; Luke 10:8). This command really teaches us the principles of priority; the idea of setting the needs of the Kingdom ahead and before our own; it is at the heart of Yeshua's very words, "But seek first his Kingdom and his righteousness, and all these things will be given to you as well" (Matthew 6:33).

The same principles are at work in the adoption of the nations into Israel. As disciples of the master, of he who is the high priest of the Tabernacle above (Hebrews 5:10; 9:11) we are adopted into his family, and thereby are allowed to eat from the table of the high priest King, which others cannot partake of (Hebrews 13:10).

As bought and adopted members of this high priest's family, we partake of his table and enjoy the bounty of his household. This should not be taken for granted. May we always show ourselves ensamples of the calling wherewith we are called and reflect the virtue of the Master of the house, of the Kingdom of God!

My Personal Thoughts

_____

_____

_____

_____

_____

_____

Colossians 2:17   יב באייר /Iyar 12

These are a shadow of things that are coming, but the body is of the Messiah.

Sometimes we make the mistake of interpreting text from the apostolic letters by the virtue of one statement instead of understanding it by the virtue of the overall context. That would be like saying that Yosemite Park is an orchard because of a couple of hazelnut trees in the middle of the vastness of the coniferous trees defining this beautiful expense of land.

When we read the verse, "So don't let anyone pass judgment on you in connection with eating and drinking, or in regard to a Jewish festival or Rosh-Hodesh or Shabbat" (Colossians 2:16) in the mind-frame that God is telling us not to pay attention to his former command concerning the Levitical calendar and diet, we are doing just that. To understand this with an anti-Torah observance twist is completely ignoring the context of the letter to the Colossians.

This epistle was addressed to the formerly pagan Colossians striving to take Torah upon them while receiving criticism from others about it. Paul encourages them by telling them that they are right to do so, because the Levitical calendar and diet concerns are a shadow of the things to come, the substance of that shadow belonging to Messiah (Colossians 2:17). Every shadow betrays a shadow caster and in this case, Messiah is the shadow caster of the festivals and diet concerns in Leviticus.

Jewish sages have put together a Midrash that compares all of Jewish history to the phases of the moon. Here is how it works,

> Thus there were fourteen generations from Avraham to David, fourteen generations from David to the Babylonian Exile, and fourteen generations from the Babylonian Exile to the Messiah. (Matthew 1:17)

If each generation from Abraham is one day, we have a full moon at the time of King David the time of the glory of Israel, darkness at the time of the Babylonian deportation, which was indeed a dark time in our history, and a full moon again at the time of Messiah. Moonlight creates a shadow. If I were to stand still during the movement of the moon during the night I would see my shadow move from one place to the other, first behind me, then in front of me. In this case, Messiah is the shadow caster whose shadow we see on earth. We see his shadow before his full manifestation in the world to come. The diet and calendar Levitical injunctions are the shadow of Messiah. Paul tells of those who would discourage the newly-born Colossian disciples' attempts at following Torah that, they are 'not holding fast to the Head' (Colossians 2:19; 1 Corinthians 11:13).

That same midrash seems to indicate the need for another twenty-eight generations for the Messiah to return in his fullness. That gives us a time of darkness somewhere during the time of the Spanish Inquisition, again another dark time in our history, to take us again to the fullness of the manifestation of Messiah at the end of this age, when he comes to reign on the earth.

May it be soon Abba, even in our days. In the meantime, may we rejoice in him in the shadow of his presence among us.

My Personal Thoughts

Matthew 24:31   Iyar 13/ יג באייר

He will send out his angels with a great shofar; and they will gather together
his chosen people from the four winds, from one end of heaven to the other.

We are still in the season of the counting of the Omer, between Pesach and Shavuot, between Passover and Pentecost. The command to count seven Sabbaths of weeks plus one day (50 days) is incumbent upon every Israelite, as in the text of Leviticus 23 it is expressed in the second person plural (Leviticus 23:15–16). The commandment to count the days of the Omer to Shavuot/Pentecost sounds very similar to the commandments of counting the years to the jubilee. The high priest (this command is given to Moses in the second person singular form) is to count seven weeks of years or forty-nine years, then to declare the fiftieth year jubilee (Leviticus 25:8–10). This declaration is made in the synagogue on Yom Kippur. The counting of the jubilee has been all but lost. Many people are trying to piece it together and we have now some ideas of where we're at, but even so, the command is not practicable at this time.

It is the duty of the high priest to count off the jubilee. At this point in time we do not have a physical high priest simply because we do not have a physical temple. The commandment also requires that on the jubilee all lands be returned to their previous owners, all debts be forgiven and slaves liberated. Today's slavery has to do with being owned by someone to whom we owe money (Proverbs 22:7). I don't think that the financial systems of today are very well geared to these practices. Can you imagine all debts being forgiven, lands returned, etcetera? Israel already had a hard time with it when it was under Rome; it would be impossible today!

Another issue with jubilees is that the Torah forbids for land in Israel to be sold in perpetuity (Leviticus 25:23). One element of the laws of jubilee states that the land should be returned to its original tribal owners. It could be used as collateral for a while, but it eventually needed to be returned. It is not our land to do as we please; it is his (Leviticus 25:23). Because of this, the sages declared that all Israel needed was to be present for the great jubilee to be practiced. Today because of the long exile, we no longer follow from which tribe people are descended. Learning about DNA has started the process, but we are far from finding all Israel. Messiah is the one who is supposed to gather all the tribes (Acts 1:6), so it was ruled that the great jubilee would happen at the coming of Messiah. We know that before he returns (Revelation 19:11–16), 144 thousand believers from all the tribes will have been sealed in his name (Revelation 7; 14:1–5). They are the firstfruits from all the eligible tribes; therefore they are the redeemed representatives for the redemption of all the tribes of Israel. They render the jubilee of the Land possible.

Yeshua will surely return to gather his people and return the Land to its rightful owners: Israel. He is the kinsman redeemer. As Boaz redeemed Ruth and thereby returned the land to Naomi, Yeshua also redeems us (The Book of Ruth). On that Day there will be a wedding and the Land will be returned to Israel (Revelation 19:9). It will truly be the jubilee of all jubilees.

May it be soon Abba, even in our days!

My Personal Thoughts

_____

_____

_____

_____

Matthew 6:12   Iyar 14/ יד באייר

Forgive us what we have done wrong, as we too have forgiven those who have wronged.

From the beginning, the Creator organized his calendar of events according to septets. The Sabbath crowns a seven-day week (Genesis 2:2–3). Creation and the coronation of Messiah are celebrated on the first day of the seventh month of the year (Leviticus 23:24). Every seven years fields in Israel enjoy a time of rest, and a jubilee deliverance of slaves and forgiveness of debts is celebrated after seven septets (Leviticus 25). In addition, festivals in both spring and fall last seven days, and Pentecost is celebrated counting seven weeks from the Feast of Firstfruits (Leviticus 23). These are our compasses in time, but the present-day Western Gregorian/Roman calendar has gotten us out of sync with Hashem's clock.

According to the Torah, after seven septets, the whole economic system has to reboot so to speak (Leviticus 25:11–17). All debts have to be forgiven and possessions retained as collateral have to returned. These possessions included individuals enslaved to creditors due to financial hardship. The jubilee provided some sort of salvation and deliverance from eternal financial servitude. Hashem said that he established this as a safeguard for the evil heart of man. He said, "Thus you are not to take advantage of each other, but you are to fear your God; for I am ADONAI your God" (Leviticus 25:17). Our sins are like our debt towards God (Matthew 6:12), and the Messiah comes on the Jubilee to restore our financial and moral balance, our credit towards Hashem.

Having rejected Hashem's wise instructions, we today have a world with a financial system based on oppressing others through eternal usury. As we see the world is more and more engrossed in an economy where the rich become fewer and richer and the poor more numerous and poorer, we see its financial base failing and being held together loosely with a paper currency that is not even worth what it is printed upon.

Endorsing the jubilee schedule doesn't seem to make good business sense but for Hashem it seems very important. In the days of King David, it is said, "The anger of ADONAI blazed up against Isra'el, so he moved David to act against them by saying, "Go, take a census of Isra'el and Y'hudah'" (2 Samuel 24:1). We are not told why God's anger was kindled against Israel, but when we look at the chronology of this, we find that in the 38th year of David, the people had failed to observe seventy rest years and jubilees. God then brought judgment upon them, causing 70,000 people to die (2 Samuel 24:15). One thousand people died for every rest year that was owed in their debt to the Torah. This judgment paid the penalty and wiped the slate clean.

Then the people failed to keep their rest years and Jubilees again. After they owed another seventy rest years (Sabbath years) and jubilees, God brought Judah into Babylonian captivity for seventy years to pay the debt. What is the reason God gave for the captivity?

> Thus was fulfilled the word of ADONAI spoken by Yirmeyahu, "until the land has been paid her Shabbats"—for as long as it lay desolate, it kept Shabbat, until seventy years had passed. (2 Chronicles: 36:21)

My Personal Thoughts

_____

_____

_____

Luke 4:18–19   Iyar 15/ טו באייר

The Spirit of ADONAI is upon me; therefore he has anointed me to . . . proclaim freedom for the imprisoned . . . release those who have been crushed, proclaim a year of the favor of ADONAI.

The sacred texts teach us about Hashem's special times (Leviticus 23: 25). Starting with spring we have the Sabbatical years every septet, a time where for the most part the land is to be given a rest and people can only eat from what they saved and of what grows of its own accord. It has been calculated that 1967, the year when Jerusalem was freed from occupation and returned to its rightful Jewish heirs was also a Sabbatical year. Another of these times is called the Jubilee year and it comes the year after seven septets.

Due to many interruptions, exiles, occupations, wars, calendar modifications, and lack of information, it is difficult to restore the exact dates of Sabbatical years and jubilees. Many have tried by collecting data from history books, such as the Book of Josephus as well as taking into consideration hints from biblical texts, and while many of these calculations have somewhat different outcomes, there is a body of them that come near to each other in their calculations. A common trend I noticed is that many put the year 28 A.D. (or around) as a jubilee year. I am not a calendar expert so I cannot say, but there are a few scholars that can agree to that.

The Jubilee year was to be announced in synagogues at Yom Kippur (Leviticus 25:8–9). During the days of the Master, jubilees were not officially kept but the first year of the Master's ministering on earth may correspond to a jubilee year. In any case, Yeshua did not miss his cue and could have announced it when he quoted Isaiah sixty-one in the Nazareth synagogue (Luke 4:18). If that proclamation at the synagogue was indeed done on a Yom Kippur, then Yeshua's forty day fast in which his virtue was tested by the enemy of his and our souls is comparable to the forty 'Days of Awe,' a Jewish tradition of spending the forty days before Yom Kippur soul-searching in order to acknowledge sin in our lives and change our ways.

If there was a jubilee during the Master's ministry, that would also explain why people had the time to leave home, travel, and listen to him. This was the point of the jubilee, to stop the daily grind of our day-to-day existence, dedicate time to God in prayer and study of the Torah, as well as to family and friends; sort of an extended Shabbat. God knows that we need help in establishing our priorities, and time to sort out problems with the people who are part of our lives.

In any case, it is evident that both Sabbatical and Jubilee years are important times in God's calendar and we better keep track of them.

Let us also remember that Yeshua is our Sabbatical Jubilee. He is the one who brings us spiritual and physical restoration, and soon his Sabbatical Kingdom will be established on earth as the greatest of all jubilees.

My Personal Thoughts

_____

_____

_____

_____

Matthew 12:37   Iyar 16 /טז באייר

For by your own words you will be acquitted, and by your own words you will be condemned.

In the sacred texts we are told of a man stoned for blasphemy (Leviticus 24:10–16). The Torah does not soil our mind with the specifics of that blaspheme, but even the Hebrew text tells us that it had to do with using the Holy Name of God, the Tetragrammatons in a common manner. In this case, it seems that the blasphemy involved cussing at someone. Again we may look at this as harsh punishment, but remembering that his ways are not our ways, let us study the matter.

Our Western society seems to have grown apart from certain forms of respect that have been common to the world for millennia. This makes it difficult for us to relate to the etiquettes of the Bible. For example, when I was a child in France, I learned that it was impolite to address adults by their first name, or even by their last name without using the title Mr. or Mrs. I was told that it was the way people of low-pedigree spoke, and that someone's name represented *them*, and that it was to be treated with respect and reverence. We carve the names of dead soldiers on marble to remember and honor them and it would be wrong to deface such a monument. A name is the personification of a human being, like a verbal effigy, and protesters burn effigies of politicians they don't like to show what they want to do to them. For the longest time, it was considered treason to criticize, or slander the name of a king or queen, or to use their name when we don't have the authority to do so. Even in the twentieth century, this practice existed in countries with autocratic governments.

If such respect is given to the name of human authorities for millennia, how much more should it be given to the name of the Almighty? The name of God was to be treated with respect, never defaced, or sullied. In the days of the Temple, the name of God was only used in prayer in the Temple or in a special ceremony to help define if a woman was guilty of adultery or not (Numbers 5).

The man in question verbally reviled another man, which was bad enough (Matthew 5:22), but then added insult to injury by using the ineffable name of God (Exodus 20:7). The Torah considers this mention of the holy name outside of the precincts of prayer and the Temple blasphemous (Leviticus 24:16).

Words may be ephemeral, but they are real. The famous saying "Sticks and stones can break my bones but words can never hurt me" is not really true. We have today countless murders committed through online bullying using words over the Internet. Teenagers commit suicide over it. It is such a problem that it now requires legislation.

In courts of law, to slander someone is called *character assassination*. In the same way, to use or misrepresent the name of God is like committing deicide in our audience's eyes and it is a very serious sin. Some very commonly used English expressions invoking God come very near to what the man in the Book of Leviticus would be guilty of.

We may need to review our ideas of respect and reverence and check our language. What may seem to us like a small thing or ethics from a distant past may be very important in the eyes of Torah, which *at the end of the day* (and at the end of days) is the standard we are judged by.

My Personal Thoughts

Acts 1:6   Iyar 17/ יז באייר

Lord, are you at this time going to restore self-rule to Isra'el?

Jeremiah is in jail sustained and supported only by Baruch his faithful scribe and friend. The Babylonian army is concluding the siege of Jerusalem and marching on the city. Against all common sense, Jeremiah is asked to buy a piece of land. Hashem tells him,

> Hanam'el, the son of your uncle Shalum, will approach you and say, "Buy my field at `Anatot; you have next-of-kin's right to redeem it; so buy it." As ADONAI had said, my cousin Hanam'el came to me in the guards' quarters and said, "Please buy my field at `Anatot, in the territory of Binyamin; because you will inherit it, and you have next-of-kin's right to redeem it, so buy it for yourself." Then I was certain that this was ADONAI's word. (Jeremiah 32:7-8)

As far as the outlook, Jerusalem is doomed. There is no point in buying a piece of land in all of Judea. This doesn't seem to make sense until we learn about the details of the transaction. In those days two deeds were drafted when a transaction was made. One deed was the open deed to be referred to at any time, but in the case of forgery, there was always the possibility to go to the second deed that was sealed, hidden, and only to be opened by an official. In this case, Hashem tells Jeremiah,

> Take these contracts, both the sealed and unsealed copies, and place them in a clay jar, so that they can be preserved for a long time. (Jeremiah 32:14)

Jeremiah was to hide both deeds. He was to do so as a prophetic sign that the land would not be rejected forever. That one day these deeds would make a claim of ownership by a Jewish owner.

About five centuries later, another power—called Rome, but codified as *Babylon* in Talmudic writings—also laid siege against Jerusalem. As Babylon of old did, Rome burned the Temple and destroyed the city. Was there at that time a deed of redemption hidden somewhere?

Several decades before the Roman destruction of Jerusalem, Yeshua, the redeemer of Israel, he that is the avenger of blood and the redeemer of the land, the Spirit of the Almighty hidden in a vessel of clay, was hidden in a cave. He is waiting for such a time when "Houses and fields and vineyards shall again be bought in this land." At that time he will return as the original document sealed by the father and he will claim the land for his people.

May it be soon Abba; even in our days!

My Personal Thoughts

_____
_____
_____
_____
_____
_____

Mark 11:25   יח באייר /18 Iyar

And when you stand praying, if you have anything against anyone, forgive him;
so that your Father in heaven may also forgive your offenses.

"Thus you are not to take advantage of each other, but you are to fear your God; for I am ADONAI your God" (Leviticus 25:17). This command comes to us from within the context of *shemitah* שמיטה (remittance year) and jubilee regulations, a time when debts are to be forgiven and lands returned to their previous owner.

The rulings concerning debt release caused much heart searching. The temptation for one to ask for a loan near the year of release knowing that the debt will soon be forgiven was as great as the one for lenders to either refuse the loan, or regulate price and interest in view of the coming year of release. Due to our evil nature, much instruction is given concerning these things (Leviticus 25). The fact that Hashem has to specify all these parameters is in itself a testament to our wicked hearts and evil inclination.

The whole prohibition regarding shady business deals in view of remittance years is summed up in, "You are not to take advantage of each other, but you are to fear your God." This is repeated several times. The systems of debts and usury are a form of oppression and slavery. The Israelites were a people that Hashem freed for a great price. They shouldn't let themselves be enslaved anymore, especially not by their brothers who were also freed slaves. In remembrance of their former slavery, Israelites were also to be kind to their employees from the nations, to the foreigner in the land. The freedom of the Israelites came at great cost of life. Jubilee laws served as a reminder that *freedom is not free*. The Israelite's stay in the land was contingent on their just and merciful interaction with each other, not oppressing each other. Even now many rabbis compare this present exilic stage with the internal oppression and conflict within Israel in the first and second century CE.

The laws of jubilee also served as a preservation of the family farm against the monopoly of big *corporations* who would otherwise ruthlessly swallow small businesses and take over the land. We need to remember that these laws are only relevant as per the Land of Israel. The jubilee also gave second chance to those who had lost everything, as well as time for people to reconnect with their relatives, make things right with friends, follow an itinerant rabbi, and study the Torah.

The application of the laws of jubilee definitely creates financial loss. This teaches us that financial success is not at the top of God's priorities. What matters most to him is the welfare of his people, of all his people. We must not complain for loss because of the jubilee, but instead remind ourselves of the great debt we owe the God of the universe. At the Father's request, our debt of sin was paid in full in Mashiach who now stands as the redeemer of our soul against the unforgiving creditor who would otherwise enslave us. Yeshua said, "Forgive . . . so that your Father . . . may also forgive your offenses. *[But if you do not forgive, your Father . . . will not forgive your offenses.]*" (Mark 11:25–26). In the biblical sense, forgiveness is the renouncement of restitution for debt incurred. King David reminds us of the Father's mercy when he penned, "He has not treated us as our sins deserve or paid us back for our offenses" (Psalm 103:10).

My Personal Thoughts

Revelation 21:13   יט באייר /Iyar 19

Three gates to the east

When Moses was on the Mount, ADONAI told him to take everything he had been shown and replicate it for all of Israel (Exodus 25:9, 40). It stands to reason therefore that the Tabernacle, its furnishings and encampment, are the shadow of the Almighty's throne room and its surroundings.

On the mountain, Moses was also given the tablets of the testimony of the renewed covenant. These were to be placed in an ark of acacia wood within the vicinity of the elements of worship. This was called the *Tabernacle* and constituted the *throne room* of Hashem. This throne room was to be surrounded by the Levite camp, and this camp was surrounded by the twelve tribes, three tribes on each side. When Balaam saw the whole encampment from afar he was so moved by the spirit of Hashem that he exclaimed, "How lovely are your tents, Ya`akov; your encampments, Isra'el!" (Numbers 24:5), which is until this day a praise mentioned each Shabbat at synagogue liturgy.

From the Book of Leviticus we learn that the three concentric circles around the Tabernacle are three concentric circles of holiness or ritual purity. To have God in their midst was great but it was also dangerous. Protocol could not be broken; we remember what happened to the sons of Aaron Nadab and Abihu (Leviticus 10). Levi was therefore a sort of a buffer zone between the presence of God and the children of Israel.

A similar pattern is found in the city of God. John describes New Jerusalem for us in the last two chapters of the Book of Revelation. The whole city is holy and has no need of the light of the sun for Hashem himself is its center giving it light and his lamp is the Lamb (Revelation 21:23). Like the camp of the *Shekinah* שכינה in the desert, the city is surrounded by the tribes of Israel as its gates. By way of imagery, this teaches us that just as one can only enter the redemptive covenant of Israel through Yeshua of the tribe of Judah, one can only enter the city by way of one of the tribes of Israel. We are told also that the city rests on the foundation of the disciples of Yeshua when he was on earth.

The sages of Israel often compared the whole idea of the Tabernacle into the human body. In their view, the Tables of the Testimony in the middle of the Shekinah camp represented the place of the heart.

In this world, we can only find sense, purity, and holiness if the word, the lamp of the Lamb is at the center of our lives, focus, and attention. When our lives seem disoriented or even a little off-center, may we consider that perhaps we have diverted our attention to other things from that which is most important: Hashem and the Torah.

We use the word *disoriented* when we lose our sense of location. It means to *lose the East*. The Tribe of Judah where our Master is from was placed on the east side of the Tabernacle. Messiah is our east helping us make sense of life.

May we never lose our *east*!

My Personal Thoughts

_____

_____

_____

Colossians 2:14   Iyar 20/ כ באייר

He wiped away the bill of charges against us.

There is a common teaching out there that claims that in his death and resurrection, Yeshua conquered and annulled the curse that comes through disobedience and that only the blessings remain. In essence, this would mean that the Torah has lost its *teeth*; there is no more retribution for sin.

This view of the Torah is due to misinterpretations of Paul's letters, especially the one written to the believers in Galatia. This is partly due to the influence of a translation done under an erroneous theology that discarded the writings of Leviticus, assuming that the ancient Hebrew Scriptures were obsolete. The translators obviously were not familiar with the religious, theological, cultural, and social context of Paul's letter to the Galatians.

One of the statements in question is, "The Messiah redeemed us from the curse pronounced in the Torah by becoming cursed on our behalf" (Galatians 3:13), which most people interpret to mean that the Torah itself is a curse. How can the Torah be a curse to us when its purpose is to revive our souls, to make us wise, to rejoice our heart, and to enlighten our eyes (Psalm 19:7–8)? It would go against everything King David said (Psalm 119). In addition, it is recorded in biblical and historical records of the life of the disciples, that they actually were very religious. Torah observance was in fact part of their testimony. Either Paul's statement is a forgery, Paul was wrong, the translators got it wrong, or there is a misunderstanding of its meaning. I stand for the two last options.

John the Disciple taught much about the nature of sin. He said that sin was the actual transgression, or breaking of Torah commands (1 John 3:4), and those who say they don't sin deceive themselves (1 John 1:8). The Torah with its definition of sin is supposed to be life-giving to us (Deuteronomy 4:1). When it does not, could it be that it is because we are wrong? I have travelled to many places, and have very often seen people transform the good that is given to them into a curse or something evil.

I heard a statement on the news the other day. Some lawmaker claimed that crime would go down if they decriminalized a certain activity currently considered against the law. The argument being: when the law is altered, the once labeled "criminal" is no longer a criminal. On the other hand, it doesn't change the behavior or the heart of the law-breaker, and it endorses criminal activity. In a Roman court of law, the prosecutor brings a record of debts, or law-breaking activities, to the judge. It is the same in the heavenly court but this time, it is the Accuser of the saints who brings legal charges against us, and he does so demanding the death penalty. The death mentioned here is not the biological death that we all partake of, but the *death* that separates us from God forever. We must never forget though that the only reason we do not get the punishment of this death is because Mashiach takes it for us in a settlement out of court. The *charges* against us are not *deleted*; they are just paid by someone else. The credit found in the virtue of his innocent suffering is enough to pay for our debt. He is the only one whose righteousness successfully defied *death* and conquered it. In Yeshua, The *prosecutor* found its match.

We owe him our lives. Our lives belong to him and we should live in a state of eternal gratitude. When asked, "How are you?" a famous radio show host always answers, "Better than I deserve." That should be the sentiment that runs through our being day and night, for we certainly are "better than we deserve"!

248

John 5:24   **Iyar 21/** כא באייר

Yes, indeed! I tell you that whoever hears what I am saying and
trusts the One who sent me has eternal life—that is,
he will not come up for judgment but has already crossed over from death to life!

The Torah is a contract. It is a contract that defines our affiliation with our heavenly Father. It tells us how we belong to him and his Kingdom (Leviticus 26:10–12). A contract usually tells of benefits for those faithful to its terms, but it is useless unless it is also fitted with *teeth* for those who break them. Within the Torah contract are imbedded two major texts of curses designed to come upon those who dishonor it (Leviticus 26:3–13; Deuteronomy 28). These two chapters of the Torah have often been erroneously understood as what Paul referred to as the *curse of the Torah* (Galatians 3:13), which had been *nailed to the cross* (Colossians 2:14), and therefore is now obsolete.

How could it be that these Torah instructions that Moses proclaimed to be our very "life" (Deuteronomy 32:47), that the statutes in which David found great rewards (Psalm 19:11), and what the writer of the Book of Hebrews called the Good News (Hebrews 4:2), are all of a sudden nailed to a tree (God forbid)? The Torah is an everlasting covenant, and even when covenantal addendums are made, they do not replace the former but are built upon them (Galatians 3:17).

Upon closer examination we realize that this so-called *curse of the Torah* 'nailed to the tree' spoken of by Paul is not the Torah contract itself. The salary of sin (breaking the Torah) is death (1 John 3:4; Romans 6:23). The word 'mavet,' death' in Hebrew, actually refers to separation from God. The curse spoken of here is the condemnation to separation from the Father by the eternal courts of judgment, a form of banishment from the kingdom for breaking the rules. Paul also speaks of a *written code* (NIV), of a *handwriting of ordinances* (KJV) nailed to the cross, which is often erroneously interpreted as being the Torah itself. The truth is that it only refers to a legal document used in courts, which is also called a *certificate of debt* (ESV). It is the document containing the list of legal charges against us. The Master often used financial and legal when he spoke of sin (Matthew 6:12). This list, this *certificate of debt* is the evidence against us that we broke the Torah. It is this list that is nailed to the cross with Messiah. Basically what it means is that Messiah pays our fine to the Judge and gets rid of the evidence that stands against us. We are given a clean slate, a chance to start again.

In Messiah, we are given a new chance to learn to live by God's standards. The idea is that like the children of Israel were rescued from the angel of death in Egypt, we also are saved from HaSatan, so we may go and learn to live for Hashem in his way. We don't obey the Torah in order to get redeemed; we do it because the Lamb of God, Yeshua HaMashiach, redeems us!

My Personal Thoughts

_____

_____

_____

_____

_____

_____

John 9:3

Yeshua answered, "His blindness is due neither to his sin nor to that of his parents;
it happened so that God's power might be seen at work in him."

The Torah teaches us the notions of right and wrong according to the Father, Creator of the universe. It sets before us the rewards of obedience and warns us of the chastisements for breach of contract. Hashem says this to his children who know his name, have witnessed his power, and lived of his bounty,

> But if you will not listen to me and obey all these mitzvot, if you loathe my regulations and reject my rulings, in order not to obey all my mitzvot but cancel my covenant; then I, for my part, will do this to you: I will bring terror upon you— wasting disease and chronic fever to dim your sight and sap your strength. You will sow your seed for nothing, because your enemies will eat the crops. I will set my face against you—your enemies will defeat you, those who hate you will hound you, and you will flee when no one is pursuing you. (Leviticus 26:14–17)

As the Messiah was the executer of God's will at creation (John 1:3; Proverbs 8:22–31) so will Messiah be the executor of God's judgment on the disobedient (Revelation 19). He will come in his time.

In the meantime, should we deduct that all diseases, fevers, and business and military failures are the direct consequences of our sins? Should we assume that one who is sick with cancer sinned more than one who is healthy? It is neither safe nor true to come to such conclusions. The Torah instructs us in this matter.

The book of Job, for example, tells us of a man who was righteous and yet suffered affliction without measure. The fact that Hashem calls someone *righteous* doesn't necessarily mean that they do not sin for "all have sinned" (Romans 3:23). To be called righteous by God simply defines our status with him.

The whole purpose for the story of Job seems to be to create a Messianic analogy. Messiah, the true righteous one, like Job, unduly suffered, was condemned by his friends for it (Isaiah 53:3–4), but at a later time is justified and vindicated by Hashem in plain sight of those who accused him (Revelation 19). It seems like Job's suffering was so God could tell us of his work through Messiah. This is echoed in the account of the healed blind man.

In a sense, the wise and safe conclusion we can make from our passage in the Book of Leviticus is that, *whereas sin and disobedience always result in calamities, calamities are not always the direct consequence of sin and disobedience.*

My Personal Thoughts

_____

_____

_____

Matthew 23:39   Iyar 23/ כג באייר

For I tell you, from now on, you will not see me again until you say,
"Blessed is he who comes in the name of ADONAI."

Leviticus 26 tells us the woes Hashem puts on his children for disobedience. The first woe tells of sickness, and military and agricultural failure. The second woe speaks of the Temple. Then Hashem says,

> If these things don't make you listen to me, then I will discipline you seven times over for your sins. I will break the pride you have in your own power. I will make your sky like iron, your soil like bronze—you will spend your strength in vain, because the land will not yield its produce or the trees in the field their fruit. (Leviticus 26:18–20)

The prophet Ezekiel used that theme just before the destruction of Solomon's Temple "to speak to the house of Isra'el and say that this is what ADONAI Elohim says: 'I am about to profane my sanctuary, the pride of your strength, the delight of your eyes and your heart's desire. Your sons and daughters whom you have left behind will die by the sword" (Ezekiel 24:21). At that time, because of sin in the land, the first temple was destroyed by the Babylonian king, Nebuchadnezzar.

Israel's history tells us that another Temple was built after the Babylonian exile. It was not as beautiful and glorious as the first one but in an effort to win the favor of the Jewish people, King Herod, the one who tried to have the Master killed at birth, transformed that second Temple into one of the marvels of the ancient world. As beautiful as it was, that Temple was also destroyed, this time by Titus, a Roman general. On Titus' victory arch, you can see engravings of enslaved Jews bringing their riches to Rome. You can even see someone carrying the Temple menorah. What an ironic monument now that Israel had resurrected from the ashes of Rome's attempted Jewish extermination.

There is a story in the Talmud that tells of a king who twice gave a beautiful coat to his son but twice the son irresponsibly spoiled the coat. The king then decided that he will again buy for his son the most beautiful coat he could get, but will give it to him when he has learned to be more responsible.

As in the story, the Father has a beautiful third *garment* in store for Israel (Exodus 4:22). It will be the most glorious of all and it will be given to him, when he has matured and learned to say again, *Baruch habah b'shem ADONAI* יי ברוך הבא בשם, *Blessed is he who comes in the name of ADONAI* (Matthew 23:29).

May it come soon, Abba, even in our days!

My Personal Thoughts

_____

_____

_____

_____

_____

1 John 1:9   **Iyar 24/ כד באייר**

If we acknowledge our sins, then, since he is trustworthy and just,
he will forgive them and purify us from all wrongdoing.

In a world where the concepts of right and wrong have become not only blurry but at times even reversed, it is very important to keep track of our spiritual walk. First of all, we must remember the definition of sin. The Hebrew word for it is *chatah*, which literally means to *miss the mark* or the *bull's eye*, and refers to disobeying the commandments of Torah (1 John 3:4). Of course, our human nature makes it impossible for us to keep all the commandments, so we are continually separated from Hashem. This is where the Levitical service comes in handy. Through it, we learn to approach Hashem by proxy. The whole Levitical system teaches us that we are insufficient and that we are dependent on another to approach the Almighty, but it does not absolve us of responsibility to do our share and the best we can to flee from sin. Here are three ways the Torah teaches us to do our part: studying the Torah, living as part of a community, confessing, and making restitution.

STUDYING THE TORAH: King David once said, "I treasure your word in my heart, so that I won't sin against you" (Psalm 119:11). We must store the words of our Father in our heart by constantly reading, listening, and memorizing them. If we have a good conscience, they will lead and guide us. The idea of disobedience will then be repulsive to us and we will feel *dirty* in our heart for doing the wrong thing. It is important to listen to the voice of this conscience led by the words of the Torah. When we ignore it for too long, our conscience eventually becomes burned and we become numb to its voice (1Timothy 4:2).

COMMUNITY: The Torah is not meant to be lived alone. It requires community. That is why it is important for believers to actively seek to live near other believers. When we go off on our own without the accountability, support, and positive peer-pressure that fellowship offers, we have the tendency to develop our own form of godly walk and therefore go astray. Wise King Solomon knew about it and said, "Just as iron sharpens iron, a person sharpens the character of his friend" (Proverbs 27:17).

CONFESSING AND MAKING RESTITUTION: Moses taught the people about the benefits of confession before Hashem. He said,

> Tell the people of Isra'el, "When a man or woman commits any kind of sin against another person and thus breaks faith with ADONAI, he incurs guilt. He must confess the sin which he has committed; and he must make full restitution for his guilt, add twenty percent and give it to the victim of his sin." (Numbers 5:6–7)

We are to concretize our repentance through audible confession (Romans 10:17) of our sins and shortcomings before Hashem, even the smallest ones. If need be, we are also to provide restitution above and beyond the worth of the offense. A person may even have to go to Jerusalem to make acknowledgment of their trespasses before God through a sin offering. In these ways, sin becomes a personal moral reality as well as a financial liability. God knows that we respond more meticulously to rules that deplete our pocket books when we break them.

Herein is the grace, the mercy and the compassion of Hashem: He teaches us personal accountability and responsibility for our sins, to make the right decisions and obey, but he also is able, through our humble confession, to help us learn our lesson and start again.

Matthew 4:4   Iyar 25/ כה באייר

Man does not live on bread alone, but on every word that comes from the mouth of ADONAI.

The fourth book of the Pentateuch is called *Numbers* in English. In Hebrew the title of this book is the first principal noun in the text, which in Hebrew is *Ba'midbar* במדבר, "in the wilderness." In today's Hebrew, the word *midbar* means "desert." The Book of *Ba'midbar* tells us of the thirty-eight years spent by the children of Israel in the desert.

The Hebrew for the word *midbar* מדבר, wilderness, reveals a very interesting truth. Most Hebrew words are based on a three letter verbal root. This verbal root is vital to us because no matter what the variation in the spelling of the word, the verbal root reveals its etymological meaning. This system becomes important in order for us to understand what the Father is trying to convey to us in the words of the Torah.

The verbal root of the word *midbar* is composed of the three Hebrew letters, *daleth, beth,* and *resh.* Strangely enough, these letters are also the verbal root for the Hebrew verb *ledaber* לדבר: to speak, from which we derive the word *davar* דבר. Today *davar* means either "word" or "thing," but it is also the ancient Aramaic word used in the Targum (Aramaic layman's version of the Hebrew Scriptures) to refer to the concept of Messiah. *Davar* is the word John used in his narratives of the Master when he said, "In the beginning was the word" (John 1:1).

Where does all this take us? These interesting facts concerning the word *midbar* have certainly not escaped the attention of Jewish sages and we find elucidation in some of their commentaries. Looking at the relationship between the Hebrew words for *wilderness* and the idea of the *spoken word,* the sages have concluded that the wilderness is the place where God speaks. Hashem surely may speak in any place, but the wilderness is usually the place where we are the most dependent on him and where we can give him our full attention. Sometimes this *wilderness* can also be the spiritual or emotional wilderness of difficulty or trying times in our lives, and these are times when we seem to hear him best.

The idea is certainly carried in the Torah. John the Immerser defined himself using the prophet Isaiah's words, "The voice crying in the wilderness" (Matthew 3:3). While fasting in the wilderness for forty days, the Master himself said, "Man does not live on bread alone, but on every word that comes from the mouth of ADONAI" (Matthew 4:4).

The wilderness is certainly a place conducive to hearing the voice of Hashem; the place of total undistracted dependency. May we learn to benefit from our wilderness times, hearing his voice telling us to "Turn from your [our] sins to God, for the Kingdom of Heaven is near" (Matthew 3:2). May we not complain against the *manna* or at the water shortage. May we learn to use those times for growth, maturation, and consecration as the children of Israel also learned to do.

My Personal Thoughts

_____

_____

_____

_____

_____

Matthew 4:1   **Iyar 26/** כו באייר

Then the Spirit led Yeshua up into the wilderness to be tempted by the Adversary.

"ADONAI spoke to Moshe in the Sinai Desert" (Numbers 1:1).

Maybe you are going through a dry spiritual season, a time of wilderness. Don't fear or despair, for it is the Creator of your soul who brought you there.

Wildernesses hold special places in our lives. They become reference points forever. They often represent places of refuge (Revelation 12:6), provision (Deuteronomy 8:16), revelation (Revelation 17:3), and maturation (Deuteronomy 8:2–3).

Our fathers' crossing the desert was really their honeymoon with Hashem. Relatively speaking they had very little cares or worries. Supplied with a constant provision of the healthiest food you can get on this earth and a fountain of water that followed them, they were under Hashem's never failing trust fund. On top of it, through the person of Moses, they had direct access to Hashem. It is no wonder they did not want to enter the Land. They were going to have to start planting and sowing fields, reaping harvests, organize a government as well as an effective army.

ADONAI remembers these years in the desert with the nostalgia of a husband remembering his early espousals. Through the prophet Hoseah he speaks of alluring his bride to a desert place where she could give him her full attention (Hoseah 2:14), then he says, "I remember your devotion when you were young; how, as a bride, you loved me; how you followed me through the desert, through a land not sown" (Jeremiah 2:2). Each year at the Feast of Tabernacles we are to remember these simple beginnings of our walk with Hashem (Leviticus 23:41–43).

Just like our fathers spent forty years in the desert learning to lean and depend on God in obedience and trust for even their daily food, Yeshua spent forty days and forty nights in the wilderness learning the same lessons (Matthew 4:1–12). If both our Fathers and the Master had to go though these things, why should we feel slighted when Hashem decides to have us to endure what seems to be a dry time?

Cherish your wilderness times. They are times for you to focus your attention on the only things that really matter which are Hashem, his will in your life, and his words. May we, like our Fathers and our Master also learn, grow, and mature from our wilderness times.

My Personal Thoughts

_____

_____

_____

_____

_____

_____

_____

_____

_____

Matthew 10:31   Iyar 27/ כז באייר

So do not be afraid, you are worth more than many sparrows.

In the first chapter of the Book of Numbers we read about a census taken of the children of Israel. It is not the first census in the Torah and neither will it be the last. Censuses are conducted with different parameters and for different purposes. This census in the Book of Numbers was a military census (Numbers 1:3).

One could be left to wonder, "What is it with God and censuses?" It can be compared to a man collecting precious pearls. Each day he dives to the bottom of the abyss to gather oysters. After opening the shell, he puts all the pearls into a box. He then rubs each one against his teeth to verify its purity, and sorts them by sizes. One can go through a ton of pearls to get three or four very valuable ones. These are precious to him. They come at the price of very intense and dangerous labor. In the evening he sets them before him and counts them. He admires and loves his pearls; they are his pride. It is the same with Hashem: censuses are a sign of his affection for his people.

Here is what Rashi, a famous sage of Israel, said about God's censuses:

> Because of Israel's dearness before Him, he counts them all the time. When they departed from Egypt he counted them (Exodus 12:37). After some fell from the sin of the golden calf, he counted them to determine how many remained (Exodus 38:25–26). And when his Shekinah came to rest upon them, he counted them again.

There is an ancient teaching that on ten occasions Israel was numbered. First when they went down to Egypt (Deuteronomy 10:22), second when they came out of Egypt (Exodus 12:37), and a third time after the incident of the golden calf (Exodus 30:12). They were counted twice in the Book of Numbers, once in connection with the standards, once in connection with the division of the Land, and twice in the days of Saul (1 Samuel 11:8; 15:4). The eighth time was in the days of David (2 Samuel 24:9) and the ninth in the days of Ezra after the Babylonian captivity (Ezra 2:64).

Prophet Jeremiah tells us that there will be a tenth census in the future,

> ADONAI-Tzva'ot says, "In this place, which is a wasteland without people or animals, and in all its cities, there will once again be pasture-lands where shepherds can let their flocks rest. In the cities of the hill-country, in the cities of the Sh'felah, in the cities of the Negev, in the territory of Binyamin, in the areas around Yerushalayim and in the cities of Y'hudah flocks will again pass under the hands of the one who counts them," says ADONAI. "Here, the days are coming," says ADONAI, "when I will fulfill this good promise which I have proclaimed for the house of Isra'el and the house of Y'hudah." (Jeremiah 33:12–14)

In those days, the whole of the Israel of God, the last harvest of the souls of the world will be counted. See you there!

My Personal Thoughts

_____

_____

255

Revelation 14:4   כח באייר /Iyar 28

They have been ransomed from among humanity as firstfruits for God and the Lamb.

In the beginning of the Book of Numbers, we learn about the redemption of the firstborn (Numbers 3:43–51). Joseph and Miriam brought Yeshua, their firstborn to the Temple to be redeemed. The functioning priest who performed the redemption that day was Simeon (Luke 2:22–26). Since there is no Temple today there cannot be a functioning priest so the redemption ceremony that Jews currently practice is only a ceremonial one as they wait for the days of the third Temple. Though non-applicable at this time, the principle is still rich.

Israel, as the biological descent of Jacob is called God's firstborn (Exodus 4:22), and according to the Torah, the firstborn has a special status in the family. They receive a double inheritance and carry the role of patriarchs of the family, clan, or tribe. The role of firstborn is not necessarily according to chronological birth. God often usurped it because of the unrighteousness of the actual firstborn. We see this principle at work in the cases of Isaac against Ishmael, Jacob against Esau, and Joseph against Reuben.

The idea of firstborn is linked to the idea of firstfruit. A harvest is dedicated to God by the waving of the firstfruit, of the first harvested omer. In the very same manner, a family of sheep or goats is consecrated to God by the giving up and consecration of the one who opens the matrix. The Book of Revelation tells us about the consecrated firstborn of the harvest of the earth. They come from the twelve tribes of Israel (Jacob's descendants). They have been chosen and sealed by Hashem with his name and that of the Lamb. In essence, they are Messiah believers from the twelve tribes of Israel and they represent the harvest of believers from the whole world before the Father (Revelation 7; 14:1–4). Yeshua himself is their firstborn who represents them before the Father (1 Corinthians 15:20).

We are approaching the end of the season of counting the Omer. On the first day of the counting of the Omer the first sheave of barley was brought to the temple for the dedication of the harvest. Messiah rose on the Day of Firstfruits. Later during the counting of Omer he appointed his intimate disciples, his firstborn, harvest from the land of Israel as his representatives to the rest of the tribes in Diaspora, and to the world (Matthew 28).

The fiftieth and last day of the Omer, which is Pentecost, is the time for the firstfruit of Israel's wheat to be brought to the Temple. On that day also, Israelites and God-fearers from other countries brought their firstfruit to Jerusalem, as they did during the time of the book of Acts. These became the firstfruit of Diaspora Israelites (Acts 2). Through them the words of the Master were carried to the rest of the world until today. Hallelujah!

My Personal Thoughts

_____

_____

_____

_____

_____

_____

Matthew 6:9   Iyar 29/ כט באייר

Our Father . . .

In many synagogues, above the ark containing the Torah scrolls, you find and inscription saying, "Know before whom you stand." This proclamation serves as a reminder that it is a serious thing to come into the presence of the very Most-High God. We call him "Our Father," and it is right. The Master taught us that, but somehow because of our contemporary Western perspective of fatherhood, we forget the ideas of respect and awe that such a title entails.

In ancient times in the East, and even in the not so distant American past, parents, and more particularly fathers, were the object of high reverence and respect. Looking back less than a hundred years ago, households were essentially run by fathers who held the key to the pocket book and disciplined their children. Their words were often few but final and certainly not to be crossed. Mothers could count on their support; all they had to say was, "You'll see when your father comes home . . . !" All this changed in America with the industrial revolution when people left the farms to live in cities, and also during WWII when women started working. As machines allowed women to do what before only men could do, it seems that men felt that they lost their usefulness and reason for existence. The Great Depression also hit city employer dependent people who lost it all. It is in the natural make-up of a man to run his family, to care and provide for them; when he can't, it will eat him up.

As many men lost their leadership place in society, as post-WWII modern-days and the sixties arrived, especially in the West, people lost all sense of respect and reverence for the family structure. This in turn reflected in our attitude towards religion and faith in general. We call adhering to certain rituals to approach God pompous, frivolous, and even legalistic. Somehow though, we understand the protocols involved in approaching a judge. We would never dare call him by his first name. We learn to call a judge, "Your Honor," a president "Mr. President," and a King, "Your Majesty." Why is it then that we resist the idea of protocol and respect with God? He is our Father yes, but familiarity breeds contempt, even with God. In fact, with God, to break with protocol brings death (Numbers 4:20).

As we lost reverence for our families, we also lost reverence for Hashem, and as we lost reverence for Hashem we lost reverence and fear to disobey his commandments. We say, "God is not legalistic; he understands," but what is the difference between *legalism* and *reverent obedience*? It seems to me that in the end, we are judged by our obedience to what he taught us to do, not by our doctrinal position or wise rhetoric, by how we live and not by what we proclaim (Matthew 25).

The question remains, how do we change this? How do we restore our respect for the holiness of God? I believe that as we learn to reinstate the parameters of respectfulness within households, as mothers enjoy again the fulfillment of motherhood, as fathers become respectable and fully endorse their paternal responsibilities, as we do these things, we will restore our ideas of the greatness of God. As children learn to obey their parents, they learn to obey God later in adult life. It may take the whole messianic age to do it though, so let's start today.

My Personal Thoughts

_____

_____

Sivan

We heard it
We felt it
We saw it
Earthquake, wind, and fire in Horeb,
And again in Jerusalem.
As from Egypt the people came
From around the world they come again!

Hebrews 4:1

Therefore, let us be terrified of the possibility that, even though the promise
of entering his rest remains, any one of you might be judged to have fallen short of it.

Working alongside the idea of a census of Israel in Numbers 1, we have a section in the text of the prophet Hoseah that tells us that Israel "will number as many as the grains of sand by the sea, which cannot be measured or counted" (Hoseah 1:10). Today, according to Jewish accounting, there are about 15 million Jews worldwide. Despite being one of the smallest religious entities in the world, it is still quite a miracle. We must remember that from the onset of their history, from barren mothers to international threats of annihilation, it seems that the Jewish people were not destined to survive. A friend of mine who has worked much of her life to promote Jewish identity told me once that in the Holocaust it was not 6 million people who were killed, but 100 million. Her notion about this was that along with these people, were destroyed all the generations that should have come out of them. If we applied this principle all the way back to when the Romans killed millions of Jews in the first century CE, Hoseah's prophecy should have been fulfilled by now.

Moses foresaw the present-day Great Exile when the children of Israel would become few in numbers. He said,

> When you have had children and grandchildren, lived a long time in the land, become corrupt and made a carved image, a representation of something, and thus done what is evil in the sight of ADONAI your God and provoked him; I call on the sky and the earth to witness against you today that you will quickly disappear from the land that you are crossing the Yarden to possess. You will not prolong your days there but will be completely destroyed. ADONAI will scatter you among the peoples; and among the nations to which ADONAI will lead you away, you will be left few in number. (Deuteronomy 4:25–27)

But using the promise in Hoseah, Jewish sages concluded that "In the Messianic Age, the sons of Israel will 'be like the sand of the sea, which cannot be measured or numbered'" (Numbers Rabbah 2:14;20:25).

Hoseah tells us in his prophecy that in that day, "The people of Y'hudah and the people of Isra'el will be gathered together; they will appoint for themselves one leader; and they will go up out of the land [Exekiel 37]; for that will be a great day, *[the day]* of Yizre`el (Ezekiel 37) for great shall be the day of Jezreel" (Hoseah 1:11). This *head* is none other than Messiah, the only legitimate king to sit on the throne of Jerusalem. Even now he is doing his work that he started 2,000 years ago of re-gathering all the tribes of Israel into one flock to serve Hashem under his command.

As of the 20th century, entire families who have been lost under the forced conversions of the Inquisition rediscovered their Jewish identities. Whole villages of people with Jewish ancestries in places such as India, Ethiopia, Russia, and China are returning to their ancient roots. Through DNA testing, people's lives are being changed as they discover their Jewish lineage. And best of all, is the latest Jewish trend to recognize the head that will lead them to their glorious destiny: Yeshua, the Jewish Messiah.

Hoseah speaks of a time when Hashem turned his face and said to the Northern tribes, "You are not my people," but in our Messiah is certainly fulfilled the rest of Hoseah's prophecy, the part when Hashem calls them again, "children of the living God Children of the living God" (Hoseah 1:10).

Matthew 2:6   Sivan 2/ ב בסיון ב

*And you, Beit-Lechem in the land of Y'hudah, are by no means the least among
the rulers of Y'hudah; for from you will come a Ruler who will shepherd my people Isra'el.*

At the birth of the Master the Powers that be were moved to take a census. As a result, while Miriam was great with child, she and her husband had to go back to their hometown of Bethlehem where she eventually delivered.

The Messiah was prophesied many years before to be born in the Judean city of Bethlehem (Micah 5:2), but the fact that it actually happened is nothing short of many miracles. Let us go back together through history and discover the story.

Joseph and Miriam were Judeans from Bethlehem; why did they live in Nazareth, Galilee (Luke 2:4)? This all started with the story of Hanukkah when the sons of Matthias Maccabees, who defeated the armies of Antiochus Epiphanes became kings over Jerusalem. Because the Maccabees were not from the House of David, the people of Jerusalem rebelled against them and a long civil war followed. In the end, the hostilities between opposite factions in Jerusalem became so great that Rome was sought out to help solve the civil war issues. Rome obliged and little by little took control of not only Jerusalem but of the whole country of Israel. It was to the point where it was the Romans who elected the high priest and the king. This is how Herod, who was not even really Jewish and even less Judean ended up on the throne of Jerusalem.

Herod knew that those faithful to the House of David were not happy with him so he tried to kill them. Many of them fled to Galilee including the family of the Master. From what we can gather so far, it seems that fate itself was determined to keep Micah's prophecy of the Messiah born in Bethlehem from being fulfilled. Not only many Judeans had to flee Judea, but the King of Israel wanted to kill them.

Going over these events, we can see the great cosmic plan at work. So many things have happened from the Hanukkah events when a would-be anti-Messiah wanted to take over Jerusalem as its king and god, to the birth of the true King of Jerusalem who will reign in it and rule it in the name of Hashem. Even Rome became a mere tool in the hands of Hashem by declaring a census that will bring Joseph and his wife Miriam back to Bethlehem for the birth of Yeshua.

That very same Yeshua will return to take over Jerusalem for good and fight against the Anti-Messiah himself in Jerusalem. At that time, he will also conduct a census as is prophesied by Jeremiah,

> ADONAI-Tzva'ot says, "In this place, which is a wasteland without people or animals, and in all its cities, there will once again be pasture-lands where shepherds can let their flocks rest. In the cities of the hill-country, in the cities of the Sh'felah, in the cities of the Negev, in the territory of Binyamin, in the areas around Yerushalayim and in the cities of Y'hudah flocks will again pass under the hands of the one who counts them." (Jeremiah 33:12–13)

My Personal Thoughts

Romans 11:33   **Sivan 3/ ג בסיון ג**

O the depth of the riches and the wisdom and knowledge of God!
How inscrutable are his judgments! How unsearchable are his ways!

Numbers 5 tells us of a very strange ritual concerning the 'woman suspected of adultery.' The ritual is very different from all others because it depends on a miracle. In those days women were not to be seen alone with someone of the opposite sex who is not a relative or their husband. Here is a scenario: A man sees his wife several times alone in the company of another man. He does not witness any indiscretion but finds it very strange that his wife should break protocol in this way. He suspects her of adultery. Immediately he has to stop marital relationships until she is vindicated. To vindicate her, the man has to bring his wife to Jerusalem where an officiating priest will unbind her hair and make her drink a potion of water, ink, and dust from the Tabernacle (reminiscent of the Golden Calf episode in Exodus: 32:20). If she is guilty, her womb will swell and her thigh will drop, but if she is not guilty of adultery, she will conceive and have a child (Numbers 5:14–31). At first glance it all seems chauvinistic and even ludicrous, but the whole thing depends on the operation of a miracle for either vindication or condemnation. The sages of Israel teach that the whole point was to protect the woman from an over jealous husband, to exonerate her, as well as to preserve marital harmony.

How Hashem shows his concerns about the preservation of matrimonial vows tells us about his relationship with us. He who is married to Israel also preserves marital harmony with his bride even at the cost of his own name, as part of the ritual is for the officiating priest is to write Hashem's name and then dilute it in water, mix it with dirt and give it to the woman to drink. This erasure of the divine name comes against and despite the torahtic forbiddance to do so (Deuteronomy 12:3–4). This teaches us that in order to bring marital peace in Israel's families, Hashem is willing to let his own name be erased and dragged through the dirt.

Pondering on this point, I am saddened when I realize the flippant attitude many have towards marriage. Whereas the Father of all compassions seems to go to the nth degree to preserve marital peace and harmony, I see (and you probably do too) many marriages broken because of trivial and mostly selfish reasons; sometimes even because of theological differences. Whereas Paul, the chosen apostle of the Master, advises marriages between believers and idol-worshipping pagans to remain together (1 Corinthians 7), nowadays people even divorce because they can't agree on how to worship the same God. Such a sad reflection of Hashem.

The way I see it, we would be destroyed if he treated us the way we treat each other; we would be lost if he judged us the way we judge each other (Psalm 103:10). If only we would realize the sanctity Hashem places on marital harmony, on *peace in the home* called in Hebrew: *shalom Bayit* בית שלום, we would understand the infiniteness of his love and compassion.

My Personal Thoughts

263

Romans 3:23

All have sinned and come short of earning God's praise.

The Torah presents us with a simple way of dealing with a woman's suspected adultery. It involves the drinking of a potent mixture and a miracle. If a man suspects his wife to have been unfaithful to him, he is to take his wife to the Temple in Jerusalem for her to be tested by the trial of *bitter waters*. This consisted of a Scripture/curse written and diluted in a mixture of water and dust from the Temple. The woman was to drink it then go to the hill country. If she survived the mixture, she would be immune from the bitter waters and later, conceive. If not, she would quickly die of a loathsome disease (Numbers 5:19–31). Hashem had Moses conduct a similar operation in the desert; "But the moment Moshe got near the camp, when he saw the calf and the dancing, his own anger blazed up. He threw down the tablets he had been holding and shattered them at the base of the mountain. Seizing the calf they had made, he melted it in the fire and ground it to powder, which he scattered on the water. Then he made the people of Isra'el drink it." (Exodus 32:19–20).

Marriage constitutes the cornerstone of a civilization. It must not only be kept pure, but also peaceful (Colossians 3:18–19). We see the importance of this in the story of the King of Persia and his wife Vashti who defied her husband in the sight of all his princes. For the sake of domestic peace in every family in the Empire, she was not allowed to remain queen and her place was given to a more deserving one (Ester 1).

We have a bit of similar case in the apostolic texts. Miriam, a young bride-to-be receives a visitation. She then leaves to visit her cousin for three months only to return pregnant to the dismay of Joseph, her betrothed who has never been with her. One could hardly blame him for not believing the *angel story*. Why didn't Joseph bring Miriam to Jerusalem for the trial through bitter waters? There was no suspicion. Miriam stood right beside him pregnant and he knew that he had nothing to do with it. There was no need for the test. In his eyes, Miriam was already guilty.

The remarkable parallel is that whereas Miriam was not subjected to the trial of bitter waters, she was still exonerated through heavenly intervention. Had it not been for the angel that spoke to Joseph, she would have been stoned to death (Matthew 1:18–25). When a suspected woman drinks the Temple mixture, she drinks the word of God in the form of his name written in ink. If she is not guilty, she later conceives, Miriam did not drink the potion but she still gave birth to the one who would be called *The Memrah*, The Word (John 1).

In a certain way, like the woman suspected of adultery, we are all also guilty. As we drink the Torah it condemns us to death. But in Messiah, as the Shield of our Salvation (Psalm 18:35), we are also exonerated by heavenly intervention.

My Personal Thoughts

James 5:16   Sivan 5/ ה בסיון ה

Openly acknowledge your sins to one another.

It doesn't seem to be something very practiced today especially in Protestant circles, but the Torah encourages us towards the art of confession. It is a very good humility exercise, and it helps us to be nicer to those whom we feel are not as good as we are. It certainly challenges our own natural arrogance.

In the fifth chapter of the Book of Numbers, we find the following text,

> Tell the people of Isra'el, 'When a man or woman commits any kind of sin against another person and thus breaks faith with Adonai, he incurs guilt. He must confess the sin which he has committed; and he must make full restitution for his guilt, add twenty percent and give it to the victim of his sin." (Numbers 5:6–7)

On Yom Kippur also the sins of Israel are to be confessed upon the goat that is to be sent in the wilderness (Leviticus 16:21). It could be that modern Protestantism has distanced itself from the idea of confession because of its negative Catholic connotation, but the difference between that and what the Torah teaches, is that confession is to be made before Hashem, not before men.

King David was great at confessing his sins before Hashem. He said, "Against you, you only, have I sinned and done what is evil from your perspective; so that you are right in accusing me and justified in passing sentence" (Psalm 51:4) and "When I acknowledged my sin to you, when I stopped concealing my guilt, and said, 'I will confess my offenses to Adonai'; then you, you forgave the guilt of my sin." (Psalm 32:5).

James, the brother of the Master, actually connected the principles of healing and confession together. He said,

> Is someone among you ill? He should call for the elders of the congregation. They will pray for him and rub olive oil on him in the name of the Lord. The prayer offered with trust will heal the one who is ill—the Lord will restore his health; and if he has committed sins, he will be forgiven. Therefore, openly acknowledge your sins to one another, and pray for each other, so that you may be healed. The prayer of a righteous person is powerful and effective. (James 5:14–16)

Maybe when someone asks for healing prayer, they should also confess and acknowledge their sins. Finally, John the beloved disciple teaches us to use confession in order to keep the reality of our sinful nature in front of us. He says,

> If we claim not to have sin, we are deceiving ourselves, and the truth is not in us. If we acknowledge our sins, then, since he is trustworthy and just, he will forgive them and purify us from all wrongdoing. If we claim we have not been sinning, we are making him out to be a liar, and his Word is not in us. (1 John 1:8–10)

Happy confessing!

My Personal Thoughts

Acts 2:3 Sivan 6/ ו בסיון

Then they saw what looked like tongues of fire, which . . . came to rest on each one of them.

It has been fifty days now that Israel left Egypt. They have learned to trust Hashem for their deliverance from oppression, for their food, for their water, for their military might, and also to make a way for them though the wilderness and even through the sea if necessary. Now they are getting ready to meet the mighty one who did all this for them.

For two days the children of Israel have been getting ready. They have obeyed Hashem. They washed their clothes, immersed themselves regularly, and refrained from intimacy with their spouses. The camp is becoming completely ritually sanctified. The spirits are high, the anticipation is great, and everybody is wondering what will happen next. Hashem did tell them to

> prepare for the third day. For on the third day, ADONAI will come down on Mount Sinai before the eyes of all the people. You are to set limits for the people all around; and say, 'Be careful not to go up on the mountain or even touch its base; whoever touches the mountain will surely be put to death. (Exodus 19:11–12)

All of a sudden it happens. Hashem reveals himself. How does he reveal himself? With words. He starts speaking and everybody listens. Not only do the people hear the words but they see them, each one in his own language in flames of fire amidst the sound of the loud trumpet, of the wind, and of the quaking earth. The Torah tells us that the people could not bear it so they ask Moses to hear for them.

When all the people saw the flashes of lightning and the mountain smoking and heard the thunder and the sound of the trumpet, they were afraid and trembled. They stood far off and said to Moses, "You, speak with us; and we will listen. But don't let God speak with us, or we will die" (Exodus 20:18–21).

Let us time travel now 1,400 years later to another sixth of Sivan. This time we are in Jerusalem.

Because of the persecution against the followers of Yeshua, the Nazarene rabbi, Jerusalem is a dangerous place for the disciples. They are only staying in Jerusalem because ten days before, when the Master ascended in front of them, he commanded them

> not to leave Yerushalayim but to wait for what the Father promised, which you heard about from me. For Yochanan used to immerse people in water; but in a few days, you will be immersed in the Ruach HaKodesh! (Acts 1:4–5)

For several days the disciples of the Master witnessed the throngs of people coming for the festival of Shavuot/Pentecost. Caravans of people and goods already came from all around Israel and from countries. The city was buzzing with activity but the disciples were quiet in their houses. They had spent the whole previous night studying and reading the Torah, especially the texts about the giving of the Torah at Mt. Horeb on that day 1,400 years before.

Suddenly, a wind blew inside their house. It was blowing in the house but not outside. It got even more exciting when flames of fire appeared on their heads. People from all around heard the commotion so they came to see what was happening. Peter then took the lead and told them not to worry, that it was only the fulfillment of Joel's prophecy (Acts 2:17–21).

And what more, as they started speaking, the disciples realized that they could share what they had to say in all the languages of the many people present.

The day went on in festivities and joy as is usual on this festival day and in the evening the disciples retired and shared notes about the events of the day. It is then that, as they thought about the tongues of fire, the wind, the earthquake, the speaking in many languages, that they realized that they experienced a repeat of what happened at Mt. Horeb 1,400 years before. As they realized their new boldness and abilities to share their message, they also realized that the *promise of the Father* had come.

266

John 3:14

Just as Moshe lifted up the serpent in the desert, so must the Son of Man be lifted up.

When Jacob blessed his twelve sons, he told them each what would happen in the future. When it came to Dan, the old patriarch said,

> Dan will judge his people as one of the tribes of Isra'el. Dan will be a viper on the road, a horned snake in the path that bites the horse's heels so its rider falls off backward. I wait for your deliverance, ADONAI. (Genesis 49:16–18)

The text of the prophecy seems to be disjointed. The sages of Judaism commented on this and said, "Our forefather Jacob foresaw Samson and thought that he was the Messiah. But when he saw his death he exclaimed, ' For your salvation I wait for your salvation, ADONAI.'"

Samson was a descendant from the tribe of Dan and a Nazirite by birth. He is the fruit of a miraculous birth announced to his parents by an angel (Judges 13:3); his ways left his people wondering about him; he even lived outside of Israel with the Gentile Philistines for a while. He was a Nazirite but seemed to carelessly come in contact with what should be considered unclean to him. In the end, Samson vanquished the Philistines, the powerful enemy of Israel, by giving his life.

Jacob was not out of his mind when he thought he saw Messiah in Samson. As iconoclastic as he was, Samson foreshadowed David's victory over Goliath. David did not die in battle giving his life, but he did spend some time living with the Philistines when he was in disfavor with Saul.

Further down the messianic genealogies, Samson does foreshadow Messiah, Messiah whose miraculous birth was announced to his parents by an angel, who spent some time ministering outside of Israel, who took a nazirite vow before he died, and who gave his life defeating the enemy of our souls forever.

What about the snake in the prophecy?

Jacob may have seen how through Jeroboam, the tribe of Dan led the Northern Kingdom to idolatry and heresy. They even used the brazen snake Moses was asked to make in the desert (Numbers 21:9).

Come to think of it, Yeshua also compared himself to that snake. As we look up to him raised on the wooden pole, we live (John 3:14).

My Personal Thoughts

_____

_____

_____

_____

_____

_____

_____

Matthew 26:29   Sivan 8/ ח בסיון

I tell you, I will not drink this 'fruit of the vine' again until the day
I drink new wine with you in my Father's Kingdom.

If a man wanted the privilege and honor to serve in the priesthood but wasn't from the tribe of Levy, all he had to do was take a Nazirite vow. As such, he could legitimately perform all the duties of a Levite priest. The Nazirite vow required a rather restricting lifestyle (Numbers 6), so it was only to be done on a voluntary basis. The Mishnah informs us that people were discouraged to make such a vow for more than six months. To end the vow was also very expensive and sometimes people couldn't afford it.

Samson was an exception as he was a Nazirite from the womb of his mother (Judges 13:2–5). When reading the stories of his life, it is important to keep that in mind. John the Immerser was also a Nazirite from the womb of his mother; we know that because the angel told his father that his miraculous child is to drink no wine or strong drink (Luke 1:15). In *Eusebius, Ecclesiastical History,* we are also informed of James' Nazirite status. It says that "James drank no wine or intoxicating liquor and ate no animal food; no razor came near his head." As such he could operate as the main priestly representation in the Temple for the Nazarene Sect. James was revered by all in his days. Even non-believers called him, Ya'akov HaTzaddik, James the Righteous. In the Book of Acts, we learn that Paul had a Nazirite vow on him, and that he paid the expenses for four Jerusalem Jewish believers to end theirs (Acts 18:18; 21:23).

It seems that taking a Nazirite vow was quite common in the early days of our messianic movement. I think that aside from needing to attend to priestly duties, people may have done it to emulate the Master who also seems to have taken one before he died. He said, "I tell you, I will not drink this 'fruit of the vine' again until the day I drink new wine with you in my Father's Kingdom." (Matthew 26:29). This sounded very much like what would have been in those days the declaration to start a Nazirite vow.

It makes sense also that Paul took a vow. He went and started congregations in Diaspora. He may have needed sometimes to perform priestly functions but he was not from the tribe of Levy; he was from Benjamin, so he would have had to take a vow.

Today, people may take a Nazirite vow, but until the time when we have a Temple, there is no way to shed it. So any Nazirite vow taken today, unless Messiah comes soon and rebuilds the Temple, is a lifelong vow.

My Personal Thoughts

_____

_____

_____

_____

_____

_____

_____

Matthew 5:21–26

You have heard that our fathers were told, 'Do not murder . . . I tell you that anyone who nurses anger against his brother will be subject to judgment; that whoever calls his brother, 'You good-for-nothing!' will be brought before the Sanhedrin; that whoever says, 'Fool!' incurs the penalty of burning in the fire of Gei-Hinnom! . . . Go, make peace with your brother. Then come back and offer your gift. If someone sues you, come to terms with him quickly, while you and he are on the way to court; or he may hand you over to the judge . . . and you may be thrown in jail! Yes indeed! I tell you, you will certainly not get out until you have paid the last penny.

> ADONAI said to Moshe, "Tell the people of Isra'el, 'When a man or woman commits any kind of sin against another person and thus breaks faith with ADONAI, he incurs guilt. He must confess the sin which he has committed; and he must make full restitution for his guilt, add twenty percent and give it to the victim of his sin.'" (Numbers 5:5–7)

This is a very interesting verse. Sin here is viewed as "breaking faith with ADONAI," like breaking the terms of a contract. John actually teaches us that we "'trespass against ADONAI," by breaking Torah commands (1 John 3:4). *The Complete Jewish Bible* (CJB) reads the verse from Numbers correctly.

Sin here is viewed not only as the breaking of Torah command, but in the mishandling of people or of people's property. Sin then becomes the trespasses against another human being made in the image of God. Along the same lines, Judaism teaches that because man is made in the image of God, in murder we actually commit deicide.

In translating the verse this way, the CJB follows the translation given in Jewish texts. This translation may not seem literal, but it accurately follows the context. Notice here that the next verse speaks of *restitution* because of sin. *Restitution* implies that a trespass against another was committed. The text even follows in that context in telling us about the mishandling of someone's wife.

This teaches us that when we mishandle he for whom Hashem cares, we mishandle Hashem who is the faithful avenger of his children. This section also teaches us about repentance according to the Father. In true repentance, we first admit guilt privately to God, but audibly (Psalm 32:5). But when we sin against others causing them some loss, it is not adequate to merely confess the sin the God. We confess sin, and then we repent by making restitution, even restitution above and beyond the cost of the trespass (Numbers 5:7).

In this matter, Yeshua gave us warnings about verbal offenses. How many times do we verbally trespass against God through uncontrolled and unjustifiable anger, sarcasm, mocking, or condescending remarks towards loved ones, other drivers, store cashiers, restaurant waiters, even towards our children or our parents? The Master warned about that. He said, "By your words you will be justified, and by your words you will be condemned" (Matthew 12:37).

How it must pain Hashem to see how we treat each other so proudly and so arrogantly. By Torah's restitution standards, we should all be totally broke and spend a lifetime of servitude to each other in restitution. Maybe that's what the world to come is all about.

May it come soon, Abba, even in our days!

Revelation 5:6

Then I saw standing there with the throne and the four living beings, in the circle of the elders,
a Lamb that appeared to have been slaughtered. He had seven horns and seven eyes,
which are the sevenfold Spirit of God sent out into all the earth.

As we read into Moses' Tabernacle assignments, we must never forget that what he was told to make was an earthly replica of what he saw on the Mount (Exodus 26:30). Looking at the Tabernacle tells us what God's throne room looks like. It actually does correspond to the throne room vision of all the prophets including that of John in the Book of Revelation.

We read in the text of Aaron being in charge of the seven lights shining before the Almighty (Numbers 8:2; Exodus 25:37; 37:18–19, 23; 40:25). We are not directly told very much about the function and property of these lights, but studying the Torah in a thematic manner sheds some light (pun unintended) on the matter.

These lamps are to burn continually before God (Leviticus 24:1–2) so In the Tabernacle, they are placed in the anteroom before the Holy of Holies. The apocryphal Book of Tobit tells us of the seven holy angels, which present the prayers of the saints, and which go in and out before the glory of the Holy One (Tobit 12:15). In Enoch, another apocryphal book early believers were familiar with, we are given the names and functions of these angels (Enoch 20:1–8).

These go in and go out Tobit says, just like the seven eyes in Zechariah's vision that run to and fro through the whole earth (Zechariah 4:10). In the Book of Hebrews, it is revealed to us that he (Hashem) makes his angels spirits, and his ministers a flame of fire (Hebrews 1:7). Finally, Zechariah tells us that these were like seven eyes in a stone (Zechariah 3:9). The stone is Yeshua (Psalm 118:22), the heavenly high priest who tends to the light, a function foreshadowed by Aaron in the Book of Leviticus (Hebrews 8–9; Leviticus 8:2).

These angels/spirits/lights roam the earth and bring our prayers to God. An ancient tradition tells us that on Friday evenings, angels enter the home of God's people and see how much priority they have given to the Sabbath. That is why we sing the famous Sabbath angel welcoming song, *Shalom Aleichem* עליכם שלום. Whether that really happened or not, I do not know, but I do know that Hashem's looks at how we remember and set-aside his Sabbath. I also know that these seven angels go in and out before the glory of the Holy One roaming the earth. They are like God's little *spies*. They come and look upon us and tell God what they saw, how we react to each other, how we carry our responsibilities as members of his Kingdom, as husbands, as wives, and as parents. They also report to him on the priority that we give to Torah study.

Does this scare you? It shouldn't unless you know in your heart that you have failed to prioritize your life according to Hashem's commandments. Maybe it is time to take stock of things and start living a life Hashem can brag about even to the devil like he did Job (Job 1:8).

We all could be older than we think; anyone of us could die tomorrow and miss a good chance at repentance in this realm.

My Personal Thoughts

_____

_____

_____

Matthew 18:21–22   Sivan 11/ יא בסיון

Then Kefa came up and said to him, "Rabbi, how often can my brother sin against me and I have to forgive him?" . . . "No, not seven times," answered Yeshua, "but seventy times seven!"

As they were leaving Egypt, God gave Israel commands concerning their lives in their Land. One of them was to celebrate the Passover/Feast of Unleavened Bread (Exodus 12:19). If this command was already given in Exodus and in Leviticus 23, why is it repeated in Numbers (Numbers 9:1–5)?

The distance from Mt. Horeb to the borders of Israel is not great and at the times of Numbers, the children of Israel should already have been in the Land. The problem was that they were delayed at least three months by the golden calf incident. The Torah allows second chances. We may orchestrate the most elaborate fail-safe plan against sin, but life has a habit of throwing curve balls at us. In spite of our loftier dreams and ideals, at the end of the day, we have to deal with the reality on the ground, and it seems that Hashem is fully aware of it.

In Numbers 9 we also have the case of a family who would miss the precious Passover celebration because of a death. In this case, Hashem again gives them the chance to celebrate Passover on the following month. This case foreshadowed Joseph of Arimathea and Nicodemus. The two men cared for the Master's body on the night of Passover 2,000 years ago. Therefore, they were ritually contaminated and could not eat of the Passover lamb that year. It was a traditional belief with the early Jerusalem believers that the two men reclined at the Passover table this year on the second month of the year for what is called: Pesach Sheni: The Second Passover.

It takes maturity and godliness to not be frustrated at the way things are compared to the way they should be. I know someone who when things do not work out the way he has dreamed he says, "It is what it is." I think sometimes that Hashem looks at us with empathy and says, "It is what it is," and then, he tries to give us a second chance. He tells us that we can celebrate the Passover in the desert instead of in the Land, or that we can celebrate it on the second month if reality kept us from doing it on the first. The whole idea of redemption and atonement is in fact about second chances.

Again we stand in awe at the perfect Almighty God, Creator of the universe, as he seems to be able to bend to the bare facts of our lives on earth. He proposes and offers us the great ideals of his Torah with the full knowledge of our imperfectness towards it and seems to say, "It is what it is."

How much more then should we be able to bear with each other's imperfection? How much patience and forgiveness and bending ability the Father has for each one of us should be the standard of ours towards others? The novice forgets about his own imperfections and looks at others condescendingly wondering how come they don't toe the line better. The seasoned mature leader and disciple of the Master knows life, that "It is what it is," and deals with it not according to his lofty dreams but according to the realities on the ground.

May we learn from Hashem, the great Father who loves us so much that he gave us a second chance in his Messiah. May we also have the maturity to accord that second chance to those we meet in this life's journey.

1 Corinthians 10:11   Sivan12/ יב בסיון

These things happened to them as prefigurative historical events,
and they were written down as a warning to us who are living in the acharit-hayamim.

It seems that few things exacerbate the Father more than his people griping and complaining. He can freely set before us the best food ever concocted in the kitchens of heaven, but we will still complain and would rather have the dainties brought by slavery. And why do we complain? There is really nothing wrong with the food Hashem gives us except that, it is not what we want.

Woe unto us and to our evil inclination! This tendency to complain and always wanting more was the basic lusting nature behind the sin in the Garden of Eden. We always seem to want what Hashem in his goodness and wisdom withholds from us, and like today's manufacturers of *goods*, the devil is always happy to oblige. The worst of it is that today's worldly merchants know about our natural bend to whine and gripe and they constantly play on it in order to make a profit. They constantly tell people, "Aren't you tired of this or that, behold I have the solution that will help you not to have work so hard, be more comfortable, or here is the food that will delight your palate, all for only $ . . . ! How can you live without it?" They make a profit and feed on our complaining nature.

It is so easy to look at the children of Israel in the desert and wonder how they could complain so much, but in reality, we complain as much as they do and about the same things. Food, hard work, leadership, and the sometimes-monotonous daily grind of life seem to be our main areas of complaint. We feel that the way God does things is not good enough. We must improve on his plan for us and make every decision in our lives from the color and consistency of our hair to whether or not to have children. We even want to decide the day of our death and call it *Death with Dignity* as if Hashem was not able to do that for us. We always think that we deserve more than the simple life our Father would have us live according to his will, so we enslave ourselves to another master: the Master Card! But Yeshua told us that we cannot serve two masters, that we cannot serve God and Mammon (Matthew 6:24, KJV).

The area of complaint that seems the most destructive in the congregational body of Messiah seems to be each other. Whereas we complain about having to put up with others, we seem to forget that also others have to put up with us. We always feel that *people* should have learned certain lessons by now so we show ourselves intolerant and impatient. We forget that in the Father's eyes, we probably should be a bit more advanced ourselves in our spiritual growth and that we only exist by the mercy of his great compassion.

May we learn from the lessons of the children of Israel in the desert and realize that these things happened to them as prefigurative historical events, and they were written down as a warning to us who are living in the acharit-hayamim (1 Corinthians 10:11).

My Personal Thoughts

_____

_____

_____

_____

_____

Matthew 6:33   Sivan 13/ יג בסיון

But seek first his Kingdom and his righteousness,
and all these things will be given to you as well.

There are two main ways the Father uses our finances to teach us: He either withholds them, or punishes us with abundance.

On the second month of their exodus the children of Israel complained about their manna diet. They wanted fresh meat. Our fathers' desire for meat made them complain about their blessed situation and look back at Egypt with nostalgia (Exodus 16:3). A year later they did it again (Numbers 11:4) and this time the Father from whom all blessings flow did not take too kindly to it and he addressed the issue by punishing them with abundance.

Abundance is not always a sign of God's blessing and approval. Abundance has a tendency to steal our hearts from God. In abundance we spend foolishly, become preoccupied with the things of the world, and find it difficult to dedicate to God in the same proportions as we did before. Avarice and greed are quick to follow and a society that has too much usually becomes fat, lazy, selfish, and insensitive to the needs of others. It seems easier to emanate godliness when things are lean. Maybe that is why many of God's children are blessed with *leanness*.

Whether we live in leanness or abundance, we should never complain. The apostle Paul was a good example of this. When addressing his own situation he said, "I have learned to be content regardless of circumstances" (Philippians 4:11). James, the brother of the Master did not hold too much respect for wealth either (James 5:1–6) and the Master himself encouraged us to not worry about our food and raiment but to busy ourselves with the affairs of the Kingdom. Housing is not even in the deal (Matthew 6:31–34).

May we learn from this lesson from our fathers in the desert and realize that abundance can be a punishment as much as poverty. Poverty usually drives us to desperation and to Hashem; abundance steals our hearts away from he who is the Fountain of everlasting life.

> And don't grumble, as some of them did, and were destroyed by the Destroying Angel. These things happened to them as prefigurative historical events, and they were written down as a warning to us who are living in the acharit-hayamim. (1 Corinthians 10:10–11)

May we pray the wise prayer from King Solomon,

> Keep falsehood and futility far from me, and give me neither poverty nor wealth. Yes, provide just the food I need today; for if I have too much, I might deny you and say, "Who is ADONAI?" And if I am poor, I might steal and thus profane the name of my God. (Proverbs 30:8–9)

My Personal Thoughts

_____

_____

_____

_____

_____

Ephesians 5:20   Sivan 14/ יד בסיון

Always give thanks for everything to God the Father in the name of our Lord Yeshua the Messiah.

The old saying, "Be careful what you pray for, you may just get it" is true. When the children of Israel complained about their diet in the desert Hashem gave them exactly what they asked but sent a wasting disease among them (Psalm 106:15).

The lifestyle of the disciples of Yeshua is not generally one of abundance. The Nazarene sect of the early Israeli disciples of the Master were nicknamed the *Ebionites*, the *poor ones* (Galatians 2:10). There is nothing wrong with abundance as it certainly can be a sign of blessing. The problem is not abundance, but our attitude towards it, an attitude very well described in the episode of the children of Israel and the quails (Numbers 11).

If there is anything Hashem hates I think it is whining, grumbling, and complaining, especially against the blessings he gives us. The children of Israel had experienced the miracles of miracles since coming out of Egypt. From an enslaved people, they were going to be established as a sovereign nation in a country flowing with milk and honey, but all they could think about was a little more variation in their present diet. The problem was not *Manna*, fish, abundance, or poverty, the problem was a spirit of entitlement.

Hashem does not owe us anything, except maybe a good whooping. The attitude that needs to emanate from our spirit is, "Naked I came from my mother's womb, and naked I will return there. ADONAI gave; ADONAI took; blessed be the name of ADONAI" (Job 1:21). The minute we approach life in a spirit of entitlement, we are bound to disappointment, discouragement, and eventual failure. I think this to be the problem behind depression, sadness, and discouragement. We have been mistreated and it's oh so unfair, so we give up and curl up in self-pity licking our wounds.

There is something very special about food. We think that we are entitled to eat whatever we want in the quantity that we want. Nothing in life works that way. In everything we need to learn the discipline to choose the good and eschew the evil. But when it comes to food, we think we are entitled to whatever suits our palate. As a result, America, for example, has an epidemic of obesity. It is amazing that the first notion of sin ever taught to us was about the consumption prohibition of a certain food (Genesis 3:2–3). A big part of the Torah is concerned about what to eat and what not to eat.

May we make the difference between what Hashem has promised and what he did not promise. Hashem never promised us skies ever blue or flower-strewn pathways for all of our lives. He has never promised that we would have sun without rain, joy without sadness, or even peace without pain. What he did promise though was strength for each day, grace for all trials, and light for our way. Also, rest after labor, help from above, unfailing sympathy, and undying love.

May we learn that we are not entitled to protection, health, or wealth, only to redemption, and eventual resurrection in the world to come.

May it come soon Abba, even in our days!

My Personal Thoughts

_____

_____

Hebrews 9:13–14 **Sivan 15/** טו בסיון

For if sprinkling ceremonially unclean persons with the blood of goats and bulls and the ashes of a heifer restores their outward purity; then how much more the blood of the Messiah, who, through the eternal Spirit, offered himself to God as a sacrifice without blemish, will purify our conscience from works that lead to death, so that we can serve the living God!

Unlike all the other offerings, which are performed by the altar of the Temple, the offering of the red heifer is to be done outside the Temple. This alludes to Yeshua who was also *offered* in a figurative way outside the Temple.

In the second half of the first century CE, the Sadducee leadership executed James the Righteous, the brother of the Master and leader of the Israeli community of believers. This event initiated a severe persecution against the followers of the rabbi from Nazareth. As the Master had prophesied, the disciples became outlawed in the synagogues and in the Temple where they had until then worshipped side by side with other Jews (Luke 21:12; John 16:2). They also faced official excommunication from the rest of the Jewish community.

The writer of the Letter to the Hebrews desperately tried to encourage Yeshua's disciples. As they lost their rights to attendance in the Temple, along with representation by its earthly high priest, the author encourages the Nazarenes to look to the Temple and high priesthood that are above. He contrasts the offerings on earth, which serve to purify the flesh for attendance at the earthly Temple, with the offering of Yeshua, whose blood cleans their conscience for attendance at the heavenly Temple (Hebrews 9:13–14; 4:16). In this light, their loss seemed like a gain.

Today Jewish Messianic believers still face excommunication from Jewish orthodoxy at large. Some very small but very vocal orthodox minorities actively work to deny present-day Jewish believers their emigration rights to the Land or to its social benefits. It is noteworthy that Paul, the apostle to the Gentiles, came from a similar anti-Yeshua circle of people. Hashem does seem to have a sense of humor.

In the same manner as the first century believers did, we the Jewish believers of today must also allow our eyes to, for a moment, forego the temporal realities below and embrace the eternal realities above. We must also, as the Master taught us, respond to evil with good (Isaiah 53:7; Romans 12:21). Because we are sure of our rights, commission, and destiny, we know that we can, and should stand firm for who we are, even while turning the other cheek (Matthew 5:39; Ephesians 6:13–14). We absolutely must refuse to ourselves the indulging temptation to answer evil with anger and hatred.

Even so, as the red heifer offered outside the Temple, let us go to Yeshua outside the camp and bear the reproach he endured (Hebrews 13:13). As offered firstborns of the congregation of the Firstborn (Revelation 7:4; 14:4; Hebrews 12:23), let us follow him and be offered as he was, excommunicated, and allow the Father to work through us his plan of universal redemption to the Jews first, then to the Gentiles (Romans 1:16).

My Personal Thoughts

Matthew 5:12   Sivan 16/ טז בסיון

The prophets before you.

"Is it true that ADONAI has spoken only with Moshe? Hasn't he spoken with us too" (Numbers 12:2)? This was Miriam's complaint. Though the English text tells us that both Miriam and Aaron complained, the Hebrew text uses the verb in the feminine form.

The complaint had to do with prophecy but also with Moses' Cushite (Ethiopian) wife. The Torah is not very generous on details concerning the situation with the Cushite woman, but we can certainly read in the text an issue of jealousy concerning Moses' prophetic gift and elevated position in the camp. Right away Hashem solved the issue by establishing what I would coin as the *Dynamics of Prophecy* (Numbers 12:6–8).

Similar problems seem to prevail in congregations today. To understand the issue, we must understand the nature, function, and property of prophet and prophecy. A prophet is not someone who tells the future or who is given messages for the benefit of everybody else. A prophet is simply someone who hears God to a certain extent.

Samuel started his career as a prophet when he heard God in the middle of the night; because all Israel heard the voice on the mountain, they were all prophets. Yeshua called his disciples prophets because they heard him (1 Samuel 3:4; Exodus 20:18; Matthew 5:12). Prophecy is also part of the 'earnest of the spirit' each one receives as believers, just as Peter reminded us using the prophet Joel's prophecy (2 Corinthians 1:22, KJV; Acts 2:16–18). But whereas everybody has the ability to hear God's voice either in a dream, vision, through studying the Torah, or even in a voice in their hearts, it doesn't mean that they should strut around as prophets saying, 'ADONAI told me,' in order to give weight to their personal views and opinions. Only certain ones are given the divine command to share a message with the body and even when that happens, the congregation is to weigh the message (1 Corinthians 14:29).

In this sense, Miriam was right in her question to Moses. But the issue here was that in her misplaced jealousy, she did not recognize Moses' status. Maybe as his older sister, she was a bit familiar with him. Hashem seemed to communicate with Moses like with no one else before. Whereas everybody else was given riddles, dreams, and visions to decipher, Hashem's communication with Moses was less ambiguous. The Torah tells us, with him I speak mouth to mouth, clearly, and not in riddles, and he beholds the form of ADONAI (Numbers 12:8). Yeshua is prophesied as the "prophet like Moses" (Deuteronomy 18:15). That is because as Moses, the Master has open communications with Hashem.

In their innate craving for self-importance, people often ignore these basic principles of prophecy and thus like Miriam cause many problems in congregations. To drop Hashem's name to share a personal opinion or view on something is very dangerous and akin to *using the Name of God in vain*.

May we remember that while Paul spoke highly of the gift of prophecy, he also concurred with the sages of old who taught that there was something even higher than prophecy: Love (1 Corinthians 12:31; 13).

My Personal Thoughts

_____

_____

John 17:11   Sivan 17/ יז בסיון

So that they may be one, just as we are.

The Torah leaves us with much to discover. It may be that the Father in his great wisdom designed it that way, so we could spend our time in studying it. We may feel also like we forever learn without coming to the complete understanding, but learning the Torah is not like learning a mathematical formula. What we are talking about here are the elements through which the worlds were created.

"Show me a man who can understand God, and I'll show you a worm who can understand man!" Said my wife to her atheist ninety-nine year-old aunt who, while facing imminent death, is starting to consider the option that after all, there might be a God.

Claiming to be able to understand the Torah to the point of being able to define it in a clear doctrinal document and established statements implies that one completely understands the fullness of God. But can God or the Torah truly and fully fit in the human brain and be explained in human words? What pride and arrogance we as people can have. This is why the Talmud, which is the Jewish commentary to the Torah, is a discussion, not a document establishing doctrine.

The Torah teaches us that there is one commandment for the Israelite-born, and for the *ger* גר, the stranger in the Land (Numbers 15:14–15). In this manner Hashem established how he wants to be acknowledged and worshipped by all the people in the world. It is not up to us to decide how to honor him. In this day and age, people go away from worshipping in the spirit and truth of Torah, and go establishing their own righteousness; but as has proven time and again, spirituality outside of the parameters of Torah leads to heresy and idolatry.

The Torah teaches distinction between person and person even within the Israelite nation, so while provoking homo-ethnicity, the fact that the same rituals are to be observed by both Israelites and non-Israelites doesn't erase distinctions. What Paul coined as the "one new man" is as 'one' as a man and a woman are 'one flesh' (Genesis 2:24) while remaining two distinct genders and personalities (Ephesians 2:15). The same principle applies to Yeshua and the Father who while "one", remain two distinct personalities even in power and knowledge (John 14:28; Mark 13:32).

Come to think of it, while being under the Torah may provoke ethnic coalescence, the beauty of it remains in the fact that we are all unique individuals. Unity is not the absence of diversity, but the working together in spite of, and within our diversity. Paul explained this principle of Israelite/gentile unity in diversity, but still called it a "mystery," so maybe we should also just leave the issue rest there and be happy with a "mystery" (Ephesians 3:1–7).

Yeshua coined it very well though; peering into the future of the international ministry of the disciples he said,

> The glory which you have given to me, I have given to them; so that they may be one, just as we are one—I united with them and you with me, so that they may be completely one, and the world thus realize that you sent me, and that you have loved them just as you have loved me. (John 17:22–23)

My Personal Thoughts

_____

_____

Hebrews 11:13–16   Sivan 18/ יח בסיון

All these people . . . while acknowledging that they were aliens and temporary residents on the earth . . . are looking for a fatherland . . . they aspire to a better fatherland. . . . This is why God is not ashamed to be called their God, for he has prepared for them a city.

The generation in the desert refused to enter the Promised Land. The writer of the Letter to the Messianic Jews of the first century CE compared entrance to the Promised Land to entering in the world to come at the Shabbat at the end of days, but for the people of the generation who lived under the bounty of Hashem's welfare system for some time may have felt differently. They were now going to have to fight to inherit the Land. The manna would cease falling, and they would now have to start landscaping, seeding, planting, irrigating, all to sustain themselves. They were also going to have to build houses, establish a government, and continue to train their army. Doesn't sound like much rest to me.

The *rest* the apostle refers to in his epistle is not a rest from activity. It is a rest from wandering in a strange land. It refers to the idea of finally arriving home. When you are home you may still have to work, but you are home. You have the right to lock your door and enjoy privacy, to eat and live the way you want to. In essence, home is where you have the freedom to serve Hashem the way he desires it.

In that respect we are, as the writer of Hebrews also said, "aliens and temporary residents" (Hebrews 11:13). As the children of Israel in the desert, we wander though this life and this age while receiving a foretaste of the bounties of the world to come through the daily provisions he allows us to partake of. We also learn to live by the legislative Constitution of the future Kingdom, which is the Torah.

The day comes when we will also cross the Jordan into that Promised Land of the Kingdom of God established "on earth as in heaven." We will then finally be home eating the grapes of our own vine seating under our own fig tree in a place when none shall make us afraid anymore (Micah 4:4). "Today, if you hear God's voice, don't harden your hearts, as you did in the Bitter Quarrel on that day in the Wilderness when you put God to the test" (Hebrews 3:7–8 quoting Psalm 95:7–8, which is read every Friday night at the welcoming of the Shabbat).

Jewish sages use the word *Today* to refer to the Shabbat. In a sense the Shabbat is a glimpse of the world to come. Why would one refuse to enter the Shabbat of the world to come? At the welcoming of the Shabbat we have to consciously stop our feverish personal activities in order to focus our attention on the awesome moment. We have to change gears. What is not done is not done. It's *half time*, and some find it difficult to stop. Maybe also like in the case of the children of Israel there is a sense of loss and fear, the loss of the comfort of the familiar lifestyle mixed with fear and apprehension of entering into the new.

May we learn today to live under the rules and principles of the world to come so that it will not feel so strange to us when its righteousness covers the earth as the waters cover the sea.

May it be soon Abba, even in our days!

My Personal Thoughts

_____

_____

Hebrews 3:14

For we have become sharers in the Messiah, provided, however, that we hold firmly to the conviction we began with, right through until the goal is reached.

As it is said, "Today, if you hear God's voice, don't harden your hearts, as you did in the Bitter Quarrel" (Hebrews 3:15).

Many look at the day of their redemption , the day they recognize Messiah as their redeemer, as an end in itself. They do not recognize that it is actually a means to an end, the beginning of a process to be completed. The program of full redemption is very well illustrated for us in the story of the exodus from Egypt to the Promised Land. This is where we find what I will coin as the Four Steps of Full Redemption.

First we are rescued, or saved from the angel of death coming upon the land. This salvation is purely by God's choosing. Jew or Gentile who obeys the instruction concerning the lamb's blood on the doorposts of their houses will be saved from the death of the firstborn and eligible to leave Egypt that very night. The Torah has not been given yet so this salvation, so to speak, is not dependent on anything personal: virtue or works. Only one thing is required regardless of who we are or of our past: the blood of the lamb on the doorposts of our houses. That's the first step.

Second, we must cross the Red Sea. This step takes us out of Egypt. With the help of mighty miracles from God, we have left our old life and culture behind. Paul referred to the crossing of the Red Sea as a national immersion, or baptism (1 Corinthians 10:1–2). That's the second step.

Third, we go to Mt. Horeb to receive the Torah. We have left our old life, culture, and country behind. We need a new life, a new identity in a new country, a new culture under a new king, with a new set of rules. Going to Mt. Horeb provides us with the instructions for our new life in our new kingdom.

Finally, after experimenting and learning to live under this new set of rules, we enter the Promised Land, receiving full citizenship of the Kingdom. This is the fourth and final step.

In Hebrews, the writer warns us about not making the same mistake the first generation did in the desert fearing to accomplish the last and final step of entering the land because of unbelief. I do not know what this exactly means but the warning remains. The children of Israel seemed to have been like the bride who got cold feet. She went through the whole ordeal and the great expense of getting married but in the end feared to move in with the groom.

The writer of Hebrews speaks of entering the Promised Land as the Shabbat. We have to make a conscious effort to enter the Shabbat. We have to agree to stop our personal activities; we have to trust that God will supply if we stop working. To enter the Shabbat we have to literally surrender ourselves to God. Is this what the children of Israel feared? Without surrender there is no peace, and there is no Shabbat.

May we learn to surrender to him every Shabbat so that we do not harden our hearts at his voice when he calls us to enter the Promised Land of his Kingdom when it is established on earth as it is in heaven.

My Personal Thoughts

---

3 John 1:4   **Sivan 20/ כ בסיון**

Nothing gives me greater joy than hearing that my children are living in the truth.

To refuse entering the Land seems to have been an unpardonable sin. Right there and then Hashem condemned the children of Israel to die in the desert. Why is it then that after the sad episode of the spies the narration in the Book of Numbers continues with, "When you have come into the land where you are going to live, which I am giving to you" (Numbers 15:2)? Rashi the Jewish sage notices, so he points out that though that generation will not enter the Promised Land, Hashem was suggestiing that their children might.

Here we have an example when Hashem fulfills the promises made to the fathers in the children. The fathers had been negative examples of grumbling and murmuring even to the point of wanting to elect a new leader who would lead them back to Egypt as they refused to enter the Land. This is a very natural reaction and we shouldn't self-righteously blame them. How many of us are guilty of settling in the comfort of familiar surroundings fearing to venture into the new unfamiliar terrain of something Hashem may have us do? These were parents who also feared for their children (Numbers 14:31). I say we shouldn't blame them because if we honestly look at the components of our lives, if we honestly look at ourselves the way Hashem looks at us, we are probably doing the same thing. Very few of us have the courage required to go face the *giants* of the unknown Promised Land of God's will for our lives. We don't, and our lives still go haywire. What we fear the most in life is the one thing none of us has control over: death, and death happens anyways.

Here we learn about the mercies of Hashem. After he finished telling the children of Israel that their carcasses will rot in the desert (Numbers 14:28–35), he continued the narration in the second person plural referring to them, not in the third person plural referring to their children who will undergo forty years of obedience training. He says, "When you have come into the land where you are going to live" (Numbers 15:2).

I thank and honor Hashem for his everlasting providence that whereas children receive the promises made even to the disobedient fathers, fathers seem to also benefit from the virtues of the retrained children. In this way, the children of disobedient Israel who received the promised Messiah are portent to the salvation of their parents. Hashem has provided us with children who by his words, will fulfill the promises that we have failed in. Could it be that this is the meaning of the promise made to Eve about her *seed:* "the woman who, on being deceived, became involved in the transgression. Nevertheless, the woman will be delivered through childbearing" (Genesis 4:25; 9:9; 1 Timothy 2:14–15)?

My Personal Thoughts

_____

_____

_____

_____

_____

_____

_____

Matthew 26:27–28

Also he took a cup of wine, made the b'rakhah, and gave it to them, saying,
"All of you, drink from it! For this is my blood, which ratifies the New Covenant,
my blood shed on behalf of many, so that they may have their sins forgiven."

Reflecting upon his work and trying to foster unity in the midst of the Philippians' congregations, Paul exhorts his congregants with,

> Do everything without kvetching or arguing, so that you may be blameless and pure children of God, without defect in the midst of a twisted and perverted generation, among whom you shine like stars in the sky, as you hold on to the Word of Life. If you do this, I will be able to boast, when the Day of the Messiah comes, that I did not run or toil for nothing. Indeed, even if my lifeblood is poured out as a drink offering over the sacrifice and service of your faith, I will still be glad and rejoice with you all. (Philippians 2:14–17)

In this statement Paul exhorted the people towards unity, but anticipating the possibility that his exhortation may fall on deaf ears, as they often do, he compared his efforts to the wine libation poured upon God's altar (Numbers 15:7).

R. Kipling said in his famous poem, *If*, "If you can meet success and failure and treat these two importers the same way . . . you'll be a man, my son." It is in that same spirit that Paul toiled teaching Torah to the nations thus fulfilling the promises found in the prophecy of Amos (Acts 15:15–18 quoting Amos 9:11–12). He worked tirelessly without any assurance of success. His only joy and reward was the knowledge of answering Hashem's call.

We must learn to emulate that attitude. "I serve an audience of one" should be the all-encompassing theme behind all we do. Our sole and only pleasure should be Hashem's satisfied look and approbation at our feeble attempts to serve Him.

While waiting for Nero to utter his death sentence, for Paul the *wine libation* theme reflected an even deeper imagery. He wrote to Timothy,

> For as for me, I am already being poured out on the altar; yes, the time for my departure has arrived. I have fought the good fight, I have finished the race, I have kept the faith. All that awaits me now is the crown of righteousness which the Lord, "the Righteous Judge," will award to me on that Day—and not only to me, but also to all who have longed for him to appear. (2 Timothy 4:6–8)

In all these things the faithful apostle emulated his beloved Master Yeshua.

May we also in this life and within the framework of our divinely appointed responsibilities learn to emulate our Master whose blood was poured as a wine libation on the altar of the Father's will and work of universal redemption.

My Personal Thoughts

_____

_____

_____

Hebrews 4:1   Sivan 22/ כב בסיון

Therefore, let us be terrified of the possibility that, even though the promise of entering his rest remains, any one of you might be judged to have fallen short of it.

The writer of the Book of Hebrews uses the children of Israel's fear of entering the Land as a platform to encourage a disenfranchised first century community of Jewish believers in Israel (Numbers 14:1–4; Hebrews 3–4).

The two situations are truly analogous. The children of Israel hear about the giants in the Land so they refuse to fight for it. As a result, they died in the desert and never entered God's rest, the rest of finding a home where they can build and settle their families. They can never enter the homeland where they can finally put their travelling gear down; where they live, exist, and multiply in a place that is their own by right. They were at the borders of receiving the fulfillment of that promise but they turned back due to fear fomented by lies (Numbers 14:2–3).

The first century Israeli believers were in the same predicament. They were ostracized by their brethren; excluded from Jewish communities, synagogues, and the Temple. They had lost all civic privileges because of their discipleship to Yeshua. All they had to do to change their woeful predicament was to recant and they would be restored into Israeli society, which sadly some did. The Book of Hebrews then uses the story in Numbers as mentioned in Psalm 95 (vs. 95:7–11) to encourage these first century Jewish believers to not lose faith like their predecessors did. The Psalm says: "If only today you would listen to his voice: Don't harden your hearts. . . . Therefore I swore in my anger that they would not enter my rest" (vs. 7–11).

Let's go over that passage. 'Today' is a Talmudic way of talking about the Sabbath. In Hebrews, the Sabbath rest of entering the Land is analogous to the idea of living in obedience to God through his Messiah. In essence a similar situation of obedience was presented to that new generation of first century Jewish believers, and through the epistle, they were being warned of the dangers of turning their back on God's promises because of fear just like their fathers did fourteen centuries before.

This warning works for us today. So many hear the truth of Yeshua the living Jewish Messiah, but when they realize the havoc obeying him will create in their lives, they refuse him. They fear being ostracized from their families and their friends as their lifestyle changes. Obeying his words in eating according to the Levitical diet and observing the Sabbath will certainly change their lives in many drastic ways: socially and even financially. Some people fear going through that.

Come to think of it, it is quite amazing because these are the things the early Gentile believers were faced with all over the Roman Empire. Their new faith in the God of Israel took them away from their idolatrous environment to obey Hashem's commandments and as a result, they lost all civic privileges in Greek and Roman society.

The days are coming and are already upon us when the text of the Book of Hebrews will resound like a distant shofar: "Today, if you hear his voice, do not harden your hearts . . ."

My Personal Thoughts

_____

_____

_____

Hebrews 4:16

*Therefore, let us confidently approach the throne from which God gives grace,
so that we may receive mercy and find grace in our time of need.*

Whereas our Father loves to bless us with the most exquisite gifts, he is also thrilled when we trust him in spite of all the obstacles that may stand between us. As a result, he often hides his gifts behind seeming walls of difficulties, obstructions, and impossibilities. Such was the case with our forefathers as they arrived in Kadesh and saw the Anakim, a race of people who were supposedly extinct from the earth by the Flood. The Torah doesn't bother to explain how these people still existed after the flood. A fanciful explanation in Jewish literature suggests that a fellow named Og clang to the roof of the ark.

Along with their giant owners, the children of Israel could also see the giant clusters of grapes of the area of Eshcol (meaning: cluster of grapes), a sign of the land's promising fertility. The clusters were so full with giant grapes that it took two people to carry one on a pole between them. Jewish eschatology teaches that in the world to come, the Land will again give grape clusters of that caliber. In the meantime, the giants stood between the people and the grapes. This is when the test of real faith comes. Those who looked at the giants felt dwarfed to locust's size. Joshua and Caleb saw God instead which in their eyes dwarfed the giants. We know what happened next: ten spies discouraged the generation of Israelites, which had to then die in the desert waiting for their children, a less cynical generation raised under Moses and God's care, to grow and conquer this Land.

Will we ever know the blessings we may have inherited had we looked at Hashem instead of sizing the difficulties? We often complain about the way things are but how many initiatives for improvement go by un-attempted because we "count the cost," forgetting to include the God factor in the equation. It seems that often our own faulty perspective is our personal giant; we downsize Hashem to the dimensions of our fears. It must make him feel insulted; what if your three-year old child downsized you to his level of trust and didn't think you, his father, could protect him against an eight-year old?

May we ponder on this sad chapter in the history of our fathers in the desert. Mostly, may we learn to recognize our unfounded fears and return Hashem to its proper perspective in our minds. Knowing that the time to favor Zion has come and that we live in a time of unprecedented fulfillment of the promises of Hashem towards us his children, may we approach him boldly with our requests knowing that he is more willing to grant them to us than we are willing to receive them.

My Personal Thoughts

_____

_____

_____

_____

_____

_____

_____

Romans 12:10   **Sivan 24/** כד בסיון

Set examples for each other in showing respect.

> Now Korach the son of . . . Levi, along with Datan and Aviram, the sons of . . .
> Re'uven, took men and rebelled against Moshe. Siding with them were 250 men
> of Isra'el, leaders of the community, key members of the council, men of
> reputation. They assembled themselves against Moshe and Aharon and said to
> them, "You take too much on yourselves! After all, the entire community is holy,
> every one of them, and ADONAI is among them. So why do you lift yourselves up
> above ADONAI's assembly?" (Numbers 16:1–3)

Such a common story. The House of Korah resented Moses only appointing those of the House of
Aaron as priests. One may understand jealousy when men seem to make biased decisions, but
this was not the case. Moses wasn't in any way making any decisions. He was just obeying and
the decisions that were made had cosmic effects that went beyond the dimension of time itself. So
this was absolute rebellion. Korah not giving respect to Moses' divine appointment and decision-
making shows his rebellious nature.

Another point is that Korah confederated with others who had nothing to do with the priesthood.
They had no claim to it whatsoever. They just jumped on the bandwagon against Moses, and
Korah was happy for the inflated *troops.* Jewish history texts tell us that Dathan and Abiram were
the same people who constantly challenged Moses and made his life miserable from even the
days when they were in Egypt. This also shows Korah's total lack of spirituality and submission to
God.

Only a small man insecure with himself, who is only concerned with his own posture and tenure
acts this way. This Korah-like attitude seems to be the plague of society today. It keeps people
from working together in consensus under any form of authority, much less under God's. I
certainly do not see how one could claim to be able to submit to God when he cannot submit to
the authorities made in God's image, which he has set around him.

You may ask, "What are these authorities that God set around us?" First of all, I would say our
spouses, the friends who know us best and who are not afraid to tell us the truth, spiritual leaders
who have known us for a long time; those are some of the authorities he has set around us. We
do well to listen to them and be sensitive to their advice because by the time Hashem has to get
involved, like in the case of Korah, things can get pretty messy (Numbers 16).

My Personal Thoughts

_____

_____

_____

_____

_____

_____

Jude 1:10–11

However, these people insult anything they don't understand; and what they do understand naturally, without thinking, like animals—by these things they are destroyed!
Woe to them, in that they have walked the road of Kayin, they have given themselves over for money to the error of Bil`am, they have been destroyed in the rebellion of Korach.

Moses takes his case to Hashem. After all, he did not ask for the job; he has tried to get rid of it several times. He knows that as a leader you get it all: all the work, and all the blame.

When he heard Korah's proud open complaints joined with 250 people, in front of all Israel, Moses, "fell on his face, and he said to Korah and all his company, "When Moshe heard this he fell on his face. Then he said to Korach and his whole group, "In the morning, ADONAI will show who are his and who is the holy person he will allow to approach him. Yes, he will bring whomever he chooses near to himself." (Numbers 16:4–5).

Moses knew how Hashem worked. Only those he accepts can come to him, and even they have to do it his way. We have seen it in the episode with Aaron's sons, Nadab and Abihu (Leviticus 10; 16:1–2). So all he had to do to prove his point is to let them come in and see what happens.

He also prayed,

> If these men die a natural death like other people, only sharing the fate common to all humanity, then ADONAI has not sent me. But if ADONAI does something new—if the ground opens up and swallows them with everything they own, and they go down alive to Sh'ol—then you will understand that these men have had contempt for ADONAI. (Numbers 16:29–30)

And when he was done,

> The moment he finished speaking, the ground under them split apart—the earth opened its mouth and swallowed them up with their households, all the people who had sided with Korach and everything they owned. So they and everything they owned went down alive into Sh'ol, the earth closed over them and their existence in the community ceased. (Numbers 16:31–33)

Where are they? In Greek, the word *she'ol* is translated as *Hades.* It is the biblical place to tell when the dead go. Many people wrote about trying to define it. The Hebrew root of the word is שאל, to ask a question. Basically, this She'ol could be referred to as the great *question*, or the great *unknown.*

I think it a terrible fate to be in an unknown place not knowing anything about it. Worst of all, no-one else either may know anything about it except that it is somewhere below the walking earth. The Torah tells us that Korah and his band went there alive.

It seems that Hashem doesn't take challenge to his leaders very easily. Sudden punishing death also happened to Ananias and Sepphira when they lied to Peter about the sale of their property (Acts 5:1–11). I think these stories should teach us a healthy fear of Hashem. When Moses speaks of the future *prophet,* to come, exhorting us to obey him he says, "ADONAI will raise up for you a prophet like me from among yourselves, from your own kinsmen. You are to pay attention to him" (Deuteronomy 18:15).

John 15:12–13

This
This is my command: that you keep on loving each other just as I have loved you.
No one has greater love than a person who lays down his life for his friends.

I heard it said one time, "If you're going to go to hell, don't drag somebody else with you." In the case of the Korah rebellion, after all was said and done, the Torah tells us that the next day all the congregation of Israel grumbled against Moses and Aaron accusing them of having provoked the death of the people of God. Again Moses and Aaron conferred with Hashem who told them to "get away from the midst of this congregation, that I may consume them in a moment" (Numbers 16:45).

At that time, Moses and Aaron showed what great responsible leaders they were. If anything should vindicate Hashem's choice of leaders, these next few lines of the narration should,

> But they fell on their faces. Moshe said to Aharon, "Take your fire pan, put fire from the altar in it, lay incense on it, and hurry with it to the assembly to make atonement for them, because anger has gone out from ADONAI, and the plague has already begun!" Aharon took it, as Moshe had said, and ran into the middle of the assembly. There the plague had already begun among the people, but he added the incense and made atonement for the people. He stood between the dead and the living, and the plague was stopped. (Numbers 16:45–48)

As parents always plead for their children no matter how bad they have been, though they had incurred the spite and contempt of these people, Moses and Aaron did not take it personally. They remained in character and responded like responsible shepherds in trying to protect the people from an angry God by going through an atonement ritual. Then the most wonderful thing happened, when Aaron "stood between the dead and the living, and the plague was stopped" (Numbers 16:48).

In this instant, Aaron showed that he understood the Messianic role of the Levitical service. Like the children of Israel who asked Moses to be the mediator between them and Hashem, Aaron now stood between the people and a fearsome angry God.

We have in those two brothers the perfect picture of our Messiah: Moses the prophet and legislator, and Aaron the priest.

As followers of the Master, we are also called to be a royal priesthood (1 Peter 2:9). May we have the gumption when the time comes to stand between "the dead and the living" for the sake of those we are meant to lead.

My Personal Thoughts

_____
_____
_____
_____
_____
_____

John 11:25 Sivan 27/ כז בסיון

I am the resurrection and the life.

Moses and Aaron proved themselves to be godly leaders. They used their power and authority not to control others in a condescending manner, but rather to save and give life. They did not try to prove themselves but rather to prove Hashem. May we emulate their example.

Moses played the role of intercessor, while Aaron stood between the living and the dead. What teamwork (Numbers 16:45–48). But people are usually stubborn and not easily convinced. Hashem then decided to help Moses and Aaron in convincing the people. He said,

> Speak to the people of Isra'el, and take from them staffs, one for each ancestral tribe . . . twelve staffs. Write each man's name on his staff; and write Aharon's name on the staff of Levi, for each tribe's leader is to have one staff. Put them in the tent of meeting in front of the testimony, where I meet with you. The staff of the man I am going to choose will sprout buds—in this way I will put a stop to the complaints the people of Isra'el keep making against you. (Numbers 17:2–5)

These *staves* were not just pieces of wood they collected from the wilderness for the occasion. These were their tribal staves with markers of authority. We remember Judah leaving his staff with Tamar as a pledge of payment (Genesis 38:18). It was like leaving his ID.

These staves were big pieces a wood, of wood that was dead. Each represented the identity of the bearer. Each staff representing its owner was going to appear in the tent of meeting, in the presence of Hashem who would chose one. And what was going to be the sign of Hashem's choice? "On the next day Moses went into the tent of the testimony, and behold, the staff of Aaron for the house of Levi had sprouted and put forth buds and produced blossoms, and it bore ripe almonds" (Numbers 17:8). Yes, the sign of resurrection.

Hashem resurrected a dead piece of wood and made his choice very clear. We therefore have no doubt about who is to be the true king, priest, leader of Israel: the Resurrected One!

My Personal Thoughts

1 Corinthians 9:3 Sivan 28/ כח בסיון

That is my defense when people put me under examination.

Samuel came from a Levitical family that descended from Korah (1 Chronicles 6:19–28). Apparently he learned from Korah's mistakes, as Samuel was certainly a man yielded and moved by Hashem.

In Samuel's days there was also a rebellion. The people rejected Samuel's leadership and requested a king. Samuel was getting old and his son did not walk in his ways so the people's complaints could have been legitimate but Hashem still told them that in requesting a king they rejected his leadership (1 Samuel 8:1–7). Maybe it was because of their worldly motives as they said to Samuel, "Appoint for us a king to judge us like all the nations" (1 Samuel 8:5).

In any case, Hashem in his great mercy, granted the people their request and gave them a king. Along with helping with the choosing of this king, Samuel was going to give one last address establishing his legacy, his records as leader of Israel, as well as parameters for the new kingdom. As part of his address, Samuel rehearses in front of the people all the time when Hashem rescued them from their enemies because they repented from their idolatries. Then he said to them, "When you saw that Nachash the king of the people of `Amon was attacking you, you said to me, 'No, we want a king to rule over us'—when ADONAI your God was your king" (1 Samuel 12:12). In essence, in spite of Samuel's success, they didn't want God's style of leadership anymore. They wanted to put their trust in a king, like the nations around them.

This episode is reminiscent of Korah's rebellion against Moses and Aaron. In the Korah's episode, Moses claimed, "I haven't taken one donkey from them, I've done nothing wrong to any of them" (Numbers 16:15). Samuel claimed, "Does any of you think I have taken your ox or donkey, defrauded or oppressed you, or accepted a bribe to deprive you of justice? Tell me, and I will restore it to you" (1 Samuel 12:3). As part of his vindication, Moses leans on a miracle. In the same way, Samuel will also ask for a miracle in order to vindicate his words to the people (Numbers 17; 1 Samuel 12:16–18).

In the first century B.C., Paul's leadership was challenged by the Corinthian congregation he established. As his defense, he declared that even though he had the right to claim being in charge of the congregations, he never used that right. It seems that he followed the examples of Moses and Samuel and stayed clear from these things that could be considered abuse of power (1 Corinthians 9).

Moses, Samuel, and Paul are good examples of leaders who served the people and did not abuse them. May we pray for more of the same!

My Personal Thoughts

_____

_____

_____

_____

_____

Revelation 19:16

And on his robe and on his thigh he has a name written:
KING OF KINGS AND LORD OF LORDS.

In Samuel we discover the tension between theocracy and monarchy. Hashem should be our ruler but we want a king. Israeli monarchy is stained with blood and sin.

Samuel succeeds to convince the people that their sin was great, but as they ask for mercy he says to them,

> Don't be afraid. You have indeed done all this evil; yet now, just don't turn away from following ADONAI; but serve ADONAI with all your heart. Don't turn to the side; because then you would go after useless things that can neither help nor rescue, they are so futile. For the sake of his great reputation, ADONAI will not abandon his people; because it has pleased ADONAI to make you a people for himself. (1 Samuel 12:20–22)

This should teach us about the great mercy and compassion of Hashem. It seems that whatever we do, he finds a reason to remain favorable.

As a good shepherd he also assures them that, "far be it from me that I should sin against ADONAI by ceasing to pray for you, and I will instruct you in the good and the right way" (1 Samuel 12:23).

As a last address he adds, "Only fear ADONAI, and serve him faithfully with all your heart; for think what great things he has done for you! However, if you insist on doing wicked things, you will be swept away—both you and your king" (1 Samuel 12:24–25). He tells the people that they can still incur Hashem's favor if they and their king serve him faithfully. These last statements really define the history of Israel throughout the centuries.

Throughout the millennia, our desire for godly leadership has gone down even more. Not only do we refuse God's theocratic rule, but we don't even want a king who has the power to tell us what to do. What we want now is a president that we can lobby into what we want him to do, one who rules by the majority of the people no matter if it is in agreement with God or not. Is it a sign of our moral decadence or maybe even the reason for it?

As humans, we always do better under good leadership, even sometimes hands-on leadership. This tension between theocracy, monarchy, and democracy will exist in our governments until the arrival of the true one who is the true king who rules according to God's ways for the welfare of his people. Didn't Yeshua have compassion for us when he saw us as "sheep without a shepherd" (Matthew 9:36)? He said,

> I am the good shepherd. The good shepherd lays down his life for the sheep. The hired hand . . . sees the wolf coming, abandons the sheep and runs away. Then the wolf drags them off and scatters them. The hired worker behaves like this because that's all he is, a hired worker; so it doesn't matter to him what happens to the sheep. I am the good shepherd; I know my own, and my own know me. (John 10:11–14)

May it be soon Abba, even in our days!

My Personal Thoughts

Romans 11:28–31   **Sivan 30/** ל בסיון

With respect to the Good News they are hated for your sake. But with respect to being chosen they are loved for the Patriarchs' sake, for God's free gifts and his calling are irrevocable.

Just as you yourselves were disobedient to God before but have received mercy now because of Isra'el's disobedience; so also Isra'el has been disobedient now, so that by your showing them the same mercy that God has shown you, they too may now receive God's mercy. How wonderful that in spite of sin, disobedience, and rebellion, Hashem never leaves us without comfort and hope for renewal.

The refusal to enter the Land and the Korah rebellion brought the Exodus generation to a physical and spiritual end. Would the future generations miss out on the promises made to Abraham because of a few jealous and disgruntled Levite priests? Let us remember that the promises of God are irrevocable.

These may have been the Exodus narrative's last words, but they were not the last words of he who actually has the proverbial *last word*. When Moses' divinely appointed leadership was challenged, the humble prophet went along with it and told everyone, "Let's ask God what he thinks." He then proceeded to collect the leadership staff of each tribe to place them in the Tabernacle. "The tribe whose staff buds overnight will be our leader," he said. Everyone agreed. The next day, the sight of dead wood resurrected to life and confirmed the choice of the house of Levy with Aaron as the high priest.

May we take the time to look at this miracle in a Messianic light? A generation questioned God's leadership and refused to follow the divine command to conquer the land. The Exodus generation Israelites were annihilated but not without the hope of inheriting through their children. Three days after a few disgruntled priests got together to challenge Moses, Hashem confirmed his choice of leadership by resurrecting the stuff of Aaron to continue leading the children of Israel to the eventual conquest of the Promised Land. In the same manner, 1,400 years later, another few disgruntled priests convened to challenge the leadership of the 'prophet like Moses.' Three days after his execution, life came back to his dead body to lead the fires of a new generation of Jewish Messianic believers, inheriting the promises leaving behind the corpses of the old generation forty years later.

From the beginning of its turbulent history, Messianic Judaism has suffered near annihilation. After the model of Yeshua, it is now resurrecting in a worldwide fire spreading from country to country, even in Israel. May we never lose hope! Hashem's word is eternal and doesn't change. The promises that escape us, our children will inherit.

My Personal Thoughts

_____

_____

_____

_____

_____

_____

שדי

TAMMUZ — תמוז

Tammuz

Breaking of tablets?
Breaching of a wall?
Did Tammuz really cease his offerings?
Hear now of Jephtah'svow
Of Pinchas' zeal.
All telling us of Mashiach!

2 Corinthians 5:21   **Tammuz 1/ בתמוז א**

God made this sinless man be a sin offering on our behalf,
so that in union with him we might fully share in God's righteousness.

The Hebrew Scriptures tell us about the laws of the red heifer, the laws that provide ritual purification to those who have been contaminated by contact with a carcass of some sort (Numbers 19). These laws have a problem in themselves. The priest who slaughters the red heifer becomes himself ritually contaminated, therefore unable to continue to perform the ritual. After 2,000 years of Diaspora we do not have any solution, so even if the Temple were to be rebuilt today, it would not be able to operate because along with the priesthood, it needs to be purified with the ashes of a red heifer.

Whereas we may not fully understand the reasons for these instructions, we must always remember that the psalmist said that Hashem's Torah is perfect, pure, and right altogether (Psalm 19:7–8). So whether we can figure it in our own mind or not, whatever it teaches is right and beneficial for us. Here is something we can glean from the mystical rulings concerning the red heifer.

Priests usually tried to avoid the state of ritual contamination. In the days of the Master they had become obsessed by it. That is why in the story of the Good Samaritan, the priest did not want to help the dying man on the road to Jericho (Luke 10:30–36). It is also why people could not conceive that a holy man like Yeshua would agree to go to the house of Matthew, or even of Zaccheus, who, while being Jewish, were people who were unparticular concerning issues of ritual contamination

Because pagans often buried their dead within the walls or under the floor of their houses, Rabbis declared that entering the house of a non-Jew automatically made one ritually contaminated. That is why Peter had to be given permission by Yeshua himself to go to Cornelius' house (Acts 10). Sexual relations also provoked that same type of contamination, so the sages tell us that Moses, who was to be ready to enter in the presence of God at any time, forewent sexual relations with his Cushite wife, which caused those who did not understand this process to murmur criticisms about him (Numbers 12:1).

Contrary to that attitude, in the laws of the red heifer, just like in the procedures of Yom Kippur, the priest voluntarily makes himself unclean by the slaughtering of the chosen animal. This teaches us a great lesson. Yeshua also went contrary to the extreme attention the people of his days gave to ritual purity. Instead of avoiding ritual contamination, he allowed himself to become contaminated. Just like the priest would perform the ritual slaughter voluntarily allow himself to be contaminated for the sake of purifying Israel, Yeshua voluntarily put on the sinful cloak of humanity and voluntarily became contaminated for our sake so he could provide us with the cleansing needed to return us unto God.

As we try to keep ourselves pure from the world and its death, we should always remember that spiritual purity is not an end in itself, but a means to an end, and the end is service. Like Peter, the Master tells us to not be afraid to enter the house of the ungodly and bring him the Good News.

My Personal Thoughts

_____

_____

1 Corinthians 10:4   **Tammuz 2/ ב בתמוז**

> *They all drank the same drink from the Spirit—for they drank from a Spirit-sent Rock which followed them, and that Rock was the Messiah.*

> The people of Isra'el, the whole community, entered the Tzin Desert in the first month, and they stayed in Kadesh. There Miryam died, and there she was buried. Because the community had no water, they assembled themselves against Moshe and Aharon. (Numbers 20:1–2)

In the Talmud, Jewish sages always associated the lack of water with Miriam's death. Could it be because these two events are recorded one right after the other?

The children of Israel must have been desperate for water. They were afraid for their flocks and for themselves. It became a mutinous crisis in the camp. Didn't Hashem know? Didn't Moses know? Let us engage together in a little messianic interpretation of these events.

Moses, Aaron, and Miriam were very much like a full expression of the identity of Messiah. As a legislator, Moses was the king. Aaron was the priest, and Miriam had always been seen as the prophetess. The word of prophecy is also often represented as water (Deuteronomy 32:2; Isaiah 55:1; Jeremiah 2:13; 14:3). Messiah also came as a source of the water of life (Deuteronomy 18:18; John 4:14), officiated as our high priest (Hebrews 9:11), and he will return as our king (Revelation 17:14; 19:16).

Jewish tradition reports that Miriam died on the 10th of Nissan. If the water sources dried up right away, why did Moses and Aaron wait till the situation had culminated to a crisis? Ancient Jewish traditions say that the first seven days of the month of mourning are set aside for sitting and grieving. It is called *shivah* שיבה. So after seven days, with water running out and Moses mourning, the situation could have escalated. It was remedied when Moses and Aaron hit the rock with, according to tradition, Aaron's staff which had budded.

The 10th of Nissan is the day when the Passover Lamb is chosen. It is also the day Yeshua entered Jerusalem with people rejoicing, singing, and dancing, very much like Miriam was known to do. As Yeshua came to Jerusalem on that famous 10th of Nissan, it was nearing the end of the first phase of his ministry, the prophetic phase. The last *drops,* so to speak, were coming out. Within four days he would be crucified, and resurrect three days later. All in all, seven days after the 10th when he entered Jerusalem, which would also have been the day that Miriam died, he would resurrect and enter his priestly ministry, the very day when it is likely that Moses hit the rock with Aaron's *resurrected* staff.

Again, these things are merely a midrashic interpretation using the traditional understanding found in the writings of the sages in Jewish literature. They cannot be taught as fact, but there is a similitude between the two events, if not exactly in time, in spiritual analogy.

May we continue to draw waters of life from the resurrected one, our prophet, high priest, and king.

My Personal Thoughts

_____

_____

_____

Hebrews 9:13–14

For if sprinkling ceremonially unclean persons with the . . . ashes of a heifer restores their outward purity; then how much more the blood of the Messiah . . . will purify our conscience from works that lead to death, so that we can serve the living God!

Here is an eschatological piece. Many Endtime enthusiasts speak passionately about the rebuilding of the Jewish Temple in Jerusalem. There is a whole organization called *The Temple Mount Institute* dedicated to reinstitute its functionality. So far, due to the Golden Dome Mosque, this vision remains an impossible dream. Let's suppose now that by a supernatural political or diplomatic feat, the Temple was rebuilt. Even if that were to happen, due to the lack of a red heifer to purify the priesthood, technically it couldn't function. But let's suppose again, that along with our supernatural political or diplomatic feat, a suitable red heifer was produced? The problem would remain that only a person already purified by the ashes of a red heifer can administer the purification ritual on another person or even prepare the solution. In a way, due to the inexistence of previous ashes as well as of a priest already purified, like the Mobius strip, the purification requirements in this day have stalemated each other (Numbers 19).

Was God oblivious to this possibility when he allowed Israel to go in exile? The texts certainly speak of a functional third Temple (Ezekiel 40). How, then, could that be?

To find the answer to that question, all we need to do is find a precedent, and we have one. The situation was similar when in the wilderness after the first generation from the Exodus had died off, Eleazar was to prepare the first red heifer solution. There was not a single person in the whole camp including Eleazar, who could meet the purity requirements. Eleazar therefore performed the ritual under the authority of Moses.

Moses had a very special relationship with God. Unlike other prophets who received dreams and visions, Moses communicated with the Almighty face to face. The sages conclude that it was the reason why Moses kept in a state of constant ritual purity, refusing to even have a sexual relationship with his Cushite wife, which caused him to be criticized by his sister Miriam (Numbers 12:1).

It is important here to notice that the establishment of the red heifer ritual only happened following the death of the first generation. Ritual purification is concerned solely with corpse contamination, so it is almost like, before entering the Promised Land, the new generation had to be purified from the 'death' that plagued it for nearly forty years. In the Korah rebellion incident, by way of Aaron's rod budding, Moses showed virtue of victory over death. That is why he was eligible to authorize Eleazar to prepare the solution (Numbers 17:8).

In the same manner, Yeshua, who has conquered death with his resurrection on the third day, will also come at the end of days with the authority to authorize the high priest of the new temple to prepare the red heifer solution.

May it be soon Abba, even in our days!

My Personal Thoughts

_____

_____

_____

Romans 12:1   **Tammuz 4/** ד בתמוז

> *I exhort you, therefore, brothers, in view of God's mercies, to offer yourselves as a sacrifice,*
> *living and set apart for God. This will please him; it is the logical "Temple worship" for you.*

The children of Israel are asked to bring a "young red female cow without fault or defect and which has never borne a yoke." They are to "give it to Eleazar the priest who will take it "outside the camp" and slaughter it before Aaron. Then, Eleazar the priest is to "take some of its blood with his finger, and sprinkle some of its blood toward the front of the tent of meeting seven times." The red heifer is then to be "burned to ashes before his eyes" (Numbers 19:2–5).

Offerings in the Book of Numbers are described with three different terms: 1) My offerings (Korbanot), 2) My food for my fire offerings, 3) My soothing aroma (Numbers 28:2). By these appellations, the Levitical worship system offers something to each of the senses. We touch and handle them, smell them as they burn on the fire, and taste of the peace offering. As the ceremonies are conducted, we hear the priestly choir while our eyes witness the whole event.

It seems that God obtains sensory gratification from receiving the offerings. As we read these and any other similar texts, we must understand that any wording crediting God with a body enjoying sensory activities is only a metaphorical and poetic tool employed solely for the sake of the human readers' understanding. When speaking of Hashem, Yeshua said, "God is spirit" (John 4:24), and he defined "spirit" as incorporeal: "a ghost doesn't have flesh and bones, as you can see I do" (Luke 24:39).

If an offerer was actually sanctified by the offering, he could theoretically, at that moment, fearlessly enter the presence of God, but he still can't. Even in our redeemed state, we only enter the glorious presence vicariously through the high priesthood of Yeshua, the Messiah (Hebrews 4:14–16). This reflects the idea of the Hebrew word *korbanot*, usually translated as 'sacrifice' or 'offering' and which means: 'a vicarious token by which I approach Hashem.' So if God does not get any sensory gratification from these offerings that really do not perfect our conscience (Hebrews 9:9) enough that we may approach God, what are they for? At one point, God even seemed to refuse offerings (Micah 6:7). The offerings represent a token of our submission and obedience, which is why our Father delights in them (1 Samuel 15:22; Hoseah 6:6). One who offers is as one who offers himself.

The pure red heifer completely and willingly offered outside the camp, is the true image of our Master, the 'Pure One' who was also willingly offered outside the camp.

My Personal Thoughts

_____

_____

_____

_____

_____

_____

_____

1 Corinthians 15:46   Tammuz 5/ ה בתמוז

Note, however, that the body from the Spirit did not come first, but the ordinary human one.

We are told about the person who sprinkles the red heifer water for purification,

> This is to be a permanent regulation for them. The person who sprinkles the water for purification is to wash his clothes. Whoever touches the water for purification will be unclean until evening. (Numbers 19:21)

In other words, the one who purifies others defiles himself in doing so.

Blood is ritually unclean and the red heifer water is blood based. Therefore he that even touches that water is made impure by it. But yet, while it is unclean, it purifies others, and while he who touches it defiles himself, he purifies others. How can an impure element purify others? It may seem like a contradiction but is it really?

To what can it be compared?

When I clean my house I usually get dirty and I have to wash myself afterword. Some of the cleaning agents that I use are even dangerous to me. When I do dishes the old fashioned way in a sink, I put my hands in dirty dishwater to scrub plates and silverware then rinse the dishes clean onto a dish drainer. I dirty my hands to clean a dish.

While this seems to be a contradiction, it is very consistent with the principles of God's Kingdom. It is impossible for one to ascend unless he first was below, or descended from above. Before being first, we must hold the inferior position.

In the same manner, serving leading, lowliness comes before exaltation, and poverty before wealth. The carnal comes before the spiritual, the corruptible before the eternal. Adam was the first, Yeshua the last, but in the end, the first becomes last and the last becomes first.

Please, Abba, may he who was first and made himself last to take us back as firsts with him return soon to establish a first-class kingdom on earth in these last days.

My Personal Thoughts

_____

_____

_____

_____

_____

_____

_____

_____

_____

_____

John 3:14–15

Just as Moshe lifted up the serpent in the desert, so must the Son of Man be lifted up;
so that everyone who trusts in him may have eternal life.

For forty years the children of Israel wandered in the desert under Hashem's heavenly care. They were protected from wild beasts, snakes, they ate heavenly food, and a rock followed them to supply them with water. The narrative even tells us that their shoes and garments did not even go threadbare. It would be easy for that new generation of Israelites to become self-righteous against their fathers, but as the old adage says, 'The apple did not fall far from the tree,' and as is generally the case, the new generation failed some of the same tests that were presented to their fathers.

Soon after Miriam died, the water dried up, which caused the children of Israel to rebel against Moses. They complained so much that they wished to have met the same destiny as their fathers. They even questioned Moses about bringing them out of Egypt (Numbers 20:1–5). The dynamics of complaint are very strange. Being a generation born in the desert, they were complaining, wishing for something they never experienced, something they had no frame of reference for. After Moses provided the people with water, the Edomites refused passage to Israel, which caused the people to complain again. We can certainly relate to their reactions. We, who are often carried on the Father's wings of care, often omit to see the mighty miracles of provision and protection he does for us daily and are quick to complain about daily inconveniences, problems, and setbacks.

Because of their complaints, God allowed snakes to afflict the people. The miracle here is not that the snakes appeared, but that though this region was infested with snakes, we hadn't heard of snake problems before. Like the parent of the whining children wants to give them something real to complain about, Hashem temporarily removed his protection (Numbers 21:4–9).

When the people repented from their complaining, they asked Moses to intercede for them. Hashem then said to Moses, "Make a poisonous snake and put it on a pole. When anyone who has been bitten sees it, he will live" (Numbers 21:8). Hashem was redirecting their vision upward. They were learning not to look at Moses for their daily needs and protection, but upward toward their heavenly protector. The Hebrew word used for pole is the word nes נס meaning "miracle." God certainly did a redemptive miracle on that day as the people looked at the brazen snake and were healed. Yeshua compared himself to that life-giving snake on a pole and said, "Just as Moshe lifted up the serpent in the desert, so must the Son of Man be lifted up; so that everyone who trusts in him may have eternal life" (John 3:14–15). The symbol of as snake on a pole has now become an international symbol for pharmacies.

As we read these stories of the true pioneers of the faith, let us remember that these things took place as prefigurative historical events, warning us not to set our hearts on evil things as they did (1 Corinthians 10:6). May we then learn also to not look to man for direction, protection, and provision, but as Moses told the people on that day, 'Look up, and live!'

My Personal Thoughts

_____

_____

_____

Matthew 21:42

> *Yeshua said to them, "Haven't you ever read in the Tanakh,*
> *'The very rock which the builders rejected has become the cornerstone!*
> *This has come from ADONAI, and in our eyes it is amazing?'"*

Jephtah was an illegitimate son. He was the son of a harlot and as such had been rejected by his family. The narratives in the Book of Judges tell us that he "fled from his brothers and lived in the territory of Tov, where he enlisted a gang of rowdies who would go out raiding with him (Judges 11:1–3).

When Israel was in need of a brave soldier to counteract the Amonites threat, they went to Jephtah for help. He responded, "Didn't you hate me so much that you forced me out of my father's house? Why are you coming to me now, when you're in trouble? . . . If you bring me back home to fight the army of `Amon, and ADONAI defeats them for me, I will be your head" (Judges 11:7; 9). Israel agreed.

Jephtah's first encounter with the Ammonites was far from diplomatic. He challenged the Ammonites land claims with a little Torah lesson, a message that was almost verbatim to Moses historical text from the Book of Numbers (Numbers 21:21–25; Judges 11:19–22). Ammon did not agree so Jephtah started to raise an army.

Jephtah went to war and won, but not without a loss. Before leaving for war he made what some would consider a foolish vow. The biblical narrative tough tells us that,

> Then the spirit of ADONAI came upon Yiftach . . . Yiftach made a vow to ADONAI:
> "If you will hand the people of `Amon over to me, then whatever comes out the
> doors of my house to meet me when I return in peace from the people of `Amon
> will belong to ADONAI; I will sacrifice it as a burnt offering." (Judges 11:29–31)

As he returned victorious, his virgin daughter rushed out to greet him. We are told that Jephthah went through with his vow. People find this difficult to read. How come he knew the Torah so well as to be able to use it to challenge Ammon on territory disputes, yet he did not realize that humans are not fit for the altar? He did not have to offer his daughter as a burnt offering.

Is there more to the story left us by the sages of Israel in the Book of Judges? Could it be that one day, one who has been rejected as illegitimate by Israel will be called to help in the land ownership dispute between Israel and its neighbors? In fact, this rejected and dejected strong man has already defeated the enemy of Israel but at the cost also of the loss of Jerusalem, the daughter of Zion, 2,000 years ago.

In the end, the mourning of Jerusalem ceases as she is revived from the ashes and becomes fruitful again.

May it be soon Abba, even in our days!

My Personal Thoughts

_____

_____

_____

2 Peter 2:15   **Tammuz 8/ ח בתמוז**

These people have left the straight way and wandered off to
follow the way of Bil`am Ben-B`or, who loved the wages of doing harm.

The story of Balaam in the Book of Numbers leaves many details up to the reader. Aside from a donkey arguing with his master and Balaam seemingly being punished while obeying, we also have to wrestle with this man who, being a non-Israelite well sought after sorcerer, related to the God of Israel as 'ADONAI my God' (Numbers 22:18). Who then is Balaam?

We have here the perfect example of a polytheist who adheres to a large spectrum of deities. Balaam is probably an expert in the mysticism of the day, keeping tabs on all current religious news and fads, including the fresh stories coming from Egypt of a Jewish Egyptian shepherd who brought an empire to its knees along with its pharaoh and princes.

Whatever is not told us in the Hebrew Scriptures about Balaam is indicated by the writers of the apostolic letters written by John (Revelation 2:14), Jude (Jude 1:11), and Peter (2 Peter 2:15). These writers all had inside information from other Jewish texts and they all looked at Balaam as a *prophet for profit*. They describe him as the typical picture of the importunate mercantile religious man who transforms religion into a business venture. Sad to say, looking at it in that light, we can see how today from East to West, religion has given way to many 'Balaams' who, with elitist profit in mind, run their spiritual offices in a corporate manner with the same ethics and understanding as a business.

While this is bad enough, there seems to be an even worst factor in this story. We have here a man who calls upon the name of Hashem, who confesses with his mouth the God Creator of heaven and earth, the God of Israel as his God, but who is also a renown sorcerer on his way to curse Israel, the people of God. This implies that we cannot believe someone's sole verbal confession of faith, especially as in the case of Bala'am, when godly works do not accompany this godly confession.

Sad to say, through the last two millennia, Jews who believe in Yeshua have seen many 'Balaams' in Christianity. Many of these include those who are today called, 'Church Fathers,' who while confessing to believe in Yeshua the King of the Jews, the Messiah sent from he who is the God of Israel, found it to be their duty to malign and persecute the Jews.

They forgot that the same God they claim to serve said that one day he will restore the Jewish people as an independent entity in their own country of Israel. That will happen when the time of the Gentiles (non-Jews) is fulfilled, when Jerusalem is no more trampled by the nations (Luke 21:24) but is again under Jewish authority.

May we learn from the story of Balaam and take upon ourselves the rebukes from John, Jude, and Peter and examine our hearts for spiritual inconsistencies.

My Personal Thoughts

_____

_____

_____

_____

Revelation 2:14

Tammuz 9/ ט בתמוז

Nevertheless, I have a few things against you: you have some people who hold to the teaching of Bil`am, who taught Balak to set a trap for the people of Isra'el, so that they would eat food that had been sacrificed to idols and commit sexual sin.

When the princes of Moab approached Balaam, he conferred with ADONAI as to whether he should go with them or not. At that time his orders were clear; he was to stay put. Upon this refusal, King Balak thought that the business-minded *prophet for profit* was bargaining for a better offer, so Balak sent an even more distinguished embassy to make the same request. Seeing the caravan of pompous dignitaries and blinded by the prospect of lifelong wealth, Balaam returned to the Lord who this time told him, "If the men have come to summon you, get up and go with them; but do only what I tell you" (Numbers 22:4–20).

The Torah continues with the story of Balaam and tells us that on his way to Balak, the prophet encountered the Angel of ADONAI ready to slay him with a sword. Whereas Balaam, the great seer was blind to the heavenly apparition, his donkey could see the danger of his master's ways (Numbers 22:21–35). Balaam in his desire for gain had only heard one part of ADONAI's command, the one that said, "If the men have come to summon you, get up and go with them." Sad to say, he ignored the rest of the heavenly message, the part that said, "But only do what I tell you."

This is called selective listening, a 'disease' common with children (especially teenagers), but also often found in people of faith (sarcasm intended). How many times do we try to support our theological position stringing verses together that agree with us and justify our tendencies, all the while ignoring the segments of Torah that disagree with us? This is a very dangerous practice. We should read the whole counsel of God, trying to understand what it tells us, not use it to support our own form of belief instead. While we must read the Torah, we must not read into it.

It certainly is an honor to have one's name written in the Torah, but in the case of Balaam, his name is written as one who is a dandy-bad example. Balaam is a man who tried to build his treasures on earth where moth and rust destroy and where thieves break in and steal (Matthew 6:19). He did it even at the cost of putting a stumbling block in front of God's people (Numbers 25; Revelation 2:14).

This story is not all about Balaam. 2,000 years later, Yeshua still used Balaam as an example of what some in the new Nazarene movement tried to do. History also tells us about the perfidy, violence, hatred, and hypocrisy of many *Balaams* who stood against the people of Hashem for gain.

Will there be more?

May we read the story of Balaam and be warned!

My Personal Thoughts

Matthew 2:1–2

Magi from the east came to Yerushalayim and asked, "Where is the newborn King of the Jews? For we saw his star in the east and have come to worship him."

Two thousand years ago, Persian astronomers came from the East in order to pay homage to the newly born Messiah (Matthew 2:1–2). How did they know, and why did they care? They were not Jewish and the Messiah really was a Jewish concern.

Is it possible that Daniel taught them? Daniel was one of the captives of Judah brought to the palace of Nebuchadnezzar in order to teach Israeli knowledge in the Persian courts. Daniel was especially knowledgeable in messianic prophecies. He actually prophesied the exact year of our Master's crucifixion (Daniel 9:24–27). One of the prophecies Daniel was certainly familiar with was about a star that would represent the Messiah. It was called the "star . . . from Ya`akov" after Balaam's prophecy (Numbers 24:17).

Astronomy had always been a very important part of the Torah. Festivals are calculated according to the phases of the moon, and one had to be an expert astronomer in order to define the calendar. Josephus writes in his historical accounts that it is Seth, Adam and Eve's third son, who was the first to define the understanding of astronomy.

Daniel, as a prophet from Judea who knew when Messiah would come, would have been very familiar with the movements of the stars. He would have certainly been able to help the Persian astronomers with understanding when the king of Jews, he who will also call the Gentiles into the covenant of Israel, would be born.

After several hundred years, the knowledge had not vanished. These Persian astronomers arrived in Herod's court in Jerusalem claiming to have followed a star, the Star of Jacob. When they asked Herod if he knew of the great tidings that the King of the Jews was finally born, Herod, who until that time thought that he was the King of the Jews, had no knowledge of this. Herod must have known about Balaam's prophecy as he associated the astronomer's star claim with the coming of the Messiah. He called his personal Torah advisers and asked them where the Messiah was to be born. They told him, "And you, Beit-Lechem in the land of Y'hudah, are by no means the least among the rulers of Y'hudah; for from you will come a Ruler who will shepherd my people Isra'el" (Matthew 2:5–6).

What else do we know about this *star*? It might be nice to know as it concerns our history, our time, and even the present-day situation in the Middle East. Here is the full oracle,

> I see him, but not now; I behold him, but not soon—a star will step forth from Ya`akov, a scepter will arise from Isra'el, to crush the corners of Mo'av and destroy all descendants of Shet. His enemies will be his possessions—Edom and Se`ir, possessions. Isra'el will do valiantly, From Ya`akov will come someone who will rule, and he will destroy what is left of the city. . . . First among nations was `Amalek, but destruction will be its end. . . . the Keini . . . is firm, your nest set on rock, Kayin will be wasted while captive to Ashur. . . . Oh no! Who can live when God does this? But ships will come from the coast of Kittim to subdue Ashur and subdue `Ever, but they too will come to destruction. (Numbers 24:17–24)

Like the Persian astronomers, may we continue to follow the star, the star from Ya`akov!

302

John 4:10 Tammuz 11/ יא בתמוז

Yeshua answered her, "If you knew God's gift, that is, who it is saying to you, 'Give me a drink of water,' then you would have asked him; and he would have given you living water."

As Balaam continued his impromptu messianic oracle he spoke of water. He said, "Water will flow from their branches, their seed will have water aplenty" (Numbers 24:7).

When Moses told the children of Israel about the Promised Land he said, "But the land you are crossing over to take possession of is a land of hills and valleys, which soaks up water when rain falls from the sky" (Deuteronomy 11:11). A land which soaks up water when rain falls from the sky?

The notion of a land drinking water from the sky may not be far-fetched to us, but for the Israelites coming out of Egypt, it was a brand new concept. Egypt was used to getting its waters from the snowmelts of African mountains, which caused the yearly overflowing of the Nile. Egypt, in a sense then got its waters from what seemed to be *below*. Israel by comparison will be a country that will get its water from rainfall from *above*. This created a huge paradigm shift for the Israelites.

We must also realize that water represented a very valuable commodity. In these arid Middle Eastern countries, an economy can be very quickly ruined with one failing rainy season. This therefore puts Balaam's prophecy in perspective. The prophecy of course is Messianic as Israel still has to be very careful with its water, but even today, it is a common expression in Israel to say that they are the only people who can use a drop of water twice.

On a midrashic level, this prophecy represents an abundance of the word of God. The word of Torah is represented as rain as Moses said,

> May my teaching drop as the rain, my speech distill as the dew, like gentle rain upon the tender grass, and like showers upon the herb. (Deuteronomy 32:1)

Rain comes down and returns to its heavenly home only to come back again. Yeshua, the "seed" of Israel (Numbers 24:7), he who has often been coined as the Torah made flesh, referred to where it is said, "No one has gone up into heaven; there is only the one who has come down from heaven, the Son of Man" (John 3:13). Yeshua told the Samaritan woman that, "whoever drinks the water I will give him will never be thirsty again! On the contrary, the water I give him will become a spring of water inside him, welling up into eternal life" (John 4:14).

My Personal Thoughts

1 Corinthians 6:18   Tammuz 12/ יב בתמוז

Run from sexual immorality! Every other sin a person commits is outside the body,
but the fornicator sins against his own body.

Balaam, the *prophet for profit*, missed his chance for a healthy reward from Balak. The evil seer had been hired to curse Israel but God took over his mouth, and he began to pronounce blessings that are used today in both Jewish liturgy and in Christian teachings. Balaam was not done.

Jewish history books tell us that after failing in the use of prophecy to curse those whom Hashem has blessed, Balaam, still hungry for a lofty reward, went to Balak and told him that no-one can curse Israel because Hashem wants to bless them. The only way to hurt Israel would be for them to incur the wrath of Hashem by themselves. Knowing that Hashem is a jealous God, Balaam then suggested that instead of making war against Israel, Balak should provoke them to sin; that he should send beautiful girls into the camp of Israel to lure the people to come to a feast to Ba'al Pe'or. They did and we know the rest of the story from Numbers 25.

Israel joined itself in idolatry with Ba'al Pe'or (Numbers 25:2–3). The practices involving the worship of Ba'al Pe'or are absolutely degrading and have a sexual nature. Hoseah the prophet mentioned this when he said, "I saw your ancestors . . . But as soon as they came to Ba`al-P`or, they dedicated themselves to something shameful; they became as loathsome as the thing they loved" (Hoseah 9:10). The idea of idolatry is detestable to Hashem.

When people from the nations joined in the community of the believers through Yeshua, it seems that Paul and the other apostles didn't make things too complicated for them except in the area of idolatry. In Acts 15, Paul comes to James, Peter, and John, the elders of the new Nazarene movement and asks them what should be the requirement for these people of the nations who want to enter the covenant of Israel through Yeshua. The answers he receives concerned issues of participation in idolatry. After deliberation with them all, James' answer to Paul was,

> Therefore, my opinion is that we should not put obstacles in the way of the Goyim who are turning to God. Instead, we should write them a letter telling them to abstain from things polluted by idols, from fornication, from what is strangled and from blood. (Acts 15:19–20)

Today the issue of idolatry may not be so relevant but the perverted practices that are an intricate part of ancient idolatry are very much around us. From its early beginnings, the history of Christianity has also been plagued with syncretism, to the abhorrence of the Jewish Nazarene disciples.

Even today, through computers, TV, radio, magazines, advertisements, and i-phones, we and our children are inundated with subtle gateways to these practices. May we remember the story in Numbers 25 and, like Joseph of old who fled leaving his coat in the hands of she who tempted him (Genesis 39:11–12), show Pinchas-like zeal in shunning these things.

My Personal Thoughts

_____

_____

_____

_____

Revelation 3:19 Tammuz 13/ יג בתמוז

Exert yourselves, and turn from your sins!

When Israel sinned in joining itself to Baal Pe'or, a man stood against this iniquity as a court of one. When Pinchas saw one of the princes of Israel bring a Moabite priestess into his tent, without due process of law, he rose as a witness, judge and executioner, took a spear in his hand, and pierced both of them through. As a result, the plague on the people of Israel was stopped (Numbers 25:7–8), and Hashem blessed Pinchas for his zeal with a 'covenant of peace' (Numbers 25:12). This story has serious ramifications as it promotes violent religious fundamentalism, something which plagues our present world within most major religions. Reading this story could justify the actions of violent terrorist extremists.

If we try to justify our actions by saying 'so-and-so did it in the Bible and God blessed him,' we stand the risk to rationalize many other anti-social behaviors such as murder, incest, and polygamy. This is not the way we are supposed to process the narratives we read in the Torah.

In the case of Pinchas, Hashem rewarded him for his zealousness. In Hebrew the word 'zealous' is *kana'ee* קָנִאי, zealot, and is a synonym to the word, jealous. Not jealous in the sense of obsessive possessiveness as the word is used today, but jealous in a protective manner as a parent willing to do anything to protect his family. Pinchas was jealous for Hashem and it hurt him greatly to see these people flagrantly defying Moses and God with their vile actions. The worship of Ba'al Peor includes some very shameful practices.

There is a right and a wrong type of zealousness. In the case of Paul, we find a mislead type of zeal when he persecutes the believers (Philippians 3:6). A misplaced zeal is still found in some ultra Orthodox communities of Israel who still persecute the Jewish believers in the Jewish Messiah. In the case of Yeshua, zeal for Hashem's house was noted when he cleaned the temple from the mercantilism (John 2:14–17). The apostolic letters also tell us that the early Jerusalem believers had great zeal for the Torah (Acts 21:20).

In any case, we must also be careful lest our zeal is misplaced. We should always strive to be zealous for the standards of the kingdom, and this means to ruthlessly root out of our lives those things that could provoke us to sin. We are safer to let God take care of others, as vengeance is his (Deuteronomy 32:35), not ours.

Paul taught the Galatians congregation that it is good to be zealously affected in a good thing (Galatians 4:18, KJV) and reminded Titus that Messiah gave himself for us to redeem us from all lawlessness and to purify for himself a people for his own possession who are zealous for good works (Good works in Hebrew: *mitzvoth* מִצְוֹת– obedience to Torah commandments). Peter also reminded us: "Who will hurt you if you become zealots for what is good?" (1 Peter 3:13).

My Personal Thoughts

_____

_____

_____

_____

Titus 2:14   Tammuz 14/ יד בתמוז

He gave himself up on our behalf in order to free us from all violation of Torah and purify for himself a people who would be his own, eager to do good.

As explained in the former entry, the story of Pinchas in the text of Numbers 25 has dangerous ramifications. People read the story and too easily decide that they are to exercise Pinchas-like zeal. As a result, they start excommunicating people whom they define as 'idolaters in the land.' Sad to say in the end, more people and families are broken due to ignorance and spiritual pride than by the type of zeal God would have us display. As examples, we see that Hashem may have vindicated Matthias' zeal, (1 Maccabees 2:26), but on the other hand, Paul's zeal to persecute and destroy the followers of the rabbi from Nazareth was evidently misplaced (Philippians 3:6).

It is important to remember the context of the actions reported to us in Numbers 25. This judgment was executed on someone who was totally aware of their Torah responsibility, which cannot be said of most people today. A leader of Israel also did these actions in public. Thus it represented not only an act of total arrogance, rebellion, defiance, and disobedience, but also of negative influence on the people.

The context of the time Israel spent in the desert was that of boot camp training of our nation, a training experience that was to become a reference point for us today (1 Corinthians 10:6). In the military for example, boot camp training is hard and merciless. Whereas boot camp doesn't represent the exact 100% lifestyle of a soldier, it is a time to strengthen, train, and teach, as well as establish a proper reference point in a soldier's life. In the same manner, in the desert, Israel was a nation in spiritual boot camp to establish reference points for the generations to come, even for us today. Reading through the text, we are told of a man stoned to death for breaking the Sabbath, of the earth swallowing thousands for challenging God's ordained and appointed leadership, and of invasions of snakes for people complaining for lack of basic needs such as food and water in a dry and desert place. I doubt any of us would do better under the same conditions.

The actions of that prince of Israel represented a total challenge to Moses' leadership and to God and did so in full view of everyone. Whereas challenging Moses' leadership carried the same repercussions as challenging Messiah, it is certainly not the same as challenging the leadership and teaching of any other congregational leader, especially when self-appointed, which seems too often to be the case.

We are to show zeal for Hashem, but may we follow the example of those early believers in Jerusalem. At a time when God seemed to increase the congregation of believers both in numbers and influence, James reports that they were all zealous for the Torah (Acts 21:20).

May we always live according to the wishes of our beloved Rabbi, Yeshua from Nazareth, who wants nothing more that we be zealous in our obedience to his commandments (Philippians 2:14). May we follow the example of zealousness left us by he who exceeded Pinchas' zealousness so that he died for us that we may live.

My Personal Thoughts

_____

_____

_____

Luke 18:5–7

But because this widow is such a nudnik, I will see to it that she gets justice—otherwise, she'll keep coming and pestering me till she wears me out! Then the Lord commented, "Notice what this corrupt judge says. Now won't God grant justice to his chosen people who cry out to him day and night? Is he delaying long over them?"

Even though extreme, there is something to be said for Pinchas' zeal. Hashem certainly blessed him so there is something we can learn about it.

Hashem blesses our zeal for him, especially when it is done with wisdom. How did Hashem bless Pinchas? Hashem blessed Pinchas by making him like an everlasting priest with priestly descendants just like Aaron. Why? We are not told. Could it be that, because in the affair of the golden calf, Aaron and the Levites who showed zeal for ADONAI in punishing those who partook in the hideous idolatry were blessed with the priesthood? (Exodus 32:26–28). Hashem said of Pinchas,

> I am giving him my covenant of shalom, making a covenant with him and his descendants after him that the office of cohen will be theirs forever. This is because he was zealous on behalf of his God and made atonement for the people of Isra'el. (Numbers 25:12–13)

This zeal that Pinchas showed was very important, so important indeed that it turned Hashem's wrath from Israel. Hashem called it making atonement for the people of Israel. This should be so important to us. I am not suggesting that we operate in the way that Pinchas did, but somehow there must be something important in what Pinchas did that we can learn from.

We all have our share of troubles—families in need or children for whom we feel things could be different, and we wish that we could do something. Pinchas was just a man like any other man, but he changed the mind of Hashem. It wasn't because he killed idolaters and defiant rebellious people that Hashem rewarded him; it was because of his intense love for Hashem. His zeal was born of love, not hatred and violence. Pinchas was a man intensely and passionately in love with God.

This is something we can relate to. How do we act when we are in love? We want to be with that person all the time; we want to please them at any cost; our thoughts are always wandering towards that person and when we are absent from them, we count the seconds until when we are with that person again. That's how Pinchas was with Hashem. That's the mind frame of a man who changed God's mind.

James tells us of another simple like man whose zeal helped change things for God's people. He said, "Eliyahu was only a human being like us; yet he prayed fervently that it might not rain, and no rain fell on the Land for three years and six months. Then he prayed again, and heaven gave rain, and the Land produced its crops" (James 5:17–18).

How many things could be different in the lives of our brethren, loved ones, and relatives if we show Pinchas-like zeal in prayer?

My Personal Thoughts

_____

_____

Revelation 7:4; 14:1, 4　　　　　　　　　　　　　　**Tammuz 16/ טז בתמוז**

I heard how many were sealed—144,000 from every tribe of the people of Isra'el: Then I looked, and there was the Lamb standing on Mount Tziyon; and with him were 144,000 who had his name and his Father's name written on their foreheads . . . they have been ransomed from among humanity as firstfruits for God and the Lamb.

After the Ba'al Pe'or incident, five sisters came to Moses with an inheritance question (Numbers 25:27). This event confirmed to Moses the continual need for hands-on leadership. After Hashem informed him that he would soon be gathered with his people, Moses anticipated the need for a new leader over Israel (Numbers 27:16–17).

God's people are often compared to sheep or children. Sheep do not survive very well without the help of a shepherd. They do not know where the green pastures and the still waters are (Psalm 23). Also, since they are not equipped with a defense system, they need protection from predators. Children also are vulnerable and easily led astray, sometimes by others, but very often by their own inclinations. Time and again Moses saw that just having the commandments was not enough. A strong and faithful leader was always needed to embody these commandments and lead the people to them, and without it, they are scattered each one towards their own ways (Judges 17:6). Our present leader-less day marked with divided theologies and many raising themselves as self-appointed prophets or leaders proves this point.

From the time the original disciples of the Master died, the Congregation of Messiah has been plagued with teachers of all kinds teaching all sorts of things. Much of it is done through ignorance, but it is also sadly because of an anti-Semitic worldview, which rejects the original teachings of the sages of classic Judaism. As a result, as the children of Israel ready to lose their leader, we in this generation also find ourselves in dire need of the 'appointed' leader over Hashem's congregations. As we pray with Moses for the appointed leader over the congregation (Numbers 27:16–17), we pray for the return of Messiah. It is interesting that Joshua and Yeshua are the same name, the Master's name simply being a shorter Aramaic version.

With the appointment of Joshua, a military census was taken, and the children of Israel were reminded of their responsibilities towards the appointed festivals (Numbers 28–29). This census counts the fighting force of the congregation of Joshua.

In the same manner, we see today a worldwide phenomenon of the followers of Yeshua being reminded of their responsibilities towards the biblical festivals, and as the Master returns, a census of the tribes is also taken (Revelation 7:4–8). This census is of the Israelites believers who, as the ancient tribes followed Joshua over the Jordan on to the Promised Land, will follow Yeshua into the world to come of the Kingdom of God on earth. These are the firstfruit, the 'omer' dedicated to God and representing the rest of the harvest of the world (Leviticus 23:10; Revelation 14:4). It is redemption by representation. It is no wonder that throughout generations the devil has tried to get rid of the Israelites: believers from the tribes are the 'omer' representation to be brought before Yeshua the high priest to represent the harvest of the world.

My Personal Thoughts

_____

_____

_____

Romans 11:16   **Tammuz 17/ יז בתמוז**

Now if the hallah offered as firstfruits is holy, so is the whole loaf.

After Elijah is through with the contest of the prophets at Mt. Carmel (1 Kings 18), he realizes that Jezebel, who had been persecuting the prophets of ADONAI, does not appreciate getting some of her own 'medicine.' Discouraged and feeling that, in spite of these glorious events, he was unsuccessful in bringing Israel back to Hashem, Elijah retreats in the desert and complains to God, "It is enough; now, O ADONAI, take away my life, for I am no better than my fathers" (1 Kings 19:4).

Hashem denies Elijah the desired death but instead sends an angel to strengthen him. (Aren't we thankful for unanswered prayers sometimes?) The weary prophet then decides to return to where it all started: Mt. Sinai. There he has conversation with the 'word of the Lord' who came to this prophet of doom and gloom in the 'quiet, subdued voice.' Elijah's eyes then are opened and he sees a remnant of 7,000 faithful men for whose sake God will not destroy Israel (1 Kings 19:1–18).

This remnant principle is a very important one in the redemption program. Abraham understood it and even used it when pleading for the life of his nephew Lot. Then ADONAI who would destroy Sodom said, "For the sake of ten [righteous people] I will not destroy it" (Genesis 18:32).

In his thesis on the subject of God not rejecting Israel in spite of unbelief, which he gave at the time when the Roman noose was getting tighter and tighter around Israel, Paul comforted himself and others by remembering this remnant principle. In Paul's mind, the remnant in question was the growing Jewish community of believers. For their sake, he says, Hashem had not rejected Israel (Romans 11:1–4). This represents a very different theology than the usual one claiming that God rejected his people to replace them with another.

Even so, in these ends of time, Israel at large, along with the world, is sanctified before God by the 144,000 remnant believers from all the tribes of Israel. They are called the 'firstfruit ' for the Lamb who is himself a 'firstfruit of those who have died' (Corinthians 15:20; 15:20; Revelation 7:4; 14:4). Yes, if the dough offered as firstfruits is holy, so is the whole lump, and if the root is holy, so are the branches (Romans 11:16). From the beginning it was, is, and shall always be: redemption by representation.

Another reality is that like Yeshua, the firstfruit is also the one who takes the brunt of the punishment for the nation. Even though it did nothing to deserve such a fate, as the firstborn, it is consecrated to God and sometimes offered for the sanctification of the rest.

May we, when the time comes, be willing offerings after the sample of the Master (Romans 12:1).

My Personal Thoughts

_____

_____

_____

_____

_____

_____

Romans 12:1   **Tammuz 18/** יח בתמוז

I exhort you, therefore, brothers, in view of God's mercies, to offer yourselves as a sacrifice, living and set apart for God. This will please him; it is the logical "Temple worship" for you.

Hashem loves our times of prayer. All too often though we pray because we need something. Hashem actually has appointed times of prayer for us. They are the morning and afternoon times of prayer.

The morning and afternoon times of prayer are the times of the morning and afternoon lamb offering. This twice-daily offering in the temple provided a constant lamb presence on the altar. We do not have a temple with an altar anymore, but should we stop praying?

The Jewish people have not. They have continued the practice in synagogues around the world. The morning prayer is called the Shacharit שכרית, and the evening one is called the ma'ariv מעריב. One does not even have to be in the synagogue to implement these prayer times in their lives. It can be done from home. The tradition is to face east towards Jerusalem when we pray.

The sound of regular prayer times with established liturgy may sound strange to Protestant ears, but this is Hashem's system; a safeguard against only coming to pray when we want something.

These morning and evening prayer times are as important as the rest of the other commandments. Hashem calls them, "the food presented to me as offerings made by fire, providing a fragrant aroma for me" (Numbers 28:2).

Daniel was known to pray three times a day facing Jerusalem (Daniel 6:10) even under the threat of death, and it is pretty certain that the Master was in the habit of observing the official prayer times.

We do not have the temple nor all the systems required in order to offer daily offerings, but the apostle Paul spoke of another type of offering that could replace the twice-daily offering. He said, "I exhort you, therefore, brothers, in view of God's mercies, to offer yourselves as a sacrifice, living and set apart for God. This will please him; it is the logical 'Temple worship' for you" (Romans 12:1). Peter also urges us in the same way with,

> As you come to him, the living stone, rejected by people but chosen by God and precious to him, you yourselves, as living stones, are being built into a spiritual house to be cohanim set apart for God to offer spiritual sacrifices acceptable to him through Yeshua the Messiah. (1 Peter 2:4–5)

May we also never forget Hosea's exhortation, "For what I desire is mercy, not sacrifices, knowledge of God more than burnt offerings" (Hosea 6:6).

My Personal Thoughts

_____

_____

_____

_____

_____

Matthew 25:10   **Tammuz 19/** יט בתמוז

But as they were going off to buy, the bridegroom came.
Those who were ready went with him to the wedding feast, and the door was shut.

The Sabbath is probably the most important of Hashem's appointed times. It comes first in the Leviticus 23 list.

The Sabbath is a sign of the grace of Hashem. Most of us are not finished with our work by the time Sabbath comes, but yet we are to stop. It's a commandment.

I am reminded of some young people who loved to tell me that they couldn't do such or such because of the Sabbath, but there is another side to this coin. The commandment "not to do any kind of work—not you, your son or your daughter, not your male or female slave, not your livestock, and not the foreigner staying with you inside the gates to your property. on the Sahabbat, is preceded by, "You have six days to labor and do all your work" (Exodus 20:9). Both of them are to be obeyed.

There are many things that we are not meant to do on Sabbath; one of them is cooking. The idea then is to prepare ahead of time. There were double altar duties at the Temple on Sabbath, which meant that by Friday afternoon everything needed to be ready. All in all, it took preparation to take a day with Hashem.

The sages ask, "What will a person eat on Sabbath if he did not prepare ahead of time?" This may be a simple question, but it has enormous theological as well as eschatological repercussions. The apostle compares Sabbath to entering the Promised Land or entering the Kingdom of God (Hebrews 3 and 4). If then we are supposed to prepare for Sabbath, if the children of Israel had to prepare for entering the Land, it stands to reason that there are preparations involved in entering the Kingdom. The children of Israel prepared for entering the Land. They took a census, trained an army, spent the previous forty years learning to obey and trust, and they brought that baggage with them into the Land.

Maybe we need to think about the obedience and trust lessons we need to learn. We need to organize ourselves as a coherent functional body; make preparation for this kingdom of God Yeshua told us was "at hand."

Like the foolish virgins in Matthew 25, may we not be caught unprepared when the bridegroom arrives.

My Personal Thoughts

_____

_____

_____

_____

_____

_____

_____

_____

James 3:2   Tammuz 20/ כ בתמוז

If someone does not stumble in what he says, he is a mature man who can bridle his whole body.

They say that 'communication is the essence of being human.' The truth of this statement is reflected in the fact that like a garden, communication allows for the growth of both good and evil, an attribute that also pertains to our humanity.

That is why the way we communicate with each other is very important to God. He who created us demands that we perform quickly not only our vows, but according to all that proceeds out of our mouth (Numbers 30:2). Solomon, the wisest man in the world wrote many proverbs about the benefits and the pitfalls of speech (Proverbs 12:18), and Yeshua, the one wiser than Solomon, told us that we should mean exactly what we say (Matthew 5:37), which means that in essence, we shouldn't use the sarcasm, exaggerations, understatements, or double-speak that political and commercial advertisements are guilty of. Furthermore, James, the brother of the Master, teaches us that one's ability to yield to God is tested by his ability to hold his tongue in subjection to the Spirit of God (James 3:2). Paul, Yeshua's emissary, exhorts us that our speech should be 'seasoned with salt,' meaning 'gracious' and able to turn the bitter of tasteless into flavor (Colossians 4:6).

The apostolic texts tell us quite a bit about the attributes that should be witnessed in the lives of the people allowed to lead in the Congregations of the Master, and honorable and truthful speech seems to be at the top of the list. This means no mocking, demeaning, disrespecting, and certainly no use of foul language. It is also the opinion of this writer that these attributes and habits should be an integral part of the private life of any person in a place of spiritual responsibility in the congregations. If their speech is contemptible in private and nice in public, they are just a fake, a sham, and no better than a regular con-man, one who pretends to be something he is not, which is also the definition of a hypocrite, and we know how the Master felt about those.

Here is a story to illustrate the point between private and public life. It is the story of a British soldier who was one night caught outside of his quarters in the nearby woods. His officer held in suspicion of passing information on to the enemy, which implied court-martial. He was taken before his commanding officer and charged for being a traitor. The soldier desperately pleaded that he had only gone into the woods to pray by himself. That was his only defense. Upon hearing this, the commanding officer asked, "Are you a praying man? Do you regularly spend time in private prayer?" The soldier said, "Yes, Sir!" Upon this answer, the commanding officer roared, "Then down on your knees & pray now! You never needed it so much." The soldier knelt in prayer, in a way that could have only been inspired by the power of a man in the habit of pouring out his soul to God. "You may go," said the commanding officer simply when he had finished. "I believe your story. If you hadn't been often at drill, you couldn't have done so well at review."

My Personal Thoughts

312

Hebrews 12:1   **Tammuz 21/ כא בתמוז**

So then, since we are surrounded by such a great cloud of witnesses, let us, too, put aside every impediment—that is, the sin which easily hampers our forward movement—and keep running with endurance in the contest set before us.

After his victorious challenge of the prophets of Ba'al on Mt. Carmel, Elijah thought that surely he now had won over King Ahab. So much so, that he went with the king back to his palace (1 Kings 18:46). King Ahab naively thought that Jezebel, his wife, would be impressed, but instead, when she heard that Elijah killed all her dear beloved prophets of Ba'al, she sent a message saying, "So may the gods do to me and more also, if I do not make your life as the life of one of them by this time tomorrow" (1 Kings 19:2). Elijah again had to flee.

We are told that

he himself went a day farther into the desert, until he came to a broom tree. He sat down under it and prayed for his own death. "Enough!" he said. "Now, ADONAI, take my life. I'm no better than my ancestors." (1 Kings 19:4)

There, discouraged and tired of the fight, angels fed him and cared for him. On the strength of that food, Elijah walked forty days and forty nights to where it all started roughly 1,200 years before, Mt. Horeb. On Mt. Horeb, Elijah had a discussion with Hashem who asked him,

He answered, "I have been very zealous for ADONAI the God of armies, because the people of Isra'el have abandoned your covenant, broken down your altars and killed your prophets with the sword. Now I'm the only one left, and they're coming after me to kill me too." (1 Kings 19:10)

It was during that time of utter discouragement and despair, when he was weary of the battle, that Elijah learned that Hashem doesn't only speak in the wind, or in the earthquake, or in the fire, but in a quiet, subdued voice (1 Kings 19:11–13).

A drama student was telling me about how he was supposed to be Hashem calling Moses during a Torah play. The drama student called, "Moses; Moses!" loudly and with a slight sense of frustration. The teacher shook his head and said, "No, no; you don't get it. Hashem doesn't have to scream to get our attention!"

When after fasting for forty days and forty nights Yeshua, in a physically weakened state, had a face-to-face confrontation with HaSatan. It is also at that time the quiet strength of the living word within him helped him withstand the tempter (Matthew 4:1–11).

The sages of Israel teach that troubled times provoke growth and maturation. As we go through our personal tragedies and times of despair, discouragement, darkness, trial, and tribulations, may we always keep a channel opened to the soft whisper of the voice of Hashem. It is at these times that he shows us that we are not alone, but that we have a cloud of witnesses cheering for us in the heavens (Hebrews 12:1).

My Personal Thoughts

_____

_____

_____

Matthew 5:34   Tammuz 22/ כב בתמוז

But I tell you not to swear at all.

We all sin with our mouths, and sad to say this sin often takes the shape of not keeping commitments, breaking promises, and not fulfilling our vows. This can happen when we don't pay our bills on time, when we arrive late for an appointment, or break a resolution. Of course there are times when excuses can be made, but I would say that more often than not, we too easily rationalize our vow breaking with absolving justifications. This has the effect of exponentially multiplying the sin, as now we are guilty of lying, deceiving, and making light of Torah commands. Others will see us as hypocrites and we will reap the sad result of losing their trust. The issue of not keeping one's word becomes all the more dreadful for spiritual leaders and teachers, which would include each and every parent.

The issue of vow-breaking is so serious in the Tanach that Yeshua advised us to not even make vows (Matthew 5:34), and James taught us to say, "If ADONAI wants it to happen" (James 4:15). After all, why should we voluntarily and consciously add to our sinful state by making unprayerful vows that we may not be able to keep.

Whereas right and wrong cannot be altered, Hashem is aware of our human sinful nature. He has therefore provided us with a way out. The Torah teaches that a father or a husband has the right to absolve a vow foolishly made by his daughter or his wife on the day he hears it. This would apply if a daughter or a wife unwisely pledges money, or herself, or even binds herself for too long of a fast, which the father/husband knows would not be healthy or appropriate at the time for her. The father or husband can then annul the vow, but here is the twist: he will bear the guilt of its breaking, thus, we are introduced to the idea of vicarious suffering for sin (Numbers 30:15).

This patristic male approach for the propitiation of the absolution of vows doesn't sit well in our modern western society but it seems that each of us desperately needs that Messianic male figure to stand for us and propitiate for our foolish vows. By way of our foolish words, we, the 'Daughter of Jerusalem' or the 'Bride of Messiah,' have foolishly pledged ourselves to others and we need someone to free us from the traps of our own foolishness.

In that way, the Father gave Messiah all power and authority to bind and to loose us from our sins, but like a debt, sin does not just disappear: someone needs to bear the guilt for it. Its annulment still requires payment and in this case, the payment is done through the suffering that was laid on Messiah. Every lie—and there are no such things as 'little' or 'white' lies—and every broken promise is an added stripe on the body of Messiah.

I am reminded of a mother who couldn't get her son to stop being mean with his mouth. She then decided to have the little boy slap her hand every time he said something bad. At first he thought it was funny, but he loved his mother and he didn't want to hit her all the time, so he stopped being mean with his mouth.

My Personal Thoughts

_____

_____

_____

Matthew 18:7

Woe to the person who sets the snare! !

Moses had unfinished business to take care of. Before relieving him from office, Hashem gave him one last assignment, "On behalf of the people of Isra'el, take vengeance on the Midyanim. After that, you will be gathered to your people" (Numbers 31:2).

The children of Israel were guilty of having disobeyed in the Ba'al Pe'or affair and they were certainly punished. They lost 24,000 people in the plague (Numbers 25). Nevertheless, Hashem also knew that Israel, who was at the time not even yet a fully organized nation, had disobeyed because a very powerful and devious enemy had snared them. Why does Hashem call this war, "ADONAI's vengeance" (Numbers 31:3)? Rashi, the Jewish sage, explains that, "He who stands against Israel is as one who stands against the Holy One; Blessed be he." Whether Rashi was right or not, it is certain that Hashem thought of vengeance for himself in the issue of Midian, having caused Israel to bring a curse upon itself (Numbers 31:3).

As Israel in the wilderness, we believers in this world sometimes stand alone against a very powerful and devious enemy who tries every trick of the trade to make us fall and bring Hashem's displeasure upon us. Sad to say, this enemy often succeeds. In the accounts of Hashem's war against Midian, we learn that whereas we may sin because of our human frame and weakness, Hashem does not count he who causes us to sin blameless. He will certainly also become the recipient of Hashem's vengeance on the day of reckoning.

Yeshua taught something along the same lines. He said,

> Whoever ensnares one of these little ones who trust me, it would be better for him to have a millstone hung around his neck and be drowned in the open sea! Woe to the world because of snares! For there must be snares, but woe to the person who sets the snare! (Matthew 18:6–7)

This idea should send chills through our spine. It is easy to look at others and blame them for affecting us, and our children, in negative ways. But as we study these events, it is important that we also point the finger towards ourselves. How does our speech, mannerism, and overall way of life affect others: our children, our spouses, our colleagues, and all those we come in contact with? What happens when we look at ourselves through their eyes? Can we go down memory lane and feel very comfortable about ourselves? Have we caused some of his children to sin because of our example? Are we in for trouble in the day of reckoning? Probably yes.

May we use this exercise to learn and grow, applying the words of the Master, "Always treat others as you would like them to treat you; that sums up the teaching of the Torah and the Prophet" (Matthew 7:12).

My Personal Thoughts

_____

_____

_____

_____

Hebrews 7:17   **Tammuz 24/** כד בתמוז

You are a cohen FOREVER, to be compared with Malki-Tzedek

As mentioned in the former entries, Pinchas had shown himself very zealous for Hashem. The punishing plague against Israel stopped when he skewered Zimri and Cozbi (Numbers 25). As a result, his family was given a priestly lineage.

When time came to avenge Israel, Moses called onto Pinchas to vest him with a very special position, which the Talmud refers to as *The Priest Anointed For War.* This special title is derived from the following statement:

> When you go out to fight your enemies and see horses, chariots and a force larger than yours, you are not to be afraid of them; because ADONAI your God, who brought you up from the land of Egypt, is with you. When you are about to go into battle, the cohen is to come forward and address the people. He should tell them, 'Listen, Isra'el! You are about to do battle against your enemies. Don't be fainthearted or afraid; don't be alarmed or frightened by them; because ADONAI your God is going with you to fight on your behalf against your enemies and give you victory.' (Deuteronomy 20:1–4)

Pinchas, in a single act of zealous love for Hashem, atoned for Israel and stopped the deathly plague from destroying the people. Later, though not a high priest, he was chosen to lead the armies of God to avenge Israel against the Medianite who maliciously caused Israel to sin.

In these events, Pinchas foreshadowed the ministry of Messiah.

In the same manner as Pinchas, Yeshua, in a single act of zealous love for Hashem, atoned for Israel and stopped the deathly plague of spiritual death that is upon each of us. Though not a son of Aaron, he has been chosen to be *The Priest Anointed For War* to avenge us from the Adversary who entices us to sin.

Psalm 110, the messianic Psalm, by excellence, speaks of the priesthood of Messiah as a priesthood of war,

> ADONAI has sworn and will not change his mind, 'You are a priest forever after the order of Melchizedek.' ADONAI is at your right hand; he will shatter kings on the day of his wrath. He will execute judgment among the nations, filling them with corpses; he will shatter chiefs over the wide earth. (Psalm 110:4-6)

Again, the events we read in the Torah point to a future time, to the time of Hashem's vengeance against all those who have caused his "little ones" to sin. Yeshua will then bring the day of vengeance of our God (Isaiah 61:2).

As we look forward to that time of vindication, may we remember to watch our steps, our words, and our deeds, that we may not cause any of his "little ones" to sin.

My Personal Thoughts

_____

_____

_____

Revelation 19:11

> *Sitting on it was the one called Faithful and True, and it is in*
> *righteousness that he passes judgment and goes to battle.*

This whole episode of the war with the Medianites, the killings, capturing, enslaving, and looting, may seem difficult to study. We may be left to wonder, "What are these texts doing in our Torah? What's the use in studying these over and over each year as we go through the Parasha? What does all this 'war' business have to do with God? Didn't John say that, "God is Love?" (1 John 4:8).

These are certainly valid questions, and indeed, God is love. What we may need to review is our definition of Hashem's love. Hashem often gave himself the attribute of being a "jealous" God (Exodus 34:14). He also says, "I ADONAI your God, am a jealous God, punishing the children for the sins of the parents to the third and fourth generation of those who hate me" (Exodus 20:5).

If somebody were to hurt our children, or even our spouses, would we, in the name pacifism, stand still, not defend, retaliate, or attack if need be? Would it also be right for a murderer of your loved on to not be brought to justice? Wise King Solomon said, "because the punishment decreed for an evil act is not promptly carried out; therefore people who plan to do evil are strengthened in their intentions" (Ecclesiastes 8:11). As parents, we can certainly understand that.

What we need to read in these texts is that Hashem is faithful to avenge his children who are like the apple of his eye (Deuteronomy 32:10). In Hashem's eyes, the Medianites were like one who would stand in the street corner offering your child drugs or membership in a violent gang. The child would certainly be wrong to follow such things, and should certainly be punished, but he who enticed him is the real criminal who deserves justice.

On the Isle of Patmos, John had a vision of the disciples under persecution crying onto Hashem saying, "Sovereign Ruler, HaKadosh, the True One, how long will it be before you judge the people living on earth and avenge our blood?" (Revelation 6:9–10).

Reading these texts, may we be comforted that he who vexes our souls, whether on this earth or in the heavens, will one day receive his due. John saw it. He said,

> Next I saw heaven opened, and there before me was a white horse. Sitting on it was the one called Faithful and True, and it is in righteousness that he passes judgment and goes to battle. His eyes were like a fiery flame, and on his head were many royal crowns. And he had a name written which no one knew but himself. He was wearing a robe that had been soaked in blood, and the name by which he is called is, "THE WORD OF GOD." The armies of heaven, clothed in fine linen, white and pure, were following him on white horses (Revelation 19:11–14)

My Personal Thoughts

_____

_____

_____

_____

Luke 4:18   **Tammuz 26/ כו בתמוז**

*He has sent me to proclaim freedom for the imprisoned and
renewed sight for the blind, to release those who have been crush.*

Today, when a crime or an offense is committed, we defer to the civic authorities in charge and in most cases this is the local police. In biblical times, there was no such police. Crime was handled by either the religious authorities or the army.

When the children of Israel were getting ready to enter the Land, to divide it and build cities, Hashem first gave them a class on civic responsibilities. Crime is always with us, and Hashem was teaching his people how to handle it. One of the civic requirements Hashem put on the children of Israel was to "designate for yourselves cities that will be cities of refuge for you, to which anyone who kills someone by mistake can flee" (Numbers 35:11).

Moses had been a first-hand witness to the hot temperament of the Israelites. If it hadn't been for the protection of Hashem, he might have been lynched several times in the course of the forty years leading them through the desert. Moses was wise and he knew that "the anger of man does not produce the righteousness of God" (James 1:20). Moses understood the system of refuge cities. It worked hand-in-hand with the redeemer status.

If a person was killed, one of his kin was to take on the role of blood-avenger. His first priority would be to find the guilty person and administer justice. The problem was that not all cases were that simple and black and white. The said accused would need to go through a trial in the presence of the proper Sanhedrin. Maybe it was involuntary, or an accident; or maybe they got the wrong person, and in the heat of anger and desire for vengeance something went wrong. The defendant is therefore given a place where he cannot be touched until such a time when the Sanhedrin can be convened.

If the person is found guilty, he is released to the blood-avenger who will execute justice himself. He will not rely on someone else to do this dirty work for him. If the person is found guilty, but of involuntary manslaughter, he can find safety for the rest of his life in the city of refuge. He is not to leave the city of refuge. He cannot go back home. The Torah commands that in this case, "after the death of the cohen hagadol the killer may return to the land he owns" (Numbers 35:28).

Why does the death of the high priest allow him to go back home free? No rational explanation is given to us. Mothers or wives of city of refugee residents were often found being good to the high-priest, bringing them food and taking care of them as if he died, they could easily be accused of killing him.

Though we are not told why the death of the high priest brings freedom to one accused of involuntary manslaughter, there are still things we can learn from the process. We learn for example things pertaining to Hashem's sense of justice mixed with mercy. Through this process, we see that someone who commits even an involuntary crime is punished but with measure. This ruling also contains the messianic principle of someone's death, in this case, the death of a high priest, atoning for someone else's sin.

We are guilty of many crimes, mostly because of our innate sinful nature. Yeshua is our high priest and his death also brings us out of the confinement of guilt.

Romans 7:4

Thus, my brothers, you have been made dead with regard to the Torah through the Messiah's body, so that you may belong to someone else, namely, the one who has been raised from the dead, in order for us to bear fruit for God.

We often call Yeshua our *go'el* גאל, "redeemer." He is even called the "Redeemer of Israel" (Isaiah 49:7), but do we really understand the role of 'redeemer'? When we do, it may change our view as to who Yeshua is, and as to what is his mission. The redeemer policies seem to be buried under several millennia of societal changes. We can read these laws and feel that they belong to a far-away time that is hardly relevant to us. But if it is part of Torah, it certainly has relevance. We must maybe look at them from a different perspective.

A *go'el* is one who is usually a next of kin. He has four major functions representing four different types of redemptions. He is the blood avenger; he redeems lost family interests like lands or properties; he redeems relatives from slavery; and he even is to marry the childless widow of a deceased kinsman. Maybe as it stands now, the redeemer laws are not so much about us and the role we are to play in society, but rather about "him" and the role he plays in our lives and most important in that of Israel. I would like to take the time to look at it from the standpoint of his role towards Israel as a people.

Yeshua, as the avenger of blood, seems to be very pertinent as far as Israel is concerned. The 2,000 year persecution of Jewish people will culminate with the whole gathered around Jerusalem. At that, the Messiah is said to come and fight against the armies who would annihilate us. Vengeance and vindication will come for a people who have been maligned for 2,000 years.

2,000 years ago, the Land of Israel was taken from the Jewish people. Since that time, it has been occupied by various powers. Those who want to occupy the Land forget the Torah, which said that the land should not be sold in perpetuity but that it shall return to its original tribal owners. I do not know if we are to the point where the Land of Israel is returned to its tribal owners, but it is certainly returned to the Jewish people at large, which is a miracle that can only be attributed to Messiah's workings behind the scenes of the politics of men.

When Yeshua was in Israel, he came upon a fruitless fig tree. It seems that he cursed the tree for not having fruit even though it was not yet the season for figs (Mark 11:13). The fig tree is often a representation of Israel.

Yeshua explained the parable,

> A man had a fig tree planted in his vineyard, and he came looking for fruit but didn't find any. So he said to the man who took care of the vineyard, 'Here, I've come looking for fruit on this fig tree for three years now without finding any. Cut it down—why let it go on using up the soil?' But he answered, 'Sir, leave it alone one more year. I'll dig around it and put manure on it.' (Luke 13:6–8)

Yeshua later explained, "Unless a grain of wheat falls into the earth and dies, it remains alone; but if it dies, it bears much fruit" (John 12:24). Yeshua, the seed of the woman, became that corn of wheat who died and bore fruit for Israel, in the form of a messianic community still thriving until this day. Yeshua himself became that corn of wheat in the deep waters of the Torah. He came to bear fruit to the spiritually barren land of Israel. His fruit became a very large congregation of believers, Jewish believers alive until this day. May Yeshua our redeemer and the redeemer of Israel be blessed forever and ever!

319

Luke 19:41   כח בתמוז **/Tammuz 28**

When Yeshua had come closer and could see the city, he wept over it.

Hashem recruited Jeremiah to be a prophet. Jeremiah had the unpleasant task of going around as a prophet of doom telling people what they don't want to hear about themselves. Though many look at Jeremiah as a prophet of doom, he was called *the weeping prophet.* He felt so bad for the people that he said, **"I** wish my head were made of water and my eyes were a fountain of tears, so that I could cry day and night over the slain of the daughter of my people" (Jeremiah 9:1). This reminds me of Paul's feelings as he spoke of Israel, "my grief is so great, the pain in my heart so constant, that I could wish myself actually under God's curse and separated from the Messiah, if it would help my brothers, my own flesh and blood" (Romans 9:2–3).

This is certainly a different vision of Jeremiah. Moses was in the same trend. Moses seems absolutely implacable with the people. Always making them tow the line, exposing their weaknesses and expecting more of them. On the other hand, when he came to Hashem, he always spoke kindly about Israel. It's almost like in front of Israel he played the 'father' role, but when with Hashem, he was more like the 'mother' pleading the Father for mercy for the child.

Before giving Jeremiah the hard message to Israel, Hashem started with a nostalgic remembrance of early espousals. He said, "I remember your devotion when you were young; how, as a bride, you loved me; how you followed me through the desert, through a land not sown" (Jeremiah 2:2). Since these early days, Israel's love has cooled off and she became guilty of spiritual adultery. Many say that Hashem rejected Israel because of its attitude, but nothing could be further from the truth.

Hashem loves Israel but he is also, shall I say, "hurt" by its harlotry. Hashem is like one who loves his wife even though she has hurt him very much.

Numbers Rabbah 2:15 gives an excellent parable on the idea,

> It may be compared to a man who took a wife. He told the matchmaker, 'There is none more beautiful, none more excellent, none more faithful and steadfast as she!' The matchmaker decided to visit the home. He found the woman neglecting the home and indulging herself in idleness. The beds were not made, the home was disheveled, and the woman took no thought for her own appearance either. The matchmaker thought, 'If only she could hear how her husband praises her! If he treats her so kindly when she is undeserving, how much more would he praise her if she made an effort to live up to his words about her.'

As Jeremiah wept at the coming destruction of Jerusalem, so did Yeshua (Luke 19:41).

My Personal Thoughts

_____

_____

_____

_____

_____

John 8:31–32

So Yeshua said to the Judeans who had trusted him, "If you obey what I say, then you are really my talmidim, you will know the truth, and the truth will set you free."

In his rebuke to Israel, Jeremiah uses the ever-analogical motif of water. He sais, "For my people have committed two evils: they have abandoned me, the fountain of living water, and dug themselves cisterns, broken cisterns, that can hold no water!" (Jeremiah 2:13), and then continues with, "If you go to Egypt, what's in it for you? Drinking water from the Nile? If you go to Ashur, what's in it for you? Drinking water from the *[Euphrates]* River?" (Jeremiah 2:18).

Water represents Torah, teaching, doctrine, and religious ethics (Deuteronomy 32:2). Speaking of the fountain of living waters, Jeremiah alludes to the rock in the desert at a time when the teaching Israel received was pure and unadulterated. It was a time when Israel followed Hashem wherever he went and there was very little if no distraction. In Jeremiah's prophecy, Hashem nostalgically looks back at that time (Jeremiah 2:2).

In the Middle East, water is very important. Cities usually were built around springs or other sources of water. The alternative was to build cisterns. In cisterns, the water would stagnate, and sometimes the cistern would have holes where the water would escape. Hashem compared Israel's idolatry to Israel preferring stagnant water to living water, to Israel preferring to use uncertain cisterns rather than relying on Hashem's living waters.

It sounds a bit like that analogy Yeshua gave the Samaritan woman between the water of the well, where she would thirst again, and the water he would give her, where she would never thirst again (John 4).

We may laugh at Israel's choice, but how many in this day and age prefer an unsatisfying man-made religion to the purity of principles offered us in the Torah? How many whom Hashem has freed return to the spiritual slavery of Egypt or Babylon (Jeremiah 2:18)?

As Jeremiah did for forty years before the fall of the first temple, and also Yeshua forty years before the fall of the second temple, today both are calling onto us to let go of the adulterated waters that fill man-made Egyptian or Babylonian cisterns and return to the Rock, the Rock that gives us the pure waters that will set us free indeed.

My Personal Thoughts

321

Av

Let us now enter the Land
Let the resurrected high priest reign
In the messianic era
The curse of Av is reversed.

John 13:20

*Yes, indeed! I tell you that a person who receives someone I send receives me,
and that anyone who receives me receives the One who sent me.*

Moses starts his preamble to Deuteronomy talking about 'The Great River,' the northern arc of the Euphrates in Lebanon that would form the Northern border of Israel (Deuteronomy 1:7). Why the 'Great River'? The Nile is far greater. The Euphrates is even mentioned last when listed in Genesis 2. The question is valid. Not only is the Creator familiar with the geography of his own creation but so was Moses who in is former days campaigned for Pharaoh.

In Hashem's eyes, greatness is not necessarily ascribed in reference to size or any personal attributes. Greatness is usually ascribed to a person, or in this case to a thing, as per their affiliations. Here is how two renowned rabbis from the Talmud explain it, "Touch a person anointed with oil and you will also become anointed with oil" (Rabbi Shimon Ben Tarphon). Also, "The servant of a king is like a king" (Rabbi Yishmael). We need to note here that being a king means to be anointed with oil, which is the literal definition of the word 'Mashiach/Messiah.'

We can understand that if I shake hands with someone with oil on their hand, I automatically receive oil on mine. We also know that the ambassador of a king carries that monarch's authority. In the same manner, not only is this river mentioned in relationship to Eden, but it 'touches' the Holy Land in that it is meant to form its northernmost border. Because it 'touches' the Holy Land, it also becomes 'Holy.' Of course this river doesn't presently 'touch' the Land, not right now according to the present-day defined borders of Israel, but neither did it when Moses spoke these words in Deuteronomy. The greatness of the Euphrates was thus spoken of in a prophetic way.

This is an important principle. Whereas this 'greatness by association' may seem like nonsense to our modern mind, it is the principle by which our Messianic faith works. When we reject that truth, we reject the spiritual mechanism that operates our persuasion. Messiah is the servant of the great monarch who has created heaven and earth. He himself receives all authority from this monarch and part of this authority is then passed on to us when we confess his name and put our faith in him (John 5:27; Matthew 28:18; Matthew 19:28; Mark 13:34). In this manner, our 'holiness' is not a matter of personal goodness, but of association and relationship. Of course, any association or relationship carries in itself certain behavioral requirements, which in the case of our relationship with Messiah is where the Torah comes in.

The beauty of this whole principle is that the Master also said, "I tell you that a person who receives someone I send receives me, and that anyone who receives me receives the One who sent me" (John 13:20). The Master left his glorious realm and came to us to live in a way that we could understand and receive him and thereby return to the Father. May we also shape our lives in a way that others receive him through us, and as a result, may also return to Hashem.

My Personal Thoughts

_____

_____

_____

_____

_____

325

1 John 4:8   **Av 2/ ב באב ב**

God is love.

From the time the first generation of Israelites out of Egypt refused to conquer the Promised Land, the Ninth of Av (in the Jewish calendar) has been the 'Day of Woe' in Jewish history.

As the second generation of Israelites out of Egypt arrived at the same spot where their fathers tested ADONAI, Moses was determined not to have a repeat of the same situation. For five weeks he prepared the people for the conquest of the Land with a long exhortation called in Hebrew *Sefer Dvarim*, ספר דברים, the "Book of Deuteronomy." In his exhortation, Moses explained the Torah to this desert generation of the children of Israel (Deuteronomy 1:5). In light of the upcoming battle with the Sons of Anak (giants), Moses reminded the people of their recent military victories, especially with the giant Og (Numbers 32:33). Herein is a lesson for us: to avoid repeating the mistakes of the past, we must devote ourselves to the study of the Torah.

It was essential that Israel understand and dedicate themselves to the Torah in order to successfully conquer the Land. The camp in the desert also counted other people from other nations, so ancient texts propose that when Moses 'expounded' or 'explained' the Torah, he did it in all the 70 languages of the world. This is reminiscent of the day of Shavuot/Pentecost where it is believed that Hashem spoke the Torah in all the languages of the world through tongues of fire (Exodus 20:18). This also reminds us of the other Shavuot/Pentecost when God sent tongues of fire on the disciples of the Master enabling them to speak the mysteries of the Kingdom of God in the languages of all the pilgrims who had come to Jerusalem for the festival (Acts 2). This is usually referred to as the 'gift of tongues' or 'languages.'

Moses may not actually have spoken the sermon of the book of Deuteronomy in the main 70 languages of the world, except prophetically. As the children of Israel of old stood at the entrance of the Promised Land, we, in this *Endtime*, also stand at the door of the kingdom established on earth as it is in heaven, and most everyone in the world has access to the book of Deuteronomy in his own language, just as if Moses spoke it to them.

This teaches us another lesson. Sometimes in our hasty zeal to communicate the words of the Kingdom, we forget to make sure we expound them in a language that people understand. There is more to language than linguistics. We may speak the same tongue but if our body language, intonations, and style are abrasive, we actually lock the message in a language foreign to the hearer. It has been said that love is an international language and love was the language of the Master, which he learned from the Father.

As the Master emulated his Father in all things, may we also emulate the Master in learning to share the word in the *language of love*, which all men understand; love with our words, but also in deeds.

My Personal Thoughts

_____

_____

_____

_____

_____

Luke 10:42   Av 3/ ג באב

But there is only one thing that is essential . . .

The children of Israel set up camp on the East side of the Jordan in the Plains of Moab. A conquest of the Land was imminent. Moses remembered what had happened 40 years earlier, on the ninth of Av, three days from this day, when the former generation refused to enter to conquer the land.

Moses understood that without the prophetic word in our hearts to lead and guide us, we tend to indulge in our own carnality, fear, and laziness. We then lack the courage to do these things that we are to do. As a result, we perish. This could be a good diagnosis of what happened to the first generation, and why they did not conquer the land.

Moses was certainly not going to have a repeat of this. The text tells us that he took it upon himself to expound this Torah to the people. He knew the prophetic word would give people strength and courage to conquer the Land (Deuteronomy 1:5). Moses sat down and made sure to ingrain in this new generation the reason why they were there, and the reasons for the upcoming battles.

Why did Moses need to 'expound'? The Torah seems to be skimpy on details.

The plain literal text often leaves much unanswered. The Talmud abounds with commentaries providing plausible answers, but Jewish sages always knew that when the Messiah comes, he would provide us with the final answers.

They were right! 3,400 years ago Moses undertook the task of elucidating the Torah to a second generation of Israelites out of Egypt. He sat to teach about the plagues, the opening of the Red Sea, the events at Mt. Horeb, and all the lessons learned in the desert to a people who had not seen Egypt. Moses explained to them the reasons why Hashem saved them out of Egypt, immersed them into a new nation, and gave them the Torah at Horeb. In the Plains of Moab, he was getting the people ready for the final step of their full redemption, for the conquest of the Promised Land. Two thousand years ago, Yeshua also came to us. He came to teach his generation, and through them, us. He started his ministry with John on the east side of the Jordan—not far from where Moses was teaching the Israelites—and then he spent his life teaching people who hadn't seen the miracles in Egypt, once and for all elucidating the Torah for them and for us, in order to prepare us for our final entry into the world to come.

The main component Yeshua used to elucidate the Torah was to remind us of the Father's love, mercy, and compassion (Exodus 34:6–7). People followed Yeshua wherever he went drinking his words of wisdom. May we also, the generation of the remnant, take time from our busy schedule to sit at the feet of Yeshua that he may elucidate the Torah for us and prepare us for the world to come.

My Personal Thoughts

_____

_____

_____

_____

Matthew 19:28

Yes. I tell you that in the regenerated world, when the Son of Man sits on his glorious throne, you who have followed me will also sit on twelve thrones and judge the twelve tribes of Isra'el.

When Moses arrived near the borders of the Promised Land, the aged leader knew that the time for him to be gathered with his people had come near. As a father does before the moment of his death, Moses gathered the people of Israel around him, a people that had grown as numerous as the stars in the sky (Deuteronomy 1:10), to give them his final word of advice.

Except for himself, Caleb, and Joshua, who were to succeed him, the whole generation that came out of Egypt had now died. Moses was surrounded by a people who had been raised in the desert under the sole nurture and admonition of Hashem through him. Their only diet was manna; their sole drinking water came from the Rock that 'followed' them. Egypt was a distant echo they had only heard of.

Moses knew that the people were difficult to lead (Deuteronomy 1:12). He knew that after his departure they still needed leadership so he reminded them of their leadership structure. These had been trained under Moses to take charge over the different matters between people, and they would need to continue to do so when in the Land.

The Father has often compared us, his people, to sheep. Sheep need human leadership and so do we. We may rebel and chaff against it but we do need leaders to define the right way for us and even enforce it at times. The saddest words in the Tanach could be, "In those days there was no king in Israel. Everyone did what was right in his own eyes" (Judges 17:6). The book of Judges is a sad testament to what happens to us when we are left to our own devices, without authoritative central earthly leadership.

Today our congregations and communities are scattered and divided, and like in the days of the book of Judges, everyone does that which is right in his own eyes, trying to obey the words of the Torah each one according to his own perspective. This has caused deep division within the congregational body of Messiah.

Hopefully, this state of affairs will not last too long. Soon, the King will return and along with his disciples as the appointed new Sanhedrin, and as Moses did in the desert 3,400 years ago, he will sit and judge the twelve tribes of Israel (Matthew 19:28) and their myriads of disciples throughout the nations (Matthew 28:20).

May it be soon Abba, even in our days!

My Personal Thoughts

_____

_____

_____

_____

_____

_____

Matthew 5:45

Then you will become children of your Father in heaven. For he makes his sun shine on good and bad people alike, and he sends rain to the righteous and the unrighteous alike.

A great *mixed multitude* accompanied Israel out of Egypt (Exodus 12:38). These were non-Israelite people from different countries who had seen the power of the mighty God El-Shaddai in Egypt and had cast their lot with Israel. They were the 'stranger' in the midst of Israel.

From the beginning of time, God formulated a redemption plan for humanity. This plan implied that Israel would be chosen as a messenger and would cradle his own Redeemer, who would also invite the multitude of the nations to come to Mt. Horeb (the Torah) and eventually follow him to Mt. Zion (the Promised Land).

Israel had been an abused stranger in the land of Egypt and forever the Father wanted that experience to motivate his firstborn (Exodus 4:22) to never abuse the stranger living within its borders. It is actually a commandment for Israel to be loving to the stranger in its midst (Deuteronomy 10:19), and therefore a contingence to Israel's acceptance in the Land of the Almighty. One who is kind to strangers, one who is hospitable, imitates God, and imitation is the core process of discipleship.

On the other hand, the stranger who took refuge under the wings of the God of Israel was required to abide by the Torah of the Land. He was not to bring other gods in the Land or to desecrate the Shabbat, the Temple, or the Holy Days. The stranger was also to be careful not in any way to be a spiritual stumbling block to Israel.

In the apostolic letters, a non-Jew, whether he is in Messiah or not, is called a Gentile. Today this word has obtained a negative connotation but it is because of the way people use it. It was not so in the Bible. The Gentile is simply someone who is not of biological Israelite descent. These come under the blessing of Abraham of whom it was said, "By you all the families of the earth will be blessed" (Genesis 12:3). That is why Gentiles who became Jewish were called "Sons of Avraham" (Acts 13:26).

There is actually a mighty blessing for the Gentile/stranger who of his own volition adopts to live under the Torah covenant. Isaiah pronounces it in these beautiful words,

> A foreigner joining ADONAI should not say, "ADONAI will separate me from his people"; likewise the eunuch should not say, "I am only a dried-up tree." For here is what ADONAI says: "As for the eunuchs who keep my Shabbats, who choose what pleases me and hold fast to my covenant: in my house, within my walls, I will give them power and a name greater than sons and daughters; I will give him an everlasting name that will not be cut off. And the foreigners who join themselves to ADONAI to serve him, to love the name of ADONAI, and to be his workers, all who keep Shabbat and do not profane it, and hold fast to my covenant, I will bring them to my holy mountain and make them joyful in my house of prayer; their burnt offerings and sacrifices will be accepted on my altar; for my house will be called a house of prayer for all peoples." ADONAI Elohim says, he who gathers Isra'el's exiles: "There are yet others I will gather, besides those gathered already." (Isaiah 56:3–8)

1 Peter 1:14–16　　　　　　　　　　　　　　**Av 6/ ו באב**

> *As people who obey God, do not let yourselves be shaped by the evil desires*
> *you used to have when you were still ignorant. On the contrary, following the*
> *Holy One who called you, become holy yourselves in your entire way of life;*
> *since the Tanakh says, "You are to be holy because I am holy.*

The idea of mankind reaching holiness can be quite a daunting conundrum. First we are told that we are in a constant unalterable sinful state (Jeremiah 17:9), but then we are required to be holy (Leviticus 11:44). Could it be that holiness is not about being sinless? What could or should a man do to attain holiness?

Let's use the Sabbath for example. Why is it holy? Why is it sanctified? Does it possess any properties that make it different from the other days of the week? Does the Sabbath day have two suns? Or two moons? Does creation stop its work on that day? Is there some sort of *magic* that fills the air on the Sabbath day? No. The Sabbath day is a day like any other day; it is holy/sanctified on the sole authority of the word of God who made it holy. By his commandment, it is holy.

The words *holy* and *hallowed* come from the Latin root *sanctified* and all come from the Hebrew *kodesh* קודש, which presents the idea of being *set-apart* or *separated*. The Sabbath day is separated from all the other days of the week solely because of a command that proceeded out of the mouth of Hashem. It is holy simply because God said so. In the same manner therefore we are separated by the commandments of God.

The injunction to be holy is mentioned as the conclusion of the dietary laws in Leviticus eleven. No other reason, concerning health or otherwise, is given to us in the Torah for following these food rules. On a general level, someone's culture and even of fellowship boundaries are largely defined by what they eat and how they eat. In the same manner our dietary laws often separate (sanctify) us from society at large who is not always biblically particular about they eat.

The solution to the holiness conundrum could then be found in the most common of Jewish Hebrew blessings which refers to the Almighty as the One, *asher kideshanu bemitsvotav* במצותיו אשר קדשנו, "who has sanctified/separated us by his commandments." Then, all that makes us holy, sanctified, or separated unto him is not some form of ascetic lifestyle, the ability of extreme self-denial, or the performance of miracles, but simply obedience to the commandments uttered by the mouth of Hashem. In essence, we are separated unto whom we obey.

His commandments that sanctify us are given to us because of is grace and mercy, not because of our works or worth. So to simplify the equation further, we are holy solely because of his mercy and grace.

My Personal Thoughts

_____
_____
_____
_____
_____

Hebrews 13:8 Av 7/ ז באב

Yeshua the Messiah is the same yesterday, today and forever.

In his mystical Gospel while attempting to explain the nature of Messiah, John the Disciple began his thesis with the following words, "In the beginning was the Word" (John 1:1). This "Word" John speaks of is actually the *Memrah* presented to us in the Targum, the Aramaic version of the Pentateuch. John then continues with, "The Word became a human being" (John 1:14). By all recognitions, this *Memrah* that became flesh to dwell among us is the Torah itself, which is not only a legal document but also the direct revelation of Hashem's nature and character to mankind.

The problem we face today is that the Torah was given about 3,600 years ago to a Semitic nomadic desert tribe of the Middle East. As such, it addresses issues relevant to its time such as slavery, the buying and selling of children, and the vendetta style of justice prevalent in those days. Though these concepts may seem archaic to us today, their form of application in the Torah came as a great improvement when it compared to the general social governance of its days. Sad to say, instead of judging the document according to its own values, many have resolved the Torah's seeming irrelevancy issues by adopting the idea that it has since been annulled by Yeshua and is therefore now obsolete. But how does this fit with the words of John? John speaks of this Torah becoming flesh through the Messiah who himself proclaimed that he came to teach us how to obey it better. How could it then be obsolete?

A proper contextual study of these commandments helps us discover the beautiful nature and character of the Almighty. We discover that in fact, his rulings constitute the same basic ideals for which many of us we fight today. They include healthy concepts of child protection, women's and worker's rights, proper criminal justice, equal opportunity, financial integrity, as well as affordable healthy dietary standards. These are, in essence, all things we find in the Torah. Why consider them obsolete and then go on re-inventing the wheel by recreating these same laws by our own means? Something is wrong with that picture.

However we feel about some of its injunctions, we need to remember that the Torah is the revelation of God's nature and character. Each and every commandment should be looked upon as a distillation of his essence, a pure revelation of his person. The study of the commandments is the study of God. When we imply that it is now annulled and obsolete, technically speaking, we abolish God. Maybe this is why the world cannot get control of its social issues. Through their misguided theology, they've rendered God obsolete.

Our so-called evolution has distanced us from the oracle given on the mountain but without it we are as stars endlessly roaming through space in search of an orbit. It may take a lifetime, but may we repent from the heresy that denies the value of God's commandments even in our day. May we also learn to find our orbital stability within the beautiful words spoken at Horeb.

My Personal Thoughts

_____

_____

_____

_____

_____

Matthew 19:14 Av 8/ ח באב

Yeshua said, "Let the children come to me, don't stop them."

The Torah requires that we teach its laws to our children and grandchildren. Yes, after we are done raising our children, as grandparents, we are also responsible to teach our grandchildren. When we fail to do so, we break the system and eventually raise a generation that does not know Torah, a world oblivious to the ways of Hashem. The ramifications of this are extensive. The idea is that the Torah contains the message of godliness within itself, as well as ethics, godly living, warning, and prophecy for every generation. When we fail to pass it on, we break the chain and take a chance on those of future generations.

Jewish sages declare that teaching the Torah to one's son is the one thing for which a man is rewarded in this world and in the world to come. Our sages also lament that Jerusalem and the Temple were destroyed only because people failed to teach Torah to their children. May we reverse that trend. In a world where the idea of faithful obedience to God's commandments is viewed as old fashioned, and even according to some religious views, obsolete, I'd like to bring forth the fatherly advice of renowned biblical sages such as Solomon who prefaced Torah teaching to his son with,

> My son, keep my words and treasure up my commandments with you; keep my commandments and live; keep my teaching as the apple of your eye; bind them on your fingers; write them on the tablet of your heart. Say to wisdom, "You are my sister," and call insight your intimate friend, to keep you from the forbidden woman, from the adulteress with her smooth words. (Proverbs 7:1–5)

Solomon knew these things from his father David who taught him,

> The Torah of ADONAI is perfect, restoring the inner person. The instruction of ADONAI is sure, making wise the thoughtless. The precepts of ADONAI are right, rejoicing the heart. The mitzvah of ADONAI is pure, enlightening the eyes. The fear of ADONAI is clean, enduring forever. The rulings of ADONAI are true, they are righteous altogether, more desirable than gold, than much fine gold, also sweeter than honey or drippings from the honeycomb. Through them your servant is warned; in obeying them there is great reward. (Psalm 19:7–11)

As Moses addressed his spiritual children in the desert he even assured them of the wisdom of Torah with,

> Look, I have taught you laws and rulings, just as ADONAI my God ordered me, so that you can behave accordingly in the land where you are going in order to take possession of it. Therefore, observe them; and follow them; for then all peoples will see you as having wisdom and understanding . . . For what great nation is there that has God as close to them as ADONAI our God is, whenever we call on him? What great nation is there that has laws and rulings as just as this entire Torah which I am setting before you today? (Deuteronomy 4:5–8)

Our world falls deeper and deeper into moral darkness, abjectness, confusion, and instability as it distances itself from the Godly wisdom that would preserve it. As the two pillars of God's way and man's way grow apart, the roof suddenly falls on their temple of confusion (Judges 16:29–30). May we, by clinging to his commands, be a light shining in the darkness, a witness to his greatness, order, beauty, and wisdom.

1 Peter 2:12　　　　　　　　　　　　　　

> *But to live such good lives among the pagans that even though they now speak against you as evil-doers, they will, as a result of seeing your good actions, give glory to God on the Day of his coming .*

With literacy now almost universal, the word of Torah is made available almost to all. Through the Hebrew language, Jews have been able to preserve its text. They have also developed easy ways to learn Hebrew so that many of us can actually study the words of God in their original language. In a way, this should save us from the divisive curse of so many translations. Jews do not have this problem because they study their Scriptures in their original language, and the language of the Torah is not Elizabethan English, nor even Greek, but Hebrew.

Reading the Torah in the culture of its original tongue is a first step in properly comprehending it, but how do we know whether we properly understand, live, and apply its words? The litmus test is in this exhortation given by Moses to the Israelite generation ready to enter and conquer Canaan at God's command;

> Therefore, observe them; and follow them; for then all peoples will see you as having wisdom and understanding. When they hear of all these laws, they will say, 'This great nation is surely a wise and understanding people.' For what great nation is there that has God as close to them as ADONAI our God is, whenever we call on him? What great nation is there that has laws and rulings as just as this entire Torah which I am setting before you today? (Deuteronomy 4:6–8)

There is s popular saying among secular folks these days that says, "Lord, deliver me from your children!" I would like to think that people who say these things are incorrigible atheists, but the truth is that this saying is popular even among believers. It is the feeling often uttered by people who have been scorned and abused by some of the self-righteous, cold, and unloving manner of some of God's people who are supposed to represent Hashem through their societal mores.

It is true that at times living by the instructions of the Torah may cause us to receive adversity from our social circles. People often refer to this as *persecution* (2 Timothy 3:12). On the other hand, not all opposition is due to *persecution.* Sometimes it is the just reward of our being obnoxious, pushy, and unwise. In the meantime, people fail to know Hashem as he would be portrayed, would we walk out Torah knowledge the way Yeshua taught us to do it. It is worthwhile to note that whereas Yeshua was so sociable that people sought and followed his uncertain ways for miles.

Yeshua sent his disciples in the same manner he was sent (John 20:21). Their life in Israel and even in the nations, which is well documented in the Book of Acts and other historical accounts, had the desired effect of creating a hunger for God in the people they came in contact with. The question we now need to ask ourselves is, "When people come in contact with us, do they see Hashem's wisdom as the Torah say they should?" (Deuteronomy 4:6–8).

My Personal Thoughts

_____

_____

_____

James 2:18

Show me this faith of yours without the actions, and I will show you my faith by my actions!

Yeshua said, "Let your light shine before people, so that they may see the good things you do and praise your Father in heaven" (Matthew 5:16). The words spoken by the Master should be understood within the Judaic matrix in which they were spoken. In the mouth of a Jewish rabbi, to shine your light means to practice Torah commandments (Psalm 119:105), and the expression "good works" often employed by the Master and other apostles comes from the Hebrew original *mitzvoth* מצות, "commandments." It is the plural of *mitzvah* מצוה found in the term *bar-mitzvah* בר-מצוה, "son of the commandment."

In essence, in his words, Yeshua tells us is to practice Torah in front of men that it may cause them to glorify the Father. This amounts to the same statement made by Moses as he foresaw the positive reaction to our relationship with Hashem. Contrary to their gods, these people will notice that our God is near to us to answer us when we call. They will also notice that the rules and statutes we are given to observe are just to satisfy the capricious whims of a deity, but for our own good and benefit (Deuteronomy 4:6-8).

Practicing Torah commandments therefore is Hashem's evangelization program, so to speak. When we show love, forgiveness, compassion, generosity, and care, which are all Torah commands, we show God's true nature to the world. When we observe the Sabbath, he gives us rest from our labor so we can spend time with him in the company of family and friends. When we eat according to his diet it shows that he cares that we remain consecrated to him. It also shows a disciplined mind, as we must remember that the first sin was all about disobedience to a certain food (Genesis 3:6). Celebrating the festivals reminds us of his goodness for us, past, present and future, and managing our finances according to the word benefits the whole community.

Today, whenever we talk about obedience to God's commandments many, as if they were Torah experts, start screaming legalism. The six million dollar question here is to know what is the difference between obedience and legalism. Someone else may have paid the price of our redemption, but it doesn't absolve us from obeying the rules of the Kingdom outlined in the Torah. Attempting to express the gratitude of the redeemed towards their redeemer, the apostle Paul said that the works of Torah obedience should be practiced, but out of love, not out of duty (Galatians 5:6).

We are his bride. As we enter his household and Kingdom it behooves to start behaving like it. This reminds me of a queen who when she publicly disobeyed her husband, for the sake of the people present he had to banish her from the kingdom, because if the queen herself did not obey her husband neither will the common folks (Esther 1). Unlike worldly kings, God is covenant keeping and he does not retract from his covenant with his people. Therefore in regards toward his everlasting and gracious compassion towards us, we should learn to do his will and obey his commandments out of love.

May we learn to live in a manner that the world will glorify our God!

My Personal Thoughts

Luke 11:10

He who goes on seeking finds.

Before entering the Promised Land, Moses sternly warned the children of Israel,

> When you have had children and grandchildren, lived a long time in the land, become corrupt and made a carved image, a representation of something, and thus done what is evil in the sight of ADONAI your God and provoked him; I call on the sky and the earth to witness against you today that you will quickly disappear from the land that you are crossing the Yarden to possess. You will not prolong your days there but will be completely destroyed. ADONAI will scatter you among the peoples; and among the nations to which ADONAI will lead you away, you will be left few in number. There you will serve gods which are the product of human hands, made of wood and stone, which can't see, hear, eat or smell. However, from there you will seek ADONAI your God; and you will find him if you search after him with all your heart and being. (Deuteronomy 4:25–29)

Judging by the 2,000-year exile that is now coming to an end, this prophecy has certainly been fulfilled. For 2,000 years, the children of Israel have been exiled, scattered mostly within the largely Christian based nations of Western and Eastern Europe. There, Israel served gods of wood and stone, the work of human hands that neither see, nor hear, nor eat, nor smell.

Then, the Torah says, "However, from there you will seek ADONAI your God; and you will find him if you search after him with all your heart and being" (Deuteronomy 4:29). Oh, how Hashem, in his great compassion, never leaves us without a redemptive promise. We do not see it in the English text, but in Hebrew this whole section plays with the singular and plural form of the pronoun 'you.' Sometimes it refers to Israel as many people, sometimes as one nation, or one man.

Does Hashem mean that only if each and every one of the people of Israel seeks ADONAI, they will find him? Each and everyone, yes, but we are also talking of Israel as a nation (Romans 11:26). Will Israel find its God again only if each and every Jew seeks him with all their hearts? In the knowledge of humanity, Hashem has established a system of redemption through the representation of a remnant (Romans 11:1–5). The first century CE has given birth to a vibrant and fruitful Messianic Jewish community that spread the teachings of Yeshua throughout Israel and the world of their day. This community almost died through persecutions, but in a sense, resurrected in our days. So we find in today's Jewish believers of Israel and of the exile a vibrant messianic force ready to play its Endtime role (Revelation 7:4; 14:4).

Yes, like James of old, those who seek him with all their heart also seek intercession for their fellow brothers and sisters, and the prayer of a righteous person has great power (James 5:16). Yeshua also reiterated Moses' words when he said, "He who goes on seeking finds" (Luke 11:10).

May we, by living a life of simple godliness, inspire others to seek him too!

My Personal Thoughts

335

Ephesians 3:10   יב באב / Av 12

> *For the rulers and authorities in heaven to learn,*
> *through the existence of the Messianic Community,*
> *how many-sided God's wisdom is.*

Moses continued his exhortation to the children of the "children of Israel" who left Egypt. He outlined Hashem's credentials: "Indeed, inquire about the past . . . has there ever been anything as wonderful as this? Has anyone heard anything like it?" (Deuteronomy 4:32). Then he goes on expounding the events surrounding the exodus of their fathers.

The Exodus is God's testimony to mankind of his preeminence over all the gods and powers in heaven and on earth. It is the testament of his ability to fulfill the promises he made to Abraham, in spite of any unforeseen developments in the dynamics of the history of his people. If Hashem says so, he is able to bring back his people from abject slavery in the lowest cultural strata of Egyptian societal gutters, and make them a free sovereign people, which eventually became the light of Hashem to the nations around them. That's what Moses wanted the children of the children of Israel to understand as they readied to conquer the Land before them.

Paul interjected the events of Exodus that showed Hashem's superiority over the gods of Egypt into his own time and work as an emissary to the Gentiles of Ephesus. He conjectured that, though it was not previously known by the ancients, in his days, according to Hashem's eternal purpose realized in Yeshua HaMashiach, through the messianic congregations God's manifold wisdom has been revealed to rulers and authorities in the heavenly places (Ephesians 3:5–6; 10–11).

In other words, our fathers didn't know it, but as the gods of Egypt learned the superiority of Hashem through the Exodus of the children of Israel, the gods of Greece and Rome were going to learn the same lesson through the exodus of their children into the Messianic Congregation of Yeshua Hamashiach. That is Hashem's universal plan, not only to redeem his children from slavery to the world, but also to demonstrate his ability to deliver them to all the powers in heaven and on earth. We are like the cherished prize of two contenders, only the game is thrown, as we already know the winner.

In the same manner that the God of Israel delivered the children of Jacob from slavery and showed the rulers and gods of Egypt *a thing or two*, he now delivers his children from the other nations and shows their rulers and gods *a thing or two*. As the children of the children of Israel were to look back at what happened to their fathers in order to mature in their faith, the children of Israel of today, along with those of the nations, are also to look back to these events as a testimony of Hashem's power to save us all from this idolatrous and wicked world. That is why it is important to celebrate the Passover Seder.

May we all learn in this day and age the many lessons of trust, faith, and obedience that can only be learned as we sit at the feet of ADONAI in the *wilderness* times of our lives, as we hear from him at his Holy Mountain.

May we also learn to fear Hashem, the Creator, the ruler of the universe, the deliverer of his people, and fear him only!

My Personal Thoughts

Mark 12:29 **Av 13/ יג באב**

> *Yeshua answered, "The most important is, 'Sh'ma Yisra'el, ADONAI Eloheinu,*
> *ADONAI echad [Hear, O Isra'el, the Lord our God, the Lord is one]."*

Yeshua astonished Sadducee priests on the subject of the resurrection of the dead, so some impressed Pharisees (not all were antagonistic) came and asked the Master, "Which is the most important mitzvah of them all?" (Mark 12:28).

Right away we must conclude from this question that not all commandments are equal in importance. This can be recognized by the fact that the breaking of some commandments only requires an immersion—like eating something not kosher—while some invoke the death penalty—like murder, idolatry, adultery, and breaking the Sabbath. Yeshua agreed to the idea of least and great commandments when he said, "So whoever disobeys the least of these mitzvot and teaches others to do so will be called the least in the Kingdom of Heaven. But whoever obeys them and so teaches will be called great in the Kingdom of Heaven" (Matthew 5:19).

Yeshua our Master answered this simple question, by quoting what has been agreed by Jewish sages for centuries before his manifestation on earth, as being the creed of Judaism, "The most important is, 'Sh'ma Yisra'el, ADONAI Eloheinu, ADONAI echad [Hear, O Isra'el, the Lord our God, the Lord is one]'" (Mark 12:29; Deuteronomy 6:4).

The word "hear" is this case, as it is also in English, not solely related to a sensorial experience but rather means *to listen with the intention to obey*. In most religions, even in Christianity, the theory and the doctrine of God is the most important thing. In the Torah, however, the most important thing is not to define or quantify God as usual creeds and statements of faith do, but to emulate his words through tangible actions and more importantly, to 'hear' and 'obey' the belief and idea that Hashem is the one and only, and that there is no other before, after, or beside him. Unless we do that first, there is no point in going any further. It is interesting to realize that from early forms of polytheistic religions to modern Western religions, which are mixed with elements of Greco-Roman paganism, this is the elementary truth that the Adversary has fought the most.

Yeshua then continues by quoting Moses' words in Deuteronomy, words that teach us how to express that belief: "And you are to love ADONAI your God with all your heart, with all your soul, with all your understanding and with all your strength." (Mark 12:30).

After that Yeshua added his own *halacha*, or application to this commandment and said, "The second is this: 'You are to love your neighbor as yourself.' There is no other mitzvah greater than these." (Mark 12:31).

In essence, we are taught here that the expression of our belief in the supremacy of Hashem is to love him first and foremost with all our hearts (our emotions), with all our souls (our life in this body), and with all our might (our substance) (Deuteronomy 6:5), and that the expression of this love is to love our neighbor as ourselves.

My Personal Thoughts

Matthew 22:37   Av 14/ יד באב

You are to love ADONAI your God with all your heart
and with all your soul and with all your strength.

In Deuteronomy, Moses sat on a mountain and exhorted the people who were soon to enter the Promised Land. He used the following words, "Sh'ma, Yisra'el! ADONAI Eloheinu, ADONAI echad *[Hear, Isra'el! ADONAI our God, ADONAI is one]*; and you are to love ADONAI your God with all your heart, all your being and all your resources" (Deuteronomy 6:4–5). In Matthew, Yeshua, who taught that the Kingdom of God was upon us , also sat on a mountain and exhorted his disciples how to live these higher standards of Torah (Matthew 12:28). The Master warned his friends with the following words, "Unless your righteousness is far greater than that of the Torah-teachers and P'rushim, you will certainly not enter the Kingdom of Heaven" (Matthew 5:20). In other words, the deeds of righteousness of the religious leaders of his days were recognized as righteous acts, but they were not enough. What did Yeshua mean?

Let us take a look at the words of the Master from the Sermon on the Mount, but through the perspective of a Jewish teacher. In Judaism, "prayer is the work of the heart" (b.Ta'anit 2a) and fasting is the afflicting of the soul (Leviticus 16:31; Isaiah 58:5). The word in this verse translated in English as *might* in Hebrew is 'me'od' מְאֹד, *much*. Our *much* therefore is our worth, our substance. To love Hashem with all our *might* then is to love him with all our substance, as in the giving of charity for example.

Yeshua's Sermon on the Mount consisted of instruction on things such as prayer (Matthew 6:7–8), fasting (Matthew 6:17–18), and the giving of charity (Matthew 6:3–4). It therefore represents instructions on how to practice loving God with all our heart, with all our soul, and with all our might in a higher manner than the religious people of his day.

As we ponder the Master's words, we discover that they teach us to obey Torah commands, but with the right motives; not just in an outward show or for social prestige.

It is so easy for our righteousness to be an outward hypocritical display of religiosity. The Master teaches us instead, "Let your light shine" before others (practice the Torah openly), in order that people see your "good works" (good works = practicing of the Torah) and give glory to our Father who is in heaven (so that people will praise and glorify Hashem, not us) (Matthew 5:16).

In other words, whatever we do should be done for the glory of God, not to increase our own value in the sight of men, a sentiment also expressed by Paul, Yeshua's emissary (1 Corinthians 10:31).

As we practice, for example, the keeping the Sabbath this week, may we do it in a way that brings praise to Hashem in the heart of others.

My Personal Thoughts

_____

_____

_____

_____

Philippians 2:13   טו באב /Av 15

For God is the one working among you both the willing and the working for what pleases him.

As they readied to enter the Promised Land, Moses addresses this second generation of Israelites from Egypt. He reminds the people of all that happened during the last forty years of wandering. He debriefs them on all the lessons learned and on how not to repeat the same errors. Knowing that he would not enter the land, he was giving them his departing address. Promises of wealth, prosperity, fertility, and military victories fill this address, promises that all hang on one phrase, "Because you are listening to these rulings, keeping and obeying them" (Deuteronomy 7:12).

From this we can define the role of Torah in our lives. Our fathers in the desert had already experienced salvation from Egypt and entered a relationship with El-Elyon, the Almighty God on the Mount. They had been chosen not for their goodness and works but because of the promises Hashem made to their fathers Abraham, Isaac, and Jacob (Deuteronomy 9:5). The Hebrew word translated as *grace* is *chesed* חסד, or, covenant loyalty. We have a God who, unlike man, keeps his promises and does not repent from them. The covenant was 'cut'; they were the redeemed on their way to the land God calls his own. The Torah was simply the contract on how to live and prosper in that Land. If they kept it, they would prosper in it, if they disobeyed it, he would take them out. Was this good news or bad news?

It was both. If our success is to be measured only by our obedience, we are all doomed as we are desperately wicked (Jeremiah 17:9). As human, not only do we need to be shown the way, but we also need someone to walk it for us, and we have it: Yeshua our Mashiach. True, some people seem more virtuous than others. Some rationalize stealing and lying as good business ethics while others keep their integrity, even at the cost of incurring loss. Some people lie while other's word is as good as gold. There are also those who easily break promises (especially in marriage) while others wouldn't dare. Some are proud and some are humble. Some find it easy to use foul language while others never would. All these virtues, though, have nothing to do with any personal goodness of our own. They are solely the results of the indwelling of the spirit of Hashem within us, which is given to us though the atonement of our Adon Yeshua. This was the promise that was given to the people at the Mount when he said he would walk "within" us. Take that presence away from us and we are again as wicked as the most wretched criminal on the planet.

When Yeshua walks within us, he is the shield that in a way blinds Hashem to our iniquities. In the name of his virtuous sinless life we are redeemed, and it has nothing to do with any good works of our own, no matter how much we try to obey Torah. Our wicked human nature will always fail us. We need the atonement of the righteous one, of the Tzaddik Yeshua as they say in Hebrew, to intervene between us and the Father. All Hashem sees then is the atonement of the Master for us, and it is this grace which then gives us the ability to perform the good works, the obedience of Torah (Titus 2:11–14; Ephesians 2:10).

My Personal Thoughts

_____

_____

_____

_____

James 3:1

Not many of you should become teachers, my brothers,
since you know that we will be judged more severely.

In his exhortation to the children of the children of Israel, Moses makes a point about the benefits of keeping the commandment. He says, "All the mitzvot I am giving you today you are to take care to obey, so that you will live, increase your numbers, enter and take possession of the land ADONAI swore about to your ancestors" (Deuteronomy 8:1).

It is a simple concept. I rent the downstairs part of my house. When a potential renter shows interest in the apartment, I give them a rental agreement which is basically a paper telling them that they can only live there as long as they follows certain rules, i.e., no smoking, no big pets, and pay the rent on time. In the same manner, the Land of Israel, being Hashem's land, he reminds the potential future tenants, the children of Israel, of the 'rental agreement' (Genesis 20:15).

The word commandment in this sentence is used as a collective word referring to the Torah commandments as a whole. It points to the whole exhortation Moses was giving to the children of Israel in his Deuteronomy address. The aforementioned verse is often used to motivate people. If they live more concurrent with Hashem's commandments, he will bring blessing upon their land. Whereas living by the Torah certainly brings blessing upon our land and our lives, this verse was contextually directed towards the children of Israel, in the Land of Israel.

The same collective form of the word commandment referring to the Torah as a whole is used in Proverbs 6:23 and 13:13. Paul also used it in his exhortation to Timothy, to keep the commandment unstained and free from reproach until the appearing of our Adon, Yeshua HaMashiach (1 Timothy 6:14). Timothy was the son of a Jewish woman and a Roman man. His Jewish grandmother raised him in the ways of the Torah (2 Timothy 1:5). In his leadership-training epistle, Paul asked Timothy not to just keep the commandment, but to keep it "unstained and free from reproach."

May those of us whom the Father has placed in positions of responsibility also serve keeping the commandment "unstained and free from reproach" and remain untainted by the reproach caused by the rationalization of our evil inclination to selfishness, pride, and deceit.

It is a tall order, but whereas those of us in position of responsibility and teaching receive double honor, we are also liable to greater condemnation (1 Timothy 5:17; James 3:1). Remember the warning of the Master towards those who through their staining of the commandments cause his little ones to stumble: "Whoever causes one of these little ones who believe in me to sin, it would be better for him to have a great millstone fastened around his neck and to be drowned in the depth of the sea" (Matthew 18:6).

My Personal Thoughts

_____

_____

_____

_____

Matthew 6:26 יז באב /Av 17

Look at the birds flying about! They neither plant nor harvest, nor do they gather food into barns; yet your heavenly Father feeds them. Aren't you worth more than they are?

While in the desert, Israel was under Hashem's complete care. Their food and water was miraculously supplied, the clothes on their back did not wear out, and their feet did not swell (Deuteronomy 8:4). Every morning as they prepared food, they handled the bounty of Hashem in their hands, and even ate it. Under these circumstances, it came naturally to bless Hashem after eating (Deuteronomy 8:10).

Now they were going to enter the Land and manna would eventually stop. They were going to have to till the land, sow, harvest, dig wells, irrigate, build houses and even train an army to protect their borders. It would then be easy to forget that Hashem is the great provider of all bounties, the protector of his people, and think that all they have is due to their own efforts.

Moses warned the children of Israel,

> For ADONAI your God is bringing you into a good land, a land with streams, springs . . . a land of wheat and barley, grapevines, fig trees and pomegranates; a land of olive oil and honey; a land where you will eat food in abundance . . . a land where the stones contain iron and the hills can be mined for copper. So you will eat and be satisfied, and you will bless ADONAI your God for the good land he has given you. "Be careful not to forget ADONAI your God by not obeying his mitzvot, rulings and regulations that I am giving you today. Otherwise, after you have eaten and are satisfied, built fine houses and lived in them, and increased your herds, flocks, silver, gold and everything else you own, you will become proud-hearted. Forgetting ADONAI your God - who brought you out of the land of Egypt, where you lived as slaves . . . who brought water out of flint rock for you; who fed you in the desert with man, unknown to your ancestors; all the while humbling and testing you in order to do you good in the end—you will think to yourself, 'My own power and the strength of my own hand have gotten me this wealth.' . . . If you forget ADONAI your God, follow other gods and serve and worship them, I am warning you in advance today that you will certainly perish. (Deuteronomy 8:7–19)

This is the age-old cycle: obedience to Torah brings success, success brings complacency, complacency leads to neglect of Torah, and neglect of Torah brings failure. Nations who once were successful because they strove to govern themselves on godly principles are now falling from very high as they forget the God who allowed them to exist.

Poverty may build character but wealth tests it. It certainly is at the times when we don't feel so dependent on the Father that our motives are tested. Our grown-up children have the same reaction. Once they feel they don't need us, we sometimes don't hear from them much. Someone told me once that if you want your children to communicate, send them a letter announcing your enclosed gift and then 'forget' to insert the check in the envelope.

Hashem has the big 'check' for us, but he also 'checks' our motives. He knows how to slow the river of his provisions and remind us that we are but dust; that we need him to even exist. He wants us to love him not just because of the 'check' though, but because we are grateful and are a bride responding to his loving advances towards us.

1 Corinthians 4:7

After all, what makes you so special? What do you have that you didn't receive as a gift?
And if in fact it was a gift, why do you boast as if it weren't?

While the whole world sat in the darkness of idolatry and superstition, Israel received the light that enlightens everyone (John 1:9; Psalm 119:105). At that time, only Israel knew about the Creator of heaven and earth. Only Israel had the light of Torah and was given the parameters of morality, of right and wrong, of pure and impure, of edible and non-edible.

As the people made ready to conquer the Land, Hashem reminded them not to think highly of themselves; that they would not be victorious because of their own righteousness and knowledge of Torah. He tells them that it is solely because of the wickedness of the current inhabitants of the Land that they will conquer it. Yes, while in the desert they learned all about righteousness, but reminding them of their failings and those of the previous generation, Hashem tells them that they are a *stiff-necked* people so to not glory in themselves (Deuteronomy 9). Later, in his apostolic letters, Paul uses the same rhetoric as he exhorts the Corinthians with, "What do you have that you didn't receive as a gift? And if in fact it was a gift, why do you boast as if it weren't?" (1 Corinthians 4:7).

At our son's graduation party, my wife's ninety-nine year-old aunt from Sweden commented, "I don't understand Americans and their graduation parties. You don't deserve a party because you were faithful to go to school and graduated, you go to school because you must!" In the same way our obedience to study the word or obey Torah doesn't deserve any accolades. Rabbi Yochanan Ben Zacchai, a sage who lived at the time of the destruction of the second Temple and who certainly knew about Yeshua said, "If you have learned much Torah, do not claim credit for yourself, because for such a purpose you were created."

Our Rabbi and Master also taught along the same lines. Using the Talmudic idea that the Torah is our yoke of service comparable to that of an ox serving his owner he said,

> If one of you has a slave tending the sheep or plowing, when he comes back from the field, will you say to him, 'Come along now, sit down and eat'? No, you'll say, 'Get my supper ready, dress for work, and serve me until I have finished eating and drinking; after that, you may eat and drink.' Does he thank the slave because he did what he was told to do? No! It's the same with you— when you have done everything you were told to do, you should be saying, 'We're just ordinary slaves, we have only done our duty.' (Luke 17:7–10)

As we learn, mature, and as we benefit from Hashem's miracles of supply and protection, may we always remember that the righteousness to whom we owe our blessed state is not ours, but that of our Master, Yeshua.

My Personal Thoughts

_____

_____

_____

_____

John 4:23

But the time is coming—indeed, it's here now—when the true worshippers will worship the Father spiritually and truly, for these are the kind of people the Father wants worshipping him.

Words are so important. Much of our theology seems to be lost in translation. Call it nit-picking if you may, but the exact meaning of Hebrew words used to describe our service to Hashem in Hebrew should be translated correctly in order to understand Torah and the concept of service to Hashem. Sad to say though, translations usually reflect the cultural and ethical understanding of the translator, which is why a preliminary knowledge of Hebrew is strongly advisable if one who desires to understand the Torah and its concept of service.

Words describe feelings but they also describe tasks that we must do. If, as manager of a company, I give a man some instructions, I expect him to do exactly what I ask. If he disobeys because to him the words I speak have a different meaning, we are going to have problems. We can imagine what happened at the tower of Babel work site when ADONAI came to confuse their languages.

English has the word *worship*. It is a good word but it is a very subjective. It fails to represent a specific action. It can mean anything from the act of singing and praising to charitable giving. In Hebrew there are words for, *to give; to thank; to sing; to pray; to praise* or *to shine something*; *to magnify* or *to make something bigger in our eyes*; *to serve* or *to work*, which means to practice any of the Torah commands; *to cleave* as to be glued to something or someone. The Hebrew word translated as worship is: *shacha* שחה, to prostrate.

To serve in Deuteronomy 10:20 uses the word *to work*. To serve God means to do the commandments and since many of the commandments are Temple related, Jewish sages have concluded that praising in prayer takes the place of temple offerings, thus we are taught about the *sacrifice of praise*, "the natural product of lips that acknowledge his name" (Hebrews 13:15).

Moses exhorted the people to "fear ADONAI your God." He said, "You are to fear ADONAI your God, serve him, cling to him and swear by his name" (Deuteronomy 10:20). Yeshua gave further instructions on this commandment. As he foresaw the coming long temple-less era, he said that the hour was coming "The true worshippers will worship the Father spiritually and truly" (John 4:23).

This little vocabulary lesson may give extra meaning and sense to Yeshua's words that can now be understood as (my narration) "the hour is coming when the true ones who obey his commandments will prostrate in spiritually and truly." This statement follows Yeshua telling the Samaritan woman that Samaritans didn't know what they were doing because salvation "comes from the Jews" (John 4:22). Yeshua was not saying, as it is usually taught, that Temple worship would be over but he was prophesying about the soon coming time of the destruction of the Temple and of the Diaspora when all those who worship ADONAI would have to do it using prayers from the heart or the "offering of praise."

My Personal Thoughts

_____

_____

_____

_____

343

Luke 1:17   כ באב /Av 20

He will . . . turn the hearts of fathers to their children and the
disobedient to the wisdom of the righteous, to make ready for ADONAI a people prepared.

Until the age of machinery and industrialization, life in the world had been the same from generation to generation. Julius Caesar and George Washington traveled at the same speed: on a horse or on something pulled by an animal. Agricultural techniques hadn't changed very much either. Older folks had more experience than the younger generation and children needed the advice of their elders. How different it is today when parents sometimes need the help of their children just to use a telephone.

The second generation of the children of Israel that came out of Egypt was getting ready to conquer the Promised Land. This was a generation that hadn't witnessed Pharaoh's cruel decree, the plagues, or the parting of the Red Sea. They never heard or saw the voices and the thunders at Mt. Horeb. They weren't witnesses to the golden calf debacle or to the retributions on those who were complaining. Moses then pointed them towards their elders: Joshua and Caleb. Being the only ones still alive who witnessed these awesome events, Moses was charging these two old warriors of the faith with the commission to teach these important lessons to the next generation. He said,

> Consider today (since I am not speaking to your children who have not known or seen it), and consider the discipline of ADONAI your God, his greatness, his mighty hand and his outstretched arm . . .

And then he goes on with reiterating the events of Exodus (Deuteronomy 11:2). It is still the norm in religious Judaism to refer back to Mt. Horeb as the signature events of the faith.

As a generation who has not seen Egypt, we should do the same and look back to these events. They do not solely teach us about the nature and character of the Father, but also about his universal redemption plan, and about Messiah. Without the story of the Exodus, we cannot fully understand Hashem's divine redemption plan, and without a working knowledge of Leviticus, we cannot properly understand Yeshua whom the apostolic letters compared to every type of Levitical offering.

In every generation, religion tries to repackage itself into relevancy by trying to adapt to its current culture. As a result, because they feel that they are more in touch with the modern times than their parents, children think that they know better than their more mature and experienced elders. As it distances itself from the original matrix that created its faith system, the world is going backwards in its moral values. No wonder we talk of a *generation gap*. Nowadays, children do not feel that they need to look back to their elders anymore, so as the apostle foresaw, the generation that sees Yeshua's return shall be disobedient and rebellious to parents (2 Timothy 3:2).

As Moses was doing in his exhortation to Joshua and Caleb, part of John the Immerser's ministry of repentance was to provoke a return of the hearts of the fathers (meaning *elders, teachers* and *rabbis* in Talmudic language) to the children. May we, as children, remember the second part of the verse, in Luke's account and follow the wise counsel we inherited from King Solomon, "Do not move the ancient landmark that your fathers have set" (Luke 1:17; Proverbs 22:28).

My Personal Thoughts

344

James 5:7–8

So, brothers, be patient until the Lord returns. See how the farmer waits for the precious
"fruit of the earth"—he is patient over it until it receives the fall and spring rains.
You too, be patient; keep up your courage; for the Lord's return is near.

Egypt received its water from below, from the regular flooding of the Nile leaving fertilizing sediments behind. Anyone could grow a crop in Egypt; success was almost guaranteed (Deuteronomy 11:10). The children of Israel were now going to a place where their increase and their success would require them to be on good terms with *heaven,* so to speak (Deuteronomy 11:11–14).

I live in Western Oregon, a place that receives its fair share (and more) of rain from September to May, sometimes even June. I drink water from my own well tapping an underground spring from melted snow. Water is never an issue here but in the Middle East downpours and water rights are at the heart of economics, politics, and even religion. Water rights were often even the source of wars.

Grain, wine, and oil speak of abundance and form the imagery of Messiah and of the Messianic Age. In the Promised Land this abundance will be dependent on obedience, and on the early and late rain from above. As well as being a natural reality, this natural process serves as a reminder of where our attention should be.

These two seasonal downpours have particular names in Hebrew: *yoreh* יורה, and *malkosh* מלקוש, which could respectively be translated as *spring,* and *autumn* rain. They refer to the rains that come around the spring season of Passover, and that of the fall season after the Feast of Tabernacles.

Messiah manifested himself to the world at the time of the *Yoreh,* the time of the last winter rains in Israel in the spring season, which comes around Passover. It is significant that the word *Yoreh* originates from the Hebrew verbal root *to teach, to instruct,* and therefore is related to the word *Torah: Instruction.*

The prophets often make poetic Hebrew word-play in the text of the Torah, alluding to rain, teaching, and Torah, all coming down from heaven, as did also Mashiach (Deuteronomy 32:2; Joel 2:23; Hoseah 6:3; 10:12).

After the spring rains, come the long hot summer of Messiah's absence, a time of harvesting wheat and barley, ending with the fruit harvest and the Feast of Tabernacles, also called *Ingathering* because this is when the harvest is gathered into barns. As the fall festivals introduce us to the crowing of Messiah and the kingdom of heaven on earth, so also comes the harvesting of olives, which produce the oil for the anointing of the king.

As reliable servants, may we be faithful with the harvest of souls he has entrusted with at his first manifestation (Matthew 28:18–20), that when he returns in the fall, he may receive his own with interest.

My Personal Thoughts

_____

_____

_____

Romans 4:13   **Av 22/ כב באב**

*For the promise to Avraham and his seed that he would inherit the world
did not come through legalism but through the righteousness that trust produces.*

Much is revealed about Hashem's plan for his people in the Book of Deuteronomy. Whereas he says that the prosperous success of our sojourn in the Land of Promise is contingent to our obedience to the Torah, we do not get the chance to inherit it because of our personal righteousness (Deuteronomy 7:12; 9:4–6). It is because the wickedness of the Canaanites was worse than that of Israel and also because of the promises made to our fathers. Hashem always keeps his promises.

Whereas the idea of proper retribution for good and evil is biblical, it is a mistake to assume that the success of our endeavors always marks a personal divine endorsement, or that the lack of it is the sign of a curse because of sin. The Book of Job is a testament of the opposite. This notion particularly leads to error when we apply it to our standing with Hashem.

The apostle Paul reiterated this concept in his diatribe about the role of Torah in our lives. When he said, "For in his sight no one alive will be considered righteous on the ground of legalistic observance of Torah commands, because what Torah really does is show people how sinful they are" (Romans 3:20), he is not teaching us about a new theological concept that Hashem had initiated with his people by the manifestation of Yeshua's work on earth, but he was teaching the actual concept of Torah as it was taught by Moses in Deuteronomy.

It is ludicrous to think that because of sin and so-called rejection of Messiah, Hashem has rejected and replaced his people with a nation taken from the Gentiles. That would mean that Hashem does not keep his promises. If our standing with the Father is a question of personal righteousness, then it is all of mankind that deserves to be rejected. Israel as a political entity may have been blinded to Yeshua's mission and ministry, but much of the Gentile believers at large have rejected the Torah that Yeshua taught as he said, "If you love me you will keep my commandments" (John 14:15).

And did all Israel reject Yeshua? Actual historical records, including those found in Luke's narratives in the Book of Acts, tell us that the Jewish people received Yeshua gladly and that Jerusalem was filled with the apostle's doctrine, so much so that the temple's Sadducee leaders feared to harm the disciples. The disciples were all Jewish believers, along with those from Acts 2 who were Diaspora Jews coming to Jerusalem for the pilgrimage festival of Pentecost. These very people, Jews, were those who propagated Messiah's Good News message around the Mediterranean Sea. They were also those who led the first congregations of believers and taught those so-called church fathers, who for the most part would later reject their Torah teachings.

I thank Hashem that he is a covenant-keeping God. The proof is that he has returned us to our land. So no matter what anyone tries to do or day about it, Hashem has kept his promises.

Those world politicians who try to defeat his purpose had better beware; they may be poking the apple of God's eye!

My Personal Thoughts

_____

_____

_____

Philippians 1:27   Av 23/ כג באב

Only conduct your lives in a way worthy of the Good News of the Messiah.

The text of the Torah in Deuteronomy 12 tells us about the reverencing of Hashem's name. When the children of Israel entered the Land, they were to shun all forms of idolatry. God told them to tear down pagan temples and sites, burn trees used for worship, destroys groves; in a sense, to obliterate the name of pagan gods before establishing Hashem's name in the Land (Deuteronomy 12:1–4). They were told specifically that they were not to worship Hashem in the way these nations worshipped their idols (Deuteronomy 12:4).

This wasn't meant to be a worldwide campaign against idolatry; these commands were only incumbent to the Land of Canaan the children were soon to possess (Deuteronomy 12:1). To establish Hashem's name on the Land meant to establish his character, his ways defined in the Torah, his culture, and his authority. To obliterate the names of idols would then consequently be to obliterate their character, ways, culture, and authority.

The nations had not yet been introduced to Hashem. They were allowed to worship other gods like the sun, the moon, and the stars (Deuteronomy 4:19). It wasn't necessarily a sin to them since they didn't know any better. It was the way they did it that was despicable unto ADONAI (Deuteronomy 12:30–32).

In order to keep Israel as far away as possible from any of the vile idolatrous practices of the Cana'anites, Hashem gave very specific instructions as to how he should be honored and worshipped. This teaches us that religion without the instruction of Torah leads to idolatry. As soon as they were in the Land, the children of Israel were to implement these instructions concerning their worship of Hashem in a very detailed manner, and not to live according to their own thinking anymore (Deuteronomy 12:8–11). Of course, the place where Hashem would write his name would not be fully revealed until the days of King David who purchased the piece of land where the Temple should later be built (2 Samuel 24), a place established for that purpose by divine decree long before.

There is another place where the Father writes his name: our hearts (Numbers 6:22–27). Yeshua also told us that he declared Hashem's name in us, and he does so by revealing to us Hashem's character, his ways, his culture, and his authority (John 17:26).

As the children of Israel were to ensure the sanctity of the name by cleaning the Land of all forms of idol-worship, we should also make sure that the name of Hashem is sanctified in our hearts, and we do that by cleansing ourselves from any selfish and proud ways that don't testify of his presence in us. To claim the presence of his name in us while at the same time denying it though our daily walk renders us worse than the pagan who doesn't even know God. This is what Yeshua had against some of the Pharisees: not their teachings, but their practices. They didn't walk their talk (Matthew 23:2–3), which is the essence of hypocrisy.

Let us not be the same, and may we learn to sanctify Hashem's name, not just in verbal praises, but also in deed and in truth from our hearts.

My Personal Thoughts

_____

_____

_____

1 Peter 5:5

Likewise, you who are less experienced, submit to leaders.
Further, all of you should clothe yourselves in humility toward one another,
because God opposes the arrogant, but to the humble he gives grace.

When the children of Israel entered Canaan, Hashem asked them to sanctify the land from all forms of idolatry. They were to ruthlessly and zealously destroy temples, shrines, and groves; even sacred trees were to be cut down and burned. If there is anything Hashem does not tolerate with his children, it is idolatry. He is indeed a jealous God who does not allow us to have divided loyalties.

It is important to notice though that this commandment specifies "in the Land and in that place" (Deuteronomy 12:1–3). It is therefore not incumbent on us to start destroying and defacing idolatrous structures that are not in Israel. At this point in time, while in Diaspora, the only other place where it is pertinent for us to rid ourselves of idols and idolatrous practices is our hearts, and by extension, our homes. The difficulty with that is that it is often much easier to see the idolatry in others than to see it in ourselves.

Our nature is such that we have a natural tendency to mercifully analyze and rationalize ourselves. To be able to see our own lifestyle in its proper perspective and analyze according to its own unbiased values requires a very special instrument. It is the same one as the one we use to see if our face is clean: a mirror. In the case of our lifestyle, this *mirror* is the Torah (James 1:23–24) and its parameters of worship. Religion defined by Torah is clean from idolatry, but religion away from Torah becomes idolatrous.

The problem today is that Torah is in the form of a written text. This is difficult because, as a person's culture defines his worldview and perspective, that same person also processes any given texts though the lens of his own cultural worldview. To see ourselves as we truly are therefore takes the *mirror* of Torah, but in the form of a faithful brother or a sister (Proverbs 27:17). This brother or sister whom Hashem's Spirit will use and speak through, in the same manner as it spoke through Balaam's donkey (Numbers 22:28), is usually someone just like ourselves who sees the wrong in others easier than the wrong in himself. This all makes for a perfect match because then, to listen to such a person requires a certain element of submissive humility, which in itself is a pertinent exercise against stubbornness and pride, which is by extension idolatry (1 Samuel 15:23). Many of us wouldn't mind Hashem descending from his throne to talk to us in a vision or a dream about our problems. That actually would feed our pride, so he usually doesn't do that. Most of the time, he likes to use the agency of an imperfect brother or sister, a spouse, a child, or even a random unbeliever to speak to us.

This reminds me of Na'aman, the leprous Syrian general. First, his wife's young Jewish slave advised him to seek healing from Elisha, the prophet in an enemy country. When he arrived at Elishah's place of residence, and after having first tried to see the king of Israel, Elisha would not even see him personally; he just sent his servant to tell him to go bathe in the dirty Jordan River. Proud Na'aman took offense and it is again his own servant who had to bring him back to his senses (2 Kings 5).

May we learn to look in the Torah from within our brothers and sisters. And as we find it, may we also, as the apostle says, "be quick to listen but slow to speak" (James 1:19).

My Personal Thoughts

Ephesians 4:4–6   **Av 25/ כה באב**

There is one body and one Spirit, just as when you were called you were called to one hope.
And there is one Lord, one trust, one immersion, and one God, the Father of all,
who rules over all, works through all and is in all.

When Hashem revealed himself to mankind, he thoroughly explained himself to the point of what would seem to us redundancy. He said it, repeated it, and as if to prove his point, he made sure that people recorded the history of both those who obeyed and those who didn't. If we would take the time to review the spiritual parameters established for us by Abba, we would avoid much confusion.

From very early on, there was to be one central place where Hashem would write his name (Deuteronomy 12:5). People could love and serve Hashem anywhere, but the altar and the Holy Ark had their own place of residence. One place also was the spiritual center of the universe: the Temple Mount in Jerusalem. Ancient Jewish writings submit that Hashem chose that place for his name to reside in from the times of creation.

When the children of Israel entered the land, they saw the pagans build altars. They saw the inhabitants of the Land set up poles and worship by trees everywhere they pleased, but Hashem told his people to not follow that example (Deuteronomy 12:2–7). He had one place and one form of worship in mind. Along with right and wrong forms of worship, this teaches us about centrality and leadership. The way Hashem has it is that he is the *Boss*, and whereas he may have governors in provinces, his orders come from one central place, and people have to come to that place at the times of his choosing to worship, to hear the Torah, to present their gifts and their tithes, all within the parameters and in the ways he instructed to follow.

Hashem told the people before entering the Land,

> You will not do things the way we do them here today, where everyone does whatever in his own opinion seems right . . . But when you cross the Yarden and live in the land ADONAI your God is having you inherit . . . then you will bring all that I am ordering you to the place ADONAI your God chooses to have his name live. (Deuteronomy 12:8–11)

That Place where the Temple was to be built is the place where Abraham, through whom all the families of the earth are blessed, offered Isaac (Genesis 12:3). It is the Place where Yeshua, who became light to the Gentiles and glory to Israel, was crucified (Luke 2:32).

It is in Jerusalem that Mashiach will establish his central global reign on the earth forever. At that time not just Israel, but all nations will be required to come to Zion and attend the Feast of Tabernacles (Zachariah 14:16–19). Gone will be the spiritual anarchic madness of today where everyone likes to interpret the Sacred Texts according to what is right in his own eyes (Deuteronomy 12:8). One of the saddest verses in the Bible may be: "At that time there was no king in Isra'el; a man simply did whatever he thought was right" (Judges 17:6; 21:25). The Book of Judges is a testament against man left to his own devices without kingly central authority.

Our congregational realm today seems to be in the same predicament as Israel was in the days of the Judges. We are therefore eagerly waiting for the King to come and take central authority of his Kingdom.

He will come; may it be soon, even in our days!

1 Corinthians 8:4 כו באב /Av 26

An idol has no real existence in the world, and there is only one God

Moses continues preparing the children of the children of Israel to enter the Land. He gives them commandments such as what to do with its idolatrous temples, about the jubilees, and instructions concerning worship.

We need to have discernment with these commandments as they all are technically relevant to the Land of Israel and do not necessarily apply in the Diaspora. In Asian countries people have statues of gods in their houses. In Thailand people hang spirit houses on their walls with a statue or a picture of one of their deities or ancestors inside. In front of it is a little platform to place a bill or a fruit symbolizing an offering. People pray towards it. These people use these spiritual houses as religious objects. When I came to America, I saw people use the same type of spirit houses as garden decorations. People who had traveled outside the U.S. had even brought back statues or symbols of African or Asian gods as decorations. These people are probably atheists, or believers with poor discernment in their choice of art, but they do not use these statues as objects of veneration. Many youth in the West also use the Taoist Ying-Yang sign not knowing that it is a religious symbol widely used in China.

Whereas I would not personally opt to use such things to decorate my home or garden, I don't think that it is up to us to judge and condemn every household with a symbol we consider idolatrous. First of all these commandments are land of Israel dependent. Also, symbols are nothing in themselves. They travel through time and cultures and only reflect the power we give them. The cross that reminds many people of Messiah is to Jews an object of persecution and forced conversion under torture.

On the other hand, someone could deck himself, his house, and his garden with the right *symbols*, wear the right clothing, use the 'in' religious lingo, and yet have an idolatrous heart. In the ancient world, people used trees, rocks, semi-precious stones, silver, and gold as objects of veneration. The rainbow, which used to represent peace and covenant with God, today is a symbol for homosexuals. Do all these things represent the identity we give them? Satanic cults use five pointed-stars in their rituals. Is every star then a pentagram? Sadly, this is also what has happened to the six-pointed star.

Christian anti-Semitism really started with Roman hatred of Israel and Domitian's efforts to exterminate the House of David. This anti-Semitism transferred to the Roman Catholic Church through the Crusades, the Inquisition, and later to the Protestants through Martin Luther, the writing of the Protocols of the Elders of Zion, and eventually the Holocaust. The favored propaganda tool was (and still is) to associate Judaism and its symbols with all kinds of satanic evil. This developed into the still lingering image of the conspirator Jew, personified by an evil Star of David, taking over the world. There might have been some Jewish bankers with an agenda, but to justify the condemnation of a race or religion on the sole basis of the actions of some is the prelude to racism and bigotry. The six-pointed star is used today by many organizations, Jewish and not Jewish. It is even used by Satanists, and some even proclaim it to be the mark of the beast of Revelation (Revelation 13:16). It is very clever and the resurgence of these lies could bring about a persecution bigger than the Holocaust, again led by people swallowing these lies and viewing Jews as the enemy. Sad to say, those who don't learn from history are doomed to repeat it. Will history repeat itself?

While being a Torah practicing believer, Paul also addressed this issue of idolatry. He said, "An idol has no real existence in the world" (1 Corinthians 8:4).

350

1 Corinthians 14:32   Av 27/ כז באב

Also, the prophets' spirits are under the prophets' control.

A long time ago in Ephesus a prospective believer asked John to teach him to do miracles. The old apostle answered that it was impossible because a disciple doesn't perform miracles; Hashem does.

Part of our redemption package includes a certain measure of spiritual gifting such as wisdom, discernment, and prophecy. Because of it, there are those who, finding these new *gifts* within themselves, automatically assume the position of spiritual advisors or prophets among the body of Messiah. These people usually feel the compulsion that they should be very generous with their word of exhortation and advice. Today, with the Internet giving us a quick, easy, and cheap way to propagate beliefs and messages, we are inundated with would be prophets of doom, creating much unnecessary anxiety and worry. One does not have to be a prophet to know the direction the world is taking. Real prophets, including Messiah, told it to us a long time ago. Even unbelieving honest politicians, economists, historians, scientists, and ecologists can see the proverbial *handwriting on the wall.*

When Moses was alive, people already were trying to supplant him and his prophetic role. The God of Israel knew that it wouldn't get better after Moses', or even and Joshua's, death, so he instituted parameters for prophets. He said that even if someone's prophecies were accompanied with *signs and wonders* (miracles), to be valid and considered, that supposed prophecy also had to be conformed to the parameters of Torah commandments. Moses actually taught that when a supposed prophet performs signs and wonders before you, if his words promote disobedience to Torah, it should be considered a test of our obedience and loyalty to Hashem (Deuteronomy 13; 1–5).

It seems that like is happening in our days. The believers of the first century CE didn't lack *would-be prophets* so Paul also had to establish parameters to the prophetic gift, which he did especially in the case of the very spiritual Greek Corinthian believers (1 Corinthians 12 and 14). Paul suggested that before acceptance, prophecies directed to the body should first be tested by the congregation elders (1 Corinthians 14:29).

I sometime wonder if this attraction towards the prophetic gift is not born of people trying to validate themselves; people trying to compensate for their sense of inferiority by making themselves a job for which no one appointed them. Things would be very different if a would-be *prophet* would be humble enough (Torah lifestyle is all about humility, not self-promotion) to first submit his prophecy to a mature and level-headed body of elders or to peer-review in his congregation before publishing it for the world through the Internet.

Even Hebrew prophets were not lone-ranger types of people; they lived in the college and the School of Prophets. Many of them like Jeremiah and Ezekiel came from priestly families and were very knowledgeable of the Torah. Would-be prophets from the apostolic era should also be knowledgeable of the Torah. One only has to read the 1 Epistle of Clement, a disciple of Peter, to see a functional knowledge of Torah worthy of a Levitical priest.

May we be wise in using the gifts given to us by Hashem. May we use them for good not evil, to build not destroy, to improve not to confuse, to give life not to kill, and to solely glorify him, not ourselves!

Matthew 19:14   **Av 28/ כח באב**

*Let the children come to me, don't stop them, for the
Kingdom of Heaven belongs to such as these.*

The most important duty of a parent is to teach the Torah to his children. When he doesn't, the next generation loses the spiritual ground gained by the previous. The enemy of our soul knows this and he makes sure that our lifestyle steals us away from this very important responsibility.

The Adversary wants the world to adore and worship him instead of Hashem, and all he needs for that is a generation of mostly unbelievers. Just a couple of generations are needed to bring it to pass and from what I can see, we are almost there. Our children today are not raised to the sounds of their parents teaching them about Hashem's plan for his people and the world, but to the demonic tireless addicting beats of Microsoft and MTV, even as they do their humanistic schoolwork. Maybe that is why Yeshua said, "But when the Son of Man comes, will he find this trust on the earth at all?" (Luke 18:8).

As a writer I find it difficult to edit and correct my own work. The problem is that I automatically read into my text what I see and hear in my head more than what is actually written on the page, so I miss my own mistakes. I need someone else, one who is removed from my text to point the mistakes out to me.

We seem to do the same thing when we read the Torah. We read it in the spirit in which it has been fed unto us from an early age. This happens when instead of teaching the Torah to our children, at a young age, we teach them already processed and theologized cute stories about it. So when the child starts reading it on his own, he is already indoctrinated and reads into the Torah what he has been taught all the way into adult life, and then he teaches the same thing to his children. This represents a perfect recipe to preserve man's teaching while killing the truth of God's word without even knowing it. To teach the child processed stories instead of the pure word of Torah has the same effect as feeding him candy bars with one percent nourishing protein and the rest fat and sugars. He really then starves to death. This has happened a lot in the teachings of the words of Yeshua. People teach already theologized stories instead of the text itself as it would be drawn from its Jewish context.

In early Judaism, a child started his religious education by memorizing Leviticus. It is even a commandment of the Torah for all males to appear before Hashem at the time of the great jubilee in Jerusalem for the public reading of the Torah by the king himself. Only after the child has been cradled by the direct word of Torah straight from Hashem's mouth is he able to have some sort of discernment and properly learn from the writings of others.

If we feel that our children are too young to understand Leviticus, there is a problem in the way we raise them, not with the word. I dare affirm that if we do not have a working knowledge and understanding of Leviticus, we have an erroneous understanding of the apostolic writings.

Soon, the King will return and again we will gather in Jerusalem with our children at the Feast of Tabernacles to hear the word read from his mouth.

May it be soon Abba, even in our days!

My Personal Thoughts

1 Timothy 3:1–9 כט באב /Av 29

Here is a statement you can trust: anyone aspiring to be a congregation leader is seeking worthwhile work. A congregation leader must be above reproach . . . They must possess the formerly hidden truth of the faith with a clean conscience.

As Israel was organizing itself into an independent nation, it developed the need for a legislative body. It started with Jethro who first advised Moses to appoint seventy elders from among the people. Later, as the second generation prepared to enter the Land, Moses continued the practice and told the congregation that they should appoint judges over the people to rule over them. This became a commandment. Moses instructed the people that these leaders were to judge using righteous judgment, not pervert justice nor show partiality, and that they were to certainly not to accept bribes, "for a bribe blinds the eyes of the wise and subverts the cause of the righteous" (Exodus 23:8) the Torah tells us. The children of Israel were to follow "justice only justice," that they may live and inherit the land that ADONAI their God is giving them (Deuteronomy 16:18–20). Of course, righteous judgments and justice were to be defined by the principles and morals established in the Torah itself, so by inference, these people were to also be experts in the knowledge, handling, and application of Torah texts.

After Yeshua's departure to the Father, the Jerusalem congregation found itself flooded with pilgrims who came for Pentecost (Acts 2). These were Diaspora Jews, proselytes, and God-fearing Gentiles, who after the particular Pentecostal events of that year decided to stick around Jerusalem to learn more from the disciples of Yeshua. In order to support these people, the Jerusalem believers established a kibbutz-like system of sharing and pooling resources for the benefit of the whole body (Acts 2:44–45; 4:32). As the disciples soon found themselves with the same leadership predicament as Moses by Mt. Horeb, they also decided that a body of elders should be elected to care for the logistical affairs of the new fledgling congregation (Acts 6). As he went and started congregations in other areas of Asia, Paul also continued the practice. We can read in the apostolic texts some of the advice he gave about the appointment of elders (1 Timothy 3:1–9; Titus 1:5–9).

Problems in a congregation seem to stem from mainly two things: a lack of decisive and wise team-working leadership, or if there is one, the people don't like it so they don't respect its advice. Many of us in the Western world seem to be plagued with an inordinate sense of independence.

The reasons for these leadership problems also seem to stem from the following two causes: the people are rebellious or the spirit of Hashem did not confirm the leadership team in their heart. Corinth is a good showcase of a congregation running amok. In Corinth everybody interpreted the Torah according to his own mind, and this resulted in certain heresies entering the congregations, heresies still present today. From Paul's letter to them, we see that they could not even produce a good leader among themselves who could keep things in check (1 Corinthians 6:1–6).

Today, as many feel disenchanted with corporate style congregations, they start forming home-groups. As we do this, we need also to remember that Torah can only be properly practiced in community, not in individuality. As these home-groups grow, we need to remember that Corinth provides us with a good example of what happens unless Moses' and the disciples' advice are followed (Deuteronomy 16:18–20; Acts 6:1–3).

Soon, Yeshua will return and himself rule over his people with a legislative body chosen from among the congregations (Matthew 19:28; Revelation 12:6).

May it be soon, Abba, even in our days!

Acts 3:22–23   Av 30/ ל באב

For Moshe himself said, "ADONAI will raise up for you a prophet like me from among your brothers.
You are to listen to everything he tells you. Everyone who fails to listen to that prophet
will be removed from the people and destroyed."

After warning the people about false prophets, Moses told Israel that they shouldn't try to obtain any prophetic messages from the spirit world using any sort of divination process (Deuteronomy 13; 18:10–14).

The patriarch then taught the congregation of ADONAI in the desert who they should go to for advice. He said that they should establish petite courts in every city and one higher court in Jerusalem for more difficult cases. Only the higher court carried the authority of life and death (Deuteronomy 17:8–13).

Moses also said that they could have a king, but that he must be from their own midst and not a foreigner. This king had to transcribe a Torah scroll for himself so he will be accountable for its every word. The king of Israel is therefore meant to be a Torah scholar (Deuteronomy 17:14–20).

Then Moses reminded the people of the day when their fathers asked for a mediator between them and the majestic power on Mt. Horeb, something Hashem agreed with. The patriarch told them that Hashem promised them a mediator in the form of a prophet, and that they were commanded to obey that prophet. We know that in many ways that prophet will resemble Moses, he will be like Moses, not in physical features of course but in his role and ministry towards Israel (Deuteronomy 18:16–19).

Moses is the one Hashem chose to lead the people of Israel into the truth of his words. Disobedience and defiance to him and his words was fatal. If this prophet is to be like Moses, he must also bring Hashem's words to the people of Israel. Defiance to him and his words should also be fatal. Moses spoke to God as a man speaks with his friend, face to face. The same should also be true of this prophet.

John the Immerser, the Sadducees, Peter, and Stephen all spoke of Moses' prophet prophecy as referring to the coming Messiah (John 1:21–25; Acts 3:22; 7:37). This shows that people gave a messianic interpretation to the patriarchs' words. So when Moses says that we should listen (hear with the intention to obey) to that prophet, Moses gave us the commandment to listen to Yeshua. It is therefore a Torah command to disciple ourselves unto Yeshua as unto a divine authority, and since he is prophet "like Moses," we should include his words as words of Torah.

May we remember these things as we read the words of the Master.

He is the prophet as unto Moses; the words of his mouth have the same validity as the words of Torah. He himself said, "Heaven and earth shall pass away, but my words will never pass away" (Matthew 24:35).

My Personal Thoughts

_____

_____

_____

_____

Elul

Fasting
Praying
Resisting
Reflecting
All that the Master taught in
preparation for the world to come,
for the Kingdom of Mashiach on earth.
May it be soon Abba, even in our days!

1 Thessalonians 5:6   Elul 1/ א באלול א

Let's not be asleep, like the rest are; on the contrary, let us stay alert and sober.

For the longest time the month of Elul has been given to reflection in order to prepare for the fall festivals, especially in view of Yom Kippur. On a messianic level, Yom Kippur is a rehearsal for the coming of the Mashiach to reign among us. Elul then, starting forty days before Yom Kippur, should each year urge us to audit our soul. It is important for us, but also for our grandchildren who may need to be ready against that day. It behooves us therefore to live lives that reflect that readiness in the sight of our children, so they will in turn teach it their children, our grandchildren.

The eschatological language of Paul and of the Jewish disciples of the first century expresses their expectation for an imminent return of Yeshua. Paul even actively busied himself with the readiness of the congregations. We have an example of Paul's idea of endtime preparation and of the sort of checklist he wrote in his letter to the Thessalonians' congregation. Oddly enough, this checklist did not have anything to do with self-preservation or survival techniques like many people teach today. Paul's idea of preparation was first and foremost concerning congregational unity, inter-personal relationships, and an unobstructed walk with Hashem. We, like the Thessalonians of the first century CE, also live in the expectation of Yeshua's return, so the counsel Paul gave them is surely applicable to us also.

After a lengthy class on how to recognize endtime (1 Thessalonians 4:14–5:5), Paul wrote, "Let's not be asleep, like the rest are." Sleep is a Talmudic expression for being oblivious to our Torah obligations. "Let us stay alert and sober." Sobriety is a Talmudic expression for being conscious of our Torah obligations. "Putting on trust and love as a breastplate" while learning to have a faith motivated by love for God and our brothers. "And the hope of being delivered as a helmet," remembering that no matter what happens, the redemptive promises of the Hashem towards his children are irrevocable. "For God has not intended that we should experience his fury, but that we should gain deliverance through our Lord Yeshua the Messiah." We are not destined to suffer the wrath of God as described in Revelation 16," who died on our behalf so that whether we are alive or dead, we may live along with him." This time *awake or asleep* is to be understood literally within the language of the day as *alive or dead* (1 Thessalonians 5:6–10).

Preparing the Thessalonians for troublous days ahead, Paul also wrote,

> Therefore, encourage each other, and build each other up. . . . We ask you, brothers, to respect those who are working hard among you, those who are guiding you in the Lord and confronting you in order to help you change. Treat them with the highest regard and love because of the work they are doing. Live at peace among yourselves; but we urge you, brothers, to confront those who are lazy, your aim being to help them change, to encourage the timid, to assist the weak, and to be patient with everyone. See that no one repays evil for evil; on the contrary, always try to do good to each other, indeed, to everyone. Always be joyful. Pray regularly. In everything give thanks, for this is what God wants from you who are united with the Messiah Yeshua. Don't quench the Spirit, don't despise inspired messages. But do test everything—hold onto what is good, but keep away from every form of evil. (1 Thessalonians 5:11–22)

Many similar exhortations are found in the other letters Paul wrote to the congregations, all within the context of Endtime preparation. On these coming days of Elul, may we truly prepare for the fall festivals auditing our souls in view of rehearsing for the return of the Master.

357

John 1:21 Elul 2/ ב באלול ב

Are you 'the prophet'?

In Deuteronomy 13:1–3 Moses taught the congregation in the desert how to discern a false prophet. He told Israel that any would-be prophet who would encourage the people to worship or serve other gods, or to serve Hashem in the ways of the pagans, should surely be qualified as a false prophet. The Torah defines for us how to serve Hashem, but the false prophet tells the people, in the name of Hashem, to do things contrary to Torah, which is equal to serving other gods (Romans 6:16).

Later, Moses also instructed the children of the children of Israel to not seek the will of God through diviners, fortune tellers, witches, or astrologers (Deuteronomy 18:9–14), but for matters too difficult for them, to establish judges and a Sanhedrin, and that they are supposed to listen to these elected judges (Deuteronomy 17:8–12). These are commandments.

Later again, Moses gives people instructions on how to choose a king, even instructions for the king himself to obey. The king of Israel is to be subject to the Torah for when he is not, he makes Israel sin and is guilty of serving other gods (Deuteronomy 17:14–17). The king is also to personally write out a copy of the Torah for his personal use (Deuteronomy 17:18).

In his Instruction through Moses, Hashem, he who made Israel a nation, told us who is the prophet we should listen to once in the land. The main attributes given about him are as in the words by Moses, "a prophet like you from among their kinsmen. I will put my words in his mouth, and he will tell them everything I order him."

Moses also informs the people that their ancestors who came out of Egypt had wisely concluded that they could not hear Hashem on their own. They wanted Moses to be their mediator. Hashem agreed and said, "They are right in what they are saying. I will raise up for them a prophet like you from among their kinsmen" (Deuteronomy 18:15, 18). It is important to notice here that any would-be king of Israel also had to be like the *prophet,* "from among their kinsmen," meaning an Israelite. It was therefore a big problem in Israel when in the days of the Master, a non-Jewish king was on the throne.

Because Joshua opened the Jordan River as Moses opened the Red Sea, some today conclude that this *prophet like Moses* was Joshua. But it was not so in the days of the Master. We remember when the Sadducees came to see John by the Jordan River asking him, "Are you 'the prophet?" (John 1:21). John later pointed to another one called Joshua, pronounced in Aramaic: Yeshua as the "Prophet" (John 1:29).

In this Yeshua, Israel has found its prophet and king *like Moses.* He is the true *prophet* who teaches us how to properly obey the Torah, and the true king who is the copy of the Torah. Even though he had to temporarily return to the Father, he has not left us alone, but has established in his disciples a Sanhedrin we can, and should listen to (Matthew 16:16; Matthew 19:28).

Living in an age of literacy, may we continually study and learn to obey the instructions the Master and his disciples left behind, that at his return, he might present the congregation to himself in splendor, without spot or wrinkle, that she might be holy and without blemish (Ephesians 5:27).

Hebrews 11:24–26   Elul 3/ ג באלול

By trusting, Moshe . . . had come to regard abuse suffered on behalf of the Messiah as greater riches than the treasures of Egypt, for he kept his eyes fixed on the reward.

One of the concerns with the children of Israel appointing a king over themselves was that he might cause the people to return to Egypt (Deuteronomy 17:16).

Because Egypt's agriculture did not depend on rainfall but on the yearly overflowing of the Nile, the country was rich and comfortable. That is why every conqueror in the ancient world wanted Egypt, including Rome, whose economy relied heavily on Egyptian goods. From the time of the Exodus, Egypt had been a snare for the children of Israel. The journey from Goshen to the Promised Land by way of the Mediterranean Sea is actually very short, but Hashem chose to take them in a way that made it practically impossible to return to Egypt, even if they wanted to (Exodus 13:17–18).

Time and again whenever the children of Israel grew dissatisfied, they wanted to return to Egypt. When they hungered, they thought about the food of Egypt (Numbers 11:5); when they were scared to conquer the giants in the Land of Canaan, they wanted a leader to take them back to Egypt (Numbers 14:4). But from the very start, Hashem forbade it. Some Rabbis today interpret this command so heavily as to declare it a sin to even make the journey from Israel to Egypt even if it just for tourism or business. How does it all work though; as two thousand years ago, in spite of the seeming prohibition for one to return to Egypt, Hashem himself sent Yeshua and his family there among the thriving Jewish community of Egypt to find protection from Herod (Matthew 2:13).

The idea of *returning to Egypt* runs much deeper than that. It seems to be more of a spiritual condition than a physical attraction. Several times when faced with wars and conquest, to Hashem's great displeasure, Israel looked to Egypt instead of him for strength and protection. Israel trusted Egypt's horses and chariots that they could see instead of the God they couldn't see. Israel may be facing the same lesson today (Isaiah 31:1–3; Jeremiah 42:15–16). Returning to Egypt has to do with the weakness of trusting the world for survival instead of Hashem. It also has to do with being dissatisfied, greedy, and desiring more than what Hashem has wisely given us. Ultimately, it has to do with despising the future eternal prospects of the Promised Land, for the instant temporal comforts of Egypt. *Egypt* provided for "the desires of the old nature, the desires of the eyes, and the pretensions of life." It was the *world*, so really, *desiring Egypt* has to do with what is "not from the Father but from the world" (1 John 2:15–16). In the movie *The Matrix*, a man quits the mission and returns to the matrix just because of lust for food. He knows the food is not even real but digital, but *it tastes so good!* That is returning to Egypt.

So when Hashem says that Israel should not return to Egypt, in essence he says, "just because you presently feel a little bit uncomfortable and you long for delicacies to satisfy your untoward appetite, don't return to the ways of the world." May we take sample from Moses, "had come to regard abuse suffered on behalf of the Messiah as greater riches than the treasures of Egypt, for he kept his eyes fixed on the reward" (Hebrews 11:24–26).

May we not look on a world with failing morals and economies for support and strength nor compromise in order to benefit from their strong armies who can't protect us. Hashem has not decreed that they should.

It is our God who owns the cattle on a thousand hills, he who will fight for us (Psalm 50:10; Nehemiah 4:20).

John 11:50   Elul 4/ ד באלול

It's better for you if one man dies on behalf of the people,
so that the whole nation won't be destroyed.

From the blood of Abel an innocent man assassinated by his own brother—humanity has been plagued with murders.

According to Moses' instruction in the Torah, murders have to be atoned for, and the only thing that can atone for murder is the blood of the person who shed it. It is not because of virtue awarded to vengeance, but because shed blood defiles the Land of Israel.

When arriving in Canaan, the Children of Israel were to cleanse the land by ridding it of all the people who practiced idolatrous murders. Israel failed to obey that command and it later became a snare for them. Hashem then cleansed the Land by sending Judah into temporary exile not once, but twice. We are now coming to the end of the second exile and a newly inhabited Israel probably has again unsolved murders on its hands. I do not know if religious authorities in Israel regularly clean the Land from unsolved murder, but we know that at Yom Kippur atonement is made for it on a national level.

The Torah tells us that someone needs to take responsibility for unsolved murders. The Torah actually suggests for this responsibility to be taken by the city closest to the discovered victim. We are taught of an absolution ceremony involving the decapitation of a heifer. The blood of the heifer is then poured in a river, and city officials wash their hands of the responsibility of the murder in the presence of priests. The Levites were to attend the ceremony because Hashem chose them not only as religious, but also as judicial authorities (Deuteronomy 21:5).

In the Torah system, justice is a religious matter, not civil, so, the priests are the religious and judicial authority. The role of the king is actually to enforce the rulings of the priests and of the Torah so you might say that in *God's world* the administrative, judicial, and legislative branches of government come under the dictates of the Torah: a religious document.

In today's world, everyone, guilty or not, strives in claiming their innocence. To the contrary, Torah teaches us the virtue of endorsing the responsibility of a crime for the benefit of all.

When Yeshua came, he taught that anger and character assassination were the seed of murder (Matthew 5:21–22), but he also himself assumed responsibility for every unsolved murder in the world, which makes us, humanity, responsible for his death, which he himself atones for (John 11:49–50). The Talmud teaches that very principle when it says, "The death of a righteous man atones for the sinner."

May we always remember Yeshua who, though he did not sin, took responsibility for all our heinous murders to cleanse the Land with his own innocent blood so we may drink of the River of Life.

My Personal Thoughts

_____

_____

_____

_____

2 Timothy 2:13   ה באלול /Elul 5 ה באלול

If we are faithless, he remains faithful, for he cannot disown himself.

The study of the Torah is the study of God's character. Each commandment reveals to us his gracious and compassionate nature. Take, for example, the case of the commandments concerning the captured women.

Pillage, loot, and rape have been the facts of war from the beginning of time, but the soldier in God's army is to adhere to a higher code of ethics. He cannot use rape as a weapon. If he desires a woman from the loot, he is to first give her the comfort of mourning her parents, the dignity of marriage, and most of all: freedom. She is not to be a slave in his household and she cannot be sold once he is tired of her (Deuteronomy 21:10–14). In these rulings, the Torah certainly provided an upgrade to the ruthless society of the day when it was given.

In a sense, we are like that slave woman. God set out to *capture* a nation for himself from among the people of the earth. He will use that nation to capture all of humanity for himself. Hashem first revealed his plan to Abraham using the patriarch's life to foreshadow his universal messianic redemption plan he had set in motion from before the foundations of the world. Later, as times matured, El-Shaddai actually went to war.

He bore his mighty arm and showed himself strong to liberate her who would be his bride. He impressed her with valiant mighty acts and brought down her captors' power. Then Hashem took her to a lonely place in the desert, revealed to her that he iwa a King with a great kingdom that will one day cover the earth as the waters cover the seas, and that he wants her to be his wife. He just saved her. He could have taken her just for the asking, but no. He asked her. She accepted. El-Shaddai who then went on to write a long *Ketubah* כתבה, which we call: the Torah (Exodus).

Very soon Hashem discovered that his beloved had a rebellious streak. She was stiff-necked and at times unfaithful. She was disobedient and constantly got herself in trouble. He did not want to put her away so he punished her but with measure, always leaving behind a remnant for her as a ray of hope. These principles are obvious in the story of Hagar. Hagar was a prize from Pharaoh to Sarah, the wife of Abraham. When Hagar was found displeasing, she was sent away but not without a redemptive promise (Genesis 16 and 21).

Even though we have broken our marriage contract many times; even though we are faithless and unbelieving at times, he remains faithful and through Mashiach he renewed for us the contract, "the *ketubah*," made, broken, and remade in Horeb.

No, he is has not rejected his people. Far be it from him to do that. He punished them but in measure always leaving for them a remnant so that their nation forever remains before him as a chosen one from the nations (Romans 11:1–5).

Through our nation therefore, Hashem blessed the world with Messiah. Mashiach came to live among us as the radiance of the Sh'khinah, the very expression of God's essence (Hebrews 1:3).

We therefore cling to his mercy and compassion. May we learn to be a faithful bride worthy of him who shows such great strength, love, and compassion in our favor.

My Personal Thoughts

Luke 14:23   **Elul 6/ ו באלול**

The master said to the slave, "Go out to the country roads and boundary walls, and insistently persuade people to come in, so that my house will be full."

Abraham was known for his hospitality. He used to send his servant Eleazer to search the wilderness for guests to bring to his table. Once there, Abraham served them a table that made them praise God. This was his way to introduce people to Hashem. If Eleazer came back empty handed, Abraham himself took off by the highways and byways himself, compelling them to come in.

The sages tell us that when Moses watched over Jethro's flocks, one of his father-in-law's sheep went missing. Moses immediately left the rest of the flock and did not return until he the lost sheep was found and secured in Jethro's fold. That sheep had probably strayed because of disobedience to the shepherd.

From his throne up above, Hashem saw the whole thing and decided that if Moses was so faithful with Jethro's flock, he could be assigned to Israel: Hashem's flock. Whether these mishnaic legends are true or not, they certainly found their way as parables in the mouth of the Master (Matthew 18:12).

The Torah teaches us that we should return lost items (Deuteronomy 22:1–3). On the strength of this command, sages instituted that if you find something, you are to be the guardian over it until you find its owner and are able to give restitution. A story is told of an old rabbi who found a bag of seed forgotten by a traveler on his property. The rabbi who found it secured it in his barn. After a year, fearing the seed would spoil, he sowed the seed, then harvested it and stored the proceeds in his barn. When later the rightful owner came to inquire about this lost bag of seed, the old rabbi returned it to him, with a profit.

Even so, through centuries of bad politics and history, Israel has lost the identity of its Messiah. Christians on the other hand, have lost the Torah. Like the old rabbi in the story, we who have found the *seeds* of the Kingdom of the true King of Israel and of his Torah are responsible to return it to those who lost it.

The seeds of Messianic Judaism have been sown into the world and have produced a beautiful culture among those who practice it. The Master charged us also to "go and make people from all nations into talmidim" (Matthew 28:19). In these words, he taught us the virtue of leaving the ninety-nine behind to go rescue the one lost one (Matthew 18:12–14). Like Abraham did, the Master also told us to go "out to the street-corners and invite to the banquet as many as you find" (Matthew 22:9).

After all, isn't it what he did? Hasn't he left the realm of glory by the side of the Father in order to walk our dusty roads and find us who were lost and wandering, that he may return us to his father, with a profit?

My Personal Thoughts

_____

_____

_____

_____

1 Corinthians 7:21–22   Elul 7/ ז באלול

Were you a slave when you were called? Well, don't let it bother you; although if you can gain your freedom, take advantage of the opportunity. For a person who was a slave when he was called is the Lord's freedman; likewise, someone who was a free man when he was called is a slave of the Messiah.

Here is an interesting story from the first century CE.

Onesimus, a slave, had escaped from the house of Philemon. He found refuge in Rome where, per inadvertence, he met with the apostle Paul, who at that time was under house arrest. Meanwhile, Philemon was introduced to Yeshua, the *slave-redeemer*, and became a member of the Roman community of believers, as well as a substantial helper to Paul.

This caused a dilemma. The Torah commands that asylum be granted to runaway slaves (Deuteronomy 23:15–16). This Middle-Eastern practice is as old as Abraham who took Eleazer, a runaway slave from Damascus, under his wings (Genesis 15:2). But Roman law on the contrary required that Paul, a Roman citizen already in trouble with the authorities, immediately return the slave to its owner.

Surely Paul was no maverick going out of his way to deliberately create problems by breaking man's laws just to prove a point. Some people like to portray the Master as some sort of radical revolutionary always challenging the system just for the sake of it. This attitude is often born from one's own worldview and personal issues with authority.

How Paul handled the situation not only shows us his wisdom, but is a good example on how to juggle torahtic and secular obligations when they conflict. Paul obeyed Roman law and sent Onesimus back to Colossi with a letter to Philemon, a letter that today is part of the apostolic texts. In the letter, Paul asked Philemon, the slave-owner, to show mercy on both Onesimus and himself. For the sake of Yeshua who spiritually freed him, and for his own sake as an apostle in dire need, Paul asks Philemon to free Onesimus who by now had become quite essential. It is like the story of Miriam obeying the Pharaoh's command to put her baby in the Nile. She did it, but she also put the baby in a basket.

In books detailing the history of early believers, we read of an Onesimus who was a great leader in Ephesus. He seems to have been Paul's personal secretary and the one who preserved the Pauline epistles. Was it the same person?

Whether this is the same Onesimus or not, what will it be said of us that we did with the freedom the Master obtained for us?

My Personal Thoughts

_____

_____

_____

_____

_____

_____

Revelation 19:11   ח באלול /Elul 8

Next I saw heaven opened, and there before me was a white horse. Sitting on it was the one called Faithful and True, and it is in righteousness that he passes judgment and goes to battle.

Moses foresaw that the establishment of judges was not enough for the governance of the emerging country of Israel. A king would also be needed to enforce Torah and the ruling of the judges.

There is nothing wrong with authority as long as that authority rules by the Torah. Under Hashem's inspiration, Moses commanded the people that any king appointed to rule over them should be a descendant from Jacob (Deuteronomy 17:14–15). Later, because of the prophetic blessing, Jacob uttered upon his son Judah (Genesis 49:10), it was even understood that the king ruling from Jerusalem should be a descendant from the tribe of Judah. To understand this context is essential if we wish to properly understand the politics behind the life, death, and resurrection of Yeshua, the true King of the Jews from the lineage of Judah.

The king, though the legislative authority of the country, was not above the Torah. He had to be obedient to the rulings established by God himself over whose people he ruled. To remind him of his Torah responsibilities, Moses commands,

> When he has come to occupy the throne of his kingdom, he is to write a copy of this Torah for himself in a scroll, from the one the cohanim and L'vi'im use. It is to remain with him, and he is to read in it every day, as long as he lives; so that he will learn to fear ADONAI his God and keep all the words of this Torah and these laws and obey them; so that he will not think he is better than his kinsmen; and so that he will not turn aside either to the right or to the left from the mitzvah. In this way he will prolong his own reign and that of his children in Isra'el. (Deuteronomy 17:18–20)

Along with being a legislator and a soldier, this king of Israel was to be an expert on Torah matters. He was to live and rule by it. None of the kings of Israel or Judah attained this level of obedience. The closest one would have been David who as a soldier was also a legislator, a prophet, and a priest. Hashem led him to build a new Tabernacle on Mt. Zion, to revamp the priesthood and create the liturgy of what would become the future temple. This was known as the *Tent of David* (Acts 15:16). But even king David broke the Torah, as we all do.

Yeshua is the only one true King of the Jews who is sinless. He is the Torah written in flesh. He is the one who did not come to do his will, but solely the will of Yeshua. When he comes to judge the world, he will do it according to the Torah, and he will not take bribes (Deuteronomy 16:19). Luke 4 shows how Yeshua handled the bribes HaSatan tempted him with.

Behold, the only true and legitimate King of Israel is coming and he will judge the world in the righteousness and justice of God's Torah.

> Pay attention! *[says Yeshua,]* I am coming soon, and my rewards are with me to give to each person according to what he has done. I am the 'A' and the 'Z,' the First and the Last, the Beginning and the End. (Revelation 22:12–13)

May it be soon Abba, even in our days.

My Personal Thoughts

John 3:16

For God so loved the world, that he gave his only and unique Son.

Some people boast that they believe in obeying all the commandments in the Torah. It is a noble thing and we should certainly try to be obedient, but we should also know that it is impossible to obey all the commandments in the Torah. If it weren't, there would be no need for the twice daily offering of a lamb, for the fall feasts, and for Yeshua in our lives.

Whereas the Torah requires our obedience, without condoning sin, it also provides for our human frailty. Divorce for example. Whereas Hashem is against it, guidelines are provided in case of it because of the hardness of our hearts. Whereas we appreciate God's mercy and compassion for our human state, it is important to keep them in their proper place. To say that because of these accepted guidelines Hashem condones divorce, would be like saying that because of the cities of refuge Hashem condones involuntary manslaughter (Deuteronomy 24:1–4; Mark 10:2–9; Numbers 35:6).

Upon their claim that they obey all the Torah, I like to ask people, "If it were legally permissible, would you stone your wife if you found her in an inappropriate relationship? Or should she stone you if you were the guilty one? Would you stone your son if he fit the bill for Deuteronomy 21:18–21?"

Even Jewish writings tell us that no one ever came to the Sanhedrin for the law of the rebellious son. Today though, not only it is illegal to personally claim and administer the death penalty on the sole basis of disobedience to Torah, but even if it were, the whole Torah death penalty procedure requires the presence of a legal Sanhedrin and of a Temple in Jerusalem. In the absence of such, these laws, while not obsolete, are presently non-applicable. Some may heave a sigh of relief, but the absence of a legal Sanhedrin does not absolve us from judgment from heaven as we read, "God will indeed punish fornicators and adulterers" (Hebrews 13:4).

The law of the rebellious son may seem the most difficult law to observe especially when we look at it as a father towards his son. I personally like to change the perspective and look at it remembering that as a father, I am also somebody's son. I may not fit the bill where my earthly father can accuse me of being stubborn and rebellious, a glutton and a drunkard, but as far as my Heavenly Father is concerned, I do fit that bill and more. I concur with King David who rightly commented, "Yah, if you kept a record of sins, who, ADONAI, could stand?" (Psalm 130:3).

This law may seem harsh and condemning, but come to think of it, if Hashem did not punish iniquity he would be unjust. Justice must be given its due to expunge iniquity. There is no other way. If justice is not expunged through us, it has to be done through someone else. In this case, this harsh justice is executed on Yeshua HaMashiach, the only obedient Son. If we were to be executed we would deserve it because we are guilty, but it was Yeshua who was executed while he was actually innocent. His death therefore serves as atonement for the sinners that we are.

In this light, we can say again that all the commandments tell us of the glory of Hashem, even those that seem the most harsh and cruel.

Blessed be his name!

Matthew 12:12   Elul 10/ י באלול

Therefore, what is permitted on Shabbat is to do good.

Due to ignorance of Jewish Law in the days of the Master, many have erroneously deprived themselves of one of the most beautiful gifts Hashem bestowed on to mankind: the Sabbath.

Most people, when reading the controversies between Yeshua and the Judean leadership conclude that Yeshua abrogated the whole Torah, and nullified their Jewish Talmudic interpretations in favor of a more *mature* sola-scriptura approach. Deeper readings though quickly prove both these notions wrong. The problem people have when they read the apostolic texts is that many people read them anachronistically.

They put the whole Jew vs. Christian and Law vs. Grace conflicts into their reading of the altercations between Yeshua and the leaders of Israel. It does not work simply because these issues did not even exist in the first century CE.

First of all, if Yeshua had abrogated the Torah, not only would he not be the Jewish Messiah, but he would have taken away all sense of decency, morals, honor, and justice from the world. He did not remove the ancient boundary stone set up by your ancestors (Proverbs 22:28). Of the traditional teachings of his days, the Master actually said, "The Torah-teachers and the P'rushim. Sit in the seat of Moshe. So whatever they tell you, take care to do it. But don't do what they do, because they talk but don't act" (Matthew 23:2–3). Through these words, Yeshua may not have agreed with their practices, but he certainly condoned their teachings.

As a first-born, when he was a young man, Yeshua studied the Torah and the traditions and he was well aware of them. He also understood that according to the teachings of the Pharisees, life and death superseded most commandments. Moved by Hashem's great compassion (Exodus 34:6–7), Yeshua could also argue that the alleviating of human suffering was acceptable in breaking, for example, the Sabbath.

Last but not least, having done his *homework*, Yeshua also understood that in Jewish Law, when a positive commandment (you shall . . .) and a negative commandment (you shall not . . .) conflict, the positive supersedes the negative one. Based on this accepted legal understanding, Yeshua could argue that the positive commandment of showing mercy, in this case by healing, overrides the Sabbatical prohibition to work. In this way, Yeshua neither broke the Sabbath, the Torah, nor brought anarchy in the country by undermining spiritual leadership, which is actually an abomination to Hashem (Proverbs 6:16–19). In asking, for example, whether or not it was permitted to do good on the Sabbath, Yeshua simply reminded the Judean leadership of their own teachings.

To live by the Torah gives us an anticipation of the world to come, of the age when Messiah will reign on a Torah legislated earth. On that day the earth will be as full of the "knowledge of ADONAI as water covering the sea" (Isaiah 11:9). May it be soon Abba, even in our days!

My Personal Thoughts

_____

_____

_____

_____

Luke 6:35   Elul 11/ יא באלול

But love your enemies . . . and you will be children of Ha`Elyon.

Many scoff at Yeshua's injunction to love our enemy. I heard a politician one time make a poke at Yeshua's Sermon on the Sermon on the Mount saying that it was such a radical teaching that it is doubtful that any country's defense department could survive its application.

We need to remember who it was who said these words. It was not a prophet or an apostle who said that we should love our enemies, but it was Yeshua himself who said it in the name of the Father, and he said it at a time when his own country was oppressed and afflicted by a ruthless foreign power. Yeshua actually fished the elements of his teachings on the mount from another sermon on another mountain: the oracle of Mt. Horeb where it was said,

> If you come upon your enemy's ox or donkey straying, you must return it to him. If you see the donkey which belongs to someone who hates you lying down helpless under its load, you are not to pass him by but to go and help him free it. (Exodus 23:4–5)

To comment negatively or mockingly on these passages of Yeshua's teachings is to comment negatively or mockingly on the very nature and character of God.

Reading the legal injunctions and terms of the Torah, we obtain a formidable peek at the very nature, essence, and heart of Hashem. The idea is that he expects these things of us because they are him; they are his nature. Just as if someone lived in my house, I would expect them to live by the same standards I do. Hashem, who takes us into his great family, expects us to live by the ideals he condones. His commandments reflect his very nature so when he tells us how we should respond to our enemy's misfortune, we are given a peek at the way God is and he tells us to be like him.

You might say, "Oh, but when I read the Torah; I see God dealing with his enemies in very harsh manners." Look at Amalek for example (Deuteronomy 25:17). God was sure to extract vengeance from Amalek's perfidy against Israel, but to annihilate Amalek was an act of mercy towards Israel.

The Torah has to be understood by balancing the principles taught in it. Take Jonah's story for example. It is the story of an Israeli politician whom God asked to go as an emissary of peace to Nineveh, a city that was stealing territory from Israel and harassing its northern villages. If Nineveh didn't change its ways towards Israel, God was going to punish them. Of course Jonah didn't want to go. He wanted God to punish those who were persecuting his country. Jonah didn't want them to have a chance at repentance.

When people asked Yeshua for a sign of his Messiahship, he didn't mention Hashem's war against Amalek, but rather his dealings with Jonah. The only sign he offered was the "sign of the prophet Jonah." Through Jonah, this story tells us of Hashem sending the Messiah as an emissary of peace to us, God's enemy's because of sin. He sends us a message to repent before the end comes (Matthew 12:39).

Again this is all measure for measure. Yeshua taught us to ask the Father to forgive us our debts (sins against the Father), but only as we forgive our debtors (those who sin against us). So if we can't have a merciful attitude towards our enemies, how can we expect God to have mercy on us who through sin have set ourselves in enmity against him?

367

Matthew 25:34–36, 40   **Elul 12/ יב באלול**

Then the King will say to those on his right, "Come, you whom my Father has blessed, take your inheritance, the Kingdom prepared for you from the founding of the world. For I was hungry and you gave me food, I was thirsty and you gave me something to drink, I was a stranger and you made me your guest, I needed clothes and you provided them, I was sick and you took care of me, I was in prison and you visited me." The King will say to them, "Yes! I tell you that whenever you did these things for one of the least important of these brothers of mine, you did them for me!"

The biblical tithing system was rather complex but very efficient. It provided a fund for the maintenance of the Temple in Jerusalem, as well as for the Levites, and the poor. Local rabbis who spent a lot of time teaching Torah worked, and their income was supplemented by the voluntary offerings of their congregants. Here is how it worked: The tithe of the first, second, fourth, and fifth year of the seven-year sabbatical cycle was set aside from the farmers in the land to be paid to the Levites, who themselves tithed from what they received to the priests (Numbers 18:30). But the tithes of the third and sixth year, farmers either gave to the poor, or spent it on themselves in Jerusalem, thus supporting the Holy City through their business (Deuteronomy 26:12–15). These are commonly called first, second, and third tithe. In this way, all Israel had a share in the support of the Temple, the priests, and the poor. This did not include voluntary offerings.

If people failed in their tithing obligations, the Levites would then not be able to do their job of teaching and caring for the Temple. This would result in a spiritual and moral downfall. The poor also would be affected, and Hashem always hears the cry of the poor against their oppressors. Following the words of the Master, the first believers in Jerusalem responded to their responsibilities towards each other and pooled resources so everyone would be cared for. Other communities of believers outside the Land did the same thing in order to survive (Acts 2:44–45; 4:32).

Since we have no more Temple or offerings at the altar, each congregation today seems to have their own adaptation of the tithing commandments. In the case when a congregation owns a building, the great majority of the tithe either goes to the mortgage, the upkeep, upgrades, utilities, equipment, taxes, salaries, and insurances. Through the prophet Malachi, Hashem accuses the people of Israel of "robbing God" but they replied, "How have we robbed you?" "In your tithes and contributions," Hashem replies (Malachi 3:8).

These are good questions to also ask ourselves. Do we rob Hashem? Do we rob Hashem by investing in fancy buildings rather that people made in his image? We may not have much money but what about time? Time is a very precious commodity. Singles and young people should invest time in those families with several children struggling to keep a schedule together. They sure could use help with housework, repairs, or home schooling. What about taking the kids for a day and giving the poor parents a break?

Do we rob Hashem of our money, time, or even of a talent we are supposed to exercise for the benefit of others? In my knowledge and experience, there are three cries that get priority in heaven's halls: those of the children, the poor, and the widows.

My Personal Thoughts

1 Corinthians 3:13 Elul 13/ יג באלול

But each one's work will be shown for what it is; the Day will disclose it, because it will be revealed by fire—the fire will test the quality of each one's work.

In the text of Deuteronomy the children of Israel promise to follow his ways; observe his laws, mitzvot and rulings; and do what he says (Deuteronomy 26:17).

On many levels, this is a generic statement. Many people, each living different lifestyles, claim to live in keeping with God's commandments and statutes. To walk in someone's way is a Hebrew idiom for imitating them. Discipleship in the Torah is not to learn someone's knowledge, but to imitate their lifestyle. So to walk in Hashem's ways means to imitate him. How then do we imitate God?

An ancient Hebrew text puts it in very simple terms. It says that just as God clothed the naked (Genesis 3:31), we should also clothe the naked; that as God visited the sick when he came to Abraham in the plains of Mamreh as he was recovering from his circumcision, so we should also visit the sick (Genesis 18:1). The text also mentions that as God appeared to Isaac after the death of his father Abraham, in the same manner we should comfort those who mourn. Finally, we learn from this text that as God buried Moses in the plains of Moab, we should also give proper attention to the dead (b.Sotah 14a). Another ancient text mentions,

> Just as the Holy One, blessed be He, is called Merciful, so shouldst thou be merciful. Just as He is called Gracious, so shouldst thou be gracious. Just as He is called Righteous, so shouldst thou be righteous. Just as He is called Devout, so shouldst thou be called devout. (Sifre on Deuteronomy 10:12)

The Master followed this imitation principle of discipleship. He said,

> I do nothing, but say only what the Father has taught me. Also, the One who sent me is still with me; he did not leave me to myself, because I always do what pleases him. (John 8:28–29)

According to the model of the ancient Jewish sages, Yeshua also encouraged us to, feed the hungry, clothe the naked, and visit those in prison (Matthew 25:35–36). In fact, this is the type of righteousness he will look for in us as we meet him at the end of days. James also taught the early Hebrew congregations that, "the religious observance that God the Father considers pure and faultless is this: to care for orphans and widows in their distress and to keep oneself from being contaminated by the world" (James 1:27).

To sum it all up, acts of compassion and mercy seem to have much more to do with the biblical way of walking after God's commands than head stuffing of doctrines and accurate statements of faith.

As we walk through life, may we always remember that when all is said and done, at the end of days, our life's work will be revealed by fire (1 Corinthians 3:13). At that time all the wood, hay, and straw of pride, self-righteousness, selfishness and vanity will burn. At that time, only the gold, the silver, and the precious stones of the positive treatment of those made in Hashem's image will count in our Master's eyes.

My Personal Thoughts

1 John 4:19 Elul 14/ יד באלול

We ourselves love now because he loved us first.

On Mt. Gerizim the children of Israel entered the covenant of God and became his people. The Gerizim covenant wording contains the following curse, "A curse on anyone who does not confirm the words of this Torah by putting them into practice" (Deuteronomy 27:9–10; 26). Paul takes up this statement: "For all who rely on works of the law are under a curse; for it is written, 'Cursed be everyone who does not abide by all things written in the Book of the Law, and do them'" (Galatians 3:10).

Sadly, this passage is commonly interpreted to mean that if a believer begins to observe the Commandments, he *falls from grace* and places himself under the curse of the Law. Of course, this interpretation of Paul's writing about the curse of the Torah totally omits his other statement: "Anyone who does these things will attain life through them" (Galatians 3:12 on Leviticus 18:5). This style of misreading in Paul's writings is at the root of what has been Christian anti-Semitism throughout the centuries.

The Torah does teach us that we *live* or *die* as pertaining to our obedience to the Torah (Leviticus 18:5; Deuteronomy 27:26). These are not teachings of men but oracles from the mouth of God, which Paul would not dare to disagree with. What did Paul mean then in his teachings about the Torah? The problem is simple: ignorance of Judaism and reading the text with an already established theology. This problem caused the translators of the English texts of Galatians to fail in making the difference when Paul speaks about a trusting obedience in the Law of God, or about the legalistic perversion of it often promoted in certain religious circles. A legalistic perversion of Torah turns the commandments into a sort of ladder by which we obtain Hashem's favor, regardless of whether we have a loving trust and relationship with him, a type of ritualistic obedience that is found in many faiths, including in Christianity.

Paul is Torah observant, but he also knows how to balance verse with verse. Follow me here through a rabbinic exegesis of the definition of a life of faith as defined in the Hebrew texts. These texts work to complement each other's understanding, not against each other.

As Paul did, the old rabbis recognized the absurdity of basing eternal life on absolute obedience to the 613 Commandments. So Rabbi Simlai brought up King David who trimmed the Torah commandments to eleven (Psalm 15), Isaiah who condensed them to six (Isaiah 33:15–16), Micah who simplified the whole thing to three (Micah 6:8), and Amos to one (Amos 5:4), to which Habbakuk agreed (Habbakuk 2:4). This is the very statement Paul used in his contention for a trusting obedience as opposed to a legalistic faithless one.

As you can see, to attain life through trusting faithfulness, while remaining within obedience to Torah, is not something that Paul invented but was often brought up by the prophets to remind people that ritualistic obedience is not the main principle. Actually, some of the prophets claim that Hashem would rather do without the offerings when done in the wrong spirit (1 Samuel 15:22).

As we discover the beauty of serving Hashem through obedience to Torah, may we never forget that our service is nothing without our love.

Alongside with the prophets of old, this is what Yeshua came to remind us and tteach us: the dimension of love and trust in our service.

Luke 8:17   **Elul 15/** טו באלול

For nothing is hidden that will not be disclosed,
nothing is covered up that will not be known and come out into the open.

There are many commandments in the Torah; some are of outwardly visible obedience, some are of a more internal nature. It is easy to pride ourselves with obedience by mostly concerning ourselves with the outwardly visible commandments, the physical manifestations of obedience everybody can see.

Everyone can see what we eat, sometimes. Everyone can hear the words we say, sometimes. Everyone can see our tzitzits, if we wear them outwardly. Not everyone can see and hear what goes on in the privacy of our homes, our bedrooms, much less the things that go on in our hearts, or in our souls. Pride and self-righteousness are often difficult to detect in someone, and most of the time, the last person to notice them in ourselves is us.

When the children of Israel arrived near the Land, they were asked to climb up on two mountains and renew their covenant (contract) with Hashem. They were to conduct an elaborate ceremony pronouncing a carefully selected series of curses and blessings. Looking over the curses in this ceremony, it seems that they were concerning hidden sins; the things we do in private. In this ceremony, heaven and earth were called as witnesses as to how the children of Israel will live while in the Land (Deuteronomy 27:11–26).

Yeshua often rebuked religious individuals for hypocrisy. He rebuked those who made a big outward show of religion in spiritual pride reflecting self-righteousness, prejudice, and intolerance. As we search our hearts in this season preceding Yom Kippur, may we make sure to attend to our hidden sins.

Solomon, the wise king of Israel, taught us that iron sharpens iron (Proverbs 27:17), so if we cannot find the things we need to work on in our lives, we may engage the help of close friends, spouses, or teenage children. These people know us best. May we not resist the hard truth Hashem's spirit may inspire them to tell us. This is the only way to grow.

Hashem already knows these things about us. We are the only ones who need to discover them. As we open our hearts to rebuke and correction, Hashem who sees in secret will reward us openly (Matthew 6:18).

My Personal Thoughts

_____

_____

_____

_____

_____

_____

_____

_____

_____

_____

Matthew 10:28　　　　　　　　　　　　　　　　　　　טז באלול /**Elul 16**

Do not fear those who kill the body but are powerless to kill the soul.
Rather, fear him who can destroy both soul and body in Gei-Hinnom.

In his exhortation to the children of Israel towards obedience to God, Moses reminds them of the sin of the Golden Calf; he warns them against idolatry with the words, "For Adonai your God is a consuming fire, a jealous God" (Deuteronomy 4:24). The writer of the Book of Hebrews admonishes his readers to obedience using this same passage (Hebrews 12:29).

For you have not come to a tangible mountain, to an ignited fire, to darkness, to murk, to a whirlwind (Mt Horeb) … On the contrary, you have come to Mount Tziyon (in Jerusalem where Messiah was crucified) (Hebrews 12: 18, 22). This whole chapter is usually read as an antithesis between Mt Horeb and Mt Zion. It is usually interpreted in the assumption of a spiritual opposition between the two mountains: "you haven't come to Moshe, but to Yeshua; not to the Torah, but to 'grace'; not to the Old Testament, but to the New. God was mean before, but now He is nicer!" This is a flawed understanding and even a minimal understanding of not only the context of the chapter, but also of the style of Jewish writers.

In this passage the writer makes a point for people to obey and fear God's discipline (Hebrews 12: 1-17) using the traditional 'kol v'homer' argument—so often used by Paul, Yeshua, all the prophets, and apostolic writers. In the same manner that Yeshua said (my narration) "If God clothes the lilies of the field which are here today and burned tomorrow better than even King Solomon in all his glory, won't he also clothe you," the writer of Hebrews declares, "You think Mt Horeb, the mountain of Moses and of the congregation in the desert was so awesomely terrible that people who disobeyed died a terrifying death? Mt Zion, the mountain of the firstborn (Yeshua) in Jerusalem is even more deserving of your respect." He said to see that you do not refuse him who is speaking. For if they did not escape when they refused him who warned them on earth (Moses), we will not escape if we reject him who warns from heaven (Yeshua) (Hebrews 12:25). Now we get the intended message: "You saw what happened to those who disobeyed at Mt Horeb? Mt Zion is even more terrifying!"

In this day and age people tend to have a very familiar relationship with Yeshua; they remember the baby born in Bethlehem, he who cried at the death of his friend Lazarus, the gentle Lamb who opened not his mouth as he was reviled by both his brothers and the pagans. We tend to forget though that the baby grew up to be the returning King clothed in a garment dipped in blood, and vested in all the authority and power of God to execute judgment and vengeance on his enemies and on all those who defy his rule (Revelation 19). He is able not only to kill the body, but he can destroy both soul and body in Gei-Hinnom (Matthew 10:28).

May we stand and be warned, serve Adonai with fear, and rejoice with trembling. Kiss the Son, lest he be angry, and you perish in the way, for his wrath is quickly kindled. Blessed are all who take refuge in him (Psalm 2:11-12).

My Personal Thoughts

_____

_____

_____

_____

_____

Hebrews 12:15

See to it that no one misses out on God's grace, that no root of bitterness
springing up causes trouble and thus contaminates many.

In their wonderings from Egypt to Canaan, our fathers learned to become a new nation. Birthed in a worldwide culture of idolatry they learned to become a people with a sense of morality and humanity: Hashem's people. Israel also learned that both good and evil have consequences and retribution not only in the sight of man, but in the sight of God, and that he is the one who establishes what is justice and righteousness.

One of Moses' main points as he readied the people to enter the Promised Land was that being God's people does not absolve us from the punishment of sin; to the contrary, adoption into God's Kingdom legally binds us to his rulings. Moses especially warned against the rationalization of sin. He said,

> So let there not be among you a man, woman . . . whose heart turns away today from ADONAI our God . . . Let there not be among you a root bearing such bitter poison and wormwood . . . saying to himself, 'I will be all right, even though I will stubbornly keep doing whatever I feel like doing . . . ADONAI will not forgive him. (Deuteronomy 29:18–20)

Many years later, the apostle uses the same imagery to warn the Israeli Messianic community of believers about the dangers of disobedience and sin (Hebrews 12:15–16).

Many people see Hashem's abundant grace as some sort of divine unswerving ability to forgive our sins and wickedness. Any would-be deity who absolves iniquity, sin, and injustice without proper recompense and retribution is certainly not the God of Israel (Deuteronomy 29:20); neither is he who Yeshua claims to be united with in spirit and principle (John 17:11).

The Corinthians' congregations had a difficult time pulling out of their Hellenistic sensual culture. They often argued with Paul trying to rationalize sin and disobedience, especially along the lines of sexual immorality. They had a hard time obeying so Paul explained the purpose of God's grace saying, "God has the power to provide you with every gracious gift in abundance, so that always in every way you will have all you need yourselves and be able to provide abundantly for every good" (2 Corinthians 9:8).

The expression *good works* refers to charity, but only in the context that charity is one of the commandments in the Torah. This *grace* the apostle speaks of could be coined as an extra spiritual *boost* to help us obey Hashem's commandments, such as charity but also the other ones such as the dietary laws, Shabbat observance, etc. Grace therefore has nothing to do with forgiveness and absolution of obedience, but everything to do with the ability to perform the commandments. In fact, if we claim to have the grace of God, we take away our excuse for disobedience.

May Hashem help us in properly evaluating our lives. May he deliver us from the evils caused by the rationalization of sin. May he give us his abundant grace that we may please him through our obedience towards his will and commandments.

My Personal Thoughts

Romans 1:19

Because what is known about God is plain to them, since God has made it plain to them.

Hashem has divided all things into two categories: the hidden, and the revealed. The hidden he says belongs to him, while the revealed belongs to us that we may observe all the words of his Torah (Deuteronomy 29:29). While many try to define the work of Messiah, Paul seems to categorize it in the category of the hidden, as a mystery.

The revealed on the other hand can also be divided into two categories. Even though it is faced with linguistic issues, we have what is revealed to us through a literal surface reading of the text of Torah, and then, we have what is revealed to us through logical deduction, midrash, historical, and cultural knowledge.

The strangest thing though, is that the things that divide us the most are not the revealed but the hidden, which by definition, being hidden, we do not know about. Questions about Hashem's nature, the nature of Messiah, understanding the day of the Lord, and the properties of the world to come define our theological boundaries and divide believers into denominational pigeon-holes each seeing the other as heretics. Of all the hidden things the Torah also tells us about, it mentions God's deeds, his greatness, his wisdom, his knowledge, and judgment. Wise King Solomon also tells us that hidden is the heart of kings, which would include the riches of the Messiah King (Job 5:9; Psalm 150:3–4; Proverbs 25:3; Romans 11:33; Ephesians 3:8).

Paul who spent his life as a Torah student and teacher gave us a little clue as to those undefined hidden things of God. He said,

> What is known about God is plain to them, since God has made it plain to them . . . his invisible qualities—both his eternal power and his divine nature—have been clearly seen, because they can be understood from what he has made. (Romans 1:18–20)

Early narrations of creation agree that God created man in his own image (Genesis 1:27). That's all we're told about him, so that must be all we need to know, and we have not yet exhausted what we can discover of God "from what he has made."

Of all the things that would help us in our research of the things of God, the most important ones may not be so high, so deep, or so far. We are made in his image and as such the sages teach that each person represents a whole universe. By learning therefore to understand each other and work together, we may inadvertently discover the heart of God.

So before we fly so high, swim so deep, or travel so far to discover the mysteries of Hashem, may we learn to walk the distance necessary to meet a man halfway, or even to walk in his shoes.

We may then understand the hidden things of God in Messiah.

My Personal Thoughts

_____

_____

_____

_____

_____

_____

_____

Luke 17:2   Elul 19/ יט באלול

*It would be to his advantage that he have a millstone hung around his neck
and he be thrown into the sea, rather than that he ensnare one of these little ones.*

The *Sh'ma* שמע, one of the most well known prayers in Judaism tells us,

> You are to teach them carefully to your children. You are to talk about them
> when you sit at home, when you are traveling on the road, when you lie down
> and when you get up. (Deuteronomy 6:7)

As the Torah tells us of the events in Exodus, several times, the text refers to our children asking questions about it in the future: "And when your children say to you, 'When your children ask you, 'What do you mean by this ceremony?'" (Exodus 12:26).

Hashem wants us to teach our children. He wants us to teach our children in a way that each generation feels as if they are the children of Israel coming out of Egypt and meeting God at Mt. Horeb. It seems in fact that Hashem desires greatly that our children be included in all aspects of our religious life and that they be taught early on to have a healthy fear of the authority of God.

If we content ourselves to sit down and study the Torah but do not make it a requirement in our own lives to at least teach its elementary principles to our children, we commit spiritual and cultural genocide. The movement stops with us and we become responsible for it before Hashem. The whole idea is for the message to be passed on so that the generation that arrives at the end of days can recognize good from evil, make the difference between the false Messiah against the real one. When we stop teaching our children the word of Torah, we kill the last generation.

This commandment to teach our children presents us with inferred obligations. Children are great critics; in their simplicity they smell hypocrisy, especially teenagers. Children are also great mimics; they learn more by watching us than by listening to us. If therefore the life we lead is in contradiction with the sermons we preach, they will see it and will learn that the words of the Bible are a cultural fairy tale that, just like you do, they can chose to keep or dismiss. This commandment to teach our children is made to keep us on our spiritual toes. If by our sloppy example we negate the importance of the Torah in our children's lives, we will be found guilty of relaxing its authority and as the Master says, "Whoever relaxes one of the least of these commandments and teaches others to do the same will be called least in the kingdom of heaven" (Matthew 5:19).

Our modern anti-God materialistic society presents many problems when it comes to teaching the principles of the word to children. But if our teenagers go away from God, is it because of society, or because our sample as parents does not convey a message consistent with our words? These are serious things to think about. In our rationalizing mind we may excuse ourselves, but Hashem may not excuse us.

May we take these things to heart and clean up our living example so that we may not be guilty of neglecting the greatest gift and responsibility Hashem has given us: our children.

My Personal Thoughts

_____

_____

_____

Luke 14:33

So every one of you who doesn't renounce all that he has cannot be my talmid.

It was after that famous Pentecost when the *Shekinah* appeared on the disciples of the Master anointing them for the task at hand of revealing him to the whole world. Many of those who had come from abroad to Jerusalem for the Feast of Pentecost decided to stay and learn from those who had lived closed to the Master (Acts 2). To financially support the fledgling Nazarene movement, the Jerusalem disciples adopted a Kibbutz type of lifestyle (Acts 2:44–45; 4:13).

Barnabas was the first to set the example by setting his enormous fortune at the feet of the disciples. He received great honor for that. Those like Barnabas who gave all became destitute, but having nothing left, they had access to the common pot. It was not a communistic forced sharing of wealth; it was a voluntary work of love for the sake of the community. I heard it said one time that the difference between what the early Jerusalem believers did to survive and what is called *Communism*, is that the Communists says, "What's your is mine and I will take it from you at the point of a gun," but the Master's disciple says, "What's mine is yours and I will share it with you because I love you."

Like the Master suggested, in general, the disciples adopted the *word of honor* system. People were bound by their word, not by vows or swearing to give all (Matthew 5:37). People declared by their own word of honor that these were all their possessions, and thereby had access to the common pot. No one came to check that what they laid at the apostle's feet was actually the sum total of their wealth. Asking someone to bind their word by swearing as suggested in Numbers 30:2 denotes a certain lack of trust in one's integrity, and lack of trust is never healthy in any type of relationship. That is the problem with the idea of pre-nuptial agreements. Right away it shows you don't trust each other. Why even get married then?

Ananias and Sapphira decided to use this system of trust to their own advantage. They were going to pretend to share all and thereby have access to the common pot, but in actuality, they kept a hidden reserve. This was wrong in so many ways but mostly of breaking and taking advantage of the principle of trust built on the word of the honor system. It was lying and, in this case, the same as breaking an oath. The Father saw through their wicked heart and executed them as they faced the disciples (Acts 5:1–11).

We may look at Ananias and Saphhira with disgust wondering how one could do such things. In the same manner though, it is important to remember that discipleship to the Master implies a promise to give all (Luke 14:33).

It is not right when partners decide to share all but one keeps a reserve. Yeshua gave his all, so likewise we owe him our all. When we come to the Master with our lives, everything must be on the table. If we have *reservations*, he will surely find us out.

By the way, the same principle works in marriage. It doesn't work very well when one gives all and the other has *reservations*.

May our lifestyle always reflect our words!

My Personal Thoughts

_____

_____

Romans 3:30 כא באלול /Elul 21

*Therefore, he [God] will consider righteous the circumcised on the
ground of trusting and the uncircumcised through that same trusting.*

Hashem told Abraham to circumcise his boys: Isaac and Ishmael. Isaac was circumcised at eight days, and Ishmael at thirteen years old. Later Hashem instituted that all the children of Jacob should be circumcised at eight days. The children of Ishmael who united with the children of Esau to make the Arab nations still circumcise their children at thirteen years old.

Circumcision is an outward sign of an inward reality. It serves as a branding in the flesh so people know we have a Master, that we belong to a family of people who has been redeemed, that we belong to a redeemer. Whereas this *branding* is applied on our *secret parts* allowing us to blend, it also reminds us that we are not our own: that we are responsible to the Torah of our Master and not to do these things that are done in *secret*.

Moses spoke of a second circumcision, but this time of the heart (also Jeremiah 4:4). It isn't to replace the circumcision of the flesh but it rather works as an addendum. The heart is the seat of the will. A person with a circumcised heart is one whose *flesh* has been removed from his will; carnality does not dictate this person anymore. Jeremiah also spoke of the circumcision of the ear (Jeremiah 6:10).

As Paul wrote of circumcision, he did not need to write to the Jewish believers who already had instructions in the matter. He referred mostly to this promised circumcision of the heart to give us a "heart to understand" (Deuteronomy 29:4; 30:6). Physical circumcision was only given to the children of Abraham and particularly imposed on the children of Israel. Given the fact that when Abraham was still uncircumcised he was made the 'blessor' of all the families of the earth, Paul then spoke to the uncircumcised Colossians (Gentile believers) of the circumcision of the heart (Romans 4:10–11; Colossians 2:11) whereby they would be grafted-in to Israel (Romans 11) though Messiah. As circumcision in the flesh changes our body showing that we have a Master and rules to abide by, so should the circumcision of the heart. One who claims to belong to Messiah should show the signs of being a different person, one not subject to his evil inclination but subject to the spirit of Hashem.

Hashem has promised that in the time of the end, when he gathers his chosen people from the four corners of the earth, he will circumcise their hearts. There is no *if* in there. This promise is unconditional (Deuteronomy 30:5–6). One may wonder, "How can it be unconditional?" For millennia before the world ever knew about God and the Messiah, the Chosen People have carried the persecution of being chosen and separated. We cherished and preserved the Torah that the world today enjoys through the effort of the early Jewish disciples of the Jewish Messiah. I told a young woman who told me that her parents were Jewish but that it meant nothing to her, that to be Jewish is like being the inheritor of a vast wealth of future blessings, and that we should not throw away our glorious inheritance because of discomfort in this present reality, like Esau.

May we all, biological Jews and grafted-in Gentiles, remember that this appurtenance to our Messiah means an unconditional promise in the world to come. As the early Jewish martyrs starting with Moses who considered the riches of Messiah greater than Egypt (Hebrews 11:24–26), may we never let go of that hope. This is the very hope, *Hatikvah* התקוה that kept the children of Israel for 2,000 years, and it will keep us until that Day comes.

May it be soon Abba, even in our days!

Philippians 1:6　　　　　　　　　　　　　　　　　　　**Elul 22/** כב באלול

And I am sure of this: that the One who began a good work among you
will keep it growing until it is completed on the Day of the Messiah Yeshua.

Moses seems to peer into the future as he warns the congregation in the desert of their future apostasy and exile. He seems to know that Israel will eventually forget the God that delivered her from Egypt. He knows that she will pervert the beauty of Torah observance, and go after idols according to the willfulness of her own heart (Deuteronomy 29:16–29). According to these passages, some people claim that Hashem forsook the children of Israel when they deviated from the straight and narrow path of obedience to Torah, and as a result, rejected Messiah. I find this strange because Hashem's oracle through Moses doesn't stop there. It continues. It continues with a prophecy of Israel's repentance and return to the Land (Deuteronomy 30:1–14).

As a new bride who carelessly played the harlot in her husband's house while he was away, Israel has been ravished, raped, used, misused, and abused. The nations kidnapped her and made her house desolate: a result of her own willful choices. I don't know about you, but I believe in the God who inspired Paul with the words, "The One who began a good work among you will keep it growing until it is completed on the Day of the Messiah Yeshua" (Philippians 1:6).

After the Holocaust, Israel said, "That is enough!" As the prodigal son of the Master's parable, she assessed her fate and made a decision to return home where Hashem was there for her with open arms and tears of joy (Luke 15:14–24). As with Jacob returning from exile at Laban's, angels waited for her at the entrance of the Land. Hashem now also gives her wisdom on how to deal with Esau's evil intentions (Genesis 32 and 33). As with Nehemiah's crew rebuilding the walls of Jerusalem, Hashem protects her from the Samaritans who try to intimidate her from rebuilding. She works hard at rebuilding her home, one hand with the work tool, and the other holding a weapon (Nehemiah 1–6).

Many look at Israel today and can hardly think of it as a godly nation. It is because the Israel Hashem so carefully nurtured in the desert has returned soiled with the spiritual, moral and idolatrous filth she has collected during her sojourn in the nations. It is like going to jail and living among criminals. One will surely be affected by such a sojourn.

Hashem knew all that would happen. But her returning to the home God had appointed for her through Abraham and rebuilding herself as a sovereign nation is the mustard seed of faith that precipitates the rest of the prophecies spoken by Moses, Isaiah, Jeremiah, Ezekiel, and many others (Isaiah 27:13; 56:8; Ezekiel 37:21–24; Jeremiah 31:31–40). After this extensive punishment that God claims would be "double for all her sins" (Isaiah 40:2; 61:7), like Job, Israel is restored twice above her former glory as in the days of Solomon's reign (Job 42:10).

Israel also regains her place as a light to the nations, and nations even flock to her for the Feasts of Tabernacle, that they may hear the "word of ADONAI from Yerushalayim" (Zechariah 14; Isaiah 2:3; Micah 4:2). Thus goes the story, a beautiful story that indeed ends well. We must be patient and not draw a premature ending. All things truly will be restored.

May it happen soon Abba, even in our days!

My Personal Thoughts

_____

_____

_____

Matthew 19:14   כג באלול /Elul 23

Let the children come to me, don't stop them,
for the Kingdom of Heaven belongs to such as these.

Moses declared to Israel, "I am 120 years old today. I can't get around any longer" (Deuteronomy 31:2). This could be interpreted to mean that because of his age, he was decrepit and no longer ambulatory but how could it be when the Torah also said that, "Moshe was 120 years old when he died, with eyes undimmed and vigor undiminished" (Deuteronomy 34:7).

What this meant was that Moses simply realized that time had come for him to pass the baton on to Joshua. Wisdom was going from him. He was not able to *get around any longer* teaching the Torah. He knew that he needed to get out of the way and surrender the leadership of Israel to his faithful and devoted disciple Joshua. Moses had given his life for the cause. He saw all the works of God with Israel. He was the instrument, what they call in Greek, the *pedagogue* of God's parenting.

As he now readied to be gathered with his fathers, Moses knew what was to befall the people he so faithfully led. He knew of their future disobedience and apostasy; he saw their defeat at the hand of their enemies; he saw multiple exiles, but he also knew that in the end, Hashem would fulfill his covenant with them.

This can be compared to our own parenting. We tenderly care and nurture our children for, let's say twenty years or so, then we send them to their own destinies. We see their first steps towards independence and how badly we want to keep them from falling as we did when they first started walking or riding a bike. We look with apprehension at their future and as we see the gloom and doom of their potential irresponsible decisions. We instinctively want to grab the steering wheel of their lives and put it back in our own secure hands. But we have to let go. We have to let God take over the leadership of our children's lives. In fact, the quicker we let go, the better it will be for them.

What do we see when we let go? We see the same things Moses saw will happen to the children of Israel. We see that our children will disobey the *Torah* we have taught them and will have to learn obedience through the things that they will suffer, just like we did with our parents. We might even wonder at times if God is really at the controls, but he most certainly is.

We can imagine that Hashem may have gone through the same thing when he created mankind. He knew that as he turned them loose in the world, they would make the wrong decision. That is why he prepared atonement for us from even before the foundations of the world (Revelation 13:8). This atonement was available for the children of Israel of old, and it is available for our children of Israel of today. We are therefore sure of this, that "And I am sure of this: that the One who began a good work among you will keep it growing until it is completed on the Day of the Messiah Yeshua" (Philippians 1:6).

As Moses did, may we with confidence turn over the leadership of our grown children to the Almighty God, knowing that he cares for them more than we even do. He even gave his only begotten son to secure them a place in the world to come!

My Personal Thoughts

_____

_____

Matthew 19:20

Where do I still fall short?

It is very difficult to explain that the recipe for eternal life is, "To keep the commandments and follow him" (Matthew 19:16–21), as proclaimed to us by the mouth of Yeshua himself. Whereas people may later understand, for the most part many have their mind stuck behind a very strong and tall barrage of 'Law-phobia.'

Since the days of Martin Luther's Reformation, people have been accustomed to the *freebie* version of the faith. As soon as they hear the slightest mention of *Mosaic Law,* they suddenly become expert watchdogs of the faith and make sure that you are not teaching the false doctrine of a redemption that would cost them something.

It is true that my redemption cost me nothing, but I cannot say that redemption was free. The facts are that if it is free, it is because someone else paid the tab, so in essence it is really not free. Justice has to be paid for God to be a just God. So the old adage is true, "There is no such thing as a free lunch."

But even if it did cost something, what would we be willing to give? Is our appreciation of Hashem's redemptive work for us only in an entitlement kind of spirit, just because it's 'free'?

Didn't Yeshua teach the parable of the man who, when he found the Kingdom, was happy to invest all that he had to obtain it (Matthew 13:44)? It seems that this man fell onto the *pro version*. The version that requires to pay, but the one which then answers the question of our rich young ruler in Matthew 19, "Where do I still fall short?"

As we come to the Kingdom through the *free version* program, we are also introduced to the pay *pro-version* option, which brings us deeper into the Kingdom and closer to the Master. The entrance to the kingdom is free, but the measure of our rewards is estimated by our personal investment, by the bread we cast upon the waters and the use of our talents (Ecclesiastes 11:1; Matthew 25:14–30).

We are certainly free to remain in the *free-version*, but wouldn't we want to get closer to him who gave everything so we could enter the kingdom? Are we just in it for the *free* stuff?

We are supposed to emulate him and he did not balk at the cost.

Do we?

My Personal Thoughts

_____
_____
_____
_____
_____
_____
_____
_____
_____
_____
_____
_____

Titus 1:7–9   כה באלול /Elul 25

For an overseer, as someone entrusted with God's affairs, must be blameless—he must not be self-willed or quick-tempered, he must not drink excessively, get into fights or be greedy for dishonest gain. On the contrary, he must be hospitable, devoted to good, sober-mindedness, uprightness, holiness and self-control. He must hold firmly to the trustworthy Message that agrees with the doctrine; so that by his sound teaching he will be able to exhort and encourage, and also to refute those who speak against it.

Establishing leadership alongside Moses had its benefits but also its dangers. When God starts speaking directly to people, eventually they think they are spiritual enough in their own rights and assume that they may now answer to God only. It is the classic prophet syndrome where people believe themselves exempted from submission to authority even when ordained. This creates anarchy and goes diametrically against the idea of appointing judges, as what Moses tried to do was establish the validity of clerical authority (Exodus 18:21).

A congregation leader I know took an informal poll of his congregation with the questions. "Do you believe in submission to spiritual leadership and authority?" The congregation answered affirmatively. The next question was, "What happens if you disagree with a ruling or a decision from that leadership?" Some answered, "I won't follow," others, "I'll leave." While everyone does have free will, to submit only when you agree is not submission. If it is, it is submission only to yourself; you then become your own leader, which makes you, as Yeshua put it, a "blind guides" (Matthew 15:14).

Submission to an earthly authority is a divine exercise that teaches godly humility. It is impossible for one to say, "I submit to God's authority only!" That very claim is born of pride because it infers that one has a private personal connection with God and his will that supersedes that of anyone else. We only learn to submit to God by learning to submit to the earthly authorities he has set upon us especially when they disagree with us. Paul encouraged it (Romans 13:1), and was subject to the council of elders in Jerusalem (Acts 15). He even went to check with them to see if what he was doing was right (Galatians 2:2).

This is why spiritual leaders have a great responsibility and therefore need to be men of integrity. They need to be able men from all the people, men who fear God, who are trustworthy and hate a bribe (Exodus 18:21).

Paul also advises that whereas they can receive gifts from people, they are not to be at charge to the people but earn their own keep (1 Corinthians 4:12). Many spiritual leaders claim tithes as their due, but that tithe was originally designated for Hashem in the service of the Temple and helping the needy of the congregation. What priests and rabbis received were voluntary gifts and offerings.

May God provide us today with such leaders for the flock of God. Leaders with the wisdom of Solomon, the insight of Daniel, the teaching style of Ezra, the sagacity of Abraham, the courage of David, the strength of Samson, and the love of Yeshua and may we have the wisdom to submit to such.

My Personal Thoughts

_____

_____

Acts 4:32–35   Elul 26 /כו באלול

> *All the many believers . . . claimed any of his possessions for himself, but*
> *everyone shared everything he had. . . . No one among them was poor, since*
> *those who owned lands or houses sold them and turned over the proceeds to*
> *the emissaries to distribute to each according to his need.*

Our world is plagued with economic instability. The specter of the Great Depression hangs over Presidents and nations, especially in the Western hemisphere. Even though measures have been taken to avoid a repeat, these seem to be nothing more than band-aids attempting to keep an overinflated balloon from bursting.

The world gages that a healthy economy is one with much movement. Whereas movement is a proof of life, one can still move and go in the wrong direction. A healthy economy should be one where everyone has enough, and more, without the use of the oppression and slavery of credit cards. Any economy based on credit and interest is based on economic oppression, which God hates (Leviticus 25:17). Like an old farmer of an Eastern European country told me many years ago, "In our country, we don't have much, but everybody has some." On the other hand, a diseased economy is one that shows a polarization of wealth, where a very few have the very most, and the very most have the very least. The Anti-Messiah of the end will provoke such economy that he will use as a form of control of the masses and persecution of those who obey God's commandments (Revelation 6:5–6; 12 and 13).

There seems to be two major economic philosophies in the world: on the one side, the ultra capitalistic system, and on the other side, the ultra communistic way. In reality, the only successful government will not be one of man's leading but that of a theocracy.

The economic system of the Bible actually provides a good model. It is funny that people don't want to use it. Hashem teaches us an economy based on capital, but balanced by a social system of tithes and offerings, which support both the religious community and the poor. Also, the system is to reboot every seven years with all debts being forgiven (Leviticus 25), which creates an automatic re-balancing of wealth where no one becomes too rich, and no one becomes too poor.

I believe this will be the system used in the world to come when Messiah rules the earth. At that time, he will force moneylenders to forgive debts every seven years and thereby abolish economic oppression.

May it come soon Abba, even in our days!

My Personal Thoughts

_____

_____

_____

_____

_____

_____

_____

2 Corinthians 6:16

*For we are the temple of the living God—as God said, "I will house myself in them . . .
and I will walk among you. I will be their God, and they will be my people.*

In ancient Israel when a man desired a woman in marriage, he would close the deal with her father around a covenantal glass of wine. This way of *closing a deal* has travelled far and wide. In France, when people agree together towards a certain action, they serve everybody involved a glass of wine that each person gently taps with the others before drinking, known also as *toasting*.

In the case of marriage, after closing the deal, the future husband then would go and "prepare a place" for him and his bride (John 14:3). He would usually do so as an addition to the house of his own father, where he lived. He may engage the help of friends and experts, especially if he were not necessarily gifted in carpentry skills. This is exactly what happened in the twenty-fifth chapter of the Book of Exodus. Hashem who betrothed Israel engaged *friends* to build a tabernacle that as he said, "that I may live among them" (Exodus 25:8). The Hebrew of that text is very interesting. It says, *oosh'chenti betocham* ושכנתי בתוכם", which carries the more literal translation of, *that I may live among them.*

Hashem doesn't want to live in a *little box* somewhere in a building where we come and pay him a friendly visit once or twice a week. As any husband would, he wants to live within the close intimacy of our hearts. There are two words in Hebrew for knowing someone, *Makir* מכיר , and *yode'ah* יודע. *Makir* is a word that relates to a casual acquaintance, but *yode'ah* is the word used in: "And Adam knew Eve his wife, and she conceived" (Genesis 4:1, ESV).

From these verses, Jewish scholars developed the notion that each Jewish home is actually a small Temple, and that each individual is also a miniature Temple. The apostolic writers were familiar with that notion. We read it in the apostolic texts,

> What agreement can there be between the temple of God and idols? For we are the temple of the living God—as God said, "I will house myself in them . . . and I will walk among you. I will be their God, and they will be my people. (2 Corinthians 6:16, quoting Leviticus 26:12)

This idea is erroneously interpreted as the body of believers replacing the Temple, but its concepts were actually an endorsement of the role of the temple in our lives, the sign of the presence of God among us. The same applies to the Tabernacle that was the mobile Temple in the desert. God had his people build the Tabernacle, which later became the Temple, which Yeshua claimed was a "house of prayer" (John 2:16). We also know that the Master was disgusted at the lack of reverence people had for the Temple.

The same ungodly hands that killed Messiah also destroyed the Temple. We are told that one day Messiah will return to take vengeance on a world who tried to up-throne him. On that Day, he will rebuild the Temple. On that Day, the light of the world will have returned. And nations will flock once a year for the feast of Tabernacle to offer their gifts at the Temple (Zechariah 14:16).

May it be soon, Abba, even in our days!

My Personal Thoughts

_____

_____

Hebrews 1:3 **Elul 28/** כח באלול

This Son is the radiance of the Sh'khinah, the very expression of God's essence.

When Moses was on the Mount, either physically or in a vision, he saw Hashem's eternal dwelling place. Moses was able to observe every detail of it and then was asked to replicate it on earth. The purpose was for Hashem to be able to dwell among his people Israel. Hashem told Moses, "They are to make me a sanctuary, so that I may live among them. You are to make it according to everything I show you—the design of the tabernacle and the design of its furnishings. This is how you are to make it" (Exodus 25:8–9).

This can be a daunting task. How indeed can the corruptible recreate the incorruptible? How can the grander and majesty of the heavenly throne be replicated with mere earthly elements? How could the purity and majesty of God's dwelling place be represented for mankind to see?

A play on the words of the Hebrew text of Exodus 25:9 gives us a clue. The word *show* in the Hebrew of the verse is *mareh* מראה but it can also be interpreted as *mirror*. Moses was not asked to replicate the very thing, but a mere model for people to see. It is like using a mirror when trying to see something in a concealed location. Also, from a distance, a mirror can capture the fullness of a large area. Yes, even though God fills everything (Jeremiah 23:24), through a *mirror* we can catch a glimpse of his greatness.

In these ancient days of the Exodus from Egypt, Hashem asked his servant Moses to have the people build a replica of his throne room as it appeared to Moses on the Mount. This would be the place from where his light would shine to speak with Moses. Moses who enjoyed direct contact with Hashem, speaking face to face with him (Exodus 33:11; Deuteronomy 34:10) became for the people of Israel the very representation of the heavenly presence in the camp. Today we do not have Moses, a Tabernacle, or an ark, but we have the earthly image of the Father in the Son Yeshua, for he is "the radiance of the glory of God and the exact imprint of his nature, and he upholds the universe by the word of his power" (Hebrews 1:3); "It is through his Son that we have redemption — that is, our sins have been forgiven. He is the visible image of the invisible God. He is supreme over all creation" (Colossians 1:14–15).

Yeshua commissioned us to our worldwide mission with the words, "Just as the Father sent me, I myself am also sending you." (John 20:21). This means that in the daily walk of our life, we are to exemplify the mission of our Master. His mission was to show us the Father; our mission is to show the Son to the world.

It represents indeed a tall order and it is doubtful that we are up to the task, but we can and should try to do our best trusting that he will do the rest. It is important; the world needs it. We cannot live for ourselves; we have been sent on a mission.

My Personal Thoughts

_____

_____

_____

_____

_____

John 5:22

The Father does not judge anyone but has entrusted all judgment to the Son.

The children of Israel couldn't bear to hear the holy voice (Exodus 20:18–21). Who can blame them? I think any of us would have felt the same.

As the people stood at a distance, Moses received rulings. These rulings are just as valid and pertinent today as they were when they were first uttered (Exodus 21–23). These rulings took on the judicial tone of civil cases.

In order to justify their *Torah is obsolete* theology, modern-day believers have divided the commandments into three categories: civil, moral, and ceremonial. This categorization does not appear anywhere in the biblical text. The division of God's rulings into these categories seems to be a reflection of our modern society where some things are considered civil (secular) and other things are considered religious. In the days of the giving of this Torah, everything was religious. In fact, for most of history, atheism was unheard of, and at certain times and places it was even a crime.

The Hebrew text tells us that Hashem was the one before whom the Children of Israel were to appear for any and all judicial cases (Exodus 21:6; 22:7–8). We do not realize this because the English text uses the word: *judges* when the Hebrew says, *Ha'elohim* האלהים, God. Looking at the text in its Hebrew context, we now see that all cases are of a religious nature. The reason the translators used the word *judges*, is because as the people appeared before the Sanhedrin court established through Jethro's council (Exodus 18), it is as if they appeared before God. Later, we are told that disobedience to this court is liable for a death penalty.

This puts a heavy responsibility on these men. No wonder the Sanhedrin shied away from the death penalty. It is told that member of the Sanhedrin who would rule in favor of a death penalty even once in seven years would be considered murderous. Because of this heavy responsibility, Jewish lawmakers only accepted eyewitness testimony. They refused circumstantial evidence.

The Sanhedrin that convicted the Master was a kangaroo court held in contempt of all the safeguards applied in Jewish courts. The Sadducees wanted Yeshua dead. They did not even allow the Pharisees in the court, as they would have stopped the process.

Human courts are bound to make mistakes. Thus is the nature of humanity. With the advent of DNA testing, many sentences are being reviewed, and after decades in jail, people now are found to have been wrongly incarcerated.

One day, our Messiah will return and to him judgment has been given (John 5:22). He will judge righteously (Isaiah 11:1–5). And he will even share the judging with his faithful ones to whose judgment the world will have to submit, as is written,

> Then I saw thrones, and those seated on them received authority to judge. And I saw the souls of those who had been beheaded for testifying about Yeshua and proclaiming the Word of God, also those who had not worshipped the beast or its image and had not received the mark on their foreheads and on their hands. They came to life and ruled with the Messiah for a thousand years. (Revelation 20:4)

GLOSSARY

Aleph	The first letter of the Hebrew alphabet
bar-mitsvah	Rite of passage ceremony for Jewish twelve year old boys.
bet-din	Biblical Jewish court of law in charge of administrating Torah rules
Brit-milah	Circumcision
Chesed	'Covenant keeping faithfulness'; commonly translated as 'grace'
Chupah	Traditional Jewish marriage canopy
Davar	From Hebrew meaning, 'word', as in the 'Word'
Ger	Non-Jewish resident in the land of Israel
go'el	Redeemer
Halacha	Spiritual walk;, personal religious observance application
HaSatan	The Adversary; the Devil
Kabalat Shabbat	The beginning of the Sabbath on Friday night
kana'ee	Zealous; jealous
Kaphar	Atonement
Kasher	Biblically edible
Ketubah	Marriage contract
Kiddush	Sabbath sanctification prayer
Korban/ Korbanot	Altar offering
Malkosh	Latter rains of the Israeli rainy season
Mashiach	Hebrew word for 'Messiah'

Memrah	Aramaic word used to explain Messiah in ancient targumic texts
Me'od	Much; substance
Me'or	Luminary
Mitzvah/ Mitzvot	Commandment
Mo'ed	Levitical festival season
Motzei Shabbat	Ending of the Sabbath
Nes	Miracle
Olah	Burnt offering
Olam HaBah	The world or age to come
Olam hazeh	This present world or age
Or	Light
Rosh	Head, beginning, leader
Ruach	Breath, spirit
Ruach Hakodesh	The Holy Spirit of God
Sh' ma	Hear ye!
Shacha	To prostrate
Shavuot	The festival of Weeks; Pentecost
Shemen	Oil
Shevet	Sceptre; staff; rod
Simchat Torah	Last day of the Feast of Tabernacles
Sukkhot	The Feast of Tabernacles
Tahor	Ritually sanctified
Tamei	Ritually contaminated
Tamid	Perpetual; name for the twice daily lamb offering
Tanach	Hebrew acronym for the Old Testament

Tareph	Non-biblically edible
Tephilims	Payer boxes Jewish people wrap on their arms and head
Teshuvah	Repentance
Tevilah	Baptism
Tzit-tzits	Fringes Jewish people hang at the corners of their prayer shawls
Vayikrah	"And he called…"
Yoreh	Early rains
Zerah	Seed